EVENING ROUNDS

DAILY DEVOTIONAL STORIES

A Collection of Stories, Essays, & Insights

by Students, Alumni, Faculty, and Friends

of

Loma Linda University School of Medicine

Compiled to Commemorate
the Centennial of the School's First Graduating Class

1914-2014

Edited by Donna R. Hadley

Volunteer Chair, Centennial Celebration Planning Committee

2009-2014

Published by
Loma Linda University Press
Office of Academic Publications
Loma Linda University
Loma Linda, CA 92350
Printed in the United States of America

Copies may be ordered from
Loma Linda University Campus Store
11161 Anderson Street, Suite 110
Loma Linda, CA 92354
Tel: (909) 558-4567
E-mail: campusstore@llu.edu
http://llu.bncollege.com.

Publisher: Loma Linda University Press
Cover layout: Kristina Benfield
Front cover:
    Hand models: Dorothy Zane (left) and Shelley Andersen (right)
    Photographer: Spencer Roy Lim
Back cover:
    The Good Samaritan statue on the LLU campus serves as a constant reminder of the University's mission to continue the teaching and healing ministry of Jesus Christ: To Make Man Whole.
    Photographer: Kristina Benfield
Compiler and production editor: Donna R. Hadley (née Olson)
Project manager: Alice Wongworawat
Project coordinator: Julie Lee
Copy editor: Duane Fike
Printer: Sinclair Printing Company, Los Angeles, CA
Typeface: Adobe Jenson Pro

This book is printed on acid-free paper.

Library of Congress Control Number: 2013953840

ISBN 978-159410-021-5 (paperback)
ISBN 978-159410-022-2 (hardcover)

Copyrights

Abbreviations

The following abbreviations are used throughout this book:

Loma Linda University Entities

AIMS	Association of International Medical Services
CME	College of Medical Evangelists (now Loma Linda University)
LLU	Loma Linda University
LLUAHSC	Loma Linda University Adventist Health Sciences Center
LLUBMC	Loma Linda University Behavioral Medicine Center
LLUCH	Loma Linda University Children's Hospital
LLUFMG	Loma Linda University Faculty Medical Group
LLUH	Loma Linda University Health
LLUHS	Loma Linda University Health System
LLUMC	Loma Linda University Medical Center
LLUSAHP	Loma Linda University School of Allied Health Professions
LLUSBH	Loma Linda University School of Behavioral Health
LLUSD	Loma Linda University School of Dentistry
LLUSM	Loma Linda University School of Medicine
LLUSMAA	Loma Linda University School of Medicine Alumni Association
LLUSN	Loma Linda University School of Nursing
LLUSP	Loma Linda University School of Pharmacy
LLUSPH	Loma Linda University School of Public Health
LLUSR	Loma Linda University School of Religion
SACHS	Social Action Community Health System

Degrees

BA	Bachelor of Arts
BS	Bachelor of Science
BSc	Bachelor of Science
JD	Juris Doctor
DD	Doctor of Divinity
DMin	Doctor of Ministry
DrPH	Doctor of Public Health
DTh	Doctor of Theology
EdD	Doctor of Education
EdS	Specialist in Education
MA	Master of Arts
MBA	Master of Business Administration
MD	Doctor of Medicine
MDiv	Master of Divinity
MHA	Master of Health Administration
MHIS	Master in Health Information Services
MPH	Master of Public Health
MS	Master of Science
PhD	Doctor of Philosophy
PsyD	Doctor of Psychology
RelD	Doctor of Religion

Lovingly and Gratefully Dedicated to

Wil Alexander

Whom Christ has used to bring wholeness
to patient and healer alike

From the Dean

Forty years ago in the fall of 1973, I was a junior medical student with just two months of hospital ward experience. Still nascent in even the simplest doctoring skills, I sat on unit 6100 combing through the paper medical charts of my three assigned patients, hoping to understand what seemed an unfair number of abbreviations. A tap on my shoulder caused me to look up into the familiar face of Wil Alexander, whom I knew as a highly respected minister in the church. Unlike other clergy in the hospital, he wasn't wearing a suit, but a long white coat with a name tag that read "Clinical Ministry" under his name. That coat befuddled me. Pastor Alexander asked if he could accompany me on morning pre-rounds. As a junior medical student (who looked about 14 years old at the time), I was in no position to tell anyone in a long white coat "no."

I do not remember the patients and I do not remember anything that either of us said, but I do remember that I was his first student in what would become 40 years of a remarkable journey in whole person care: the melding of "faith and medicine."

Forty years later Wil Alexander, age 92, still makes whole person rounds every week at our Medical Center. Forty years later, the "whole person care" senior medical student elective is the perennial favorite. Forty years later, he has been the leader in teaching our decades-old mission "To Make Man Whole." Forty years later our mission continues to be very real and very practical, tightly aligned with the founders of our 105-year-old school. Forty years later his imprint on Loma Linda is indelible. Forty years later we dedicate this book, *Evening Rounds*, to a man of God who found it his mission to keep Loma Linda University's mission vibrant.

—H. Roger Hadley, LLUSM class of 1974

Wil Alexander and Roger Hadley on unit 6100, forty years after their first encounter

From the Editor

A second book was never part of the plan. *Morning Rounds* was compiled, edited, and published, concluding the kickoff for Loma Linda University School of Medicine's centennial celebration in 2009. Done.

But as soon as the first copies were distributed, comments began to pour in. Everyone had a different favorite story and many were asking for more. Fifteen thousand or so copies later, the idea of a sequel just wouldn't quit.

The book you are holding is our response to inquiries, encouragement, prayers, and participation from many of you. And you're exactly right: More stories do need to be told, stories that help create a more complete picture of the history of LLUSM and its graduates. These stories make the case that "To Make Man Whole" is a mission that is as needed today as it was in 1909—perhaps even more.

May God use the stories on these pages to inspire, encourage, and bless us on our journey toward wholeness.

About the Authors

From the worlds of medicine and science come stories and insights from those who have studied and witnessed life from the moment it begins to when the last breath is drawn and thoughts emerge of what lies beyond.

Three hundred sixty-five authors, including freshmen medical students, seasoned practitioners, scientists in state-of-the-art laboratories, and others serving in primitive conditions around the globe, share their stories and insights that together weave a rich tapestry of what encompasses whole person care. The personal nature of what is written on these pages will resonate with many readers.

Pieces of Wholeness

For each month a heading titled "A Piece of Wholeness . . ." precedes a quote attributed to Wil Alexander. These quotes are a small sampling of the numerous "pieces" that constitute wholeness.

Deferred Mission Appointment (DMA) Program

This scholarship supports medical students who are committed to serve at a Seventh-day Adventist mission hospital after completing residency training. Many of the authors' biographies have reference to this program.

Wil Alexander Whole Person Care Award

This award recognizes a senior medical student who has demonstrated to his/her peers and colleagues, during the clinical years, a growing excellence in the physical, mental, emotional, spiritual, and relational care of patients as part of the art of medical practice. Several authors were recipients of this award as noted in their biographies.

—Donna R. Hadley

With Sincere Appreciation . . .

The School of Medicine acknowledges the following people and entities who have underwritten the cost of this book, allowing *all* proceeds to go to the LLUSM Student Spiritual Renewal Endowment Fund. This generosity will benefit current and future medical students as spirituality continues to be intentionally incorporated into their time spent at Loma Linda University.

Marjorie and James Akamine

Jackie and Ted Hamilton

Loretta and Loran Hauck

Marilyn and Raymond Herber

Sheila and Steven Hodgkin

Elizabeth Venden Sutherland

Carolyn and Ralph Thompson

Marjorie and Louis Venden

Loma Linda University Faculty Medical Group

Loma Linda University Medical Auxiliary—llumedaux.org

Acknowledgments

Kristina Benfield—LLUSM project editor for communications and design. The first-class design work associated with *Evening Rounds* including the cover, publicity, and advertisement materials is the result of her creative mind and eye.

Editorial Review Board—Numerous individuals from varied backgrounds who aided in the direction, tenor, and validity of this book.

Duane Fike—A veteran from *Morning Rounds* who once again volunteered hundreds of hours as a copy editor. His advice and recommendations were invaluable.

Audrey Howard and Eppie Manalo—Staff of LLU Academic Publications and University Press for their superb skills in the thorough reviewing of the manuscript.

Julie Lee—LLUSM administrative secretary for the dean's office, who agreed to work full time on this project for more than a year; her varied responsibilities, too numerous to mention, were each done adeptly and thoroughly making her indispensable from start to finish.

Brittany Mitchell (née Leno)—LLUSM administrative assistant to the dean, whose proficiency regarding public relations and advertising for the book was what helped launch the project so successfully.

Rhodes "Dusty" Rigsby—LLUSM class of 1987, assistant to the dean for administrative affairs; primary medical editor and lexicologist extraordinaire whose talents were used throughout the book.

Stephen Thorp—LLUSM class of 2016, volunteered to assist after he read *Morning Rounds*; his biblical knowledge and his organizational abilities were excellent.

Tamara Thomas—LLUSM class of 1987, LLUSM vice dean for academic affairs; her strict attention to detail in copy editing and writing skills helped in numerous capacities.

Marjorie and Louis Venden—Biblical scholars and "fans" of *Morning Rounds* who served as skillful and fervent volunteers in assigning appropriate Bible texts where needed.

Karen Wat Nielsen—LLUSM class of 1976-B, a volunteer whose creative writing talents were immeasurable in the copy editing process.

Acknowledgments

Carol Weismeyer—LLUSM senior administrative secretary for the student affairs office and another veteran of *Morning Rounds*; her superb proofreading skills once again made her a vital member of the team.

Alice Wongworawat—LLUSM associate dean for finance and administration, whose expertise provided seamless continuity between the two books; having been project coordinator for *Morning Rounds*, she paved a smooth road for the project coordinator, editors, and other members of the team for *Evening Rounds*.

All the "closers"—Pat Eiseman, Dana Gonzales, Craig Hadley, Kent Hansen, Mindy Morrell, Travis Morrell, Ricardo Peverini, Brittnee Quintanar, Marci Weismeyer, Michael Weismeyer, and Lynn Wilkemeyer—for their varied talents, tenacity, and time. Each of their contributions made a positive difference in the outcome of this book.

And to each of the authors, who willingly shared their personal stories and perspectives: You collectively portray a comprehensive and rich description of whole person care that is embedded in the mission of Loma Linda University School of Medicine.

And lastly . . .

Donna Hadley—my indefatigable and talented wife who conceived *Morning Rounds* and, to the delight of its readers, agreed to be the editor of *Evening Rounds*. Once again, she volunteered hundreds of hours. Her precious skills to recognize and adroitly edit a compelling story never cease to amaze me.

My profound thanks to each one of you.

—H. Roger Hadley
Dean, LLU School of Medicine

EVENING ROUNDS

DAILY DEVOTIONAL STORIES

The Loma Linda University Physician's Oath

Before God these things I do promise:

In the acceptance of my sacred calling,

I will dedicate my life to the furtherance of Jesus Christ's healing and teaching ministry.

I will give to my teachers the respect and gratitude which is their due. I will impart to those who follow me, the knowledge and experience that I have gained.

The wholeness of my patient will be my first consideration.

Acting as a good steward of the resources of society and of the talents granted me, I will endeavor to reflect God's mercy and compassion by caring for the lonely, the poor, the suffering, and those who are dying.

I will maintain the utmost respect for human life. I will not use my medical knowledge contrary to the laws of humanity. I will respect the rights and decision of my patients.

I will hold in confidence all secrets committed to my keeping in the practice of my calling.

I will lead my life and practice my art with purity, and honor; abstaining from immorality myself, I will not lead others into moral wrong doing.

May God's kingdom, His healing power and glory be experienced by those whom I serve, and may they be made known in my life, in proportion as I am faithful to this oath.

This oath is recited three times by LLUSM students in their academic journey: the White Coat Ceremony, Freshman Dedication Ceremony, and Commencement.

JANUARY

"GIVE THE EYES OF YOUR HEART
THE SHEER BEAUTY OF THE ORDINARY."

January 1

Let me introduce myself.

I am your patient. I am the King's daughter.
I am your patient. I live under a bridge.
I am your patient. I am governor of the state.
I am your patient. I fry hamburgers at McDonalds.

I am 83 years old next week. I am 17—going on 35.
I am Black. I am Chinese. I am Dutch.
I'm a Muslim. I'm a Buddhist. I'm a Christian.
I'm a woman ... a man; gay ... straight; rich ... poor.

I am fat. I am tall.
I am skinny. I am short.
I shop at Nordstrom. I shop at the House of Thrift.
I drive a Porsche. I ride a bus.

I'm powerful. I'm not.
I'm funny. I'm dull as bones.
I am rebellious. I am sensible.
I am sympathetic. I am negligent.

I am dying. I hurt—bad.
I am expecting my first child. I'm on drugs.
I was shot in the abdomen. I was raped.
I need my teeth fixed. I need my life fixed.

I need you.

I need your knowledge. I need your skill.
I need your respect. I need your attention.
I need my dignity to survive—in addition to my body.
I need to know your name. I need to know you care.

I need to understand what you are talking about.
I need information. I need to make decisions.
I need you to protect my privacy. I need your smile.
I need you to not give up on me when things look discouraging.

When I see you, I need to know I am not just a number.
When I see you, I need to know I am not in this alone.
When I see you, I need to know I am getting first-class care.
When I see you, I need to know I am your most important patient.

I am a free being. I do have the power of choice.
I may come to Loma Linda ... I may go elsewhere.
Are you happy to meet me?
Do you want me to stay?

I am your patient.
Let me introduce myself.

Wil Alexander is a professor in LLUSM department of family medicine and an emeritus professor of relational studies in LLUSR. He received a PhD degree from Michigan State University in 1962. He was founder of the concept of "whole person care" for thousands of medical students and founding director of LLU Center for Spiritual Life and Wholeness. In 1990, he received the LLU Distinguished Service Award.

You have turned my mourning into dancing; you have taken off my sackcloth and clothed me with joy, so that my soul may praise you and not be silent. O Lord my God, I will give thanks to you forever. Psalm 30:11-12, NRSV

Our daughter, Svea, was born on Sunday morning, January 2, 2011. She was delivered three months ahead of schedule and weighed 1 lb. 0.9 oz.

Around Thanksgiving, the perinatal specialist told my wife, Heidi, and me that our pregnancy would need to be delivered much earlier than our April 1 due date. At that time, the idea of a viable birth was something we only dared hope for. Results from another prenatal ultrasound raised concerns. Our radiologist informed us that our baby might have a congenital condition that could shorten her life expectancy to no more than one year.

Further tests over the next several days dismissed the radiologist's diagnosis. By the time of her birth, Svea's restricted growth appeared to be the result of the placenta being abnormally formed, not the result of any significant disorder of her own body's structure or function.

One morning between visits to the neonatal intensive care unit, I read Psalm 30. I looked it up because of a chipper tune that had been repeating itself in my head with the words taken from the above text, "You have turned my mourning into dancing."

Three thousand years of human ingenuity have brought significant successes in mediating the burdens of disease and death for many. But despite the accelerating proliferation of technological adaptations, we human beings continue to experience situations that can shake our confidence in our life's foundations.

A lyricist thousands of miles and tens of centuries removed from our Seattle hospital room captured a sense of unbounded amazement at God's work. I felt that awe alive in my own chest as I beheld my daughter: Impossibly small! Impossibly beautiful!

Jeffrey T. HansPetersen, LLUSM class of 2000, is a family practitioner on Vashon Island, Washington, where he and his family live. Svea turns three years old in 2014.

January 3

I will give you a new heart and put a new spirit within you; I will take the heart of stone out of your flesh and give you a heart of flesh. Ezekiel 36:26, NKJV

From the moment I first entered the world, with only a part of my heart functioning, my world has been one full of hope. Surviving a heart transplant and being surrounded by caring and loving people have given me a positive attitude and a reason to dream. As I sorted through the cards and letters sent to my family at my birth, I witnessed an outflow of warmth, well wishes, and prayers. How did I get through all the illnesses, pain, and differences to be the happy and healthy teenager I am today?

Part of the answer is that I come from many supportive worlds. One of these worlds—the Loma Linda University Medical Center (LLUMC) Transplantation Institute—has served as my second home. It is a place that allows me to be filled with optimism and hope, surrounded by people who care. When I walk in, the receptionist, who has been there since I was born, asks me what I have been doing and how I am.

Over the years, I have been able to get to know most of the staff. Now, every visit feels like a family reunion. The LLUMC Heart Transplant Team taught me how important it is to encourage and support those around me. However, it was also there that I discovered that I was not just like everybody else. I soon learned that, because of my condition, I needed to take care of myself in ways that were not necessary for other people. Nonetheless, this extra caution did not mean that I could not aspire to a successful future. Instead, it taught me I could control my own destiny.

As I have tried to find my own way, my family has always been there, praising and supporting the decisions I have made, from my first steps to joining team sports. When times became difficult due to health issues, my mother would sit next to me; we would touch our index fingers together and she would say, "We are one. Together we can do anything."

I want to be a person who makes a difference, just like the many people who made such a positive and forward-moving impact on my life. I will be a leader, someone who can build a supportive environment as so many others have built for me. I have already started on this journey by volunteering as a coach for my community's basketball team. This position is just the beginning of what I hope I can achieve during my lifetime.

I want to inspire others to live their lives to the fullest and to follow their dreams, just as I am doing. The world around me is a great place, and I am going to live in it employing my fullest potential, as a testimony to that greatest of gifts given to me by another—a new heart.

Matthew Krugler is a communications major at the University of La Verne. He expects to graduate in 2017. This was the author's response to the essay prompt, "The world I come from and how it shapes my dreams/aspirations." He was born on April 18, 1995, and his heart transplant at Loma Linda University Medical Center occurred on May 9, 1995.

Praise the Lord, my soul, and forget not all his benefits—who forgives all your sins and heals all your diseases, who redeems your life from the pit and crowns you with love and compassion, who satisfies your desires with good things so that your youth is renewed like the eagle's. Psalm 103:2-5, NIV

"When I grow up, I will be a scientist!" blurted the five-year-old boy.

"Scientists don't come from the *caseríos*," some pragmatic relatives would remind me. Growing up in the *caseríos*, as the low-income housing projects are called in Puerto Rico, I knew my chances of even attending college were negligible.

When I reflect upon the twists and turns of my amazing journey from the *caseríos* to Loma Linda University School of Medicine (LLUSM), I look beyond my own capabilities and recognize a loving God, guiding me along the way; humble parents who valued education and faith; and a tiny Adventist church that encouraged me to go to college. It takes a church to raise a child!

As a student at the University of Puerto Rico (UPR), scientific research was off my radar until my senior year, when a professor invited me to join her cancer research laboratory. Becoming a scientist was now a reality! Years later, near the end of my PhD degree education at the University of California, Davis, I shared with my pastor the wonders of how God had shaped my life. He then posed a question that would haunt me for years, "Have you ever considered serving at LLUSM?" I replied that I had never been to the school, was not aware of its research programs, and that my dream was to be a scientist in a world-renowned medical research institute.

One evening years later, after coming home from my "dream job" at the Scripps Clinic and Research Institute in La Jolla, California, I received a phone call from two scientist friends who were both being recruited to LLUSM. They told me that the school was looking for a professor with my academic background. I visited to learn more about its mission, research, and teaching needs. This visit deeply impressed and moved me!

While driving back home, I prayed and wondered if God was calling me to give up my "dream job" and come to LLUSM. At the time, I was being considered for highly coveted faculty positions at Scripps and the UPR. My wife and I prayed for guidance, and the answer came soon and in a surprising way. The UPR cancelled the faculty search; and my mentor at Scripps, a world-famous physician-scientist, advised me to seriously ponder the numerous opportunities that LLUSM would offer. Sometime afterward, when the timing was perfect, I was invited to join the faculty of LLUSM and transfer my research program there.

As I reflect upon my 16 years at LLUSM, I am grateful for God's presence and guidance in the midst of the joys, challenges, and perils of academia. The endless opportunities for my family and me to grow professionally, personally, and spiritually; to mentor students from diverse backgrounds; and to serve the institution, the church, and the community have all exceeded our wildest dreams. Often in the evening solitude, I still hear my pastor asking me about serving at LLUSM. I reply: "Yes, and I have learned here the true meaning of a dream job!"

Carlos Casiano, PhD, is a professor in LLUSM departments of basic sciences and medicine and associate director of the Center for Health Disparities and Molecular Medicine. January 4 is when he began working full time at LLU.

January 5

*But those who hope in the L*ORD *will renew their strength. They will soar on wings like eagles; they will run and not grow weary, they will walk and not be faint. Isaiah 40:31, NIV*

I sometimes prayed with my patients in the family medicine clinic, but I had never had a patient ask to pray for me in clinic, until . . .

It had been a long and tiring day in clinic. It seemed as though everyone needed all their medications refilled or forms filled out; or they brought up "by-the-way . . ." and mentioned urgent problems at the end of the visit. I was already running very late when I saw on my schedule that Mrs. Pritchard was my next patient.

In addition to needing follow-up for her diabetes and hypertension, Mrs. Pritchard had survived a major cancer surgery, which had left her with chronic pain and recurrent stomach and bowel symptoms. This was not going to be a short visit. With a sigh, I opened the exam room door, walked in, and greeted Mrs. Pritchard.

I noticed immediately that she was smiling cheerfully, not just with her mouth, but with her eyes as well. She looked completely at peace, in spite of her chronic medical problems and uncertain prognosis. Now that I thought about it, I remembered that she was usually smiling at her visits, but I had no idea what was her source of strength.

"Mrs. Pritchard, you have been through a lot of challenges, yet you have the most beautiful smile," I said. "Can I ask what is helping you cope?"

"Of course, you can ask," she replied. "It is the Lord," she said, brightening even more. "When I first got sick, the Lord and I had some words. But now we have made peace and my prayers and relationship with Him get me through the day. I am so grateful to Him to just be alive. I have been praying for my doctors as well. Would you like me to pray for you now?"

"Yes," I replied, startled.

Taking my hands in her gnarled ones, she prayed the most beautiful, eloquent, and joyful prayer I have ever experienced. Tears welled up in my eyes and fatigue melted away. I found myself smiling often during the rest of clinic. It seemed as though clinic time went by quickly in an atmosphere of peace.

As I drove home that evening, I reflected on the visit with Mrs. Pritchard. She was cheerful even though she had serious medical problems and her long-term survival was uncertain. I had been grumpy because clinic ran late. But here I was, driving home to a nice dinner, which I would enjoy without pain or nausea. I thanked God for the blessing of Mrs. Pritchard.

John K. Testerman, LLUSM class of 1980-B, PhD, is chair and an associate professor in LLUSM department of family medicine. He serves as chairman for the LLUSM spiritual life and wholeness committee.

"Martha, Martha," the Lord answered, "you are worried and upset about many things, but few things are needed—or indeed only one. Mary has chosen what is better, and it will not be taken away from her." Luke 10:41-42, NIV

It was an early morning in a very busy emergency department. I was tired after working several shifts that week but had still signed up to work an extra shift with an attending physician whom I admired. The patient we were seeing was a woman with a two-year history of abdominal pain. Over that time, she had repeated diagnostic tests, multiple consults, and even surgery. It looked as if there was nothing we could truly do to help her today, other than pain control.

As we entered her room, I had a million other things on my mind. I immediately took up a post against the wall to work on discharge paperwork for her, as well as another patient, along with a preliminary attempt at orders for a third patient. Vaguely, I was aware of my attending sitting down by the bed and beginning to engage in what sounded like a very involved conversation about how the patient's life was going in general. "Great," I remember thinking, "we don't have time for this."

I gradually began to tune in the conversation. Her pain had begun slowly and she ignored it at first; then as it increased, she began to search for a diagnosis. As specialist after specialist tried and failed to give an adequate answer, discouragement set in. She had to quit her job as a teacher because of symptoms, and she had also amassed numerous medical bills. Her husband, who was in the room, also expressed frustration and a desperate need for answers.

My attending listened to it all with compassion and empathy, expressing her own regrets that modern medicine had thus far failed to help. The couple admitted they knew there was nothing we could truly do today; they just thought Loma Linda University Medical Center would be their last hope. With the true reason behind their visit in mind, my attending gave them contact information for our outpatient clinics, pain medication, and, most importantly, a prayer for healing and answers.

As we left the room, with the couple's thanks ringing in my ears, my mind no longer dwelled on my paperwork. While I felt as though we had spent forever with them, by looking at the clock, I realized it had been only 15 minutes. I stepped aside into a hallway for a moment to think. What I had just seen went against everything commonly thought in regard to modern medicine—that you have to rush through patients in order to see all of them, that you cannot take time to connect.

The conversation made a significant impact upon our patient, truly addressed her deeper needs, and yet took no more time than seeing any other patient. I confronted my own cynicism and reminded myself that everyone has real concerns, worries, needs, and desires. As I went back to work, with a different perspective, I realized this lesson would make a lasting impact on my life and career. Just as Christ had time for the individual in the midst of the masses, so we, too, must take time to connect with our patients on an individual level.

Molly Estes, LLUSM class of 2013, is an emergency medicine resident at Stanford University Medical Center in California.

January 7

For nothing is impossible with God. **Luke 1:37, NIV (1984)**

While sitting in my rental car in an unknown parking lot in Oregon, I learned a valuable lesson about how philanthropy has the power to change the future and to save lives. I had been employed by Loma Linda University Health (LLUH) for about a year-and-a-half when this experience happened. I always had great respect for Loma Linda University (LLU) and the professionals it produced for the world, but I knew the institution only distantly. However, in my short time as an employee, I realized that I was privileged to serve in a truly special place, a place the Lord designed for a unique calling and mission. I can confidently say LLU is one of the world's little-known gems. It has a rich heritage of making the "impossible" happen.

This particular day, I was visiting carefully selected alumni of LLU, as well as some former grateful patients, to get their feedback and to see if they had an interest in potentially supporting a project.

I had three appointments that morning; two went incredibly well, but one individual felt the plan was too big to accomplish. Thus, contemplating my next visit and knowing the enormity of the tasks needed to complete the vision, I sat quietly and prayerfully until my cell phone shattered the silence.

On the phone was the sweet voice of Jan, a long-term friend of Loma Linda University. She had recently attended a small group where Richard Hart, LLUSM class of 1970, a few others, and I had shared our vision for the future. She said, "Rachelle, I have been thinking about the meeting and the incredible plans Loma Linda has and decided to call and share my thoughts."

She went on to say: "At first, I thought this was too big and improbable; but then I thought about the people who, more than a hundred years ago, made significant sacrifices to start Loma Linda from nothing but a bold vision. To see how lives are saved every day through professionals at home and those we send around the world is nothing less than miraculous."

I was caught up in her every word as she further shared, "I have been thinking that now is my time to stand up and support an incredible vision that will shape the next 100 years at Loma Linda." She then said, "I just wanted to call and let you know that I am committed to help take Loma Linda into the future." My throat caught as I thanked her for her call and expressed my appreciation to her.

She had no idea how much her call and message meant at that specific time. Jan, already a friend, became an inspirational teacher that day. She had experienced first-hand the miracles that happen every day at LLU, and she lit a fire of confidence and encouragement for success that, together with the Lord's leading, can make the "impossible" happen again.

The above text from Luke—"nothing is impossible with God"—rang clear. With friends like Jan, I am confident that LLU will continue to change the future of health care through its alumni, patients, and friends, as they help accomplish its mission, "To Make Man Whole."

Rachelle B. Bussell is vice president of advancement for LLUH. Her husband, Mark, is a 1989 physical therapy graduate from LLUSAHP. January 7 is the date her daughter, Clarissa, started nursing school.

He answered and said, "Whether He is a sinner or not I do not know. One thing I know: that though I was blind, now I see." John 9:25, NKJV

I have been blessed in a profession where God does the healing, and I collect His fee. As an example, after the thaw in the Cold War, an evangelistic team from Oregon traveled to Russia. A beautiful young Russian, Marina, was the talented translator for their meetings. The team was surprised to discover that their translator was blind!

A team member, Ruthie Jacobson, immediately recognized Marina's outstanding talents and imagined what it would be like if Marina could see. Ruthie then rallied an Oregon women's ministry group to help Marina. They went on to raise the necessary funds to bring her to the United States to see if her vision could be improved.

After arriving in Oregon, she was brought to my Salem office for a consultation. She said she had gradually lost her vision at an early age, a cause that was said to be due to cataracts. But she was reluctant to have the cataracts removed, because, in her city, there was only about a 50 percent success rate due to infections and other complications.

Upon examination in our office, she was found to have no other eye diseases except the cataracts. She elected to have the surgery in my surgery center. It was a privilege to remove her dense bilateral cataracts and to replace them, at no charge, with intraocular lenses. God did His healing, and she went from hand motions to 20/20 vision!

After Marina returned home, I received a letter. I will never forget that letter of gratitude and her recounting of how she anxiously awaited to see her husband for the very first time. She wondered what he looked like. She was not disappointed, as she wrote, "He was just as beautiful as I had always imagined!" Now that is what I call collecting His fee!

Gordon Miller, LLUSM class of 1975, practices ophthalmology in Salem, Oregon. He is married to Julie Deegan, a 2007 LLUSPH graduate, and they have three children. He dedicates this devotional to his late father, Donald B. Miller, CME class of 1945.

January 9

Again, the kingdom of heaven is like a merchant looking for fine pearls.
Matthew 13:45, NIV

When I began medical studies at Loma Linda University, I sought "pearls." These were experiences not available anywhere else and that shimmered most attractively. A month's rotation through the proton facility seemed to me a real gem, as it was the only facility of its type on the planet. With just a little finesse, the appropriate permission was obtained and the experience was scheduled. As a student with a keen interest in the physical sciences, the opportunity would not be squandered.

The first day of the rotation proved well worthwhile. There was a tour of the technology behind the therapy, including a room where low-melting temperature alloys were cast into beam-modifying materials. My pearl seemed found!

As an added bonus, working with the resident doctors was quite enjoyable. They were optimistic and, within a very short time, I felt fully accepted. They showed me all sorts of exciting things and explained that they had the best job in the world because "our patients get better." When asked what they meant, they explained that, because radiation oncology often leads to good outcomes, they were blessed with a population of patients who often returned to say thank you, occasionally bringing boxes of candy. It was like a heavenly dream: cutting-edge science, appreciative patients, and delectable treats.

In the midst of this rarified experience, I found myself one day in a room with an attending physician, a resident doctor, a father, and an adult patient with the intellectual capacity of a small child. In spite of being intellectually challenged, the patient was emotionally astute and understood hierarchical social status with exceptional keenness. He was good-natured enough but took fiendish pleasure in passing out insults.

I watched as the attending settled into the more mundane aspects of the clinical visit and began discussing the patient's situation with the father. During this time, the patient looked on through uncomprehending eyes that were becoming increasingly sad and fearful. The prognosis was not great. The worried father asked a question, and the patient instantly recognized that the attending physician, embarrassed, was not in possession of an answer.

With a sudden exuberant expression on his face, the patient broke into a cackle and bellowed, "He doesn't know; find someone smart!" The father and attending both blushed. The room went silent. The patient was devastated, despairingly grappling to comprehend his blunder. To this day I remember the color and intricate thread patterns in the carpet. I did not dare look up.

Out of the corner of my eye, I caught the attending physician slip his arm around the patient, look the father square on, and heard him say, "My friend is absolutely correct." The patient's face burst with radiance. He was no longer sad and scared; he was correct and now a friend of an important person!

It then occurred to me that I had been hunting for pearls of the wrong type—and demanding rarity. Real pearls of kindness are not rare at Loma Linda University. They are the gems that shimmer in the setting of the University's educational endeavors.

Paul Herrmann, LLUSM class of 2000, PhD, is an associate professor in LLUSM department of pathology and human anatomy and in LLUSAHP department of clinical laboratory science.

I will say of the LORD, "He is my refuge and my fortress, my God, in whom I trust." Psalm 91:2, NIV

We were serving at Yuka Hospital, a very remote institution in western Zambia, during the time when Rhodesia (now Zimbabwe) declared its independence from England. Zambia's economy primarily relied on the importing/exporting of goods via Rhodesia. However, due to their Unilateral Declaration of Independence (UDI), the international community attempted to crush Rhodesia with a trading embargo—creating a "blockade." Subsequently, most of our staples and supplies, including fuel, were airlifted in from Tanzania.

Because of this political situation, our personal and hospital supplies became very difficult to obtain and were always unsure. Prior to the UDI, we had become accustomed to the convenience of electricity in the evenings; propane for our home stove and hospital autoclave; and fuel for the generator, water pump, and vehicles. We had sugar and flour, matches, flashlight batteries, candles, and many other items. We had really been spoiled!

As supplies of these "essentials" dried up for periods of four-to-nine months at a time, we carefully conserved our meager supplies. Crystal, my wife, transitioned back to a wood stove for cooking, and when the propane was completely exhausted, we closed down our autoclave. All scheduled surgeries were cancelled; our few sterile supplies were reserved, and eventually used only for emergency cases.

Then, one Sabbath afternoon, I was called to see a full-term, pregnant leprosy patient who was in labor. She had a living fetus, but it was failing to progress. A Cesarean section was needed for a favorable outcome. What to do? We decided to move ahead and do an immediate C-section while the sun was still shining (our lighting source)—but without the luxury of sterile gowns, drapes, or instruments (we still had a few sterile gloves).

Pausing first, as usual, to send a petition to our Heavenly Father, asking for His care and blessing on this event, we administered a spinal anesthetic, laid the patient on the operating table, and then scrubbed her abdomen in preparation for the incision. All our unsterile instruments were laid out on a metal table, doused with a generous splash of alcohol, and then ignited (treating our eyes to a spectacle, even if we knew it was questionable sterilization).

My assistant and I put on our hats and masks, scrubbed our hands and forearms with (nonpotable) tap water, dried them with the suds still on, and gloved up. We walked to the table, barefooted and bare-chested, and proceeded with the C-section.

God blessed us with a healthy Sabbath baby. Postoperatively, we prudently covered the mother with our available second-generation antibiotics, and she recovered free of infection or other complications. We thank God for this and many other experiences that demonstrated His care over us. We thank Him for those we were privileged to serve during a difficult era.

Charles L. Wical, CME class of 1960, is a retired anesthesiologist and was an LLUSMAA 1991 Honored Alumnus. He served for 15 years at various hospitals and clinics in Africa. He and his wife, Crystal, live in Prescott, Arizona. January 10 is Crystal's birthday.

January 11

Jesus gave way to tears. John 11:35, NWT

It wasn't all right. My father thought it would be and wrote that in his *Morning Rounds* devotional. But the cancer came back, this time with a vengeance. What had originally been confined to his kidney spread to his aortic lymph nodes, esophagus, clavicle, brain, adrenal gland, lungs, liver, and pancreas. That last cancer was the official cause of death.

After his surgeries, my father had been on units where patients went to recover and return home. This hospital stay was on the unit "where people go to die," he stated to my mother as he was wheeled from the emergency department (ED). He knew this would be his final hospitalization.

He drifted in and out of consciousness for the next couple of days. He had made his wishes known to my mother, the ED staff, and his doctors: He wanted to be comfortable, even if that meant he wouldn't be alert. For so long he had masked his pain but not anymore. He knew the end might be excruciating and if there was a way to avoid most of that, it was worth not being able to interact with others.

My mother, brother, and I wanted those last couple days to cram in things we meant to say but hadn't since we took our cues from my father. If we said them, the elephant in the room would finally be recognized for what it was and the inevitable—his impending death—might come up. My father had a wonderful attitude and fought long and hard. If we talked about how bad things actually were, about what was going to happen, would he give up? Would he die faster? We didn't know and we didn't take the chance of finding out.

We didn't want him to spend his final days in agony, so, as much as it saddened us not to be able to talk to him, we knew he had made the right decision. Finally, the pain got so bad that the doctors were going to administer the strongest pain meds. We knew this would make him unconscious for the rest of his life. He knew it too. This was our last chance to talk with him—our chance to say goodbye.

My father refused pain meds for hours so he could be alert. When my brother and I arrived at the hospital that day, my parents had already said their "I love you's" to each other. Then it was our turn. We noticed tears in my father's eyes. Other people thought it was from the pain; we knew better. He never cried from the pain before; he wouldn't be starting now. No, the tears were tears of sadness, of saying goodbye to his beloved children. They were a father's tears.

In today's text, Jesus is crying over the death of His good friend Lazarus. Jesus knew that He would soon raise Lazarus from the dead, so why was He crying? He, of all people, should not be. Yet crying is a very human emotion, and Jesus was fully human, besides being fully Divine. He was sad for His friends as they mourned the loss of their brother. God, Jesus' Father, must have been saddened to see His Son grieve, although He, too, knew Lazarus would soon be alive again.

God is also our Father. When we experience sadness and grief is He also not sad for us? He knows that someday our loved one will be raised again, but He still aches for His children as they mourn. If Jesus cried over the death of His friend, how much more must God cry over our grief? The tears in His eyes are a Father's tears.

Marci Weismeyer is the daughter of Richard (Dick) and Carol Weismeyer. For more on the backstory refer to the April 9 Morning Rounds devotional. January 11, 2011, is the day Marci and her brother, Michael, said goodbye to their father; he died the next day. Dick was the executive director of university relations for LLU and started working full time for LLU in 1966. Carol works for LLUSM dean's office.

God is our refuge and strength, an ever-present help in trouble. Therefore we will not fear, though the earth give way and the mountains fall into the heart of the sea, though its waters roar and foam and the mountains quake with their surging. Psalm 46:1-3, NIV

After many long hours in the operating room, I walk down the dimly lit hallway of an austere Haitian hospital. I have to carefully watch my step because patients are everywhere. A few are on mattresses, most are on pieces of cardboard, while some are lying on nothing at all. This is *evening rounds*, a few days after the Port-au-Prince earthquake on January 12, 2010, that claimed the lives of more than 200,000 people. Few, if any, moments in world history have witnessed more orthopaedic emergencies at one time and in one place.

The scene is surreal. Patients line the hallways, fill every corner of the corridors and patios, and cover the grounds outside the building. Most are waiting for surgery; some have already been operated on. There are people of all ages who have lost limbs and sustained crush injuries and fractures of nearly every bone in the body, including the femur, tibia, ankle, and elbow. And, in the midst of all this, a few newborn babies, who have yet to experience the dawn of their first full day of life.

I have been operating for more than 90 hours, catching just a few moments of sleep between cases by resting my head on a duffle bag in the corner of the operating room. Comfort and corporal desires are not of concern. Only a small portion of all the cases have been completed. I continually remind myself that this apocalyptic circumstance is not a disorienting, hallucinatory dream.

There are no notes to write. No orders to change. In fact, there are no charts. Pre-op and post-op patients are differentiated by a piece of masking tape on the forehead. Pre-op patients read OR1 or OR2, depending upon their urgency, and post-op patients are marked with a date and abbreviated title of their operation. Wound care orders are written on the dressings. And, in spite of limited availability of pain medication, very few are complaining.

Under these adverse conditions, the beauty of the human spirit is brought forth, and, in spite of horrific tragedy, God's love is felt. In pursuit of survival, life is boiled down to its most simple elements. All of the things that normally cause us stress and worry seem trivial and silly. In these first several days after the earthquake, money is meaningless, banks are closed, gas stations are inoperable, restaurants are giving away food, and people are helping people.

Each of these patients has a story involving loss of life, suffering, and tragedy. One patient lies with her Bible open to Psalm 46. And at the end of the hall, a woman lying on the floor, who has been operated on for a severe pelvic fracture, begins singing, "How Great Thou Art."

Scott Nelson, LLUSM class of 1996, is an assistant professor in LLUSM department of orthopaedic surgery. In 2010, he was LLU Alumnus of the Year and the LLUSM commencement speaker, and in 2011, he was awarded the Outstanding Contribution to the Community Award by the San Bernardino County Medical Society.

January 13

And the prayer of faith shall save the sick. James 5:15, KJV

The reality that I was becoming paralyzed due to a condition called Guillain-Barré disease was frightening. I was unable to stand or turn over in bed, had difficulty swallowing, and my condition was rapidly getting worse. While some cases of this condition are mild with a rapid complete recovery, it was evident early on that I did not have a mild form of this disease.

When I was nearly completely paralyzed, I requested special prayer and anointing, hoping for a miraculous healing. The prayers were a blessing, as prayers always are, but I continued to deteriorate and the days and nights in the ICU seemed long and unbearable. I was uncomfortable, required respiratory support by a ventilator, and could not change my position in bed. My inability to move seemed like eternal torture and I wondered if I would ever get better. While most of my nurses were very helpful, considerate, and moved me when I became uncomfortable, it seemed, however, that the nurse I usually had at night was *always* exhausted. She even remarked how nice it would be to just lie in bed and rest and felt it was unnecessary for me to be moved frequently.

For the next few weeks while still on a ventilator, I seemed to have no improvement and was getting worse rather than better. One morning I felt that I was not getting enough air even though the ventilator seemed to be functioning. I had the sense I was going to die—and I hoped the end would come soon. A nurse told me to not be so nervous.

Shortly thereafter, it was observed that I was cyanotic and unconscious. Providentially for me, the surgery team was on morning rounds in the ICU when this occurred. They immediately corrected the problem which was an obstructed airway. When I awakened from unconsciousness, I couldn't see and had a terrible headache due to lack of oxygen, but I was aware of several people around me who seemed to be excited about something! In a few minutes my vision returned and my headache went away, but of course the reality of being totally paralyzed was still present.

I believe the special prayer and anointing service by the ministers saved my life because the respiratory malfunction occurred when the surgery team was on morning rounds in the ICU rather than at night when the drowsy night nurse was on duty. If the malfunction had occurred at night I probably would not have survived, or if I had, I would likely be in a vegetative state.

In the course of a few months, I made a slow recovery to full time activity and employment. My prayers and those of the ministers were answered, but not in the manner I had expected. We should be thankful every day that our prayers are answered even though sometimes they are answered differently than the way we request or hope for.

Donald Peterson, CME class of 1947, is an emeritus professor in LLUSM department of neurology and was previously an associate professor in LLUSM department of basic sciences. He received the LLU Teacher of the Year Award in 1972, the Macpherson Clinical Teacher of the Year Award in 1974, and the LLU Distinguished Service Award in 2007. This experience occurred in 1964 when he was 42 years old.

There will be the shout of command, the archangel's voice, the sound of God's trumpet, and the Lord himself will come down from heaven. Those who have died believing in Christ will rise to life first; then we who are living at that time will be gathered up along with them in the clouds to meet the Lord in the air. And so we will always be with the Lord. So then, encourage one another with these words.
1 Thessalonians 4:16-18, GNT

I was on my way to clinic with a thousand things on my mind. How could I see all these patients on time and get to my next appointment? I had so many tasks that had to be done before the next day.

The first patient on my schedule was Don. He had jaundice and had been diagnosed with cancer of the pancreas. His particular cancer was one of the more difficult ones to treat. However, because the scans did not show any evidence of spread yet, I suggested that he might have a chance to be cured with surgery.

As we began talking, he told me that he was 58 years old and had a lovely wife, as well as three children who had all just finished college. Obviously, he wanted to be cured of his cancer; but he added that if he ended up dying of this dreaded disease, he had lived a full life.

Wow! I walked out of his room amazed by his optimistic spirit. The problems that I thought I had before I came to clinic seemed artificial and superficial. And they were.

Part of my job over the years has been to take care of thousands of patients with cancer. Many people have asked me how I can keep from being depressed by this. Actually, not only are cancer patients not depressing, but also they are some of the most inspirational people in the world. Sure, many of them end up not winning their battle with this disease, and that always hurts. Yet, I continue to be amazed at how courageous and altruistic they are.

I cannot count how many times they have told me things similar to what Don said: I have lived a great life, and I am the luckiest man alive. Is there any way that I can be in a research trial so that I can help others who may get this disease? Can I assist with a support group to help others with cancer?

As I said before, there are many that do not win the battle; but so often they have figured out what the really important things in life are. In addition, many of these patients have found true comfort and rest in a Higher Being.

So the next time you think you have problems, come with me to one of my clinics; you will come away from it realizing three things:

1. No matter how many problems you think you have, you have nothing to complain about. You do not have cancer.
2. You do not have to wait until you have a life-threatening disease to discover the important things in life. Go home and hug your spouse and kids today.
3. We can thank God for the hope that we will see all of our friends and patients again someday.

Mark Reeves, LLUSM class of 1992, PhD, is director of LLU Cancer Center and an associate professor in LLUSM departments of surgery and basic sciences. January 14 is the birthday of his wife, Michelle, LLUSM class of 1986.

January 15

Seek the LORD and his strength, seek his presence continually.
1 Chronicles 16:11, NRSV

During my intern year at the VA Loma Linda Healthcare System, I had an inpatient named Mr. W. I rounded on this young Iraqi Freedom veteran every day for an entire month. Mr. W had been given opiates while in military service and had become addicted to them after he was discharged. This addiction led to his falling into the wrong crowd when he returned to the States. But he had completed a drug rehab program and had been "clean" for a few months before he was involved in an accident.

Mr. W became a "hit-and-run" victim as he walked along a road. Some hours after the accident occurred, an anonymous Good Samaritan found him unconscious in a bush next to the road and called 911. He was taken to the hospital and admitted to the ICU. During his first night, he had three cardiac arrests.

Some days later, he was found to have compartment syndrome in his left leg and had an emergency above-the-knee amputation. He also had "road rash" all up and down one side of his body. After surviving his stay in the ICU, Mr. W was transferred to our internal medicine team at the VA.

It was a long, uphill battle for him from the start. It was difficult to wean Mr. W off his IV pain pump after the amputation. He also complained of depression and posttraumatic stress disorder. Due to the antibiotics Mr. W was receiving to treat his road rash skin infections, any prescription of antidepressants was contraindicated.

I discussed the plan for his care and tried to encourage him on a daily basis. I noticed his mood shifted as he battled depression after the amputation. His facial expressions and tone of voice would change when he was having a bad day. Weeks after the amputation, my patient would state that he had severe pain and would plead for more IV opiates for pain relief.

His family was often at his bedside when I pre-rounded on him and as I encouraged him to get off the opiates. Toward the end of my rotation, I did notice a Bible at his bedside; but, regretfully, I never took the time to talk to him about it until my last day while on call.

I was on my way to the emergency department for an admission around 9 p.m. and decided to say goodbye. I went to Mr. W's room and started talking to him. We talked about this and that; but at the very end of our conversation, Someone was prodding me in the back of my mind to pray with him. I offered, and he immediately said, "Yes."

I said a 30-second prayer and, afterward, looked up to say goodbye. As I raised my head, I could not believe my eyes! Mr. W had a bright beaming smile and his face seemed to be glowing with joy and peace. My quick prayer had done more for this patient than all the antibiotics, opiates, and bedside counseling he had received during his entire hospital stay!

This incident demonstrated to me the healing power of prayer. I learned first-hand that our requests to the Great Physician go far beyond man's trivial attempts at physical healing.

Jonathan Zumwalt, LLUSM class of 2012, is a resident in dermatology at LLUMC. His wife, Brittany, is a pediatric nurse at LLUCH. January 15 is the author's birthday.

January 16

Then their father Israel said to them, "If it must be, then do this: Put some of the best products of the land in your bags and take them down to the man as a gift—a little balm and a little honey, some spices and myrrh, some pistachio nuts and almonds." Genesis 43:11, NIV

On January 16, 2001, as the plane banked to line up with the Tirana runway, curiosity overcame dread. I looked out and saw ragged peaks looming over city sprawl. Albania! What had we done?

I had earned a late-life law degree; only six weeks before that graduation, my doctor husband, Jack, LLUSM class of 1962, and I attended a Christian Legal Society meeting in Washington, DC. There we met an American lawyer, Bob Baker, who was on a mission to find a physician with time to sacrifice for the sake of a small Christian clinic in Albania's capital. I suspect "Someone" arranged to seat Bob across from my husband, the only nonlawyer in the room, because Bob had a problem: the ABC Clinic in Albania was required to have on staff a physician with either American or British training. One such person was on the way but could not arrive until October. Would Jack fill in until then? Bob felt sure that he had been led to Jack; Jack was persuaded that God had invited him into a faith adventure. I was aghast.

Only 15 years released from the grip of Enver Hoxha, the insane Communist dictator, Albania was in turmoil: impoverished, crime-ridden, and with a vestigial infrastructure. And it was a cold place; we would live in the unrelenting chill that penetrates unheated, concrete-block apartments.

Did I want to spend almost a year in Albania? Well, no. But there was that "coincidental" luncheon. We had been missionaries before, called by an official committee and sponsored by our well-organized church. This call, however, was a venture bolstered only by our prayerful conclusion that God wanted us to work in Tirana with a group of Evangelical Christians.

We knew we seemed alien on that first Sabbath in our "own" church ("rich doctor from the U.S. and his snooty lawyer wife"). Determined to be friendly, we discovered young English learners whose curiosity overcame their preconceptions. A sense of purpose ignited, and I pled that God would lead me to the arduous spiritual project for which I had surely been called. I had so much to offer . . . all that education!

One day there came a question I could not escape: "What do you like best about Albania?" ("Best? Is there anything of value here, Lord?") And then I remembered Jacob. When Jacob reluctantly sent his sons into Egypt to buy food, it was because famine stalked the desiccated Middle East. What was left that could be offered to the man who controlled Egypt's abundance? Take "some of the best products of the land . . . as a gift—a little balm and a little honey . . . some pistachio nuts and almonds." In the midst of deficiency and drought, Jacob found, and shared, something valuable.

Thus, that became my assignment: find the worth; learn to appreciate and praise; and practice loving a broken country and its confused new Christians. It was not glamorous and had nothing to showcase the "gifts" I wanted to present to God. But He wanted my heart, not my law degree. Slowly I learned to find and give balm and honey: encouragement. Our October goodbye was my reward: "The best thing you did was to like us."

Sharan Bennett, JD, was president of LLU Medical Auxiliary from 2009 to 2010. She and her husband, Jack Bennett, LLUSM class of 1962, have four children. January 16, 2001, is the date they arrived in Tirana, Albania.

January 17

And he laid his hands on every one of them, and healed them. **Luke 4:40, KJV**

A young Loma Linda University School of Medicine student attended a conference in San Francisco and heard an impressive lecture by a physician from Harvard School of Medicine. The speaker seemed to have a deep appreciation for the concept that humans have a triune nature. A person is made up of a physical body and also has unique mental capabilities. But more than just body and mind, humans have the dimension of a soul or spirit. To ignore this component is to miss treating the whole person.

A chance meeting with the speaker in the lunch line provided an opportunity to chat. The speaker asked the student where she was attending school. Almost apologetically, considering the speaker's credentials, she said, "I'm from Loma Linda University."

The lecturing doctor's expression lit up as she said: "Oh my goodness! How fortunate you are! Do you realize that you are at one of the few institutions in the world that teaches you how to treat the whole patient? They have a Christian perspective, and that makes their graduates generally more caring for the person behind each diagnosis!"

What does it really mean to be in the ministry of healing? So much of a doctor's practice can feel like a mundane repetition of handling so much of the same kinds of problems, day in and day out. In trying to truly hear the patient, much of a visit can consist of just being there and grieving with patients who are in pain—not the pain of the body, which often is the easier type to deal with, but the pain of the soul.

We do not really have ointments, pills, or surgical procedures to deal with the agony of a patient who has just lost a child or a spouse. We do not have diagnostic tests or scans for loneliness in a solitary orphan without kin during the holidays, or for despair in those who cannot afford the best medicine for their chronic illnesses.

But somewhere, somehow, without even knowing it, we linger a bit longer in the exam room with these hurting patients of ours and just listen to them and empathize with their situations. Sometimes we are frustrated, feeling that we are making no difference in near-hopeless cases. But the presence of a caring Christian doctor at the side of a patient in desperate straits seems to bring healing to the spirit, though perhaps not right away, and certainly not in every case. In taking these cases home with us, and including them in our evening prayers, we offer them what the world cannot give.

The young medical student stood just a bit taller after this affirmation from the impressive lecturer who wished that she, too, could have had the type of training that recognizes that each patient is a whole person.

Ron Evans, LLUSM class of 1982, has practiced ophthalmology in Placerville, California, since 1986. January 17 is the birthday of his daughter, April Evans, LLUSM class of 2011.

January 18

Let us be concerned for one another, to help one another to show love and to do good. Hebrews 10:24, GNT

In the busy emergency department of the Children's Hospital, I stepped around nurses and residents and entered my next patient's room. I found a 13-year-old boy who looked small enough to be 10. He was on his back sitting slightly upright with his hands over his belly. He was yellow.

I introduced myself, and he smiled weakly and said hello. I explained my role to his parents, who spoke little English, and, with their approval, started asking him questions. "Hello, how are you feeling?"

"Not that great," he responded.

"Can you tell me what's going on?"

"My stomach hurts, and my eyes and skin have been turning yellow," he replied.

"How long has this been going on?"

"Almost a week," he said. I continued asking all of the questions I had learned over the past three years as a medical student. We admitted him several hours later for hepatitis of unknown etiology.

We ran the full battery of tests; every single one was negative. That is not uncommon, I was told. Since I was the student who admitted him, I had the privilege of checking on him each morning. His mother was always by his side, and his father came when he could. Through the translator, we explained to his parents what we thought was going on.

I watched him get progressively worse over the next three days while we did everything we could think of against an enemy we could not identify. His liver was failing; he was dying, and we did not know why. Because Loma Linda University Children's Hospital does not do liver transplants, it was decided to transfer him by ambulance to another children's hospital (where he quickly became number one on the national transplant list).

The transport team hooked him up, strapped him in, and wheeled him downstairs. "Sorry, Dad, there's only room for one parent in the ambulance," the transport team instructed him. "Mom, you can go, but Dad, you'll have to drive yourself. Do you have the directions we printed for you? Good. Any questions? No? See you there, then."

The father and I stood in the parking lot and watched the ambulance drive away with his wife and dying son inside. As I searched for something to say, silent tears rolled down the father's cheeks. He told me he could not remember how to get to his car. I started to give him directions about how he needed to go back through the hospital, but realized I probably could not follow them myself. "I'll walk you there, okay?" We rode the elevator up to the main floor in silence.

In the hospital foyer, he said he knew how to get to the parking lot from there. I put my hand on his shoulder and said, "They'll take good care of him." I offered my hand to him, but he reached out and hugged me, leaving a few moist tear spots on my short white coat. "Thank you for everything," he said. Then he smiled, turned, and walked out the door.

Ryan Eggers, LLUSM class of 2014, is in the combined MD/MA bioethics degree program. He is from Whidbey Island, Washington. He graduated from Walla Walla University with a BSE degree in civil engineering. He was president of his LLUSM sophomore class. He met his wife on January 18, 2008.

January 19

You are the light of the world. A city on a hill cannot be hidden. Neither do people light a lamp and put it under a bowl. Instead they put it on its stand, and it gives light to everyone in the house. In the same way, let your light shine before men, that they may see your good deeds and praise your Father in heaven.
Matthew 5:14-16, NIV (1984)

The United States health-care system is undergoing one of the most monumental changes of any industry in its history. While the new extended coverage of health care is certainly going to alter the nation, the spirit with which it is administered does not have to evolve adversely with it.

One of the main reasons I was drawn to Loma Linda University 17 years ago was its Christ-centered mission, "To Make Man Whole." Where in today's working world can you go and openly declare your devotion to your Savior and offer yourself up in His service?

I have witnessed and received the blessed compassion and aid of "angels on earth" who demonstrate Christ-like love to those in need. From the curing of my son's leukemia, the successful brain tumor operation of my niece, the treatment of my brother-in-law's heart condition, the birth of my grandson, and everything in between, I have been completely entwined in the loving care of many individuals. Truly, when "ye have done it unto one of the least of these my brethren, ye have done it unto me" (Matthew 25:40, NKJV).

It is this sincere Christ-focused service that sets this organization apart from the world now and into the future. The strength of any organization is the people who represent it. So important to the success of Loma Linda is the heart of its people. From the board and senior leadership, to the doctors and nurses and all the clinical support staff, to all the remaining administrative support staff and departments, each plays an important role in the success of this institution. Everyone here can and does make a difference in the patient care experience.

If each individual harbors a genuine concern for the welfare of his fellow being, in whatever capacity, be it patient or fellow employee, everyone who sets foot on this campus will feel that spirit of love permeate the very walls of this institution. Anyone who enters the doors will sense a difference in the atmosphere of the environment, as he or she seeks assistance.

The visitors or patients may not be able to put their finger on it, but the feeling will be noticeable. It will be tangible. A feeling of love, peace, and caring will embrace them like the warmth of a down comforter on a cold winter's night. Such will be the condition when each of us exhibits this love for our brothers and sisters.

No doubt, tough times are ahead of us. But with the help of our Lord and Savior, Jesus Christ, we can make it through. We can make a difference in the lives of others, no matter where we serve in this organization. Let us each decide today to make a difference—that we will engage in the great cause of doing good. Let us be kinder, more loving, more forgiving, and more Christ-like. If we do this with a desire to serve, we will find peace and happiness in our own lives. Then it may be said, as in the verse above, that others will "see your good deeds and praise your Father in heaven." May it ever be so with us is my hope, prayer, desire, and sincere commitment.

Troy Holmes is vice president of contracting for LLUAHSC and an assistant professor in LLUSPH department of health policy and management.

January 20

Be kind to one another, tenderhearted, forgiving one another, as God in Christ forgave you. Ephesians 4:32, ESV

Despite the late time and her confusion (which was manifested daily), she smiled, but her voice seemed strange. As I looked closer into her eyes, I was stunned to see a clarity that I had not seen for weeks. I apologized for the lateness of the hour; after all, it was two hours since her evening medications. "How are you doing?" I asked.

She turned toward my voice and smiled again, a smile that I had come to know well. It was the same gentle smile that had been captured for posterity in the Women's Army Corps black and white 8" x 10" portrait that hung on her bedroom wall to my left. I should know, as I had commented on the photo, which showed her as a lovely 20-something-year-old carefree woman, many years ago.

In a halting voice she noted, after staring at me for almost a minute, "I think I may have been good to you."

While serving patients, I have certainly heard many utterances—some kind, some not. I answered carefully, "What makes you say that?"

She continued as if I had not spoken: "I think I was kind to you, wasn't I?" She frowned and looked expectantly at me as if my answer had great importance.

Nonplussed, I replied, "I believe you have been kind to me."

She relaxed back onto her bed and again smiled, "I believe I was. At least I allowed you to go to school."

Starting to have an idea of where this was going, I replied quietly, "Yes, you certainly did."

Looking satisfied, she replied, "Well, look at you now—a doctor! You did well."

It was my turn to smile, "Yes, ma'am, I think I did."

She closed her eyes and relaxed. Before my examination was over, she had slipped into a comfortable sleep. And, despite the hour, I called her daughter to update her on her mother's condition.

Her daughter was absolutely mortified and apologetic when I relayed to her our strange conversation, but I was not insulted. She quickly realized that I was more interested in who her mother thought that I was. Her daughter conveyed that her mother had been born in rural Georgia and told stories of social injustices and racism toward people of color during her childhood prior to the family's moving to California in the 1950s.

I felt grateful for this insight into the life of a patient whom I had been privileged to care for—insight to which I ordinarily may not have been privy. My patient died in her sleep less than two weeks later, those clear green eyes closed forever.

Gayle V. Mitchell, LLUSM class of 1997, practices internal medicine in Los Angeles, California. January 20, 2014, is Martin Luther King Jr. Day.

January 21

And they brought young children to him, that he should touch them . . . and [Jesus] said unto them, Suffer the little children to come unto me, and forbid them not: for of such is the kingdom of God. Mark 10:13-14, KJV

It was my first night volunteering in the neonatal intensive care unit. It was quiet, in spite of the bustle of activity. As I walked toward the charge nurse, announcing that I was the new "cuddler" assigned to the Saturday night shift to help soothe any of the babies who needed holding, a look of relief washed over her face. She grabbed my arm and quickly took me to the bedside of a beautiful baby girl.

"You are just in time," the nurse said to me. "This is Sydney. She has been shaking and crying all evening without any respite. Put on a gown and hold her if you like; maybe you can help her calm down."

As I did so, the nurse began to explain Sydney's medical condition. At first glance, I was puzzled because she looked healthy and full term. She had been lying in a crib, unlike the other premature newborns beside her—some in incubators and some on ventilators. But the nurse then told me that Sydney, born to a mother addicted to heroin, was now experiencing extreme withdrawals in spite of the slow detoxification process. I was shocked that the nurses actually had to administer methadone in order to safely wean Sydney from the drugs. The nurse then told me that the mother rarely came in to see her. This sweet, precious angel was alone and in agony.

As I picked her up, gently swaddled her, and rocked her in my arms, tears streamed down my face. I sat in the chair and held her tightly to stop the shaking. My heart raced with prayers, and upon instinct I began to softly sing the song "Amazing Grace." The sound of my voice soothed her and her cries subsided. She wrapped her little hand around my finger tightly and would not let go. Every time I whispered her name, her eyes fluttered and she looked up at me. I sat with her for my entire shift, letting her rest within my arms.

This routine went on for a few weeks. Every time I arrived for my shift, I was happy to see "my" girl, and the nurses were happy to see me.

I realized that although I have not become a physician and am unable to help in the medical capacities that I so deeply desire, I am still a healer. The simplicity of human touch, warmth, and closeness provides comfort and wholeness. My prayers for this precious child of God and the soothing melodies that I sang over her may do more than I might have initially expected for her healing, growth, and overall well-being.

Several weeks later, I saw Sydney's mother come onto the unit, and everything within me wanted to be angry and questioning. Instead, I greeted her with a warm smile; and as I watched her pick up her baby girl, my heart filled with compassion and any judgment melted away into empathy and hope.

Through this experience, I learned never to underestimate the power of a gentle touch, as well as the effect of time spent simply *being* with another. And, regardless of how unforgiveable someone's decisions or actions may seem, they too are human—with the same basic needs of love, forgiveness, and care.

Sydney taught me how to love without words.

Narges L. Horriat is a 2011 graduate of Azusa Pacific University. January 21 is the day this story occurred.

Therefore, if anyone is in Christ, he is a new creation. **2 Corinthians 5:17, NKJV**

She came to our lifestyle center on the verge of a crisis. Morbidly obese, hypertensive, arthritic, diabetic, and with heart failure, she knew she would not live much longer if something did not change—drastically!

Leann could barely walk from her bedroom to the car in her garage. Each time she did, it would take about 10 minutes of heavy breathing to recover. On Sabbaths, she would drive to church an hour early in order to secure the parking spot next to the door. Otherwise, she would not have been able to make it inside.

With pleading eyes, she looked across the desk at me, searching for answers to her problems. I did what I have made it my habit to do with each person I treat: I prayed with Leann, asking the Great Physician to take her situation in His hands and work out His will in her life as she cooperated with Him. Then we developed a plan.

Within a couple of days of simple poultices on her knees, her arthritis pain resolved. A whole-food, plant-based diet began the process of weight, glucose, and blood pressure control. Time outdoors in the fresh air and sunshine improved her mood and encouraged further healing.

During the first couple of days at our lifestyle center, Leann had difficulty getting from her room to the dining room for meals, but she made it with the assistance of her cane. After a few days, she ventured out the front door of the center and walked a lap under the veranda. The following day she made a single lap around the parking lot. As the days progressed, she began to walk more laps around the parking lot, laps around the lifestyle center, and then forays down the road.

By the time Leann had been with us for more than a month, she was walking over two miles at a time, and without a cane! At the same time, her arthritis pain was resolved, her blood sugars were under control, her blood pressure was markedly improved, she had lost 30 pounds, and she was off all medications!

The Great Physician transformed Leann's body, and this body transformation mirrored the spiritual transformation He was working in her life—the same transformation He desires for you and me. We are all suffering under the fatal disease of sin; but God offers us healing, strength, and victory if only we will work in His strength.

Leann would never have improved had she not made the effort each day and then increased her effort as her strength increased. Neither will we. Without the Great Physician, any effort she made would be useless, and so it is with us. "The secret of success is the union of divine power with human effort. Those who achieve the greatest results are those who rely most implicitly upon the Almighty Arm" (Ellen G. White, *Patriarchs and Prophets*, p. 509).

The Great Physician is still alive and has a simple remedy for your fatal condition. Trust in Him, cooperate with Him, and you, too, will be transformed.

Mark Sandoval, LLUSM class of 2005, practices lifestyle medicine at Uchee Pines Institute in Seale, Alabama. He was the recipient of the Wil Alexander Whole Person Care Award in 2005.

January 23

And the King will answer and say to them, "Assuredly, I say to you, inasmuch as you did it to one of the least of these My brethren, you did it to Me."
Matthew 25:40, NKJV

I paused in the midst of the operation and looked at the resident doctor beside me, momentarily caught off guard by his comment. "Why are we wasting our time, and taxpayer money, operating on this kid? Wouldn't it be kinder to just let him get aspiration pneumonia and die? I think it would be a much more responsible thing to do."

I looked down at the twisted little body on the operating table. We had finished an anti-reflux operation and were creating a feeding gastrostomy for this little boy, who was severely neurologically impaired. He had been born with a genetic disorder that doomed him to a near-vegetative state and a short expected life span. His uncoordinated swallowing was making it difficult for him to take in the formula that his mother patiently tried to feed him.

All these conditions, combined with frequent vomiting, had left him very thin and emaciated. His spasticity had caused his arms and legs to become markedly contracted, and his spine twisted with scoliosis. The small patient could not even appreciate the taste of the little bit of formula he was actually able to swallow.

This poor boy would never be able to play hide and seek, go to kindergarten, ride a bicycle, or enjoy flying a kite. He certainly would never be a productive member of society; instead, he would require a large amount of expensive medical support. In fact, he probably would not even be able to respond, in any sociable way, to the ministrations of the health-care team, or even his mother.

I briefly considered those facts, realizing exactly what prompted the resident's questions and comment. I then thought of the boy's mother, who was fully aware of her child's severe limitations but who had chosen to devote her life to caring for his needs. I knew that doing this operation would not only make feeding safer for the child, but would also make the process infinitely easier for his mother. In essence, it was as if this one operation was for the benefit of two patients.

And then I was reminded of the words of Jesus, "Inasmuch as you did it to one of the least of these." With those simple words, Jesus charged us with the responsibility of caring for all God's children, regardless of material worth or social value. Sometimes, it is obvious who needs help, such as the twisted child on my operating table, or the homeless teenager in the park.

But sometimes the need, while just as real, is not quite so apparent. Individuals with a spiritual or emotional void may not outwardly demonstrate their inner distress, but on the inside they may be crying for a sense of purpose, a mentor, or even just a friend. May each of us realize that everyone we meet may be in need and that they merit being treated with all the love and respect that a child of God deserves.

Don Moores, LLUSM class of 1987, is an associate professor in LLUSM departments of surgery and pediatrics, and is head of the pediatric surgery division at LLUMC.

And he said unto them, The sabbath was made for man, and not man for the sabbath. Mark 2:27, KJV

Shabbat Shalom! Late every Friday afternoon, as I gather my books and papers to head home at the end of the week, I receive this parting greeting from my colleague Steven M. Yellon, PhD. Steve, a fellow faculty member, is a world-renowned neuroendocrinologist and member of the conservative Jewish faith. Even when he is away at a scientific meeting on the East Coast or overseas, Steve calls with a *Shabbat Shalom* for a peaceful and restful Sabbath with God. A blessing, *Shabbat Shalom* is a promise that the Sabbath will be a day of meaning and renewal, for refocusing our priorities on life, and for rejoicing in our uncountable gifts from the Supreme Creator of the Universe and Life.

In his 1951 book, *The Sabbath*, the Jewish scholar Abraham Joshua Heschel (1907-1972) observed that Sabbath is a "Sanctuary in Time," a "Palace of Time," and a "Great Cathedral" with which we are blessed. In His wisdom, God bestowed the Sabbath upon us—a time to reflect upon the grandeur of His creation and goodness. Heschel noted the manner in which much of our mundane existence consists of the technological, "thing-oriented" aspects of life, our drive to amass accoutrements and wealth, and our subjugation to the tyranny of materialism.

Heschel contrasts this with the "Higher Goal of Spiritual Living," to experience the sacred, to celebrate and become attuned to God's holiness in time. Sabbath is the day on which we are called upon to share that which is eternal, to set our consciousness in tune with transcendent verities, to honor our Lord, and to care for that "Seed of Eternity" planted within our soul.

In *Home-Sick*, the English poet Samuel Taylor Coleridge (1772-1834) expressed similar thoughts of the Sabbath as a time to experience peace with our Creator: "'Tis sweet to him who all the week/Through city-crowds must push his way,/To stroll alone through fields and woods,/And hallow thus the Sabbath-day."

Pierre Abélard, the French theologian-monk (1079-1142), foresaw, in his *Hymnus Paraclitensis*—"O what their joy and their glory must be, Those endless [S]abbaths the blessed ones see!"

The Torah reminds us that at Creation, "God saw everything that he had made, and behold, it was very good. . . . And God blessed the seventh day, and sanctified it: because that in it he had rested from all his work which God created and made" (Genesis 1:31; 2:3). Thus, the Sabbath is a time to turn to and celebrate the mystery of God's creative genius. From the miracle of a single cell, with its dazzling array of 20,000 plus genes and 10,000 plus different proteins and molecular complexity, we can wonder at the several billion cells functioning in concert that form a sentient human being, and other glories of the universe.

As one who attempts to understand the mysteries of the developing brain, and what we as healers can do to prevent its damage, I continually am mystified at the creativity of the "Celestial Design Committee." What peace and joy to be with God in experiencing a day of rest, contemplation, refreshment, and rededication. It is His hallowed Sanctuary in Time. *Shabbat Shalom!*

Lawrence D. Longo, CME class of 1954, is a distinguished professor in LLUSM departments of basic sciences, gynecology and obstetrics, and pediatrics. He was director of LLUSM Center for Perinatal Biology from 1995 to 2012. He was LLUSMAA 1974 Alumnus of the Year, received the LLU Distinguished Service Award in 1994, and was awarded the LLUH Lifetime Achievement Award in 2013.

January 25

Put on the whole armor of God, that you may be able to stand against the wiles of the devil. For we do not wrestle against flesh and blood, but against principalities, against powers, against the rulers of the darkness of this age, against spiritual hosts of wickedness in the heavenly places. Ephesians 6:11-12, NKJV

We sat in a church in Togo, West Africa—the very birthplace of voodoo—little realizing we were about to witness a very real battle between good and evil. Our team from the state of Washington had conducted a field school, training 40 gospel outreach workers for two weeks. Each morning we presented that evening's program to the local evangelists, who then went to eight sites throughout the capital, Lome, to feed the gospel to their spiritually hungry listeners.

Now it was the last day of the series, and baptismal candidates had been bused to the central church. One woman told how she had been dedicated to the devil as an infant and instructed in the art of voodoo. She was given powers to destroy property, kill, and cause terror. At night, she could leave her body and be transported by the devil long distances to bring disease, destruction, and death to those who were cursed.

Prior to today's baptism, she admitted she was sent to destroy certain Christian neighbors but found she was powerless to harm them. Realizing there was a force greater than the devil, she asked her Adventist neighbors about their all-powerful, loving God. She studied the Bible with them and eventually requested baptism.

However, on the day originally scheduled for her baptism, the devil afflicted her with abdominal pain so severe she was unable to attend. She made two more attempts, only to be stricken with worse pain each time.

Now, after attending the gospel outreach series, she again requested baptism. When she explained her past experiences to the pastors, they decided they should all unite in prayer for her during this baptism. As she approached the front of the church, her pain began, and her fellow candidates had to actually carry her into the baptistry. The pastors interceded fervently for her from an adjacent room. The pastor baptizing her sensed the power of evil as she came toward him in the water.

With all the pastors and congregation praying for divine intervention, this previous slave of the devil was baptized into God's family. The moment she was immersed, her pain left and the evil presence surrounding her vanished. Rising from the water, she radiated pure joy. The congregation spontaneously stood up and began singing "Praise God, From Whom All Blessings Flow."

Standing by the door of the room where the pastors had been praying, I watched as they hugged and pounded each other's backs excitedly. Christ had won another victory! The devil was defeated, and this woman was free—free from the devil's power and free to worship the God of salvation she loved so much.

We may not live in voodoo-land, but be assured the devil is just as real wherever we are. And no matter what evil may be sent our way, we must remember who the powerful Victor is on this battle-torn planet. As we surrender ourselves completely to Him, we can trust our loving Savior to carry us through to the end.

John Rogers, LLUSM class of 1974, is a family practitioner in Caliente, Nevada. This story occurred in January and February of 2000.

Your ears shall hear a word behind you, saying, "This is the way, walk in it,"
Whenever you turn to the right hand Or whenever you turn to the left.
Isaiah 30:21, NKJV

Most of us do not feel that we have had a "Damascus Road" experience. Neither did I. But then, on further reflection, perhaps I did.

I had finished teacher's college in Iceland, where I grew up. My father had recently passed away and I was pondering what direction my life should take. A Norwegian graduate of the SDA Seminary, who recently arrived in Iceland said to me, "Helgi, go to college in the USA for a year. Washington, DC, is the best place to go, because you can always find work there."

Taking his advice, I earned a BA degree at Columbia Union College and then an MA degree in school administration at Andrews University. During my year at Andrews, I began to dream of going to medical school. But I did not have any of the science premed requirements and certainly none of the money that was needed.

Nevertheless, that spring I went back to Washington, DC. During that summer, the next school year, and the following summer, I finished the premed requirements. I earned my way by driving a taxicab in DC and working nights in a psychiatric hospital.

That autumn, I met with Loma Linda University School of Medicine's (LLUSM) dean for admissions, Walter Clark, about possible acceptance into the next medical class. In January, a letter came from the LLUSM admissions office saying, "Not this time, but maybe next year." Not wanting to waste time, I applied to the University of Iceland where the tuition was free; I was subsequently accepted.

After the semester ended, I sent a letter containing my science grades to Dean Clark, not expecting anything to change. But in early March, I received a phone call from him saying I would be accepted to LLUSM that autumn if I finished the current year successfully. I was speechless, and my tongue became twisted as I told him about my plans to attend medical school in Iceland. I did manage to say that I was very happy about his call.

When I first arrived in DC, I had contacted a family friend who was living there. Henry E. Andren, CME class of 1937, had been stationed with the U.S. Army in Iceland during World War II and had visited our home several times. Now I needed advice, so I called him and told him about Dean Clark's phone call. He asked me how I had responded. "Call him right back and tell him you're coming," he instructed. "I will lend you the money for the first year."

Where does this kind of generosity originate? Both Henry's Christian faith and Loma Linda likely played a role. Wherever one goes in this world, there are testimonies like mine of LLUSM graduates changing lives of others for the better. Attending medical school at Loma Linda University was a dream come true—a reality better than the dream. Meeting a wonderful Wisconsin girl—the love of my life, added to the wonder of it all. But I will never forget Henry's act of kindness and generosity. That was my "Damascus Road" experience. My eyesight was not affected, but I have seen life very differently since then. Let us recommit ourselves to these kinds of deeds that are the legacy of LLUSM graduates. My life was changed. And I will be forever grateful.

Helgi Heidar, LLUSM class of 1967, is a retired ophthalmologist who co-founded Pacific Cataract and Laser Institute in the twin cities of Centralia and Chehalis, Washington.

January 27

Each of you should use whatever gift you have received to serve others, as faithful stewards of God's grace in its various forms. 1 Peter 4:10, NIV

Mrs. Santiago and her husband came to see me in my office for her to be evaluated for advanced bladder cancer and to discuss a radical cystectomy and urinary diversion. Her physical condition and prospects for major surgery were complicated by multiple medical problems.

They both knew that she was in a difficult situation. She had 16 grandchildren and she and her husband lived for their family. The matriarch of her family, at only 59 years of age, she was not prepared to leave her family behind.

We had a candid discussion about the gravity of her situation and the potential options, as well as the risks and complications of each one. She was anxious to go ahead with surgery as soon as possible and told me that she had a strong faith in God and was putting her trust in Him to lead my healing skills in giving her the best care possible. The surgery went smoothly, and she was discharged home sooner than expected.

However, over the next two weeks she developed a superficial wound infection. Although caring for this infection would be difficult, it was decided that it could be treated at home. Her husband was a receptive pupil for teaching. He repeatedly used the illustration that he would be "an instrument" to extend our knowledge for his wife's care and that he could learn anything we were willing to teach him. He emphasized that he would do *whatever* we asked him to do.

Quickly, her wound developed granulation tissue and closed as a result of the aggressive dressing changes and care administered by her husband. Given all of the medical barriers she had against healing, it was a remarkable recovery. It was made possible by her husband's meticulous and timely care. I was delighted with her progress, and she told me that her prayers had been answered and that her faith had been justified.

I am reminded that we should be as humble as Mr. Santiago and be willing to allow our "gifts" to be used as instruments for God's healing touch. I paused from this encounter and reflected on the thought that the knowledge we have acquired and the talents we have developed represent a powerful force for good in this world.

Simply, this force is the healing ministry of Jesus Christ, and it can and should represent the best of what our faith has to offer. It is our obligation as teachers in the Loma Linda University School of Medicine to live it, teach it, and protect it.

Herbert Ruckle, LLUSM class of 1986, is chair and a professor in LLUSM department of urology. He and his wife, Carol Lau, LLUSM class of 1978-B, live in Redlands, California.

And now these three remain: faith, hope and love. But the greatest of these is love.
1 Corinthians 13:13, NIV

I am moving my mother into assisted living. No complaints have been registered against this facility, the public areas and the individual rooms are clean, the staff is courteous and professional, the food is nutritious, and there is even a cockatiel in the lobby to add a bit of color and sound. There is no question that the move is a step up from her previous situation—no issues with housecleaning or cooking or yard work or falling with no one able to help. And, she is ready for and wants to make this transition; so we all agree this is a good thing, the right thing to do.

So why are tears creeping out of my eyes as I drive through the long, empty stretches of I-10 between Tucson, Arizona, and Redlands, California, with my mother dozing in her seat and my 16-year-old daughter in the back?

Part of the reason, I suppose, is that this experience is a glimpse into my own mortality—the circle of life, and all that it implies. I already know that my hair now requires treatment to be a color other than gray, that my eyesight is not what it used to be, and that I am not running with the same Lopers pace group that I did a few years ago. The conversations with my physician have changed. But this . . . this is different.

Another part of the reason, certainly, is the memories, and with them, a sense of loss for what is no more. All relationships are somewhat complicated, I suppose; at least the long-term ones are, so it is a mixed bag. We grew up with next to nothing; yet I was given piano lessons and swimming lessons, whether I wanted them or not. The wonder of this did not hit me until well after I became an adult; I now realize how many years she must have gone without, say, new shoes, so that I could have some of the experiences and skills that she desperately craved.

Mom was incredibly determined and hardworking, unwilling to take an answer of "no" from her family or anyone else. For example, she bucked her family's expectations and a complete lack of resources to earn a college degree in education, though it took her 10 years to do so. While this uncompromising approach did not always sit well with me as an adolescent, I see it now as a gift that made the impossible possible. And now this educated, determined, and strong-willed person is riding quietly to a place where others will do for her what she can no longer do for herself.

If I shift my head just right, I can see Mom's features in the rearview mirror. Another shift and I see my own. There are similarities; I think about the genes, the memes (ideas and ways of thinking), and the experiences she has given me—many very good, some perhaps not so good, and some—who knows? If I shift once more, I can see my own daughter's beautiful face, cradled in the headphones that connect her to her world of YouTube, forums, and Minecraft. The circle of life continues turning. How can any of us fully appreciate or value what Mom gave to us, and what we in turn pass on to our children?

I love my mom and I love my daughter—three generations, each of us lost in her own world of thoughts, yet bound together in ways that none of us fully realizes. And I realize anew how precious is this moment—every moment—that I spend with someone I love.

Penelope Duerksen-Hughes received her PhD degree in biochemistry from Emory University in Atlanta, Georgia. She is associate dean for basic sciences and translational research, chair and a professor in LLUSM department of basic sciences, and vice chair in LLUSM biochemistry division. January 28 is the author's mother's birthday.

January 29

I stretch out my hands to you; my soul thirsts for you like a parched land.
Psalm 143:6, NRSV

It appeared to be an ordinary morning as I got into my Volkswagen to attend a friend's graduation exercises at University of California, Los Angeles (UCLA). Eight months pregnant, I had just completed my residency in obstetrics and gynecology at Los Angeles County/University of Southern California Medical Center (LAC+USC) and was studying for my board exams. My husband and I were also preparing to go to Nigeria.

My habit was to use a seat belt while driving; however, that particular morning, I sensed a strong urge by the Holy Spirit not to use the seat belt, so I did not. While driving west on the Santa Monica freeway at 65 miles per hour in the fast lane, I suddenly saw in my right peripheral vision a white car veering toward me. I remember thinking, "I hope he gains control of his car so we can avoid an accident." Then everything went blank until I opened my eyes and saw two men hovering over me. They told me, "You have just been in an accident, and we are on our way to UCLA Medical Center." I wondered why UCLA since I had just finished my residency at LAC+USC. I lost consciousness again.

The driver of the car that hit mine had lost control of his car while trying to avoid a car whose driver was making an unsafe lane change. My car crashed into the center divider; I was ejected from it and ended up in the middle of the Santa Monica freeway during the busiest hour of the day. It was a miracle I had not been hit by another car while lying there, or that I had not been crushed inside my car. Had I been strapped into my seat, survival was doubtful because the car's front end was totally demolished.

The next painful 24 hours were eased by a nurse who never said a word but just squeezed my hand as if to say, "Everything will be all right." In addition to the concussion sustained, I had a broken scapula and rib, a subluxation of the right hip, an extensive laceration to the face, and multiple wounds and abrasions. But worst of all was an abruption of the placenta with fetal demise. Being unable to be placed in stirrups, a difficult induced labor ensued; our little girl was delivered stillborn. *How sad the day and dark the night.*

Through God, my nightmare turned into a series of miracles. The plastic surgeons repaired the large facial laceration; the scar remains almost invisible. While hospitalized, at the urging of my husband and with the assistance of a close friend who reviewed with me the night before, I took my ob-gyn board examination. A proctor was provided by the USC department of obstetrics and gynecology. God enabled me, in spite of extreme pain and fatigue, to take the exam—using my right hand to write and my left leg to support the clipboard. I passed the exam successfully.

Subsequent to discharge, and because I was unable to stand and do surgery or deliveries, I took a residency in anesthesiology. This decision enabled me to combine all the skills learned into obstetrical anesthesia, a field that resulted in employment at three medical schools: Martin Luther King Jr.–Drew, Loma Linda University, and Michigan State University.

As I became pain free and able to practice obstetrics and gynecology, my dream of becoming a medical missionary materialized. God has allowed me to practice in the Ivory Coast, Ghana, Nigeria, Lesotho, Kenya, Malawi, and Jamaica. No matter how dark the night, *God can turn it into a brighter day.*

Evelyan Thomas, LLUSM class of 1962, specialized in obstetrics and gynecology as well as anesthesiology. She and her husband reside in Redlands, California. They previously spent time in West Africa as missionaries. She is an active member of the PAPS Team International. January 29 is her birthday.

Blessed be the God and Father of our Lord Jesus Christ, the Father of mercies and God of all comfort, who comforts us in all our affliction, so that we may be able to comfort those who are in any affliction, with the comfort with which we ourselves are comforted by God. 2 Corinthians 1:3-4, ESV

"Clop, clop, clop . . ." My heavy, ugly shoes announced my arrival. Mustering up my courage, I nervously entered my new patient's room. "Good morning. My name is Ingrid, and I am a medical student here to examine you." In order to inspire patient confidence, I purposely omitted two important facts. Fact #1: Ingrid Wahjudi, Medical School Year 2 (MS2) had changed to MS3 only one week ago. Fact #2: Ingrid was frantically trying to stay afloat amidst the inundating, relentless waters of internal medicine at the county hospital.

My introduction was greeted with a dismissive roll of the eyes as the patient turned her head away to face the window. As I fumbled through the physical exam, I attempted friendly small talk with no success. I did not blame her. My patient, Ms. V, was 29 years old. Her distended abdomen, pregnant with metastatic stage IV cancer, left her painfully immobilized, short of breath, and emotionally reeling. Each morning before I visited her, I prayed for wisdom to make a difference. "How's your family?" I asked, while percussing her abdomen. "What are your girls learning in school?" I inquired as I checked for pitting edema.

One day I noticed she was wearing makeup, so I told her she looked pretty. I soon learned she had just gotten married the day before in that hospital room. As the walls began coming down, my questions became more personal: "How did you find out you had cancer? Do you feel hopeless? What are you afraid of?" She told me her fears: scary medical procedures, her daughters' futures, the unknown.

Before I knew it, it was my last day. While rounding at her bedside that morning, my attending told her the grave prognosis: she had months to live, not years. She lay there stunned, speechless. As he continued to explain the medical mumbo-jumbo, she abruptly interrupted him, and asked, "Can you take a picture of me with her?" She pointed at me.

Overwhelmed, I managed to compose myself as the attending paused and took the picture. I then turned to her and grabbed her hand. As I looked into her face, I forgot about my attending's unfinished speech, the residents in the room, and my composure. I broke down and began to cry with her. The team left to continue rounds while I stayed.

We talked about how to spend the remaining months, plans for her daughters, and God. . . . I told her that I had been praying for her. I admitted that I did not know all of the answers for suffering, but I did know from personal experience that God is always there and He gives hope. Soon it was time to go. As my heavy steps carried me out of the hospital doors, my slightly more worn-in shoes were as hideous as before, but I was leaving a changed person from three weeks ago. Yes, my clinical skills had improved and my courage had strengthened. But most important, my commitment to showing God's compassion to others grew deeper and more fervent on my journey to follow in the footsteps of Jesus' healing ministry.

Ingrid Wahjudi, LLUSM class of 2014, is from Loma Linda, California. Before pursuing medicine, she was an elementary school teacher and photographer. She is happily married to her high school sweetheart, Devon Lowry, LLUSD class of 2012. They are both deferred mission appointees.

January 31

For the LORD takes delight in his people. Psalm 149:4, NIV

Our God is a God of love. He enjoys showering His beloved ones with little gifts, just to say, "I love you." Perhaps you have lost hope of finding a parking spot in time to meet a critical appointment. You send up a desperate prayer and suddenly a space appears. A worried mother wonders where her son is and sends up a quick prayer. Just then the phone rings and she discovers all is well. Millions of believers around the world have similar experiences every day. God is real and He loves to make His presence known to those who are open to it.

But just now the skeptic in you is saying, *Wait a minute! Are you trying to tell me that God manages the little comings and goings around the world? What about women who are raped and whose cries for help go unheeded? What about men who contract terminal cancer in the prime of their life and feel as if their prayers reach no higher than the ceiling?*

These objections have serious weight. Believers often fail to realize how trivial their experience of God's presence may seem to others who have suffered deeply in this life. Our glib expressions of how God is working in our everyday lives can be like a knife in the heart to someone experiencing the absence of God. It can feel as if God answers only trivial prayers.

The story of Job makes it clear that at least in this life, there is no answer to most of the specific objections raised above. The tragedies in Job's life were unexplainable in earthly terms. Perhaps God's intervention in Job's situation would have upset the whole space-time continuum of the universe in a way even quantum physicists could not understand. God cannot explain what we cannot understand.

What we do understand is that larger divine interventions can change things in a way that causes collateral damage at some unspecified time in the future. The good we hope God will do in the present could cause greater harm in the future. In the context of the cosmic conflict between God and Satan, major interventions in people's lives are very complicated. The ramifications are usually way beyond our understanding.

Having said this, I still want to argue that a believer's experience in a parking lot is not necessarily imaginary. I cannot explain the timing and the effort involved in God's actions. But I do believe that God would answer every prayer in a positive manner, if pleasing us were the only consideration.

I guess what I am saying is that the lower the ultimate stakes, the lower the potential consequences of any particular divine intervention. Then the more likely a loving God can use the circumstances of life as a token of his love. We serve a God who delights to please His children, whenever doing so would not cause harm to anyone. However, those of us who have experienced this kind of intimacy from God need to be careful when and how we share such experiences with others. Our well-intentioned testimony can do harm even when God's gift did not.

Jon Paulien, PhD, is dean of LLUSR. He earned his MDiv and PhD degrees from Andrews University, where he taught before joining LLU's faculty in 2007. He enjoys spending time with his family.

FEBRUARY

"TO LOVE TAKES TEARS!"

February 1

Look unto me, and be ye saved, all the ends of the earth: for I am God, and there is none else. Isaiah 45:22, KJV

So often people ask the question, "Is there a God in Israel?" They see all the trouble and strife on planet Earth and they allow disbelief to creep in. This doubt is the playground of the archenemy of God. As a Seventh-day Adventist physician, I want to remind myself and everyone else that there is still a God in Israel. On multiple occasions, I have had the opportunity to watch Him work not only in Scripture (1 Kings 17:17-24 and 2 Kings 4:14-37), but also for me personally.

Elijah and Elisha, both strong men of God, demonstrated beyond a shadow of a doubt that there is truly a God in Israel. On separate occasions they were each used by God to bring life back into a young child. I am no Elijah or Elisha; however, God has revealed Himself to me in a similar manner.

I was working in the emergency department when a call came in that a family was en route with a lifeless child. The child had no pulse or respirations for an unknown length of time. No cardiopulmonary resuscitation had been initiated. This type of scenario always brings mass chaos to the emergency department, with everyone running about preparing for what was to come. It brought tears to my eyes, and it also brought a prayer to my mind to the God of the universe for wisdom and skill to be able to handle this case.

Upon arrival, the child was cyanotic and lifeless. The respiratory therapist could not find the correct endotracheal tube or ambu bag for the child. I looked into the emergency cart and something told me to use a #5 tube. I quickly grabbed the tube and inserted it between the vocal cords on the first attempt while the nurse was doing chest compressions. But there was no ambu bag on hand for a pediatric patient.

I breathed into the tube while others continued to look for the bag. After several breaths, the cardiac monitor showed an immediate rapid heart rate. The color of the child began to show improvement. The child was stabilized and transported to the children's hospital, where a full and uneventful recovery was made.

I know for certain that there is still a God in Israel. We so often forget that God is not human, and we need to be reminded that He is eternal. He says, "I am God, and there is none else" (Isaiah 45:22, KJV). Every one of God's children needs to remember that He is only a prayer away. "Prayer is the key in the hand" of the faithful believer that unlocks heaven's storehouse" (Ellen G. White, *Steps to Christ*, p. 94).

Keeping that in mind, let us *all* pray for the *soon return* of our Lord and Savior. Even so, come quickly Lord Jesus.

Lloyd Ruff, LLUSM class of 1976-A, specialized in general surgery and completed an internal medicine gastroenterology fellowship. He currently works in emergency medicine in De Queen, Arkansas.

What shall I return to the LORD for all his bounty to me? I will lift up the cup of salvation and call on the name of the LORD. Psalm 116:12-13, NRSV

The day after, ESPN SportsCenter designated it as the greatest play in Super Bowl history. "It" was the overhead grab made by New York Giants wide receiver David Tyree during Super Bowl XLII (2008), where he pinned the ball against his helmet as he was tackled to the ground. As Tyree was quoted in USA TODAY January 29, 2008, "As great as that catch was—as great as that moment was—I knew I wasn't going to have a moment that eclipsed that. It gave me a sense of peace as far as moving on." He never caught another pass. His NFL career was over soon thereafter, but his real work was merely beginning.

According to Mark Earley, "It was not the most pivotal moment in young David Tyree's life. That would be what happened four years earlier when Tyree found himself behind bars in a jail cell, arrested for drug possession." Tyree told the New York Times, "What looked to be the lowest point in my life ended up being the greatest thing that ever happened to me. . . . I had no joy. I had no peace. . . . My life was in disarray." Shortly after his release from jail, his pregnant girlfriend demanded that he choose between her and his criminal lifestyle. It was then he began reading the Bible in earnest. This time though, the words made "sense" to him. Battling alcohol addiction since eighth grade, he soon had his last drink. He and Leilah were married that same year.

Steadfast in his commitment to Christ, Tyree says that His story is "bigger than [my] Super Bowl catch. It is about destiny and purpose." He is more concerned with "changing lives." He and his wife have been doing this since 2006 when they founded "Next in Line," an organization which counsels teens.

What a moving story, but what does it have to do with us? Similar, but less spectacular events happen to us as individuals, and to those who come into our lives. A few come in the form of personal tragedy that are catapulted into pivotal points—how do we respond? How do our patients respond when at their lowest in a hospital bed? Can we be the instruments God uses for positive change in their lives?

As we make rounds, diagnose, and treat, another question to ask ourselves is: Do we demonstrate compassion and whole person care because it is expected, or does it flow out of us as in Tyree's case, because our commitment is to serve Christ passionately and make an enduring difference?

David Tyree's impossible third-down "helmet catch" in the final minutes of Super Bowl XLII fueled the New York Giants' winning touchdown drive in a 17-14 victory against the New England Patriots.

D. Leigh Aveling, DMin, is a chaplain at LLUMC and an associate professor in LLUSR. He holds a doctorate in pastoral counseling and ethics and is a licensed marriage and family therapist. February 2, 2014, is the day of Super Bowl XLVIII.

February 3

Be still, and know that I am God. Psalm 46:10, NIV (1984)

I arrived in Port-au-Prince, Haiti, nine days after the January 2010 earthquake that killed hundreds of thousands, injured countless others, and decimated the limited infrastructure previously present. The medical needs of the injured were overwhelming. When I reached the hospital, patients with open fractures were still finding their way to the operating room for initial treatment. Femur fractures were just starting to be addressed.

On the medical level, the needs were massive. From a practical standpoint, the patients had no place to go after being treated, as their homes had been destroyed. There was lack of food. Supply of drinking water was limited. Grief was pandemic, as nearly every person had lost family or close friends.

As days passed, hospital resources began to improve, with the exception of one glaring deficiency—we had no transfusable blood available. One particular femoral intramedullary rodding took longer than anticipated, with more than expected blood loss. Although I was not part of the initial procedure, I became involved when the patient was brought back to the operating room later in the day for resuscitation. He had to have blood—now!

We did everything possible to acquire some blood from the surrounding institutions, but failed. We kept the patient alive for several hours, but, without the needed transfusion, he eventually died.

The next day, a patient returned to the operating room for a wound debridement. The attending surgeons felt they had an adequate debridement, but blood continued to ooze from the open wound. The operative team placed a tourniquet to temporarily stem the flow, until transfusable blood could be procured. Even though they were assured that blood would be available, none was forthcoming. The tourniquet had to be left in place to save his life, but in the process, the limb viability was lost.

I was devastated. A death from a preventable cause one night, followed by an arm amputation from another preventable cause the next day was just too much. Although I had not been involved in either surgery, and the damaged arm, later amputated, would have had a likelihood of poor function, this "medical practice" was still not the way it should be. I was trained to save lives and protect injured extremities. Preventable deaths and amputations were so unnecessary.

Finally, I could not take it anymore. The weight of the needs was too great, and I was overwhelmed with the despair of failure. I was going home. At this point, God reminded me that it was true—I could not make a difference. Only He could make that difference, if I allowed Him to work through me.

I finally realized that when things did not work out the way I had planned, prayed, or wanted, the results were not in my hands, but in His. After I had done my best through His strength, and prayed for His blessing, if things did not meet my expectations, I had to step back and let Him be God.

DuWayne Carlson, LLUSM class of 1989, practices orthopaedic surgery part time in Nebraska. He also manages New Beginnings Ranch in southwest Colorado and promotes a healthy lifestyle for himself and others.

Do not be conformed to this world, but be transformed by the renewal of your mind, that by testing you may discern what is the will of God, what is good and acceptable and perfect. Romans 12:2, ESV

"After you see this patient, let me know if you think this is a man ... or a woman," the nurse said to me. I was seeing internal medicine walk-ins on this afternoon. Over the years, I have seen thousands of patients and worked with dozens of different nurses, but I have never had a request quite like this before.

I look at the front of the chart. "Jennifer." "F." I turn to Heidi, the nurse, and say, "This is obviously a woman. Her first name is Jennifer and her gender is female."

"After you see this patient, you'll know why I asked you this question," Heidi counters. Intrigued and puzzled, I head down the hall to see Jennifer.

Sitting very upright on the exam table is a patient about 30 years of age. The patient has stringy, dirty-blonde, shoulder-length hair, and is wearing (only) beige shorts and a yellow tank top. The chest is flat without need of a bra. There is stubble on the chin. The face has strong masculine features. And there are muscles everywhere—chest, abdomen, back, neck, upper and lower extremities. Rippling, bulging muscles with lots of "cuts."

This is Jennifer, and she is a body-builder. In fact, Jennifer is so into body building that she has been injecting herself with male hormones she received from a friend in order to look buff. Unfortunately, I am seeing her today for an abscess, caused by a recent injection with a dirty needle. After drawing a syringe-full of thick yellow pus from her left deltoid muscle, I call the surgeon on call. He eventually takes her to the operating room for an incision and drainage.

We are a society obsessed with appearance. We go "gaga" over the looks of the hottest Hollywood star or singing idol. Between skin products, hair products, clothes, shoes, accessories, supplements, diets, Botox injections, and plastic surgery, we spend billions of dollars a year attempting to look good. We do all this to transform ourselves into something that we think is better. Some of us, like Jennifer, even risk health to look great.

The Apostle Paul speaks of a different, better, and more enduring transformation in Romans 12:2. The effects of all the creams, dyes, fabrics, leather, gold, silver, hormones, and procedures in the world cannot even come close to the transformation that Paul is promoting.

This transformation comes about by the renewing of the mind. It starts on the inside and is manifested by joy and peace and calm on the outside. And it is not just a "makeover." The word in Romans translated as "transformation" is the same word used in the Gospels to describe the transfiguration of Christ.

Would you like to be really attractive? Seek the transformation described in the Bible. It will turn you into a most beautiful person.

Erin Stone, LLUSM class of 1982, is an internist in Woodland Hills, California, and is pursuing a master's degree in interreligious studies.

February 5

Is anyone among you sick? Let him call for the elders of the church, and let them pray over him, anointing him with oil in the name of the Lord. And the prayer of faith will save the sick. James 5:14-15, NKJV

Just ask any fledging doctors of today if they have ever seen a case of measles in a kid. Most likely they will say "No." And chances are, they never will. "Red measles" (nine-day measles) was all too familiar before John F. Enders and his almost miraculous vaccine. Now, measles are rare and for the most part deleted from the diagnostic radar screen.

When I made a house call on little Dee Dee, measles was not far from my mind, for it had been epidemic in our little town for several weeks. As I stood by her bedside, the rash had faded. Gone also was the vexing cough and the red eyes so characteristic of measles. Mother and Father had coaxed their little daughter through the acute illness. But now, to their dismay, Dee Dee had quit eating and would swallow no water, not even ice chips. Her happy smile had disappeared, and for the past two or three days, she lay in her bed barely responsive. It did not require an astute clinician to come up with the diagnosis— Dee Dee had measles encephalitis.

I called our small-town hospital and spoke with the director of nurses. Together, we arranged for a pediatric bed, and my orders included a nasogastric (NG) tube for nourishment. At my request, a visiting consultant drove out from the city, confirmed the diagnosis, concurred with the treatment regimen, and departed—leaving me with a dismal prognosis. That was four weeks ago.

Now, I was making my evening rounds, and I noticed that Dee Dee's mother had pinned a pink ribbon in her golden hair, adjacent to the ugly NG tube—our little patient's link to survival. I stood there thinking hopeless thoughts.

And then it struck me: This should be a case for the Apostle James and his advice to anoint the sick among you. Why had I waited so long?

The next day I stood again by her bedside, this time with our hospital chaplain, the administrator, and Dee Dee's mother and father. We prayed as the chaplain anointed our little patient. We prayed again. As I left the room, I glanced back, half hoping to see her sitting up in bed smiling.

Early the next morning as I stepped off the elevator, the charge nurse asked me if I had come to see Dee Dee. I wondered what she knew and if her smile augured well for the little patient in that somber room close by the nurse's station. As I walked in, Dee Dee, sitting up in bed, spoke for the first time in more than six weeks. "Hi, Dr. West," she beamed. "Can you take this nasty thing out of my nose yet? I think that my mommy is coming to take me home soon."

Some may call it a coincidence. But those of us who observed the event believe that we witnessed a Heavenly healing and that our Dee Dee was indeed a miracle girl!

Raymond West, CME class of 1952, is an emeritus professor in LLUSM department of family medicine. He taught in LLUSPH departments of epidemiology and preventive medicine for two decades. This event occurred while he was practicing at the Seventh-day Adventist hospital on Vancouver Island, British Columbia.

And he shall turn the heart of the fathers to the children, and the heart of the children to their fathers. Malachi 4:6, KJV

"I just can't stand it anymore!" a plethoric Dr. Whistler bellowed at his cowering adult daughter, Maureen. "Here you are calmly reading this garbage"—only he used another word. "This is my wife. This is your mother. Where are your feelings?" Maureen showed that she indeed had feelings and yelled back, "I'm leaving!" And she bolted for the door. "No, you're not!" her father shouted back. "You're staying till we work this out." Maureen hesitated; then her well-practiced reflex of running away from her father's angry outbursts took over and she dashed out of the room, slamming the door behind her.

Dr. Whistler broke the sudden silence by saying softly, "I blew it. You know, the last time we had a blow-up like this, she didn't talk to me for over three months. I don't know what will happen now. We may have to decide without her."

Decide what? Decide whether someone lives. Maureen's mother, Nancy, had been in poor health. One week earlier she was hospitalized with internal bleeding. She had stabilized with blood transfusions and an endoscopy suggested colon diverticulosis as the reason for the bleeding. Then she had hemorrhaged again. A central venous line was hastily placed in order to quickly give her blood and fluids.

Then Nancy turned blue and suffered a cardiac arrest. She was resuscitated and placed on a respirator. A chest x-ray showed partial collapse of the lung on the side of the central line. She did not awaken after the cardiac arrest and appeared to have suffered brain damage.

Dr. Whistler was sure she would not want the collapsed lung treated or to have life support continued. However, he told me that his daughter had been agonizing over whether withdrawal of life support was in accordance with Jewish teachings. She had been reading from material provided by a rabbi when the outburst occurred. "To remove a pillow from under the head of the dying person so that they will die is not permitted. To remove a source of constant noise that is keeping them alive is permitted."

That night the dysfunctional family was on my mind. I prayed that God would somehow bring them healing through Nancy's final illness.

Two days passed, with no change in Nancy's condition and no sign of Maureen. Dr. Whistler requested another family meeting, uncertain if Maureen would attend. Surprisingly, Maureen did show up. Her father apologized for his outburst. She replied, "It's very scary when you yell like that." Father and daughter discussed Nancy's situation calmly and agreed that:

1. Nancy would want life support stopped.
2. It was okay ethically and morally, and in accordance with Jewish beliefs, to make Nancy comfortable and withdraw life support.

A short time later, father and daughter embraced as we made Nancy comfortable, stopped life support, and watched her life slip away. Through prayer and patience, God used Nancy's death to bring healing and reconciliation between father and daughter.

David Bland is an associate professor in LLUSM department of medicine and medical director for the medical intensive care units at LLUMC. He is a specialist in pulmonary and critical care. His medical degree is from the University of New South Wales in Sydney, Australia.

February 7

Because of Christ, we give off a sweet scent rising to God, which is recognized by those on the way of salvation—an aroma redolent with life.
2 Corinthians 2:15-16, MSG

Christian health professionals are sometimes unaware of the far-reaching impact that even routine interactions can have on patients. An incident in my own experience has enabled me to trace the course of such an influence.

Employed at the United Nations (UN) as a bilingual secretary many years ago, I was assigned to the Office of Program Planning, Budgets, and Accounts. On my first day at work, my supervisor explained that employees needed to be flexible enough to work on weekends, especially during General Assembly. I told her that I was happy to work whenever necessary, except on Friday evenings and Saturdays. In that case, she graciously explained, it would be necessary to reassign me to another office where this issue would not arise.

Later that day, the departmental director asked if I was a Seventh-day Adventist. When I responded in the affirmative, he said: "I was told that you would be reassigned to another department, but you are not going anywhere. We need you in this department." I, of course, was happy to remain in a department where, from the first day, the chief himself so explicitly valued me. But what does this have to do with Christian physicians and other health professionals?

Paraphrasing Paul Harvey, the rest of the story comes later. While stationed at the UN offices in Thailand some years before, this director—a career UN diplomat—was hospitalized in Bangkok Adventist Hospital. During his stay in that facility, he had been so impressed by the professionalism, warmth, and personal touch the staff provided that the positive impact remained with him over the years as an unforgettable experience. He associated that unique professional care with Seventh-day Adventists. I became one of the beneficiaries of the ripple or "halo" effect generated by the interactions of Christian physicians, nurses, and others with this patient—so routinely, so long ago, so far away, and with so much care.

Because I decided to go on to graduate school for studies in educational psychology, I remained at the UN for only three months. The director encouraged me in my pursuits and offered a personal recommendation. He placed a note in my file stating that, as a valued employee, he wished that I would return to the UN and suggested that on completion of my studies I should apply for a position at UNESCO (United Nations Educational, Scientific and Cultural Organization). Further, at a farewell party, I was presented with a set of Cross pens engraved with my name.

Was all this because of Lenoa? Of course not! It was because of the far-reaching impact of Christian health-care professionals who, in their daily rounds, served as competent and compassionate extensions of the right arm of the Great Physician, Jesus Christ.

Lenoa Edwards is assistant dean for admissions in LLUSM where she has worked for more than 20 years. She was born in Nicaragua and previously served as a missionary in the Philippines.

He heals the brokenhearted and bandages their wounds. Psalm 147:3, NLT

Any doctor has probably experienced it—the feeling of anxiety that comes when checking your schedule and realizing you are going to see Mr. (or Ms.) Difficult. He comes in different forms: a demanding attitude, a "poor historian," a confusing set of symptoms, or a variety of unrealistic expectations.

Although I was his primary care provider, I had not seen Mr. M in four years—since my first year of residency—so I honestly could not remember what the man was like. But reviewing a recent clinic note by a resident caught me up to speed. The patient had tested positive for methamphetamines, and the resident had written this in her note: "Patient very hostile and spoke threateningly. Please do not schedule this patient with anyone except Dr. Koh."

So it was with quite a bit of anxiety that I welcomed Mr. M into my room to see how I could help him. I began with an open-ended question, and he took advantage of this opportunity to share. He had recently begun to use methamphetamines after his grandmother passed away three weeks ago. But this death was just the most recent of a series of painful memories.

Mr. M, a war veteran, took me back in time to a particularly disturbing incident that had been etched in his memory. He described, with gripping imagery, his story of finding a wounded man on the side of the road—an enemy soldier who had been shot by his platoon—alive, but struggling to breathe. The man had lost a good part of the right side of his chest wall and was in shock from bleeding.

The last moments of this man's life were spent with Mr. M at his side, holding his hand, gazing into the pleading and desperate eyes of a dying man, with no hope to offer. Mr. M struggled to suppress his tears as he shared that not a day goes by but that he sees, in vivid flashbacks, the face of that dying man.

I did not have any profound insights to share with Mr. M; I just listened intently and then thanked him for trusting me with his story, offered some available resources for PTSD, and bid him farewell until our next visit.

But something really meaningful took place during that visit. I sensed the Spirit of God had been present with us, and the result was apparent on our faces as I escorted Mr. M out. God had shown an anxious, young physician the depth of healing He can perform through him. And, somehow, He had reminded a desperate, mentally tormented man that the healing that comes through human connection far exceeds the counterfeit of any stimulating substance.

I find it rewarding to see, through various situations with difficult and imperfect people, that the Great Physician is actively at work, bringing healing.

Shawn Koh, LLUSM class of 2008, is an assistant professor in LLUSM department of medicine practicing at the VA Loma Linda Healthcare System.

February 9

For as the heavens are higher than the earth, so are my ways higher than your ways, and my thoughts than your thoughts. Isaiah 55:9, KJV

The administrative board in Phuket, Thailand, heard "death rattles" coming from the Phuket Mission Clinic. With too few patients, it was financially drowning. They thought it might be best to close the inpatient wards and try once more to revive just the outpatient clinic. I was seeing patients in Bangkok, Thailand, and was asked to give the struggling satellite clinic in Phuket one last try.

When my family and I arrived, I discovered that only 6 to 10 outpatients were being treated a day, with 1 to 3 inpatients still being cared for in curtained-off wards on the second floor of a vacated former Chinese school. Such was the case with this "clinic," which had been reopened in 1947 after World War II by Frank Crider, CME class of 1945.

A philanthropic Chinese tin miner had kindly loaned us the building rent free. The clinic, pharmacy, and surgery were on the first floor. After surgery, patients had to be hand carried (usually by the surgeon) up narrow stairs to the second floor, which had been divided by curtains into makeshift wards. The floor had been termite food for so long that a woman's high-heeled shoe would sometimes go through it. The staff was clogged with excess employees, some of whom were dipping sticky fingers into the meager proceeds from medicine sales.

But God always has ways far above ours. In this instance, He used a woman. Shortly after I began treating patients, a new female patient came to see me. She had been to several doctors in town but none had helped her. I prescribed some medication for her symptoms. Within four hours of taking the prescription, she was pain free.

Unexpectedly, she began singing praises all over town for the new mission doctor. Because she was rather wealthy, liked to talk, and was influential, her story spread like wildfire. There was no way this medicine could have healed her in four hours; this was God's doing!

As her recommendation for the clinic flashed through the town, patients began swarming into our waiting room, and the inpatient cubicles filled up as well. Soon, the corrupt employees were eliminated, and the clinic's income began to increase dramatically. On some days, we would see as many as 100 outpatients!

About this time, another wealthy tin miner had become quite appreciative of the services of our sister mission hospital in Bangkok. So he gave the clinic in Phuket a handsome three-acre plot on Thepsatri Road, the only road on to the island from the ferry and airport.

With this gift, the board agreed that, instead of closing the clinic, we needed to build a new hospital on this property. With God's blessing and the hard work of many, including the Kettings (Samuel, CME class of 1960, and Effie Jean, CME class of 1954) and the Rodas, the new hospital was opened on February 9, 1965. In addition, a church, a school, residences, nurses' dorm, and a cafeteria were also built—some of which have been enlarged several times since then.

Truly, God's thoughts were higher than any we could imagine—even using an enthusiastic, satisfied patient!

Paul Watson, CME class of 1959, was a missionary in Vietnam and Thailand for 13 years. He then worked as a family practitioner in Knoxville, Tennessee, until he retired to Thousand Oaks, California. February 9 is his birthday and the day Phuket Mission Hospital opened.

And he passed in front of Moses, proclaiming, "The LORD, the LORD, the compassionate and gracious God, slow to anger, abounding in love and faithfulness."
Exodus 34:6, NIV

The virtue of empathy for the suffering of others lies at the root of many cultures and religious traditions. Our English language borrows the Greek word *paskhein* ("to suffer") to make our words "passion" and "compassion" and borrows the Latin word *compati* ("co-suffering") to form the word "patient," one who suffers. In describing the Good Samaritan (a prominent ethic embodied in statues on the Loma Linda University campus), Jesus used the actions of the Samaritan as a model for compassionate conduct.

At Loma Linda University School of Medicine and within the hospitals on campus, teachers and students of medicine can and should learn how to be compassionate from other traditions. Among our Jewish colleagues, God's statement to Moses, "Hashem, Hashem, God, Compassionate and Gracious, Slow to Anger, and Abundant in Loving Kindness," (Exodus 34:6) tells us all about the need to be nonjudgmental and to show bountiful love.

Our Islamic colleagues understand that each of the 114 chapters of the Qu'ran (with one exception) begins with the verse, "In the name of God the Compassionate, the Merciful," and with the word *rahmah* (the compassion a mother shows to her children).

From our Hindu colleagues, we learn that the Sanskrit word *ahimsa* is translated as "refraining from harmfulness"; and the Hindi word *daya* means compassion, charity, and self-control.

Later, St. Francis of Assisi asserted: "If you have men who will not exclude God's creatures for shelter, out of compassion and pity, you will have men who will deal likewise with their fellow men."

Ellen G. White wrote: "It should be written upon the conscience as with a pen of iron upon a rock, that he who disregards mercy, compassion, and righteousness, he who neglects the poor, who ignores the needs of suffering humanity, who is not kind and courteous, is so conducting himself that God can not co-operate with him in the development of character. The culture of the mind and heart is more easily accomplished when we feel such tender sympathy for others that we bestow our benefits and privileges to relieve their necessities" (*Testimonies for the Church*, Vol. 6, p. 262).

Albert Schweitzer, the venerated German physician-missionary, is quoted as saying: "Compassion, in which all ethics must take root, can only attain its full breadth and depth if it embraces all living creatures and does not limit itself to mankind."

Tenzin Gyatso, the Fourteenth Dalai Lama, wrote in 2008: "True Compassion is not just an emotional response but a firm commitment founded on reason. Therefore, a truly compassionate attitude toward others does not change even when they behave negatively" (*Buddha Vacana*).

What do these statements from revered teachers have to do with LLU? I believe that Christ's message of "Blessed are the merciful" applies to all of us in our great diversity of cultures, religions, and value systems. Compassion is taught by example, and such examples need to be internalized by medical students and residents in their daily learning of realities within their practice of medicine.

Thurman Merritt is a professor in LLUSM department of pediatrics and LLUSAHP department of cardiopulmonary science. He received his MD degree from the University of Kansas in 1972. February 10 is the birthday of his son, Bryce.

February 11

Wisdom is the principal thing; Therefore get wisdom. And in all your getting, get understanding. Proverbs 4:7, NKJV

In 1966, I took my first pop quiz as a clinical student. I turned in my short, written answer to Jack Kennedy, CME class of 1954, then associate professor of ob-gyn at Loma Linda University. I had read the assigned chapter in Williams' *Obstetrics* and listened intently to Professor Kennedy's cogent lecture. I was confident. The single question was, "How would you care for a pregnant patient who was brought to the emergency department (ED) with vaginal bleeding but no pain or evidence of uterine contractions?"

The next day, I waited for my graded quiz to come back—the one I had answered with pride. It came, and there, scrawled across the top of my paper in brilliant red, was the grade—"F." Annotating the failing grade was this humbling question: "Figure out why the patient and her baby might have died with the care you suggested! Do not do a pelvic exam unless you are ready to intervene with blood, surgery, and have others to help, such as anesthesia!"

In 1976, a decade after my "F" grade, I had an urgent call in the middle of the night from the ED at the 97th General U.S. Army Medical Center in Frankfurt, West Germany. An enlisted soldier had just carried in his pale, limp wife, who was bleeding heavily and near term. By the time I entered the ED, the resident on call was holding a vaginal speculum in his gloved hands. He told me he was trying to do a vaginal exam "to see where the bleeding was coming from."

"Don't do a vaginal exam!" I urgently ordered the ED doctor. A hostile look crossed his face. I ordered that the patient be taken immediately to surgery, and preparations made for an emergency C-section. The nurses, anesthesia, and surgical techs worked rapidly as my team. Within minutes, a limp but alive baby girl was delivered, and the mother was no longer hemorrhaging from placenta previa.

Almost two decades passed after this incident, and in 1994 I retired from Army medicine. My wife, Tina, and I moved to Silverdale, Washington, where I enjoyed salmon fishing from the banks of Puget Sound. In the summer of 1996, about three decades after Dr. Kennedy's pop quiz, I was fishing beneath the massive Tacoma Narrows Bridge.

A man came up to me, himself dressed in the scruff of a salmon fisher. He asked, "Are you Dr. Thomsen?"

"Yes," I replied, somewhat incredulously. "How did you know?"

"In Frankfurt, in 1976, during the night, you saved my daughter's life." He explained that after his wife had started to bleed heavily, he carried her into the ED at the 97th. A doctor ordered the ED physician to stop trying to do a vaginal exam. "That doctor," the salmon fisher said, "was you!"

The next day, we again fished for salmon at the same site. Quietly, an attractive young woman joined us. "Dr. Thomsen," the same scruffy salmon fisherman said, "I wanted my daughter to meet the doctor who saved her life in Frankfurt that night in 1976. She leaves tomorrow to start her first year at the University of Washington!"

Russel J. Thomsen, LLUSM class of 1968, is a retired obstetrician and gynecologist residing in Silverdale, Washington. He served in the U.S. Army (active and reserves) for 31 years after completing his residency at the University of Utah.

For you know that it was not with perishable things such as silver or gold that you were redeemed from the empty way of life handed down to you from your ancestors, but with the precious blood of Christ, a lamb without blemish or defect. **1 Peter 1:18-19, NIV**

I have spent my career as a family physician, emergency physician, and in a variety of medical administrative roles. Along the way, I have had the privilege of diagnosing and treating a myriad of illnesses and injuries, delivering a few hundred babies, and caring for victims of trauma and devastating disease. Perhaps I have even been part of saving a few lives that would otherwise have been lost, although I am not sure about that.

- Nine years old. Nine birthdays, nine Christmases, nine seasons of winter snow and summer sunshine. Then she was diagnosed last month with acute leukemia. She is under intense treatment, and a remission is anticipated. In fact, there are realistic hopes for a full recovery. But today, she needs platelets to prevent untoward bleeding. And she will get them. I made sure of that.
- He was almost home, 20 miles down, 2 to go, peddling along at a 16 mph clip when the car ahead made an unexpected turn into his immediate path. He was thrown across the hood of the car and crashed to the pavement on his left side. Somewhere along the way, his helmet took a hard enough lick to crack it down the middle, along with his clavicle, humerus, seven ribs, and spleen. He needed packed RBCs upon arrival to the emergency department. He got them. I made sure of that.
- They say she has disseminated intravascular coagulation (DIC). Her blood-clotting factors are being used up at an alarming rate. She cannot survive this situation very long. Her doctor has ordered fresh, frozen plasma. It is on its way to her now. I made sure of that, too.

What is clear to me is that the life-saving contribution of my medical care and treatment, however appropriate and effective, is dwarfed in comparison to the impact of the blood that I have donated over the past half century. I have lost count of the number of units, but I believe that it is somewhere in the 10-gallon range by now.

I was feeling a bit proud of that amount until I attended a blood donor recognition banquet in our town—only 10 gallons (and above) donors were admitted. There were several hundred people in the grand ballroom. Among them were many 25-gallon donors, several 50-gallon donors, and the grand champion donor: a woman in her seventies who had donated 80 gallons of blood over her life-saving lifetime!

Our regional blood bank maintains an inventory of two-to-three days' supply of blood and blood products. That is all. That is also the reason the blood bank is open for business every day. And that is why I will be standing in line to fill out the paperwork, roll up my sleeve, and do my part to save another life when the Big Red Bus rolls into my neighborhood. When the nine-year-old leukemia patient and the wounded cyclist and the desperately ill patient with DIC need blood, I will help make sure it is there.

Ted Hamilton, LLUSM class of 1973-A, specialized in family medicine and is vice president of medical missions for Adventist Health System. He resides in Ocoee, Florida. His blood type is O positive.

February 13

Simon Peter answered him, "Lord, to whom can we go? You have the words of eternal life." John 6:68, NRSV

Is it always necessary for us to mean exactly what we say? If you are honest, it seems, the answer is easy. Of course, you should never say anything you do not mean. The essence of integrity is to be true to your word, to be sure that your feelings and your language perfectly agree. But the truth is more complicated. There are times when insincerity is a virtue, when what we feel and what we say may be miles apart, and there are certain things we need to say whether we mean them or not.

In the first case, we should use words insincerely when they express feelings we do not have, but wish we had. As we ordinarily express it, words follow feelings. We feel a certain way, and that determines what we say. But there are also times when feelings follow words.

My wife and I had a little girl, Alison, during my fourth year of graduate school, just as I was trying to finish my dissertation. During a good part of the week, Alison was mine to look after. But with all that was on my mind, it was not easy to be the gentle, caring father I wanted to be—especially to a demanding little girl who cried and squirmed and fussed.

To settle Alison down, I tried talking to her in a quiet, reassuring voice. I cannot remember what I said, and I do not remember how much my words helped her, but I know they helped me. The words did not express what I actually felt, but saying them helped me acquire the feelings I wanted to have. Sometimes saying things insincerely, I discovered— saying things you do not really mean—can help you mean the things you say.

There are other times, too, when what we say is more important than whether we are perfectly sincere in saying it. My father-in-law collapsed several years ago while saying his prayers one Sabbath evening. My mother-in-law called us from their downstairs apartment and said there was a problem. We rushed to help him, but it was clear he was slipping away.

The ambulance came. The paramedics saw his heart had failed, looked at his advance directive—he was 95 years old—and decided there was no reason to take him to the hospital. So, they left. Then the police came. They determined that he had died from natural causes, and they let the coroner know. Then they left.

Finally, around 2 a.m., two men came from the mortuary to remove the body. Before each of these groups left our home—the paramedics, the police, the undertakers—one of them paused and said exactly the same thing: we are sorry for your loss.

We are sorry for your loss. How sorry were they? None of them knew the man. They had never met us. They were all doing what they were paid to do. I am sure none of them felt deep grief. So, how sorry were they? I do not know, but I did not care. They said those words for us, not for them. They were words we needed to hear. And I will always be grateful that they said them.

Whether you are a health professional or not, there are things people need to hear you say. And you can say them whether or not they perfectly reflect the way you feel. Sometimes, insincerity is a virtue. When you sense that people need your voice, speak to them. Trust your words, and do not worry about your feelings. You have the words we need to hear.

Richard Rice, PhD, is a professor in LLUSR. His latest book, Suffering and the Search for Meaning, *will soon be published by Intervarsity Press. His wife, Gail, EdD, is on faculty in LLUSAHP and is director of faculty development for LLU. They have two children and four grandchildren.*

February 14

Beloved, let us love one another: for love is of God; and every one that loveth is born of God, and knoweth God. In this was manifested the love of God toward us, because that God sent his only begotten Son into the world, that we might live through him. 1 John 4:7, 9, KJV

One of my first patients after I completed my residency was a vivacious elderly lady, Dorothy. I treated her breast cancer surgically and followed-up with her every few months thereafter for signs of recurrence. While our visits over the ensuing years were ostensibly hers, it was her husband, Bill, who came increasingly to prominence.

Bill was the quiet one—always there, sitting in the corner, nodding at the appropriate time in coordination with his wife's gestures. She was the animating force between them. More often than not, Dorothy would ask me to listen to his lungs because he was not feeling well, and most of those times I sent him down to the emergency department for admission due to congestive heart failure.

The week Dorothy appeared sans Bill, I was alarmed. She allayed my fears, excitedly sharing that he was doing the best he had in years with his new pacemaker. A few months later, she gushed about how his heart rate had quickened from 60 to 70 bpm and how EVERYTHING was so much better, wink wink! She even giggled that she was considering asking the cardiologist to set him to 80!

Eventually, Bill needed his pacemaker leads replaced; and, because they lived far from the hospital, the two of them stayed in a nearby hotel the night before his procedure. Technically all went well, but the physicians, unable to awaken him, placed him in the ICU on a ventilator. This was the first in a stepwise deterioration, which proceeded to sepsis.

After days keeping vigil by his bedside, Dorothy finally saw his eyes flicker open and look at her for the first time since the procedure. She was beside herself with excitement, grasped his hands, and talked of her love for him. He was unable to speak, of course, but with a free finger pointed toward the foot rail of the bed.

She was confused about the gesture and asked him various yes/no questions until she deduced that he wished her to look down toward his feet. She explained that she found nothing of note, save for a bandage around a toe. She next understood that he wanted her to remove it, which she did. A small, hand-torn strip of paper fell, coiled on the laundered sheets.

Her trembling fingers unfurled the note, which read: *I love you. I love you. I love you.* Their eyes met, both pairs filled with love and liquid. He then closed his eyes and passed away. . . .

Hearing this story from my newly widowed patient left me speechless, both due to the large lump in my throat and the thought that anything I could say would somehow distract from the power of their love in life and in death. Yet, we as Christians have our own love story—a love so strong as to die to save the object of His love, a love that foresaw that event before the world was even made. More than all other stories, *that* is love.

Marvin Atchison, LLUSM class of 1998, is a general surgeon in Orange County, California. This story occurred while he was working at Kaiser Permanente in Fontana, California. February 14 is Valentine's Day and the day of the 2014 Freshman Dedication Service for the LLUSM class of 2018.

February 15

Wisdom is with the aged, and understanding in length of days. Job 12:12, ESV

It is evening. The sun has dipped below the horizon to the west. Below him, the lights of the Medical Center compete with the last blushes of rose and purple on the mountains. For more than 50 years, he has sat on this hilltop watching his beloved College of Medical Evangelists transform into a bustling, world-renowned institute. Why did he come here so long ago, and why has he never left?

Is it the once peaceful, sleepy valley, with its orange groves and winter haze of smudge? Is it the noon whistle blowing from atop the hill or the broadcast of chimes at sundown on Friday evening that still echo in his mind? Or the town where everyone knows your name? He can hardly distinguish the old campus now, with its new bookends of Medical Center and Centennial Complex.

Is it because of the giants who walked the halls before him—such as Evans, Mortensen, Macpherson, and Shryock? His eyes are dimming, but their vision never failed as they continued in faith to establish a school for healing and medical evangelism. Providence after providence showed that the little lady who had stood on Mound Hill and proclaimed that such a school was needed had the inspiration of One who could see all things, know all things. He thinks of his own colleagues like Small, Hadley, and Smith who helped the school to continue to be a light into the twenty-first century. Has he helped to fulfill their dreams?

Is it the challenge and excitement of making diagnoses that will ever after affect the course of a life—the relief of "benign" or the sinking thud of "malignant"? He has seen so much change as new technologies probe ever deeper into the body and help to clarify the nature of each cell. When he began his career, autopsies were the "final answer," but who even does them any longer?

Is it the joy of shaping eager young minds into future physicians, dentists, nurses, and therapists? Countless students have sat through his lectures and listened to his soft-spoken "pearls" of wisdom. His face lights up as he remembers their visits during the Annual Postgraduate Convention and other homecomings when they recall his help and concern in guiding them along the path to their professions. He is amazed that he has even taught the offspring of some of those students. Is that why he never wished to leave?

"So I saw that there is nothing better for a man than to enjoy his work, because that is his lot. For who can bring him to see what will happen after him?" (Ecclesiastes 3:22, NIV).

It is evening. It is enough.

"He" is Bo Ying Wat, CME class of 1949. He began his career as an instructor of pathology at CME/LLUSM in 1952, serving on the faculty for more than 50 years. He was an LLUSMAA 1993 Honored Alumnus and received the LLU Distinguished Service Award in 2002. He passed away on April 19, 2013. This account was written by his daughter, Karen Wat Nielsen, LLUSM class of 1976-B. She is married to Virgil Nielsen, LLUSM class of 1980-A. February 15 is the birthday of the author's father.

What is man that You are mindful of him, And the son of man that You visit him?
Psalm 8:4, NKJV

One Sabbath morning, I received an urgent phone call. My 30-year-old patient, Mrs. Brown, was going into labor. "Both sides of my family are driving down right now! They're all excited to meet their first grandchild!" she exclaimed when I arrived at the hospital. The day she had been eagerly anticipating had finally come, and everyone was anxious to welcome this new life into the world.

As an intern at Florida Hospital, I first met Mrs. Brown when she was 12 weeks pregnant. I learned that she had been unsuccessfully trying to have a child for more than 10 years, so she treated her unborn baby as a prized treasure. She faithfully came for every appointment and was soon the clinic's model for expectant mothers.

Her shelves were lined with numerous books on pregnancy and parenting, and she even played classical music tapes on her belly. Her prenatal preparation was exemplary. I knew she was fully equipped and ready for motherhood. What a lucky baby, I thought.

Receiving the news of her labor that Sabbath morning filled my heart with happiness. This was the day that her diligence would pay off! After 15 hours of agonizing labor, Mrs. Brown's baby boy was born around midnight. The hospital room erupted in tears and shouts of joy! The extended family engulfed me in hugs, expressing tearful thank you's, and I gladly reciprocated their sentiments.

And then I looked at her newborn baby. Suddenly, my smile wilted as I sensed that something was wrong. The child was limp. As I looked into his precious eyes, I knew he had Down syndrome. Seeking a second opinion, I quickly called a pediatrician to confirm the diagnosis. My heart sank as my suspicions were verified. Delivering the news to this happy group was one of the most difficult things I have ever had to do.

"Why? Did I do something wrong?" she asked me. What once were joyous tears now stained her cheeks with concern. I asked myself the same questions. A look of worry was painted on each family member's face in the room. Fumbling for words, I silently prayed for something to say.

For a moment, my mind began to race. I recalled a 19-year-old patient, who had delivered her fifth healthy child without any prenatal care. I remembered women who rejected the idea of motherhood altogether, but who went on to give birth to babies in perfect condition. What if this were the sixth child of my 19-year-old patient, I thought. What kind of care would this baby get in the hands of an incompetent, uncaring mother?

Instantly, with the help of God-inspired thoughts, I knew what to say. "Mrs. Brown," I began, "of all the patients that I've followed for pregnancy, you've been the best and have done nothing wrong. Although you deserve the ideal baby, you are the perfect mother for this child. You're the most qualified, because he needs someone like you to be his mother—someone responsible, caring, loving." I stood in silence as she began to nod her head in agreement.

As expected, that little baby was the healthiest and most cared for child that I saw during my internship.

Like Mrs. Brown, our God is the perfect parent. Although He deserves ideal children, we need a responsible, caring, and loving God like the One we have.

John Y. Chung, LLUSM class of 1988, is a dermatologist in Dalton, Georgia. He and his wife, Linda, have three children.

February 17

Blessed is he who considers the poor; The LORD will deliver him in time of trouble.
Psalm 41:1, NKJV

The day's routine activities at Fletcher Hospital (in the Blue Ridge mountains of western North Carolina) had not prepared me for what was about to happen. Starting at 7 a.m., we had surgeries, then rounds and consultations, followed by afternoon appointments.

Around 6 p.m., two itinerant painters showed up at my office—one having severe abdominal pain. They had been to a hospital about 25 miles away, only to be turned away for lack of insurance and money. Then they went to the VA Hospital in Asheville but were again denied care because they were not veterans and had no insurance or money. Examination revealed right lower quadrant tenderness with rebound, so a diagnosis of acute appendicitis was made.

The patient was taken to surgery and after our usual and customary practice of praying with the patient, an appendectomy incision was made. Upon opening the peritoneal cavity, the appendix was found to be normal, but gastric contents were found indicating a ruptured gastric ulcer. The appendectomy incision was closed and an upper midline incision was started. At this point the patient went into cardiac arrest.

In 1960, we did not have defibrillators and CPR had not come into vogue. So I opened the left chest and began rhythmic manual heart compressions, all the while praying silently and earnestly for the Lord's intervention. In about 5 minutes (it seemed like 20) the patient's heart resumed normal activity.

Once the heart regained function, I closed the chest wound, completed the abdominal incision, identified and closed the gastric perforation, washed out the abdominal cavity, closed the incision, and sent the patient to the floor because we had no ICU. The patient never spiked a degree of fever, made an uneventful recovery, and after 10 days was discharged to resume his normal activities and travels!

This was another amazing illustration of how the unseen presence of our Divine Physician provides and guides His willing servants with skill and talents that we and our patients would not otherwise benefit from. The Lord has blessed our humble efforts in a self-supporting home mission, where never a patient was refused care for lack of insurance or money. We averaged about 500 surgeries a year with no post-op wound infections or complications. Our only scrub nurses were Fletcher Hospital School of Nursing students.

Dear Lord Jesus, Whatever my day holds, I choose to remember that my time is in Your hands. I trust You for the details of my day and know that You always know what's best. I rest in the safety and security of Your everlasting love for me. In Jesus' name, Amen.

Pierce J. Moore, CME class of 1944-B, is a retired surgeon residing in Hendersonville, North Carolina. He was an LLUSMAA 2012 Honored Alumnus.

Above all else, guard your heart, for everything you do flows from it.
Proverbs 4:23, NIV

Carefully place your stethoscope over the second right intercostal space and listen. Tune out the sounds of the office, the voices of other patients, the voices of the nurses in the hallway. Eliminate all the clanking of keys and the clicking of footsteps. Filter out the everyday distractions, and tune into the sounds the heart is making. Doing so could save your patient's life.

And if you tune out all the things that are daily vying for your attention, if you filter out the multitude of noises that are clouding your hearing, and tune into God's heart—it could save your life.

"And it repented the LORD that he had made man on the earth, and it grieved him at his heart" (Genesis 6:6, KJV). For a being as immortally steadfast and eternally resilient as God, what could cause his heart to break? The Trinity had not lost a member, a member of the angelic host had not gone flat, and the stars had not fallen from their places in the sky. There was no disconnect in Heaven that caused God's angina, so He would have to focus on something here on Earth.

A father loses his son. The thrills of the world captivate the boy and lead him to abandon his father and his home. The boy hardens his heart against reason and trades in all the father's favor for frivolous friends and short-lived happiness. But—like an ebbing tide—as quickly as everything comes, everything goes. The boy, soon abandoned and alone, finds himself lost. The father, though rejected and mistreated, tirelessly yearns over his lost child—heartbroken. Here is what could break the heart of an immortally steadfast and eternally resilient God—losing His child. Losing you.

A mitral stenosis is an example of a severe heart problem caused by the left side of the heart that can show manifestations on the right side of the heart. Sin, however, is such a severe cardiac defect that it does not just affect another side of the heart; it affects another heart altogether. The child hardened his heart and ran away, and it broke the father's heart. And when you and I harden our hearts and run away, the same happens to our Father's heart.

However, the beauty of redemption's story is not that a sin-polluted heart was diagnosed; the beauty is that a cure for it was found. "A new heart also will I give you, and a new spirit will I put within you: and I will take away the stony heart out of your flesh, and I will give you an heart of flesh" (Ezekiel 36:26, KJV). God offers you and me heart transplants. Complete renewal. Total rebirth. A second (third, fourth . . . or six hundredth) chance.

With our new and renewed hearts, we can learn to truly love the Lord our God with all our heart, all our soul, and all our mind (Matthew 22:37). As we do that, we begin to better understand what it means to love our neighbor as ourselves (Mark 12:31). And when we truly love our neighbor as we love ourselves, we will know what it means to help make man whole, because we ourselves will have been made whole.

And thus, by surrendering our hardened hearts, we put in motion a cascade that will enable us now to effectively continue the healing and teaching ministry of Jesus Christ, one patient's heart at a time.

Vincent M. Spellman Jr., LLUSM class of 2016, was born and raised near Reading, Pennsylvania. He graduated from Oakwood University. February 18 is his birthday.

February 19

Be joyful always; pray continually; give thanks in all circumstances.
1 Thessalonians 5:16-18, NIV (1984)

She was a young, bright, active adolescent; but life for Erin took an unexpected turn. She developed a rare disorder of the central nervous system that resulted in extensive demyelination, primarily involving the motor system. She became completely paralyzed—unable to move her arms, legs, or her face; and she could not talk or swallow. And yet, she was fully awake and alert, had normal sensation over her whole body, and could hear and see. All her cognitive functions, including memory and thinking ability, were intact. She was completely aware of her surroundings and could see everyone around her and hear what they were saying; but she had no ability to reply. She was trapped in her own body, a condition often described as being "locked in."

In Erin's words: "It's as if I woke up from a very deep sleep or from a dream and for a second you are confused, not knowing where you are, but you hear laughing and talking. It is like seeing the world through a screen door, knowing your vision is fine, but something is making it hazy. My awareness is still, yet the world around me whizzes by on either side of my head, like two conveyor belts on high speed."

Just how did this young teenager react to such a devastating physical disability? I was privileged to be one of her physicians during her acute illness 16 years ago. After a period of rehabilitation, she regained some very slight movement in her left arm; it was just enough to control the joystick of her electric wheelchair and slowly point with her index finger to letters on a letter board on her lap tray. As Erin pointed to individual letters, an observer was able to record her unspoken words.

Then, at the age of 16, she wrote about her incredibly difficult situation with these surprising words: "I wake up every single day and thank God that I'm still here and that I'm me. My life is wonderful. I am surrounded by friends and family who love me just as I am." Erin's spirit, her positive attitude, and a profound faith in God soon became an inspiration to all.

Although severely disabled, Erin still exuded an engaging personality; liked to socialize; and had a warm, good-natured, and friendly demeanor. She wore a constant smile. She could have become depressed or bitter and angry at her fate. Instead, Erin was determined to make the most of her life.

She went back to school and graduated from high school at the top of her class. She took college classes and became interested in recording her thoughts and feelings. With her mother's support, Erin is currently writing a memoir about her life's experiences.

She shares with her family a strong faith in God, and has written some spiritually inspiring essays that she refers to as mini sermons. Several of these have been read by her mother to the congregation in her church. Erin has become an active ambassador for Free Wheelchair Mission, an international Christian charity that provides mobility to physically disabled individuals in poor countries.

Her life today is a source of inspiration to all those who know and love her. Now as a mature, wonderfully wise woman of 30, Erin still attends my clinic regularly, dispensing warmth and inspiration as I dispense her medicine.

Murray Brandstater, MBBS, PhD, is chair and a professor in LLUSM department of physical medicine and rehabilitation. He received his medical degree from Melbourne University in Australia. February 19 is the date of the onset of Erin's illness.

February 20

In humility count others more significant than yourselves. Philippians 2:3, ESV

Josh visited the emergency department occasionally due to problems from his heroin use. His visits usually began in the parking lot smoking area—his unofficial waiting room—and then we would roll him into the emergency department in his wheelchair. He was paralyzed from his mid-back down.

Today, however, Josh and his wheelchair were in the actual waiting room. Unusual. He was sleeping, also unusual. His wavy, shoulder length hair begged a washing. His left leg and knee were swollen and red—I had never seen a knee effusion so large. He mentioned that it had been a bit larger the past few days. He did not realize that his temperature of 103 degrees, his low blood pressure, and his fast pulse could all be from that infected knee.

Tests and treatments began. We withdrew more than a cup of pinkish-tan fluid from his knee joint, finding not only that it was filled with pus, but also that both bones were shattered from some forgotten fall. We stabilized his temperature and blood pressure; however, he would not heal with antibiotics alone. The toxins from the infection were poisoning him, killing him. The specialist arrived and informed Josh that his leg needed to be amputated—now.

Josh was angry. "I'm leaving. Take this IV out."

I was surprised. Was it not clear to Josh that he was dying? He felt that the specialist was demeaning him, did not care about him, and had not considered saving his leg. "I would rather die, than have my leg cut off by that ____." I decided to try to talk to him. He wanted to smoke, so we loaded him in his wheelchair with the IV and rolled him back outside. As the sun set, he told me how he became paralyzed.

It was a summer day, eight years earlier. After sweating all day on the cattle ranch, a group went to the river to cool off. A rope swing was the culprit. From high on the bank, he jumped and hung on. But as his weight came to bear, the rope broke, and he landed on the rocks, just short of the water. He was paralyzed immediately, losing the use of his legs and control of his lower body.

After our conversation, he agreed to stay in the hospital, still swearing he would never let that other doctor talk to him or touch him again. But he would consider treatment by someone who cared about him, reinforcing the old adage about a patient's view of doctors: "They don't care how much you know until they know how much you care."

Some patients are harder to provide care for than others. While Josh was offended by the other doctor, he is kind to most patients, some of whom I am impatient with. True treatment and healing begin with the miracle of selflessness. In humility, I need to count others more significant than my interests, my time, and myself.

Victor Wallenkampf, LLUSM class of 1976-A, is an emergency medicine physician in Humboldt County, California. February 20 is his wife's birthday.

February 21

Do not repay evil for evil or reviling for reviling, but on the contrary, bless, for to this you were called, that you may obtain a blessing. 1 Peter 3:9, ESV

I had at one time worked in a midwifery clinic that was established by midwives and run by them for more than 15 years. When the sponsoring hospital decided to hire an ob-gyn physician, Dr. Chan, to be the medical director of the clinic, the midwives were extremely unhappy. First, they resented having an MD overseeing them. Second, they did not like the fact that he was male. Third, they did not like that he was a Christian, and they strongly disapproved of his praying with his patients. They did everything they could to make life miserable for him. There were days when Dr. Chan would go home, drop to his knees in his living room, and ask God why He had sent him to this clinic. This continued for many months.

One day as we were sitting around the conference table discussing various issues, the midwives complained directly to Dr. Chan about how they did not appreciate some of the things he was doing. The atmosphere was tense. Dr. Chan sat quietly and took it all in stride. He finally said, "I am sorry." The attacks stopped.

Later, I asked Dr. Chan why he apologized to them when he had done nothing wrong. He said, "The best way to have them stop complaining is to apologize." I asked him what went through his mind when the midwives were assaulting him with their words. He said, "I was praying for them."

That incident made a big impact on me. It made me think of today's Bible text: "Do not repay evil for evil." What a role model! It also reminded me of another role model. When the Roman soldiers and the crowd mocked Christ while He was hanging on the cross, He prayed, "Father, forgive them, for they do not know what they are doing."

Dr. Chan continued working as the medical director of the clinic for six years until he accepted an administrative position in another state. His Christianity permeated every aspect of his daily interactions with the midwives, his colleagues, and his patients. He left indelible impressions on all with whom he came in contact, especially me.

Before he left, the midwives gave him a farewell party in one of their homes. After dinner, they had a little ceremony during which each of them lit a candle and placed it standing in a container of sand. Many gave tributes to Dr. Chan, complimenting him and thanking him for his leadership and friendship.

The most touching of the testimonials was by a midwife who confessed that when Dr. Chan first started working in the clinic, she disliked him intensely because of his Christianity. However, over the years because of his consistent exemplary leadership, she and the other midwives had grown to respect and love him, and they would miss him greatly. It was such a touching scene as the midwives hugged him farewell. His Christianity had finally won them over. His secret: a consistent daily walk with the Lord.

This close relationship with the Lord is free and available to every one of us. May today be the beginning of your deeper relationship with your Lord and Savior Jesus Christ, so that you, too, may radiate His love to those around you.

Caleb Liem, LLUSM class of 1970, is an obstetrician and gynecologist practicing in Salinas, California. He and his wife, Doreen, live in the neighboring city of Marina.

February 22

They also will answer, "Lord, when did we see you hungry or thirsty or a stranger or needing clothes or sick or in prison, and did not help you?"
Matthew 25:44, NIV

An "Ah ha!" moment happened when I was in my first intense inpatient clinical rotation. I was very overwhelmed during that service. Would I forget to check something important on my patient? Would I be able to see all my patients before rounds? In the midst of all this internal anxiety, I was assigned to care for a patient named Mr. Jones.

Mr. Jones was a minimally responsive patient who would only open one eye when his name was called loudly. Otherwise, he would lie in bed throughout the entire physical exam not moving a muscle. As the intensity of the rotation began to bear down on me, my morning visits with Mr. Jones became very impersonal. I was solely focused on accomplishing the physical exam maneuvers I needed to perform and then moving on to the next patient.

Then, one morning, Mr. Jones scared the life out of me! I walked into his room, just as I always had. But this time as I started the examination, he suddenly grabbed my arm, looked straight at me with both eyes wide open, and shouted "HEY!" As my tachycardia resolved, it hit me. I had been so focused on my own priorities and needs that I was no longer taking care of Mr. Jones; instead, I was taking care of me.

Jesus spoke of a group of people who fed the poor and clothed the naked but did not even realize that they were serving Him. They were not concentrated on the goal of qualifying for Heaven or impressing Jesus with their good works. If that were the case, they would have been keeping track of all the times they had done "good deeds." Instead, they were focused outside of themselves, caring for the world around them. They were attuned to the needs of others, not on any internal desire to improve themselves or to better their standing before God or others.

Ever since that experience with Mr. Jones, I have become aware of the danger of the goal-oriented approach to life. By focusing on lofty aspirations, much can be accomplished; but there are limitations. The downside to internal goals is to become so focused that we stop looking outside of our little universe of accomplishments; we fail to see the world around us or even to see Jesus.

By taking a page from the lesson Mr. Jones taught me, I have realized the value and importance of living outside of my own agenda for success and allowing Jesus to help me concentrate on the priorities of the broken people around me.

Gene Conley, LLUSM class of 2013, is an internal medicine resident at Mayo Clinic in Rochester, Minnesota. This story occurred during his third-year internal medicine rotation.

February 23

Therefore we do not lose heart. Though outwardly we are wasting away, yet inwardly we are being renewed day by day. For our light and momentary troubles are achieving for us an eternal glory that far outweighs them all. So we fix our eyes not on what is seen, but on what is unseen, since what is seen is temporary, but what is unseen is eternal. 2 Corinthians 4:16-18, NIV

After walking out of the operating room, just having performed a bilateral mastectomy, I thought about the journey that had led my patient to this point. I also thought about all that she yet must go through to even hope for survival beyond the next five years, a marker that most cancer patients know. The difficultly of diagnosing *two* sisters with breast cancer on the *same* day was hard enough. One sister, though, would have it much worse.

It was to have been a normal day for me in the office, but that day would end differently than I anticipated. It would also end differently for two sisters. I had two females on my schedule, and both were flagged as "breast conferences." This title was set aside for special hour-long sessions during which I would discuss a new breast cancer diagnosis. And this day, I would have this conference with two sisters and the same immediate and extended families.

Both sisters, that day, would receive their diagnosis of breast cancer. I told them this with some familiar faces sitting around that conference room table. I had seen them crowded into the exam room prior to the biopsy. It should be explained that sometimes breast cancer runs in a family; but to diagnose two sisters with breast cancer on the same day, and have to explain the exhausting treatment regimens and the expectations for both, was overwhelming. There was not a dry eye in the room.

One sister, however, would have a much longer course. The older sister received her diagnosis first. She had localized cancer, and most likely would need just a small portion of the breast removed, followed by radiation therapy. The younger sister, however, would then receive the news that she had a very advanced and aggressive disease that would require multiple rounds of chemotherapy, major surgery, and a longer stay in the hospital. And after that, she would need radiation therapy to the entire breast and armpit.

As a physician, I was able to explain, medically and surgically, everything that was about to happen. But how do I help put this experience into the context of God's undying love for each one of us? I was blessed to have spiritually uplifting conversations with my two special patients, and we often had time to pray together.

Probably the most encouraging work to me, the surgeon, was the presence of a chaplain immediately outside the operating room, praying. The importance of this gesture was immeasurable, both spiritually and in its meaning to the family. Seeing the patient and the patient's family receive physical, emotional, and spiritual care, to me, is the difference that Christ can make as He uplifts His people to be closer to His image.

"The Savior is present in the sickroom, in the operating room; and His power for His name's glory accomplishes great things" (Ellen G. White, *Manuscript*, 1899, p. 159).

Stephen Waterbrook, LLUSM class of 2004, is a general surgeon in Kettering, Ohio. This story was written in honor of his wife, Katie, and those affected by breast cancer. February 23 is his birthday.

Then Gideon said to God, "In order to see whether you will deliver Israel by my hand, as you have said, I am going to lay a fleece of wool on the threshing floor; if there is dew on the fleece alone, and it is dry on all the ground, then I shall know that you will deliver Israel by my hand, as you have said." Judges 6:36-37, NRSV

It was a dreary winter quarter my sophomore year at Pacific Union College in central California. It had been raining nonstop for the past two weeks. I was sitting in my dorm room that afternoon, really anticipating spring break. Among other things, I was looking forward to seeing my girlfriend back home and had two tickets for a performance of "The Phantom of the Opera."

Just then, my mother called and asked: "How would you like to go on a mission trip to Honduras during your spring break? They're building an orphanage and there is also a local hospital there where you can spend some time during the week. We'll pay for the trip!" While the idea was intriguing, it did not outweigh my desire for a relaxing break at home. I told her I did not have plans for anything that ambitious. She told me to think about it for a few days, and then let her know.

I was conflicted and leaning toward not going. However, it did seem like a good opportunity to test my premedical desires. I decided to turn to God for guidance. If only He could make my choice clear, without any doubt, that would be ideal.

The two weeks of solid rain gave me an idea. In the spirit of Gideon, I asked God for a sign. *If You would like me to go to Honduras, please let it not rain tomorrow.* If God really wanted me to be there, this was the chance I would give Him to show me. I also thought that would be a good way to get out of going, without feeling too guilty about it.

The next morning it was unusually quiet. When I looked out the window, I saw nothing but a clear blue sky. Not a single cloud all day! Needless to say, I was impressed. I also remembered that Gideon had prayed twice, and I also felt the need to press my luck.

Dear Lord, It really seems like You want me to go to Honduras. But for me to be sure, please let it rain again tomorrow. Amen. When I woke up the next morning, I heard the familiar pitter-patter outside my window.

So, during my spring break, my parents enjoyed a date night seeing "Phantom" in Los Angeles. My girlfriend, who was very impressed by my story, graciously understood. I went to Honduras and had a very good experience. I spent most of the time shadowing physicians in the hospital. I was humbled by the positive attitudes of the local people, despite the poverty and illnesses surrounding them.

In the end, the experience helped solidify my desires to proceed with medical training. To be completely honest, I am not sure what, or if anything, in the course of history was changed as a result of my going on this trip. What I knew for sure is that God wanted me to be there, and that feeling of confidence goes a long way.

Edward Javor, LLUSM class of 1998, is an endocrinologist in Riverside, California. His wife, Gina, is an LLUSM graduate, class of 1999.

February 25

And it shall come to pass, that whosoever shall call on the name of the Lord shall be saved. Acts 2:21, KJV

Elton was a rather crusty, 60-year-old curmudgeon who entered my office in my third year of practice. His opening remark was: "You have a bunch of religious books in your office. Do you believe in God?" I assured him that I believed in Him with all my heart.

"How can you believe in God when you know man evolved through the Darwinian Theory of Evolution, and that eliminates the need for a creator?" Elton questioned. Remembering what H. M. S. Richards Sr., the venerated preacher, once told me of his retort to a query like this, I responded: "I don't have that much faith."

Elton came in two to three times each year, and each conversation started the same way. However, after about seven years of these types of verbal exchanges, he surprised me one day and said: "Maybe you could be right." He seemed to be softening his position on evolution and God.

One morning at 5:30, he called me and said: "Doctor, I have some chest pains and it is difficult for me to breathe." I sent an ambulance to his home while I started for the hospital. We arrived at the emergency department (ED) at the same time. An EKG revealed a serious problem.

A local cardiologist happened to be passing by the cubicle and I motioned to him. He stopped, glanced at the EKG and without a word left the room. Outside the patient's vision, he motioned me to come. He looked at me and said: "Dr. Benson—*he's dead.*" I responded that he obviously was not since he was still talking. But the cardiologist replied that the man's life was down to minutes because the major coronary arteries were occluded.

When I returned to Elton's room, he asked: "Am I dying?" I could not lie, so I had to tell him, "Yes, Elton, you are." His response was, "Oh my God, my God!" He repeated it louder a second time, "Oh my God, my God!"

He then requested that I pray for him. I answered in the affirmative and then described Christ's experience on Calvary with the dying thief, to whom He gave the promise of salvation. I pointed out to Elton that the thief had done no good work. I said: "We don't lose salvation by what we do; nor do we lose it by anything we don't do." Personally, I believe we are saved only by grace, through faith, through the righteous blood of Christ. We only have to ask for salvation in our sincerest plea, believing that He can save our soul for eternity. We are reminded in 2 Corinthians 5:21 that the sinless Christ took our sin and gave us His righteousness. What a trade!

At Elton's request, I prayed for him a short heartfelt prayer, stating that he could rest in Jesus if he would only believe. The short prayer ended with Elton's response, "I am resting in Jesus. I am resting in Jes . . ." He never finished the second attempt at saying Jesus' name.

I believe we will see Elton in Heaven.

Douglas L. Benson, CME class of 1959, was a general practitioner in Eagle Rock, California, for 35 years before retiring. He and his wife ministered to many through their medical practice and the youth program at their church. February 25 is the birthday of his late wife, Lynn.

February 26

And when Jesus went out He saw a great multitude; and He was moved with compassion for them, and healed their sick. Matthew 14:14, NKJV

During my second year of medical school, our class had the opportunity to follow physicians in local clinics one day a week for several months. While this routine was a welcome break from studying, those clinic days were sometimes long and monotonous, mainly because we did not know anything about medicine except how to study it.

I was assigned to a clinic in a very poor community in the middle of San Bernardino, California, working with an extremely dedicated physician who truly cared about her patients and demonstrated Christ's love to each of them. No matter how disheveled, how unhygienic, or how ignorant her patients were about their health, she gave them the best care and the most compassion she could offer. Because this daily opportunity to deliver compassion as Christ did was the reason I chose medicine, I decided to look for those moments when I could be compassionate. After all, as a lowly student, this was all I could offer these patients.

Some patients were only interested in quick, efficient visits, while other patients needed a kind word or a reassuring touch. I spent as much time as possible to make them feel cared for, while the physician attended to their medical problems.

My favorite day at that clinic began like all of the rest, very routinely. But our last patient for the day was a special one. She was an elderly Hispanic woman who was brought in by her caregiver. The patient only spoke Spanish, so the caregiver did all of the talking—not because the physician did not speak Spanish, but because the patient rarely spoke. Her husband had died recently and she was extremely depressed.

As I examined her, I gently patted her on the shoulder and smiled. She saw me but would not acknowledge my presence through her sad eyes. Throughout the interview, I tried to convey something to her, although I am not sure what. But I wanted her to know I cared, even though she still would not look at me. Once the visit ended, the physician and I sat down at our work area to finish the paperwork.

A few moments later, the caregiver led our patient out of the office. Just as they were passing us, the patient raised her hand and gave me a slight wave, while the corners of her mouth turned up into a shy smile. I waved back and smiled, trying to contain the joy in my heart. I had thought my efforts were useless. After all, I was *just* a medical student.

But this sweet woman showed me that what medical students have to offer begins long before our training is complete. She showed me that we can impact our patients' lives, even as students, by showing them compassion, if we just look for the opportunities to do so.

Tiffany Earle, LLUSM class of 2014, is from Charlotte, North Carolina. She graduated from Southern Adventist University with a BS degree in chemistry.

February 27

Whether therefore ye eat, or drink, or whatsoever ye do, do all to the glory of God.
1 Corinthians 10:31, KJV

"Sorry, but I don't mix my personal life with my work life," I replied to John Chung, LLUSM class of 1988, after he asked me if I wanted to attend his weekly home Bible study group. Several months later, he asked me to bring a few surgical case photos to his Bible study meeting, telling me that he had "forgotten" them at the office. That was how he got me to start attending his Wednesday night Bible studies, and what a rich blessing it has proven to be! I met like-minded friends, and the studies led me to appreciate the Bible and *Spirit of Prophecy* books.

One year prior to this, I had found myself questioning the way I lived my life—an uncertainty that stemmed from a personal relationship that failed. It was a humbling experience to realize that, while my professional life flourished with hard work, dating did not work the same way. A good friend told me: "You need to let God write your love story for you. He is the one Who knows you best." That humbling dating experience caused me to fall on my knees and pray a prayer of surrender.

Until that time, I had compartmentalized my life. There was minimal overlap of my personal, spiritual, and work lives. My priorities were different in each area of my life, and there was no overriding objective. It took a life-changing event for me to recognize this hypocrisy. A change happens because, sooner or later, different areas of your life that are out of sync start clashing with each other.

In retrospect, God had been working for a very long time to help me see my problem. When I gave my life to Jesus, life became much less complicated. There was peace in my heart, which meant fewer emotional roller coaster rides. I began to trust God more in His leading, a trust that resulted in gaining freedom from certain sins with which I struggled. And He also led me to my wonderful husband. Best of all, the Cross finally had personal significance to me. I am undeserving, and yet He has blessed me to the brim. For that I am forever thankful.

I am so grateful for the physician mentors in my life, doctors who have shared Christ in the workplace and have told me: Our office is a mission field, and we need to reach people not just physically, but also spiritually. Pray with your patients; the Holy Spirit will tell you which patients need prayer. Out of the hundreds of patients I have prayed with, I've only had one person say no to prayer. Have prayer with your nurses at the beginning of the day to ask for guidance. Be faithful in the little things; then God can entrust you to the bigger things. My passion is not just dermatology; it's planting the seeds so we can help bring as many people to Heaven as we possibly can.

As I have witnessed dedicated mentors take the time to call anxious patients, provide prayer, and give their hard-earned money to benefit others, saying, "It's all God's anyway," they have made a large, indelible impression upon my life. I hope to pass on the torch and be a mentor to other young people, so they also may see a glimpse of God's persistent love and guidance.

Jane Yoon Clark, LLUSM class of 2005, practices dermatology in Dalton, Georgia. She is married to Chester Van Clark III. February 27 is her mother's birthday.

February 28

But seek first the kingdom of God and His righteousness, and all these things shall be added to you. Matthew 6:33, NKJV

The summer between my first and second year of medical school I had the opportunity to go on a mission trip through the SIMS (Students for International Mission Service) program. I traveled to Ile-Ife Seventh-day Adventist Hospital in Nigeria. It happened to be the same hospital where I was born and reared during the first part of my life. While I was growing up in Nigeria, my father served as a missionary physician in the hospital. Returning to this site, I had many nostalgic moments as I walked around the hospital and in the compound that houses the hospital, as well as during visits to the living quarters of the staff.

As a medical student I was able to shadow the other physicians who were working and training in the hospital. I was also able to get some hands-on experience, including suturing one patient and inserting a catheter into another. But above all, I had the opportunity to grow in my walk with God.

While there, I became very close to five patients who, sadly, passed away. Two of them were twin baby boys, less than five days old. Life that had barely begun for them was so quickly gone. I started thinking about what really matters in this life. Is it the opportunity to go to school and get various degrees and different letters after my name or to start a successful business or to get married and have children? Where should my priorities really lie?

I realized that, at the end of the day, what really is important is my relationship with God and being able to spend all eternity with Him. I also want to share Him with others, so they may do so as well. This objective, however, does not mean I should quit school or stop living on this earth. I realize that everything that God allows us to do, every opportunity He brings our way, is another chance for us to get to know Him more, to truly grow in Him.

If we were idle on this earth, doing nothing but waiting for Christ to return, we can only imagine the chaos there would be. So God, in His infinite mercy and grace, gave us work to do to keep us occupied until He comes back for us.

My end goal and my success are not defined by my work, but rather my work should be an opportunity to develop my Christ-like character and truly minister to others. What an awesome privilege I will have as a medical professional to minister in a way that others cannot. I must remember that as I tend to my patient's physical needs, I can also minister to them spiritually. And, ultimately, it is this spiritual impact that will do the patient the most good.

Adegbemisola Daniyan, LLUSM class of 2015, is from Paradise, California. She graduated from Oakwood University with a BS degree in biology. February 28 is the birthday of her father, Samuel A. Daniyan, LLUSM class of 1979-B, who has served as a missionary physician in Nigeria and Guam.

MARCH

"Keep in constant touch with Jesus.

Keep in close touch with others.

Keep in careful touch with yourself."

March 1

Look at the birds of the air; they do not sow or reap or store away in barns, and yet your heavenly Father feeds them. Are you not much more valuable than they? Even the very hairs of your head are all numbered. So don't be afraid; you are worth more than many sparrows. Matthew 6:26; 10:30-31, NIV

Sarah wanted to talk to me on the phone last night, which is unusual because Sarah prefers face-to-face conversations. I will take a conversation with a seven year old any way I can get it, but I also sensed she had something important to say. "Hi, Daddy. Tweetie is dead." Sarah tends to get to the point.

She had adopted the orphaned baby bird only the day before but had been mothering it nonstop with overwhelming compassion. Sarah embraces life with a compelling intensity.

"I'm so sorry. I know you took good care of her, and I'm so proud of you," I said.

Sarah interrupted, speaking quickly: "We need to bury her in the backyard, but I don't want a cross or anything with her name on it because that will just make me think of her and be sad."

"All right," I responded, then paused trying to think of something comforting to say.

But Sarah does not abide silence. "I will help you dig the hole. Bye-bye Daddy," she said and handed the phone to her mother.

I later learned the rest of the story. Sarah had been feeding the little bird faithfully every 15 to 20 minutes. Caring for her and caring about her. When Tweetie died, Sarah cried. The tears of a little girl can break any heart.

When I arrived home Sarah was already in bed. I went upstairs to kiss her goodnight and found she was still awake. "Daddy, I changed my mind. I don't want to bury Tweetie."

"Okay. Would you like me to do it?"

"I want you to put her in the trash."

"Oh. Are you sure? Why?"

"Because I don't want to think about her every time I go into the backyard."

"Okay, we'll do it in the morning," I agreed. "Goodnight, sweetie." Sarah went right to sleep.

In the morning when Sarah woke up, we went downstairs for the "funeral." We gathered up Tweetie in her Avon-bag casket. I asked Sarah if she would like to say anything. She just shook her head. Nothing needed to be said.

"Would you like me to pray?" I asked. Sarah nodded and bowed her head.

Dear Jesus, Thank you for allowing Sarah to care for Tweetie for the past day. Thank you for making Sarah such a caring little girl. Thank you for letting Tweetie have such a peaceful and loving last day with Sarah. Please bless Sarah and Tweetie so they can be friends again in Heaven. Amen.

Sarah and I then walked into the garage, where Sarah remained as I continued toward the trash bins sitting out at the curb by the street. I opened the trash bin and glanced back toward the garage. Sarah was peeking out from behind the car. She waved at me to "go ahead." I gently placed the Avon bag in the trash and Sarah went back into the house. Time to move on. Sarah grieved with amazing grace. There are many lessons in the love of a little girl for a baby bird.

Chris Johnston is an associate general counsel for Loma Linda University and LLUMC. His daughter Sarah was born on March 1 at LLUMC.

March 2

You, Lord, hear the desire of the afflicted; you encourage them, and you listen to their cry. Psalm 10:17, NIV

The greatest privilege we have as medical professionals is the opportunity to hear people's stories. And when we stop to listen, truly and sincerely listen, we just might be amazed at what people share.

Lily was one of those stories. She had bounced around in foster care, was adopted and subsequently abused, and was separated from her sister. She finally ended up at Loma Linda University Medical Center because of a brain mass. When I asked this preteen where she lived and heard her nonchalantly and honestly tell me that she was not exactly sure, it made me want to leap across the room and hug her.

That same desire to comfort her occurred when she shed tears over a potential CT scan. I explained that the brain scan would not hurt. I told her that we were trying to figure out the best way to help her get better. I encouraged her to ask questions. Then I just sat there quietly.

It was then that, in the most innocent way possible, she asked: "Will I still be able to listen to my music? Will fixing my brain keep me from hearing music?" These questions humbled me. As a medical team, we had focused intently on giving her a proper diagnosis and treatment plan. But Lily's concerns were about simpler things.

Another story was Ralphy, who was a six year old who would dance himself to sleep. He was watching the same movie every time I came to see him—and rewound it to show me the identical scene every day before allowing me to leave. Then came the day we had to tell his family that he didn't have tuberculosis; he no longer had to remain isolated from everyone but his mother. Instead, we found that Ralphy had a rare lung tumor.

The next morning, he was the happiest I had seen him in the two weeks I had been following him. I asked him why he was so happy. While standing on his bed dancing, he said: "Because my grandpa can come visit me now, and no one has to wear a mask!" I had cried when I read the devastating pathology report, but Ralphy had reasons to be thankful.

As student physicians, we have countless opportunities to practice our skill as clinicians. Infrequently, though, I have utilized those opportunities to revel in the beauty of my patients' stories. But if we are to care for people the way God cares for us, we must hear our patients for more than their hypertension and back pain. We must choose to hear their hearts.

Cory Mitchell, LLUSM class of 2014, is from Camarillo, California. He graduated from Pacific Union College with a BS degree in exercise science. These stories occurred during his third-year pediatric rotation at LLUMC. March 2 is the birthday of his late grandfather, Eldon Dickinson, LLUSD class of 1964.

March 3

The kingdom of heaven is like what happens when someone finds a treasure hidden in a field and buries it again. A person like that is happy and goes and sells everything in order to buy that field. The kingdom of heaven is like what happens when a shop owner is looking for fine pearls. After finding a very valuable one, the owner goes and sells everything in order to buy that pearl. Matthew 13:44-46, CEV

I was disturbed. No, I was angry, when I read the following passage [abridged] by Jack London in his story, *The Sea-Wolf*.

"Harrison had been sent eighty feet aloft to fix a jammed sheet at the end of the gaff and while on the rigging, almost fell to his death."

Van Weyden, the narrator of the tale, asked the Captain, "'But you, who make a mock of human life, don't you place any value upon it whatever?'

'What kind of value? How do you measure it? Who values it?' replied the Captain. 'Why should I be parsimonious with this life which is cheap and without value? There are more sailors than there are ships on the sea for them, more workers than there are factories or machines for them. Take the man I had aloft. He held on as if he were a precious thing, a treasure beyond diamonds or rubies. To you? No. To me? Not at all. To himself? Yes. But I do not accept his estimate . . . And what have you to say?'"

In economic literature, the value of an object or thing is determined by what we are willing to give up to acquire it. The stories of the "Hidden Treasure" and the "Costly Pearl" found in Matthew 13:44-46 reflect this concept.

If the price is too high, no one (or very few) will purchase the item. If the price is too low, the manufacturer will not be able to stay in business and continue to produce the item. It is the purchaser who ultimately determines the value of the item and whether or not the producer will remain in business.

How much do you value your education? Is its value determined by the amount of tuition dollars? Is it the time equivalent spent studying and going to classes, when you could have been earning an income in another job? Is it the income you were able to make in your profession, subsequent to your education? Is it the "good" that you have done, as a result of the knowledge you have obtained, regardless of the remuneration? Just how valuable is your education?

But how do we answer Captain Wolf Larsen? Unless we recognize that an individual has value because Christ died for that life and the cost is irreplaceable, then Captain Larsen was right: Life has no value except to further our own personal goals. Nothing is of value unless it costs you something.

Tomorrow, when those of you who are doctors "see your patients," will you see them as just more people in a never-ending queue, who need to be taken care of before you go home? Or are they individuals for whom Christ died, and are you, as their physician, there to provide something of value that they cannot get anywhere else? That will determine the value of *your* services.

Is personal security the ultimate goal of your practice, or is it—according to your reason for attending school—to help "Make Man Whole?"

Burton Briggs, LLUSM class of 1966, is a professor in LLUSM department of anesthesiology. He was president of LLUSMAA from 1997 to 1998, received the School of Medicine Distinguished Service Award in 2002, and was an LLUSMAA 2010 Honored Alumnus.

And after the earthquake a fire; but the LORD was not in the fire: and after the fire a still small voice. 1 Kings 19:12, KJV

The beeper buzzed. The emergency department was already calling with another admission. It was March of my internship, and I was starting another 36-hour call. The snow was still on the ground outside, and my mood inside was blue. I went into the trauma room to see why they were calling, and my heart sank. It was an elderly woman who was comatose. I looked to see if she was breathing but was not sure. I raised her left arm to check for a pulse, and her arm flopped toward me in an unnatural manner. The humerus was completely fractured.

I started doing the resuscitative procedures while thinking, thankfully, she was comatose and not feeling any pain. She had a history of multiple myeloma that had eroded the bones away in several places. In addition, she had sunken craters in her forehead. The steroids she was on had induced a hyperosmolar hyperglycemic state.

As each lab report was returned to me, it contained another problem that needed to be addressed. I worked through them, one at a time, thinking my goal would be to provide comfort measures until the cancer had run its natural course. However, the Lord had other plans.

She was moved to the ICU and lived through my 36 hours on call. To my amazement, she was alive the next day, and the next. A few days later, the nurses told me she was speaking, which I could not help but question. However, her vital signs stabilized to the point she was ready to be moved to the floor.

As always is the case in an internship, my turn for call came again. I was patrolling the hallway and raiding the fridge when I heard music coming from her room. The voice was broken and halting, but it was my patient singing with friends and family, "Shall We Gather at the River?" To a tired and lonely intern, it sounded like angels singing from Heaven.

When I looked in her room, she had her Bible in her hand, trying to hold it up with her good arm while the broken arm was in a makeshift splint. The picture was inspirational, and I could envision angels helping her hold the Bible. I had missed church many times due to my internship, but this scene was the most powerful sermon I had heard in a long time.

God speaks to us in many ways. I have had the privilege of meeting many dynamic people in my career who have truly inspired me. However, none have influenced me the way this lady did at a time when I needed it. I received praise from my fellow residents for making the great "save" on this patient. But I knew in my heart the reason this lady lived. She had one more sermon to preach before she was going to rest—waiting to be "gathered at the river."

T. Martin Kelly, LLUSM class of 1985, is an attending physician in the emergency medicine residency program at Carl R. Darnall Army Medical Center in Fort Hood, Texas.

March 5

I will instruct thee and teach thee in the way which thou shalt go: I will guide thee with mine eye. Psalm 32:8, KJV

Whenever we travel on the Earth's surface, whether by foot, sea, or air, we are assisted by landmarks (trails, peaks, streams, sun, moon, or stars) and are sometimes also helped by compasses and maps. Navigational assists such as GPS (global positioning system) have been available in automobiles since the 1990s. However, they have been used in ships, airplanes, and missiles since the 1970s.

This system, using 24 orbiting satellites, is intended to locate your GPS device on Earth and then assist you as you move toward your desired destination by showing maps on a screen or giving voice directions. The device follows your movement, and if you take a detour, it will note your deviation and give you instructions to reach your desired destination. It is like magic!

On a recent trip from Nevada to California's San Francisco Bay Area, I used my GPS to assist me. I noticed that Bakersfield, California, appeared to be about halfway to my eventual destination; that seemed like a good place to stop for a while. I needed a convenient place to stay just off Highway 99, food to sustain my wife and me, and fuel for the rest of the trip. But since I had not visited Bakersfield for more than 20 years, I was in unfamiliar territory.

I consulted my travel information sources (AAA maps and their hotel-motel and restaurant guide book). But the information on Bakersfield was about 20 pages, providing me with too many options for places to stay, available restaurants, and possible gas stations.

On previous trips on Highway 99, I had enjoyed countryside vistas of gorgeous farms, ranches, and animals. These were now replaced by hundreds of houses and shopping centers. Such formerly simple decisions of where to stay, where to find a decent meal, and where to buy fuel suddenly became one big confusing decision. What should I do?

I am happy to report that I have been blessed with a daily lifetime positioning system, GGS. God's Guidance System has assisted me with the proper selection of whatever is needed for the occasion. In this case, the GGS came through again and helped me select a hotel that was only one block off Highway 99; it located an excellent restaurant as well. Also, the Costco gas station was just a block away from the hotel. I thank God daily for His promise: "I will guide thee with my eye."

Francis Lau, CME class of 1947, is an emeritus professor in LLUSM department of medicine. He previously taught medicine and cardiology at LA County General Hospital for CME and USC. He has four children, all of whom graduated from LLUSM.

March 6

And by his light I walked through darkness. Job 29:3, NRSV

As I walked through the doors of my unit, ready to start my shift, I met my co-workers, who were sobbing tears of sadness. My assignment that day was the honor of being the nurse for a family whose child had just passed away on night shift. Over the past year, I had taken care of their son many times. I had much in common with the parents: the father was a surfer, world traveler, and adventurer; it would have been hard for us not to become friends.

I saw their emotion that day first hand. Sobbing. Screaming. Begging. Pleading. Holding their child tightly. Rocking back and forth. Brokenhearted. The pain they felt that day, I felt. When they were ready, I gently lifted their son from their hands . . . clenched hands.

Together, we bathed him for the last time. I cleaned the room, removed all the silent, life-sustaining equipment, and scrubbed his blood off the floor. I cried every time another family member arrived, and we started the sobbing process over again with the parents. I brought the family coffee, water, and chairs, in order to provide comfort in their hour of mourning.

Hours later, I woke the mother, cuddling her son, and told her we needed to take him downstairs, and she would need to leave. After thousands of times, this would be her last trip down our hallway. Her son was swaddled in his favorite blanket, surrounded with his favorite stuffed animals, and she would never hold him again.

Their walk down the hallway was interrupted by many hugs from my co-workers. Even our monitor technician embraced them and cried some more with them. I knew I would have to return to the room for the worst thing I have had to do in my life. I had to prepare the small body for the morgue. As I opened the door to his room, I turned around to see four of my co-workers standing behind me. "We would never let you do this alone," one of them said.

We have kids die occasionally, but this time was different. This was my friend's son. It felt like my own son. It hurt. I was not numb like before. I had let them in, and they felt like family. I struggled for months after that day, but I hugged my own boys more, and I complimented my wife more. I appreciated my friends and family more.

The nectar of life seemed sweeter after that. That day not only changed the way I carried out my job, but it changed the way I felt and loved, because it gave me a deeper meaning of love. Before, I put up defenses to avoid feeling the pain my patients' families felt. Now, I love every family I take care of, and it feels so much happier, and means so much more when I send them home safe and sound.

You cannot truly understand love until you have experienced the depths of pain. And we might never truly appreciate Heaven if we had never lived on this earth.

Greg Eiseman has been a pediatric cardiac ICU registered nurse for five years at LLUCH. He is married to Heidi, LLUSM class of 2010. They have two sons and hope to serve overseas in the future.

March 7

But when he heard it, he said, "Those who are well have no need of a physician, but those who are sick. Go and learn what this means, 'I desire mercy, and not sacrifice.' For I came not to call the righteous, but sinners."
Matthew 9:12-13, ESV

Skin and bones writhed in the bed, fighting for life, gasping for air. The hospital was quiet and dark with the thick silence that lies over everything at night, except in this little corner, surrounded by a curtain.

"No! No!" Mr. D yelled, "I don't want an IV. Why am I tied down?" He was pulling at the restraints and twisting. In a way, he looked very much alive—like a fish does when it is pulled up and dropped in the bottom of a boat.

I watched the physician deftly giving orders, listening to the patient's heart and lungs, assessing his mental status, and dispensing advice to the nursing staff as the patient tried to undo everything the team was working to accomplish. He had squirmed out of his gown and was barely covered by a sheet. There were no family members by the bed, and I thought, "This is how man has been dying for thousands of years: naked, alone, fighting for every final breath."

I felt incredibly removed, trying to avoid being trampled by the traffic surging in and out of the doorway. I looked behind me and caught a glimpse of what was playing on TV. I felt caught in space and time between this corner in the hospital where a naked man was fighting to keep himself alive for just another minute and the beautiful characters on the screen who never even spared a thought for how this was all going to end someday. What was I doing here?

But then I thought, who needs a doctor? Certainly not the well—it is the poor, the naked, the sick, the old. These are the people I set out to serve when I began my journey through medical school. Even though they are not the elite, I want to treat all of my patients with compassion—even the demented, noncompliant ones. They are immensely, intrinsically valuable, even if our society does not see them that way.

But my job does not stop at acknowledging that their life is difficult; my job is learning how I, as a Christian physician, can make my patients' burdens easier and express to them unconditional love and kindness. It is about serving the people whom I have no desire to serve; the amazing part is when God opens my eyes to see that even under the residual smell of tobacco, vomit, and soiled clothes, there is a beautiful person who is His child.

At that point at Mr. D's bedside, I want to say that I went forward to take his hand and be with him while the tumult surged around him. But I did not. I was too timid about getting in the way or being scolded by an irascible nurse. I just stood there—mute, trying to learn and absorb so that next time I would know how to move in coordination with the funny dance circling the bed of a dying man.

Next time though, I pray to God that I will see the patient with His eyes. I will take his hand, squeeze it gently, and say: "I'm with you; we're doing everything we can."

Hayley Hunt, LLUSM class of 2014, is from Carnation, Washington. She graduated from Wheaton College with a BS degree in biology. This story occurred during her third-year internal medical rotation.

And whoever receives one such child in My name receives Me.
Matthew 18:5, NASB

The voice on the other end of the phone line sounded familiar, a sound that always thrills a grandpa's heart. "Grampy, what are you doing?" It was Argy, proud to be able to dial by herself, now calling from Sri Lanka. As she chatted on, my mind went back some eight years.

The emergency department was already full of accident victims from a bus crash, so the police came directly to the administrator's home with a new problem. Chandra and Charlie had just returned to Ethiopia from home leave and were relaxing that evening, getting acquainted with Judy Schmidt. She was a maternity expert and CDC consultant who had just arrived in Gimbie on assignment to the government for a few months. Unable to find a decent hotel in town, she had come to their home looking for a place to stay.

The police message was brief. A newborn baby had been discovered in a community latrine—hypothermic with a weak sucking reflex. The outlook was grim.

With sensitivity and concern, the team of three began their work—now immensely grateful for Judy's expertise as they went about warming, bathing, trying to feed the baby, and wondering: "Who is this? Where is the mother? Will this frail baby make it or be just another sad statistic? And if she does survive, what will happen then?"

Through that night, the next day, and several more nights, the outcome was uncertain. But, gradually, the baby started eating, responding, and embracing life. As her survival became more certain, her story became more complete. She was the result of a teenage pregnancy, and the mother—rejected by the child's father—made a quick delivery in a local latrine, and then fled in fear. Others finally heard the weak cry and tried to retrieve the baby from deep in the muck. Then the police were called and, after tearing off the sides of the latrine, they were able to pull the struggling baby out and head immediately to the hospital.

As the days and weeks went by, the hourly care became easier; feelings started to grow in Chandra and Charlie. The thoughts started coming: "What if we never find the mother? Should we consider adopting this baby? How would that be done here in Ethiopia? Are we really ready for this?"

After a few months, Charlie and Chandra posted a notice on a tree in the community, as the law dictated, asking if anyone claimed the baby. With no response, they dared to think of adoption. But first a name was needed. Chandra had started taking the baby with her to the office each day, where her secretary, Berhane, suggested naming her Aregane, a term meaning, "we found her," in the local Oromifa language.

Several months later, I visited Gimbie Adventist Hospital and met Aregane for the first time. Over the next year, as the paperwork was completed, Argy became my granddaughter. Rescued from a latrine in Ethiopia, she is now a bubbly eight year old, currently living in Sri Lanka with her brother, Karl, and her parents.

Out of rejection to being claimed. From abandonment to now being cherished. Through a series of miracles, God saved this baby and delivered her to our family. Her life became a testimony to His care for the least of these. And I am forever grateful for His gift.

Richard Hart, LLUSM class of 1970, DrPH, is president of Loma Linda University. He received his DrPH degree from Johns Hopkins University in Baltimore, Maryland. He was an LLUSMAA 1994 Honored Alumnus, 2008 AIMS Global Mission Award recipient, and LLUSMAA Alumnus of the Year in 2012. March 8 is Aregane's birthday.

March 9

Praise be to the LORD, for he has heard my cry for mercy. The LORD is my strength and my shield; my heart trusts in him, and he helps me. My heart leaps for joy, and with my song I praise him. Psalm 28:6-7, NIV

Even though the Korean War was going on, I was deferred from military service during college and medical school. But with the conscription still in force, I knew that eventually I would be drafted; so I elected a military internship and surgical residency. Upon completion of my surgery residency at the U.S. Naval Hospital in San Diego, California, I was assigned to the naval hospital on the island of Guam.

On one ordinary tropical morning, just two weeks after we arrived on the island, the telephone rang. It was the commanding officer ordering me to come immediately to the hospital. A Lockheed Super Constellation with 90 passengers aboard had crashed into Mt. Barrigada. Soon our hospital halls were filled with screaming, crying, and badly burned people. Where to begin? I lined up the nurses and corpsmen to give injections of morphine for pain relief.

Since many were burned over 80 percent to 90 percent of their bodies, a condition beyond our capability to help, I knew I could only relieve pain and do tracheotomies for airways. Even though Guam's temperature was at 99 degrees, with 98 percent humidity, there was only one air-conditioned room on my floor. With so much heat, it was important to get fluids into the burn patients quickly.

I looked around for help from my fellow doctors. None was available. Only nurses and corpsmen were with me. We had to open the emergency supplies maintained on site in the event of war, as we had run out of fluids and pain medications very quickly with these patients. I began to take each man—one by one—and calculate the fluids required and do "cut downs" for intravenous access and perform tracheotomies as needed.

I was overwhelmed with the magnitude of the tragedy; but the words "men as true to duty as the needle to the pole" (Ellen G. White, *Education*, p. 57) kept ringing in my ears. I continued cutting off the charred clothing and doing "cut downs" and tracheotomies.

Many did not survive the first 24 to 36 hours. I stayed on my floor 24 hours a day for the first week and slept when I could. I silently prayed over and over that the Lord would give me strength, courage, and wisdom.

The Lord answered my prayers. "We" were able to save all those who had body surface burns of 65 percent or less with no other significant injuries. A letter of commendation from the commanding officer of the U.S. Naval Hospital in Guam recognized our efforts; however, my real reward will come when I hear, "Well done," spoken by the Master Physician.

Allen Botimer, CME class of 1955, is a general surgeon who practiced in Seattle, Washington. Now retired, he resides in Nampa, Idaho.

Casting all your care upon him; for he careth for you. 1 Peter 5:7, KJV

"We have three patients for you," the nurse practitioner said, as I walked through the door.

"Two are on the floor, and one is in the emergency department," she added, as I glanced at the clock; it was 5:40 p.m. I was late! I was flustered and felt terrible that the day shift resident doctors had been waiting for so long. They gave me all the pertinent points about the patients and quickly left.

Three admissions are not that many, but three at the same time is a different story.

"This is going be a fabulous night," I thought, sarcastically. Not only was I late and had three patients who needed immediate attention, but I had not had time to go home to grab my two call-night essentials—a pair of sneakers that I usually had stashed in my bag and my cell phone charger. So, I would have to walk around all night in slippery ballet flats.

I headed downstairs to see the patient in the emergency department, slipping and sliding as I went. I really needed some more comfortable shoes. After assessing the patient and leaving admission orders, a small voice said, "Check your car." Check my car? I knew I had not picked up my sneakers that morning, but I obliged.

I quickly headed to the parking lot to look in my car trunk. Inside, tucked in a corner, was a pair of sneakers! I could not believe it. I grabbed them and ran back inside. At least I would be more comfortable while trying to get everything else done.

I ran upstairs and headed to the call room to change into my scrubs. As I bent down to tie my laces, I saw something sticking out from the wall. I had seen it before but thought it was the charger for our pagers. I picked it up and tried sticking it into the USB port on my phone. It fit!

Things were looking up! There were still three admissions to type though and two patients still to assess. I decided to glance at the histories for the other two patients before I went to see them. They were return patients with straightforward histories who were being admitted for routine chemotherapy. Both were stable with no complaints. Maybe this night was not going to be that bad after all.

When I had a quiet moment later that night, I reflected upon what had happened. Everything I was concerned about when I walked through the door, God had rectified. We often think we can go to Him only with "big" things—such as sickness, deaths, important life choices, or spiritual struggles. But His word says to cast ALL our care upon Him, great *and* small. He is never too busy to attend to our needs.

The same God, who brought comfort to the families of those in the hospital, found time to provide me with sneakers and a phone charger, as trivial as that may seem. May we cast *all* our cares upon Him today, be they great or small.

Nicole Haughton is a pediatric resident at LLUCH. She is originally from St. Catherine, Jamaica. March 10 is her birthday.

March 11

For the Lord himself will come down from heaven, with a loud command, with the voice of the archangel and with the trumpet call of God, and the dead in Christ will rise first. After that, we who are still alive and are left will be caught up together with them in the clouds to meet the Lord in the air. And so we will be with the Lord forever. Therefore encourage one another with these words.
1 Thessalonians 4:16-18, NIV

Is anyone prepared for death? Occasionally, death is expected, one last step at the end of a long road, allowing for funeral arrangements and last farewells. Just as often, death arrives without warning, a lightning strike on a silent summer night.

At graduation, we new doctors are confident that we can care for the 90-year-old retiree just as easily as we can tend to the 16-year-old accident victim. We are taught the significance of palliative care and the five stages of grief.

Somewhere in the evolution from medical student to physician, however, the training that was formerly black and white morphs into something significantly more gray and hazy. Countless patients have made this clear to me, but one patient particularly comes to mind.

He was a retired pediatrician from up North, spending a few weeks vacationing with his family in the South. Earlier that day, he had been splashing in the ocean with his granddaughter, but that evening he developed shortness of breath. Soon after arriving at the emergency department, he went into cardiac arrest; his implanted defibrillator began firing, and CPR was initiated. He was intubated and given multiple doses of epinephrine; circulation was eventually regained, and he was admitted to my team.

His wife, children, and grandchildren moved into the cardiac care unit. They stayed with him day and night—holding his hands, reading the Bible, and streaming YouTube videos of Lady Gaga, for whom he had recently developed a great liking.

His progress was slow; but after several weeks, he began to open his eyes, follow commands, and write a few words. The family and the medical team were ecstatic (we had become close after caring for their husband-father-grandfather for so long) and decided it was time for extubation. As the tube was joyfully removed, our patient smiled and greeted his family. The medical team stepped out to allow more space for the family celebration.

Ten minutes later, the son exploded from the room. "Come quick," he said, "Dad's not doing well!" We rushed in to find our beloved patient apneic and bradycardic. We immediately began CPR; however, this time, and despite our best efforts, we were unable to bring him back. We cried. We cried for our patient, we cried for his family, we cried for each other. The family choked out thanks for our efforts; we could hardly respond due to our own tears.

Did my training prepare me for the desolation I felt as we trailed from the room? No. Does it help knowing he had those last sweet moments with his loving family? Maybe. What I do know is that I am fairly certain I will never feel entirely comfortable with death; but as long as I can provide compassion to my patients and their families, it will be enough. "And so we will be with the Lord forever." Therefore, please encourage each other with those words found in the verses above.

Lisal Folsom, LLUSM class of 2009, is completing a combined internal medicine-pediatric endocrinology fellowship at Indiana University and Riley Hospital for Children. She lives in Indianapolis with her husband, Nathan.

March 12

Neither height nor depth, nor anything else in all creation, will be able to separate us from the love of God that is in Christ Jesus our Lord.
Romans 8:39, NIV

My eyebrows furrowed as I read the words, "*Leg pain for over 40 years.*" It was the referral reason for my last patient at the end of a long day, and my shoulders slumped as I imagined how this visit would go. In truth, it was the end of a particularly grueling week, and I was feeling worn out and a bit sorry for myself. What occurred during this simple encounter, however, reminded me how our calling to serve at Loma Linda University allows us to nourish spiritual lives—not only those of our patients, but also our own.

When I entered the room, my patient was sitting alone. She was an elderly woman with a rounded and pleasant face. She smiled and attempted to stand up in greeting but winced in obvious discomfort at the effort. Touched by this gesture, I smiled back, introduced myself, and told her, "Please, no need to stand."

As we sat and talked about her medical concerns, I was struck with how composed and normal she seemed—despite the reason for her referral, which hovered worrisomely in the back of my mind. As it turned out, her chronic leg condition arose from an episode of physical abuse that had occurred when she was a young teenager. Despite this traumatic event, her attitude was not one of self-pity or entitlement. Instead, her experience had inspired her to live a life dedicated to helping others.

Life at home now was filled with turmoil: a daughter battling drug addiction, an abandoned teenaged granddaughter with bipolar disorder, and an alcoholic husband. She brushed aside concerns about her chronic leg pain and, in its place, described a straightforward bout of low-back pain. Yet, instead of seeking prolonged medical leave, she asked me if she could return to work so she could provide for those who depended upon her. Her attitude was the complete opposite of what I had anticipated!

Near the end of the visit, I was somewhat surprised when she looked at me and said, "I really feel blessed that God has given me the chance to care for my family." This woman felt comfortable bringing up her faith because she knew that our health mission is based on God's healing ministry. At the same time, I felt ashamed that my professional struggles were so trite, compared to what this woman faced on a daily basis. And yet, she was able to maintain a spiritual connection at its most valuable level.

As we bowed our heads together and asked God to infuse His love and strength into her life, I inwardly thanked Him for this encounter that reminded me of His promise to be with us always. Nothing in this world can separate us from God's love.

Bryan Tsao, LLUSM class of 1996, is chair and an associate professor in LLUSM department of neurology. He and his wife, Juna, LLUSM class of 1996, live in Redlands, California, with their two sons.

March 13

And he said: "Truly I tell you, unless you change and become like little children, you will never enter the kingdom of heaven." Matthew 18:3, NIV

"**R**iley!" I tried my best stern voice, as I nonchalantly galloped down the hall after my patient, "Come back here!" He giggled as I grabbed the sleeve of his gown, gave a tug to turn him around, and headed back toward his room. "You caught me sneaking off!" he said, happily plodding behind me as I kept a firm grip on his gown.

"I caught you!" I responded, trying to resist the urge to laugh with him. I knew that if I responded as if this was some sort of game, then I would be chasing him all night.

We walked around the circle about a million times, with a couple of exploratory journeys down hallways, and finally Riley was ready to go back to his room. I sat him on the edge of the bed and distracted him by telling him he needed to hold my important piece of paper where I wrote down his vitals. While he contemplated this task, I got his medications ready and brought him a glass of water.

"Swallow these," I said, handing over a little cup filled with colorful pills. He grinned excitedly, as though I had handed him candy, and he downed them obediently.

"Great job!" I said happily, and we grinned at each other over the accomplishment of this task. Then for the remainder of the evening, I had a shadow as I completed the rest of my nursing tasks. While I charted, Riley stood off to the side and patiently watched. When I went into another patient's room, he waited for me outside the door. If I walked down the hall to get supplies, he was right behind me.

Unobtrusive, innocent, and curious as a child, this 250-pound, 20 year old trailed me like a faithful puppy. If I smiled, he smiled. If I whisked hurriedly by him on a mission to get something down the hall, he whisked after me without asking any questions, only knowing that we must work quickly!

"Riley, we need to go to bed now," I said finally.

"We? Who's we?" he questioned impishly.

"YOU," I clarified, trying not to smile, "You need to go to bed! I am not going."

"Well, I'm not either!" he began rebelliously. "I am going to stay up and watch TV all night!"

"Okay, let's go put you in bed and we'll turn on the TV." I led the way to his room, "You lie down there, and I'll be back in just a second to help you turn it on." I stepped outside the door and then went back in less than five minutes. Riley was asleep. "Riley," I whispered, "I thought you wanted to watch TV!" The peaceful face on the pillow was the only answer I got.

Sometimes patients make you cry, sometimes they make you laugh, and sometimes they walk right into your heart.

Allison Thorp (née Westermeyer) is a student in the master of science family nurse practitioner program at the University of Maryland. She is married to Jonathon Thorp, LLUSM class of 2012.

March 14

Heal me, O Lord, and I shall be healed; Save me, and I shall be saved, For You are my praise. Jeremiah 17:14, NKJV

My grandfather is 74 years old. If you caught sight of him sitting still, you might think that he was a typical elderly man who relies on a cane and walks slowly and carefully. Truth is, he can run and jump and would win a knee bend competition with me. He has no trouble matching pace with my brothers and me on hikes and walks.

My grandmother, equal in age, can nearly keep up with him! They have a computer business out of their home, exercise regularly, and eat fresh and canned food from their acre-large garden and various fruit trees. It would be difficult to accuse them of abusing their bodies.

At our family reunion, I solicited volunteers for an exercise to improve my physical examination skills. My grandfather volunteered, saying that he had not visited the doctor in more than 20 years. He was his jovial and curious self, so the exam took much longer than ordinary because he told me stories, and I explained what I was doing along the way.

There were no problems or issues until I reached the heart exam. Lub-dup, lub-dup, good and strong. Lub-dup, Lub . . . dup, lubdup lubdup lubdup . . . still strong, but irregularly irregular. I called my aunt, who has worked as an emergency department nurse, over to listen. She agreed with my assessment; and after questioning him about symptoms, which he denied, we both began to explain what this could mean to my grandfather. Atrial fibrillation. Possible stroke. Clots in the legs.

To my dismay, I also found severe pitting edema in both ankles. I explained to my grandfather the various possible causes of swelling in his feet. All throughout our explanations, he listened carefully and asked questions. We explained what we could, and he wrote down the information we gave him so he could research it for himself.

The next step was obvious to us; he should visit the doctor to figure out what was causing the edema. We reiterated the information and strongly encouraged him to do something about it. We all knew that it was unlikely he would make an appointment; my grandparents do not have health insurance.

When we were all heading to our respective rooms for the night, my grandfather was so appreciative. He said: "I thank you, Katrina, for explaining to me what you found. I was not sure what I was going to do about it, but now I know." He was so calm and unworried. I went into the bathroom and cried. I felt so helpless. I am training to become a doctor, and now my own grandfather needs help, and I cannot give it to him.

In reflecting on that thought, I realized that my active, intelligent, excited-about-life grandfather was not worried about what I had found wrong with his body because he does not have to put trust in me or any doctor to take care of him. God is his strength. He is the Healer; I am not, and I never will be.

I prayed that night that God would use the discoveries I made to benefit my grandfather—not just frighten him or my grandmother with a possible diagnosis that they could not afford to uncover. I let go and let God hold my grandfather, just as He always has.

Katrina Stewart, LLUSM class of 2015, is from Georgetown, Tennessee. She graduated from Southern Adventist University with a BS degree in psychobiology. March 14 is her birthday.

March 15

For You formed my inward parts; You covered me in my mother's womb. I will praise You, for I am fearfully and wonderfully made; Marvelous are Your works, And that my soul knows very well. Psalm 139:13-14, NKJV

She was very quiet each time she entered the exam room. That was typical for a 17-year-old girl who was pregnant. From the time she entered the waiting room to the time she walked out the door, she never spoke unless spoken to. No questions, no comments. Just silence. She was never elated, but rather bewildered, seeming to ask, "What will happen to me next?" She never came with anyone else, and each time she just quietly returned for her routine exams and followed her doctors' advice.

At 26 weeks, she had the usual blood work drawn: a complete blood count checking for anemia and a one-hour glucose tolerance test checking for diabetes. These were all routine tests, and I fully expected routine results. When her test results came back, her white blood cell count was 25,000—indicative of a major problem! She was referred to an oncologist who performed a bone marrow biopsy and diagnosed her with chronic myelogenous leukemia.

So here she was—17, pregnant, and now with a serious diagnosis. My heart went out to her. When she began chemotherapy, I began to wonder whether this mother-to-be would survive to care for her baby—this miracle of life she carried.

At 34 weeks she delivered early—a healthy baby girl who did not need the ventilator, was not in the neonatal intensive care unit, and was stable enough to room in with her mother. I remember coming into the patient's room one day and seeing her holding her baby in her arms. That little baby girl had the exact same copper-colored hair as her mother's hair, the same small turned-up nose, the same thin lips, the same pale-colored skin.

I noticed the baby's grandmother was sitting by the window, and the baby's father was by the side of the bed. And I pondered again—how precious this baby must be to everyone in the family, particularly to the patient's mother and boyfriend. Amidst a terrible diagnosis and an uncertain future, that baby was a lasting reminder of this patient—a gift, a miracle.

I was reminded that God provides signs of healing and rebirth, even in the midst of sorrow and disease. The rebirth of the mother in her child was a wonderful sign. More wonderful still, in Christ we are born again to the likeness of our Father, to daily become like Him—in the image of God.

Kathleen Lau, LLUSM class of 1982, is an assistant professor in LLUSM department of gynecology and obstetrics. She and her husband, Ricardo Peverini, LLUSM class of 1984, live in Loma Linda with their two sons.

And he said to all, "If anyone would come after me, let him deny himself and take up his cross daily and follow me. For whoever would save his life will lose it, but whoever loses his life for my sake will save it. For what does it profit a man if he gains the whole world and loses or forfeits himself?" Luke 9:23-25, ESV

I always thought coming to medical school would make me feel very smart—it is an easy assumption to make. After all, as medical students, we have battled thousands of other competitors for our spot and have emerged victorious. We have "supposedly" neared the pinnacle of our educational pursuits, approached yet another height of knowledge, and are now surrounded by brilliant ideas and people.

While all that may be true, the feelings of any grandeur that could be expected to come along with that "superiority" are often sadly lacking. I can honestly say that in my two years at Loma Linda University School of Medicine, I have never felt more exhausted, weak, and inept.

The reality of the medical field is one of a constant drive to perform, to succeed, and to compete. While so many good things come along with it, much of the time this all-out effort is just plain exhausting. There have been times when it took all I had just to lie on the floor and breathe in and out. In these moments, as awful as they often are, I have seen God more vividly than in any other place in my life.

God does not ask us to "get our lives together" all of the time. He does not withhold His love or His will from us until we achieve certain scores or milestones. So often we get caught up in thinking of God as too much like us.

Unfortunately, we forget that He does not act according to the world, nor does He act according to our own plans (as much as we wish He would). He loves us even, and especially, in our weakest, most broken down, and selfish moments. It is the beauty of who He is. It is why He is not just our Friend and Teacher, but also our Savior.

I confess I often fall into the trap of trying to control my own life. Medical school is a great environment to foster that temptation. While it feels great to do well on an exam or to be praised by my peers, I must constantly remind myself that it is not by my own power or for my own glory that I am here.

God calls us daily to deny our own ambitions and follow Him. When we faithfully choose to trust His strength and goodness above our own, we can let go of the many pieces of our lives that we struggle so hard to keep in their perfect places. We can find a true, joyful, and purpose-filled life. Is not that what we are all looking for anyway?

Clare Richardson, LLUSM class of 2015, is from Paradise Valley, Arizona. She graduated from Arizona State University with a BS degree in biochemistry. She was vice president of her sophomore class and is currently president of her junior class.

March 17

Being confident of this, that he who began a good work in you will carry it on to completion until the day of Christ Jesus. Philippians 1:6, NIV

"Every artist must learn that even the failed pieces are essential."
—Rob Bell, *Drops Like Stars*

A sudden jerk and rattling rumble awakened me from the almost-sleeping state I had been in on a bus ride from Kenya to Tanzania. I kept my eyes closed, wanting to fall back asleep—until the driver's hard turn of the wheel, in an attempt to get back onto the tarmac, tipped the bus on its side. The jolt threw me against the ceiling where I heard the earth and rocks scrape against metal until the bus slid to a stop. My eyes were very much wide open now, and my heart was racing!

Panic hovered over me until I looked up to see the window that had served as my pillow up until a few moments ago was now my escape. Just a few moments more and I was safely out of the dust-filled cabin and sitting under a tree next to the two pastors I was traveling with. We had left Nairobi two days earlier and was supposed to reach Heri Hospital that evening. Now, I would not arrive until the following afternoon.

As I looked back at the bus, I saw people gathering behind it and realized that others might need assistance. My feet stopped moving after just a few steps toward the bus as I saw the cold reality of the situation: one child's life shortened; two women being carried out of the bus in blankets with their faces covered. I was later informed that a fourth had died as well.

I found myself conflicted. My mind went through phasic motions, between wanting to help and being too afraid. I doubted what help I would even be able to offer; there were no bandages or gloves and I did not speak Swahili. Doubtful and afraid, I turned around to continue to watch rather than act.

After a few more steps, I dispelled my reservations and emboldened, turned around to go back toward the bus. But it only took a few steps and more sights of reality for the doubt and fear to return, halting me once again.

And so it went, walking toward and away from the crashed bus. Several steps forward, several steps back. Turn, walk, stop. Courage, assertiveness, compassion, action. Fear, doubt, inadequacies, discouragement.

I never made it to the bus. My feelings of ineptness, doubts of my own abilities, and fear kept halting me. But while I felt guilty for never reaching it, I kept trying. And perhaps that is just as important as having reached it.

There are sure to be more opportunities in life, and I may miss many of them; it is an imperfect process. But it is this imperfect process of trying and failing, of turning back toward the bus that will eventually enable me to finally reach it.

Zach Taylor, LLUSM class of 2015, is from Fairfield, Montana. He graduated from Walla Walla University with a BS degree in biology. This story occurred while he was volunteering abroad prior to starting medical school.

March 18

She stretcheth out her hand to the poor; yea, she reacheth forth her hands to the needy. Give her of the fruit of her hands; and let her own works praise her in the gates. Proverbs 31:20, 31, KJV

Our mother, Earla Gardner Aagaard, graduated from the College of Medical Evangelists (CME) in 1946 and retired in 1995 at age 73. She received an invitation to write a devotional for *Evening Rounds* in 2012 when she was 90 years old, but she chose to decline. However, we, her daughters, thought we would write it for her and about her.

Earla was the youngest child of medical missionaries, Jonathan Earl Gardner, CME class of 1919, and Ethel Swing Gardner, a nurse. Earl and Ethel served on the island of Penang, off the coast of Malaysia, and started a clinic that eventually became Penang Adventist Hospital. Earla was born in the mission field, joining her sister, Martha June Gardner, CME class of 1945. Earla and June's parents were insistent that their daughters become doctors rather than nurses, despite Earla's fondness for the starched white aprons worn by nurses in those days. Thus, both girls enrolled at CME after graduating from Pacific Union College.

In their first year of medical school, Earla married another student, Carl Aagaard, CME class of 1946. She always told us that Carl was the only reason she made it through medicine. Earla chose anesthesia as her first specialty area and was skilled in doing ether drip with pediatric cases, but she found this stressful and searched for something she would like better. She settled on psychiatry, much to her parents' distress, who felt that particular specialty was not "real" doctoring, or at least not the kind that did people any good.

Earla persisted, nevertheless—completing her residency at Langley Porter Clinic in San Francisco and starting a practice in Ukiah, California. In what was not typical psychiatric treatment, she occasionally brought teenage patients to our home to stay. They shared our bedrooms, meals, and worships, just like one of the family.

Part of Earla's work was done free of charge for needy community members and for the church. She provided mental health services to conference pastors and their families, as well as to students referred from Rio Lindo Academy. Each week for years, she taught a well-attended Sabbath School class for mothers of Cradle Roll children, going over parenting advice from books, such as *Child Guidance*, as well as explaining associated psychological ideas related to mothering.

Earla's paternal grandfather was bipolar, and her father had always feared that he himself would develop similar symptoms; this anxiety became stronger as he aged. When he finally confided his dread to Earla, she was able to explain to him that if he had not already shown any signs, it was unlikely that he was going to develop the disorder so late in life. He was greatly relieved by this.

And at that point, Earla's father, who had protested her choice of psychiatry as a specialty, reconciled himself to her calling because of her ability to help him get past his own distress. He told her that he believed he had been wrong and that she was indeed doing good for people.

We thank God for our mother and the life of service and ministry she has given Him.

Lola Aagaard Boram and Carla June Aagaard wrote this devotional as a tribute to their mother. March 18 is the birthday of their father, Carl.

March 19

But God was merciful! We were dead because of our sins, but God loved us so much that he made us alive with Christ, and God's wonderful kindness is what saves you. Ephesians 2:4-5, CEV

I was born in Shattuck, Oklahoma, to a father who was a wheat farmer and milked cows, and to a mother who raised five sons and cooked meals outside the home to make ends meet. I would have returned to the farm as my occupation, but my mother would have none of it. She thought I should be a doctor, so I took premed, was accepted to Loma Linda University (LLU), and became first a physician, and then an obstetrician and gynecologist.

My spiritual life was up and down, but I always knew my grandmother and parents were praying for me. During the early years, I was busy starting a practice, taking call, and raising a family. The day I finally went to church I felt out of place, but I decided to stay and make my spiritual life a priority.

In my practice, I was always under the conviction that I should pray with my patients; but I did not know how to start. Then I thought, "I could pray before surgery." So, after the pre-op visit, I would say, "Whenever I do surgery, I have prayer with my patients. Would that be okay with you?" Then, I would pray for the patient, caregivers, family, and a good outcome. Prayer connected them to God.

After the delivery of a baby, I would tell the mother, "The Lord has blessed you with a beautiful baby." This routine became a real blessing to the patient and to me. I became known as a "doctor who prayed with patients," and my practice flourished.

As I neared retirement, I considered what I would do next. I decided to become a volunteer chaplain at the hospital. After visiting with patients, I would pray for them.

One day, I prayed a prayer that God would do with my life whatever He wanted. A short time after, I was diagnosed with parotid gland cancer. I had surgery, chemotherapy, and radiation; but the cancer recurred. So I came to LLU as a patient and had radical neck surgery performed by Paul Kim, LLUSM class of 1998. I received wonderful, compassionate care. So many loving people visited and prayed for me.

One day, during my recovery, God gave me a song about my future; I named it, "Jerusalem, My Happy Home." It was a real miracle to me, because I had never written a song before. God showed me that my hope is not in this life, but with Him in our eternal home.

After returning to my home in Texas, I became convinced that God had healed me. Then I had a PET scan which revealed that the cancer had recurred. So how was I healed? God showed me that I was healed one day at a time. Every morning He assures me that I am healed for that day. What a blessing!

As I look back, and see how God has answered prayers in my life, I am amazed. He has used the prayers of family, friends, and people all over the world to heal me, spiritually and physically. God always answers prayers, including mine, in His wisdom for what is best. Jesus said, "Ask." If we do, He will answer! So, please pray!

J. Barry Siebenlist, CME class of 1961, practiced for 40 years and delivered nearly 9,000 babies before he retired in 2001. He lived in Killeen, Texas, with Joan, his wife of 47 years. He submitted this entry on December 26, 2012, and passed away on July 16, 2013. He is survived by his wife, two children, and five grandchildren. March 19 is his wedding anniversary.

I pray that God, the source of hope, will fill you completely with joy and peace because you trust in him. Romans 15:13, NLT

T he future is so close now. My whole universe is tightly focused upon one simple piece of paper—I will read it in 12 hours.

My soul is quiet. No more doubts, no more uncertainty. The residency matching process* is so hectic that perhaps it's only human to place hope in a Greater Power guiding the chaos. Even so, I cannot deny how faith has supported me.

Reflecting back on my journey, it is irrefutably clear—God placed the people and events in my life that have led me to this quiet, monumental pause. I am humbled by His plan . . . you know when I entered college I vehemently stated I would NEVER become a physician? Now look at me, 12 hours from stepping into my future as a young doctor, and utterly grateful that my college-age self had some celestial sense knocked into her. I'm laughing, and I find myself saying:

"Okay, fine, God; You win this round of life planning. I suppose I'll trust You for the next adventure too."

As I watch the hours tick by, my faith and peace grow. It is ever so comforting to look back and see the wonders God has given me at Loma Linda. His hand was guiding my path the whole time. It's undeniable—I did not get here alone. And no matter where I go next year, I will not go alone.

Wish me luck.

---

*The residency matching process culminates every year on the third Friday of March. On this day (known as Match Day), over 20,000 senior medical students across the U.S. simultaneously receive notice of where they will go for their residency training.

Tamara Moores, LLUSM class of 2012, is an emergency medicine resident in Salt Lake City, Utah. March 20, 2014, is the eve of Match Day for LLUSM class of 2014.

March 21

Ask and it will be given to you; seek and you will find; knock and the door will be opened to you. Matthew 7:7, NIV

My wife and I have been involved with Canvasback Missions, which provides specialty medical teams to the people of the Marshall Islands and the Federated States of Micronesia (FSM). In 1997, on one of our earliest trips to the FSM, we were asked to provide care for patients suffering from chronic ear disease, and we primarily focused on this need. But when we arrived, we found that an islander in the hospital had a fairly large three-pointed fish bone stuck in his larynx, and it had been there for more than two weeks! His local medical personnel knew of our soon arrival and had kept him in the hospital, hoping we would be able to help.

Being an otolaryngologist, one would think that removal of a fish bone would be a routine procedure. But because we anticipated treating only ear diseases, we did not bring any laryngeal instruments that would be useful for this problem. These islanders are extremely poor and have little, if any, of their own medical equipment and supplies. That lack requires visiting specialty teams to bring everything they need for their work.

We searched the hospital for any possible tool that might aid in removing the fish bone, but to no avail. There were numerous drawers in several rooms that were completely empty of any supplies, let alone something that could reach down and grab a fish bone.

That evening, our team discussed the case and what we might be able to do, including having the patient sent to Honolulu or the Philippines for definitive care. We prayed earnestly for help and guidance that night; the next morning, after worship and further prayer, we went to the hospital.

The patient was wheeled into the operatory with no obvious instruments available other than a headlight and a tongue blade. I was impressed to ask the anesthesiologist to place him under anesthesia without intubation (as the fish bone was directly obstructing the view of his vocal cords) so that I might look at the problem while the patient was asleep.

At the very moment the patient was going to sleep, my surgical technician "happened" to look again in one of the same drawers we had searched frantically the night before. In that drawer, miraculously, there was an old but functional McGill forceps! Using the anesthesiologist's laryngoscope and my newfound tool, I was able to locate the fish bone and remove it easily and without incident.

We were all amazed by the obvious answer to our prayer in such an incredible way. It brought to life God's promise in Isaiah 65:24 (NIV): "Before they call I will answer; while they are still speaking I will hear."

James Reese, LLUSM class of 1974, has practiced otolaryngology in Sonora, California, for more than 35 years. This story occurred on a trip to Pohnpei.

*For the L*ORD *will comfort Zion; he will comfort all her waste places, and will make her wilderness like Eden, her desert like the garden of the L*ORD*; joy and gladness will be found in her, thanksgiving and the voice of song.*
Isaiah 51:3, NRSV

"You need to turn on the news! . . . Oh, no, no! It can't be! . . . Were they on the plane? . . . Is it really true?" These were my initial stunned reactions to that tragic day (March 22, 2009) that changed the lives of our families forever. There was an outpouring of care and concern from many friends, family, and the general public, as news reports and videos depicted the plane crash, which claimed the lives of three families, including my nephew Brent and his family.

I have such fond memories of Brent. I liked his thoughtfulness, warmth, and ingenuity throughout his years as a child, teenager, young adult, husband, and father. And his wife, Kristen, added such love, sparkle, and spontaneity to our lives. We loved their precious Hailey, with her beautiful smile, loving hugs, and wise insights; and their spunky Caleb, who, with his mischievous, radiant smile, charmed everyone through his welcoming spirit and favorite words, "I love you."

Through all of this, I often had to ask myself, "Why? Why God? Why did this have to happen? Why were so many lives cut so short?" Each person lost that day was so very precious and special to their families and friends; even today, that loss is still overwhelming and incomprehensible.

I have to admit that there is no answer; but I am reminded of the words: "I know not how, nor when, nor why, I can but this on God rely. His love, His grace, eternally . . . God is." I have had to accept that on this earth, we may not know all the answers; but we just have to trust completely that God, who knows the end from the beginning, is love.

For the parents and grandparents of the families who were on the plane, their extended families, and their friends, the song "When We All Get to Heaven" is especially meaningful. It reminds us that nothing on this earth really matters. We cling to the "Hope" that is made possible only because Christ gave His life for us. "What a day of rejoicing that will be!"

∞

In memory of the love and lives of the three families who died in the plane crash on March 22, 2009: Vanessa Feldkamp Pullen, LLUSM class of 1998, husband Michael Pullen, LLUSD class of 1999, children Sydney (age 10) and Christopher (age 7); Amy Feldkamp Jacobson, LLUSD DH class of 1997, husband Erin Jacobson, LLUSM class of 2000, children Taylor (age 4), Ava Grace (age 3), Jude (age 2); Kristen Mautz Ching, LLUSN class of 2000, husband Brent Ching, LLUSD class of 1998, children Hailey (age 5) and Caleb (age 3).

Shirley Chang (née Ching), LLUSN class of 1965, PhD, is Brent's aunt and a member of the board of trustees for LLUAHSC. Brent's father, M. Robert Ching, LLUSM class of 1970, is an orthopaedic surgeon in Oroville, California, where he practices with his son, Brian, LLUSM class of 1996.

March 23

Indeed, we felt we had received the sentence of death. But this happened that we might not rely on ourselves but on God, who raises the dead.
2 Corinthians 1:9, NIV

Awakening before the alarm went off, I could feel my eyes rotating abnormally as a gradual paralysis enveloped my right side. Alarmed, I reached over to awaken my wife, and haltingly spoke: "Judi, ... something ... is ... terribly ... wrong ... with ... my head." As she dialed 911, I reminded her that there was no 911 at that time in Dayton, Ohio, so she called the operator. My mind was working fine, but I was becoming trapped in a paralyzed body. She called my sister, who heard the siren of the ambulance coming for me as it passed her home.

Judi also called our neighbor, classmate Peter Haynal, LLUSM class of 1976-B, who came over as the paramedics arrived. He noticed that I had an upgoing, right Babinski sign, an indicator of possible neurological damage. This was terrifying to me, an interventional radiologist.

Halfway to the hospital, I tried using my left hand to raise my right arm, but the arm fell to my side as dead weight. Noting that this "stroke" was progressing rapidly, I wondered if I would live to reach the hospital. In that deadly downhill spiral, I spoke with God: *Lord, You have given me life, and I have tried to do my best with it. I will accept whatever You have in store for me. If it's my time to go, I'm ready. But if You give me life, please give my right side back so that I won't be a burden to those about me, and so that I can continue to serve You and my patients. Amen.*

I felt the reassuring comfort of His loving hands, knowing He was in control; I was willing to accept whatever the future held. In seconds, without any "trumpet blast," my right side was back. I lifted my right arm and spoke normally, as if nothing had been amiss. When I arrived at the emergency department, I was the happiest patient imaginable; God had answered my prayer with a miracle!

The positive Babinski and rotatory nystagmus (rolling eye movements) persisted for several days. But the CT and MRI were negative; as I came out of the MRI, I heard a soft roar. The condition was tinnitus, a noise in the ear that sounds like a radio station off channel.

I also heard the roar of a large crowd that had gathered in the waiting room, showing their concern. I was admitted to the ICU, but as an amazingly healthy patient compared to other severely impaired neurosurgical cases. Five days and many tests later, I was discharged with the diagnosis of viral encephalitis.

Yes, you can explain this as a localized inflammation near my brainstem, causing spasm of arterial branches supplying the nerves to my right side, with the spasm relaxing after 45 minutes. But I believe my improved state was a miracle—that God answered my prayer from the depths of despair, giving me my right side back. He left me with a little hearing loss and tinnitus to remind me of His power to answer prayer with a miracle.

Robert Hewes, LLUSM class of 1976-B, is medical director of imaging and interventional radiology at Florida Hospital Memorial Medical Center in Ormond Beach, Florida. March 23 is his wedding anniversary.

March 24

You will keep in perfect peace him whose mind is steadfast, because he trusts in you. Isaiah 26:3, NIV (1984)

She was frail, elderly, and "addicted" to benzodiazepines. No one liked her; in fact, she even annoyed me. Three days earlier, I had discharged Ms. Jones, and now here she was again—what is called a "bounce back." With a quivering voice she described her latest malady, and as usual, it was nothing specific.

But one thing that did not change was her consistent request, "Doctor, please give me some Ativan."

Argh, I said in my mind, *that is all she wants!* "No, Ms. Jones," I responded, "your outpatient doctors decided to slowly bring you off those medicines because they aren't good for you." Three hours later, while we were rounding on another patient, I was paged: "Dr. Thorp, Ms. Jones is having a seizure."

This case will forever leave an impact on my mind. People's bodies externalize the innermost needs, even to the point of having a psychogenic seizure! Later in the afternoon, I returned to see her—determined to find the root cause of her behavior. Over the next three hours, I had one of the most comprehensive conversations I had ever embarked upon with a patient. It was terrible, tragic, and painful.

At the surface, she lived with her son, who was verbally abusive. But as I "dug down" layer after layer, I found out that she had been widowed and then had remarried into a physically abusive relationship. Some of her children and grandchildren had died. She had other children who were on drugs. Recently, a sister had died. She was a lady who was filled with inner pain and turmoil.

Using whole person skills and religious/spiritual care questions that I learned as a student at Loma Linda University School of Medicine, I kept "digging." I asked her, "What brings you hope?" "Nothing," she replied. So then I said: "Many people say that they aren't religious but that they are spiritual. Would you describe yourself as a spiritual person? And, if so, does God play a role in your life?" With hesitation in her voice, she responded: "Well, I believe there is a God, and I wish I knew Him better."

Through the Holy Spirit's leading, I carefully kept asking questions and discovered that she had turned away from going to church because of a pastor who had tried to sexually abuse her. She explained that she had never told anyone this before. She had turned away from God because of a human's misrepresentation.

I decided to open up and share with her my faith in the God I knew. She looked at me and asked me to pray a prayer of rededication for her. I did; and when I opened my eyes, her face was the calmest I had ever seen. She took my hand and said, "Thank you; that's what I needed." A relationship with God was the anxiolytic she needed.

Many people in this world have a distorted view of God, and, concurrently, have an intense desire to know Him. Isaiah 26:3 comes to my mind when I think about the peace that this lady realized when she recommitted her life to Christ. At first I did not like Ms. Jones, but I learned an incredibly important lesson that day: Encourage patients to tell their story. And through their story, you might see them for who they really are and bring them into a new/renewed relationship with our Savior, Jesus Christ.

Jonathon Thorp, LLUSM class of 2012, is an internal medicine resident at Johns Hopkins Bayview Medical Center in Baltimore, Maryland. March 24 is the birthday of his wife, Allison.

March 25

A man who has friends must himself be friendly, But there is a friend who sticks closer than a brother. Proverbs 18:24, NKJV

Let me tell you about my friend. In God's providence, our friendship developed during the last four-and-a-half years of his life. He lived to be 103 and died shortly after we had celebrated that special occasion.

In 1933, he graduated from the College of Medical Evangelists. On page 65, in the predecessor to this book called *Morning Rounds,* you will find a gem he wrote for the *Alumni Journal.* At the bottom of the page are a few words describing who he was. I would add that he became my treasured friend.

His name was Albert F. Brown. And if you knew him, you are remembering ways in which his life blessed yours. For me, the following recollections are just a glimpse of our time together. When we met, Dr. Brown's eyesight was severely compromised. However, using every available aid, he tenaciously kept in touch with the world of print, sight, and sound.

We regularly got together on Thursday afternoons for a couple of hours to share our journeys. Marjorie, my wife, joined us for many of these visits and loved listening in. We became acquainted by sharing our stories. And what a storyteller he was! We chose books and articles that I would read aloud—then we would discuss with vigor. Conversations were wide ranging. He was quick of mind and wonderfully witty.

Once I unloaded a big burden, created by a rancorous debate over some small matter. He patiently heard me out, asked a few questions, then softly said: "Oh Lou, I don't hoist my sail for every wind that blows."

My friend was crystal clear on what matters most. Many times he quoted words from Whittier's poem, "The Eternal Goodness":

> Yet in the maddening maze of things
> And tossed by storm and flood
> To one fixed trust my spirit clings;
> I know that God is good!

Through sunshine and shadow, Dr. Brown's confidence and trust in God were unshakable. He would talk about "the School of the Hereafter" in a way that just grabbed me. He became genuinely excited about boundless time and unlimited resources to explore the treasures of the universe.

He considered the marvelous human heart—kept in order and activity by the power of an ever-present God—the ultimate marvel of Creation. According to him, each of us has our own personal operating model that is "cheerily tapping out signals," echoing our Maker's glory upward of two billion heartbeats in a lifetime.

Speaking of his own heart he wrote: "When my working model finally stops, a better model will take over at the sound of a shout, without missing a beat, as far as I would be able to tell, and my heart and I will just go on singing."

Friendship is our greatest treasure, indeed. What a friend this man was to me and to a host of others. The text above also speaks of "a friend who sticks closer than a brother." It points us to the wonder of Jesus Himself welcoming us into a growing and eternal friendship.

Louis Venden, PhD, is an emeritus professor in LLUSR where he was on the faculty for over 25 years. He served as senior pastor of the Loma Linda University Church from 1977 to 1989 and was director of the Center for Spiritual Life and Wholeness from 2001 to 2004. March 25 is the birthday of his mother, Ivy Ruth Blackenburg.

GOD, your God, is the God of all gods, he's the Master of all masters, a God immense and powerful and awesome. He doesn't play favorites, takes no bribes, makes sure orphans and widows are treated fairly, takes loving care of foreigners by seeing that they get food and clothing. Deuteronomy 10:17-18, MSG

Glancing at the list of afternoon patients, I saw that her name had been scribbled in as a walk-in. I knew exactly what she would be coming in for: her pain meds, an allergy med (that was probably no longer on the market but which she insisted was the only one that worked), another medication for her chronic diarrhea, and, of course, her "nerves" medication. Darlene was like clockwork—only she was 65 years old, cachectic, homeless, and a broken timepiece.

She was living out of a van filled to the brim with belongings, trash bags, bits and bobs, and her beloved cat, Apollo. Oh, and she shared the van with her aging brother, who spent most days of the week trying to get to his multiple appointments with specialists at VA Loma Linda Healthcare System. They were an odd pair. Despite his crusty demeanor and constant ranting that his "docs don't know what they're doing," he always managed to say something that was actually funny, and I'd laugh without expecting to.

But today I was tired, had skipped lunch because I was still writing in charts from my morning patients, and saw that my afternoon list had grown surreptitiously. The last thing I needed was having her squeezed into my afternoon. No one else would see her since her medical chart had expanded to volumes 1, 2 and 3.

Looking at her last chart note, I realized she had not seen me in two months. I walked into the room and was greeted with, "Doc, I was so sick these last few weeks!" She told me she had gone to Urgent Care with abdominal pain; and while waiting, her brother had keeled over and was rushed to the VA Loma Linda Healthcare System emergency department. They both ended up being admitted as inpatients, he at the VA and she at Loma Linda University Medical Center East Campus Hospital. But it was what she told me next that touched me and made me realize how a simple act of kindness can impact a person's life.

"I didn't know what would happen to Apollo, all by himself in the van. There was no one I could turn to, Doc."

"What happened?" I asked.

"A woman security guard came by the van, saw Apollo by himself, and found me in the hospital. She said she would take him home for a few days until I got better. Oh, she was just wonderful!" Darlene had tears in her eyes.

What that security guard did that night for Darlene was a precious gift—knowing that her one pet companion was in safe and caring hands brought her peace of mind. Sometimes it takes something other than medicine to help our patients through tough times.

Juna Tsao, LLUSM class of 1996, is an assistant professor in LLUSM department of preventive medicine. She and her husband, Bryan, LLUSM class of 1996, live in Redlands, California, with their two sons.

March 27

And after you have suffered a little while, the God of all grace, who has called you to his eternal glory in Christ, will himself restore, confirm, strengthen, and establish you. 1 Peter 5:10, ESV

Alleviating human suffering will one day be my job. I know that I will not always succeed. Several years ago, however, while living in the jungles of Peru, I learned a powerful lesson about finding meaning in the midst of human suffering.

I was out visiting my elementary school students in their humble homes one afternoon. On this particular day, one of my favorite mothers invited me in and insisted on serving me some rice. As I ate, she filled me in on the neighborhood gossip. Her 13-year-old sister was sleeping with a neighbor man in his twenties. Her brother had recently stolen several hundred dollars from her husband.

As if we needed some more drama, we both heard a loud cry piercing the quiet evening. It sounded like the cry of a young boy. I cringed. She leaned closer to me and whispered: "That's Gerald. His mother beats him just about every evening at this time. There is no love in that home," she added.

Gerald, I realized, was one of my own second grade students. He was a good student. He was always the first to blurt out some sort of answer in class, and he always wore his pants too high. I liked Gerald, and I could not bear the thought of him being beaten.

I finished eating, thanked the mother, and left. As I was leaving her home, the cries were still coming from several doors down. I walked away, trying to push out the thought of Gerald hurting, when another terrible thought took its place. I remembered the news I had received just that week. One of the other student missionaries from my university had been raped and murdered as she was serving on an island in the Pacific.

It was more than I could bear. I hung my head and cried aloud, "This world is lost!"

No sooner had those words left my mouth than three small children, who had been playing in the gutter, saw me and came running toward me. They smiled and shouted, "Professor Mateo!" They were younger siblings of my students.

They gathered around me and wrapped their arms tightly about my waist. I am not normally one to give hugs, but that evening I clung to those children for a long time. God seemed to be saying to me: "No, Mateo, the world is not lost just yet! There is still love left in it, and I will always remind you of that when you need it most."

Yes, God will one day put an end to human suffering. He will take us to a world where even the memories of child abuse, rape, and death will fade away. Yet, until that day comes, He makes absolutely sure that there is love left in this world, that there is a light at the end of every tunnel, that somewhere, somehow, there is someone to give you a hug at the end of a very long day.

Matt Hartman, LLUSM class of 2015, is from Portland, Tennessee. He graduated from Southern Adventist University with a BA degree in chemistry. This story occurred during the 2009-2010 academic year while he was a student missionary in Pucallpa, Peru.

For everyone to whom much is given, from him much will be required; and to whom much has been committed, of him they will ask the more.
Luke 12:48, NKJV

ost of us reading this book are extremely blessed. If you have more than two pairs of shoes and a hot meal to eat daily, research data indicates that you are doing better than a large portion of the world. The Bible is full of Scriptures asking us to share of ourselves with others who are less fortunate. I mentally categorize this "giving back" into three types of sharing: time, resources, and knowledge.

Often it is our time that seems the most difficult to spare. When did we last visit a shut-in, widows and orphans, or a prisoner? Matthew 25 reminds us that when we visit the sick and those in prison, it is the equivalent of visiting God. Can you imagine? And Hebrews 6:10 (NIV) reminds us that God is not unjust, and He does not "forget your work and the love you have shown him as you have helped his people."

Sharing our resources can mean donating goods to charity or food to the local food bank. Luke 3:11 (NKJV) quotes John the Baptist, who said that he "who has two tunics, let him give to him who has none; and he who has food, let him do likewise." And Jesus reminds us that "whoever gives one of these little ones only a cup of cold water in the name of a disciple, assuredly, I say to you, he shall by no means lose his reward" (Matthew 10:42, NKJV). Those who have been blessed financially can donate to worthy causes that provide help to those in need.

Last, and dare I say most important, are we sharing our knowledge? Are we sharing God with others? God has asked us to make disciples of all the nations and to go into the world and preach the gospel to all (Matthew 28:19, Mark 16:15). We are called to be the spice of life, the salt of the earth, and the light of the world.

Therefore, let us answer the call and let our light, our spiritual light, shine before men that they may glorify God in Heaven (Matthew 5: 13-16). It is easy to feel inadequate and ill-equipped to answer this call. But we must not let those thoughts discourage us, as God can transform our stumbling words and feeble efforts into greatness for His cause. "You shall receive power when the Holy Spirit has come upon you; and you shall be witnesses to Me . . . to the end of the earth" (Acts 1:8, NKJV).

Let us not despair if we have been falling asleep in handling our blessings responsibly; we can start today. Let us not view it as a guilt trip, but a reality check. Ultimately, we are accountable to God alone. Let us invest wisely so that when Christ returns, He may say to us: "Well done, good and faithful servant; . . . Enter into the joy of your lord" (Matthew 25:21, NKJV).

Anna Gomez Bowman, LLUSM class of 2007, is a forensic psychiatrist and also an instructor at the Medical University of South Carolina. March 28 is the birthday of her husband, Jerry.

March 29

A brother is born to help in time of need. Proverbs 17:17, NLT

The rewards of being Jesus' hands and feet for service as a physician are many but have never been more evident than what I experienced several years ago on the African continent. My wife, Donna, and I and our three children had gone to Tanzania to assist with an Adventist Development and Relief Agency (ADRA) project, which was to provide medical care among the Masai tribe.

An African physician and his family had built a small house in the area and were using one of its only two bedrooms as a clinic/office/hospital for treating the Masai people of the area. Our teenage children were to help with the construction of a new medical clinic while my wife and I would see patients.

Lines of people came daily—warriors, mothers, children, and the aged. Some had diseases we could treat, but others had complicated problems beyond our abilities and resources. One day I noticed a 10-year-old boy hopping through the village on one leg using a stick for a crutch. Upon quizzing a helper, I learned the boy had been unable to walk for many days.

With much encouragement, he finally came into the clinic; the cause of his lameness was clearly evident. His massively swollen right knee caused severe pain with any attempt at motion, and on palpation, it proved to be warm, tender, red, and fluctuant. My conclusion was that he had an intra-articular joint infection, which was *not* something to treat in an African bush clinic!

I explained, through our interpreters, that he needed immediate orthopaedic care, and I learned that the nearest care was five hours away in Nairobi. I asked that his transport be arranged. I was told it was impossible—no car, no gas, no money to pay to enter the hospital, no one to go with him to cook for him—and he would not leave his village! The only care he would receive would be at this bush clinic.

After much thought and prayer, I opened the skin over his knee; out poured a half liter of purulent, foul-smelling material. Upon probing the abscess, my six-inch Kelly clamp could have been easily lost inside. I had no idea if the joint space had been entered; but I placed a drain, bandaged it, gave him the only oral antibiotic we had, and asked him to return.

Each day he came for a bandage change, and daily more fluid was expressed from the wound. Never did he moan or cry or complain regarding this painful ordeal, as the Masai are very stoic. Instead, as the days ticked by, whenever he left, he would put his hands up to give me high-fives, along with a big smile.

By God's grace, he began to walk—first with a limp, then a normal walk, and by the time our three-week project was ending, he was running though the village. That was reward enough, but I will never forget the last day he came for his daily visit—now mostly a social one. As he sat on the makeshift table, I checked his healing knee and told him we would be leaving the next day. He turned his head to look me straight in the eyes in disbelief. As he stared, tears appeared in his Masai eyes and, for an eternal moment, two friends had their gaze locked on each other. Then he turned and slowly walked out the door—offering not a word and no high-fives, but with a heart full of gratitude that could not be expressed any other way except by tears.

John Shank, LLUSM class of 1970, and his family: wife, Donna; children, Greg, LLUSM class of 1999; Cristy, LLUSM class of 2004; and Heather are all active in local and international missions. March 29 is the author's birthday.

And as he entered a village, he was met by ten lepers, who stood at a distance and lifted up their voices and said, "Jesus, Master, have mercy on us." When he saw them he said to them, "Go and show yourselves to the priests." And as they went they were cleansed. Then one of them, when he saw that he was healed, turned back, praising God with a loud voice; and he fell on his face at Jesus' feet, giving him thanks. Now he was a Samaritan. Then said Jesus, "Were not ten cleansed? Where are the nine?" Luke 17:12-17, RSV

A patient at Sycamore Medical Center in Miamisburg, Ohio, was having a routine surgery when something went wrong: a blood vessel was accidentally nicked. The resulting bleeding became quite severe, and the surgeon asked for help. A vascular surgeon, who usually does not go to Sycamore Medical Center, was called in to assist. The vessel was expertly repaired and the patient recovered fully.

Upon hearing about this intervention, I wrote the vascular surgeon a thank-you note, expressing our appreciation for his willingness to go out of his way to save a life. I thought nothing more about the incident. A few weeks later, he came up to me and thanked me personally for sending him that card. It meant so much to him. Appreciation means so much to all of us. It has deep meaning to the Great Physician, as well.

Doctors' Day is March 30. Although it was not officially recognized by the U.S. Congress until 1990, the day was established to be observed annually in recognition of members of the medical profession who daily, and often thanklessly, perform modern-day miracles for their patients.

March 30 was the day chosen because it was on that day in 1842 that ether was first used as an anesthetic agent in surgery. A Georgia physician, Dr. Crawford Long, administered it. That one intervention arguably was one of the most important contributions ever made to the field of medicine.

Saying thank you to someone is simple and cheap. In a world awash with text messages, receiving a personal letter or note in the mail is treasured. These notes are a very effective way to show our appreciation. Let us not forget to take time to thank our medical staff and our personal physician for the specifics of their competent, tender, and attentive care to their patients.

A story that still brings tears to my eyes was a thank-you note sent by the nurses of an intensive care unit to the home of a physician, who labored day and night in the hospital, caring for a critical patient. The nurses all signed this thank-you card and sent it not to the physician, but to his wife. They thanked her for her willingness to share her husband's time, expertise, and compassion over that long weekend. I am sure her husband got the message.

Gregory Wise, LLUSM class of 1973-B, served as a missionary physician at Bella Vista Hospital, Puerto Rico, in 1977 and was previously head of general internal medicine and geriatrics at LLUMC. He is currently vice president of medical affairs at Kettering Medical Center in Ohio.

March 31

No one has greater love [no one has shown stronger affection] than to lay down (give up) his own life for his friends. John 15:13, AMP

I was 15 years old when I learned that my father wished to donate his body to science when he died. "It is a noble thing to do, and someone will really benefit from it," he said softly.

I asked naively, "Dad, is it because you want someone else to get your eyes after you die?"

"No." He smiled. "I want someone to get all of me."

At the time, I did not know what he was talking about; but if he thought it was good, so did I. But as I grew older and saw the recipients of organ donors thrive after transplantation, the gift of my father's body held more meaning for me. But not until I learned about gross anatomy class did I fully grasp the nobility of his selfless gesture.

It was on October 25, 2006, that I received the call that my father had died of a massive heart attack. His body was being transported to Syracuse University where his last wish would be fulfilled.

As I made the trip back home I imagined what the medical students would learn of him in lab: "A 76-year-old Caucasian male with sudden MI secondary to thrombocythemia." They would not know how he loved Laurel and Hardy films, or that he was a world-class tuba player. They would not know how hard he worked to provide for his family; that he had a heart as soft as warm butter; or that he adored his wife of 56 years.

One might guess that his piano playing was awful by looking at his short, thick fingers that got stuck between the black piano keys. But there was no way to know he used to set his own work aside to help the neighbors get their hay baled when thunderstorms were on the horizon. Nor could they know how tenderly he walked the floor with each of his four small children, night after night, singing soothing and tender little songs to us so we could go to sleep.

When my father donated his body to science, he gave his all. It was the way he did things: 100 percent. In good faith, he surrendered his body, stories, and history into the hands of those whose future livelihoods depend upon familiarity with the body: physicians, whose lives of service would carry forward his generosity and selflessness in their work. It was, indeed, a very noble gift.

I think of my father often in my work—as I witness a physician lean over the bed of a sick child, pat the back of a waiting husband outside surgery, or give hope to a dying patient, through tired but smiling eyes. That was how my father was, and his gift lives on in the compassion of physician friends he will not know until Heaven. Loving service is fueled by the gifts of those who have gone before. God bless those who give their all.

Barbara Couden Hernandez, PhD, LLU counseling and family sciences class of 1992, is director of physician vitality and a professor in LLUSM department of medical education. March 31 is her parents' wedding anniversary.

APRIL

"WE CAN LOOK AT THE MESS THAT IS OUR WORLD TODAY AND WONDER WHERE GOD IS MOST AT WORK. OFFER HIM YOUR LIFE FOR DEEPER SERVICE AND LOVE AND YOU WILL FIND HIM AT WORK IN YOU FOR HIS HURTING PEOPLE."

April 1

The LORD on high is mightier than the noise of many waters, yea, than the mighty waves of the sea. Psalm 93:4, KJV

In the autumn of 1945, three recent college graduates boarded a transpacific ocean liner in San Francisco destined for Hawaii. Although they did not graduate from the same school, they had all received degrees in education and, by chance, were housed in the same cabin for their journey across the Pacific. As a result of their identical professional interests and the unusual circumstances that united them, they developed an intimate personal friendship.

Surprisingly, they were all assigned to teach at Laupahoehoe Elementary School, located in a harbor village on the "Big Island" of Hawaii. Two of the young future teachers, Marsue and Dottie, accepted their assignments. Pearl, though willing to join them, declined the offer at Laupahoehoe because her father "firmly opposed this assignment." Instead, she accepted a teaching job at Ewa Elementary School on Oahu.

In the spring of 1946, an earthquake originating in the Aleutian Islands produced a huge tsunami that impacted Laupahoehoe. Two large tidal waves inundated the shores where the Laupahoehoe Elementary School was located. As the waves receded, the young students became wildly excited and ran to see the many fish on dry land!

Suddenly, a gigantic third wave engulfed Laupahoehoe, swallowing everything in its path, including students, teachers, and local residents. Two teachers' cottages were crushed where they stood, and two other teachers' cottages were swept out into the angry waters of the Pacific.

The third tsunami wave was estimated to be 50 feet high. In all, of the 174 lives lost, 23 were students and 4 were teachers. Two students and one teacher survived the onslaught after 10 hours of struggling for their lives in the turbulent ocean. Except for one mangled, crushed body, none of the others were recovered.

This catastrophic event occurred at 7 a.m. on April 1, 1946, a day traditionally labeled as "April Fool's Day." A monument at the site of the Laupahoehoe Elementary School includes the names of those who died. Among them is Dottie, the young first-year stateside teacher and cabin mate of Marsue and Pearl.

Clinging to a raft, Marsue was rescued by Dr. Leopold Fernandez, with whom she had become acquainted before this event. Immediately after being rescued, Marsue graciously accepted the marriage proposal of the physician who saved her from the jaws of the hideous tsunami monster. Another survivor rescued by this same physician later completed his training as a physician.

The other cabin mate, Pearl, who did not accept the Laupahoehoe teaching assignment, has been most grateful for the mercy extended by an Omnipotent Being. And I have been most grateful as well, because in 1947 Pearl became my wife.

NOTE: For details, refer to the story by Marsue Fernandez entitled "Carried to Sea by a Tidal Wave," *Reader's Digest*, March 1959.

Alfred H. F. Lui, CME class of 1945, was a thoracic surgeon who currently resides in Rolling Hills Estates, California.

Though he slay me, yet will I trust in him: but I will maintain mine own ways before him. Job 13:15, KJV

A haze hung over Port-au-Prince, Haiti. Fires were burning the remnants of uncollected water bottles, debris, and unusable items destroyed in "The Event." The smell of rotting flesh soon permeated the bus. Our masks went on, but the people outside were accustomed to the deadly reminder of the January 12, 2010, Haiti earthquake.

When we arrived at the Adventist Community Team Services (ACTS) headquarters, lines of suffering people lingered near the clinic's entrance. No sooner had we finished our orientation than an American social worker asked, "Can you come with me to see a patient who is experiencing deep emotional needs at the hospital?" We walked quickly to where our patient lay sleeping in a Coleman camping tent.

Jasmine was a gifted girl who was hoping to teach French or become a singer. She had been studying on the third story roof of her home when the fourth story of the house next door came crashing toward her. She leapt in time to avoid being killed but fell three stories, crushing her left lower leg. Amputation was the only option to save her life. Her older sister was not as fortunate and died in the collapse of the home. As a result, Jasmine was having suicidal thoughts.

Because of her posttraumatic stress disorder, it was important for her to "work through," as we say in psychiatry, the emotions and experiences she had recently suffered. She had been writing in her journal. This journaling of her precious thoughts and feelings would be essential for her recovery. I asked her, "Could you read to us from your journal?"

She began: "The day that I had my accident is engraved in my memory. It's all as if it happened in a dream. Now, I am a handicap. I live in a world of handicap. I have no house to live in, five of my family members are dead, and we are not too rich and not too poor, but I am miserable." As we listened, we wept with her. We spent time offering encouragement, validation, and support.

"I have not lost all my hope, for God is here during all my suffering, pain, chagrin, contempt, and humiliation. God my Father has sustained me, which is why I am not deprived. My Father, My Father, My Father!" Her response, as in Job 13:15, had hope and clinging trust.

"My deceased sister used to say, 'We must enjoy every part of life, because we never know what is in the future.'" Jasmine wistfully continued, "We live in a world of despair, regret, pain, suffering, and misery. For me, all my plans have crumbled. We are not responsible for what we have lost, but for what we do. Sometimes love makes us suffer when it is sincere."

What a statement, conveying the essence of Christ's suffering and the meaning of love, knowing that sincere love has depth of loss in death. She understood what survivors have: a gift of a life with dreams, not of guilt.

Thomas J. Andrews, LLUSM class of 1978-B, is a psychiatrist who works with the general and Native American populations in rural California. He was part of the first psychology team on the ground in Haiti following the 2010 earthquake. He dedicates this story to the victims, survivors, and volunteers with the hope that others will be encouraged to change our world for the better; to his wife of 30 years, Marie-Pierre, who helped translate Jasmine's journal; and to his daughter Claire-Alyce Andrews, LLUSM class of 2012. April 2 is Claire's birthday.

April 3

And we all, with unveiled face, beholding the glory of the Lord, are being transformed into the same image from one degree of glory to another. For this comes from the Lord who is the Spirit. 2 Corinthians 3:18, ESV

Since graduating in 1969 from Loma Linda University School of Medicine, I have been very busy in general practice. Having seen literally thousands of patients in seven different locations, I have been impressed by the diversity and yet the similarity of us humans. It has been a magnificent privilege to serve each patient, to listen to what they have to say, and to assist them on their journey through life. One of my patients stands out in my mind because of the text noted above.

His name is Bob; he is 85 years old. He has been a patient at our office for well over 10 years. He is a fellow church member and, according to our head nurse, "my favorite elderly man." His life has not been an easy one—with his own multiple, long-standing medical problems and caring for his now-deceased wife who had been bedridden for several years, during which she was supported by his solicitous care.

Despite these challenges, he has been an inspiration to me and to my staff every time he comes for a visit. His ready smile, his words of encouragement, and his interest in our lives and those of our families reveal a loving and caring spirit. Not only are these qualities admirable, but also his numerous acts of kindness for the community revealed the same type of interested focus.

He spends a day each week volunteering at one of our local hospitals. He keeps in touch with the "older" church members (some of whom no longer attend church) and has lunch with them on a consistent basis. He provides a monthly stipend for an outstanding student at our church school. He is a man who seeks to "add value" to each situation with which he is involved.

When he is asked what motivates him to do all these things, his answer is, "God blessed me with gifts and a giving spirit, and I am just following up on what He has done for me."

Each day, Bob beholds and becomes transformed!

Arthur Davis Jr., LLUSM class of 1969, practiced medicine for more than 40 years and was a general practitioner in Indio, California, for 28 years. He submitted this story in December 2012 and passed away on July 2, 2013. He is survived by his wife, six children, and six grandchildren.

But You, O Lord, are a God full of compassion, and gracious, Longsuffering and abundant in mercy and truth. Psalm 86:15, NKJV

As she sat across from me in the exam room, Maria looked dazed and overwhelmed. She had good reasons for that appearance, I supposed. After all, her story was tragic, but not all that uncommon.

Maria had arrived in the United States from Guatemala a few weeks before—not by plane, or by train, but by "coyotes"—men who smuggled her across the border. "I paid over $3,000," she lamented. "My daughter is still in Guatemala with my mother. The 'coyotes' threaten not to bring her to me if I don't pay them another $2,000." Like millions of other undocumented immigrants, the price tag to a better life has no limit.

But Maria wanted more than just a better life. She desperately needed medical care. She was approximately six months pregnant and had AIDS. Somehow, she managed to find her way to our San Bernardino clinic for help.

The tasks put before our team were no less daunting. A high-risk OB referral must be in order first. We had fewer than three months to reduce this mother's HIV viral load to nearly undetectable; otherwise, the unborn child would be at much greater risk for perinatal HIV transmission.

In the few ensuing weeks, Maria faithfully returned to the clinic. She tolerated her HIV medications well. Her small, cachectic daughter was soon reunited with her. How they came up with all the money I have no idea and I dared not ask. All I cared about now was that her daughter would receive the treatment she needed. A call to Loma Linda University Medical Center's pediatric infectious disease division ensured that her little girl would be able to obtain medical care there.

Prior to Maria's delivery, our team managed to collect much-needed clothing and supplies for the baby. A local six-year-old girl also learned of Maria's plight. Despite her tender age, she decided she wanted to help. Maria was extremely surprised and delighted to receive $162 that this young girl raised making and selling bookmarks!

Maria's HIV viral load eventually became undetectable—she gave birth to a son who was free of the HIV virus. Soon thereafter, Maria and her children moved to another country; I never saw them again.

There are lessons to be learned from Maria's story, including that we must avoid stigmatizing people who have certain types of diseases. In this case, HIV/AIDS did not mean an irresponsible lifestyle. Maria, along with many other women for whom I have cared, was an unfortunate victim through absolutely no fault of her own. Also, a team approach is paramount in HIV care.

But it all starts with a compassionate heart—after all, we serve a God who is the Author of compassion.

Wilfred W. Shiu, LLUSM class of 1990, is an HIV specialist in Northern California. April 4 is about the time this story occurred.

April 5

He replied, "I saw Satan fall like lightning from heaven. I have given you authority to trample on snakes and scorpions and to overcome all the power of the enemy; nothing will harm you. However, do not rejoice that the spirits submit to you, but rejoice that your names are written in heaven." Luke 10:18-20, NIV

"Wayne, how would you like to come to church this Saturday? The sermon is going to be good, because I'm preaching," I told him (hopefully with a big smile on my face). Wayne is a 35-year-old diabetic patient of mine who struggles with getting adequate exercise and maintaining a healthy diet. Intrigued that his doctor would be preaching, he accepted my invitation.

For a period of time before, Wayne had attended our church regularly; then, because of various circumstances, he quit for quite some time. Just recently, he began coming back to church on Sabbath mornings. Wayne enjoys studying the weekly lessons and frequently asks for specific needs during prayer and praise time at our church service. He is hoping to become involved in teaching the Sabbath School lesson.

Wayne also savors the vegetarian cuisine at potlucks and making friends with church members. He appreciates the Sabbaths when we go to nursing homes to sing with the residents. Just two months ago, he quit drinking alcohol and is giving God thanks for that miracle. Now he is asking for prayers to stop smoking.

The challenges of a physician are many, yet the rewards far outweigh the sacrifices. One thing that brings me happiness is seeing patients making healthy choices, and then watching them bask in the benefits of their improved health.

I get even more excited when patients realize that what they are experiencing is a gift from God, as they go on to develop a closer relationship with their Creator. This reminds me of the joy the disciples had when they returned from their mission trip and told the Lord, "Even the demons submit to us in your name" (Luke 10:17, NIV). Jesus pointed them to something far more wonderful, "Rejoice that your names are written in heaven" (Luke 10:20, NIV).

Wayne is not alone in his struggles. Noncommunicable diseases (most of which are lifestyle related) cause over 70 percent of the lost years of life in the United States. On one hand, modern medicine is continually making advances in ways to treat and prevent these chronic diseases; yet on the other hand, our poor lifestyles that contribute to risk factors (like obesity) for these diseases are increasing.

We as physicians know, in theory, how to prevent many diseases, but struggle with knowing how to motivate our patients to make the necessary lifestyle changes. One resource that I have found helpful in my medical practice is that of partnering with the local church, just as I did with Wayne. The pastor and church members can be helpful, not only in educating patients, but also in giving them social and spiritual support. My deepest desire and prayer is that the Holy Spirit will show us other ways that we can utilize the resources God has given us, in order to motivate our patients to better physical and spiritual health.

Robert Spady, LLUSM class of 1985, PhD, is a primary care provider for the Total Health Physician Group, an Adventist church-owned clinic in Moscow, Idaho.

He shall call upon me, and I will answer him: I will be with him in trouble.
Psalm 91:15, KJV

D r. Mary Small wrote the following in a letter home to her parents, Carrol, CME class of 1934, and Lucile Small, while she was serving at Ottapalam Seventh-day Adventist Hospital in India.

"Last Sunday I delivered a baby, the daughter and third child of a lady whose husband is a PhD degree student in plant breeding. His education and grasp of English made it much easier to communicate with him regarding their baby who, at 16 hours, was jaundiced, yellow as a pumpkin, and becoming much deeper yellow as time passed. The first bilirubin we did was 20 mg% (should be 1 mg%), and it subsequently rose to 34 mg%. It was obvious that something needed to be done. We three doctors pooled our collective knowledge and decided that the baby needed an exchange transfusion (this was an ABO incompatibility); we also discovered that none of us had ever done one. I saw one when I was a junior medic, and Bhaktaraj Chelliah had assisted with one once. We concluded that this was ample qualification and proceeded to do it—but, of course, not as soon as we had planned.

"Monday morning we detected the jaundice. By Monday night we had the report of 20 mg%—so we repeated the test, and it came back as 2 mg%! That was obviously wrong; but it was almost midnight before we discovered which technician had used the wrong pipette, introducing a tenfold error into the calculations. It was then too late to send a messenger to get a blood donor (we had only a 'walking blood bank'), so the next morning we sent for a donor. He came and was the right group, but the crossmatch was incompatible with both mother's and baby's blood. This required yet another donor to be found. By the time he came two hours later, the electricity had gone off, making it impossible to spin down the blood for serum; settling and clot retraction take a long time.

At 10 p.m. Tuesday, 24 hours after we should have done it, we did the first exchange transfusion. Monitoring consisted of listening to the heartbeat frequently, for we had no way to check blood pressure on a newborn. The baby was still yellow after the procedure, and the next morning it was obvious she needed a second transfusion. At least we managed to do that one in the daytime, and the next day the bilirubin started down. Today I discharged mother and baby; both had normal color. Only the father was pale when he saw the bill!"

No telephones, no Internet, no appropriate specialist to consult, and scant equipment— just pray and improvise. Can you understand why we had extra need for Divine guidance?

Mary Small, LLUSM class of 1966, served in India from 1970 to 1984, and upon returning to the States completed a maternal-fetal medicine fellowship in Los Angeles. She was on faculty in LLUSM department of gynecology and obstetrics from 1986 until she retired. She was an LLUSMAA 1995 Honored Alumna. Her mother's birthday is April 6.

April 7

God is light, and in Him there is no darkness at all. If we say that we have fellowship with Him and yet walk in the darkness, we lie and do not practice the truth; but if we walk in the Light as He Himself is in the Light, we have fellowship with one another, and the blood of Jesus His Son cleanses us from all sin.
1 John 1:5-7, NASB

This is the story of two men who came into my office and left with different outcomes.

The first man was brought in by a neighbor. His cataracts kept him from driving, reading, or seeing the faces of his family members. I offered him cataract surgery, but he declined, saying, "I see just fine." He demonstrated his vision by barely counting the fingers I held in front of his eyes. My descriptions of the speed, ease, and safety of the procedure only made him more adamant that surgery was unnecessary.

His cataracts continued to get worse until even walking became a dangerous task, with the chance of tripping and falling ever present. He came to see me once more, asking for new glasses—which I knew would be of no help to him. And, again, he declined surgery.

He never came back. I hope he allowed someone, somewhere, to help him with cataract surgery. His fear and lack of trust kept him in the gloomy shadows when he could so easily have been set free from his prison of darkness.

The second man came one Monday morning as a blind old man tapping his white cane. On Wednesday when he came for his post-op visit, he was spinning around, shouting, and singing, "I can see, I can see, I can see," as he danced his way into my exam room!

Delighted with the return of his eyesight after cataract surgery, he was completely rejuvenated. I laughed at his antics, happy to be a part of his tale, participating in the story as his eye surgeon. It was a pure joy to restore what was rightfully his to begin with, and especially so because he was such a grateful and expressive man.

He recounted to me how his life would change. For one thing, he could now navigate clearly, walking without fear of stumbling into things. He would resume driving, which meant he could be independent; and perhaps he would even travel a bit. The possibilities were astounding, and his happiness was contagious! He thanked me for the "great job" and I thanked him for being such a good patient and for the privilege of taking care of him!

These instances remind me of John 9:41, where Jesus says that He came so that the blind would see, but those who claim they can see would remain blind.

Leilani Norton, LLUSM class of 1982, is an ophthalmologist in Placerville, California.

April 8

Commit everything you do to the LORD. Trust him, and he will help you.
Psalm 37:5, NLT

This story begins in North Africa, on the shores of the Mediterranean Sea, in the city of Benghazi, Libya. During the early 1940s, Erwin Rommel, known as the German Fox, led his Nazi army across North Africa and almost to Cairo. But God said, "No farther," and he was stopped at El Alamein. When we arrived in Libya in 1966, remnants of World War II were still very much present, e.g., fortifications and live ammunition shells. These live shells were still agents of injury and death.

I was just finishing a skin graft on a patient when a nurse called me to come quickly to the emergency department (ED). When I reached our new, unfurnished ED, I saw, lying on the floor and surrounded by people, a patient I was totally unprepared to face. Jan, my 12-year-old daughter, lay on the floor, arms and legs covered with blood, chest a mottled blue, unconscious, no heart sounds, and no respirations. My mind was numb with shock. "Think what you have been trained to do," I reminded myself, while at the same time uttering a prayer for God's intervention. As I began CPR, other members of our staff arrived. The suturing of lacerations began; lab and x-ray technicians arrived; an IV was started; and a nurse anesthetist provided oxygen while blood from a staff member was given after a "quick match."

Alice, my wife, arrived and bent over Jan's head and sang softly, "Angels are watching over you." She added words from the Lord's Prayer: "Thy Kingdom come, Thy will be done, on earth as it is in heaven." She submitted Jan to God's will.

What at first appeared to be a minor half-inch laceration over her chest turned out to be a fragment of shrapnel from a 22mm antiaircraft shell that had penetrated and gone through her heart. This shell, an item collected by children, exploded as Jan was throwing what she thought were "empty boxes" into a fire. She was helping a newly arrived family dispose of their packaging boxes.

After a half hour in the ED, Jan suddenly took a deep breath and screamed; then, all was silent, except for her breathing. After we spent a long, prayerful night at her side, she awoke, amnesic, but without evidence of brain damage. She was flown to the United States, and, 10 days later, had open-heart surgery at Loma Linda University Medical Center.

The shrapnel had caused a rent or tear in the ventricular septum as it went through her heart, leading to congestive heart failure. That fragment still remains radiographically visible behind her heart; a constant reminder of God, who said, "Stop, no more death." How can we not trust Him to help us—come what may?

April 8 is a day we will always remember. It was a day of submission, trust, and gratitude to God, who knows the beginning and the end. On His providence we can rely, regardless of the outcome.

Don C. Fahrbach, CME class of 1955, is a retired family practitioner residing in Munising, Michigan. His daughter, Jan, works as an ICU nurse in Hawaii. She and her husband, Ron Sauder, a childhood playmate in Libya, are the proud parents of twins. April 8 is when this story occurred.

April 9

It was he who gave some to be apostles, some to be prophets, some to be evangelists, and some to be pastors and TEACHERS, to prepare God's people for works of service, so that the body of Christ may be built up until we all reach unity in the faith and in the knowledge of the Son of God and become mature, attaining to the whole measure of the fullness of Christ.
Ephesians 4:11-13, NIV (1984, emphasis added)

Mrs. Winifred Nakamoto Oshita, my seventh and eighth grade teacher in a little one-room Seventh-day Adventist church school in tiny Kapaa on Kauai, Hawaii, is a person I would like to honor by writing about her in this book. In 1938, she was a single lady—recently graduated from Pacific Union College's Department of Education—who ventured to this out-of-the-way place and began her career as an outstanding educator.

My father and mother had only a fourth- and eighth-grade education; but when my mother became a Seventh-day Adventist, she was impressed to send her children to that little church school on Kauai, where I was enrolled in the second grade.

When beautiful Winifred came along, she was the first college-educated teacher we had ever had. With her vivacious and loving personality, she had a great influence on all of us. I will never forget that, after teaching us a class in physiology, she took me aside and said: "Ernest, you did so well in this class, you can be a doctor if you set your mind to it." Until then, it had never occurred to me to aim high. It was a thought that remained in my mind throughout high school, military service, Pacific Union College, and medical school.

Because of her inspiration, out of that elementary school of 22 students, 4 others in addition to me became alumni of Loma Linda University (LLU): her younger siblings from Maui, Masao Nakamoto, CME class of 1955, and Ethel Nakamoto Inaba, LLUSN class of 1955; Percy Lui, CME class of 1955; and my brother, Ronald Zane, LLUSD class of 1957. When I count the spouses, the children, and children's spouses who attended LLU, it comes to a total of 19—all in two generations!

Mrs. Oshita and her husband, Elder Hideo Oshita, also a PUC alumnus, taught for many years at Hawaiian Mission Academy; later he became pastor of the Los Angeles Japanese Seventh-day Adventist Church. Mrs. Oshita emerged to be a very effective principal for a number of years at San Gabriel Academy Elementary, in San Gabriel, California, nurturing thousands of students through the years. One wonders how many of those attended LLU!

As I am nearing 52 years of practicing and teaching ophthalmology at Loma Linda University School of Medicine, I am thankful to God that I have the great opportunity to be here. Nothing is more gratifying than to be involved with the training of our young people, to be God's hands and feet in healing the sick. I certainly owe a great debt to my teacher, Mrs. Oshita. Living in Monterey Park, she is now very frail at 96 years of age; but in my mind, Mrs. Winifred Nakamoto Oshita will always be a giant in the Kingdom of God.

Ernest Zane, CME class of 1956, is vice chair and an associate professor in LLUSM department of ophthalmology. He was awarded LLUSM Distinguished Service Award in 2010. He and his wife, Dorothy (one of the hand models on the cover of this book), reside in Loma Linda, California. April 9 is the birthday of Mrs. Oshita.

And this is the confidence that we have toward him, that if we ask anything according to his will he hears us. And if we know that he hears us in whatever we ask, we know that we have the requests that we have asked of him.
1 John 5:14-15, ESV

As long as I can remember, Loma Linda University has been a part of my life. Its influence extends from being reared on amazing food that my mother always credited to Loma Linda University School of Nursing to hearing stories about my uncles, cousins, and friends who became physicians or dentists; these were the "missionaries" we prayed for every night. It was a place that I was reared to believe epitomized the "light on a hill" or the "salt of the earth" referenced in the Bible. It was a special place with a special mission.

When I had the opportunity, many years later, to move to Loma Linda, California, and be a part of that place, it was not a very difficult decision. For several years now, I have had the amazing privilege of working to support the clinical faculty of Loma Linda University School of Medicine.

Because of the nature of my work, I do not have much freedom to tell stories. But these are stories that make me laugh, cry, and keep me coming back day after day. They are also the ones that validated those told by my mother and multiple family members. There are, however, a couple I can share about the spiritual atmosphere here.

A few years back, our leadership team made the commitment to start our weekly meetings with a "thought for the day." A schedule was created, and we rotated the responsibility. Through this process, we have been able to get to know each other, support each other, and depend upon each other in ways we had never done before. Starting our time together with a focused spiritual thought and prayer has clearly changed the way we work through the many challenges that come our way.

About the same time, I became involved in a small prayer group on campus. It is just a handful of people who all are seeking a closer walk with Jesus—who get together regularly to lay before Him our personal and professional lives, as well as to pray for our attention to be directed on Him. We look forward to our shared time together and, somehow, it provides what is needed to carry us through our tasks.

For me, prayer makes all the difference. It might be as simple as sending a quick page or phone text to a colleague saying that you are praying for him or her, or asking that person to pray for you. It means being free to take time before a tough meeting and ask for guidance and wisdom, or to sit with an employee who is struggling and say a prayer—all the while knowing, without a doubt, that God hears.

A few months ago, just before a round of corporate boards started, I happened to speak with the dean of the School of Medicine. He is someone who is always approachable and kind. I knew what the day ahead would be for him and many others, and I felt impressed to pause and ask him if I could pray for him. He said, "Of course."

The freedom to pray with others is just one reason I love Loma Linda University. The institution is in my DNA, and it continues to be a special place with a special mission.

Barbara Sharp is executive director of LLUFMG office of professional employment and recruitment.

April 11

And it shall be said in that day, Lo, this is our God; we have waited for him, and he will save us: this is the LORD; we have waited for him, we will be glad and rejoice in his salvation. Isaiah 25:9, KJV

It was in the middle of the night, and we were halfway between Guam and Hawaii on a commercial flight. I had been taking my young patient's vitals every 15 minutes on our seven-hour flight. He was still unconscious, even after having an emergency bore hole placed in his skull in Guam. We were on our way to Honolulu so our patient could have emergency brain surgery there, in order to remove the subdural hematoma that he had sustained after a head injury.

Sherwin, a teenager, was involved with the wrong crowd. His father, Willie, was a good friend of ours and one of the pastors on Palau. They had been in Guam visiting when Sherwin was involved in a motor vehicle accident. Now he was lying on a cot—taking up six seats on the commercial airplane that was our "ambulance" headed to Honolulu.

We knew he had sustained a concussion; but over a several-hour time frame, his level of consciousness had deteriorated to the point that he had to have surgery or lose his life. Would we make it to Hawaii on time? Would there be irreversible brain damage? Would Sherwin be restored back to the happy, helpful teenager we all knew? At this point, all we could do was pray that he would remain stable during the long flight while the neurosurgical team waited for us in Honolulu.

When we arrived, an ambulance met the plane at the airport, and Sherwin was taken directly to the hospital. When Sherwin's father and I arrived at the hospital some time later, the neurosurgeon met us and told us that the subdural hematoma had increased in size and that Sherwin was being taken immediately into surgery. He invited me to assist him in the surgery; I was able to see that the subdural hematoma had been completely removed and that all the bleeding had been successfully stopped. Now all we could do was wait to see if Sherwin would awaken.

The next morning when Sherwin's father and I walked into his room, Sherwin was sitting up. When he saw his father, the first thing he said was, "There's my dad!" From that point on, we knew that Sherwin would be all right. He has since become a pastor, like his father.

This event reminded me of the text in Isaiah 25:9, when we will all look up and see Jesus coming in a cloud with His angels. Then we will all know that, from that moment throughout eternity, we will be all right because we will be with our Father and our brother Jesus.

Keith Hanson, LLUSM class of 1978-A, and his wife served as missionaries in Guam from 1982 to 1988. He is a family practitioner in Brewster, Washington.

April 12

For thou hast been a strength to the poor, a strength to the needy in his distress, a refuge from the storm, a shadow from the heat, when the blast of the terrible ones is as a storm against the wall. Isaiah 25:4, KJV

On Friday, April 12, 1940, after traveling from a boarding college in Norway, I was miraculously reunited with my family in the remote farmhouse to which they had fled after the Nazi invasion of Norway three days prior. We kept the Sabbath day quietly. The weather was cloudy. Sunday came and went without any spectacular happenings, except that my brother's girlfriend came up from Oslo. She had not experienced anything unusual other than the cars that had been used as roadblocks had been removed and other items now took their place.

On Monday morning, April 15, we heard the first eerie sounds of machine guns and explosions in the distance, and we knew that the enemy had arrived. The weather was overcast, so we could not see very far. Usually, on a sunny day, other farmhouses were clearly visible from our valley location.

On our property were two farmhouses and a barn. In the other house, the farmer and his wife had been sitting in the kitchen when they suddenly had an urge to move into the living room, since that room was the farthest from the valley. That decision would prove to be their salvation. Unknown to the other people on the farm, their son had gone outside with a pair of binoculars to try to see some of the action, in case the clouds partially cleared. Unfortunately, before he could see anything, the Germans saw him.

In a few moments, we heard the sudden, ear-deafening noise of an explosion outside, saw black smoke billowing up, and then heard another explosion. This time the house we were in felt as if it had been moved a foot off its foundations and then back again. More explosions followed. The window glass disappeared right in front of me; it must have been sucked out.

All in all, the Germans shot five times at our house with their cannons, probably the size of a Howitzer. The house was hit in the kitchen area, just a few feet from where we had been crouching. We knelt in prayer and pleaded with God for His merciful protection. Then we fled to a lodge in the forest to spend the night.

We were told that when a group of German soldiers came up to the farmstead shortly afterward to survey the damage and count the dead and wounded, they could not believe that none of the 20 people on the farm were killed or injured.

It is my conviction that the Germans had in mind to wipe a Norwegian outpost off the earth, and the devil intended to totally obliterate a family that served the living God, kept the Sabbath, and had the faith of Jesus. But the angels overruled his plans and moved the trajectory of the shells just a little from their projected path. Otherwise, I would not be able to share this story of God's guidance and protection over my loved ones and myself.

Praise the Lord for His merciful protection—thank God it is as real today as it was back then.

Svein R. Nilsen, LLUSM class of 1962, was a family practitioner for 34 years in San Bernardino, California, where his wife, Mildred (née Markussen), worked as office manager. He wrote this account in 2008 as a sequel to his April 12 Morning Rounds devotional. He passed away on August 27, 2010, followed by Mildred on May 31, 2012. They are survived by their three daughters and six grandchildren.

April 13

God, who got you started in this spiritual adventure, shares with us the life of his Son and our Master Jesus. He will never give up on you. Never forget that.
1 Corinthians 1:9, MSG

As the medical student rounding with a pediatric surgeon at Loma Linda University Medical Center, I stood listening to my attending physician discuss with a child's young parents a long list of problems and treatment options. I imagined the child was lying quietly, and, if awake, would be listening to muffled voices—like hearing someone talk while your head is under water. That muffled sound is logical because this child had not been born.

These parents were receiving a prenatal surgical consult in preparation for the birth of their child, at which time operations to correct the child's developmental defects would begin. Under the best of circumstances, the process to correct developmental defects can take years. These multiple stages of surgical alterations often involve a diverse team of medical specialists. Complications during reconstruction and recovery can multiply the complexity and time required. The emotional toll of the process on children and their parents is immense, not to mention the financial impact—and there is also the time commitment to surgical recovery and subsequent clinical visits.

Day after day, I would see parents and their children—some just beginning the medical journey, some in the midst of it, and some excited to be making their last post-op visit. Yet, through their long, arduous process, it was inspiring to see how loving, patient, and dedicated these parents were.

The example of these parents is a great illustration of God's love for us. I imagine that when the earth was being created, there was much anticipation. God was at work, and the other worlds watched, like watching an artist. And when the earth was complete, God and everyone else took a step back to admire—it was perfect.

But then something happened; sin entered the world. At that point, everyone realized that this world would not be like the others. The children of this world were broken, and it would take a special plan and a large amount of time to restore them. But God did not give up on them.

He put a plan in motion, and it was an expensive plan—it cost God His Son's life. But it worked. God saved the world so each one of us can have the potential to be restored to eternal life. We are works in progress though; each of us must choose to be a part of His plan for restoration. We strive to be better people, but there are many complications along the way.

Our spiritual journeys are full of ups and downs; we have good days and bad days. It is often a difficult journey, but God never gives up on us. He is loving, patient, and dedicated. He wants to see you and me perfectly whole someday.

So, I stood in that exam room, thinking about the unborn child for whom gestation and birth would be merely the first two of many steps required to reach sustainable life. And I realized, in a spiritual sense, that I am that child.

Carl Erickson, LLUSM class of 2015, was born in Loma Linda, California, and grew up in Portland, Oregon. He graduated from the University of Oregon with a master's degree in physiology and biomechanics.

April 14

And Jesus went about all Galilee, teaching in their synagogues, and preaching the gospel of the kingdom, and healing all manner of sickness and all manner of disease among the people. Matthew 4:23, KJV

The elevator makes its "ding!" sound as I step off onto the fourth floor of the children's hospital. Wearing my short, white coat, I timidly walk up to the charge nurse and ask, "Is there anyone who would be willing to let me interview them for a class project?" As I try to analyze the confused look on her face, she says, "Are you sure you're in the right place?"

I want to say, "I don't know, you tell me," but I know exactly why she is asking. A sign outside the double doors states that quiet time is from noon to 2 p.m. because the children are sleeping. Thankfully, though the nurse gives me the help I need.

I am about to enter the "bravest ward" in the hospital—a place filled with heartbreak, with joy, with thankfulness, with a maze of sobbing families—pediatric oncology, a place filled with cancer. The nurses are cheerful, and the children are more courageous than a prize fighter trying to win a championship belt.

I finally make it to my patient, Sarah's, room; the nurse said it would be fine to go in and conduct my interview. As I enter, Sarah is lying on the bed trying to sleep, so I ask her parents if they would like me to come back. Not upset, they tell me to stay, and so I begin asking my questions as if I were reading a list of orders in a drive-through.

The interchange does not feel natural at all. Sarah is a 16-year-old advanced placement student in high school, and one day she began to feel sick and a bit clumsy. Taken to the hospital for the second time, she was finally diagnosed with a huge medulloblastoma (a high-grade tumor of the cerebellum).

As her mother tells me about the medulloblastoma, she begins to cry. My heart feels as if it has dropped right through the floor. Other questions begin to flood my mind. I think about how I had spent time in neuroscience and now cannot even remember what a medulloblastoma is. I think about the fact that here I am, a medical student, and there is nothing I can do to physically help her diagnosis.

I also think about why this girl has to suffer through all of this. Why her? Why now? However, my last thought is one of excitement when I realize that I am in a profession that affords me the ability to care for those who are most vulnerable.

I put my arm around the mother as she weeps, and I tell her how devastating this must be for her. By now, I am switching my focus from my class project to the patient and her family. This is my first real test of successful doctoring. I notice at this moment that much of being a doctor has nothing to do with the medicine. It is about the patient.

I am aware that my MD degree will not serve as a symbol of intelligence or hard work, but rather as a spotlight into the lives of suffering patients, in order that I may offer them care as a "person" on medical, emotional, and spiritual levels.

Michael Hunter, LLUSM class of 2015, is from Hemet, California. He graduated from Loyola Marymount University with a BS degree in biology/biochemistry. April 14 is his birthday.

April 15

Therefore, since we are surrounded by such a great cloud of witnesses, let us throw off everything that hinders and the sin that so easily entangles. And let us run with perseverance the race marked out for us. Hebrews 12:1, NIV

I like running, and, in fact, I like racing even better. Little did I realize that on a very cool, sunny Patriots' Day, April 15, 2013, I would come within minutes of being in the blast zone of the two bombs set off by terrorist brothers in Boston. I was taking pictures with a throw-away camera as I raced the 26.2 miles; and my last picture, before finishing in 3 hours and 57 minutes, would show the crowd and race officials lining the sidewalk at the very location of the first blast. Sadly, some of these people would later lose their limbs or even their lives.

The time of the first blast: 4 hours and 03 minutes. I heard it echoing up and down Boylston Street, like the boom of a jet flying overhead. I saw the rising cloud of the burning blast powder like a funeral pall settling over runners and spectators alike. I did not see the carnage, thank God, because not being medically trained, it would have been so frustrating to see the wounded and bleeding and not know how to help them.

But I did see the immediate response of policemen and race officials in the racing chute where I was. They were running toward the first blast to provide assistance, risking their lives had there been more blasts.

My first thought was to retrieve my race gear from the storage buses parked at the end of Boylston. As soon as I had on a warm jacket, which many runners never were able to have, I tried calling my wife, Loretta. She was in Loma Linda working at her office as one of the assistant deans in the School of Medicine.

For more than an hour, all my attempts at getting through to her or anyone at Loma Linda failed. Finally, I was able to inform my frantic wife that I was okay. She knew that I was planning on finishing in four hours flat; so, when she did not hear from me, she assumed I had been injured, perhaps seriously. How comforting to hear each other's voices!

My heart still goes out to the injured, the maimed for life, the deceased, and their families and loved ones. Three died, and more than 280 were injured. Why did I not hear reports of dozens of runners being transported to area hospitals? I realized it was because the crowd of spectators, usually four or five rows deep, took nearly all the flak from the shrapnel. Later, I learned that only one runner was injured from the bombing.

I thought back to Easter weekend, a couple of weeks before the marathon. It took on a dramatic new meaning as I realized that Christ took the shrapnel hurled by the enemy so that we can successfully run the race that leads to His Kingdom. I want to finish that race. I want family and loved ones to do so as well. While the Hebrews verse above speaks of running, the secret of completing the greatest race we will ever run is found in the very next verse: "Let us fix our eyes on Jesus, the author and perfecter of our faith, who for the joy set before him endured the cross, scorning its shame" (Hebrews 12:2, NIV [1984]).

He took the flak for me!

Warren H. Johns, PhD, is an associate professor at Loma Linda University working in the University Libraries as a special collections cataloger. He has worked as an academic librarian for 25 years. The 2013 Boston Marathon was his second Boston Marathon and one of the more than 30 marathons that he has run.

April 16

"But I will restore you to health and heal your wounds," declares the LORD, "because you are called an outcast, Zion for whom no one cares."
Jeremiah 30:17, NIV

I am writing orders for a routine admission, when I hear an *okada* speed up and stop right at the door behind me. A mother rushes off the back of the motorcycle, carrying a small, limp frame of a child, and places him on one of the exam beds.

I think the worst and hesitate to get up from the chair. So many children in this part of Africa are brought in with severe malaria combined with anemia, all of them limp like this boy, many of whom are dead on arrival or die soon after.

He lies motionless on the bed, eyes shut tightly. I feel a pulse and I see his chest rising. Thank God, he is not dead, I think to myself, but I cannot wake him.

I see a large swelling on his forehead and soon discover that he has fallen from a second story building. His breathing begins to change. At times, he takes quick gasps, and at other times he takes deep breaths, almost like sighs. He then begins to vomit, a bad sign that could indicate that the pressure in his head is increasing, most likely from bleeding within his skull.

I call the neurosurgeon from the teaching hospital nearby. He advises that we intubate this seven-year-old boy, and put him on a ventilator. That will help him breath regularly and decrease the pressure in his head.

After the intubation I see the boy again. His chest rises each time the machine pushes air into his lungs. He moves slightly as this happens, but is still deeply unconscious. I shout his name into his ear. No response.

Even if we get a CT scan, will we enter his skull to remove the blood? Even with surgery, most of our head injury patients die. Even in the best hospitals in the world these injuries may be fatal. When medicine is not enough, what can we do? I pray. I ask God to give him life. I feel at peace and I know that God is in control.

Less than an hour later while I am admitting another patient, I am met by our nurse anesthetist. "Guess what?" he tells me. "I removed the breathing tube from that boy and he's awake and talking."

I cannot believe it! I finish the admission and head to the ward. Sure enough, the boy is awake, communicating. I look at his forehead. How strange! The swelling that was there before is gone. I look again. How could this disappear so quickly? The swelling was from a collection of blood under the skin. Blood does not reabsorb that quickly. It is not medically possible.

Surely, I think to myself, he must have a headache after his fall. I ask the mother, "Is his head hurting?" She asks him in the local language and he shakes his head, "no."

"What? Ask him again," I tell the mother, thinking maybe he did not understand the question. She asks him again, and receives the same reply. I ask him, using the little Yoruba that I know. Again, the same reply.

I think of all the medical possibilities that could explain his improvement, but there are none. I tell the boy and his mother that what has happened is from God; there is no other explanation. "*Oluwaseun,*" the mother shouts, "all gratitude to God!"

Jason Lohr, LLUSM class of 2001, is an assistant professor in LLUSM departments of preventive and family medicine. This story was written while he and his wife, Belen, also LLUSM class of 2001, were missionary physicians in Nigeria for five years. April 16 is his birthday.

April 17

Fear thou not; for I am with thee: be not dismayed; for I am thy God: I will strengthen thee; yea, I will help thee; yea, I will uphold thee with the right hand of my righteousness. Isaiah 41:10, KJV

The early years of my medical practice were spent in Crescent City, California. There were no emergency department (ED) physicians, so our hospital staff of only six physicians was required to take care of all ED medical problems. Around that time, the *Journal of the American Medical Association* reported the ratios of doctors to patients in the United States; they listed the county with the fewest doctors in relation to patients. It happened to be Del Norte County, where I practiced. This ranking helped explain why our staff had such an overload.

On one occasion while practicing there, I was told that a man was coming in who had been involved in an auto accident. He was drunk and had hit a tree. His face had been cut to ribbons because in those days car windshields were not shatterproof. The U.S. Army, Merchant Marine, and Coast Guard in San Francisco had me under contract to care for patients in our area and send them to San Francisco when stable. This man was from their radar facility; I needed to care for his injuries.

After examining the patient, I came to the conclusion that there were no serious internal injuries present. After a silent prayer, I went to work on his facial cuts. It took me four hours and 400 plus stitches to repair all the damage. Many areas had skin missing, making it difficult to do a good repair. Three days later he had stabilized sufficiently to be sent to the San Francisco Army Hospital for convalescence and further plastic surgery. I was certain that more reconstruction would be necessary.

I did not see the man again until two or three years later. I was walking down the street one evening on my way home when a man came up to me and said he was the one whose face I had repaired a few years before. A quick look told me that plastic surgery had left minimal scarring. I congratulated the doctors in San Francisco for doing an excellent job. Surprisingly, he informed me that all they did in San Francisco was take out the stitches and send him home. I recognized the good Lord as the Plastic Surgeon who had done a perfect repair through me.

Elmer Hart, CME class of 1953-B, is a retired family practitioner residing in Yakima, Washington. This story occurred while he was practicing in Crescent City, California, around 1970. April 17 is his birthday.

April 18

Blessed be the God and Father of our Lord Jesus Christ, who according to His great mercy has caused us to be born again to a living hope through the resurrection of Jesus Christ from the dead. 1 Peter 1:3, NASB

I was attending a Good Friday service when I received a message over my pager that a 28-year-old patient of mine had just succumbed after her long battle with acute myelogenous leukemia. Good Friday services are somber enough as the betrayal and death of Christ are contemplated, but receiving such news during this service put my mood under an even darker pall. After the service my wife and I decided to go to the hospital to console Carrie's family and friends.

Although she had a good social support structure, it was small. She had lost contact with her father and had an on-again, off-again relationship with her mother. As a single mother of a five-year-old boy, she had difficulty with her transition to adulthood. Nonetheless, she had seemed to be pulling her life together.

She had done odd jobs as a waitress, and with income from part-time acting in Hollywood, she had just enrolled in classes at a community college. In the rearranging of her priorities, she had put the rearing of her son at the top of her list. She had made a few good friends along the way; her life seemed to be going in the right direction. But then, suddenly, she developed profound fatigue and unexplained bleeding from her gums.

As an oncologist, I am often asked how I handle my own personal emotions when having to bear bad news to patients, especially in the face of such unfairness. Or, how is it that I can keep doing what I do when ministering to patients who have a disease from which they know that they will ultimately succumb.

Well, to be perfectly honest, I still do not have any pat answer to those questions, despite having been in the field for more than 25 years. The good news about my specialty, however, is that there are many more triumphs than failures; and that, like my patients, I always have hope that there is something better just around the corner.

But one observation that I have made is that regardless of whether one is 28 or 98 years of age, there is always unfinished business. Regardless of age, we are all on this earth for only a short period of time, in the context of all eternity.

Carrie's story is not all sad. During her many hospitalizations, she had befriended the female hospital chaplain, who happened to be a woman not that much older than Carrie herself. During Carrie's illness, the chaplain was able to guide Carrie through her spiritual awareness. When the time came that Carrie took her last breath, she was at peace.

Yes, there is Good News just around the corner. Good Friday services are always followed by Easter Sunday, when the pall is lifted and the hope of salvation from evil and physical illness is celebrated with the resurrection of Jesus Christ. And with this realization we know that whenever our time on Earth here is done, Eternity with our Creator is just around the corner.

Bruce Hayton, LLUSM class of 1984, is married to Tammy, LLUSM class of 1991, and has a private practice in Temecula, California. April 18, 2014, is Good Friday.

April 19

There is no fear in love. But perfect love drives out fear, because fear has to do with punishment. The one who fears is not made perfect in love. 1 John 4:18, NIV

I could not believe the results of this new, noninvasive screening test. Could it be that this miracle conception, this embryo that I secretly called my "little prophet," had Down syndrome?

My husband and I had previously gone through three rounds of in vitro fertilization, and that effort had resulted in one amazing boy who is 18 months old. However, the most recent trial had failed. And then—without any medications and most of the month being much too tired—I found myself pregnant. Yes, an ultrasound confirmed a beautiful embryo with a heart beating 144 beats a minute. I did think it was too good to be true!

Up to this time, I thought I was going to spend at least a few more months changing a bit more of my life. I had been rather distant from God, so I thought I might have to really present my case before Him and tell Him about this void in my soul for a second child. I would start by eating more healthily and would begin spending hours in daily prayer and Bible study, seeking the Lord. I wanted to convince Him that I deserved one more miracle among all the miracles He had worked in my life. I felt that if I could not have a baby, then I would have to mourn the loss of the love that I already had for the child. But before I could do any of that, God gave me His answer.

The amniocentesis result confirmed that the baby boy I am carrying has Down syndrome. At that point, the thought of bringing into this world a child with such challenges and differences from the "typical" was unthinkable and heartbreaking. I could not stop crying for days. As I cried, I talked to my baby and said, "I'm so sorry, baby. I'm so sorry that life will probably be harder for you than me, but I love you so much! We will get through this together."

I began reading more and more about this syndrome. I realized I knew very little about it and discovered the many health problems they might face throughout life. The mental challenges range from mild to severe. Some affected adults accomplish much and are independent; others struggle.

From all that I have learned so far, I find that this is a disability that now has more encouraging aspects. Today, individuals with Down syndrome are accomplishing more than ever before due to increased acceptance and more opportunities that are open to them.

As I am writing this, I am closing in on 20-weeks of my pregnancy. I am now exposed to many questions regarding whether or not I should be continuing with this pregnancy. I do not really know what those questions mean, and I do not think the people who ask me know, or those who propose so-called "options" know either. So I reassure them of my choice. This is my child whom I have loved before he was conceived. I will not let anyone hurt him. And whatever comes our way, I fear nothing.

Cindy Sumarauw, LLUSD class of 1998, has a dental practice in Salt Lake City, Utah. She and her husband, Derek Sakata, LLUSM class of 1999, have two boys. April 19, 2013, is the day Abram M. W. Sakata was born.

For by grace are ye saved through faith; and that not of yourselves: it is the gift of God: Not of works, lest any man should boast. Ephesians 2:8-9, KJV

Early in my medical career in the mid-1950s, I had the privilege of spending several years in the Philippines at Manila Sanitarium and Hospital. It was a very interesting time. I enjoyed meeting the Filipino people, made many new friends, and had many rewarding experiences.

One particular experience that impressed me occurred during Easter Holy Week. I was able to observe one of the week's religious rites, called flagellation, which is held every year on Good Friday. The rite is designed to commemorate the suffering, crucifixion, death, and resurrection of Jesus. It is held outside Manila in a localized area and is not widespread throughout the country.

The flagellants are thousands of young men participating in a reenactment of the sufferings of Christ. The event, which consists of a day-long procession, is intended to show gratitude for the death of Jesus on the Cross, as well as to ensure the participants' salvation. The procession starts with young men sitting while a colleague slaps their back with a leather strap, followed by beating their back, chest, arms, and legs with a bamboo-tipped whip.

If not enough bleeding occurs during this initial step, the participants then strike the back and other body areas with special paddles that have glass chips imbedded in them in order to increase bleeding. They then start their procession of several miles to the church.

Along the way, the flagellants flail themselves with bamboo whips so that the bleeding will continue. When they arrive at the church, they lie on the floor and are again lashed with a leather strap, after which they are taken to a nearby pond with dirty water where their bodies are washed.

The procession I saw also included several young men who were carrying large wooden crosses. Part of the procession had members dressed as Mary, mother of Jesus; Mary Magdalene; and John the Baptist.

As I stood and watched that day, I am sure that some may have been participating merely as part of a "show"; but there were many, I felt, who were hoping to attain eternal life through their works. I was saddened that they were unaware that all their efforts were not necessary, or even useful, in assuring eternal life. The great gift given to us by the crucifixion of Jesus is the gift of grace and assurance that, if we confess our sins, accept Jesus, and follow Him, we will have eternal life. It is our mission to convey this blessed assurance to those who are not aware of His great gift.

Roy Jutzy, CME class of 1952, is an emeritus professor and former chair in LLUSM department of medicine. In 1998, he was awarded the LLU Distinguished Service Award followed by LLU Alumnus of the Year Award in 2002. He served at LLUMC for more than 40 years and was presented an LLUMC Lifetime Achievement Award in 2006. April 20, 2014, is Easter Sunday.

April 21

Have I not commanded you? Be strong and of good courage; do not be afraid, nor be dismayed, for the LORD your God is with you wherever you go.
Joshua 1:9, NKJV

Three defining events occurred in my mother's life that served as an affirmation of her faith in God. This is the most precious legacy that she has passed on to us.

The first event began in 1912 in a remote Christian town in northern China called "Gospel Village." When she was three years old, her father passed away; and her mother—an Adventist Bible worker—worked long hours giving Bible studies and simple health treatments in the surrounding villages. As a result, my mother was frequently left in the care of relatives and faced a miserable life with a bleak future.

That all changed one day. Excitement was in the air with news that an American was coming for a visit. Elder Ezra Longway, a dedicated missionary, made the surprise announcement that he would select one young man and one young woman to take to Chiao Tou Tseng, an Adventist school with a self-supporting work program for furthering Christian education. To her surprise, my mother was chosen; this was like the dawn of a new life!

For the second event, fast forward to 1941—to the cosmopolitan city of Shanghai, then under the oppressive occupation of the Japanese Imperial Army. Now, as a young mother with a baby and a toddler, my mother was confronted with a dilemma: Should she stay in the city to face an uncertain future; or should she be reunited with her husband, who had transferred 1,200 miles away to Kunming?

She knew it would be a perilous journey, without organized public transportation or shelter, and fraught with notorious bandits, air raids, and marauding soldiers. In simple faith she opened her Bible, and her eyes alighted on the above verse. With renewed confidence, she set forth.

The third and final event occurred in Hong Kong in 1951. At that time, my two sisters—Gloria Chan, LLUSN class of 1961, and Lena Hszieh, LLUSD DH class of 1967—as well as George Hszieh, LLUSM class of 1968, and I were in our preteen years. I still remember the bombshell-like news when we heard that our father would not be coming home. He was a banker-turned-businessman who was enticed to return to mainland China, now under Communism. Once there, he was incarcerated with no prospect of release. With hard work and ingenuity, my mother was able to open a dressmaking school and provide for our family until my father's unexpected release seven years later.

On many an early morning, I clearly remember my mother's voice in earnest prayer as she knelt by the open window. By the providence of God, we survived crisis after crisis; each time our faith and trust in Him were reaffirmed by His love and protection.

Eric Tsao, LLUSM class of 1963-aff, MBBS, is a diagnostic radiologist who worked primarily in St. Helena, California, and for six years at Hong Kong Adventist Hospital. Now retired, he is on the board of trustees of LLUAHSC, LLUMC, and LLU. April 21 is his parents' wedding anniversary.

April 22

I can do all things through Christ who strengthens me. Philippians 4:13, NKJV

"I will give you a ride." Those words changed the course of my life. They came from a dental hygienist from Loma Linda University who was working at Saigon Adventist Hospital and was helping evacuate the hospital as the Vietnam War culminated in April 1975. I ran home and hastily packed a few belongings in a pillow case—my Bible, my church hymnal, two Vietnamese-English dictionaries, and an *ao dai*.* Soon, our group of 10 nursing students boarded one of the few planes remaining at the airfield.

As the plane lifted off, filled with passengers huddled on the floor, I thought of my family, whom I might never see again. I had no idea what would happen next, but I trusted in the Lord to guide me as He always did.

I came upon God and the Seventh-day Adventist church early, despite growing up in a Buddhist family. As a sixth grader, I was on my way to register for a new academic term at the local school. God nudged me to turn into the Seventh-day Adventist academy instead. The Adventist church and church family have been central in my life ever since. I eventually graduated from the academy and enrolled in their nursing school. As a nursing student, I had just started training at Saigon Adventist Hospital when God sent that messenger who helped me board the plane to a new future.

The plane stopped in the Philippines before arriving in Guam. We stayed at the refugee camp for a few days. Then Loma Linda University arranged for our group from Saigon Adventist Hospital to be taken to Loma Linda to live with sponsor families. I will forever appreciate the kindness of the families who took us in. They were our families away from home and helped us acclimate to a new culture. Through God's grace and with support from my church family, I continued my studies in California and eventually graduated as a registered nurse (RN).

After working as an RN for 17 years, I felt God's calling to become a physician. With God's guidance and my supportive husband who stayed in the U.S. to work, I attended medical school at Autonomous University in Guadalajara, Mexico. Once again, I embarked on a journey in a foreign country; but, this time, I was not alone. I had my two little girls with me. It was challenging to balance my family and a medical career. Nevertheless, I ultimately fulfilled my dream of becoming a physician.

I now have a thriving clinic in East Los Angeles, where the majority of my patients are low-income immigrants. Given my experience in Mexico, I am able to build strong relationships with Spanish-speaking patients. In retrospect, I see God's steadfast presence in my life, from the time I attended Saigon Seventh-day Adventist Academy, to my arrival in Loma Linda, to my time in Guadalajara, and now, to my daily interactions with patients. The Lord placed guardian angels in my life and shaped the opportunities for me to become a physician who has a passion for working in underserved communities. I know that no matter what circumstances I encounter, God already has a plan.

---

*a traditional Vietnamese dress

Mai-Linh Tran, LLUSM class of 2015, is from Cerritos, California. She graduated from University of California, Los Angeles with a BS degree in physiological sciences. This story was written and submitted on behalf of her mother, Ngoc-Mai Tran, MD, whose life highlights God's steadfast presence. They are most appreciate of the families that kindly opened their homes to refugees. April 22 is the day the author's mother left Vietnam.

April 23

A new heart also will I give you, and a new spirit will I put within you: and I will take away the stony heart out of your flesh, and I will give you an heart of flesh. Ezekiel 36:26, KJV

The "school of life" was in session. A vibrant and polished patient was informing me that she had decided to donate a kidney to an acquaintance. I knew this lovely woman was an educated person. I scratched my head and wondered aloud why on earth she would do such a thing? Why, I wondered, would she risk her career as a teacher? Why would she risk her health? And why would she do this for someone she herself described as a virtual stranger?

Her answer taught me a lesson about overcoming adversity that made me want to be a better man, a better physician, and a better servant for Christ. I listened, spellbound, that afternoon as she described the incredible events of her life. I learned of the violence and pain she endured as a child in the chaos of a shattered family—the countless foster homes, her brushes with death, a horrific car accident, and a life barely worth surviving.

But she shared how, in the midst of it all, when she should have felt worthless, when many would have given up, she felt called by God to rise above the desperate circumstances of her past and to live with courage and purpose. She claimed the promise in Isaiah 40:31 (KJV): "They that wait upon the LORD shall renew their strength; they shall mount up with wings as eagles." And she knew she was meant to fly!

She told how she had surrendered her life to God and allowed Him to do whatever He wanted with her. So far, He had called her to teach incarcerated youth. She explained that, because of her own past, she was uniquely able to identify with those hurting young people. She was able to work with them because she was ready when God needed her.

And now, she felt God needed her again. She was ready to give this life-saving organ because her life had already been saved—and *that* was really the lesson. All of the medical information I would go on to share with her that day about kidney transplants truly paled in comparison to her desire. Her life had already been saved.

I often contemplate the education I received during that office visit, and I remind myself that my life has also been saved . . . on a hill called Mt. Calvary. I want to be ready the next time God needs me. Don't you?

Lewis Barker, LLUSM class of 1981, is a family practitioner in Turlock, California.

April 24

Therefore my heart is glad and my tongue rejoices; my body also will rest secure.
Psalm 16:9, NIV

Although I had always intended to go to medical school, I found myself wanting to dive into medicine sooner, to learn earlier what it takes to care for someone. So, I chose to study nursing. One of my favorite semesters of nursing school was community health. For that study, our team of students was assigned to monitor the residents of a building for government-sponsored, underprivileged, independent seniors. Our day consisted of visiting our patients, speaking with them about their health status, and helping them with any educational or social needs that we could.

I always felt extraordinarily privileged when stepping into their homes, where I could get a glimpse of their story and possibly improve their quality of life. I still remember every story and every patient, but one I'll never forget was named George. He was 92 years old, although I would have guessed he was in his seventies.

"How are you doing? What do you have planned today?" I asked, trying to make that all-important good first impression.

"Well, I have a lady friend in the building who I'll play some cards with. She is quite lovely, a pleasure to be around. I also need to help set up downstairs for the exercise clinic," he said with a smile.

However, my delight at his cheery demeanor quickly turned to worry as I examined him. I did not then have the same knowledge of heart sounds and their associated pathologies as I do now, but as I placed my stethoscope over his heart, I knew that it was a small miracle the patient was so animated and alert. The patient insisted that he felt fine, and he also insisted that he would not be seeking any further care.

"I've lived enough, loved enough, and it is no problem for me to go when it is time," he responded. "I just want to play some cards and spend some time with Lorelai." George had, in fact, lived an eventful life. He was a war veteran, and I looked forward to hearing about his life, both in and outside of the military.

When we returned the following week, I wanted to hear George's stories. Our short first interaction with him had painted a picture of a grandfatherly figure, full of wisdom, wrapped in a vibrant demeanor. As the students gathered to plan their visits for the day, I found out that George had passed away in his sleep that weekend.

Saddened, I decided to find out who Lorelai was and pay her a visit. She was a bright, sweet lady whose face lit up when she spoke of George. "He was a lovely gentleman, so caring and thoughtful, even after a very difficult life," she said as she shuffled her cards for a game of solitaire.

Though I never heard his stories, his attitude spoke of the ultimate lessons he had learned from life more convincingly than any story George himself could have articulated. Even through hardships, he chose love and compassion.

Giovanna Sobrinho, LLUSM class of 2016, is from Shrewsbury, Pennsylvania. She graduated with a BS degree in nursing from York College of Pennsylvania. April 24 is the birthday of her father, Glimar.

April 25

Finally, all of you, be like-minded, be sympathetic, love one another, be compassionate and humble. 1 Peter 3:8, NIV

I was expecting my first grandchild, a granddaughter. My husband and I had the pleasure of being at our daughter's 20-week ultrasound session and watching little Nisha kick and wiggle around. We were ecstatic and could hardly wait for this next phase of our lives!

In April, when my daughter was in her third trimester, I got the phone call that no mother or grandmother wants to receive. The voice on the other end said, "No heartbeat . . . Nisha has no heartbeat!" I felt numb.

I was able to take a plane and be by my daughter and son-in-law's side as my first grandchild came into this world, silently, on April 15, 2010. We gathered together as a family and had a small funeral for our darling granddaughter, Nisha.

Returning home in mid-May, I struggled daily with this profound loss. It was during this time that so many friends, acquaintances, and strangers shared their compassion so openly with me and our family. I was touched by others who had experienced similar situations, and they reached out to me. So many stopped and took the time to listen and understand. Stillbirth is a very confusing loss. The grief process seemed harder to relate to, to interact with. Yet many did.

Looking back at Nisha's birth brings waves of sadness, but woven into that sadness are small acts of incredible love and compassion. These gracious gestures of care have been a source of healing. To those who sat and listened, to those who shouldered my tears and felt my ache, and to those who took the time to share of yourselves to show the healing power of compassion, I thank you.

Many of you who comforted me walk the halls of Loma Linda University Medical Center daily. And on a regular basis many of you, liberally and without hesitation, show compassion.

Duane Elgin eloquently writes, "Compassion will no longer be seen as a spiritual luxury for a contemplative few; rather it will be viewed as a social necessity for the entire human family."

Padmini Davamony is executive director of information services and decision support services at LLUHS. She earned an MBA degree from La Sierra University and an MS degree in health informatics from LLUSAHP.

Be kind to one another, tender-hearted, forgiving each other, just as God in Christ also has forgiven you. Ephesians 4:32, NASB

I could see him limping into the exam room from my computer station. His clothes were wrinkled and stained, he leaned heavily on his cane, and the smell of cigarettes wafted down the hall as he walked by. My medical assistant handed me his record as she plugged her nose and waved her hand back and forth in front of her face. She did not need to say a word.

As I walked into the room, the patient smiled at me. He was missing several teeth, and a few more were clearly rotting. As we went through his history and physical evaluation, it was clear he had lived a hard life, full of poor choices. He looked to be in his seventies, but was only 61 years old. He had quit drinking and doing drugs nearly 10 years ago. But he had not been able to give up smoking yet.

Surprisingly, he had a 10-year-old son at home; and when he talked about him, his face beamed with pride. He spoke about all the things he wanted to do with his son but was not able to do because of the pain he was having in his hip.

Getting him onto my operating schedule was like the proverbial "pulling teeth," but we were able to do it following his medical workup. Right before surgery, he thanked me profusely. I smiled and told him, "Don't thank me yet."

"Doc," he said, with tears in his eyes and a near toothless grin, "you don't know how much this means to me. I want to be able to fish, hunt, and just play with my son without so much pain." He had been dealing with a severely arthritic hip for nearly five years.

His hip replacement went well, and when I went out to the waiting room to talk with his family, a bright-eyed, chubby boy of 10 came bounding over to me: "How's my dad?"

This interaction with this patient really made me reflect upon the love our Savior has for us. No matter the choices we have made or where we find ourselves, God is able to restore meaning to our life. What a wonderful God we serve!

Chad Harbour, LLUSM class of 2004, is an orthopaedic surgeon in Spokane, Washington, specializing in hip reconstruction and trauma. April 26 is his wedding anniversary.

April 27

So I saw that there is nothing better for a person than to enjoy their work, because that is their lot. For who can bring them to see what will happen after them? Ecclesiastes 3:22, NIV

I came to Loma Linda University School of Medicine from the hills of Virginia; and although I made good grades, I had great difficulty adjusting to Southern California and longed to be back in Virginia.

At the end of my freshman year, I went to the dean and asked to be transferred for my sophomore year to the Medical College of Virginia. He looked at my transcript, saw that I had good grades, and agreed to support my transfer.

Once I was back in Virginia, I called the registrar at the Medical College and was told by a secretary that my transcript was there; however, the registrar was away for three weeks. The dean would not look at any students wanting to transfer in until the registrar said all requirements were met.

I waited three weeks, then called the registrar again. She was in but told me the dean was away for a month, and no decision could be made until he was back.

A month later, I called her again and was told that the dean was trying to catch up from his month away but would make a decision within two weeks.

About a week later, while having lunch in my father's used furniture store, the phone rang and my mother answered it. She turned to me, put her hand on the mouthpiece, and silently said: "It's Loma Linda." I answered the phone, and it was the dean on the line. He said to me, "I must know if you are coming back to Loma Linda now as I have told a young man who wants to transfer in that I would let him know tomorrow." I knew that it was possible for the Medical College not to accept me, so I told the dean I would come back to Loma Linda.

I hung up the phone, turned around, and there was the postman handing me a registered letter from the Medical College. I opened it and read, "Welcome to the Medical College of Virginia." I was bitterly disappointed and wanted to call Loma Linda back and say I wouldn't be returning. But I had a code that said once I told someone that I would do something, I always kept my word.

I returned to Loma Linda, where I met and married my wife that year. Now after 50 plus years of a happy life, I nearly weep to think of the difference about 10 seconds had made in my life. I cannot imagine a life without Jan, our three children, and eight grandchildren—and from a professional viewpoint, it's impossible to imagine not working all my life for Loma Linda University School of Medicine and experiencing the joy and satisfaction that this has brought me.

I can only thank God that He always does what is best for me even though it may take a few years for me to see it. That letter that was 10 seconds late and so disappointing at the time has been the greatest blessing of my life.

John Mace, LLUSM class of 1964, is a professor in LLUSM department of pediatrics, of which he was chair from 1975 to 2003. In 1994, he was LLUSMAA's Alumnus of the Year and in 2007 was LLU Alumnus of the Year.

Never again will they hunger; never again will they thirst. The sun will not beat down on them, nor any scorching heat. . . . He will lead them to springs of living water. And God will wipe away every tear from their eyes.
Revelation 7:16-17, TNIV

My wife, Ann, and I were part of a medical team responding to the humanitarian crises in Ethiopia that had resulted from nearly two years without rain in some parts of sub-Saharan Africa. Surrounding our feeding center and humble "hospital" were encamped an estimated 20,000 starving and weakened refugees, living in makeshift shelters. We waged a constant war against typhoid, typhus, malaria, pneumonia, cholera, and other infectious diseases that spread easily in the camps.

While we saw many children, who could forget little Esmara? Her unconscious, small frame was carried into our hospital by her parents, who had looks of pleading desperation on their faces. We learned she was the last living child of the five children they had when the famine began, and they had walked 60 miles across the desert in hopes of saving her.

In her weakened condition, it seemed unlikely she would survive. In equatorial Africa, the leading differential diagnoses of an unconscious child would be cerebral malaria or meningitis, which we could treat. We drew some blood for a malarial smear, which came back negative. I performed a lumbar puncture, which was crystal clear, making bacterial meningitis unlikely. After further talking to the parents, we learned she had been recovering from the measles; we made a presumptive diagnosis of postmeasles encephalitis.

We explained to the parents that with every nurse taking care of an average of 60 patients per shift, it was humanly impossible for us to provide the intensive care Esmara needed, without neglecting others. We placed a nasogastric tube (NG) and showed the parents how to mix and administer small, frequent feedings, and how to keep her head up afterward to prevent aspiration. We explained pressure sores and the need to rotate her unconscious body frequently.

Three times a day, Ann or one of the nurses would drop by to administer an antibiotic for the pneumonia that seemed to be rattling in one of her lungs, but her parents faithfully did all the nursing duties. We never saw a moment when one of them was not by her side. Every morning on rounds my eyes would immediately find the corner of the room where she lay to see if she had survived the night; amazingly, she would still be there.

One morning on rounds, I walked in to find the NG tube pulled out. Her parents were smiling broadly as they held a cup up to her lips and showed me how she could weakly open her eyes and swallow small sips of formula. A few days later, Esmara was propping herself up by standing and holding on to her father. On an impulse, I knelt on the ground in front of them and opened my arms to see if she would come to me. After some reassuring words from her smiling father, she released her grasp on him and with her spindly little legs wobbled over to me and gave me a shy hug, the memory of which lingers nearly three decades later.

Yet, for every Esmara, there was a weeping mother of another child who we could not save. So we were comforted by the promise of Revelation mentioned above: "And God will wipe away every tear from their eyes."

Rick Westermeyer, LLUSM class of 1983, is an anesthesiologist in Portland, Oregon. He received his diploma in tropical medicine from the London School of Tropical Medicine and Hygiene.

April 29

We believe that Jesus died and rose again, and so we believe that God will bring with Jesus those who have fallen asleep in him. For the Lord himself will come down from heaven, with a loud command, with the voice of the archangel and with the trumpet call of God, and the dead in Christ will rise first. After that, we who are still alive and are left will be caught up together with them in the clouds to meet the Lord in the air. 1 Thessalonians 4:14, 16-17, NIV (1984)

In the symphony of sounds in the neonatal intensive care nursery (NICU), beeping is a good thing. Ventilators hiss, providing breath for the infants born ahead of their time—infants with skin transparent from being thrust into the world prematurely, who are at the mercy of man-made machines instead of experiencing the warmth of their mother's womb. Silence is the enemy—when there is no beeping, hissing, or blast of an alarm. Silence is not a good thing here.

In 1973 Loma Linda University Medical Center was establishing its own NICU with life-saving technology. Babies would soon arrive by helicopter or ambulance and go to their transparent cocoon within the walls of the nursery. They would be wired to the life-saving sounds. The fight would be on!

But victory does not always come in that unit. "Doctor, would you please baptize our baby?" I was talking with the parents of a newborn who was losing his fight. Too little. Too sick. Too weak. "But I'm not a Catholic," I replied. "We know, Doctor. It's okay you're a Seventh-day Adventist," they urged with their Hispanic accent. "*Por favor*, Doctor. Now. Baptize our baby before he dies." Their eyes were wet; their hands clutched tightly to mine.

I slipped back through the door of the NICU and went to the tiny form in the incubator. Despite all efforts, the heart rate was slowing rapidly, irreversibly. "Please get me a Dixie cup with warm water," I asked a nearby nurse.

Behind her mask I could see her eyes talking, as if to say, "What . . . why the . . ?"

"Please hurry," I said, my voice expressing the urgency of the seconds remaining in which to work.

Dixie cup in hand, I dipped my finger into the warm water and thrust it through the incubator opening. I glanced up briefly at the faces of the mother and father, now pressed hard against the fine chicken-wire reinforced glass wall of the NICU. Their tear-filled eyes strained to see their baby. Time was running out.

I moved my wet finger over the tiny, motionless chest in the sign of the cross, and, in barely audible sounds, muffled by my mask, uttered those familiar words, "I baptize you in the name of the Father, the Son, and the Holy Ghost." The alarm sounded, like a blaring horn. The nurse pressed the button of the EKG and it went dark. It was over. My eyes met those of the parents and I nodded, "It's over."

I walked outside the nursery, to where the parents were, and they thanked me. It was as if they were trying to console me. Strange, but true. We huddled for a time, our arms entwined. No words. No sounds. Silence. That dreaded sound of silence.

I look forward to the day when those parents and their baby will be reunited. I want to be there with them and their special baby, baptized with water from a Dixie cup.

Linda Dixon, LLUSM class of 1972, is a pediatric anesthesiologist who practices in Hawaii and Nevada. This story occurred during her pediatric internship at LLUMC from 1972 to 1973.

April 30

Uncover my eyes so that I may see the miraculous things in your teachings.
Psalm 119:18, GW

Sometimes patients really have more going on than meets the eye. I was on my third-year surgery rotation as a medical student. My patient came in to the emergency department that day because she could no longer hide from her sister, with whom she lived, the bleeding from her left breast. I took an extensive history which revealed a positive mammogram many years prior, but with no follow-up due to loss of insurance. I asked about all the characteristics of her lesion before I ever laid eyes on it.

When she finally revealed the wound, her sister gasped! A menstrual pad had covered the inner aspect of her obviously swollen breast. Removing the pad revealed a large ulcerated lesion. Her history had been so unimpressive and so imprecise. She believed "it" had been there for "only a few months." As I surveyed her skin, I observed peau d'orange and said that this was what I was inquiring about when I asked if her skin looked like an orange peel. She mumbled something about "never looking at it with glasses on."

It presented to me, a medical student, as textbook cancer, yet, my story was less convincing to my resident who felt that the patient had an abscess that might need incising and draining. However, upon seeing the pathology that was so profound on this woman's breast, he no longer considered this option for treatment.

I wondered how anyone could let something get this serious without seeking help. I knew that even a non-medical person could see that there was something horribly wrong! Then it hit me—this is how sin creeps in—slowly and quietly but persistent and unrelenting. Over the course of time, we gradually become desensitized to this non-medical cancer.

We need to constantly re-evaluate our lives and motives so that those things that keep us from wholeness do not grow in and on us. If they do, may we see them for what they really are and seek the Great Physician for the healing that only He can give.

Sarah Killian, LLUSM class of 2011, is a resident at In His Image family medicine residency program in Tulsa, Oklahoma.

MAY

"One wonders what would happen if all health-care givers were to more carefully add the serving of life and sharing of spiritual stories to their attempts to live up to what they feel called to be and do."

May 1

But my God shall supply all your need according to his riches in glory by Christ Jesus. Philippians 4:19, KJV

During my second year at the College of Medical Evangelists, I was informed that all students were required to pay their bills in full by a certain date in order to qualify for taking the final exams. I had been trusting God for paying my bills during medical school. Now my statement showed a balance due of $400.

My classmate, Ali Mohamed from Iran, was auditing classes to help prepare him for taking the California state board exams. He knew my situation and suggested I write a letter, which he would then give to his contacts for possible financial aid. I wrote the letter, reluctantly, after telling him I was trusting God to meet my needs. "I believe in Allah," he said, as he took my letter written: "To Whom It Concerns."

As an international student from British Guiana (now Guyana), I was accustomed to having immigration department agents visit me regularly to ensure that I was actually enrolled in school and not violating immigration laws. A few weeks after I gave the letter to Ali, I went to the dean's office because four men had shown up to evaluate my situation. I felt sure they were immigration agents coming to deport me since I could not pay my bill. But to my surprise, they were businessmen delegated by the Rotary Club of Whittier, California, to investigate my situation. They had received the letter Ali had delivered to them.

My story of God's faithfulness impressed them. They invited me to speak at the Rotary Club in the fall of that year, with no promise of immediate help. I had plans to spend the summer doing colporteur work (selling religious books door-to-door) in Texas, but looked forward to that fall speaking engagement.

Unexpectedly, 10 days after I saw the men in the office, I learned from the LLU financial department that the Whittier Rotary Club had sent $400 to apply toward my account—the amount was exactly what I needed to clear my debt and take the final exams! These men were never told of my pressing need.

With a thankful heart, I promptly went to the Rotary Club to express my gratitude and to ask them what made them send that amount when no help was promised until they had heard my speech that coming fall. They immediately responded, "We were so touched by your story and decided to send something in the meantime."

"Why $400?" I asked. They could not fully explain but were positive God was in the decision after I informed them of the recent school financial policy.

Does God watch over a poor foreign medical student in dire need? Of course He does! God's promises are as sure as the sun that rises every morning. He is the God of Abraham, Isaac, and Jacob. By faith, even while in medical school and through the present, I believe I could humbly add my name to those spiritual heroes of Hebrews 11. May His name be forever praised!

Claude Chan, CME class of 1953-B, born in Guyana, returned there to serve at Davis Memorial Hospital in 1959 before working in private practice in Van Nuys, California. He was the director of emergency medicine at White Memorial Medical Center from 1971 to 1974 and a flight surgeon in the U.S. Air Force from 1974 to 1995, serving in 1991 as commander of the largest MASH Hospital during Desert Storm. Dr. Chan, now retired, is 86 years old. May 1, 2014, is the National Day of Prayer.

May 2

By thee have I been holden up from the womb: thou art he that took me out of my mother's bowels: my praise shall be continually of thee. Psalm 71:6, KJV

It was during my gastroenterology (GI) fellowship at the University of Iowa Hospitals and Clinics that my wife, Serena (Saw) Kam, LLUSN class of 1982, became pregnant with our first child. It was in the midst of her pregnancy that her obstetrician told her to come in ASAP for an ultrasound because her tests showed an elevated alpha-fetoprotein level (AFP). We both knew such a diagnosis meant that our baby could be born with severe neurological problems.

An ultrasound was expeditiously done, and we were relieved when we learned that our baby did not have any neurological problems. Unfortunately, it did show that our baby, who we now knew was going to be a boy, did have gastroschisis (a birth defect in which an infant's intestines protrude out of the body through a defect in the abdominal wall). I was struck by the irony of a GI fellow having a baby with a gastrointestinal problem.

A friend, Ken Lombard, LLUSM class of 1982, who was a pediatric nutrition fellow also at the University of Iowa, insisted on becoming my son's primary pediatrician. Other specialists were soon lined up, including a pediatric gastroenterologist and, amazingly, a pediatric gastrointestinal surgeon. The surgeon explained to us that the best scenario for our son would be if they could operate on him as soon as he was born. They would place his intestines back into his abdominal cavity and sew the cavity shut (not unlike stuffing a turkey).

Unfortunately, this surgery is not always possible when the abdominal cavity is too small, when the intestine is too swollen, or if the timing of the surgery is delayed. The sooner the operation could be performed after his birth, the better were the chances of having a successful outcome.

However, it was also explained to us that if he was born during the day, the surgery would be performed right away. But if he was born during the night or early morning hours, then the surgery would have to wait until the usual daytime operating room hours.

Of course, my son decided to come prematurely and during the early morning hours of the Sabbath. We were resigned to an operation later that day. To our surprise, however, our son's surgeon walked into my wife's delivery room. He said the surgery team had just finished doing a gastroschisis operation on a newborn baby girl, who had been born the day before and had been helivaced in for an emergent surgery. He added that they were now ready for our son.

The operation was a success; and despite being one month premature and weighing less than 5 lbs., our son made remarkable progress. In fact, he was discharged sooner than any other gastroschisis patient the hospital had ever had. We could only attribute this success to a miracle from God. To honor what the Lord had done for us and our son, we named him Christopher, "the one who bears Christ (in his soul)."

Nathan Kam, LLUSM class of 1983, is a gastroenterologist in Hayward, California. May 2 is his son's birthday.

May 3

The wind blows where it chooses, and you hear the sound of it, but you do not know where it comes from or where it goes. So it is with everyone who is born of the Spirit. John 3:8, NRSV

Air China flight 1509 banks eastward on its approach to Xiaoshan Airport, flying over the strips of crops squeezed among the farming villages, canals, and freeways. I gaze out the window, daunted by the immensity of the numbers: 8.7 million people in the city of Hangzhou; 55 million people in Zhejiang province; 1.34 billion people in China.

I am coming to this vast country for a week of board meetings and consultations on accreditation requirements, which, I found, would be interspersed by lavish vegetarian meals. I wonder if a real medical missionary like Dr. Harry Miller in 1903 felt equally daunted as he approached the shores of China with the assignment to evangelize 400 million people of the Qing Empire.

As he set up clinics, hospitals, nursing schools, and soy milk factories, did he tabulate each precious baptism? Then, in 1948, when Communist revolutionaries swept away all of the institutions he had nurtured and severed communications with the 40,000 Seventh-day Adventist Christians in mainland China, did he, even for one moment, wonder if it had all been in vain?

Perhaps Dr. Miller took solace in the fact that he had eased human suffering by performing thousands of surgeries. He did not know that one of his patients from Zhejiang had a son who would become a Hong Kong film mogul and philanthropist. Fifty years later, when officials of Zhejiang Medical University approached that son to fund a new teaching hospital, Sir Run Run Shaw remembered Dr. Miller's care of his mother and added a stipulation: The new teaching hospital must be operated by Loma Linda University for five years to create a model teaching hospital that fused Western and Chinese insights.

In the 1990s, a stream of Loma Linda University administrators, physicians, nurses, allied health providers, and teachers helped build Sir Run Run Shaw hospital. People like David Fang, LLUSM class of 1971; Gordon, CME class of 1944-B, and Alphie Hadley; Robert, CME class of 1946, and Betty Rosenquist; and hundreds of others worked and lived with their Chinese colleagues to create what is now a 1,600-bed academic medical center that hosts thousands of administrators from other Chinese hospitals who come to learn administrative and educational innovations.

Dr. Gordon Hadley and his colleagues knew that the heirs of the revolution monitored how these "church people" conducted themselves as they built Sir Run Run Shaw Hospital. A decade later, when Adventist leaders approached the Chinese State Religious Affairs Bureau in Beijing, officials welcomed them: "We know about you Seventh-day Adventists. We have observed your work in Hangzhou and know you to be trustworthy."

As of 2012, there are an estimated 700,000 Seventh-day Adventist Christians in China. There are no officially credentialed missionaries in the country, no public evangelism, and no church organization. But as each of us—Harry Miller in 1903, Gordon Hadley in 1993, and perhaps even I taxiing down the runway—respond to God's calling to relieve suffering, His Spirit blows like a gale throughout the earth.

Dan Giang, LLUSM class of 1983, is associate dean for graduate medical education in LLUSM and is a professor in LLUSM departments of medical education and neurology. He is married to Sarah Roddy, LLUSM class of 1980-B. May 3 is the birthday of the late G. Gordon Hadley, CME class of 1944-B.

For we do not have a High Priest who cannot sympathize with our weaknesses, but was in all points tempted as we are, yet without sin. Let us therefore come boldly to the throne of grace, that we may obtain mercy and find grace to help in time of need. Hebrews 4:15-16, NKJV

After donning my student white coat, I stepped into the Medical Center elevator and pressed the button for the third floor. During my two weeks of "shadowing," I was assigned to the neonatal intensive care unit. As I stepped off the elevator, I noticed that the midmorning hum had simmered down as rounds had finished.

I strode back to chat with Baby H's parents. "Hi, I'm a student physician." The father nodded solemnly. His uncle, along for support, immediately turned to me with concern and questioned in broken English, "Baby doin' good? Heart, everything . . . okay?"

Putting my hands up in a helpless gesture, I explained, "I'm not the doctor, just a medical student."

He nodded as if he understood, then continued, "Heart, uh?" He turned to his nephew, the baby's father, and said, "*¿Cómo se dice, el ritmo cardíaco subió?*"

Smiling at him, I said, "*Hablo un poquito de español. Usted pueda hablar en español si quiere.*" ("I can speak some Spanish. You can talk in Spanish if you like.") I silently thanked God for the gift of languages. Just a single word in one's mother tongue opens floodgates previously barred to connection.

Their eyes lit up with relief, and the emotional wall crumbled. The Spanish came in rapid fire. Eyebrows furrowed, the father began to tell me the story: "This is my first baby. I was really excited that it was a boy. Everything was going great, but then there was this heart thing . . ."

My mind remembered the scene from the earlier visit. As completely "green" medical students, we were rounding with the team when suddenly pagers beeped incessantly, announcing an emergency C-section. A dignified stampede ensued. We medical students squished into a corner, observing the blur.

The attending physician barked orders as the baby changed hands at the window. No heart rate. Intubation. Chest compressions. Umbilical line. Medications. Packages ripped open, chucked over shoulders. The tiny heart began to work. A few minutes later, the baby "crashed," and the scene was repeated. Three times the frantic team resuscitated the child.

The father finished his story: "It was real scary. I have a supportive family and I know they were all praying hard."

I smiled and said, "We were praying hard, too."

The connection had been made. They realized that there was someone who could sympathize with what they were experiencing, and speak their language. I hope they glimpsed a picture of Jesus. Leaving all glory behind, He chose our humanity. He walked through life as we do, experiencing loss, suffering, betrayal, loneliness, and the effects of sin. He understands the language of our heart. "Surely he has borne our griefs and carried our sorrows" (Isaiah 53:4, ESV).

Keri Skau, LLUSM class of 2016, grew up in the mission field. She graduated from Union College with a BA degree in French. She was class pastor her freshman year and currently is class pastor her sophomore year. She has a passion for medical missions.

May 5

Jesus said to her, "I am the resurrection and the life. The one who believes in me will live, even though they die." John 11:25, NIV

A gloomy man once said that a person is on his way to dying the moment he is born. This fatalistic view of life underscores a dangerous pessimism in the world of medicine. It is a view that doctors should be wary of throughout the course of their challenging careers, lest they fall into its grasp.

As a third-year medical student roaming the inpatient wards at Riverside County, I have seen much in the way of suffering and death. Many patients will wait until their diseases have progressed to a point of crisis before presenting, at which time modern medicine can only offer them so much in the way of care and betterment. And yet, despite having the deck stacked against the physicians by the severity of the condition, I have participated in amazing health care that has brought back the light of hope in an otherwise dimly lit world.

Mr. G was a 25-year-old patient who presented with swollen legs and uneasiness written all over his face. Right heart failure from pulmonary hypertension landed him in the ICU less than a day after admission, and on his third morning, he flatlined. The team did chest compressions on him for seven minutes before a pulse was finally felt again. Even though we resuscitated him, his prognosis was not good because his kidneys were failing and his brain had been without oxygen for too long.

During the compressions, I had seen Mr. G's father, amid tears, holding his son's hand while the health-care team frantically tried to get the young man's sick heart beating again. The speed of his deterioration had caught Mr. G's family by surprise. They were not ready to say goodbye. At the same time, the determined response of the team in the face of a seemingly insurmountable condition had not gone unnoticed by them.

When the team met with his family to let them know of Mr. G's poor prognosis, there was much weeping. However, despite the tragic news, his parents were extremely grateful that we had extended their son's life, even if only for a short time for them to say a proper goodbye. That night after an attempt at dialysis, Mr. G's heart beat its last. He passed away with his family holding vigil around him.

What I am going to call a "medical pessimist" would argue that all we did for Mr. G was delay an inevitable fate by just a few hours. Where were the healing and the hope? What the pessimist fails to see is that in those few extra hours, the family was able to spend one last evening together, create one final set of memories, say their farewells properly, and ultimately begin a process of emotional healing that transcends physical death.

Through the doctors' actions, the family lost a beloved member on their own terms. The victory was not in the prolongation of the patient's life, but in the manner of his death.

Marlen Pajcini, LLUSM class of 2014, was born in Tirana, Albania, but has lived in California for most of his life. He graduated from University of California, Berkeley with a BA degree in molecular and cell biology. This story occurred during his third-year internal medicine rotation.

Why art thou cast down, O my soul? and why art thou disquieted in me? hope thou in God: for I shall yet praise him for the help of his countenance. Psalm 42:5, KJV

It is interesting how little events in life can become meaningful milestones. On my first day of wards as a junior medical student, I was assigned to pre-round on Mr. Jimenez. I was both excited and nervous to see him since he was my very first hospital patient.

Arriving at Mr. Jimenez's room, I found him quietly snoring in bed. He appeared much larger and more austere than I had imagined. "Oh boy, am I going to have to wake this man up?" I thought. At the bedside, I saw a nurse taking his vitals. "Good morning," I whispered with a nervous smile. "It looks like he's sleeping."

The nurse briefly looked me up and down. "Yeah, Doc, but you can wake him up if you need to," she replied, seeming to know that this was my first time.

I stalled and asked the nurse a few questions, secretly hoping Mr. Jimenez would wake up on his own. He did not. "Okay, well, I am going to wake him now," I said to the nurse in an unusually decisive fashion. I tried to look as in control as possible. "Good morning, Mr. Jimenez!" I said with my best peppy grin. "Sorry to wake you; I just wanted to see how you're doing." No response.

"Ahem! . . . Good morning, Mr. Jimenez!" I spoke a little louder this time. "How are you today?" Nothing. The patient was still as a rock.

"I can't back down now," I thought. Stepping a little closer to the bed, I took my hand, gently tapped his chest, and trumpeted, "GOOD MORNING, Mr. Jimenez! GOOD MORNING!" The plump figure under the sheets finally began to shift; his quiet snoring suddenly morphed into an annoyed groan.

At this point, the bedside nurse amusedly said, "Um, that is not Mr. Jimenez." My stomach flipped! I took a step back from the bed and turned to the nurse, puzzled. "Isn't this room 8?" I asked.

"Yes, but this is bed 1. There is a Mr. Jimenez in bed 2," she replied with a smirk.

I was so embarrassed! "I passed the first two grueling years of medical school to wake up the wrong patient!" I thought to myself. After apologizing to the gentleman in bed 1, I turned around to see the real Mr. Jimenez in bed 2, looking at me with an entertained expression.

Although this would not be the last of my bumbles, I have come to realize that it is not always the big things, but, in fact, the small things that influence us the most. The following excerpt from *The Desire of Ages* has reminded me that our Lord is interested in every event, regardless of the size.

"Whatever your anxieties and trials, spread out your case before the Lord. Your spirit will be braced for endurance. The way will be opened for you to disentangle yourself from embarrassment and difficulty. The weaker and more helpless you know yourself to be, the stronger will you become in His strength" (Ellen G. White, *The Desire of Ages*, p. 329).

I am thankful our Savior has promised that as we rely on Him, He will encourage and strengthen us—even when we are most embarrassed!

Daniel Calaguas, LLUSM class of 2013, is from Loma Linda, California. He is a pediatric resident at LLUCH.

May 7

And we know that all things work together for good to those who love God, to those who are the called according to His purpose. Romans 8:28, NKJV

The orange glow of sunset lit up the western sky outside the window of the chaplain's office as I reviewed the list of patients awaiting a visit. Sunsets always remind me of God's goodness, and I breathed a prayer of thanks for the peaceful beauty. It had been a full day in the Clinical Pastoral Education program, but it was not over yet. Now I was on call!

The evening serenity was soon broken by the familiar "beep" sound, and I was on my way to the medical center. I hurried down the hall and circled the nurses' station, searching for the right room. Finding it, I slowly peeked in. A mother and her children sat holding each other's hands next to the bed.

Ravaged from a battle with cancer, the husband/father lay still and lifeless as the radio played Christian music softly. The mother wiped her eyes and we began to talk. Soon the kids joined in, telling stories about their daddy. "I know God will work it all out for good," the mother said. "He will" was all I could think to say. I wished I could take away their pain.

We held hands, prayed, and cried. "It meant so much that you came," the mother said. I smiled as I left, but inside my heart was churning. How could God let this happen to such a precious family? I had to keep moving though; many more patients were waiting.

Room after room, prayer after prayer—I did my best to comfort, in spite of my inner struggle. But then came the last stop of the night. In the back of a room, a pale-faced, but pleasant elderly woman was waiting for me. Seeing me enter the room, she immediately tried to sit up and exclaimed, "I'm so happy you came!" She began to talk. I listened. She had not had an easy life and was now too sick to go home.

But in spite of it all, she had an amazingly positive spirit. "God has been so good to me," she repeated, as she told her stories with the most genuine smile I had ever seen. After a while, she squeezed my hand and thanked me for coming. I could tell she was tired, so we prayed and said goodnight.

Walking into the cool evening, I was still wrestling with the pain I had seen. But I could not get those words out of my head: "God has been so good to me." In the midst of her pain, all alone and at the sunset of her life, that kind woman recognized the goodness of God. "God really is good," I thought. And I remembered the mother's words of confidence: "I know God will work it all out for good."

I still wrestle when I see suffering, and I do not have the answers. But I do know that I will never forget the words from those two women who sincerely believed that God really was good. I pray for faith like theirs—faith that always remembers God's goodness in a sunset, even through the tears.

Kyle Allen is the pastor at Mentone Seventh-day Adventist Church in California.

The Lord will protect him and keep him alive, And he shall be called blessed upon the earth . . . The Lord will sustain him upon his sickbed; In his illness, You restore him to health. Psalm 41:2-3, NASB

I met Mr. H the first day of my third-year internal medicine rotation. He had been a healthy 56 year old until being diagnosed with cancer a year before. By the time I met him, the cancer had been in remission for several months. However, part of his lung had been removed, and the immunosuppression from the chemotherapy had activated a fungal infection in what remained of his lung tissue. He was being treated with IV antifungals and had already been in the hospital for several weeks when he was assigned as my patient.

He was scheduled for another round of chemotherapy in a couple of months; his care was a balance of giving him enough antifungals to treat the infection, while avoiding severely damaging his kidneys. The infection needed to be treated quickly because the upcoming chemotherapy would destroy his immune system and give the infection free reign in his lungs. Unfortunately, the treatment was not working fast enough.

As a result of these problems, Mr. H was stuck in the hospital with no solution in sight. Considering his situation, he was in surprisingly good spirits. Occasionally, he seemed a little depressed, but overall, he was relaxed and positive.

One day I asked him how he stayed so calm, and his answer surprised me. He told me that when his medical problems were just starting, God told him that everything would be just fine and that this sickness would not end in death. Some mornings I would see him reading his Bible when I came in to pre-round. He told me he drew strength from that, and his faith sustained him.

I have never heard God speak to me, but I know He is telling us the same thing he told Mr. H. In Jeremiah 29:11 (NIV) we read, "'For I know the plans I have for you,' declares the Lord, 'plans to prosper you and not to harm you, plans to give you hope and a future.'" Romans 8:28 (NIV, margin) says, "And we know that all things work together for good to those who love God, who have been called according to his purpose." These verses remind me that God is always in control. I do not need to worry because anything that happens to me is subject to His will.

Also, there is an Ellen White quote that gives me comfort in difficult times. It says, "God never leads His children otherwise than they would choose to be led, if they could see the end from the beginning and discern the glory of the purpose which they are fulfilling as co-workers with Him" (*Ministry of Healing*, p. 479).

I had the privilege of caring for Mr. H for three weeks, and I talked to him more than to any other patient while I was in medical school. After my rotation ended, I learned that he had gone into surgery to clean out the infection around his lungs and that he was finally able to go home. His patient faith reminded me that God is always in control; and, if I trust in Him, I have nothing to fear.

Jonathan Schilling, LLUSM class of 2013, is from Chattanooga, Tennessee. He graduated from Southern Adventist University with a BS degree in biochemistry. His is married to Kristen (née Lloyd), an MS student at LLUSN.

May 9

Where were you when I laid the foundation of the earth? Tell me, if you have understanding. Who determined its measurements—surely you know! Or who stretched the line upon it? On what were its bases sunk, or who laid its cornerstone? Job 38:4-6, NRSV

"**W**hy am I here?"

Every once in a while, I ask myself this question in a broad sort of way: "Lord, what is your purpose for my life?" More recently, the question has become much more specific: "Lord, why did you bring me here to Loma Linda University?"

A few months into my new job—after the "honeymoon" phase—I started to realize just how big the challenges are at this place. Of course, I have had similar experiences at nearly every organization I have ever worked for, but it felt different this time. Perhaps it was the position or the level of responsibility, or both. Whatever it was, the pressure was building. I was starting to feel overwhelmed. I even started to ask myself if I was the right person for the job.

One Sabbath afternoon, I came across an old devotional book in my car. I wondered why it was there. I had last read it about 10 years ago. Remembering the huge impact it had on my life then, I decided to open it up and start reading. Then I came to page 46. It was as if the words that followed were written precisely for what I was going through.

The book suggested that I was supposed to feel this way. What?

Hmmm . . . is it possible that living by faith requires a bit—maybe a large amount—of uneasiness? There is this thing called dependence, a word that I typically do not like. Perhaps God is calling upon Loma Linda University Health to do something so great that we, as humans, and no matter how gifted and skilled, just cannot accomplish on our own.

That view leaves us with three possible paths: 1) We roll up our sleeves and work harder; 2) We ignore God's plans and create our own; or 3) We humble ourselves, acknowledge that this is not about us, and depend on Him—not for a possible option, but as our only option.

I do not know what the founders of what would become Loma Linda University felt, but my guess is that they knew a thing or two about dependence. More than 100 years later, as I look at this institution today, I see the same humble desire for God's will to be accomplished through our schools and hospitals.

And so the answer to my question, "Lord, why did you bring me here to Loma Linda University?" is simply this: "You are going to be part of something you never would have imagined possible. All you have to do is to trust Me and to depend upon Me completely."

Frightening and exciting, all at the same time, is the thought that we are attempting to do something here that is so big that we are sure to fail . . . unless God steps in!

Tony Yang is assistant vice president for public affairs at Loma Linda University Health.

May 10

Blessed be the God and Father of our Lord Jesus Christ, the Father of mercies and God of all comfort, who comforts us in all our tribulation, that we may be able to comfort those who are in any trouble, with the comfort with which we ourselves are comforted by God. 2 Corinthians 1:3-4, NKJV

Shortly before graduating from medical school, my wife, three sons (ages four, two, and newborn) and I were taking a leisurely stroll around the "hill," a prominent high point on the Loma Linda University campus. As my wife and I talked, the two older boys took turns piloting a scooter on the sidewalk.

As we rounded a corner, Micah, our middle son, was at the wheel. Fearless in his naïveté, he began picking up speed on a downhill section of rough sidewalk. Confident in his ability to slow himself down, even at such a young age, I remained unconcerned. After he had gone out of sight, with big brother following close behind, a disquieting scream brought a sudden panic!

I sprinted to where he lay, tangled in a tree after the cornering ability of his scooter had been no match for his speed. I scooped him up and, with horror, immediately noticed a lump the size of a baseball obscuring his beautiful forehead. He was obviously dizzy and near losing consciousness. As I held him close and sprinted across campus to the emergency department (ED), my thoughts were a blur of self-condemnation for free-range parenting gone awry, of prayers for his safety, and of concerns for neurologic impairment on the heels of my recently completed neurology rotation.

There in the ED, where I had toiled many hours as a student on rotations as varied as trauma surgery and psychiatry, I now sat with my most precious treasure, who was bravely gazing into my eyes for reassurance as he battled the pain of his recent smashup. And as I sat there, I wiped the tears from his eyes, watching carefully for subtle changes in pupillary size; providing stimulation so he would not slip into unconsciousness; and coaching him on his breathing for the examination.

Mopping up blood and anxiously watching the size of the knot on his forehead, I was once again very grateful for the medical profession. As I sat in all the unenviable vulnerability of a parent with an ill child (compounded by my own culpability for the accident), I became acutely aware of our powerlessness in illness, of the surging hope of a favorable outcome, and the elation of good news. Would he need a CT scan? No. Would he be okay? Yes. Would there likely be any long-term complications? No—other than a temporarily disfigured face and two very large black eyes.

Knowing my son to be extraordinarily blessed to have narrowly escaped a horrendous head injury, I thought of those whose experience has not been met with a favorable outcome. Since becoming a physician, treating the ill in longitudinal fashion, I see the wear and tear of the arduous daily battle with illness—one's own or that of a friend or family member.

I am grateful for the comfort that God, through those serving in the emergency department that day, was able to extend to me and to my son. I pray that through this experience and others like it, I, too, may be able to comfort those who are vulnerable and in need.

Mark Warren, LLUSM class of 2010, is a psychiatry resident at Mayo Clinic in Rochester, Minnesota. He and his wife have four children. May 10 is Micah's birthday.

May 11

Blessed are the pure in heart, for they will see God. Matthew 5:8, NRSV

The practice of obstetrics is an emotional business—usually joyful and occasionally devastating. Prior to the advent of ultrasound, knowledge of the unborn child was limited. Surprise at delivery was common—both good and bad.

One such occasion involved the delivery of Shawn. He was preceded by two beautiful sisters, ages 6 and 10. With the delivery of his head, I noted an extensive cleft lip and palate. This extended down his trachea; and in spite of surgery and spending one-and-a-half years in the Children's Hospital undergoing multiple procedures, the cleft was never closed. He survived with a permanent tracheostomy and gastrostomy. The family moved a trailer near the hospital so they could be near him every day.

He was the poster child for the March of Dimes when he was two years old. His sisters took him to "show and tell" when he was able to leave the hospital. They demonstrated for their classmates the proper technique for cleaning and maintaining his tubes.

Two years after Shawn's delivery, Patrick was born. We were all anxious to see his face. When I turned him over, he had a double cleft palate with angulation of his middle face—more deformed than Shawn. I agonized in that moment how to tell the mother (fathers were not allowed in the delivery room in those days). Finally I just said, "Mom, this boy is like Shawn, only worse." She responded with four words: "Give him to me."

I learned the true meaning of unconditional love.

A. Richard Graham, CME class of 1960, is an obstetrician and gynecologist who has been practicing in the Seattle, Washington, area for more than 50 years. This story occurred before prenatal diagnostic tools, such as ultrasound, were available. May 11, 2014, is Mother's Day.

May 12

For he will command his angels concerning you to guard you in all your ways; they will lift you up in their hands, so that you will not strike your foot against a stone.
Psalm 91:11-12, NIV (1984)

L ate in World War II, thousands of soldiers were being transferred to the West Coast in preparation for an invasion of Japan. I was one of them. During field training in a heavily wooded area of western Washington, an officer asked me to search for the tallest tree I could find. Then, he wanted me to climb as near as I could to the top of it to assess the direction from which another platoon would potentially be coming to attack us.

The density of the forest caused all but the top limbs of these very tall trees to rot, break off, and fall to the ground, due to lack of sunlight. This branch loss left stubs of branches projecting several inches from the tree trunk, making climbing relatively easy.

I did not sit down on the first living limb high in the tree, but rather on the next one above it. While tucking my shirt back under my belt, there was a snap, following which both the limb and I began to fall. Although I had sat down gently on this evidently rotten limb, I fell onto the limb below it. On that lower branch I found myself hanging by my knees, watching the limb I had just been sitting on float to the ground far below.

Shortly, afterwards, I discovered that all the limbs below me, and the next one above the limb I was hanging from, had rotted and fallen to the ground. In my mind, only a miracle—such as an assist by an angel supporting the remaining branch, the one that I had landed on—can account for it holding me and preventing me from spiraling to my death.

How wonderful to know that we have a Father in Heaven who loves us so much! He is so interested in our well-being that He assigns His army of angels to watch over us and to provide help when we need it—wherever we are.

Wendell H. Wall, CME class of 1953-A, is a retired family practitioner residing in Battle Lake, Minnesota.

May 13

Reckless words pierce like a sword, but the tongue of the wise brings healing.
Proverbs 12:18, NIV (1984)

In the past, I have been told that my profession as a dentist was similar to that of a tooth carpenter, chipping away painful decay and shaping the tooth back to its original design. However, I met a patient last year who totally changed my perspective about dentistry. I discovered that dentistry is not just about drilling, filling, and billing. It is about changing smiles, changing lives, and healing hurting hearts.

My patient was a married mother of three beautiful boys. When I first saw her, she was very unhappy and lacked confidence in her smile. Even though some work had been done to her front teeth previously, they were constantly chipping and fracturing away. Those imperfections, including a congenitally missing right lateral incisor, plagued her for many years.

In her own words, she wrote: "I was made fun of all my life because of my teeth. I wouldn't really smile; and if I did, it was always with a closed mouth. I developed severe social anxiety. If I ever had to do a presentation in front of the class, I would break out in hives. I hated to have any attention focused on me; the anxiety worsened and started to impact my life outside of school as well. . . . I wasn't popular for kids are mean! I didn't have any boyfriends. When one guy asked me out in the sixth grade, I found out later that he was actually playing a prank on me. When he went in to kiss me, he pulled away, laughing and saying, 'You think I would actually like you?' I was mortified. . . . I assumed everyone was in on it since they all were laughing.

"Thankfully, I no longer have to live with my anxiety anymore. My two oldest boys make me smile, because they tell me I am pretty and I look like a princess. When I became a believer, everything changed. I no longer focus on how the world sees me, but how my Heavenly Father does. I am thankful for the hard journey I faced along the way. I am very happy with the person smiling back at me in the mirror today [because she] is a very beautiful, confident, and strong woman. I appreciate all those that made this possible, including Dr. Chee. My smile wouldn't be what it is today had it not been for him!"

What did it take to create such a transformation? Four cosmetic crowns, in-office tooth whitening, and strong doses of encouragement were all that were needed for my patient. The wisest man who ever lived on earth, King Solomon, once said that our words have the ability to hurt, but words of wisdom will heal the hurting heart.

I am so glad that our profession is not just about tooth carpentry alone, but also about turning pain into purpose, hurt into healing, and trial into triumph.

Vincent K. Chee Jr., LLUSD class of 1992, is an assistant professor in LLUSD department of restorative dentistry. In 2011, he received two nominations for Smile Heroes of the Year. May 13 is his birthday and was about the same time that his patient's dental treatment was completed.

May 14

Now then go, and I, even I, will be with your mouth, and teach you what you are to say. Exodus 4:12, NASB

Every student needs at least one excellent teacher early in his learning career. Mine came during my internship at the White Memorial Medical Center. At just the right instant, when least expected, I was given a new understanding of reality.

While working in the pediatric clinic, I had nearly finished a visit with Mrs. Rodriguez and her five very robust and, in my opinion, "out of control" children. Each child had something that she wanted me to check. It seemed like a little "law and order" might help everyone in that crowded exam room.

When all their medical problems had been addressed, I spent just a moment detailing a few of the "finer points" of successful parenting. After pleasantly listening to my advice, Mrs. Rodriguez proceeded to gather her things and to usher all her children into the hallway. As the last person in the exam room, she quietly turned to me and asked, "Doctor, how many children do you have?"

"None," I replied.

Carefully looking me over, she drew a deep breath and, with an experienced smile, mused, "Oooh . . . !"

I watched in silence as she turned to herd her five bouncing bundles of energy down the hall. However, I have to admit that one sincere, well-positioned word taught me more than many long and often tedious lectures.

Since that day, I have spent an entire career practicing obstetrics and gynecology and have worked with the Total Health Lifestyle Center. Helping people make good lifestyle choices has consumed a large portion of my medical career. I have also assisted patients in implementing those choices. Countless times I have been asked, "Were you ever obese?" "Did you ever smoke?" "What addictions have you had?" My answers have been mostly negative.

Still ringing clearly in my thinking today is the lesson Mrs. Rodriguez taught me in the pediatric clinic decades ago. There are so many things we can never know about another person's circumstances and choices—so many reasons behind that person's every action.

It is also true that in order to help people change behavior, we do not need to personally experience all their habits. Never once have I been pregnant. However, in thousands of prenatal clinic visits and deliveries, I have helped women solve issues with their pregnancies.

Understanding the power of motivation is absolutely essential to helping people succeed in a lifestyle change. Fear, bribery, social pressure, and even longevity are, at best, short-term motivators.

The most effective and powerful motivator of all time is love. If the love that Jesus is showing me comes through to my patients as genuine love and concern for them, there can be tremendous hope for their progress, which is key to their success. God's love for each one of my patients can come directly to them from Jesus, through me. Oooh . . . ! Why be just a doctor when I can be a tool in the hands of the Master Physician?

Jay Sloop, CME class of 1960, is a retired obstetrician and gynecologist. He submitted this entry in November 2012. On May 14, 2013, he was reported missing while on a mission trip in Kiev, Ukraine.

May 15

As for me, I will see Your face in righteousness; I shall be satisfied when I awake in Your likeness. Psalm 17:15, NKJV

It was Tuesday morning, May 14, 2013. Linda handed me the phone—my brother Randy in California was on the line. "Dad has gone missing this morning in Kiev. He failed to return from his morning walk." My father, Jay Sloop, CME class of 1960, was on a three-week trip to Belgrade, Yugoslavia, and Kiev, Ukraine—working to help set up two Seventh-day Adventist "lifestyle" medical facilities. This was his passion. He had been in the region several times before—the details seemed routine, so how could this be?

Our son Jeff was the closest to the area—in Cairo, Egypt, at Nile Union Academy. He could be there in just a few hours. We called Jeff; and he was soon on the plane with Ron, his vice principal. One of the other Americans on the project in Kiev met them at the airport, and Jeff and Ron joined the search.

The Seventh-day Adventist church headquarters in Washington, DC, soon sent a team from Denmark that specialized in missing persons. Randy also arrived with more help from the United States. The park, where various security cameras last showed Dad entering, was searched repeatedly. Dog teams from the Ukraine and then from Germany were brought in, thousands of fliers were posted, hours of video surveillance footage were reviewed, multiple national news stories were run on TV, and trained searchers were hired.

Also, possible witnesses were interviewed, in addition to hundreds and hundreds of hours of searching by the Ukrainian Adventists and others. Nothing turned up—absolutely nothing!

It has been months now. Still nothing. We have slipped from hopefulness toward reality. And we wonder what happened? And why? We await God's answers.

And yet, as I think back over the past 40 years, I am most impressed with my dad's understanding of our mission as physicians. In our annual community heart disease-prevention seminar, Dad always gives a talk entitled "Whole Person Health." In it, he points out how God created us as three-dimensional people.

He recounts how, on the sixth day of Creation, God formed Adam from the dust of the earth; and when He was finished, Adam had a perfect face, a perfect foot, a perfect liver . . . but he was one dimensional—physical. Then God breathed into him the breath of life; and his mind came alive, and now Adam could see and think and feel and remember—now he experienced life in two dimensions—the physical and the mental. How much more fulfilling that was than a one-dimensional life!

And then, on the seventh day, God offered to spend all day with Adam and Eve—to become friends. At that point, Adam and Eve began to develop in the third dimension—the spiritual. Now how much larger and even more fulfilling their lives were—living in *all* three dimensions! If we want to live life fully, we will come to the Person who makes us *well forever* by His presence.

I will be the one giving that lecture this year . . .

Richard Sloop, LLUSM class of 1986, is a neurologist in Yakima, Washington. Dean of LLUSM, Roger Hadley, requested the author write this tribute to his father, Dr. Jay Sloop (see May 14 devotional). It was submitted August 27, 2013.

May 16

"For I know the plans I have for you," declares the LORD, "plans to prosper you and not to harm you, plans to give you hope and a future." Jeremiah 29:11, NIV

I still remember that summer day in August 2005, as I got off work in Kelowna, British Columbia. It was a particularly hot day and an anxious one, as I counted down the minutes until the end of my shift when I could begin the five-hour drive to Vancouver Children's Hospital to see my brother. It seemed like not too long before that my brother and I had been hanging out and playing hockey with no cares in the world.

My brother had always been a rather skinny and athletic kid, but he had begun putting on quite a bit of weight, despite his healthy eating habits and playing many different sports. Initially, we had not thought much about his weight gain, until one day when my brother, much to his dismay, discovered he was lactating! Over the course of a few days, our lives went from being all fun and games to discovering that my little brother had a prolactinoma pituitary tumor.

Being young, we did not exactly understand what a prolactinoma was; all we knew was that it was serious. The more I began to learn about it, the more I became worried about what might happen to my brother and my best friend. At first, he was put on medication to control his hormone levels and slow the growth of the brain tumor. This worked fine for a while and at times we would both forget completely about his hidden enemy.

However, over time, the medication began to fail and, at just 15 years old, my brother underwent major brain surgery to remove the tumor. I still remember my mother and father sitting down with him to explain some of the complications that could result from the surgery.

One of the most worrisome possibilities was that since the pituitary tumor was extremely close to the optic nerve, the procedure could result in permanent blindness. With all the terrifying possibilities of the surgery, I felt my role as brother needed to shift from being goofy and playful to being a more comforting, understanding, and compassionate older brother.

I remember thinking, "Why would God allow this to happen to someone as young and happy as my little brother?" I suppose the only way I seriously dealt with those feelings was by talking to my family. To see my brother act so strong and courageous, and to see him hold so steadfast to his belief that God would be with him, no matter what, was an inspiration to me and kept me strong in my faith.

My brother told me he was most comforted by Jeremiah 29:11 (NIV), which says, "'For I know the plans I have for you,' declares the Lord, 'plans to prosper you and not to harm you, plans to give you hope and a future.'" After seeing his attitude, I decided that if he could be strong in the face of his illness, then I should be able to be strong as well.

On that hot August 2005 day, my brother had successful surgery. He immediately lost weight and in no time we were back together doing the things we loved; hockey, fishing, and other activities. In 2012 he once again underwent surgery to remove the tumor that had recurred. This will be a life-long battle for him, but it is good to see him prepared to face the future with a strong trust in God.

Ryan Manns, LLUSM class of 2016, is from Kelowna, British Columbia. He graduated from the University of British Columbia with a degree in medical biochemistry. May 16 is his brother's birthday.

May 17

The LORD is close to the brokenhearted and saves those who are crushed in spirit. Psalm 34:18, NIV

I had come back to my first year of residency about two weeks after my son's funeral, and, due to grief, had a short attention span. During cardiology rounds, I was physically present but often barely there mentally. One morning, I was paying more attention than usual when I heard snippets of a presentation. "Mr. A . . . had an MI . . . not making progress . . . appears depressed. Plan: continue cardiac rehab, contact social services . . ." After that brief moment of acute attention, I returned to my mental haze.

Upon finishing rounds and charting, I wandered around the unit, waiting to be paged. On yet another restless lap around the nursing station, I ambled into Mr. A's room. I honestly had no idea what help I might offer. I sat by his bed, introduced myself, and we began talking. I found out his wife had died from cancer six months before, and recently his brother's wife had been diagnosed with the same cancer. His daughter's husband had abandoned her and their two daughters; his only son was a drug addict who robbed him and others.

"No wonder he's depressed," I thought. "Any reasonable person would be, given all that life's thrown at him." The conversation had been long and pleasant when he suddenly asked a simple question. "Do you have any children?" How was I supposed to answer that? It would be easiest to just say, "No"; and, technically, I would be correct. Or I could say, "Yes"; but then I would have to explain. I did not need to burden him with my problems.

The pause became uncomfortable; and before I could answer, he apologized for asking. I told him it was okay and decided to be vulnerable and honest, "Yes, I had a son; but he died three weeks ago." Then, I could say no more. We reached out and held hands and both cried silently for a long time.

Suddenly, he brightened and with renewed vigor said: "I know what I'm going to do. I'm going to sell my house, move near my daughter, and be a father to her two little girls." It was a wonderful idea. After a few more minutes of talking, I was paged and had to leave.

The next morning on rounds, the medical student exclaimed with wonder: "Mr. A's not depressed any more! He's made incredible progress in the past 24 hours. I think we can discharge him today."

The resident mused, "I wonder what happened."

As for me, I was amazed that God could use such a wounded, broken person as a healer. I then realized that I did not have to "have it all together" in order to make a positive difference. We are all fellow pilgrims on this journey of life and a sympathetic ear and words of encouragement can be just as healing as the finest medical care. I am grateful that I was and can still be a conduit of God's grace, imperfect though I am.

Delbe Meelhuysen, LLUSM class of 1987, practices internal medicine in Cleburne, Texas. This story occurred during her internship, May 1988. For more on the author's backstory, refer to her February 16 Morning Rounds devotional.

For even the Son of Man did not come to be served, but to serve, and to give his life as a ransom for many. Mark 10:45, NIV

Looking back over my life, I never imagined my ordinary life would one day become intertwined with extraordinary history.

When I was young, my family was certain that I was destined to become a minister. But later, my mother confided to me that, while she had hoped I would enter the ministry, my often-stated observation that the florist at my church "had the best job in the world—placing flowers in the house of God"—led her to correctly conclude that I would one day become a florist.

During the early days of my employment at Loma Linda University Medical Center (LLUMC), prior to the Internet's revolutionary impact, my responsibility was to collect data for research. One day, I received a unique STAT request for an overwhelming volume of materials dealing with infant heart transplants, protocols, transplant rejection, and interspecies transplant. I wondered what had prompted the assigned search.

My questions were answered on the national evening news when the anchor newscaster reported that LLUMC, with the permission of a young baby girl's mother, was attempting to save the child's life by exchanging her weak heart for a baboon's heart. I shared with my mother the exciting news that I previously had pulled research materials for this groundbreaking procedure.

The transplant recipient, "Baby Fae," achieved global name and face recognition as people worldwide fell in love with her and prayed for her survival. Sadly, she passed away, but the knowledge gained during her short life contributed to successful future infant heart transplants.

Years later, I became the owner of the florist shop that had provided the flowers for Baby Fae's casket. Her mother—who had moved out of state—contacted me and requested that every year on Baby Fae's birthday, I place baby pink roses on her grave. We became telephone friends. I assured her that I would treat her child's resting place as I would treat a family member's, and that I would keep its location confidential.

In 2009, during the LLU School of Medicine's Centennial celebration, Leonard Bailey, LLUSM class of 1969, was scheduled to interview Baby Fae's mother. When I was given the honor of providing flowers for the podium, I asked if I could present this courageous mother a personal bouquet. As I handed her the bouquet, I said, "Hi, you don't know me." At that point everything went off script. She said, "Thad! I would know your voice anywhere." Dr. Bailey then asked me to share our story.

At that moment, I felt as if a part of my life had come full circle. I had witnessed medical history from the beginning of an incredible story to the end. And I had experienced the blessing of combining my life's passion of floral design with a unique opportunity for ministry, providing a service to a major figure in that history.

Thad Mosely, owner of Premier Florals, creates floral arrangements for LLU graduations and the LLU Church. This story took place while he was working at the now closed LLU Jorgensen Library. May 18 is his birthday.

May 19

Therefore, my beloved brethren, be steadfast, immovable, always abounding in the work of the Lord, knowing that your toil is not in vain in the Lord.
1 Corinthians 15:58, NASB

Ted, a young person trying to mix a life of drugs and pleasure with a college career, was about to graduate; but he was concerned about what his future would bring.

Many colleagues were having interviews with prospective employers, but not Ted. This "snubbing" made him re-evaluate his priorities, so he started by flushing his stash of drugs and alcohol down the toilet. He pleaded with God to forgive his rebellious ways and asked Him for the roughest, toughest job He could find—to make amends for the wasted years and harm he had caused.

Things in Ted's life changed dramatically. Shortly before graduation, a friend of the dean of men had a short conversation with Ted; he was hired on the spot to work with 16- to 20-year-old men who had committed crimes ranging from petty theft to murder while involved in the illicit drug industry. He was excited and thanked the Lord, as he could not think of anything tougher to do.

Ted developed a program in which life-changing, character-building activities could be interwoven among the men's regular school work and daily chores. The most important objective was to introduce them to the Lord. However, the men were only interested in putting in their time. As Ted studied the semiannual evaluation report, he was devastated to see that his program resulted in only 15 percent of the men choosing to live without drugs and crime.

The next morning, after a restless night, Ted went to a quiet place in the woods for some counsel. As he knelt in the fresh snow, he told the Lord that this job was more than he could handle and he needed something else. Immediately, a voice from the surrounding woods gently answered, "Ted, I don't want you to work for Me anymore."

Ted responded, "But Lord, You . . . You don't understand, I want to work for You more than anything else in the world." The voice answered again, "No, you're not working for Me anymore." All was quiet for a while, and then Ted said, "Lord, if You don't want me to work for You, just tell me what You want and I'll do it."

The Lord complimented Ted on his work and then told him he was attempting an impossible job. "What I really want you to do is let Me work with you. If you allow Me to be your partner, we can do great things." All was quiet as Ted walked back to the ranch, when he suddenly stopped and said: "Lord, you're on. Tell me what needs to be done, how and when to do it, and give me the strength I need." Ted no longer had a job; he was in a partnership.

Before his conversation with the Lord that snowy morning, the ranch had an 85 percent failure rate in rehabilitating the men. Since then, the ranch has had an 85 percent success rate.

Working "for God" means you are a hired employee, working for a paycheck. Working "with God" means you are a partner, and He provides the resources.

Marvin Peters, PhD, is an emeritus professor in LLUSM department of physiology and pharmacology. He resides in Yucaipa, California.

May 20

Is anyone among you sick? Let him call for the elders of the church, and let them pray over him, anointing him with oil in the name of the Lord. James 5:14, NKJV

"Tell me about this anointing," a dental professor asked, as we emerged from our Prince Hall offices on campus and headed toward the Loma Linda University Medical Center.

We shared concern for an administrative assistant who brightened everyone's life on the fifth floor of the office building. Young, energetic, competent (and in love), she had made an impact on us. However, we were shocked when we learned that, while getting into her car in the parking lot, she had collapsed. Soon help was summoned and CPR was administered until emergency attendants arrived.

Now our fifth floor sunshine was in a medically induced coma. Her parents had arrived on an overnight flight. Machines were monitoring brain activity. Her heart was unstable. The prospects were grim. And I had received a request to conduct an anointing service on her behalf.

My colleague, a dental professor, who participated faithfully in the dedication and consecration events planned for the School of Dentistry students, was curious about this anointing—a practice unknown to him. He wanted to know if this was like the Catholic "last rites" for the dying.

And I had the good news. "Not at all," I assured him. "This is a prayer for healing. We're following the biblical injunction in the book of James: 'Is any one of you sick? . . . anoint him with oil in the name of the Lord'" (James 5:14, NIV [1984]).

There were probably 20 people surrounding Katie's bed—all quietly awaiting an invitation that God guide the physicians in their treatment. All of us placed our hands gently on the bed as I poured the oil and petitioned for the healing hand of God. There was a distinct sense that we were partnering with Divine help.

Today we are thankful for the skilled care Katie received; the procedures she survived; and the guidance of God, who promises, "The prayer of faith will save the sick" (James 5:15, NKJV).

William Loveless, EdD, is a professor in LLUSBH department of social work and social ecology. He served as senior pastor at Loma Linda University Church from 1970 to 1976 and from 1990 to 2002.

May 21

During the night Paul had a vision: there stood a man of Macedonia pleading with him and saying, "Come over to Macedonia and help us." Acts 16:9, NRSV

I remember an unusual event that occurred during my senior year in medical school, just before graduation. My classmate Jon Freed, LLUSM class of 1990, and I—along with our proctor, Brad Nelson, LLUSM class of 1968—went to Africa in May 1990 for a tropical medicine rotation. We were called to Yuka Hospital in Zambia to relieve a missionary doctor.

During our stay at Yuka Hospital, a middle-aged man showed up at the hospital. This man, who had traveled three days by foot from West Angola, had acute abdominal pain and distention. After assessing him, we realized that he needed surgery to remove a bowel obstruction. We did not have a fancy operating room or the proper medical supplies to do a major abdominal surgery; however, we knew that if we did not do the surgery, this man would die.

After saying a word of prayer and administering spinal anesthesia, Dr. Nelson and Jon started the abdominal surgery. I observed the procedure from start to finish. The surgery began in the usual manner, with a midline vertical incision. After they entered the peritoneum to determine the cause of the pain, it did not take long for them to determine that the pain was due to volvulus, a visible twist in the intestine.

As I continued to watch the operation, they followed the small and large intestines multiple times, trying to untwist the bowel. After what seemed like an eternity, I realized that no matter what they did, nothing was working. A bowel resection was not even a possibility without the IV fluids and proper supplies required for that type of intervention. We were faced with a major decision: do we close and leave the volvulus as we found it, or do we continue with the procedure?

Time was ticking and the spinal anesthesia would be wearing off soon. We whispered another prayer, and a miracle happened before our eyes. The previously twisted bowel that was in the hands of Dr. Nelson and Jon simply untwisted on its own, and the volvulus was gone! After further examining the small and large intestines and finding everything to be normal, they closed the abdomen and sent the patient to the recovery room.

With no IV fluids, we started oral hydration shortly after surgery; and the patient made a complete recovery before we left Yuka Hospital. Shortly after we returned to America, we received a letter from the hospital, sharing with us an even greater miracle than the surgery that we had witnessed with our own eyes. The man had accepted Jesus as his personal Savior, and he said that God had sent us to Yuka just for him!

What a privilege for us to have been a part of God's plan for this man's eternal salvation. This experience taught me even more about God's love for each one of us—and the extraordinary measures to which He goes to save His children. I cannot wait for His Second Coming, when I can meet this man again and talk about how God's miracles saved his life that day in Africa.

Tae-Woong Im, LLUSM class of 1990, is a family practitioner at Rancho Family Medical Group in Temecula, California. May 21 is his daughter's birthday.

And I will bring the blind by a way that they knew not; I will lead them in paths that they have not known: I will make darkness light before them, and crooked things straight. These things will I do unto them, and not forsake them.
Isaiah 42:16, KJV

oes God lead? Absolutely, and in ways that we cannot see until later. Now at age 78 I look back and realize I have been following God's leading throughout my life and have many good memories.

1930s: A coal miner father in West Virginia struggles to keep his wife and three children alive.

1934: Another son, James, is born into the family; and this son is doomed to a life of poverty. At age four, the young boy is assigned certain household chores and hoes corn in the fields. As he grows, he is happy and runs barefoot through the hills and meadows.

1946: A time of great adventure because James' family has been directed to move to Arizona. Now the boy has a chance. At age 12, he has a job as a newspaper boy; and during his teenage years, he picks cotton in the fields for $2.00 a day. He works his way through high school and graduates without money or a secure future. At age 19, he is a young Marine on his way to Korea. By age 20, he is a Marine Corps sergeant in charge of a 155 mm gun, 16-man crew.

1950s: Two weeks prior to discharge from the Marines, James is directed by his first sergeant to go to the College of Medical Evangelists (CME) and become a physical therapist. Four days after discharge, he is working in a copper mine in Arizona to depths of 5,150 feet. It is so hot and the work is so dangerous that men die. He attends Arizona State University for two years and then transfers to the physical therapy program at CME in 1959.

1960s: He meets the love of his life, Carol Anne Rittenhouse. He graduates as a physical therapist in 1961 and marries in 1962. Injured on the job, he is off work for six months. He subsequently works as a full-time therapist while attending night school at two different colleges, four nights a week, for two years.

1965: At age 31, he enters Loma Linda University School of Medicine on a scholarship, while his wife supports the family. He graduates in 1969! In those early years as a physician, he learned, by staying long nights at the bedside of his patients, how fragile life is and how much it hurts when you lose a precious soul. He made house calls for those who could not come to see him, and he did this up until the day he retired. He wrote Bible texts, as a Christian witness, on the prescription pad slips he gave to his patients.

2006: He retires and loves his three happy children, who are now responsible adult citizens.

2013: He and his wife have plans to go to Guam for a short term of mission service.

I still remember that small boy of long ago—running through the hills and meadows and down dirt roads without shoes. As I look at my feet, now aged and worn, I realize again that I was that little boy, and that God does indeed lead.

James R. Cruise, LLUSM class of 1969, practiced general internal medicine in Ukiah, California, for 35 years. Now retired, he lives in Redwood Valley, California. May 22 is his wife's birthday.

May 23

I have loved you with an everlasting love; I have drawn you with unfailing kindness. Jeremiah 31:3, NIV

It is a dark, starry African night at Mwami Hospital in Zambia, but no one is looking up as a mother walks into the courtyard, her three-year-old child wrapped to her back, actively dying with measles encephalitis. They have come from a long distance, but too late: the child is unconscious, pupils fixed, within minutes asleep until Jesus comes. It is a tragic scene, played out around the world over and over again, wherever health care is poorly accessible for want of resources, transportation, or basic knowledge of health.

The scene is sad enough on its face; and yet I, at a deeper level, and freshly graduated from Loma Linda University School of Medicine, watch my inability to engage this grieving mother in her great time of loss. As I confirm her child's death and try to comfort her, the barriers of language, customs, and social position all work against me.

In my own world, these are less obvious, but still very real—whether in cross-cultural interactions or in the more complex obstacles of emotion, anger, fear, or simple lack of compassion. Even if the language is common, the words may still be foreign—"medical speak" rolls off our tongues reflexively. If all things are equal, then our backgrounds, education, values, and spiritual journey may still be landmasses apart from others.

At the core of a healing interaction is listening with our full selves—hearing at a physical, emotional, and spiritual level. And then we need to sort the vast array of inputs in a short time to craft a stepwise plan forward that addresses immediate and then future paths toward recovery. In that sometimes short time we spend with our patients, they need to know they have been heard, their concerns addressed, their fears validated; and that there is hope when it may seem hopeless. They need to be cared for. They need to sense the uniform language that bridges all gulfs—compassion.

As this mother packs her still child on her back, she cries softly and walks into the dark night, unaware of the stars above. Our Greatest Guide through those dark nights has always been the One who made the stars to shine from the start. He cares for us and our patients with an everlasting love that breaks down all barriers; it is a love that heals completely and forever.

Keith Wilkens, LLUSM class of 1982, has practiced family medicine in Spokane, Washington, for 31 years. Shortly after completing medical school, he and his wife, Joyce, worked at Mwami Adventist Hospital in Zambia, and in the government hospital in Zimbabwe for three months before starting residency at Florida Hospital in Orlando. Their memories of Africa burn bright, and they look forward to returning.

May 24

Then Job answered the Lord: "Indeed, I am completely unworthy—how could I reply to you? I put my hand over my mouth to silence myself. I have spoken once, but I cannot answer; twice, but I will say no more." Job 40:3-5, NET

Right now, we are in the midst of a celebration of what we know. It is something we like to display. We take tests to put a number on it; we give awards for it. And after four years of slogging through information, we get to put on a long black dress, wear a decorative couch pillow on our heads, and shake hands with a superior, while being given a quarter million dollar piece of paper. We are graduating.

Of course, I am very glad for what I do know; I have learned many valuable things in the last four years (for instance, a beta blocker might help me currently). But right now, I am really focused on something else. What I am really worried about is what I do not know.

First of all, I do not know what it will be like to not be in school. That routine has not happened for more than two months at a time in the past 20 years of my life. And I do not know what it will be like to have a long-term salaried job.

There are some things that I am glad I do not know. After a tough day at the hospital, I do not know what it is like to return to an empty home; my wife has always been there for me. And I am happy to say that I do not know what it is like to have parents who push you into medicine, or would be disappointed if you did something else with your life.

And while I do not even really know what it will be like to be a doctor, give me 30 hours and then I will tell you (just a little bit of hubris for humor). At this point, I do not know too much about Utah, a place where I am headed in 10 days. And I do not know what I am going to do with 16 more inches at the bottom of a white coat.

Also, I do not know what it is like to give my signature for medications that may have harmful side effects, or to write orders for a life-saving treatment. And I am not entirely sure how to give orders to someone who may be twice my age.

I do not know how to answer all the questions I will get from patients, and I do not know exactly what I will do in three years, when I am *really* done.

I just do not know. I do not know the future, and that can be very difficult. But if I have learned one thing in the past four years—with all of the examinations, hours in the hospital, and days studying, plus all of the close calls, lucky guesses, and moments of victory—if I have learned one thing, it is that God does know; and every day is a slow revealing of what He has in store for me.

So you can prepare, prepare, prepare for years, your whole life even. But sometimes, not knowing—that is just the way it goes.

Bradley Schleenbaker, LLUSM class of 2013, is a family medicine resident in Salt Lake City, Utah. He gave this speech at LLUSM baccalaureate service in 2013. May 24 is the date of the baccalaureate for LLUSM class of 2014.

May 25

Even as the Son of man came not to be ministered unto, but to minister, and to give his life a ransom for many. Matthew 20:28, KJV

That's it! I suddenly realized that my friend, Prakash, could possibly go to medical school in Mexico. He was a young Nepalese I befriended after my arrival as a new mission doctor at Scheer Memorial Hospital in Nepal. To prepare the way, I had spoken with Ira Bailie, CME class of 1954, and his son Darrel, who attended Montemorelos University in Mexico. I wrote to Dwight Evans, LLUSM class of 1973-B, who—along with Naomi Pitman, CME class of 1936; Donald Sargeant, CME class of 1944-B; and Russell Youngberg, CME class of 1949—was teaching there.

The paperwork was frightening; but finally, with an old typewriter and snail mail service, Prakash was accepted to begin his lifelong dream. This process took more than two years, with both of us spending many hours on that typewriter. Through this effort, we had fallen in love and were now newlyweds. Shortly, we arrived in Mexico, where Prakash would begin medical school.

Soon after our arrival, Zeno Charles-Marcel, LLUSM class of 1980-aff, joined the staff to teach internal medicine. He was a graduate of Howard University but had spent time at Loma Linda University during his residency, and had recently become an Adventist Christian. He was a fine physician who loved his students and his patients.

Dr. Charles-Marcel was passionate about teaching. One time, as students encircled the patient's bed, they discussed the patient's presenting problem and past history. Now it was time for the physical examination. After listening to the man's chest, the students turned their attention to the patient's lower extremities. Very dirty socks with a distinctive odor covered his feet and ankles. No one moved to help.

At that point, Dr. Charles-Marcel reached down, carefully removed the socks, and simply looked up at his students, and said, "You have lost an opportunity to serve." Then he continued his remarks on the physical exam and diagnosis.

That moment on hospital rounds happened almost 30 years ago, but few weeks go by that I do not recall Dr. Charles-Marcel's remark. Now, when I look into a drunken face covered with blood and vomit in the emergency department (ED) on a Friday night, I realize I have an opportunity to serve. And when I listen to the tired mother of a sick child, I have an opportunity to serve. And when the ED nurse calls about yet another drug overdose at 3 a.m., God has given me another day to serve Him.

Our daughter, Christina Miller, is graduating from Loma Linda University School of Medicine in 2014. She carries an iPhone with amazing applications that cover almost any medical topic. She is conversant about ECHOs and MRIs and robotic surgery, all things that did not exist at my graduation. But I pray that, when she graduates, she will not only be schooled in the latest medical topics, but that she also will have learned the most priceless lesson from the many lives who have touched hers. May she never lose an "opportunity to serve."

Sherry Shrestha, LLUSM class of 1974, practices family medicine with her husband in Hazelton, British Columbia. This story occurred at Universidad de Montemorelos in Mexico, where her husband was studying medicine. May 25 is the date of the commencement for LLUSM class of 2014.

Therefore confess your sins to each other and pray for each other so that you may be healed. The prayer of a righteous person is powerful and effective.
James 5:16, NIV

It was January 1968, during the war, in a small army dispensary/tent hospital in Vietnam near the Cambodian border. A tank company finishing patrols rolled into camp for a rest. One of the "tankers" with abdominal pain came for aid accompanied by a skinny, homely, red-haired medic and a lieutenant. The soldier lay on a stretcher supported by sawhorses. The medic and lieutenant stood on one side and I on the other.

As I began to examine the patient's abdomen, the medic came around on my side and pressed up hard against me and placed his hands next to mine on the soldier's abdomen. I pushed his hands back, as it was not possible to do an exam this way; however, his hands came right back, pressing against mine. Now I was wondering what was happening.

Again I pushed him away, but back again came his hands; no words had been spoken by either of us. My wonderment turned suddenly to irritation; I exploded at the medic, proper words, but an improper attitude. The red-haired medic was crushed, and soon I did not feel comfortable with myself.

After I finished the exam and had sent the soldier on his way, the lieutenant stayed by to talk with me. Very politely, he told me he felt I had been harsh on his medic. He agreed with me that the medic had overstepped his bounds, but felt I had overreacted toward him. He then went on to share with me details about the character of this red-haired kid.

The lieutenant said the boy was loved by all of the "tankers." He was consistently doing acts to bring happiness and comfort to the men. He wrote home to their families to have items that the soldiers needed sent to them. He placed his life on the line for them. Now I was more uncomfortable with my response to his inappropriate act, realizing I was far more egregious than he. I determined to find the lad and ask for his forgiveness. The tankers left camp on patrol and I watched for their return.

Months later, I was on a different assignment, where my duty also involved examining the "killed in action" to determine cause of death. One day, a large number of body bags were dropped off on the helicopter landing pad. The bags had been zipped open and, as I went from bag to bag, it seemed to me the eyes from one particular bag were following me.

As I approached this bag for exam, I saw red hair; I looked down into those open eyes and recognized the person I had wanted to meet up with to ask for forgiveness. It was too late. A feeling of deep sadness consumed me. A bullet had gone through his knee, and he had bled to death; a simple tourniquet would have given him life.

I sought out his tank company to inquire what had happened. When an accompanying infantryman had been wounded, Red, true to his character, leaped from his tank without hesitation, and raced to give aid. He was hit on the run, and no one was around to treat him. He truly was one of God's jewels.

Edwin Noyes, CME class of 1959, is a family practitioner residing in Forest Grove, Oregon. May 26, 2014, is Memorial Day.

May 27

You need not fear any dangers at night or sudden attacks during the day.
Psalm 91:5, GNT

It seemed like any other Wednesday in May 1980. I was completing my neurology residency at Louisiana State University and had been assigned to Charity Hospital in New Orleans.

Wednesday afternoon meant epilepsy clinic. Rather than leaving clinic after I had completed my assigned patients for the day, I volunteered to see a patient for one of my younger associates. I called Mr. X into the very small examining room, and along came his wife. They were from Cajun country, a long trip away. They had arrived early to have blood drawn for anticonvulsant levels, as arranged at his prior visit. They were unhappy about having to wait a long time that day, especially as they watched physicians leaving the clinic rather than seeing them.

After some history and examination, I reviewed his anticonvulsant blood levels and said, "Your Dilantin level is low."

"Why is my Dilantin level low?" he asked. I gave him a list of several reasons why it might not be in the therapeutic range. "You mean you don't know why my Dilantin level is low!" he screamed.

Then he stood up, turned away from me toward the closed door, and pulled out a knife—which made him look much larger than his actual 5' 7"! I stood up. He rushed toward me with the knife and thrust the knife toward my heart. I instantly leaned backwards and twisted to the side, using my left arm to deflect his right arm and the knife away from my chest.

I landed on my back on the floor. I yelled, "Help!"—which my associates in the other clinic rooms interpreted to mean that a patient was having a convulsion. They surmised that I could handle the situation just fine, so they took their time coming. As I was lying on the floor, the patient came at me again with the knife. I remembered another karate move—a thrust-kick to the assailant's chest. That slowed him down until people started arriving at the door. When they came, the man willingly gave up his knife.

I stood up, found my glasses, examined my shirt, and saw no tears or apparent piercings; I figured I was extremely fortunate. And then I saw some blood and determined that the knife had gone between the buttons of my shirt and slashed my chest directly over my heart. Fortunately, "my" twisting, defensive karate sweep had made the knife deflect 90 degrees so that it went almost parallel to my chest. The knife had made about a 3 cm cut laterally, but only about 2 mm deep, rather than plunging into my chest and heart—then I knew I was fortunate!

Had the hand of the angel deflected that blade? Or, was it "my" karate move? Had God guided me to go to those evening karate classes during medical school and "taught" me just enough karate to defend myself that day? Did that give "plausible deniability" to this being a miracle? Or, was karate the "mechanism" for a miracle? Did God have plans for me? Or, did I attend those classes for the best exercise and best overall conditioning I have ever had? Or, as I had thought at the time, did I go to those classes just to meet girls?

Gordon Peterson, LLUSM class of 1974, is a professor in LLUSM departments of neurology and physical medicine and rehabilitation. He and his wife, Myra (née Josselyn), reside in Redlands, California.

For in the one Spirit we were all baptized into one body—Jews or Greeks, slaves or free—and we were all made to drink of one Spirit. 1 Corinthians 12:13, NRSV

There I was, my wife at my side, surrounded by 11 other ordination candidates. We had been through a full month of orientation, counsel, and even indoctrination; now we were about to be launched into an adventure of a lifetime. We were being ordained by the laying on of hands into the brotherhood of credentialed missionaries of the Seventh-day Adventist Church.

As we knelt there with the pastors and elders of the Loma Linda University Church, the Campus Hill Church, and the officials of the Seventh-day Adventist General Conference and the Institute of World Mission, we absorbed the words uttered in prayers to our Heavenly Father for guidance and fruitfulness. Yet, as we bowed reverently, my mind, in an instant, retraced a wide array of memories and thoughts that spanned many years and much space. In a bizarre kind of way, the dots were being connected, and the pronouncement of an old missionary physician became prophetic.

On May 14, 1955, I was received into the world by Robert F. Dunlop, CME class of 1944-aff, a missionary physician. He was the medical director of the Adventist medical clinic in St. Clair, Trinidad. My parents had become acquainted with him and Dr. and Mrs. David Bull when they lived in another part of Port-of-Spain, and they were very fond of these dedicated missionaries.

My parents trusted these doctors and the staff at the Adventist clinic, so they "naturally" went to the new clinic and nursing home (known as a birthing center in the United States). As Dr. Dunlop handed my father the blanketed bundle, of which I made up the major part, he said to my father: "He is one of us." As I was growing up, these words would become part of the narrative of my birth whenever it was related. Over the years, my father interpreted Dr. Dunlop's statement to mean I would be a physician. I thought the doctor had only referred to my gender.

I was raised Roman Catholic and attended Anglican schools. I became a Bible-believing follower of Jesus Christ while I was in school at McGill University, where I studied electrical engineering and later physics and physiology. But God had other plans.

By a twist of fate, I became very interested in medicine and enrolled at Howard University in Washington, DC. I knew nothing about Adventists until I met a young Adventist student who became my best friend during medical school. In 1980, we both "matched" to our first choices, to join the LLU internal medicine residency program. I had firsthand observation of how my friend Kenley Davis, LLUSM class of 1981-R, lived; and I saw that he and others were practicing what I had read in the Word. I was soon following those tenets myself, as best as I could. Thus, I joined the Adventist fellowship in 1981.

So, here I was on the platform, flooded with these thoughts; the words, "He is one of us," reverberated in my brain. Yes, I concluded, I was indeed like my birth-attending physician (whom I had hoped to meet one day): a man, a doctor, a Christian, a Seventh-day Adventist, and a missionary. I pray to be as effective and impacting as was Dr. Dunlop. By God's grace, he will hear the story when we meet in Heaven.

Zeno Charles-Marcel graduated from Howard University College of Medicine in 1980. He is currently vice president of medical affairs at Wildwood Sanitarium, Inc., and is an adjunct associate professor in LLUSM department of medicine.

May 29

If I give all I possess to the poor and surrender my body to the flames, but have not love, I gain nothing. **1 Corinthians 13:3, NIV (1984)**

The African sun was leaning toward the horizon, and all the heat stored in the earth was beginning to radiate upward. Clinic at the Gimbie Adventist Hospital had ended early, so I grabbed my camera and hiked out beyond the compound walls. Earlier I had seen a grove of acacia trees, and in them at least one colobus monkey. With a little luck and a little patience, I hoped to get some pictures of their characteristic white faces and plumed tails.

In the rural western part of Ethiopia, Gimbie was my home and school for six meaningful weeks during my fourth year of medical school. I cared for every patient I could with my limited medical knowledge, was challenged by the ravages of disease, and was blessed by a greater intimacy with God.

I found my vantage point on the edge of a dirt road, the reddish clay pushed up and crumbling. The copse of trees lay directly in front of me, filling the foreground of a rugged, yet beautiful vista. The same dirt road I was sitting on snaked around a large boulder and widened to accommodate a group of kids playing soccer. The players were from the village; I recognized a few of the orphans who were cared for at the hospital. The best dressed had torn t-shirts and shorts; none wore shoes. The ball had long ago given up on holding air and bounced around erratically.

As they played, I prayed, thanking the Lord for the incredible opportunity to be sitting exactly where I was. A thought came strongly to me, *This is what I was made for!* Indeed it was, on at least two levels. First, the challenges and rewards of medical mission work stirred a passion within me that I was only beginning to recognize. If God's plans for us are linked to our deepest desires, as some have suggested, then this was a powerful glimpse of what God had in mind for me.

Years have passed since I sat on that hill, yet I have only begun to grasp the second layer of meaning. While I was made to serve overseas, more importantly, I was made to live in communion with God. There is meaning in serving those who have almost nothing, but even more in serving with the Creator.

As Paul said, as quoted above, if I "have not love, I gain nothing." If Paul were writing to me, perhaps he would have said, "If you serve every day of your life overseas, but are disconnected from the Source of love, it will be worthless."

God's will for each of us is to continually learn of love from its Source, and then to share that love.

Brenden Hanks, LLUSM class of 2005, is an anesthesiologist in Parker, Colorado. He enjoys serving overseas.

May 30

The Lord *your God is in your midst, a mighty one who will save; he will rejoice over you with gladness; he will quiet you by his love; he will exult over you with loud singing. Zephaniah 3:17, ESV*

I remember Shaun vividly. He was a nearly lifeless three-year-old boy; his only movements were involuntary seizure-like jerks. He did not respond to my touch. His entire body was cool when I felt him. He had an innocent face, but no words came from his mouth.

The day I met Shaun, I had been running hectically around the pediatric intensive care unit (PICU). Suddenly my pager went off. The secretary said it was a transport call—but not just any transport call; it was my very first transport call! I had just finished my internship the previous month, and I was a newly minted senior resident physician. I now had the opportunity to go out on transport calls (where I get to ride on ambulances or helicopters to pick up children from around Southern California and bring them to Loma Linda University Children's Hospital [LLUCH] for further treatment). Since I had no idea what to expect, I was visibly nervous.

I arrived at the community hospital and was directed to Shaun. He had been found lying at the bottom of a swimming pool, probably 10 to 15 minutes after he had fallen in. He was near death, with seizure activity from severe brain damage and a blood pH that was essentially incompatible with life (pH of 6.6). In my conversation with his father, I told him we would do everything possible, but that we could not promise much. I remember everyone commenting that it was likely that he would not live long, and that, hopefully, he would not die while being transported.

We stabilized Shaun and took him to LLUCH. I was fortunate enough to continue taking care of him in the PICU. I gave daily updates to his father, who was constantly by his side. Amazingly enough, Shaun slowly started to make a comeback. In the course of a few days, he was able to have his breathing tube taken out and started to move his extremities.

I will never forget the moment when his father told me that Shaun had just spoken the word, "Daddy." How could that be? What an amazing thing to hear your son, who has essentially died, come back from death, hold your hand, and say, "Daddy!"

In light of that miracle, I could not help but think about another Father. I think about a Father who had a Son, Jesus Christ, who was born, lived a short life, and was put to death on a cross. What for? So that He could be raised. Why? So that we, who are as good as dead because of our sin, could be raised from the dead, like Shaun. What for? So that we can cry out, "Daddy."

My prayer is that we, too, would be able to know the joy of calling God our "Daddy." And that we would know God's delight and joy in hearing that cry from us, just like Shaun's father rejoiced in hearing his son.

Andrew Wai, LLUSM class of 2011, is in his med-peds residency at LLUMC. May 30 is his mother's birthday.

May 31

I praise you because I am fearfully and wonderfully made; your works are wonderful, I know that full well. Psalm 139:14, NIV

During my residency training in med-peds, I have encountered many individuals who are suffering. The vast majority of my patients have poor health as a result of self-inflicted injury or lack of self-care. I remember a patient I admitted to the hospital. He was 55 years old with a history of long-standing alcoholism, a recent stroke, and blindness from cataracts. He had been homeless for the majority of his life.

In his current state, he was helpless, bedbound, and frail appearing, with aged and wrinkled skin and a few patches of white hair on his head. In fact, he appeared to be in his nineties, even though he was 55. The patient in the adjacent bed was 96 years old, but looked younger and was independent in all aspects of self-care. I looked at the younger man with sadness and thought again how sin had degraded humanity far from the image of God we were modeled after.

We are fearfully and wonderfully made by a loving Creator and are modeled after His very own image (Genesis 1:27). I am always amazed at how masterfully God created us. The intricacy of the body at the cellular level, the way the organ systems work in unity, and the added component of intelligence make us unique living beings. The greatest honor is that we resemble God in image.

Knowing this heritage, we should be expected to uphold our bodies with respect and care. When Jesus did his ministry on earth, He said, "I am come that they may have life, and that they might have it more abundantly" (John 10:10, NIV). Jesus wants us to be healthy for our happiness.

Satan has given society addictions and vices that take away our freedom; and they poison the mind, body, and spirit. Many times I care for patients who use drugs and alcohol and have complete disregard for their health. I ask myself at what point in life did some of my patients make the wrong decisions.

The usual medical guidance and interventions are oftentimes unsuccessful at helping them realize the detrimental effects of their actions. I point my patients to One who has the power to break the shackles of all their habits. At Loma Linda University School of Medicine, we are trained to incorporate the cornerstone of healing, Christ.

As Christian physicians, we must first realize that medicine is guided not only by scientific research, medicine, and surgery, but also that true healing comes from Christ Himself. Sometimes sharing the encouraging words of the Bible with a patient has much more impact than explaining the pathologic effects of lifestyle and uncontrolled disease.

There is always hope with Christ to make lifestyle changes. I am encouraged when my patients are able to take control of their life and illness. I rejoice when, after many office visits and prayers, my patients decide to quit smoking, alcohol, or drugs. As physicians, we have the privilege of working together with Christ, the Chief Physician, to restore the image of God to each of his sons and daughters.

Eric C. Chow, LLUSM class of 2009, is an internal medicine-pediatric physician in Waipahu, Hawaii. This story occurred during his residency in San Diego, California. May 31 is the day he married his wife, Irene.

JUNE

"Make room for the Creator Spirit to use whatever imagination you still have!"

June 1

And He said to me, "My grace is sufficient for you, for My strength is made perfect in weakness." Therefore most gladly I will rather boast in my infirmities, that the power of Christ may rest upon me. 2 Corinthians 12:9, NKJV

She began to notice a vague numbness in her left cheek sometime during her second trimester of pregnancy. It was intermittent at first, almost imperceptible at times, and both she and her primary care doctor attributed it to a nonspecific pregnancy-related symptom. Besides, she had a toddler at home and was too busy to pay much attention to the fleeting sensation in her face.

After her delivery, the numbness increased, evolved to pain and then to a left lateral rectus palsy. By the time she came to see me, her MRI demonstrated a large mass in the left cavernous sinus, one that appeared to emanate from the nasopharynx. I biopsied the mass and then had to make a very difficult phone call. "Lauren, I'm very sorry to tell you that the results of your biopsy showed nasopharyngeal cancer. It is very extensive, involving the brain, and I recommend that you undergo treatment with chemotherapy and radiation."

Of course, she and her husband had many questions, which I attempted to answer in the gentlest way possible. The word cancer strikes a cold fear into anyone's heart and raises numerous questions. What is the treatment like? What will life be like after treatment? How long do I have to live? Nothing can prepare a person for the dreaded diagnosis of cancer.

Lauren was a fighter and refused to be bowed by her disease or her harrowing treatment. She underwent a grueling course of chemotherapy and radiation, with a partial response. She then underwent a second course of radiation, followed by several more months of chemotherapy. During this time, she experienced all of the expected sequelae of treatment—hair, weight, and hearing loss; recurrent infections; and frequent hospitalizations—all the while raising two young children with her husband.

But Lauren, a woman of strong faith and active in her Christian church, gave her testimony frequently to praise God for his blessings. She maintained a blog, which she shared with me and with many others, to give glory to God for His goodness to her, despite her cancer.

She has survived more than four years since her initial diagnosis, to the astonishment of all of her doctors, including me. We know she will eventually succumb to her disease; but by her witness, I am reminded frequently that we are all on borrowed time, having the privilege through the grace of God to live our life here on this earth for a short time.

I continue to be inspired by Lauren's faith and gratitude to Him, and she has touched countless lives through her living witness. In our daily struggles—whether with health, family, career, or finances—we need to be reminded that God is the Creator, Sustainer, and Healer, and will restore all things in the New Earth. As followers of Christ, it is our purpose in this lifetime to share that good news with those around us, to give the message of hope and salvation to a desperate and hurting world.

Marilene Wang, LLUSM class of 1986, is an otolaryngologist, head and neck surgeon in Los Angeles, California. June 1 is the date she graduated from medical school.

Remember your leaders, those who spoke to you the word of God. Consider the outcome of their way of life, and imitate their faith. Hebrews 13:7, ESV

I sat at my desk, mentally preparing myself for another sophomore exam. The room filled rapidly with my classmates. Everyone looked stressed and tired. We all had the same basic questions: "Am I ready? Will I do well? What if I do poorly?" I had studied hard but did not feel very confident that day. Like a thousand bewildered bees, drug side-effects, physiologic pathways, and diagnostic hallmarks swarmed through my tired brain.

"Are you related to Julian Howe?" asked an energetic voice behind me. I could not believe my ears. Julian Howe was my great-grandfather, but who on earth could possibly have made that connection? My answer was not long in coming, for I soon found myself talking and laughing with someone who knew him. It was the lively, 90-year-old Gordon Hadley, CME class of 1944-B, the beloved former dean of the School of Medicine—a respected physician and an administrator of international renown.

At that moment, however, he was simply a down-to-earth, personable man who quickly put me at ease as he told me stories about Julian. "You should come over for a visit some time so we can talk more," he said, as he was leaving. The test was about to begin, but he made me promise to visit him.

Unfortunately, I did not immediately pursue his invitation. Preparing for the USMLE Step 1 exam consumed my thoughts. Sadly, just weeks after I took my boards, I learned that Gordon Hadley had passed away. In retrospect, I should have tracked down his phone number and set up a time to visit right away. He would not have minded. He would have answered my phone call and made me feel like an old friend in 30 seconds.

Despite my missed opportunity, I feel honored to have met him. Obviously, he was a great man—indeed, legendary—and he helped me forge a meaningful connection with a vitally important part of my heritage. More importantly, however, this storied-old-colossus of a physician stopped by my desk to say hello, share a few stories, and put me at ease. That is a memory I will treasure for the rest of my life, and a legacy of true greatness we should all strive to emulate.

Barry Howe, LLUSM class of 2015, is in the combined MD/MA bioethics degree program. He is from Harpswell, Maine. He graduated from Southern Adventist University with a BS degree in biology. Before medical school, he spent a year in the Kyrgyz Republic researching wild walnut-fruit forests.

June 3

Then shalt thou delight thyself in the LORD; and I will cause thee to ride upon the high places of the earth, and feed thee with the heritage of Jacob thy father: for the mouth of the LORD hath spoken it. Isaiah 58:14, KJV

In 1979, when I was a medical student in Japan at Yamagata University School of Medicine, I had a dilemma. I worshipped on Sabbath and did not attend the required classes and exams on Saturday. This nonattendance became an issue with the school. Eventually, the academic dean summoned my father, who had to come all the way from Hokkaido. My non-Christian father was furious when he went to meet with the medical school deans. However, when he returned to my apartment after the meeting, he was unexpectedly quiet.

He finally spoke up, saying: "When I went to your medical school, I met many of the deans, and among them was the student dean, Professor Endo. He came to me with tears in his eyes and said, 'It is tragic to see such a great student like your son unable to continue his medical education because of this Sabbath problem.' Don't you understand how highly Professor Endo thinks of you?" I did know him. Although his class and exams did not occur on Saturday, he regularly showed kindness and compassion to me, even more than I had felt from a local church pastor. I was impressed by the professor's benevolence. The next morning, my father quietly left my apartment for Hokkaido.

Some years later, I departed Japan and reentered medical school at Loma Linda University. During my senior year at LLUSM, I revisited Yamagata with my wife. Because of the incident above, I felt obliged to find Professor Endo and thank him. He was so glad to see me and treated me as if I were part of his family!

Professor Endo then surprised me by saying, "To tell you the truth, I thought over the Saturday issue after you departed from our medical school. I finally concluded that it would be more beneficial for our school system and students if we gave them both Saturday and Sunday off. So, after multiple painstaking negotiations with the Government Health Ministry, we became the first medical school in Japan to give our students both weekend days off. You should feel free to come back to us anytime."

I told Professor Endo that as I had gone so far as to study abroad, I would have difficulty coming back. He smiled at me. Interestingly, after the changes Yamagata University made in student scheduling, they became famous for possessing the highest passing rate on the Japanese Medical National Board Examination. After all, Professor Endo and his entire medical school became partakers of the benefits and blessings that the Sabbath offers!

Now and then I find myself looking back on what might have been. If I had gone back to Japan when Professor Endo invited me, I would have experienced my medical school/residency at Yamagata University, and most likely practiced in Japan for my entire career. Subsequently, I did have to overcome several hard times, but I finally became an epileptologist. Although I did not return to the medical school to which Professor Endo brought a blessing, my heart remains with him. Several years later, I learned of his death. Reflecting on his kindness to me, it was like news of a family member's death. I long for the day when I will see him again.

Hisanori Hasegawa, LLUSM class of 1987, is a neurologist in Michigan. He arrived in the United States on June 3.

Lazy people should learn a lesson from the way ants live. They have no leader, chief, or ruler, but they store up their food during the summer, getting ready for winter. Proverbs 6:6-8, GNT

The setting was an operating room at Yuka Adventist Hospital in Kalabo, Zambia. Large windows on three sides of the room admitted bright sunlight which was the sole illumination for the surgery. Battery powered spotlights were saved for the most difficult cases.

Arthur Miller, CME class of 1942, a retired thoracic surgeon from Roseburg, Oregon, was helping me perform a hysterectomy to remove a football-sized fibroid tumor. The patient was a Losi woman who was under spinal anesthesia, allowing us only an hour or two at the most in which to perform the surgery.

My wife and I were serving, as was Dr. Miller, as temporary volunteers at this primitive mission hospital. He was a strong Christian and demonstrated this in every aspect of his life. One of the most gifted surgeons with whom I have ever had the privilege to work, his skills were legendary. I confirmed with him one story of a record-setting cholecystectomy at LA County Hospital in the days of surgical competitions between the three medical schools staffing that hospital in a bygone era—he and another surgeon had the record of seven-and-a-half minutes skin to skin—a record that may still stand today!

As I worked with Dr. Miller on this case and numerous others, I became impressed with how he always anticipated surgical events—planned or otherwise. He seemed to think 10 or 15 moves ahead. He would arrange surgical packs, retractors, and other instruments to facilitate future actions rather than only those immediately intended.

As the operation progressed, the advantages and permutations of these preparations became obvious. Where I would have mucked around, advancing somewhat inefficiently, we moved cleanly and efficiently ahead with his suggestions. All was controlled and elegant. As Dr. Miller would commonly say, "You will save yourself a lot of time in the end, if you spend a little time preparing your work at the beginning."

What an insightful principal to live by: the better the preparation, the better our execution. May God bless our efforts to carry this out, in our personal lives and in serving our patients.

George T. Simpson, CME class of 1953-A, is chief of otolaryngology, head and neck surgery at Veterans Affairs Western New York Healthcare System Medical Center, and is a professor of otolaryngology and surgery at the University of Buffalo.

June 5

For if you forgive other people when they sin against you, your heavenly Father will also forgive you. But if you do not forgive others their sins, your Father will not forgive your sins. Matthew 6:14-15, NIV

I faced the power of forgiveness while lying on the floor after my husband of 27 years tried to kill me. Up until that time, I thought I had a good marriage.

Life can change in a moment, and those moments are the times when knowing God is with you can make all the difference in the world.

I was locked in a small room, inhaling chemical fumes my husband had mixed together. As I lay on the floor, knowing I had no way out, a text in Scripture came to me as clear as if it were spoken—we must forgive; for without forgiving those who harm us, we can never enter Heaven.

As I struggled to breathe and knew I was dying, I forgave the man who was trying to take my life. I felt a peace come over me, and I knew God was with me. It is a calm that is hard to explain, but the struggle was gone, and His peace engulfed me.

At that moment, God impressed my husband to open the door, checking to see if I was still alive. I tried to pretend I was dead, but could not control the gurgling in my lungs. No longer restraining the door, he left the house. I believe God gave me the strength to cross the large field between our home and a godly neighbor, who got help for me. I found out later that the neighbors had been out of town, but, for some unknown reason, were impressed to come home early.

During the first four days of my hospitalization, the medical staff told my family that they did not expect me to live. I have been left with some residual lung and throat damage which only reminds me of how I was saved from death. I knew, without a doubt, that whether I lived or died, God was with me.

Jan Wilkemeyer attended Andrews University in Berrien Springs, Michigan. She worked at LLU in the HRM department from 1969 to 1979 and later worked in the LLUSM Continuing Medical Education office. This story occurred on June 5, 2005.

And whatever you ask in prayer, you will receive, if you have faith.
Matthew 21:22, ESV

Maybe there is a connection between cars and the testing of my faith. It was Friday, the day of my anatomy final, and I had to be in the classroom at 9 a.m. I jumped into my Honda Odyssey at 8:45 a.m., and started it. Just then, I remembered I had to bring my trash bin to the street; so I turned off the ignition, got out of my car, and ran to complete the task. After that was done, I stepped into my car and turned the key to start the engine.

To my surprise, my car would not start! I kept trying, but to no avail. Panicking, I decided to say a quick little prayer. With my eyes half-closed, I sent one up and then tried turning on my car again. As disappointment befell me, I felt the Spirit compelling me to say a *real* prayer. This second time, I closed my eyes tightly, folded my hands, and took a few deep breaths before sincerely begging God to start my car, because I really needed to get to my final.

After the "Amen," I was infused with faith that God had fixed the problem. I slowly turned the key in the ignition again and was so relieved to hear the roaring engine come to life. Though I was the last one to walk through the classroom door, I praised God that I arrived at my anatomy final just in time.

Another car incident happened when I was a student medical missionary in India, the summer before my second year of medical school. One Sabbath, we were driving an old car down a rugged mountain road to Kodai Kanal Seventh-day Adventist Church. Halfway through the trip, we started hearing weird screeching and clunking noises. Dr. Sundaram, the driver and physician I was shadowing, decided to get out of the car to check on the strange sounds.

As he and Samuel Limbong, LLUSM class of 2015, the other student missionary I went to India with, stepped out, I closed my eyes and said a prayer: *Lord, I know that the devil is trying to prevent us from going to church today. But somehow I know that we really need to be there! You are stronger than him, and I believe that You can bring us out of this and make the car work!* Just then, both of them got back in and said that they did not find anything wrong with the car.

As Dr. Sundaram started to drive again, I was amazed not to hear any more abnormal sounds! We arrived at the church safely, only to find that they wanted us to do special music for them that service. Sam and I had the opportunity to give this testimonial and sing, "In Christ Alone," glorifying our God who brought us to church that day for a special reason.

It might be cars or anything else. All I know is that God definitely answers a prayer offered faithfully and sincerely.

Carrie Lam, LLUSM class of 2015, is from Loma Linda, California. She earned a BS degree in fine arts.

June 7

Careless words stab like a sword, but the words of wise people bring healing.
Proverbs 12:18, GW

One day, our kindergartner, Steve, was terribly slow getting dressed. Since he was so engrossed in the story he was telling me, I seized the opportunity to slip a handsome new shirt over his head and hoped he would not notice. I should have known better. One glance down and he exploded. "I won't wear this shirt! I don't like it!" He raced up the stairs, reappearing a moment later, wearing his favorite old sweatshirt.

During the ensuing altercation, I was proud I never raised my voice and accepted defeat rather gracefully. I kissed him goodbye, and watched as he walked down the driveway. But I was surprised to see him suddenly stop, turn, and start back toward the house. He confronted me at the door and said, "I won't go till you talk nice to me."

Even though I still loved him when he refused to wear the new shirt, my response made him feel rejected. I had robbed him of the "soul food" he needed so much, even to the point that he was unwilling to go without it for only three hours. I am glad he came back and gave me a second chance.

But I wonder how often I have done something similar to my patients. When I must report negative test results, lack of improvement, or dire long-term consequences of their behavior, do they feel understood and accepted or judged and rejected?

We became health-care professionals because we wanted to help people. And, as Christians, surely we should go beyond providing excellent medical care for our patients; we should also feed their spirits.

The famous psychologist, Karl Rogers, identified three characteristics essential in a helping relationship—genuineness, empathy, and unconditional positive regard. I believe Rogers was right in saying that all three are critical. Yet, how unusual it is for a person to communicate all three. I think they are often packaged in a receptive gaze, warm tone of voice, smiles, laughter, and active listening.

My husband and I operate a pediatric clinic. Today, a young mother commented that her son asks to come here. Many of our patients do. I am sure the toys and books in the waiting room can take part of the credit, but we believe the staff is also satisfying a hungering of the spirit.

Five-year-old Steve told me, in no uncertain terms, what he needed from me. Patients ask for diagnoses, tests, and prescriptions, not for genuine empathy and unconditional positive regard. Yet they need those as much as my son did, because healing the body includes healing the soul; and we do not live by bread alone.

Julia B. Swarner earned her DrPH and MPH from LLUSPH. She taught clinical nutrition at LLU for 20 years. Her husband, Orville, LLUSM class of 1965, is a neonatologist.

June 8

Love suffers long and is kind; love does not envy; love does not parade itself, is not puffed up. 1 Corinthians 13:4, NKJV

Among the many teachers to whom I am indebted, one teacher stands out in my mind. I will not mention his name because I did not obtain his permission, and my guess is that he would prefer not to be named. However, many of you reading this (especially former medical students) will probably recognize this particular teacher.

I rented a room in an apartment complex where the rent was low; it was on Starr Street, very close to Loma Linda University Medical Center (LLUMC). My next-door neighbor was a middle-aged single mother with daughters, ages 8 and 10. One day she came to tell me she was being referred for biopsy of a breast lump. She was quite concerned and quizzed me about the procedure. Having recently rotated through general surgery, I did my best to give her the most pertinent medical information possible. I also reassured her that she would receive excellent medical care at LLUMC.

A few days later, she knocked on my door. Opening it, and expecting to hear the results of the biopsy, I was surprised to see that she was beaming with a big smile. I was more surprised when she told me that she had the biopsy done and the result was not good. She was to be hospitalized the next day to have a mastectomy.

I was confused initially, because she was in such good spirits. She explained that her biggest concern was about childcare for her two girls during her surgery. But that problem had been solved. She said that when she hesitated about scheduling surgery, her surgeon learned that she was concerned about her children and immediately called his wife and arranged to have her daughters stay at his house while she was hospitalized.

This teacher probably does not realize the impact that one act of kindness had on my career. While I do not recall any of the things he asked me during my oral examination as a student, this is one lesson he taught that I will never forget.

Daniel J. Won, LLUSM class of 1980-B, practices pediatric neurosurgery in Fontana, California.

167

June 9

From him the whole body, joined and held together by every supporting ligament, grows and builds itself up in love, as each part does its work. Ephesians 4:16, NIV

It seems like such a small thing—and it is. But it was mine and I miss it. And yet, it has caused me to rethink my view of "Whole Person Care."

Not too long ago, I had a too close encounter with a wood splitter. The result was that I have lost part of the tip of my left middle finger. In the grand scheme of things, it is a small loss. My clinical world is pediatric heart transplantation, so I surely cannot complain about my loss when I am with my young patients—all of whom have lost, and gained, a heart. That said, the accident has affected me more than I would have thought likely.

The constant irritating pain was expected. What I did not expect was how much I would miss that part of my finger. By "miss it," I do not mean the functionality of the finger, though that surely is irritating. For instance, even typing this short devotion is harder than it used to be. But—I miss the physical part of it.

This awareness dawned on me about three weeks into this small journey on the other side of the stethoscope. I was feeling kind of depressed, which is not my usual, sometimes pathologically optimistic self. It finally dawned on me that I was mourning the loss of part of me.

I received superb care in the emergency department and afterward. I was particularly struck by the healing power of compassion and competence that was shown to me by a wonderful fifth-year plastic surgery resident. I have nothing but praise for my surgeons and the expert therapists in the hand rehabilitation center. And, I also now know that there was more healing that needed to occur than just the knitting together of my tissue and regaining proper sensation.

I am not wise or savvy enough to be able to describe the psychological underpinnings of a human's sense of self. I do know, though, that it is complicated and likely very individual. What this experience has taught me is that I should be more sincere when I ask how a patient is feeling. They could be physically feeling fine; but within their spirit or their psyche, they could be experiencing loss, worry, sadness, dissatisfaction, or any number of other confusing or upsetting feelings.

I very much value having been trained at, and to be practicing in, an institution that has a core value that appreciates that being well is not just a matter of medicines and scalpels. It includes an understanding that humans are spiritual and emotional beings that combine with a physical being to create a whole person, created in the image of their Creator.

I also know that I, too often, am focused on the nuts and bolts of making sure my patients' immunosuppression med levels are fine, that they are not anemic, and that they are getting their proper rejection surveillance. My additional prayer is to remember that when I ask, "How are you feeling?" I make it clear that I am interested in their whole person response to that question.

Richard E. Chinnock, LLUSM class of 1982, is chair and a professor in LLUSM department of pediatrics. He and his wife, Ruthie, reside in Oak Glen, California.

June 10

May the God of hope fill you with all joy and peace as you trust in him, so that you may overflow with hope by the power of the Holy Spirit.
Romans 15:13, NIV

A strawberry red-haired 23-year-old girl, just one year older than I am, sat in front of my medical school religion class telling her story. Her left jaw had a slight depression, barely noticeable, and not at all affecting the bright smile that never left her face.

A few years earlier she had battled osteosarcoma (bone cancer). As the pictures from her surgery and chemotherapy flashed across the classroom screen, she enthusiastically—yes, enthusiastically—explained the details of her cancerous nodule, split open jaw line, and platinum blond wig. I have to admit I was skeptical of her happy attitude. She said that she was thankful for her cancer, but how was that possible? I have only known cancer to be sad, both life debilitating and life taking.

But, cancer seemed to have a different effect on this girl with the beaming smile. She told us how her life abruptly halted, yet she was glad it had. She believed God had a purpose for her cancer, although she admitted to not always feeling this way.

When she was first diagnosed, she thought the cancer was a punishment. But instead of turning away from God, she prayed fervently for healing in the weeks leading up to her surgery. And on her surgery day, she insisted on a CT scan to prove to her doctor what she already knew—the tumor had been miraculously healed. Touched by her faith in the power of prayer, her doctor re-evaluated the balance between his medical knowledge and his spiritual beliefs. He couldn't justify a CT scan, but was moved to order an x-ray.

A few hours later, she was heading to surgery. God hadn't answered her prayers. Struggling to make sense of her beliefs after the surgery, she eventually concluded that her cancer was a blessing. This transformation was difficult for me to comprehend.

However, throughout her story, she emphasized and re-emphasized that Christians do not belong to this world. Money, success, and health, even for us invincible 20-somethings, are transient and fleeting. She viewed her struggle as a way to share the gospel. When asked about her sunny disposition, she used the opportunity to spread her belief of a promised eternal life for those who cling to God rather than to this world.

I still had a few doubts. Her cancer had barely left a mark. It was probably easier to look favorably on a cured cancer. Yet in her closing remarks, she asked us to pray for her, as she would be undergoing a biopsy of several masses that had shown up on her chest x-ray the previous day. The cancer was back.

At that point, my skepticism crumbled. Her relapse drastically changed the backdrop of her story. This 23-year-old woman, just a year my senior, had lived the tough philosophical questions of life. And she had come away courageous and an amazing witness for God. Patients may be in need of help, but they can also be the ones helping others in need.

Janna M. Vassantachart, LLUSM class of 2016, is from Colton, California. She graduated from Pacific Union College with a BS degree in public relations and journalism. June 10, 2014, is her grandmother's 91st birthday.

June 11

Then Moses and the Israelites sang this song to the LORD: "I will sing to the LORD, for he is highly exalted. . . . The LORD is my strength and my song; he has become my salvation. He is my God, and I will praise him, my father's God, and I will exalt him. Exodus 15:1-2, NIV (1984)

One of the most memorable stories from the Bible is the story of Moses and the Israelites going through the Red Sea. I still remember my brother and me asking our mother to read it to us again and again. In fact, if there are to be games in Heaven, I am planning to ask God to play the "Red Sea Game" so I can walk through a sea.

You remember the story, right? The Israelites had just left Egypt where they had been slaves for more than 400 years. But as they were traveling through the wilderness and had just reached the Red Sea, they got the worrying news. Pharaoh and his army were coming after them. And you could sense the fear in the camp as they began to complain to Moses: Why did you do this to us? Why did you bring us out of Egypt? Now, the sea is in front of us . . . the army is behind us. "It would have been better for us to serve the Egyptians than to die in the desert" (Exodus 14:12, NIV).

Moses does not write this, but he was afraid, too, as he was trying to calm the people down. But then God appeared and spoke to Moses, asking him to raise his staff and to stretch it out "over the sea." And then the impossible happened! A miracle occurred! The waters were divided and the Israelites passed through the sea "on dry ground" and were saved.

But have you noticed how the story ended? We usually stop reading the story right here at the end of Exodus 14, when, in fact, chapter 15 is part of the story of the Red Sea too. "Then [after the passing through the sea] Moses and the Israelites sang this song to the LORD" (Exodus 15:1, NRSV). *The story ended with a song.* And the song was a memorial of what God had done for His people. It was a song about His mighty act. It was a song about His miracle. It was a song about God who did the impossible. And this song was recorded and sung for generations to come.

Think for a moment, now, about the story of Loma Linda University. It seems to be very similar to that of the Israelites at the Red Sea. Travel with me down through the years to the beginning of the twentieth century. Seventh-day Adventism was going through a difficult period as it faced organizational, theological, and financial challenges.

It was around that time, in May 1905, that Ellen White, the founder of Loma Linda University, received a letter from John Burden about a property near the vicinity of Loma Linda, California. As she read it, she replied immediately to him to "secure the property at once. Do not delay for it is just what is needed."

And when the church leaders could only see "the sea" and showed little enthusiasm, Ellen White pressed ahead. In 1905, John Burden purchased the property for a fraction of its original cost and since that time Loma Linda University has grown to serve the whole world, following the example of Jesus "To Make Man Whole." Today, Loma Linda University's miraculous story is our "song" to "sing."

Lord, Thank you for this "song" and the reminder that You are still God of the "impossible" things. Amen.

Theodore N. Levterov, PhD, is director of the Loma Linda branch of the Ellen G. White Estate and an assistant professor in LLUSR. June 11, 2014, marks the 100th anniversary of the first LLUSM graduation.

Observe the Sabbath day by keeping it holy, as the LORD your God has commanded you. Deuteronomy 5:12, NIV

Both my father, Jerry W. King, and my grandfather, Archie E. King, became physicians. In fact, both graduated from Loma Linda University (LLUSM class of 1977-A and class of 1953-B respectively). Certainly, their collective success was inspiring and played a large role in my own interest in the field of medicine. I was, therefore, thrilled and proud to carry on the family tradition when I was accepted to Loma Linda University School of Medicine in 2001. Those positive feelings were, unfortunately, tempered by fear. I had heard how difficult medical school would be. I was not naïve.

I remember asking my father for advice before embarking on my very long road trip from Georgia to California. "How did you do it? Do you have any tips? What was your secret to success?" He gave me a few generic suggestions such as, "Study hard," and, "Don't fall behind."

But then he said the thing that I remember most clearly. "You must stay balanced. You must eat, sleep, and exercise. But most importantly—critically—you must not be tempted to dishonor the Sabbath. The Sabbath is a wonderful gift. If you keep it holy, no matter what, and use it for spiritual renewal, you will be successful. Do not spend it studying for or worrying about an upcoming exam. Use it as God intended: for rest."

At first, that advice seemed obvious and easy. But then medical school started; and I developed a whole new perspective on the terms *busy*, *overwhelmed*, and *stressed*. I understood why my father made a point to give me that advice. I needed that day of rest during those taxing four years. It provided much-needed renewal and strength.

I am thankful that I followed my father's advice. I did not feel any temptation to use the Sabbath as extra "study time." And God indeed blessed me greatly. He gave me His invaluable wisdom. I feel certain that I could not have accomplished what I did without Him, and without the balance afforded to me by consistently having 24 hours to rest my mind and spirit.

The Sabbath truly was "made for man." What a precious gift.

Cassandra Graybill (née King), LLUSM class of 2005, practices obstetrics and gynecology in Mount Vernon, Washington. June 12 is her father's birthday.

June 13

I delight in weaknesses, in insults, in hardships, in persecutions, in difficulties. For when I am weak, then I am strong. 2 Corinthians 12:10, NIV

I was a fourth-year medical student, nearing the end of my training. It was the night before I was to take National Boards, Part 2. Anticipating an exhausting day of examinations, I headed off to bed for a peaceful rest.

Unfortunately, in the middle of the night, an insect found its way into my ear. Seemingly stuck on my tympanic membrane, it proceeded to buzz and flap, trying to free itself. It is amazing the amount of noise a small insect can make! I hoped this "noisome pestilence" would resolve itself soon. No such luck. Repeated buzzing and flapping continued, until finally I got up and drowned the menace by irrigating my ear canal. Peace at last!

Just when I had finally drifted off, my alarm sounded. As usual, my shoe-string food budget of canned soup made for a pitiful breakfast. Lack of sleep, poor nutrition, and added stress had me set up for a dubious day.

I soon headed off to the Loma Linda University campus to take my board exams. Alert enough, I made it through the first half of the examination. By noon, however, I was totally exhausted and hungry. I was looking forward to driving to a nearby restaurant for a decent meal before testing resumed.

However, upon arriving at my car, I discovered that my front bumper was stuck on the rear bumper of the car in front of me. Putting my car in reverse, I tried to disentangle the bumpers. But it proved to be futile. I quickly called to four nearby buddies to lend a hand. All of us together could not dislodge the tangled bumpers.

Shortly thereafter, an old, decrepit man, leaning heavily on a cane, approached me. He offered to "lend a hand," but I declined, not wanting him to injure himself. After all, four strong young men had been unsuccessful. Insisting on helping, he directed me to grab one end of the bumper and he took hold of the other end.

I gave it a half-hearted effort, not expecting success. To my utter astonishment, the car bumper lifted easily upward and backward enough to free my car. After a quick inspection for damage to the other car, I turned to thank the "old man." Amazingly, the "old man" had disappeared. He was nowhere in sight! Remember, I had noticed he had been barely able to walk, even with a cane.

Knowing that it was not possible for such a hobbling "old man" to go more than a few feet, it occurred to me that he had been an angel. Skeptical of angel stories, I wanted a plausible explanation. I quickly ran up and down the street, calling for him and looking behind trees, cars, and buildings, but to no avail. I never found him.

I proceeded to drive to a nearby restaurant, but my mind was no longer on food. I concluded that God indeed had sent me an angel that day in my time of need. I knew that my weakened state was an opportunity for spiritual growth. The text quoted above took on a new meaning . . . "when I am weak, then I am strong."

Jon Richards, LLUSM class of 1979-B, practices anesthesiology in Auburn, Washington.

June 14

But now thus saith the LORD that created thee . . . Fear not: for I have redeemed thee, I have called thee by thy name; thou art mine. Isaiah 43:1, KJV

The Scripture above offers so much encouragement! My Friend knows my joys and challenges and is ever near to comfort me in times of disappointments and joys. My dear wife, Wilma, also had situations that revealed God's protecting care. She was in a serious automobile accident but was unharmed. At a church swim meet, someone jumped off the dock, grabbed her from the back, and the two went down three times, nearly drowning. A young man jumped in the water and saved them both.

As to her physical health, God worked miracles, one by one. Wilma had a normal exam and mammogram in March 1992, but by June 1992 she noticed a thickening in her left breast. A biopsy showed inflammatory carcinoma. Since I was an ob-gyn physician in Pontiac, Michigan, we decided on the University of Michigan Cancer Center for treatment.

Chemotherapy was given, followed by surgery. Twenty-two positive lymph nodes were found. Radiation and a second set of chemotherapy were completed in August 1994. She was in remission until January 2000, when an MRI showed metastasis to her spine. Oral chemotherapy, with three different medications, gave her a good quality of life until the summer of 2003. She passed away on November 15, 2003.

Wilma was a very dedicated Christian lady and served on the executive committee of the Michigan Seventh-day Adventist Church Conference. Her faith in Jesus and her love for her Best Friend were shared with others, as she enjoyed giving Bible studies and being involved in church activities.

Her personal relationship with Jesus, along with medical science, kept her living 11-and-a-half years after her diagnosis. I praise God constantly for the beautiful 52 years we shared together after we met as students at Adelphian Academy in Michigan.

I delight in the promise that God knows each of us by name and has chosen us; both are daily reminders for us to grow spiritually. Having been Wilma's caregiver gave me added assurance of the love that our Heavenly Father has for each of us.

Also, Psalm 73 has strengthened my Christian experience and reminds me to not compare my life and the loss of Wilma to the good fortunes of other people. David almost gave up his faith in God when he looked at the prosperity of the wicked instead of looking to Jesus. My faith is constantly enriched knowing He is my Best Friend.

During my 80 plus years, God has worked miracles in my life and He will do the same for you. Be faithful—be faithful and trust that God will make us whole.

Raymond L. Mayor, CME class of 1955, is a retired family practitioner/obstetrician and gynecologist residing in Berrien Springs, Michigan. He married the late Wilma Cesario, LLUSAHP class of 1951, on June 14, 1951.

June 15

Their descendants will be known among the nations and their offspring among the peoples. All who see them will acknowledge that they are a people the LORD has blessed. Isaiah 61:9, NIV

The older I become, the more thankful I am for my father's blessings. The supreme blessing he gave his five sons was equipping us with an experience with an earthly father, a relationship that made an indelible impression in forming a context in which we could know, follow, and worship a Heavenly Father.

My father worked very hard at creating an environment where each son's identity could be deeply rooted in our family and in our relationship to God. He blessed us with empowerment and helped us learn that not conforming to everyone else need not rob us of our joy. I believe such a view is one of life's most important lessons. Apart from the supernatural activity of the Holy Spirit, no person within a young child's life has similar access to protect the conscience, self-esteem, and motivations like a father.

I remember well the bicycle or bus rides home from school in anticipation of what awaited. Was it the time of year to harvest the honey from the bee hives? Was the vegetable garden ready to be planted? Was it time to make our entrepreneurial wagon route door to door with fresh fruits and vegetables?

My father turned the flash cards for me at a time when multiplication seemed like calculus. He taught us to install sprinklers and program timers. He taught us to set lobster traps; to rig a catamaran; to sharpen the blades of a lawn mower; to remove an outboard prop; to frame an office wall; to lay out, pour and screed a cement slab; and to replace a garbage disposal. And he hugged us whether we were happy or sad. This show of affection made us learn about character and about God.

My father also taught by example, by not being afraid of learning with us. He worked hard, too. Emotionally abandoned by his German father, he started with nothing following the Second World War.

He was awed by Creation, fueling a curiosity with the minutest sea creature to the paradoxes of the geological record. We liked that he read to us, and he, himself, read constantly, including the Scriptures, and he prayed. He walked three miles per day, rain or shine. When prejudice within the American church and culture was rampant, he adopted into our family a boy from Ethiopia. We took trips to visit missionaries.

My father blessed my educational pursuits. When I was 28, his was the most important face I saw when I walked the aisle at my Loma Linda University School of Medicine graduation. When I was 38, his blessing was the most important part of opening our new operation in Shanghai. He blessed with his time and resources our cross-cultural medical and dental ministry in Honduras. He celebrated and blessed my marriage. He has blessed each of our six children. His legacy by the grace of God will live on through them.

Bless you, Dad. Bless you, Carsten Robert Hamann. Blessed be the name of the Lord!

Curt Hamann, LLUSM class of 1988, is president and CEO of SmartPractice®. June 15, 2014, is Father's Day.

Judge not, that ye be not judged. Matthew 7:1, KJV

It was a beautiful morning as sunlight streamed in the freshly cleaned hospital windows, providing a cheerful atmosphere for patients and staff. I had been a utilization nurse for several years and had seen many things in my career, but nothing quite as unusual as what I witnessed that morning.

One of our older pillars of the medical staff was known more for his sometimes gruff demeanor than for his tender side. One could never predict what politically incorrect or abrasive comment might come from his lips. Most considered him a competent doctor but some of the nurses, including myself, had a tinge of fear when he walked in as he made his rounds.

On that tranquil morning, my enjoyment of the peace and quiet on the "4 East floor" was shattered by the loud clatter of crashing basins and bedside tables. Immediately after I heard the sickening crash and thud, I saw the commotion of nursing staff running in and out of a patient's room!

The elderly patient in the room called out in agony. He moaned, pitifully asking for help. His nurse saw him crumpled on the floor—his left hip obviously broken judging by the direction his foot was pointed. She ran to get some IV pain medications.

The patient's attending physician, Dr. Gruff, was just down the hall when the man fell. I went to his room, but we could not immediately move the patient safely. He was lying there, suffering on the floor while we waited for the lift team.

At that moment, Dr. Gruff, without hesitation, came in and knelt down on the floor beside his patient who had fallen out of bed. I could not believe my eyes as I saw the doctor then lie down next to the man, face to face, his white coat stretched out on the tiles. He put his arm around the old man's shoulder, comforting him. "I'm sorry, Mr. Jones. I'm so sorry" he said over and over.

His words were not profound, but the whole scenario brought a tear to my eye. And to that patient, his words and actions eloquently conveyed wonderful comfort, compassion, and healing love. Dr. Gruff was powerless to help as a physician, but he showed Christ-like character by getting down to the level of that fallen patient and letting him know that he cared, reassuring him that help was on the way.

I was reminded again that day of the futility of judging people by their outward appearance. Sometimes the sandpaper façade is only skin deep, and underneath might be a heart of gold.

Vicki J. Simpson is a research nurse at the VA Loma Linda Healthcare System. She is married to James Simpson, LLUSM class of 1970. June 16 is their wedding anniversary.

June 17

Every good gift and every perfect gift is from above, and cometh down from the Father of lights, with whom is no variableness, neither shadow of turning.
James 1:17, KJV

I never thought I would be the wife of a doctor, the mother of three very active children (two girls and one boy, ages 10, 7, and 6), and a full-time graduate student—all at the same time. I look at my life and know that God has given me all of these gifts because He knew I could handle them.

On this particular day, my heart was very heavy after I had dropped off two of my children at school and headed to the doctor's office with the other one. I had experienced a "gut feeling" (mother's intuition) a few days prior and knew something just was not right with my child. Within a matter of days, I had made an appointment to see a tutor and a physician.

The tutoring appointment transpired as expected, but this doctor's appointment made me quite uneasy. However, there was no way I was going to allow my child to see the worry on my face. After my husband and I had been called into the doctor's office, a series of tests was given to our daughter; and we were told the results immediately. There was complete silence in the room.

This perfect gift I had given birth to was diagnosed with an unusual eye disease that had taken away the sight in her left eye. Not only that, I braced myself as we were told that she could possibly lose the sight in her right eye one day, too. For years, I had struggled and prayed to become the type of "perfect" mother that I admired in public with her children. How was my family going to get through this situation without it tearing us apart?

While absorbed in the shock of the moment, my cell phone rang. As God would have it, my favorite aunt was calling to have prayer with me. I excused myself to take the call in the hallway and was able to take time to compose myself so I would not "lose it" in front of my child and husband.

I walked back into the doctor's office and decided that, from that moment on, I was going to be my child's advocate and get the best help possible for her. Since the initial diagnosis, my child's good eye has been patched a maximum of 12 hours a day to try to trick the other eye into working; and she also underwent major eye surgery, but all to no avail. The sight in her left eye has not come back.

I stare at my child every morning before she wakes up, in preparation for helping her to get dressed for the day. I know that despite her circumstances, she is still God's perfect gift from above. Not only is my daughter a gift, but so are your daughters and sons, regardless of any physical limitations—*all* are precious in His sight!

Deia Williams is the wife of Nathan Williams, LLUSM class of 2000. She is the mother of three and a doctoral candidate at Capella University in Minneapolis, Minnesota. June 17 is the birthday of her daughter who is featured in this devotional.

For I am the LORD, who heals you. Exodus 15:26, NIV

It is exciting to see the working of the Holy Spirit, especially when it comes to health care. Throughout our scientifically based education, we are trained to think in specific principles of reasoning, and such reasoning allows for no room beyond the laws of nature. But, as Christian health-care providers, it is not only our privilege but also our calling to collaborate with the Holy Spirit as we work to bring healing.

While serving in our mission hospital at Penang, Malaysia, we wanted to clearly portray to our community that God was an integral part of our hospital. In a country dominated by Islam, Hinduism, and Buddhism, we wanted our hospital to stand out as being more than just a facility that provided health care. So, in gold letters above the main entrance were the words, "God Heals, We Help." We wanted others to see God by pointing them to the true Provider of life.

Two special experiences confirmed to me that God was working through the Holy Spirit in our hospital. One day, a non-Christian visitor commented to one of our staff that every time he visited our hospital, he felt a strong presence surround him. It was an atmosphere that he had never experienced anywhere else. He could not explain it and wondered why it happened. Although this particular staff member was not a Christian, she did know of and believed some in God. She shared with the visitor, "That is the Spirit of their God that fills this place."

The second moving story took place when the Loma Linda University Overseas Heart Surgery Team visited our hospital. One particular nine-year-old Muslim girl was selected to undergo heart surgery. Being old enough to understand the risks of the surgery and even the possibility of death, she was very anxious and fearful. The night before surgery, she was in tears and nearly inconsolable, so our staff prayed with her.

The next morning as she was being wheeled into the operating room, the nurse commented on how calm she was, especially after the night before. The young girl said, "I'm not afraid, because He is with me," as she pointed toward the ceiling. Then she asked: "Don't you see Him? He's right there above me, and He won't leave me."

The nurse did not clearly understand what the girl was talking about until the day she left the hospital. As she was being wheeled out through the main lobby, the Nathan Greene painting of the "Family of God" was hanging on the wall. The young girl said: "There He is. That is Who was with me, and I wasn't afraid," as she pointed to the picture of Jesus.

In the words of Ellen G. White: "The Holy Spirit never has, and never will in the future, divorce the medical missionary work from the gospel ministry. They cannot be divorced. Bound up with Jesus Christ, the ministry of the word and the healing of the sick are one" ("Come Out and Be Separate," Manuscript 21, 1906).

We clearly saw the working of the Holy Spirit in our hospital.

Kenneth Rose, LLUSM class of 1988, is a general surgeon in Enterprise, Oregon. He and his family served at Penang Adventist Hospital from 1994 to 1999.

June 19

And my God shall supply all your need according to His riches in glory by Christ Jesus. Philippians 4:19, NKJV

The impetus for my interest in nutrition and lifestyle change came mainly from my participation in a "natural foods co-op" dining situation at Oberlin College in Ohio. With new enthusiasm I read *Ministry of Healing* and *Counsels on Diets and Foods* by Ellen White.

After completing a project with the nutrition department at Loma Linda University School of Public Health, I felt a desire to obtain a graduate degree in public health but instead, I opted for medical school.

After an internal medicine residency, and then working a couple of years at City of Hope, I could not have been more excited to find a church near my home with a health center that focused on nutrition and lifestyle. This led, in the 1980s, to my working at this health center, which had been started by a church in Southern California.

The health center offered medical care with a lifestyle change emphasis—including health education (individually or in classes) and hydrotherapy, as well as Bible classes offered on Saturday mornings. Eventually, I became the only physician providing medical care there.

For several years, we had booths in the local town health fair. On one of these occasions, we met Flora. She expressed a desire for weight control. While she came to see me for a lifestyle change, she gave back far more than I ever could have imagined. She started to assist with setup and cleanup for our health education or cooking classes. She became the janitor for the health center. Flora also took charge of the bulk mailing of our informative health letter. As a volunteer, she served as an integral part of our team, even though, initially, she was not a church member.

One late afternoon, Flora came to the health center thinking she had gastrointestinal flu symptoms. Upon history and examination, I suspected bowel obstruction. After admitting her to the local hospital that evening, I called for a surgery consult. Flora did have surgery for bowel obstruction, but then ended up, post-op, sedated on ventilator support for an extended period of time.

When it came time to wean her off the ventilator, she seemed to be stuck in a semistuporous condition. Eventually, even after stretching her hospital stay, hoping for a turnaround, we had to schedule a tracheostomy to avoid damage to her throat from extended placement of the breathing tube. I prayed often for her recovery.

Flora had entered the hospital as a very energetic, active woman, with no known lung disease. To see her in her current condition was very disheartening. On my morning rounds the day of the planned tracheostomy procedure, I got a surprise. I walked in to see a completely different patient, one who was fully alert, and clearly not needing a tracheostomy!

Apparently, God had made His evening rounds the night before and changed her status just in the nick of time. Flora came off ventilatory support shortly thereafter. While some might call it a coincidence, I praised God for His timing and mercy.

Shirley Hon, LLUSM class of 1976-B, is an internist residing in La Cañada, California. This story occurred when she was working at Norwalk Adventist Health Center, which has since closed. To enhance her knowledge of whole person care, she has also obtained MA degrees in psychology and marriage and family therapy.

The LORD gave and the LORD has taken away. Blessed be the name of the LORD.
Job 1:21, NASB

Some time ago, I was asked by the parents of one of my patients to come to the bedside of their sick child and pray daily for a miracle. In one of my many visits, the mother shared with me how they had been in this same situation before. A couple of years earlier, another one of their children had been hospitalized, and, despite all the medical attention he received, the child passed away. While the family knew the health of this child was deteriorating, the parents believed God would intervene this time.

One afternoon, as I was getting ready to leave the hospital, I received a page message from one of the nurses asking me to come to the unit immediately. As I arrived, I was informed that the parents of this child had decided to withdraw all life support after he had suffered some complications. The parents had explored all options and after consulting with the medical team, they had come to this difficult conclusion. What the parents had requested at that moment was one final prayer, as a way to say goodbye, with everyone gathered at the patient's bedside.

Among all the family and friends in the room, their church's praise leader was also there. He had brought his guitar and sat in the back corner playing hymns and praise songs at the request of the child's parents. For the next few minutes, the music became the soundtrack that filled the room as we watched the medical team disconnect the small patient from all the machines, and place the child in his mother's arms.

After a few minutes, the father requested to hold his child one more time; and as he hugged him and cried, we heard the praise leader play the song, "Blessed Be Your Name," by Christian songwriter Matt Redman. The father, with tears flowing down his cheeks and one arm carrying his dying son, raised his hand to the heavens and sang the words to that song.

Sadly, after a couple hours, the child passed away. The family never saw the miracle they had prayed for; yet, before they left the hospital, both parents acknowledged that though they did not understand why this had happened, they would continue to praise God, in the good and the bad times. I went home that evening wondering if I could say the same if I were in their place.

Saul Barcelo is a chaplain at LLUCH. He is married to Susana Galaviz, LLUSM class of 2007.

June 21

One thing I do know. I was blind but now I see! John 9:25, NIV

I felt a sense of overwhelming compassion upon entering the exam room and observing Larry struggling to read the eye chart. Barely able to see the big E with his right eye, and only able to perceive light with his left, Larry was beyond legal blindness. Severe cataracts had taken away the vision of this once productive construction worker, who was now desperate and disabled by a back injury.

He was alone in his small apartment to fend for himself. Occasionally, someone would take him out for a grocery run or do simple errands. One time a "friend" helped him; later Larry found out all his possessions and his wallet, including his driver's license, had been stolen.

Late in the afternoon, on the day before his procedure, the surgery center informed our office that due to a new regulation, Larry's surgery would be cancelled unless he could produce a photo ID upon arrival in the morning—no exceptions! Bureaucracy stood in the way of help for a needy patient. I spoke with Larry that evening by phone, and we were both disheartened by the center's unwillingness to bend. We finished the conversation with Larry saying, "It's over an hour's drive, but I'm coming in the morning anyway; maybe something good will happen!"

As I worked through my morning surgery schedule, I was surprised to see Larry ready to go at the appointed time. Unknown to me, that morning the office surgery coordinator had called an "angel," Sharee, the physician/hospital liaison. She was able to gently persuade the center's management to consider sources of identification other than a photo to satisfy the regulation. His procedure was challenging but uneventful, with optimism for a successful outcome.

A wide grin greeted me at the first postoperative exam, with an exclamation, "All I know is, I was blind, but now I can see!"—and he was able to read the bottom line on the eye chart. I asked Larry if he had ever read the stories in the Bible about the sight of the blind being restored. "No," he said, "but now that I can see, I will!"

A short time later, at a mutual friend's wedding, with tears welling up in her eyes, an emotional Sharee shared how this experience had touched her. "I think most people think about glasses, eye exams, minor surgery, and some correction of vision—but not complete restoration. It could actually give someone one of their core senses back, a change that impacts their entire life—functionally, socially, and occupationally. It can also make a huge difference in the lives of others around them. What a life-changing event that must have been for him."

"I will lead the blind by ways they have not known, along unfamiliar paths I will guide them; I will turn the darkness into light before them and make the rough places smooth. These are the things I will do; I will not forsake them" (Isaiah 42:16, NIV).

Douglas Bishop, LLUSM class of 1983, practices ophthalmology in Placerville, California. June 21, 2012, was the day Larry had his sight restored.

And God shall wipe away all tears from their eyes; and there shall be no more death, neither sorrow, nor crying, neither shall there be any more pain: for the former things are passed away. Revelation 21:4, KJV

I closed the door to examination room #3 behind me, where I had just had an office visit with one of my favorite patients. She has been seeing me for chronic pain and depression, but the worst thing for her was disfiguring rheumatoid arthritis. Before we began every office visit, she would show me her gardening magazines, specifically pointing out the annuals and perennials she would love to plant. She would then describe in detail the flower beds she would create if she could turn back time and was young and healthy again. Life before rheumatoid arthritis was beautiful for her.

This sweet patient had come in today for a three-month checkup, but this office visit was unusual. She was still combing through her magazines when I entered the room, but she was more solemn than usual. The spark in her eyes was gone. It was frigid in Pennsylvania that morning, so she was in more pain than usual.

After showing me her favorite gardening plants and flowers, she quietly said, "I hope He allows me to have a garden when I get there." There was no denying who "He" was. Through tears, we talked about Heaven, where there would be no more bugs or weeds. No more harsh winters. No more rheumatoid arthritis.

When I hugged her goodbye, I could only think of one of my favorite hymns, "When We All Get to Heaven." I hummed it for the rest of that day.

> Sing the wondrous love of Jesus,
> Sing His mercy and His grace.
> In the mansions bright and blessed
> He'll prepare for us a place (in her case, a garden).
>
> When we all get to Heaven,
> What a day of rejoicing that will be!
> When we all see Jesus,
> We'll sing and shout the victory . . .

Sharon Michael Palmer, LLUSM class of 1999, is a family practitioner in Columbus, Georgia. She is married to Army Specialist Matthew Palmer. June 22 is the date her sister celebrates her remission from lymphoma.

June 23

Medical school has challenged me in many ways, yet at the same time it has drawn me closer to God. During my brief time at Loma Linda University School of Medicine, I have had the incredible opportunity to learn how to trust God with everything—my finances, relationships, and grades. While it has not always been easy for me to do so, I have learned from past experiences that He is true to His promises.

One experience in particular that helped strengthen my trust occurred at the age of 12, when my father was diagnosed with aplastic anemia. Suddenly my life changed as my family and I were transplanted to the University of Michigan Medical Center, where my father was treated. Through the weeks and months that followed, I was reminded again and again of how God can work through various circumstances to strengthen my faith in Him.

One story from this childhood experience remains especially etched in my memory. Since my father was self-employed at the time of his illness, my family was left without a regular income for the seven months while he received treatment. During this time, we had to rely completely upon God to provide for our needs. I remember praying each day for my father's health and the care of my family.

It was incredible to see how God answered my prayers. When my mother had to pay the bills each month, just enough money would come in from friends, family, and people we hardly knew; and these amounts would cover our expenses. There was never an excess of money—just enough for our needs. At this time in my life, I learned how to turn everything over to God.

This experience and others like it have helped strengthen my faith. However, there are still times when I am facing a difficult exam or stressful situation that my belief starts to waver. It is during those moments that God gently reminds me to look back at the many times He has helped me.

By looking back at how God has guided me through life, I am reminded that I can fully rely on Him to help me through each difficulty I may face in the future. Although medical school is intense, I know He will be with me each step of the way, ensuring that I have enough strength to face each new day—all He asks is for me to trust Him.

Brent Sherwin, LLUSM class of 2015, is from Berrien Springs, Michigan. He graduated from Andrews University with a BS degree in biology. He and his wife, Laura, LLUSD class of 2015, are deferred mission appointees. June 23 is the anniversary of their wedding day.

I will be a Father to you, and you will be my sons and daughters, says the Lord Almighty. 2 Corinthians 6:18, NIV

It has been said that life is made up of moments of profound inspiration. I looked through the windows of our SUV, saw men holding AK-47 rifles, and thought, "How did we get here?"

That Sabbath day in Kabul, Afghanistan, started with sunshine and bright blue sky. An afternoon drive into the gorgeous mountains seemed like a nice way to finish out an already remarkable week. We, a group of six Loma Linda University (LLU) physicians, had experienced an exceptional time in the unique culture of this country, teaching the special people of Afghanistan.

As we lectured to local physicians and toured hospitals, seeing unique medical conditions, it was both incredibly educational and heartwrenching. Our physician team had been blessed by having Borhaan Ahmad, an LLU pediatrician, with us. Borhaan grew up in Kabul and this was his first trip home in nearly 20 years. Seeing Kabul through his eyes made every experience of the trip feel personal to all of us.

We passed through Kabul and entered the countryside, seeing both spectacularly beautiful scenery and a country at war. We stopped to take pictures but Ayub, our driver, warned us not to wander far, as the red-painted side of the rocks surrounding the road indicated land mines. The majestic peaks shining in the sunlight encircled us as we saw one incredible scene after another.

Witnessing these surroundings, I almost felt that I was experiencing "time travel" back to biblical times. I saw large herds of goats and sheep in the countryside, accompanied by running children, bearded fathers, and mothers in long robes flowing in the wind.

Borhaan surprised us by saying: "My father's driver, who was like a member of our family, grew up in a village close to here." We entered the next village, and suddenly AK-47-toting men surrounded our car. I thought, "How did our idyllic journey so quickly change?"

We all exchanged concerned glances as Ayub and Borhaan answered questions from the armed men. Unexpectedly, the leader of the village men stepped forward, suddenly dropped his gun, began talking excitedly, and then embraced Borhaan. Wow! What did the words mean?

The village man in charge was the Ahmad family driver's son. He invited us to his father's home just off the road. In the shadow of the majestic peaks, we watched a frail man in long robes with his cane make his way carefully across a meadow.

Part way he stopped, dropped his cane, and, with tears streaming down his white beard, embraced Borhaan. As we all fought back tears, I thought, "I will remember this special moment forever." I experienced profound inspiration, albeit preceded by several seconds of fear!

What a difference a few moments made as we went from being held at gunpoint to being welcomed as family. We experienced a version of paradise—sitting outdoors on Afghani carpets and pillows, surrounded by orchards, and served fresh fruit, nuts, and tea. I was transported back to the time of Jesus, a time when weary travelers were welcomed. I was reminded once more what a special thing it is to be the sons and daughters of God.

Tamara Thomas, LLUSM class of 1987, is LLUSM vice dean for academic affairs and associate dean for faculty development. She is also vice chair and a professor in the department of emergency medicine.

June 25

I eagerly expect and hope that I will in no way be ashamed, but will have sufficient courage so that now as always Christ will be exalted in my body, whether by life or by death. Philippians 1:20, NIV

A MATTER OF PERSPECTIVE (WHAT DRIVES THE HUMAN SPIRIT?)

A desperate man seeking to buy a cure

A realistic man cherishing the quality of his remaining time

An elderly man with improving numbers at the price of prolonged pain

A young man choosing comfort and dignity in his final days

A conflicted son struggling to make the right choice for his mother

A mother making the loving choice for her three-month-old daughter

A young woman worn years beyond her age in her fight with metastatic cancer

A middle-aged man feeling stronger than ever, despite progression of his rectal cancer

A man turning toward God in order to save his marriage

A man who finds profound strength through the love of his wife

A man with a failing heart unwilling to hear the truth

A man on a ventilator just dying to be heard

A last thread of hope placed in chemo undone by progression to his lungs

A same man's hope redirected toward the comfort of home

A peaceful grandmother opening her eyes to see her grandchildren for the last time

A loving family beside her, reminiscing about the imprint she left on each of their lives

A sobering reflection in the mirror

A weary peer who shares the same hobbies and interests as mine

A reflection of a week spent in Palliative Care

A student physician's perspective on life forever touched by the things he has seen here

Andrew W. Choung, LLUSM class of 2013, is a family medicine resident at Kaiser Permanente in Fontana, California. This poem incorporated his patient care experience from his fourth-year palliative care elective at LLUMC.

He who is faithful in a very little thing is faithful also in much; and he who is unrighteous in a very little thing is unrighteous also in much.
Luke 16:10, NASB

Although time passes rapidly, with its passing one is also given the advantage of perspective. Henry S. Haskins wrote, "What lies behind us, and what lies before us, are tiny matters compared to what lies within us."

As I look back on my medical school days, I am thankful I took my training at Loma Linda University. I am not looking back with rose-colored glasses. But I am sincere in my belief that I had a number of godly professors who were concerned about me as a person and about my training, who emphasized integrity and faithfulness in details.

Our class of 1963 was one of the last classes to have training at both Loma Linda and Los Angeles. While we were at Los Angeles County Hospital and White Memorial Hospital, several of us junior and senior medical students worked at a hospital in Monterey Park, doing histories and physicals. We did a complete history and physical for the sum of $2.50!

One experience stands out that left a lasting impression on me. I had done a number of histories and physicals on ladies but was not completely at ease with the physical contact involved. One day I was told that the head nurse was admitted to the hospital—and it was my job to do the history and physical on her. Now, years later I do not remember why she was in the hospital, but it was not serious.

I had been taught by our Loma Linda University School of Medicine instructors that there should be no shortcuts and no "dry labbing." Therefore, I went through her long history; and the physical included a careful breast examination, which revealed a small mass in one breast. A subsequent biopsy showed an early stage cancer. She then had surgery, which was curative.

This experience taught me to be thorough and to value honesty and integrity, both of which had been stressed by our medical school professors.

I recall a sentence from the book, *Patriarchs and Prophets*: "Integrity in little things, the performance of little acts of fidelity and little deeds of kindness, will gladden the path of life; and when our work on earth is ended, it will be found that every one of the little duties faithfully performed has exerted an influence for good—an influence that can never perish" (Ellen G. White, p. 574).

Jess S. Simmons Jr., LLUSM class of 1963, is a retired dermatologist residing in Joplin, Missouri, where he practiced for 30 years.

June 27

Give thanks to the LORD, for he is good! His faithful love endures forever.
Psalm 118:1, NLT

Taking a step back to look at life and life experiences helps us to cultivate a sense of appreciation and gratitude. Often our reflections or measures of experiences are shaped through comparison with others. That may not always be the best and most satisfying way to measure our experiences or assess our own good fortunes. We are responsible for our own happiness, and perhaps we need a more standardized, objective measure.

Emily Jane Brown, CME class of 1953-A, was a longtime friend; and over the nearly 25 years of our friendship, she taught me many things. She was what many of her friends would fondly call "a colorful character." She could hold her own in nearly any situation.

She was a World War II army nurse in the famed 47th General Hospital of the U.S. Army Medical Corps, which was staffed largely by Seventh-day Adventists; and she later became an anesthesiologist (largely a man's profession at the time). She married late in life and said that her 15 years while married to her beloved Jim were the best years of her life. But what I will always most remember her for is how she characterized and quantified life experiences that were special.

Jane said that she got the idea of measuring life experiences from a college professor while at Pacific Union College. He said that there were a variety of measures to quantify academic progress and accomplishments—credit hours and grade point average. He suggested there also should be a way to quantify exceptional life experiences. He proposed adopting the designation "unit of living."

Such a measure, according to him, could be used to mark life events—experiences that were worthy of celebration and would provide the basis for later reflection. These units of living could be a day at the Huntington Library and Gardens, a special evening with friends, a day with grandchildren, a class reunion, or an evening musical concert.

On June 27, 2011, Jane celebrated her 100th birthday, surrounded by several dozen well-wishing friends and family members. It was a day that was both exhilarating and exhausting for her. Her comment at the conclusion of the day was, "Now that was several units of living." Gratitude makes our lives richer, and perhaps having a way to quantify the best life experiences makes us more likely to reflect on just how blessed we are.

H. Maynard Lowry, PhD, was a professor in and director of major gifts and planning at LLUSD from 2004 until his retirement in 2013. June 27 is the birthday of Emily Jane Brown.

Be strong and take heart, all you who hope in the LORD. Psalm 31:24, NIV

When I first started my practice, I realized how dependent I was upon the Lord to properly diagnose and treat my patients. Every day it became more apparent that I could not have a successful practice without His constant help. Many times, a diagnosis eluded me until a desperate plea to Jesus brought the correct diagnosis in answer to my prayer. The following is one of those more outstanding examples.

We had just come home at noon from church when the hospital called to inform me they had one of my patients, a little two-year-old girl, in the emergency department. She was comatose, but with normal heart rate, normal respirations, clear lungs, and no fever. She had the most severe opisthotonos (spasm with the head and feet arched toward each other) I have ever seen, with her head nearly touching her lower back.

The nurses were finally able to bend her forward so we could perform a spinal tap; and the fluid was as clear as spring water, absent of a single cell. I was completely baffled, but I silently prayed all the harder. From her parents I learned the child was perfectly normal earlier that day as they went to a picnic provided by their employer. They said their daughter had played around, over, and under the table on which they were eating.

I reexamined her, and found everything as before, except that her abdomen was hard as a tabletop. Suddenly, I was impressed that her board-like rigidity was due to a black widow spider bite.

We administered the antitoxin; and within five minutes, she opened her eyes, saw the nurses, and screamed the most wonderful (to me, anyway) wail I had heard since the last baby we had delivered! She never lapsed into unconsciousness again or had any further problems—she was discharged the next day. The family went home and had a thanksgiving prayer session that evening. Their prayer of thanks was small compared to mine, which lasted all the way home and continues to this day.

Calvin Acuff, CME class of 1956, is a retired family practitioner residing in Morganton, North Carolina.

June 29

Let your conduct be without covetousness; be content with such things as you have. For He Himself has said, "I will never leave you nor forsake you."
Hebrews 13:5, NKJV

It was to be our fourth day of flying in the jungle. We had been traveling around South America in the mission plane, screening villagers for eyeglasses and scheduling needed surgeries. We took off early in the morning from the dirt strip in Guayaramerin, Bolivia. Five of us were tucked into the Cessna 182, along with two large suitcases full of eyeglasses and examination equipment.

Only a few high clouds were visible as we climbed into the air. We were planning to visit several very remote indigenous villages before heading back toward "civilization" that evening. About 45 minutes into our first leg, the weather started to deteriorate rapidly. Our pilot tried to find a clear path to our first destination, but to no avail. A nasty thunderstorm rolled down out of the Andes. We needed to find a place to land the plane quickly.

Our pilot then remembered that, on a previous trip, he had seen a nice grass strip in the area and had marked it on the plane's GPS (global positioning system). We descended under the clouds and followed a small river to the "runway." After buzzing the area to clear the local soccer game, we landed and rolled to a stop. A group had gathered around the plane, along with one large Caucasian gentleman. In perfect English, he invited us into his log home to wait out the storm.

We learned that he and his wife, as missionaries, had been living among this small strip of several hundred people for 24 years. The dialect spoken was unique to this tribe and had no written form. And it was certainly a remote area. We were three hours by foot, and more than an hour by canoe, to the nearest dirt road.

This missionary had developed a written form for the local language and had just completed translating the New Testament for them. He proudly showed us a printed copy. As the storm cleared and we prepared to leave, the pilot discovered a low tire on the plane. Our host "happened" to have a 12V air pump. We "happened" to have a small generator with a 12V outlet on it in the plane. We were able to get sufficient air into the tire to take off.

We flew to the next small village, saw a large number of people, and then flew to Riberalta for refueling. On the long four-and-a-half hour slog from Riberalta to Santa Cruz, darkness settled in. About one hour from our destination, the engine started misfiring and losing power. As had increasingly become my habit on this day, I sent another prayer heavenward. My friend next to me also confessed that he was speaking to the "Chief Pilot." It was discovered that the carburetor was icing up. Appropriate steps were taken, and the engine found its rhythm again.

We landed at Viru Viru, and the adventure for that day was over. Every day of life is a gift from our Creator; but, on some of our days, the gifts are brought into especially sharp focus.

David Markoff, LLUSM class of 1986, has been practicing ophthalmology in Waynesville, North Carolina, since 1990.

June 30

And call upon me in the day of trouble: I will deliver thee, and thou shalt glorify me.
Psalm 50:15, KJV

First, let me say that it is hard to believe that 50 years have passed since I earned my MD degree at Loma Linda University School of Medicine. Looking back at many student and work experiences, I can see how one's professional focus is defined by many situations.

When I was a medical student serving at Los Angeles General Hospital, a patient was wheeled in still conscious with a gunshot wound to the forehead. I immediately checked his vital signs and prepared to treat him; my fellow student, Werdna Cochran, LLUSM class of 1962, was on his other side. She asked the patient, "Why do you think someone would want to shoot you?" Werdna went into psychiatry, and I went into eye surgery.

In 1969, as my tour of duty in the U.S. Navy was almost over, I was planning to extend my service. Just one hour before I was going to sign the re-enlistment papers, Robert Shearer, MD, chair of the Loma Linda University (LLU) ophthalmology department, phoned to say there was an immediate need for my services at LLU. Without that timely call, I would not have had the Loma Linda University career I have enjoyed.

When I graduated in 1962, many treatments and diagnostic tests in common use today had not yet been invented. Laser, cryosurgery, modern cataract surgery, innovative medications, operating microscopes, computer imaging, and many similar things were unknown. A long-time patient of mine vividly illustrates the contrast in outcomes. When I lasered him for macular degeneration in 1980, he suffered an immediate reduction of vision from 20/40 to about 20/60. Yet, not to treat would have meant more loss of vision. But when the same patient returned in 2003 with the same problem in his second eye, he was treated with antineovascular medications and still has 20/25 vision.

When a patient suffers from medical and health trouble, we doctors attempt to restore their health and happiness. But we do not heal anything. Instead, we try to fix things with medicine or surgery to allow natural processes to work.

To carry out this task effectively, we physicians all stand on the shoulders of those who taught us: George Kambara, LLUSM class of 1998-hon; Dale Hauck, CME class of 1946; Sidney Brownsberger, CME class of 1925; Robert Schillinger, CME class of 1949; Robert Shearer, CME class of 1943; Lewis George, CME class of 1939; and many others who have given timeless instruction to my associates and me.

Teaching skills to younger doctors who will use your techniques for many years to come provides a rare chance for achieving a kind of professional immortality; thus, teaching at LLU has been a true blessing for me. There is something special about LLU graduates, whose rare caring attitude transcends academic achievement or financial gain as they live the motto, "To Make Man Whole." May God continue to help Loma Linda University, an institution I cherish, carry out its mission.

Wayne Isaeff, LLUSM class of 1962, is an associate professor in LLUSM department of ophthalmology.

JULY

"BE STILL AND KNOW THAT HE IS GOD."

July 1

I have told you these things, so that in me you may have peace. In this world you will have trouble. But take heart! I have overcome the world. John 16:33, NIV

"Laura, Laura, open your eyes! Move your fingers, move your toes! Your mother is here to see you!" Immediately, I woke up to severe aching chest pain with every breath taken, and multiple lines connecting me to various monitors. It was 6 p.m. on Friday, July 1, 2011, and I had survived my second open-heart surgery at Loma Linda University Medical Center (LLUMC).

During my third year of medical school, I took a medical leave of absence between my clinical rotations in order to prepare for my pulmonary valve replacement. As I lay there with my chest incision and surgical drain, I thought back to all the life experiences that brought me to this point. I realized that my dream has always been the same: to become a pediatrician.

As a young girl, on March 2, 1988, I had my first open-heart surgery at LLUMC. Since I was born with Tetralogy of Fallot (a syndrome of four congenital heart defects), I had a complicated four-part surgery which included cutting open my narrowed pulmonary valve.

All the medical lingo seemed strange at the time, but one thing that clearly came to mind was that I was different from those around me, particularly my healthy younger sister. Although I could never keep up with her during swimming and tennis classes, I was still able to maintain a healthy and active life by being involved with marching band in high school and studying bioengineering at University of California, Berkeley.

In June 2008, I was accepted into Loma Linda University School of Medicine, where I truly found meaning and purpose for my life. Through my classmates, I became a Seventh-day Adventist. I learned how to cherish the importance of the Sabbath and the church's health message.

Although I gained stronger faith as an Adventist, I knew that my spiritual convictions were being tested as I was facing the need for a new pulmonary valve. Fortunately my faith grew in more ways than ever possible when I discovered a classmate who also had a heart condition. He lives his life full of gratefulness which he shows by loving God and people. After reading my classmate's testimony, I became determined to use faith and prayer in my practice of medicine.

My unique journey to become a pediatrician gives me an even stronger desire to encourage children with congenital conditions to appreciate and live life to its fullest. Sharing my surgical heart experiences with parents will allow them to have tangible hope for their child's future.

As I lie down during the quiet hours of the night, the loud S2 click of my new valve gives me comfort—and I go to sleep knowing that I have a purpose-filled life ahead of me.

Laura Huang, LLUSM class of 2013, is a pediatric resident at Kaiser Permanente in Los Angeles. She had her first open-heart surgery in 1988 performed by Leonard Bailey, LLUSM class of 1969. On July 1, 2011, he and Anees Razzouk, LLUSM class of 1982, performed her second open-heart surgery.

Blessed are the poor in spirit, for theirs is the kingdom of heaven.
Matthew 5:3, NIV

During a typical day, a general pediatrician has many opportunities to experience instances of joy and wonder. One cannot help but smile sometimes at the sight of a beautiful, innocent face, complete with big, round eyes, and a toothless grin. It is easy to laugh at times when a child will give an odd or funny reply, like when I once asked a four year old what her favorite vegetable was, and she answered, "Hot dog." Or when a five year old asked if getting chicken pox means you will turn into a chicken!

There are also inspiring stories, like the case of the 18-year-old female who grew up in the inner city raised by a single parent and still managed to earn a full four-year scholarship to a Christian university. There are sad stories, too—but often they are tempered by a child's amazing resilience.

I was reminded of this by a young boy on a relatively slow summer day in the office. As I was entering the room, the boy's mother came out to speak with me first—not a good sign. She wanted to share his sad story. She told me how the patient's father suffered from a poorly treated bipolar disorder leading to the father's suicide attempt by cutting his wrists. While the father was profusely bleeding, the seven-year-old son called 911.

Her son received counseling after the attempted suicide incident, and his psychologist recommended that he get a pet. His mother felt that having a puppy really helped him and that he seemed to be doing well. As I was examining the patient, I offered up a silent prayer for all of them. I was unsure what to expect from him, but during our conversation, though quiet and reserved, he seemed content and well-adjusted.

One of the last questions I asked him that day was, "What is the name of your dog?" He answered, "Happy."

Elizabeth Endeno-Galima, LLUSM class of 1998, is a pediatrician at a community clinic in the South Bay area of Los Angeles County, California. July 2 is the date this story occurred and her husband's birthday.

July 3

In every thing give thanks: for this is the will of God in Christ Jesus concerning you. 1 Thessalonians 5:18, KJV

It was so easy for me to take life for granted. Despite a life filled with miracles, from nearly dying at birth to my convoluted path to maturity, I still found ways to overlook special moments God had given me. That was the case until my friend John died.

It was another busy day as I tackled my ever-growing to-do list before leaving the office. Then I heard a knock on my door; before I could even look up there was John's wife saying, "My husband has been diagnosed with a rare form of cancer, and we are devastated." All of a sudden, time stopped and all my pressing deadlines paled in comparison to this news.

Immediately we searched for the best oncologist. John was admitted to one of the advanced regional cancer treatment centers. But eventually all the best efforts failed.

One evening, John walked into my office looking happier than I had seen him in months. We chatted lightly about life, things we planned to do at retirement, and our hope for a happy resolution to his cancer. Then, out of the blue, our conversation shifted. John said, with his voice a little shaky and his eyes yearning for some reassurance, "If I cannot have my previous health before the cancer diagnosis, all I ask is for God to restore my old health for only one week." Puzzled, I wondered what he thought he could accomplish in a week.

Sensing my curiosity, he continued: "There are many things I plan to do with my family and friends. I can make it the most fulfilling week of my life." I knew granting him one week of complete remission would not be impossible for God. After all, God gave King Hezekiah an extra 15 years (2 Kings 20:1-6). I prayed for John as he left my office, hoping that our next meeting would bear good news. But there was never to be a "next time" because that was the last time I saw John alive.

It made me think what a difference one week could have made. I could only contemplate on the many weeks we waste yearly by focusing on the negatives instead of appreciating the little things that make life worth living. Now, at the end of his life, my friend's only wish was that he could turn back the clock and add one week.

The reality, though, is that we are placed on this earth to live each moment only once—each is truly unique. God has called us to live every single day as if it is our last. Surely, this is not an easy task, especially when we are stressed, attending to unruly patients, helping an ungrateful friend, or just confused about life's next move. Still, God has a plan for us daily. Appreciate and enjoy each unique minute, embrace the opportunity, and bask in His promises—one moment at a time.

Samuel Achilefu, PhD, is an adjunct professor in LLUSM department of radiology and LLUSP department of pharmaceutical sciences. He serves as an LLU trustee and consultant to the Office of the Vice Chancellor for Research Affairs. He is also a professor of radiology, biomedical engineering, biochemistry and molecular biophysics, and director of the optical radiology lab at Washington University in St. Louis, Missouri. July 3 is his wedding anniversary.

So do not worry about tomorrow, for tomorrow will bring worries of its own. Today's trouble is enough for today. Matthew 6:34, NRSV

"Oh no," I thought to myself as I looked at the chart of my next patient. "It's Maria, again!"

She had come to see me multiple times in the past few weeks with sundry vague complaints, including headaches, chest pain, and muscle aches. She had also tried various medications without any improvement. After doing multiple tests, I concluded that she had fibromyalgia and recommended regular exercise.

Lately, when I saw her in the clinic, I felt very anxious, which I've learned is a good indicator to me that the patient has underlying anxiety. I asked her if there was anything going on in her life that was contributing to her symptoms, and she stated that there were many issues. She was struggling with her work as a janitor, she did not like her job, and she was worried about her elderly mother in Honduras.

I recommended she see a counselor to help her deal with her stress and anxiety, but I saw by the look on her face that this suggestion was not going over well. She did not think this would benefit her. I felt frustrated—how could I help her if she would not take my advice and seek additional care?

Then I noticed her necklace with the cross on it, and I realized that we had not really talked about her spiritual life. Because I was previously in the military and now practice in a large group, I tend to be "politically correct" and often do not talk with patients about their spiritual beliefs, perhaps being too self-conscious or afraid to impose my religious views on others.

But something came over me (perhaps the Holy Spirit or memories of Dr. Wil Alexander's Whole Person Care class from medical school). I gently asked, "Is it all right if I pray with you?" At that moment there was silence, and as her face went from anxious to surprised, I thought: "Uh-oh, major gaffe; patient grievance letter, here we come!"

But then a slight smile appeared on her face, and she said: "Yes, I would like that." So I put my hand on her shoulder and said a prayer for her, asking God to help ease her burden. A remarkable thing happened—her whole countenance transformed, and peace came over her. It was a result more effective than any pill, and without any bad side-effects. After that visit, she no longer came to my clinic every week with vague complaints. Later, she told me how much she appreciated my praying with her—no doctor had ever done that before.

Several years after this contact, Maria developed an aggressive form of breast cancer with multiple complications. But, through all the suffering from that disease, whenever she saw me in the clinic, she had a sense of calm; we prayed together at the end of each visit. In retrospect, I see that I was foolish to feel that I alone had to help her—we both found that we could consult the Great Physician, and we were both better for it.

Alan Anzai, LLUSM class of 1992, served in the U.S. Air Force for nine years after completing his residency. He and his wife, Shing Chung, also LLUSM class of 1992, are family practitioners in Sacramento, California. July 4 is his wife's birthday and is Independence Day.

July 5

For we have made lies our refuge, And under falsehood we have hidden ourselves.
Isaiah 28:15, NKJV

Any physician working in a rural hospital emergency department (ED) where he or she is the sole physician lacks the support systems that large tertiary hospitals have, such as trauma doctors, surgeons, and ICUs. A doctor in a rural setting has to call on all of his or her training to treat some of the most mundane cases that come through the doors, and also some of the most heartbreaking.

The doors of the ED crashed open as a gentleman who had been in a trucking accident was wheeled in on a stretcher. The ambulance attendant was giving a rushed report to the nurse when I overheard him stating, "And I couldn't get a blood pressure."

I stepped out of the cubicle of the patient that I was seeing and looked across the small ED at the patient. I saw an approximately 20 to 30 cm bruise across the area of his liver. Turning to the receptionist, I ordered her to call the helicopter to come and transport the man to St. Louis. She replied, "He doesn't want to fly." My reply was, "It's the only way I can get him help." She asked, "Which hospital will he be going to?" I replied: "Get started. I will have a place by the time they land."

The gentleman had been transporting log slabs along the winding back roads for which Missouri is famous when his truck left the road and crashed into a roadside bank and trees. When the ambulance crew arrived and assessed him, they wanted to helicopter him from the scene; but he had refused. They finally convinced him to allow them to transport him 25 to 30 minutes to our local emergency department.

As I was stabilizing the patient and preparing him to leave as soon as the helicopter arrived, I got acquainted with the ambulance attendant. He told me that the patient thought that nothing was seriously wrong after the accident and that the ambulance crew was being overzealous.

We finally got his blood pressure into the low normal range and his pulse into the high normal range. The helicopter crew arrived, and I was giving them the report when the patient "crashed." We immediately started CPR and all other available interventions but were unable to revive him.

To this day I have never forgotten this man and the lessons to be learned from his death. If he had accepted the advice of the ambulance crew at the accident scene and allowed them to transport him by helicopter to a large St. Louis hospital with all its available support lines, when he "crashed," it would most likely have been in their ED. He then would have been rushed to the OR, where he could have undergone life-saving surgery. But because of his decision not to believe them, he lost his life, and his children lost their dad.

How many times have our personal decisions affected not only our own lives, but also the lives of those around us? May our decisions be the ones that point us to the Heavenly Physician, who can save lives.

David L. White, LLUSM class of 1979-B, is a family practitioner working in emergency medicine in Salem, Missouri. He served as a missionary in Guam from 1983 to 1988 and has traveled to Mexico on several mission trips since then. This story took place while he was working in Potosi, Missouri. July 5 is the birthday of his wife, Linda.

July 6

And it shall come to pass, that before they call, I will answer; and while they are yet speaking, I will hear. Isaiah 65:24, KJV

God is good! There is no doubt about it. He loves us and shows us His love every day. He knows what we need before we do. I remember one particular day when I was reminded of this.

We live in Summersville, West Virginia—a small town in the heart of the state. It is surrounded by beautiful mountains, rivers, forests, and a large lake. Our church is a small, close-knit group. We also have several new members and enjoy getting to know them better. Our church not only worships and prays together, but we also socialize outside of the church walls.

Once a year, we celebrate Sabbath with a church picnic at Carnifax Ferry. This park commemorates the Civil War battle that took place there. It is a beautiful park, with picnic tables under pavilions, a playground for the kids, and trails to walk through the woods on the way down to the river where the ferry used to be. The park overlooks the Gauley River far below. From that vantage point, one can see the white-water rafters navigating down the rapids. However, by the standards of city dwellers, it seems to be out in the middle of nowhere. And it is.

Our picnic on this occasion was on a gorgeous day. Several of the members brought guitars and one had an accordion. We sang many songs of praise to God. We had testimonies that were very thought provoking, and everyone was blessed. Then we sat down to a potluck picnic feast.

My husband, Mark, and I were sitting under the pavilion, watching the kids play and fellowshipping with the adults near us. Mr. and Mrs. R were sitting out in the sun across from us. They were relatively new members of our church. Mr. R was a patient of Mark's and Mrs. R was a patient of mine. Mr. R had a history of heart disease but currently was not having any cardiac problems.

Mr. R had been talking to some other friends when he became rather quiet. We looked over at him. He was holding his chest and was pale. Mark immediately went over to him. His heart was racing and irregular. Now here we were, miles from the hospital, out in the woods, and with our cars parked several hundred yards up a hill.

Realizing the man needed help, Mark ran up to the parking lot to get the car while I sent up a prayer. When Mark reached the parking lot, he could not believe his eyes. Right in front of him was an ambulance, with emergency medical technicians we knew; the vehicle was just sitting there! We quickly got Mr. R into the ambulance and to the hospital, where, with medication, his atrial fibrillation quickly converted back to a normal rhythm.

This quick response to a need was indeed a miracle and another manifestation of God's great love. It brought to mind that wonderful verse in Isaiah, quoted above, that assures us, "Before they call, I will answer."

Susie M. Wantz, LLUSM class of 1985, and her husband, Mark, LLUSM class of 1983, along with several other LLUSM graduates, are part of a family medicine group practice. They have a daughter and live on a farm in Summersville, West Virginia.

July 7

For I have given you an example, that ye should do as I have done to you.
John 13:15, KJV

It was early in the morning, and the resident doctors I was working with were getting ready for their rounds. I had just completed my first year of medicine, and I was enjoying being back on the wards. I had been assigned to work for two weeks on the family medicine team at Loma Linda University Medical Center-East Campus Hospital. But I never imagined how much I would learn from my attending physician, Dr. Dublin.

As soon as Dr. Dublin entered the conference room, we all sat down around a table and one resident began her report, "Last night, we had—"

"Wait one minute," interrupted Dr. Dublin. "Before we begin, let us all have a quick prayer to ask God to guide us in the decisions we are about to make for each patient." I was shocked to hear that coming from a busy attending physician. I bowed my head.

After we had all finished presenting our patients, Dr. Dublin asked, "Which patient do you think might be willing and would benefit the most from Christian encouragement?" Surprised by his question, I was even more amazed that all of the residents agreed to ask Dr. Wil Alexander, the Whole Person Care teacher, to come later that day to speak with one of our patients whose CT scan showed a mass in his brain.

The next day, Dr. Dublin began with prayer again. This time, after we had finished presenting our patients, Dr. Dublin stated, "Today, before we go on to see the patients, I would like each one of you to say one thing that you appreciate about the person on your right. I know we might not all know each other well, but at least we worked together yesterday, so I am sure you can think of something. I will start."

After each of us had said our appreciations, all the residents thanked Dr. Dublin for the simple, yet very meaningful exercise. "Sometimes I feel as if I haven't done anything right, and it's so easy to forget that I am still appreciated, but I need to let others know I appreciate their hard work as well," one resident confessed.

Later that morning, as we rounded on one of our patients with chronic pain, Dr. Dublin sat close to the patient, and explained to her what the plan would be. Then, he quickly moved on to ask about her social history, and suggested she expand her social network by finding friends at a local church. He added, "You will be surprised how much a positive support system in your life can make a difference in dealing with your pain. Is it okay if I pray with you before I leave?"

After Dr. Dublin finished praying, the patient's tone of voice changed dramatically. She mentioned some of her own spiritual struggles and added how much she appreciated his praying for her. It was obvious to me that she had seen Dr. Dublin's sincere concern for her life, and not just her medical condition.

Before Dr. Dublin, I had not met a physician so committed to the physical and spiritual healing of his patients and students. I thank him for reminding me that I came to Loma Linda University for a purpose: to learn how to practice the healing ministry of Christ by following His example.

Amarilis Cornejo, LLUSM class of 2014, graduated from Southern Adventist University with a BS degree in biochemistry.

Dear children, let us not love with words or speech but with actions and in truth.
1 John 3:18, NIV

For medical students, getting through four years of college is hard enough, but then to follow that with four more years of medical school and three to five years of residency can be daunting. It is no wonder that many medical students and residents get discouraged along the way. They have late nights of studying, early mornings of patient rounds, long hours on their feet in the operating room, and, finally, evening rounds. What is their reward? They get to do it again the next day. That is their reward, but what is the reward they want?

For instance, what does every student of the surgical sciences dream of? "I want to operate!" The real reward comes when students get to experience the culmination of their educational journey. The student becomes the doctor and now, with instruments and suture in hand, the moment where "the rubber meets the road" is before him or her.

Two years after I finished my surgical training, I recognized one of those moments. A 17-year-old young man was taken to the operating room after being stabbed in the chest at a party. Initially, I thought the injury had been to the lung; but upon opening the young man's chest and having pulsatile blood shoot three feet up into the air, we quickly realized the problem was in the heart.

I had the resident put his finger over the hole while the surgical technician and operating room nurse gathered the sutures we would need to repair the heart. While they assembled the supplies, I turned to our medical student and said something I never said before but have often repeated since. "This is where the rubber meets the road!"

"What do you mean?" the wide-eyed student asked. "I mean," I replied, "I have thought about a case like this many times and have reviewed what I would do in my head. I have read about how to place the sutures so as not to tear the heart muscle and make the hole bigger. I mean this is where preparedness meets opportunity."

That experience made me think of today's verse: "Let us not love with words . . . but with actions." All the lectures, textbooks, sermons, and discussions we have ever read or listened to only matter inasmuch as we put those lessons to action. What is our reward? What is the culmination of our long educational journey in our walk with Christ? What opportunity are we being prepared for? I sincerely believe that in our journey as Christians, the rubber meets the road at every opportunity when we need to demonstrate love in a palpable, actionable way.

Two days later, I went by the ICU to check on our patient. This teenager, who was at death's door two nights before was now having waffles and scrambled eggs for breakfast!

Nephtali R. Gomez, LLUSM class of 2004, is an instructor in LLUSM department of surgery and is director of the endocrine surgery division at LLUMC. He received Teacher of the Year Award in 2012.

July 9

Then the righteous will answer him, "Lord, when did we see you hungry and feed you, or thirsty and give you something to drink? When did we see you a stranger and invite you in, or needing clothes and clothe you?" Matthew 25:37-38, NIV

I was in my first year of medical school, new to California, and still a bit startled by the differences between this state's terrain and the West Virginia mountains where I grew up. I was leery of driving in the heavy traffic, but I needed food; so I eventually ventured out.

As I waited to drive away from the store, the sinking sun glinted into my eyes, in just the right way for me to see the handmade sign. "Down on my luck, please help." I do not know how old its holder was, perhaps in her late twenties. She did not smile once in the few moments I watched as she leaned against the Walmart sign behind her. My car was stopped only three feet from her scuffed shoes, but she never really looked up. Then again, neither did I.

We do not have people standing on corners in my hometown. Even so, I am well aware that, all too often, efforts to support people in her situation are abused and monetary contributions go toward things other than food. I had learned to look the other way when people like her passed through my life; but for some reason, she was different. Something about the utter hopelessness of her life caught my attention, and it refused to let go.

I absolutely did not know what to do. I had no money. But suddenly, I wanted to roll down the window and say, "Hi," just to break the barrier of silent judgment. I wanted to ask if she was hungry or if I could take her somewhere and feed her. I wanted to know if she had a pet or if she needed a place to stay. What was her story? Maybe I should just give her my number, in case she needed someone to call and had no one else. Perhaps it was a crazy decision—but most of my life has been rational, far too rational. And it felt right to help.

But I should have acted faster. The driver of the car behind me blared his horn, and I realized that the light was green. I became the target of half a dozen impatient drivers strung out behind me in an irritated line. I hit the gas without thinking and began to move.

Her eyes darted up at the noise and met mine. And while they were just tired eyes, she was a person; I drove away from her when I did not have to do that.

Connection does not happen only when money changes hands. The value of any connection lies in people feeling that you actually care what happens to them—in this case, to her as an individual, not just a nameless face on a corner. I missed a chance to share that with someone who needed it, and I drove away. But there will be a next time. Maybe it will be a library instead of a street corner, a hospital room, or a grocery store. Perhaps—who knows? But whenever it comes, I hope I am ready for it.

Alyssa Erskine, LLUSM class of 2015, graduated from Southern Adventist University and grew up on a farm in West Virginia. July 9 is her birthday.

July 10

One of them, when he saw he was healed, came back, praising God in a loud voice. He threw himself at Jesus' feet and thanked him—and he was a Samaritan. Luke 17:15-16, NIV

There are times in our busy lives that make us stop and become mindful of how important it is to not only say thank you but also look for opportunities to practice "random acts of kindness." The following happened several years ago before my husband and I retired from medical practice; it gave us pause to think about the implications of gratitude.

One particular morning we decided to go for lunch at an intimate French café at a popular mall. Soon after we arrived, we stood in line waiting to be seated. Once at a table, we ordered our favorite soups and sandwiches. We thoroughly enjoyed our meal—especially the fresh, crispy, and delicious French bread!

We finished the meal and my husband asked for the bill. The waiter told us that the bill had already been paid. "What?" we exclaimed in surprise! We really were caught off guard and wondered what in the world . . . ? Our waiter saw that we were not sure what to think and said, "Do you see the waiter standing in the corner of the room? He paid your bill—he said that as soon as you came in, he recognized both of you as his family doctors who had treated not only him, but his whole family."

As we looked over in the direction he indicated, we recognized our former patient. His mother had brought him to our office when he was 18 years old. She was worried that he was depressed. Prior to dropping out of school he had poor grades. He no longer qualified for medical insurance, and the family could not afford medical services. We treated him at no cost and gave samples of medication for him to take home. He was seen several times on follow-up visits until his condition resolved.

We embraced our former patient and thanked him for his generosity. He told us that he had finished high school and was employed full time at the café.

On the way back to our office, we pondered what had just transpired. How could we show more appreciation for others, not only in words, but in actions? Let us not forget to demonstrate gratefulness as we get wrapped up in our busyness—above all, let us be thankful to God daily for life, peace and happiness.

Yolanda Leon, LLUSM class of 1964, is a retired family practitioner. Her husband, Hugo, is a retired general surgeon.

July 11

In all things I have shown you that by working hard in this way we must help the weak and remember the words of the Lord Jesus, how he himself said, "It is more blessed to give than to receive." Acts 20:35, ESV

After my first year of medical school, I found myself with a decision to make. What would I do with the last summer vacation of my entire life? I knew that I did not want to spend it stuck in a research lab while my body's vitamin D stores were slowly depleted. So, some friends and I decided to go on a mission trip.

We eventually found ourselves in the beautiful, tropical paradise of Brazil. We spent much of our time traversing the Amazon River in a large, two-story houseboat, providing medical care to various villages along the water's edge.

During one of our excursions, we left our main camp and traveled through the swamps by skiff to visit some of the more remote areas. One of the local villagers, a man by the name of Maizinho, was our guide. A gentleman of few words, he would sit at the bow of the boat and simply hold up his arm, left or right, to direct us through the marsh and the trees. His family was also famous in the area for making açaí juice, a delicacy made from a berry of the same name. It was a refreshing and delicious treat to have in the middle of the humid jungle.

Two weeks later we were able to revisit the same remote town. I had been joking the whole trip that I had been longing for two things: an *Amigos da Esperança* T-shirt that many of the Brazilian evangelists wore and another glass of that legendary açaí juice.

On one of our final days at the village, a friend told me that Maizinho was looking for me. I knocked on the door to his house, and inside I found him sitting at the kitchen table. Silently, he presented me with an *Amigos da Esperança* shirt, as well as one cold glass of açaí. I gladly accepted both.

Later, I found out that he had given me his own personal shirt, quite literally the shirt off his back. I also learned that açaí had been scarce in the village, and he and his wife had scrounged around to make a single cup of the juice, just for me. I did not even know that he had heard me talking about wanting those things. I was completely overwhelmed by his act of utter selflessness.

It was then and there that I realized the real reason I was on that trip. It was not to provide medical care because, to be honest, a twenty-something with only one year of medical school under his belt is basically useless. I thought I went to Brazil to help others, but I was the one who needed help.

Through a man, a shirt, and a drink, Christ was revealed to me in a real and humbling way. We often give to others when we have excess, but this gentleman taught me that true service comes when you give all that you have to another.

Bradley Cacho, LLUSM class of 2014, is from Lodi, California, and graduated from Pacific Union College with a BA degree in religion. He served for a month in Brazil as a medical missionary after his first year of medical school. July 11 is the date he departed for Brazil.

Come to me, all you that are weary and are carrying heavy burdens, and I will give you rest. Take my yoke upon you, and learn from me, for I am gentle and humble in heart, and you will find rest for your souls. Matthew 11:28-29, NRSV

The well-known verses above quoted from Matthew offer several insights. First, the words came from the lips of Jesus, who lived this human life, and they offer comfort, encouragement, and hope. Other versions enrich the meaning by using such words as *weary* and *overburdened, tired* and *heavy laden,* whose work is *hard,* whose load is *heavy.*

Does this human condition as described strike a responsive chord in the hearts of many responsible and diligent workers—especially in the medical profession? We, who have gone through medical school and residency (or are in it now), know all too well the endless studying, the long hours and sleepless nights, and the ever-changing challenges to providing better medical care.

Second, the verses are a heartfelt invitation from the God of limitless resources. *The Message* Bible has a unique paraphrase of the verse, which reads: "Are you tired? Worn out? Burned out . . . ? Come to me. Get away with me and you will recover your life. I'll show you how to take a real rest. Walk with me and work with me—watch how I do it. Learn the unforced rhythms of grace. I won't lay anything heavy or ill-fitting on you. Keep company with me and you'll learn to live freely and lightly."

Third, the text reveals the secret of entering into such an experience with Christ. The key word, a verb, is *learn.*

Sometime during my high school years I came across two Italian words that have grown in significance to me. The words, actually a phrase, were *"Ancora Imparo."* It was the motto of that renowned genius, Michelangelo, and means "Still Learning." It has stood the test of time. Whether in times of success or failure, in times of prosperity or adversity, in times of happiness or sorrow, or in times of knowledge or ignorance, it still rings true. "Still Learning" denotes not just rote memorization or the all-pervasive accumulation of knowledge, but the humble, wholehearted seeking after God—continually.

Eric Ngo, LLUSM class of 1963, is an associate clinical professor in LLUSM department of preventive medicine and LLUSPH department of health promotion and education.

July 13

He must increase, but I must decrease. John 3:30, ESV

L iving the life of a full-time student and part-time worker for three years, it seemed as if the only tempo I knew coming out of graduate school was a busy, fast-paced routine. And it did not slow down later, as I had hoped.

It was a mad dash after finishing school in June—planning and coordinating my sister's *quinceañera* in August and maid of honor responsibilities for another sister's wedding in October. And all the while, I was studying for my boards scheduled for the end of October. Then I went straight into working three jobs.

I loved all these moments and experiences and was excited for the changes in my life. But a couple of months into this schedule, I felt burned out. I had difficulty managing my time, mainly because I was still living the "routine" I had while in school. Time was precious, and in order to do everything I wanted—my quiet time with God, exercise, family, friends and hobbies—I had to fit them in somewhere.

Then the day came when I felt beyond exhausted and miserable. I thought to myself, "This is no way to live." Sure, I was doing everything I wanted, but my mind and body were spent. The reality of how I had been living those last couple of months began to set in, and it was this: My life was changing, and in order to allow those changes to have a place in my life, I could not add to what I already had on my plate. I had to clear some space to allow "life" to fit more comfortably.

I realized that breaking a three-year long habit might not be easy. I am still working on accepting that I will need to let go of the way I knew my life to be in order to allow for what it is now becoming.

One thing I have started doing is placing a pause in my day by taking "snapshot" moments. In the midst of feeling so rushed from sun up to sun down, I realized, when my head hit the pillow at night, that I could not think of a single moment in my day when I was truly happy and at peace.

So I started to purposely create those moments. I would "snapshot" the falling autumn leaves, the smiling face of a stranger, or even the sounds of the birds outside my window. As I started doing this activity, I began to recall those moments at the end of my day. Each recollected "snapshot" would bring a warm smile to my face.

This exercise reminds me of what it means to live the Christian life. Christ says, "Whoever finds their life will lose it, and whoever loses their life for my sake will find it" (Matthew 10:39, NIV). Sometimes we try to cling to those things we did before we knew Christ and had a relationship with Him. But it does not work that way. In order to allow Christ to fully transform our lives, we must die to the things we once knew, because only then, can He give us more and truly make us into everything we were made to be.

Jackeline Angulo, LLUSAHP class of 2012, graduated with a master's degree in nutrition and dietetics.

Then call on me when you are in trouble, and I will rescue you, and you will give me glory. Psalm 50:15, NLT

It was a warm July night. The freeways were clear and the drive to the Riverside County Regional Medical Center was uneventful and quick. Uneventful was fine; I just wished it was not so quick as I arrived at my job too soon. It was my first week as an intern; I had graduated from medical school only one month earlier. And I really was not looking forward to my first overnight shift as the cross-cover intern.

As I met my co-intern for the sign-out of patients, I was handed five team lists. Each team had a cap of 20 patients. I would need to serve as the on-call physician for all the non-ICU patients who belonged to the five teams. Needless to say, I was a tiny bit anxious about what the night had in store for me.

Actually, the night was a blur. I did not sleep a wink. I will admit, though, that this was partially my own fault. In theory, I could have slept in the little bit of downtime I did have. But, instead, I sat on my chair with my computer logged in, "just in case."

During that night, I remember calling my senior resident multiple times for what I felt to be "stupid" questions—questions that someone called "doctor" should not have to ask. My telephone calls were often prefaced with, "I'm sorry to bother you," or, "This is a dumb question, but . . ." Yet each time I called and woke up my senior—and I am positive I woke him up even though he tried to sound awake—he never once criticized me.

I really appreciated that he was always there to support me, whether it was joining me at the bedside of a patient, or offering advice over the phone. There is nothing quite like the sinking feeling of your first overnight shift as the cross-cover intern. There is also nothing quite like the feeling of knowing there is a senior resident ready to back you up at the other end of a phone call.

And as Christians, the feeling of finding yourself lost and confused, in a completely intimidating, frustrating, terrifying, or faith-testing situation can be utterly overwhelming. The great news, though, is that your Heavenly Father is eager, happy, and willing to support you through your time of uncertainty—and He's only a prayer away.

Jeffery Wonoprabowo, LLUSM class of 2012, is an internal medicine resident at LLUMC.

July 15

For I, the LORD your God, will hold your right hand, Saying to you, "Fear not, I will help you." Isaiah 41:13, NKJV

In July of 1953, my husband, Joe Riley, CME class of 1954, and I were driving from Loma Linda, California, to Lansing, Michigan, for his medical preceptorship with Lee McElmurry, CME class of 1942. With us were our two sons, ages 3 and 18 months. In those days, before the Interstate system, we were traveling the old Route 66. As it approached Flagstaff, Arizona, the road began winding up into the mountains, sometimes with curves so sharp that one could not see oncoming traffic for any appreciable distance.

We were driving an old, well-used 1941 Ford, purchased a short while before. It was fairly reliable on level roads, but on a steep grade, it had a tendency to stall. Traffic was busy as we approached Flagstaff. We shifted the car's gears, hoping to make it up this steep grade. In our attempt to keep moving, we began to approach the oncoming traffic ahead of us. As we slowed down, the inevitable happened—the engine stalled and we came to a stop.

Quickly, my husband put on the car's brake and said he would try to push the car and turn it around, thus heading the car downhill until we could restart the engine. He asked me to get behind the wheel and steer. I felt panic rising in my heart because a huge bus suddenly came around the curve at full speed traveling in the opposite direction.

I could not envision being able to turn around when we had no view of what would be coming toward us as we were crossing the road. I was immobilized by fear, but my husband went to the rear of the car and leaned in to push. Suddenly, a shiny, black, "old time" Model T-type truck pulled up behind us and a man jumped out, calling to my husband to stop! He came up to our car telling us not to try to turn around as he pointed to the sheer 100-foot drop beyond the edge of the road.

He said, "Let me push you the rest of the way up until your car will start." Skeptical about the power of that little truck, my husband got back in the driver's seat. As the truck crept toward us, we felt the gentle push against our bumper; we began to move slowly but very easily up the steep grade. In a few moments, we reached level ground and quickly found a spot where we could pull over and thank him for his help. However, as we turned to look for his truck, it was nowhere to be seen.

We sat there momentarily stunned by what had just happened, realizing that God had indeed sent an angel to save our lives. As the years have passed, we have recounted that story many times, always giving God credit for His mercy and protection on that mountain road. We are convinced that our guardian angel appeared to us—driving a little black truck!

Jean M. Riley's late husband, Joseph L. Riley, was a graduate of LLUSM class of 1954. He became well known at Florida Hospital as the founder and organizer of the JLR Medical Group—a large anesthesiology group serving the Florida Hospital System. Joseph and Jean were married for 62 busy and eventful years before he passed away in July of 2010.

July 16

Choose my instruction instead of silver, knowledge rather than choice gold, for wisdom is more precious than rubies, and nothing you desire can compare with her. Proverbs 8:10-11, NIV

I grew up in Virginia, immersed in the early American history of the Historic Triangle—Jamestown, Williamsburg, and Yorktown. I attended a small, conservative, loving church. When I was fortunate enough to be accepted into the Loma Linda University School of Medicine (LLUSM), many fellow church members warned me about the crazy, liberal people in California. "Watch out and return home as soon as you can, or they might change you out there!"

After I finished my pediatric residency, John Mace, LLUSM class of 1964, asked me to join the pediatrics faculty. I am sure some of "my people" in Virginia feared for my soul. I stayed in California partly because I was single and there were about 2,000 more single Adventist women in Loma Linda, California, than in Hampton, Virginia! But I also stayed because of my amazing mentors.

Lyn Behrens, LLUSM class of 1963-aff, is the most efficient person I have ever known. She demonstrated careful and complete patient care and amazing administrative skills.

LLUMC faculty physicians, Sanford Schneider and Stephen Ashwal, showed me that there are many different approaches to providing great patient care. I will never forget going on rounds with Dr. Schneider and checking on a teenager admitted with status epilepticus (unremitting seizures). I had spent much of the previous night with this patient, administering every anticonvulsant known to man, but without effect. Dr. Schneider stooped over the still seizing patient and in a stern voice said, "You stop that right now!" The patient did! I thought I had witnessed my first miracle, but then Dr. Schneider informed me: "I knew they were pseudo-seizures; no one could still be seizing after all the medicine you gave her!"

I consider John Mace my medical father. My parents have been the greatest mentors anyone could wish for, but are nonmedical. Thus, I had much to learn about being a physician. Dr. Mace had a great sense of humor. In the playroom, he once pretended a giant stuffed Cookie Monster bit his arm. A toddler did not think that was funny at all so Dr. Mace immediately held and comforted him.

Kindness and compassion were modeled each day I worked with Dr. Mace. I soon realized that he knew everything! He is brilliant, but so unassuming about it. I came to him with a difficult case one day, and he said he might have a few articles in his file to help me. When his secretary brought the articles, I found he had written one of them.

In 1994, my wife (yes, I did find the most beautiful and bright woman by staying in Loma Linda!) and I moved to Washington state. Several years later a family drove 90 miles and took a ferry across Puget Sound to see me. Their son had congenital rubella syndrome, and Dr. Mace had cared for him for years. When they moved to Washington, they were happy to make that drive just to see a physician Dr. Mace had trained.

I thank God for the Christian mentors at Loma Linda University. Indeed, Loma Linda did change me, though not in the way my friends in Virginia had feared!

Les Richards, LLUSM class of 1980-A, is a pediatrician in a multispecialty group in Anacortes, Washington. July 16 is his wedding anniversary.

July 17

Be strong and courageous, do not be afraid or tremble at them, for the LORD *your God is the one who goes with you. He will not fail you or forsake you.*
Deuteronomy 31:6, NASB

Three years after graduating from college, blessed with a husband and two children, I decided to go back to school. Initially, the "phobia" that kept me from considering medicine was my aversion to anything involving eyes. Even the thought of contact lenses or eye drops turned my stomach! With this obstacle in the back of my mind, I nevertheless enrolled in classes to complete my medical school prerequisites. I prayed for direction and realized the only way to overcome my fear was to face it.

In an effort to obtain some clinical experience, I applied for a position at an Arizona donor organization as a tissue recovery technician. This job would involve recovering skin, bone, or even a heart from cadavers. After a few months, I finally heard back—but from an unexpected department—the eye bank! I knew this was God's hand, and I heard Him challenging me. This would be my moment of truth; either I would succeed and know striving for medicine was not a mistake, or I would fail and introduce even more doubt into my mind.

I endured a month of rigorous training that involved chart review, blood draws, and cornea recoveries. I flinched and struggled my way through three training recoveries and was finally cleared to proceed alone. I had chosen to work 12-hour night shifts so I would be able to spend more time with my children. On my first shift, I was paged for a donor in Bullhead City, a four-hour drive from Phoenix. Fortified with caffeine, I started the journey alone.

After reviewing the hospital's medical chart for suitability, I headed to the funeral home to find the donor. Expectedly, the mortuary was dark and creepy, and I had a mini panic attack as I opened the body bag. In it was an elderly lady with a thin, withered body who had undergone a double mastectomy due to breast cancer. The first step was to complete a physical exam and draw blood for the required donor-screening tests.

Unfortunately, my attempts to retrieve blood were in vain. I was distressed when I thought about returning empty-handed so I desperately tried neck as well as groin veins, but without success.

As a last-ditch effort, I called the triage coordinator back in Phoenix to let him know what was happening. He calmly walked me through a "cardiac stick," where one puts the needle directly into the chest. I did as instructed and breathed a sigh of relief as the tubes of blood filled effortlessly. This was the turning point; from then on, removing corneas was no problem for me.

Something amazing happened during my time spent performing recoveries. I became proficient and satisfied that my work provided an important service to those in need of transplants. God had made His point. I knew that I would be able to deal with any difficulties in medical school. Not only did I learn to appreciate ophthalmology, but I also gained a deep respect for those who give of themselves, even after death.

Priya G. Lewis, LLUSM class of 2015, graduated from University of Maryland with a BA degree in economics. She was ocular services coordinator at Donor Network of Arizona for two years before beginning medical school. July 17 is her birthday.

July 18

Many are the plans in the mind of a man, but it is the purpose of the LORD that will stand. Proverbs 19:21, ESV

It is evident that God completely changes your life when you give it to Him. Often the change happens over time, as we allow the presence of God's love and wisdom to shape our willful flesh. Sometimes it happens because of a storm.

After high school graduation, I worked in my parent's restaurant for money, hung out and partied with my friends, and aspired to be a professional athlete. Contradictory to such a lifestyle, I often felt a desire to know more about God. I tried studying the Bible on my own but understood little of it. Thankfully, God knew my desire and provided the understanding through a willing servant.

One day while my brothers and I were helping our father load our moving truck, we noticed that our neighbor, George Detloff, was also moving. We did not know him very well but were curious enough to inquire of his plans. Amazingly, we learned we were moving to the same neighborhood, two houses down from each other.

Not long after our move, my mother was having a conversation with George and shared with him that I had been trying to study the Bible. George, a Seventh-day Adventist, took this opportunity to invite me to a Bible study at his home. After studying with George for four months, I wanted to be baptized; with that decision, the change began.

Shortly after giving my life to God, I felt convicted that I was supposed to attend college and become a doctor. Prior to this, I had no plans or desire to even attend college, but I proceeded to work hard in my classes, and God blessed.

I took the MCAT a year late and thinking I would have a free year, I took a temp job working in a machine shop. I applied to only one medical school that year for early admission—not expecting to get in.

On July 18, 1997, I was working in the machine shop and was planning to go for a mountain bike ride after work. Around 3 p.m. that afternoon, the storm made its presence. Its mighty wind and rain bellowed an assertive "no" to my plans for a mountain bike ride. Disappointed, I went directly home.

Upon my arrival home to what had suddenly become a clear afternoon, my father greeted me with a knowing smile and said, "Do you think God loves you?" I gave a questioning look in response and replied, "Yes." Dad just continued to give me that same knowing smile and instructed me to go talk to my mother.

Through her happy tears all I was able to understand was to quickly call Dr. John Thorn, LLUSM associate dean for admissions. I called him and he explained to me that he had been trying to reach me since early afternoon. His call was urgent and his question, which had to be answered by 5 p.m., was "Would you like to be a member of the Loma Linda University School of Medicine class of 2001?"

I became part of the Loma Linda graduating class of 2001 and completed a surgical residency in 2006. God has blessed me in my journey. He has opened doors for ministry through Bible studies in my office and has given me a successful practice. I have learned, from that summer day in July 1997, that God can change the direction of your life in an instant. If not for that storm, I would have gone mountain biking rather than to medical school.

Douglas W. Cook, LLUSM class of 2001, is an adjunct assistant professor in LLUSM department of surgery. He practices general surgery in Hanford, California. July 18 is the date this story occurred.

July 19

If you, then, though you are evil, know how to give good gifts to your children, how much more will your Father in heaven give good gifts to those who ask him!
Matthew 7:11, NIV

His name was Peter—an outgoing, over-achieving 15 year old, a little small for his age, a straight-A student, and soccer player. He loved body surfing and, during a day at the beach with his family, dove under an exceptionally big wave. Brutal in size and force, it churned him into the sand head-first, rendering him instantly and permanently paralyzed from the shoulders down.

A few weeks later, he was admitted to the Inpatient Spinal Cord Injury Rehabilitation Service at Loma Linda University Medical Center. Back in those days, the rehabilitation for quadriplegia took nearly six months of hospitalization, with daily grueling therapy and nursing care. There was no World Wide Web or social media to help expand Peter's world now that he could not stroll down the street to hang out with friends. The cell phone had just made its debut.

One would think Peter did not know that he would never kick a soccer ball, write a math equation, or dress himself again. He gave 100 percent to his therapies, his young face intense as he learned to use his few remaining muscles to make up for so many he had lost. With both stoicism and humor, he endured the often-painful medical challenges associated with a high spinal cord injury.

Peter's positive attitude and focus during an unimaginably difficult time impressed this young physical medicine and rehabilitation resident. It was not long before our conversations went from the "What happened?" of the history and physical examination to the "and then what?" of friendship.

He described somersaulting through the gritty ocean brine, unable to move; and I asked a sincere, but silly question: "Were you scared?" The answer was anything but silly. Peter's slender shoulders moved up and down in a gesture of acceptance. "I knew my dad would come. I just held my breath and waited for him to come get me."

Peter's father was noticeable, mainly because he was always in the background. From morning to evening, he accompanied Peter—attending therapies, offering encouragement, and doling out tough love when necessary. He was a quiet man, speaking softly in his Eastern European-accented voice. But there was no hiding the strength behind his kind eyes.

If Peter was admirable in so many ways, it was easy to guess from whom he had inherited or learned those traits. There was no doubt his father loved Peter without reserve and intended to take every step of this arduous journey with him. He would also insist Peter become the best he could be, despite his life-changing injury.

As quoted above, Matthew 7:11 says that God wants to give His children good gifts even more than earthly parents do. He loves us with abandon, walks through every dark valley with us, and has good plans for our lives, despite the crippling effects of a sin-marred world. How much peace we would have if we, like Peter, remembered that no matter what happens, our Father is with us; He is coming, and all we need to do is hold on and wait for Him.

Esther Chough Lee, LLUSM class of 1988, is an assistant professor in LLUSM department of physical medicine and rehabilitation (PM&R) and is the PM&R department chief at VA Loma Linda Healthcare System. July 19 is her birthday.

And Enoch walked with God: and he was not; for God took him.
Genesis 5:24, KJV

WENT FOR A WALK

There was a note waiting for me when I woke up.
It said, "Grace, I went for a walk. Mom."
It was a simple note, but I treasure it.
My Mom is getting to the place where her walks are taking her further and further away
    from me.

And one day she will not be coming home.
How do you tell the one that gave you birth, "Goodbye?"
I believe you really never do.
It is an unnatural thing, this thing called death.
It grates against our very nature.
It is not the way it is supposed to be.

I do not want to say, "Goodbye," to the one who has always been there.
I want to hold on.
But one day the Lord will take her.
And on that day, I will hold on to that note.
I will tell myself, "She just went for a walk."
"Soon she will be coming home."
That is how it is supposed to be.

And that is how it is going to be!
There was another who took a walk and did not come back.
God took him to His home.
It will not be long now, and all those who have taken long walks with their Lord will
    return to us.
You see, "Goodbyes" are not necessary.
"I'll see you soon" is more appropriate.

All I need to know is in that note.
"Grace, I went for a walk. Mom."
She will be back.
I know she will.

Grace E. Radoycich, LLUSM class of 1987, is a pathologist residing in Mesa, Arizona. This entry was
inspired by her mother, Helen Radoycich, whose birthday is July 20.

July 21

But the gift of God is eternal life in Christ Jesus our Lord. Romans 6:23, NIV

My earliest contact with health care at Loma Linda University was as a patient back in 1954. My parents—second-generation missionaries to India, were working at Spicer Memorial College at the time. Early on a misty morning, I was riding my bicycle at "break-neck" speed when I met with a bone-breaking accident. I refractured my left forearm in the crash. The break was compound and comminuted.

Three years earlier, when my family was at Vincent Hill School in northern India, I had fallen while on a school camping trip, breaking both bones of my left forearm. Dr. I. R. Bazliel, an orthopaedist and the medical director of the Simla Adventist Hospital, treated that injury with an open reduction and placement of Vitallium® plates.

Following the bicycle accident, a classmate and friend of Dr. Bazliel at the Indian Military College Hospital in Pune reduced the fracture and placed the forearm in a lightweight traveling cast. Fearing that I might need a bone graft, he advised my parents to take me to the United States for more definitive treatment.

Those were the days when air travel was not as fast as it is today; it took us more than two days to make the journey from Bombay to Los Angeles. There, at White Memorial Hospital, Dr. T. Gordon Reynolds, CME class of 1923, the chief of the orthopaedics department, examined me, looked at the x-rays of the reduction, and decided that he could not improve on the work that the Indian army surgeon had done. He elected to wait until the healing was complete, and then he removed the plates that had been placed at the initial injury.

Interestingly, Dr. Bazliel was in an orthopaedic fellowship with Dr. Reynolds at "the White" during that same time, and he provided "continuity of care" halfway around the world! I have often reflected on my experience, for it was while a young patient on the pediatric unit that I first expressed my intention to be a "doctor."

I remember well not only the two hospitalizations and the operation at "the White," but also the seemingly long trips between our home in Upland and Los Angeles to my clinic appointments. I also remember the concerns my parents harbored about the expense of my care. At the final visit my mother went to pay the doctor's $625 fee, which may not seem like much today, but which was more than two months' salary for her while she was working as a registered nurse at Pomona Valley Community Hospital. I can still see the expression on her face when she saw Dr. Reynold's scrawl across the bottom of the statement: "Paid in full." Tears of gratitude and relief were freely shed!

The words of an old hymn, recently repackaged and revived, come to mind: "Jesus paid it all, All to Him I owe . . ." My professional experience as a physician has been everything that I had hoped or dreamed it would be. I continue to feel a strong debt of gratitude to those who introduced me to the healing ministry of Jesus and who nurtured my professional career at Loma Linda University—and above all, to Him. "Jesus paid it all, All to Him I owe!" What comfort! What assurance! What hope!

Ted Mackett, LLUSM class of 1968, took a general surgery residency at LLUMC which was interrupted by two years of service in the U.S. Air Force. He then completed a colorectal surgery fellowship at St. Mark's Hospital in London, England. Currently, Dr. Mackett is chair of the department of surgery at Adventist Medical Center in Portland, Oregon.

Jesus said, "Let the little children come to me, and do not hinder them, for the kingdom of heaven belongs to such as these." Matthew 19:14, NIV

Recently I manned a booth for Loma Linda University at a convention in Sacramento. The centerpiece of our booth was a full-size replica of the "Come Unto Me" sculpture that stands at the entrance to our Medical Center. It represents Christ sitting on a bench, with a young boy holding a puppy sitting next to Him. There is so much emotion about the way the artist has crafted Christ's face. I cannot quite put my finger on it. Could be love, could be laughter, maybe even understanding. Whatever it is, it is definitely inviting. Looking at this sculpture makes a person want to interact with it.

During my second day at the booth, a herd of young kids came up, wanting their picture taken with the sculpture. What started out as an innocent group picture soon turned into kids climbing around the sculpture, walking on top of the bench, shaking hands roughly with the figure of Christ, and otherwise causing general mayhem. You know, typical kids.

They were soon gone, but left behind a mess of literature and other trash around the sculpture. I began to clean up, brushing the dirt and other items off the bench. On the hem of Christ was a piece of lint that I went to remove. Only, as soon as my fingers touched it, I realized that it was not a piece of lint.

It was, unfortunately, a booger. A BOOGER!—a piece of nose mucus! And I was touching it—yes, touching it! No gloves. Straight hand. Seriously? A booger? On the hem of Christ? I went to the bathroom and washed my hands, of course, followed by a quick rubdown of the sculpture.

Later I thought, "Who would wipe a booger on a sculpture of Christ?" It seemed quite disrespectful. But then I remembered that there is a pure innocence about children, with their love of animals and of other children—but most of all, a love of Jesus.

As I stood at the booth on another evening, a little girl around the age of two walked toward me. She did not seem to be with anyone, but, with rare boldness, she walked right up to the sculpture of Christ and climbed into His lap.

Quite animatedly, in her high little voice, she told Him all about her day. She gestured toward her "owies," and even told Jesus how excited she was about her new kitten. As she finished her story, she stood on Christ's lap, and with her arms wrapped tightly around His neck, leaned over and kissed Him. It was a beautiful sight to behold.

Dustin R. Jones was the associate director of the LLU public relations department from 1999 to 2013. He is now manager of marketing communications at Kalispell Regional Medical Center in Montana.

July 23

It is the same way with the resurrection of the dead. Our earthly bodies are planted in the ground when we die, but they will be raised to live forever.
1 Corinthians 15:42, NLT

Today is my oldest son's birthday. It is a bittersweet day, as we recently lost Greg to a rare form of brain cancer. He was born during my husband's senior year of medical school while I was finishing my degree in medical technology. Greg was a bright, energetic, and handsome little boy.

When Greg graduated from Loma Linda University School of Medicine (LLUSM) in 1987, he was near the top of his class. We were so proud of this fine young man who always followed the Golden Rule. He went on to become an interventional radiologist, married, and had two beautiful children.

One Sabbath after church, he shared with me that he was carrying a heavy burden. He had something growing in his left temporal lobe. I immediately called the family together at our house, and we attempted to make sense of what was beginning to happen . . . to him and to our family. Life can change drastically in a few moments.

He had GBM, the worst possible news. Glioblastoma multiforme (GBM) is a very rare, aggressive cancer. We all knew what that meant. The journey began. But Greg was a valiant warrior, exhibiting great courage and faith. The surgery was a success, with no known tumor left behind. Greg was having Sabbath dinner at his dining room table with the entire family within 48 hours after his surgery. We considered that our first miracle.

Of course, next followed proton radiation treatments, 30 of them. Neither the proton nor chemotherapy made him significantly ill—our second miracle. Following his last proton treatment, my husband and I put him on a plane to join his family at Leoni Meadows Camp in California, where he presented a lecture, another miracle.

In March of 2012, Greg hosted his LLUSM 25th class reunion and left that week for the NIH in Baltimore, Maryland. He was evaluated and chosen to participate in a vaccination research study. While there, he was told the tumor had returned so he was scheduled for a second surgery. The entire family traveled to Maryland to be with him. Again, the surgery was successful. However, in May the tumor returned once more.

That summer, all 14 Watkins traveled to Hawaii and Mammoth Mountain, California, to be together. Many conversations were held with Greg, expressing our love and appreciation and the common affirmation that we serve a sovereign God who is faithful—always. As long as Greg could speak, he declared his unwavering faith in our God.

We also learned the value of faithful friends. A warm hug and a reassuring "we are praying for you" sustained us throughout our journey. This support continued to the day of his passing, February 18, 2013. We were overwhelmed with the outpouring of love and caring at the time of Greg's death. Nearly 1,000 attended his memorial service. Greg truly would have been amazed and overwhelmed.

I would like to share what we have learned from this journey. You have to make a conscious decision to trust, no matter what, and not question the love of God. There are no earthly answers, but there is a mighty God who is in ultimate control of all eternity. We are grateful for the story of salvation and the blessed hope it brings to each of us.

Dixie Watkins graduated in 1962 from LLUSAHP's medical technology program. For years she has been a dedicated volunteer for LLU Medical Auxiliary, LLUCH, and LL Ronald McDonald House. She and her husband, Hubert Watkins, LLUSM class of 1962, have four children and five grandchildren.

For he shall give his angels charge over thee, to keep thee in all thy ways.
Psalm 91:11, KJV

Most of us have experienced Divine appointments and interventions, but often are unaware. These Divine interventions may have influenced medical decisions or other areas of our daily life.

I experienced a number of such interventions, but will share the most glaring and startling to me. This took place on the Feather River Highway, while I was en route from Quincy, California, to Oroville, California. It was the summer of 1959, between my first and second years of medical school at the College of Medical Evangelists.

My classmate, Vernon Sparks, LLUSM class of 1962, and I were doing blister rust control for the U.S. Forest Service in the Plumas National Forest. It was a Friday afternoon, we stopped work about noon and headed toward Lodi, California, to spend the Sabbath with my parents. My father and I had traded vehicles for the summer. He drove my Studebaker sedan, and Vernon and I used his 1949 Ford pickup.

The engine on the pickup had been overhauled about 5,000 miles prior, and it ran flawlessly, until, suddenly, a loud clanging noise came from the engine compartment—it awakened me, the driver. I had noticed Vernon had dozed off a few miles back, as the ambient temperature was increasing with the altitude drop. We came to a quick stop, turned off the ignition, and hurriedly opened the hood expecting to find broken metal, but all seemed in order. We then noticed we were on the wrong side of the road, and next to a 1,000-foot drop-off, where there was no guardrail.

Being nearly penniless medical students, we were not looking forward to the expense of a tow truck to Oroville and a motor overhaul. I was certain that the engine had been destroyed and driving a bit further would add to the repair bill. We decided that if we could ease the truck around the bend, we could coast much of the 16 miles down into town. The engine started, albeit with considerable clanging.

As we drove very slowly, the noises began to abate. After a few miles we drove a bit faster. We then gained the courage to drive all the way to Lodi at regular highway speeds, as the abnormal sounds had totally subsided. We drove the pickup the rest of the summer without any mechanical attention. The engine operated without any problems.

While there may be an explanation for the noise which emanated from the engine compartment, the timing of those loud sounds was, without a doubt, Divine intervention waking us to prevent almost certain death.

Harley D. Miller, LLUSM class of 1962, is a family practitioner in Chehalis, Washington.

July 25

Treat others as you want them to treat you. Matthew 7:12, CEV

It was an anxious plea for help. In fact, there was a very frantic voice on the other end of the line. It was a call one evening, out of the blue, from someone I did not know, whose name I hardly recognized. The time was about 40 years ago in the early 1970s, a time in which being gay carried much more of a stigma than it does today.

"I am just wondering if your church has any programs that can help me," were the first words I heard. This surgical nurse calling me apparently had learned of my church affiliation from someone on the hospital staff. It was clear I was not the first person he had contacted, nor was my church his initial target for help.

The voice continued. "I am gay and I am desperate. My family has judged me as evil and has rejected and disowned me. I have no friends. I have sought professional help without results. I have tried everything I know to overcome my condition, and I'm at the end of my rope. Do you think you or your church could help me?"

How should I respond? The one thing I knew for sure was that my particular church, at that time, had no program to assist him. I was recently out of training as a nephrologist, so this was not the typical consultation I was used to receiving. Nor was my own background such that I was likely to offer much relief for his pain. What to do? A fairly lengthy conversation ensued which I felt, in spite of my best efforts, was unlikely to have alleviated his despair.

After hanging up, the one thing I still remember clearly is how inept and powerless I felt to address a situation I did not begin to understand, and one for which I probably had underlying subconscious prejudices of which I was unaware. I had no further communication with this gentleman, but the news I received a week or so later was that he had committed suicide which left me profoundly sorrowful.

Coming early in my career, this experience was just the first of many incidents that left an indelible impression on my mind. Numerous biblical references regarding judging and acceptance are pertinent. Black and white answers are often inappropriate and even harmful. "Don't condemn others, and God won't condemn you. God will be as hard on you as you are on others. He will treat you exactly as you treat them" (Matthew 7:1-2, CEV). "People judge others by what they look like, but I judge people by what is in their hearts" (1 Samuel 16:7, CEV).

People are burdened by many problems they did not choose to have. Who can tell what is in their hearts? *Only* God knows the hearts of His children.

Robert E. Bond, LLUSM class of 1964, is a retired nephrologist residing in Salt Lake City, Utah. This story took place in the early 1970s near the beginning of his medical practice.

Thy gentleness hath made me great. Psalm 18:35, KJV

To be certain, many excellent, knowledgeable, experienced and dedicated individuals have helped me in my education and in my career in medicine. Those who have left the greatest impression on me, however, are not those who gave the most interesting lecture, taught the most complex principle, wowed with their spectacular God-given skills, or even spent the most time with me.

What I have enjoyed most about my experience at Loma Linda University (LLU) has been learning from and working with people who demonstrate the gentle spirit of God, the One who always desires to lift us up. I would like to comment on a few of these people, beginning with a teacher.

While I was in college, Steve Yellon, PhD, from the department of perinatal biology, was my mentor in a summer research program. As important to me as his teaching the scientific process was his willingness to collect our data (by sacrificing study hamsters) at all hours of the day and night. It was a job that should have been mine, but one that he understood was difficult for me. His kindnesses and easygoing spirit made for a memorable summer.

In medical school, there were many who devoted themselves to their students, both in the classroom and on the wards. In particular, Jeff Cao, LLUSM class of 1971, cheered us on from the trenches, selflessly devoting extracurricular time in order to help us prepare for our exams.

Later on, in fellowship training away from the LLU campus, a couple of Loma Linda University graduates continued my wonderful training. Rendon Nelson, LLUSM class of 1980-A, one of my professors at Duke University, offered enthusiastic world-class instruction in clinical and didactic abdominal radiology. He displayed a remarkable ability to take pride in the contributions of trainees and hospital staff, treating all alike from the top down, while consistently minimizing our shortcomings.

The following year in Philadelphia, I was ever impressed with the cheerfulness and even temperament of our interventional radiology (IR) section head, Geoffrey Gardiner, LLUSM class of 1973-B, who was available no matter how tight the schedule or late the hour. Never once did I hear a terse word leave his mouth or see exasperation on his face; busy weekends were merely excuses for group pancake trips nearby.

Early in my LLUSM career, when confronted with some complications that threatened my confidence, I would go sit in the office of vascular surgeon Ahmed Abou-Zamzam, MD. There I was presented with words of kindness and encouragement. Also, Rebecca, one of our IR technologists, always radiates an optimistic and easy countenance, no matter how tedious or desperate the case or how ungracious or unappreciative our patient.

And I must also acknowledge, last but not least, my father, Douglas Smith, LLUSM class of 1966, who was a teacher formerly, and is now a colleague. He has taught me to see sheep where others may see wolves.

Reflecting on the selflessness of these individuals reminds me to attempt to emulate our gentle Father. Perhaps a colleague Dan Kido, LLUSM class of 1965, summed it up well when he admonished me to not covet personal achievements, but rather strive to achieve all for the glory of God. Loma Linda University is a special place that will continue to flourish as long as humbleness thrives.

Jason C. Smith, LLUSM class of 1996, is an associate professor in LLUSM department of radiology, assistant professor in LLUSM department of basic sciences, and program director for the division of interventional radiology. July 26 is the wedding anniversary of he and his wife, Ruth.

July 27

Blessed is the man who trusts in the LORD, And whose hope is the LORD. For he shall be like a tree planted by the waters, Which spreads out its roots by the river, And will not fear when heat comes; But its leaf will be green, And will not be anxious in the year of drought, Nor will cease from yielding fruit.
Jeremiah 17:7-8, NKJV

Tromp, tromp, tromp, tromp . . . The methodical plod of my sneakers hitting the pavement on my way home had its usual soothing effect on me one late afternoon during my third-year surgery rotation. I was post-call that day, after being in the hospital for over 24 hours. I had headed home for a short nap. I needed to clear my head before I started studying for the next day's quiz.

As I ran down my well-traveled sidewalks through the neighborhood, I could not shake the feeling of something being amiss in my life. *Was it an upset stomach from something I scarfed down in the hospital cafeteria this morning between cases? Was it exhaustion from being on call all night? Was it worries about the upcoming quizzes and tests?* I wiped the sweat from my forehead, still plodding along. No, this feeling was something deeper.

"Your soul is dry."

What? My soul is dry?

"Yes, you feel you have nothing extra to give to your patients. That's because you're not getting anything from Me to give to them."

Hmmm . . . maybe You have a point there, God.

"I know you have to be at the hospital well before I wake up the sun each morning, but if you don't spend some time with Me to receive My Word and My love, then you will have none to give to My patients."

Mulling over His words, I plodded on.

I knew moving to the desert for medical school would be hard for me, a mountain girl from North Carolina, who is happiest out in the forests exploring trails or picking berries. Even harder than dealing with the location, though, was dealing with the constant bombardment of the common disease, called "busyness," that physicians experience. This disease was threatening to turn my soul into something like the raisins I threw on my oatmeal that morning.

God made it clear to me during that afternoon how essential it was to have daily time alone with Him. In order to survive in the scorching desert of the medical profession, I would need to dig deep. My roots would need to make constant connection with the life-giving water of Christ.

But how, God? Having daily devotions was easier before third year! How can I carve out room for anything more into my schedule now? I'm already exhausted all the time.

"Just let Me handle that, My child. All you need to do is spend time with Me."

I rounded the corner and turned down my favorite street in the neighborhood, the street lined with big, tall, shady . . . trees!

Tromp, tromp, tromp, tromp . . . *Okay, God, You're going to have to help me dig deep!*

Sarah Belensky, LLUSM class of 2013, is a family practice resident in Boise, Idaho. After completing residency she looks forward to spreading the healing ministry of Jesus Christ overseas. She is a deferred mission appointee.

"For My thoughts are not your thoughts, Nor are your ways My ways," says the LORD. *"For as the heavens are higher than the earth, So are My ways higher than your ways, And My thoughts than your thoughts." Isaiah 55:8-9, NKJV*

Working with the Forest Service, we had controlled the lightning strike forest fire by late night. At that point, I was told that I could head down the mountain. "Down the mountain" meant going home to get my old Chevy and an older trailer. Then I would be starting out for medical school at Loma Linda University.

I only had to go down the western slope of the mountain to reach the trail. But having no moon to guide me meant that the faint Government Issue headlamp, which was bouncing around on my Forest Service hard hat, was crucial when it came to finding my way. Ahead of me was the dense willow thicket that I had to go through, then up a small rise, and I would finally be on the trail.

Scratching my way through brush and willows, I finally broke through the last of it. The night had been moonless, but as I started to go up the rise, the moon edged up over the mountain. But it was in front of me! I was supposed to be going west with the moon behind me. Using my faint headlamp, I had completely turned around and was going up the mountain that I had just started down.

All my gut feelings told me to go straight ahead. But I had faith to believe that God was not playing tricks with the moon. So down I went, but this time with the moon behind to guide me. Coming out on the other side, I found the little rise I was looking for and descended back to the Forest Service workstation.

Why this story? Several times in medical school, and even after, I was firmly convinced that the Lord had approved my plans and goals to do great things for Him. But then He would shut the doors of opportunity that I thought were certain and good. Instead, He would put the moon at my back and show me better ways than I could have dreamed.

For as the Lord says, "Neither are your ways My ways . . . ." In fact, His way is best!

Gary H. Harding, LLUSM class of 1967, is a retired pediatrician residing in Troy, Montana.

July 29

And they took note that these men had been with Jesus. Acts 4:13, NIV

"**M**orning worship before medical rounds?" my friend inquired, with a look of surprise.

"That is exactly right!" I replied.

Even though White Memorial Hospital was the flagship of the Loma Linda University School of Medicine many years ago, for junior and senior medical students, much of their clinical experience was obtained at another medical center run by the county. Consequently, the integration of spirituality with medicine in such a secular institution of learning was out of the question.

But it was a different situation at "the White." At the discretion of the attending physician, such integration could exist, but not as a routine. So, I was extremely happy to have my short internal medicine rotation there under the tutelage of two fine Christian physicians who made it a practice to have worship prior to their medical lectures and rounds.

The worship was brief, focusing on the ministry of Christ the Healer, and was closed with prayer. These two attending physicians took turns conducting the worship. It was not their style to pontificate. But I just loved the way they prayed. It was heartwarming to hear them talk to God with a conversation-like prayer and apparent that they had a close relationship with Him.

That spiritual connection happened nearly half a century ago. My—how the brief contact with these two godly men positively impacted my life and my practice later on! The message came loud and clear that if I wanted to have a good day, start it right. And the way to do it was to talk with the Lord before getting involved in the day's activities. That became my adopted guiding principle.

There was something else I learned from my close observation of the two physicians. Their visible attitude toward patients helped me appreciate the value of every soul. Their patients were not "numbers" or medical "cases," but people—individuals in need of help, to be treated with kindness, compassion, and respect. To me, their exemplary lives were truly the personification of the motto of Loma Linda University: "To Make Man Whole."

After all these years, many of the medical pearls they gave us may have faded from memory. However, their day-by-day Christian life that made such an indelible imprint in my mind lingers on. In my opinion, the compliment accorded to Apostles Peter and John could also be descriptive of these Christian doctors: "and they [that included me] took note that these men had been with Jesus" (Acts 4:13, NIV).

Looking back, I wish I had taken the opportunity to tell them how their down-to-earth Christianity has blessed me beyond measure. Both have gone to rest, but the day will soon come when I can express my gratitude to them face to face for contributing so much to my professional and spiritual life.

Wellington O. Manullang, LLUSM class of 1964, completed an obstetrics and gynecology residency at White Memorial Medical Center and worked there from 1969 to 1976. Moving to Washington he joined a group practice with several other LLU graduates in Renton. Now retired, he is frequently involved in health seminars overseas.

Hear my prayer, LORD; listen to my cry for mercy. When I am in distress, I call to you, because you answer me. Psalm 86:6-7, NIV

When I graduated from Loma Linda University, both my wife and I wanted to go overseas as missionaries. However, I was subject to be drafted into the Army. I chose to enter the National Guard as a way to begin paying off our school debts.

Before joining, I made it clear that on Saturdays I would honor my duty to care for the sick, but I would not take part in military exercises. This request was granted. That worked well, until one Sabbath a Federal Inspection was to take place. I reminded my commanding officer of my commitment, and he replied, "You will attend and that is a command." When I refused to attend, I was made to sign my resignation papers which were sent to the Governor for his signature.

Because I wanted to stay in the National Guard, the Minnesota Seventh-day Adventist Conference service representative and I went to meet with the Commanding General for the National Guard in Minnesota. He greeted us with, "I know Adventists. My neighbor is a member, and a nice fellow when he is not drunk."

With that awkward beginning, he said, "Let's see if your papers have been signed by the Governor. If they have, there is nothing I can do." So he called the Governor's secretary, and she said he had left for the weekend. She looked, and said there was nothing on his desk.

Before long, the commander said, "There is one way this could be avoided; you could attend another unit's Federal Inspection on a day other than Saturday. Let me call the Governor's secretary again, just to see for sure that your resignation is not there."

He called and she said, "I'll look again, but I am certain that there is nothing there." She came back on the phone, surprised, and said, "Dr. Robinson's resignation is here, but it is unsigned by the Governor." The commander told her, "Hold it, and I will see to it that the doctor's resignation shall be rescinded."

I was able to stay in the National Guard until we started our mission appointment. To this day, I believe God placed those unsigned papers on the desk.

William W. Robinson, CME class of 1960, is a family practitioner in Yakima, Washington. This incident took place when he was in the National Guard in Minnesota before leaving for mission service.

July 31

The LORD is my strength and my shield; My heart trusts in Him, and I am helped;
Therefore my heart exults, And with my song I shall thank Him.
Psalm 28:7, NASB

The White Coat Ceremony is a highlight in every aspiring physician's career. It serves to mark the starting point of our professional journey and to initiate us into the role of being a doctor. My White Coat Ceremony was no different. It also provided one of the deepest spiritual lessons I have ever received.

At the ceremony, Dr. Robert Orr, a renowned medical ethicist, spoke about the professional responsibilities engendered in being a doctor and wearing a white coat—a symbol intimately associated with our role. He addressed how in trust relationships—where one party has more knowledge and power—the greater party has the ethical responsibility to prove himself or herself as trustworthy. He ended with an appeal for us to be responsible physicians and to prove ourselves worthy of the trust and respect our communities give us.

I left the ceremony that evening thinking about what an interesting analogy Dr. Orr had provided for the Christian journey. While we are in trust relationships with our patients, we are also in an analogous relationship with God. However, in the case of our spiritual relationship, we are the less knowledgeable and less powerful partners. Thus, while we have the responsibility to prove ourselves worthy of our position, God also must prove Himself worthy of our trust and respect. He must show that He deserves the faith and worship we give Him.

With this thought, I then asked, "How has God proved Himself?" While philosophers and scientists can think of many reasons for and against the existence of a personal God, the ultimate proof of God's role in our lives comes from a personal encounter with Him. Has God shown Himself to me? The answer, unequivocally, is that He has shown Himself faithful to His word over and over again.

From the time I really, truly asked God to take control of my life, He has kept His promises. He has been faithful—from helping me with a seemingly impossible college class to sustaining me through the MCAT to bringing me to Loma Linda University.

Just the fact that I am even in medical school now bears testimony to the greatness of my God! Now, I ask you, "How has God kept His promises in your life?" Perhaps you feel He has not kept them. I challenge you to open the book of Psalms, read until you find something applicable to your life today (it will not take long!), and claim that promise. Then, in faith, wait until He answers your request.

Stephen Thorp, LLUSM class of 2016, is from Oliver, British Columbia. He graduated from Southern Adventist University with a BS degree in music, organ emphasis. He is vice president of his sophomore class. He is a deferred mission appointee and looks forward to a career in medical missions. July 31, 2014, is the date of the White Coat Ceremony for the LLUSM class of 2018.

AUGUST

"IT IS EXCITING TO KNOW HOW LOVE CAN FLOW
FROM GOD THROUGH US TO EACH OTHER
SO UNIQUELY! SO JOYFULLY!"

August 1

Hearing this, Jesus said to Jairus, "Don't be afraid; just believe, and she will be healed." Luke 8:50, NIV

I would assume that one of the reasons a student chooses an Adventist medical school is to learn how to practice medicine in a Christ-centered way. That certainly was a large part of my decision to attend Loma Linda University. I wanted to be taught about medicine in a way that emphasized emotional, spiritual, and social health as important parts of maintaining ideal physical health.

And I did learn. First, I was surrounded by caring instructors, who wanted me to succeed so badly that they went above and beyond to help me study and assure my success. Next, there were attending physicians who truly practiced "whole person care." These physicians followed the biblical example of Jesus in their focus on body, mind, and spirit.

So the groundwork was laid, but how was I going to implement the lessons I had learned? Was I the doctor that prayed with every patient? Was I comfortable wearing my faith on my sleeve? Did I want patients to know that I was trusting a Higher Power to guide me in helping them? As a young doctor, I did not yet know all the answers.

A series of events helped me find my way to practice Christ-centered medicine. These occurrences began as I waited for my three-year-old son to come out of surgery for his broken arm. A minor procedure, yes, but he was my baby!

Then, it was my turn, lying pregnant in a hospital bed with 24 hour-a-day monitoring for 5 weeks, attempting to keep my little girl where she needed to be, and not in the neonatal intensive care unit. And finally, I sat with my husband in the surgeon's and then the oncologist's offices, listening to the diagnosis given him. "Yes, it is cancer." "Yes, you need more surgery." "Yes, you will need chemotherapy."

I was able to see miracles performed, right up close. It is a miracle that an anesthesiologist can put a child to sleep, that an orthopaedist can operate, and that my son now has a fully functioning right arm. It is a miracle that an obstetrician, a perinatologist, and a neonatologist can maintain a baby, who was trying to be born at 29 weeks, and keep her safe and sound and healthy. It is also a miracle that my husband has spent the last five years cancer-free.

So it finally came to me. I have a sacred calling. All doctors do. And because of that calling, it is impossible to keep Christ out of my practice. I may not pray with all my patients, but I do pray for them. And every once in a while I am allowed to see a miracle I helped perform: the suicidal patient who is now happy and healthy; the young mother who had early detection of cancer, allowing less invasive treatment and more years with her growing children; and a family at peace with the passing of a loved one, assured that they will see him again in Heaven.

So I thank God every day that I have been given the opportunity to work with Him in healing His children. And I thank God that He has blessed me, personally, with many modern-day miracles.

Amanda Rosaasen, LLUSM class of 2002, is a family practitioner in Moorpark, California. She is married to Jonathan Rosaasen, LLUSM class of 2002. Together they founded Moorpark Family Medicine.

August 2

Fear not, for I am with you; be not dismayed, for I am your God; I will strengthen you, I will help you, I will uphold you with my righteous right hand.
Isaiah 41:10, ESV

My first day of medical school was over. I had attended lectures all day; and now I gathered my books, knowing I was about to begin a lifelong learning process. As I sat there with all my notes in front of me, I thought to myself about how the Lord had been with me to this point.

He had guided me in high school by allowing a teacher to suggest a career in medicine. She talked about a program called, "Si Se Puede," which was hosted by Loma Linda University (LLU) in order to expose underserved populations to careers in the medical field. I attended that program and felt in my heart that medicine was for me.

At La Sierra University, God was there also. He allowed me to see that I was moving closer to acceptance into medical school. He blessed with a scholarship to pay for the MCAT and also a course to refresh my knowledge before the exam. He found a home for me the day before I started orientation at LLU.

But in the middle of all that, I felt scared.

I knew that God had been with me all along; but now that I was on campus, I suddenly felt alone. In my heart, I knew I was here not because of my hard work or my will, but because He had been guiding since the very beginning. Now He was telling me to keep going, but at the same time I felt like a little child.

I was afraid of what lay ahead . . . afraid to go through this challenge . . . afraid of the volume of information that was being taught. I remember that my soul was burdened with questions: Why am I here? Does God really want me to become a doctor? What is my ultimate purpose? I could not believe what I was going through. Many of my friends would have given everything for the opportunity I now had, but here I was questioning God's intention for my life.

As I struggled with these questions, I came upon a framed quote hanging in the hallway outside the School of Medicine dean's office. The words were: "We have nothing to fear for the future, except as we shall forget the way the Lord has led us, and His teaching in our past history" (*Life Sketches of Ellen G. White*, p. 196).

After reading that, I felt that even though I have unanswered questions and am still afraid about the future—not really sure where all this is going—God is with me on this journey.

Daniel Samano, LLUSM class of 2016, is from Mexicali, Mexico, and graduated from La Sierra University with a BS degree in biomedical sciences.

August 3

Do not be anxious about anything, but in everything, by prayer and petition, with thanksgiving, present your requests to God. And the peace of God, which transcends all understanding, will guard your hearts and your minds in Christ Jesus. Philippians 4:6-7, NIV (1984)

Much like a pilot does before takeoff, a surgeon has a checklist of items to review in order to assure patient safety. Some of the items on this checklist include verification of proper documents; marking the patient; and stopping, prior to making an incision, to verify with all parties in the operating room that the procedure scheduled is the one to be performed.

In the summer of 2010, I was invited to go on a two-week trip to Kenya. Most of what we did was nonsurgical, but I did see many spine-related problems. My training and practice were dedicated to spine surgery; so, after returning home, I decided to go back to Africa a second time. I researched and found a hospital that could accommodate a spine surgeon. I was introduced to a mission hospital run by the Presbyterian Church.

Arrangements were made with the sponsoring hospital, a spine company was found who would donate instrumentation, and surgical instruments were borrowed from my local hospital. Nine months later, in March of 2011, I was on my way back to Kenya to do what I love most: spine surgery.

After reviewing potential surgical candidates, I prepared to do my first case. Many orthopaedic procedures had been done at Kikuyu Hospital, but never a spine case. I had many things on my mind and wanted to make sure that our team was prepared. After the patient was prepped and draped, I asked for a "surgical time-out."

I was expecting to hear a nurse, with a clipboard in hand, do the usual question-and-answer routine I had become accustomed to at our hospital, but I heard no such thing. Instead, after a significant delay, a small voice behind the portable x-ray machine said, "I'll pray." A prayer was offered for the patient and all the people involved in the operation, as well as for God's blessing.

I thought to myself, "I'll pray." How significant that surgical time-out was. It involved not a checklist of things to do and not to do, but direct communication to our Father in Heaven, the Ultimate Healer. It has been 25 years since completing medical school, where I was commissioned to "go out into the world and make man whole." But it took a small voice, hidden behind the x-ray machine, halfway around the world in Africa, to *emphasize the importance of prayer.*

Prayer, thus, is simply pausing and asking God for guidance—not only in our medical practice, but in everything we do in life. Just think how many times you could have avoided trouble if you only would have stopped, paused, and asked God for direction. Paul, in his letter to the Philippians, writes in chapter 4, verses 6 and 7: "Do not be anxious about anything, but in everything, by prayer and petition, with thanksgiving, present your requests to God."

You do not have to be hidden to pray; you can be in the middle of your clinic, in front of a staff meeting, or in your car. Pray often—He will gladly grant you peace and guide your heart and mind.

Joseph M. Verska, LLUSM class of 1987, is an orthopaedic surgeon in Boise, Idaho. He and his wife, Desiree, have three daughters. He enjoys volunteering overseas and has worked in the Ukraine, Philippines, South America, and in Kenya where this story took place.

August 4

Then he said to them, "Whoever welcomes this little child in my name welcomes me; and whoever welcomes me welcomes the one who sent me. For it is the one who is least among you all who is the greatest." Luke 9:48, NIV

Most medical students at Loma Linda University are solidly passionate about becoming a doctor. As these idealistic students begin their years of learning, the reality of all the hard work of study and the volume of material they need to master raises the ever-present question, "Can I really make it?" Yet, the students' level of maturity grows exponentially with early exposure to patients, more book learning, countless examinations, and looming board exams.

Life will never be the same on their road toward becoming a doctor. With the exposure to the learning culture, medical students see the attending physician as the leader of morning and evening rounds, the questioner of the learners, and the confronter, who often points out areas that can be improved, polished, or refined on how a good doctor does things.

As part of the process of learning, a medical student is often fraught with self-doubt, and surrounded with questions: Will I pass my boards? Do I know enough to be a competent doctor? Will I ever be like my attending physician? Will I really be able to cure disease and help people? What is my worth as a student, anyway? But Jesus had a different perspective, when He said, "For it is the one who is least among you all who is the greatest."

After having abdominal surgery, I witnessed a number of caregivers come and go each day. But the one who caught my attention was the medical student who was always the first one present at 5 a.m. wearing a smile. "Good morning, Mr. Walters! [She did not know I was a physician.] How are you today? Are you awake yet? I am so sorry to come so early. Let me warm my hands and my stethoscope."

The student did the examination, and asked how I was handling being in the hospital. Was there anything she could get for me? This medical student always had a gentle touch, was sorry if removing the bandage caused any pain, and was sensitive to my emotional reactions to having had surgery. She never seemed rushed, and her eye contact was awesome, conveying a strong sense of genuine concern. Wow, what an experience!

I learned so much about my surgery and my condition from this student, because she took the time to talk with me and to care about me. A clear alignment of Loma Linda University School of Medicine's values was coming from the heart of this incredible physician-in-training. Interacting with this compassionate medical student was the highlight of my hospital stay.

How delightful it was to experience such care—from the least among us—who had become the greatest. I pray a special blessing on each medical student for the skills needed to master the knowledge, to keep focused on the Master's compassionate values, and to demonstrate love and appreciation, even while in training.

Clifford A. Walters, LLUSM class of 1974, is an associate clinical professor in LLUSM department of gynecology and obstetrics. August 4, 2014, is the first day on the hospital wards for LLUSM class of 2018.

August 5

Then Jonathan made a covenant with David, because he loved him as his own soul. 1 Samuel 18:3, NRSV

Inefficient and hopelessly stressed-out would be a fair description of me in August of 2003 as an intern during my first Loma Linda University Medical Center (LLUMC) medicine ward rotation. Despite an outstanding medical school performance at Universidad de Montemorelos, Mexico, and having passed the boards, I was not as ready as I thought for residency in the United States. My senior resident, similarly, was an international graduate and transferee from another residency program. Although very knowledgeable, he was not familiar with this hospital's system.

Our attending was very enthusiastic about helping with our training. This support also meant our undivided attention during very long bedside rounds, often going past 4 p.m. This situation was compounded by a generous patient load, one that kept growing as we struggled to efficiently discharge our patients. Bradley Andersen, LLUSM class of 2003, my co-intern, was also having a hard time—not because he could not do his fair share of the work, but because he seemed to be the best-equipped to carry most of the team's responsibilities.

I was starting pre-rounds at 4 or 5 a.m. and not leaving the hospital until very late at night. In the little time I did have off, I could not sleep. I was calling nurses and worrying about my patients and wondering whether I had done all I was supposed to do. I was spiraling down quickly into despair. A growing sense of inadequacy overwhelmed me with a feeling that I was dragging the whole team down with me.

My wife tried to help the best she could by encouraging me, caring for our two small children on her own, and also working as a nurse. God, in His infinite grace, knew I needed help quickly. He sent Brad, my co-intern. On one of those dark nights, postcall, after a 40-plus-hour sleepless work stretch, Brad called me. Although I do not remember the exact words, he told me he would do whatever he could to help me get through that month.

I knew he was already doing so much more than I was. But his offer meant the world to me as he agreed to take extra time to help me learn the processes, forms, templates, and organizational skills for rounds and for the work that followed. He even gave me a metal folder to help organize my papers. I use that folder to this day as I make my rounds as a hospitalist at LLUMC.

In 2006 when we both became chief residents at LLUMC, it was again a privilege to work with Brad as we helped other residents in their training. I am indescribably grateful to him and the many other LLUSM graduates and teachers he represents for the amazing mission they live and share so graciously.

Here is evidence of God's sacrificial love for us, not only through the life of Jesus in the past, but also in the present, through human instruments such as Brad. God's love for me, as evidenced through experiences like this, inspires and reminds me today to embrace and live this mission as my own—an adopted child of His Kingdom and of this institution.

Alan Michel is an assistant professor in LLUSM department of medicine, chair of utilization management, and associate medical director of operations for the direct hospitalist service at LLUMC.

August 6

Therefore, as God's chosen people, holy and dearly loved, clothe yourselves with compassion, kindness, humility, gentleness and patience. Colossians 3:12, NIV

On August 6, 1996, we were on the second day of a three-day back-country trek in the Colorado Rocky Mountains. I was descending down a shale-faced slope next to a glacier, when the boulder I stepped on gave way and, together, the boulder and I plummeted down the mountain. In the midst of my fall, the boulder crushed my left hand.

I looked at my hand in utter disbelief, as my middle finger was dangling on the dorsal surface of my hand, while my index finger was split end to end with bone and muscle exposed. I remember many things about that moment in time—the thought of bleeding to death on the side of a stormy peak pass, the intense pain of the injury, and the shock that I might never be able to do things again that I love; including losing out on the prospects of being a physician.

My father, Dennis Hilliard, LLUSM class of 1975, an oncologist, "MacGyver'd it"— making a splint out of plastic forks and knives and an ACE bandage. I think his work would have made even an orthopaedic surgeon proud! I do not remember much of the 13-mile hike out that my father and I made by full moonlight. However, I do vividly remember being in an emergency department bed, and the hand surgeon coming in to examine me.

Though it was 3 a.m., he arrived impeccably dressed in shirt and tie and a freshly starched white coat. He spoke to me in a manner that immediately provided me with peace of mind. He said that, while there was no chance of saving my middle finger, my index finger, with a bit of time, would be fine.

Knowing that I was interested in medicine, the surgeon, Dr. Tsai, informed me that his partner became a hand surgeon in large part as a result of a traumatic hand injury he had sustained to two of his left hand fingers. This surgeon, and, of course, my father, demonstrated to me kindness as they knew the words I needed to hear in a moment when I was very discouraged.

As physicians, we must never forget that there will·be times when we cannot "heal," but there will never be a time when we cannot be kind.

Anthony Hilliard, LLUSM class of 2002, is an assistant professor in LLUSM department of medicine. He completed a residency in internal medicine followed by fellowships in cardiology and interventional cardiology at Mayo Clinic in Rochester, Minnesota. He and his wife, Tammy, have two children.

August 7

For though I am free from all men, I have made myself a servant to all, that I might win the more. 1 Corinthians 9:19, NKJV

I first met Lillian, an obese 56-year-old lady, when she was referred to me to have her left leg amputated. Her great toe was totally black; her second toe was almost as bad. Her foot was pulseless and cold. On her shin was a huge, deep ulcer, exposing the main extensor tendon to the foot. All medical alternatives had been exhausted; Lillian needed an amputation.

However, Lillian did not want an amputation! She pled, she begged, she cajoled. I finally agreed, telling her, "Since there is no significant invasive infection, I will make a deal with you. If you will follow the plan I outline for you, we will wait and watch carefully to see what happens." For almost two years Lillian struggled. With sincere prayer, she changed her diet, managed to get a bit of exercise and, eventually, smoked her last cigarette. That was nine years ago. The last time I saw Lillian, she was still walking on both feet—her left foot now warm and pink.

And then—there was Mary. A colleague asked me to see a patient with him—a patient who had extensive ulcers on her feet and legs. Mary had been a patient at Cook County Hospital for months at a time during the past year, but to no avail. She was obese. She was dirty. She was loud—yelling into her cell phone as we tried to evaluate her. Yes, and she was angry and mean! I do not think she heard a word I said to her that day, but she did permit us to apply some dressings and accepted another appointment for the following week.

If ever there was a patient one might wish would go away and never return, Mary was that patient. But come back she did—the next week—and the next—and the next. By then Mary was beginning to feel a bit better, and I hoped that—just maybe—she was starting to hear what I was saying to her.

So after I had made a few suggestions, I asked if I might pray with her. Upon concluding the prayer I saw tears flowing down Mary's face. "No doctor has ever prayed for me before," she sobbed. From that moment on, Mary was a different woman. That was nearly three years ago. It has been a long and difficult road—for her, for me and for my staff. But Mary has not been back in the hospital for her legs since that day—and they are now healing rapidly.

Just two hurting people that God placed in my path. Two ladies previously enslaved but no longer responsive to the culture of this world. Both were now beneficiaries of the "whole body" training I received so many years ago at the College of Medical Evangelists.

Walter C. Thompson, CME class of 1961, is a retired general surgeon who works part time at Open Arms Free Clinic in Elkhorn, Wisconsin. He is the author of several books including Missionary Doctor *and* Health Smart. *He and his wife, Avonne, were married on August 7.*

Truly I have spoken; truly I will bring it to pass. I have planned it, surely I will do it. **Isaiah 46:11, NASB**

Jose was a typical 16 year old who loved cars, soccer, and spending time with his friends. But in March 2011 he developed streptococcal meningitis and endocarditis. Vegetations formed on his heart valves, with abscesses eroding the wall of the heart.

After two weeks of IV antibiotics, his blood cultures were negative and surgery was performed—including replacement of his damaged aortic valve with a mechanical valve. But endocarditis recurred.

Cardiology, surgery and infectious disease services all agonized over this young man's predicament. It was decided to treat Jose conservatively with IV antibiotics and allow his tissues to heal and form strong tissue for the surgeon to repair. Jose received IV antibiotics at home for three months. But his condition deteriorated and he returned to the hospital with ascites and congestive heart failure. The medical teams decided to attempt repairing his extensively damaged heart.

The heart transplant team was also consulted, and he was listed for a heart transplant, if all else failed. When one is listed for a heart transplant, the donor heart is given a medical record number and a random name that begins with the first letter of the recipient's surname.

On July 15, 2011, after an extensive discussion with Jose and his family, he was taken to the OR to again attempt a repair. Three experienced cardiac surgeons worked on this very complex operation, but the heart would not beat despite correcting electrolytes, infusing inotropes (cardiac stimulant medication), and pacing. A right, then left ventricular assist device was placed, but still no cardiac activity. The transplant coordinator was called, and a request for the highest priority for a heart transplant was submitted.

How does one tell the parents of a child that their son will not survive without a new heart? Dr. Nahidh Hasaniya, Jose's cardiothoracic surgeon, slipped into the chapel and prayed for wisdom from our Heavenly Father, whom he knows as Allah. Miraculously, a heart had been offered for another patient at Loma Linda University Medical Center (LLUMC), but it was deemed unsuitable for that patient. Another center was evaluating the heart. The transplant coordinator negotiated, saying Jose would not survive without a heart transplant right now! The other center graciously released the heart to LLUMC.

A team was sent to procure the heart, and, as they were nearing the hospital, Dr. Hasaniya began to remove the old, diseased heart. The new heart was put in place, and the patient was weaned off the heart-lung machine, with good function, good contractility, and normal sinus rhythm. Everyone anxiously watched to see if Jose would wake up and be the same fun-loving young man he had been before surgery. Two hours later he awoke, the breathing tube was removed, and he was asking for ice!

His postoperative course has been uneventful. Jose's mother is eternally grateful for this gift of life, realizing how close she came to losing her precious son. Each time she leaves our clinic, she quietly says, "God bless you!"

The name that was randomly chosen earlier for Jose's donor was "Godsent," and it surely was. This amazing story reminds me of the Scripture, "Before they call I will answer, while they are yet speaking I will hear" (Isaiah 65:24, NRSV).

Janette Whittaker-Allen is a registered nurse and pediatric heart transplant outpatient coordinator at LLUMC.

August 9

We see Jesus, who was made a little lower than the angels for the suffering of death, crowned with glory and honour; that he by the grace of God should taste death for every man. Hebrews 2:9, KJV

A small, first-grade girl, upon returning home from school one day, reported the day's happenings to her mother. A friend at school who was feeling very sad sat sobbing, with her head down on her desk. The little girl slowly continued: "I didn't know what to say to her, Mommy, so I put my head down on my desk and cried with her."

That little girl's empathetic response should become our answer to pain. When we feel another's pain, we truly share that person's lot. God suffers with us, too. He is always with us in our sorrow. It is never His will that we should be sick, suffer pain, or die.

God, our loving Father, is very badly misrepresented by Satan. Disease, sorrow, and pain remain the especially cruel work of Satan. He deceives some of us into thinking that God causes these things. But every Christian must remember that Satan and sin, not God, cause suffering. Once the Christian learns this fact, he or she will hate sin and love God. To thank God for pain and suffering is, in reality, thanking Him for sin.

In the Cross appears the demonstration of the ultimate love that comes from the heart of God. Even here, Satan tries to blind humankind to the true character of God. Satan pictures God as a bloodthirsty tyrant, demanding the life of the sinner and even demanding the life of His only begotten, beloved Son, Jesus Christ.

But the Cross does not display a picture of a demanding tyrant God. Rather, it becomes a picture of a loving Father giving Himself, through His Son, to show how far sin separates a person from the true God. In the Cross, we see God sacrificing Himself and suffering the penalty of each human's sin in order that humankind might share God's glory—a glory that the human race does not truly deserve.

So why do we have suffering? Because under the circumstances of the great controversy between good and evil, God cannot abolish all suffering just yet. The good news is that evil can never permanently triumph over God. That issue got settled, once and for all, outside an ancient city on a hill where a Cross once stood.

That event happened so that we can enjoy His love now and forever. And we can return that love by comforting and sharing the pain of others, just as that young girl did.

Virchel Wood, CME class of 1960, is a professor in LLUSM department of orthopaedic surgery. He was LLUSMAA Honored Alumnus in 1999, received the LLU Distinguished Service Award in 2004, and was named LLUSMAA Alumnus of the Year in 2007.

August 10

You're blessed when you care. At the moment of being 'care-full,' you find yourselves cared for. Matthew 5:7, MSG

The morning sun began to filter through the blinds as my alarm sounded. I quickly jumped out of bed, wide-eyed and slightly jittery in anticipation of what was to come. It was my first day of medical school, and I would be following a third-year medical student during her anesthesiology rotation. I had no idea what to expect, but I knew it would be an unforgettable experience, shadowing the anesthesiologists at Loma Linda University's Outpatient Surgery Center.

I felt invincible wearing the dark blue scrubs and the shiny new ID badge I had received only a few days prior. My third-year student and I matched the quick and determined steps of the anesthesiologist as she introduced herself to her patients of the day. I had never been in an operating room, and I was beyond excited to finally get a chance to see a surgery firsthand!

As I stood behind the sterile field of the operating room, the smell of the Bovie began to waft toward my direction. At first, I decided to hold my breath in hopes that the smell would pass. I soon realized what a horrible idea that was, and, upon breathing again, I caught a huge whiff of the smell of cauterized flesh. I began to get tunnel vision as the room began to go in and out of focus.

I excused myself from the operating room, thinking I just needed some air. With each step, I felt weaker and weaker; I finally grabbed the sink in an attempt to stabilize myself. From then on, everything became blurry and a whirlwind of events. A physician nearby came over to check on me and called for help when I was unable to respond. Suddenly, nurses and physicians came to my side as they helped me into a wheelchair and transferred me to a gurney.

I had gone from a medical student to a patient in a matter of minutes! When I had regained consciousness, they did their best to make me feel comfortable as they explained to me that I had experienced a vasovagal response. Seeing how embarrassed I was, both the nurses and physicians jokingly told me stories they had heard about other students, even residents, who had had similar experiences. In a place where I knew no one, I felt as if family surrounded me.

We were told during orientation that at least one first-year medical student faints each year. Who knew that I would accomplish this feat on my very first day of medical school!

Emilie Nguyen, LLUSM class of 2016, is from Claremont, California. She graduated from University of California, San Diego with a BS degree in biochemistry and cell biology.

August 11

And this is the testimony: God has given us eternal life, and this life is in his Son. Whoever has the Son has life; whoever does not have the Son of God does not have life. 1 John 5:11-12, NIV

Being born is nice. Being born into the "Family of God" is better, but being adopted (drafted) into the "Family of the U.S. Army" is scary. After three years in that latter "family," I was free to choose, and I adopted the "Family of the College of Medical Evangelists." That decision has been exhilarating!

I was born in Nevada, Iowa, where I was a village kid at Oak Park Academy. That status allowed me to become acquainted with students from every class at that school from my birth until I graduated and went to Emmanuel Missionary College (now Andrews University). From there, I went to basic training at Camp Barkeley in Texas.

None of the recruits at camp could understand how I recognized so many of those there. (You guessed it—I was a village kid back home in the "Family of God.") On D-Day plus four, I landed on Utah Beach with the 45th Infantry Field Hospital. On the day after arrival, a Tuesday, I decided to search for a Seventh-day Adventist church in the city of Verviers, Belgium. I noticed a 12-year-old boy standing at the bottom of the steps of the theater where we were billeted. I said to him, "I bet you can't speak English."

He replied, "I can."

I said, "I bet you have never heard of a Seventh-day Adventist."

He said, "Yes, I have and I will be here at 8 o'clock Saturday morning to take you to meet some."

To my surprise, he was there on Saturday. After an hour of walking, he pointed to an apartment and said, "They are on the second story." I turned around to say, "Thank you," but he was gone. (Guess you know Whose "Family" he belonged to.)

So what was my next "Family?" It was CME, where I graduated in 1953. I practiced in Sunnyvale, California, for 45 years. While there, I started to realize what "CME" stood for, so I decided to go to Brazil for a summer (it became two summers) and practiced medicine on the *Luziero*, an Amazon River medical mission launch. During our second summer there, we adopted a seven-year-old girl. (Which "Family" made that possible?)

While busy on the *Luziero* one afternoon, a young barefoot boy came and asked my translator if I could go with him into the hot, wet, rainy tropics to see something. He took off like a rabbit and I followed. We finally came to a clearing with a house where he pointed to some steps and said: "Sit there. I will be back." After quite some time, he came back and handed me a beautiful grapefruit and said, "Pastor Halliwell* planted that fruit tree." (What a large "Family!")

After several years' hiatus, the "CME" bug kicked in again, and I took five trips to Romania, where I conducted three-week evangelistic outreach services and, with the help of my brother, built five churches. Now, at age 88, I have a "call" to go back to Romania and reap some of what we sowed at each of those five churches. And then soon and very soon, I will be joining another "Family"—the "Heavenly one."

---

*Leo B. Halliwell was a Seventh-day Adventist missionary who ministered aboard the first *Luziero*.

Willard D. Regester, CME class of 1953-B, is a retired family practitioner residing in Williams, Oregon. He regularly visits Romania to build churches. August 11 is his wedding anniversary.

August 12

And the very God of peace sanctify you wholly; and I pray God your whole spirit and soul and body be preserved blameless unto the coming of our Lord Jesus Christ. Faithful is he that calleth you, who also will do it.
1 Thessalonians 5:23-24, KJV

August 12, 2003, is a date I will never forget. I was rotating through the neurology clerkship as a fourth-year medical student at Loma Linda University. On this specific date, I followed Daniel Giang, LLUSM class of 1983. He is the multiple sclerosis (MS) specialist in the department. I had a special interest in learning more about MS, as my father had been battling this disease for the past 21 years.

By this time, I also knew that my father was doing poorly. He had been in a nursing home for the past three years and had been admitted to the hospital two days prior for complications from pneumonia. I had just seen him 12 days earlier on a quick trip home to Tennessee while on a short break between my third and fourth year of medical school. I knew, due to his declining condition, that each visit home could be the last.

My father had been a big inspiration in my life. He was a godly physician and wonderful father, and his work ethic encouraged me to follow his footsteps into medicine. As I observed Dr. Giang evaluate and treat several patients, and talk to their family members that day, it was an emotional flashback for me of what my father had been through, and what we, as his family, had gone through as well.

Early in my fourth year I had settled on specializing in internal medicine. At the start of my neurology rotation, I had prayed to God and asked Him that if He wanted me to choose a different career specialty other than internal medicine, He would give me a clear sign. I was not prepared for the sign that would be given.

After returning home from clinic that August afternoon, I had a voice message from my mother. I sensed that something was wrong. When I called back, she gave me the sad news that my father, John McNulty, CME class of 1945, had passed away. It was not shocking, as I knew he had a poor prognosis from the pneumonia, but losing him was still painful. Yet, I knew that God was with me and our family.

I traveled home the next day for the funeral and was blessed to spend time remembering my father. One week later I was back at Loma Linda University to finish my neurology clerkship.

During this period, I sensed that God was leading me into the field of neurology. By His grace, I matched into the neurology program at Loma Linda University, completed my residency in 2008, and then finished a clinical neurophysiology fellowship in 2009. I went on to serve for two years at the Adventist Hospital in Trinidad and am now practicing in Tennessee.

I am thankful for the mentorship I received from Dr. Giang and many others in the neurology department at Loma Linda University School of Medicine. I also know that my father would be thankful for where God has led me today.

Norman L. McNulty, LLUSM class of 2004, is a neurologist in Lawrenceburg, Tennessee. The last verse that his father quoted to his family was 1 Thessalonians 5:23-24.

August 13

And He said to me, "My grace is sufficient for you, for My strength is made perfect in weakness." Therefore most gladly I will rather boast in my infirmities, that the power of Christ may rest upon me. 2 Corinthians 12:9, NKJV

As a doctor, I am so privileged to watch life happen daily and over time. I go to my office every day, do my work, and the most amazing people walk into my life. Some are loud, some are quiet, some troubled, some want advice. Some are heroes.

They don't think of themselves as heroes. No one cheers when they walk into a building. They don't have multi-million dollar contracts, and you would never recognize their names. These heroes bring with them the example of a life lived with grace, dignity, and integrity.

Among the number of heroes I have met, one stands out above the rest. John was in his thirties. He had several tumors in his brain that were technically benign (that is, not rapidly growing nor immediately life-threatening), but were large enough to affect his ability to walk—John walked with a cane. Initially, there had been hope that a combination of treatments might shrink the tumors, but the location and potential side effects made any treatment modality difficult.

I cannot think of John without the broad smile on his face and his gentle, joking manner. His easy laugh rang down the clinic hall every time he came in for care, and he always had a handshake and a compliment for staff and doctors alike.

One day I asked him what made him so happy. He said he loved his work (as a physical therapist) and felt he had a special calling in that area because of his own physical problems. He worked full time, lived independently, and was even able to drive. He told me how he couldn't wait to see his patients every day and how happy he was when they improved.

Many months later, he began struggling more than usual to walk. He had to enlist the use of a walker. His hearing was also deteriorating. Eventually, John could no longer drive. But, he still wanted to care for patients. He worked out an arrangement for a ride to and from work each day even though he couldn't work a full day.

Then, his eyesight began to wane and the tumors grew enough to seriously alter his balance so that he could not walk at all. He became dependent on a wheelchair. Shortly after that, it became obvious that John not only could not work, but he also could no longer live independently. He had to move closer to family.

The last day I saw him, John came in with the same broad smile, this time straining to see and hear me as I leaned down to touch his arm and talk to him. He had a joke for me. I don't remember the joke, but I do know he thought it was really funny! He agreed to live with assistance if he could just get back to seeing patients. He told me his goal was to stay with his parents for a little while until he could get back some mobility and then get on with his *real* life.

I remember standing in the empty exam room, tears blurring my vision, and feeling like I'd lost a hero as John was wheeled out the door.

Rima Bishara, LLUSM class of 1986, is an internist in Waco, Texas. She is married to Brett J. Bolte who completed his physical medicine and rehabilitation residency at LLUMC in 1991.

August 14

And he said: "I tell you the truth, unless you change and become like little children, you will never enter the kingdom of heaven." Matthew 18:3, NIV (1984)

Have you ever found yourself caught up in the hustle and bustle of the world you live in? There is so much to do on a daily basis—between work as a physician, home as a wife and mother, and, oh, yes, a social life, if you have time for friends. How do people do it all?

I was only a few years out of residency and had a young family. We lived on the second floor in a quaint two-bedroom apartment. My son was almost two years old at the time and full of energy. What a joy he was to us! It was such a pleasure, after a long day at work, to come home and see his smiling face. He would usually run up to me and give me the world's biggest hug! All of my cares seemed just a little less important after that greeting.

One Sunday we were headed out to do some house hunting. My son was big enough to go down the stairs by himself. He rushed down them with no trouble at all. Then all of a sudden, he stopped on the sidewalk and lay on his tummy. Being a first-time mom and germaphobe physician, I became quite concerned.

I asked him what he was doing, and he responded, "I'm looking at the flowers, Mommy!" He had the biggest smile on his face and a twinkle in his eye. I quickly reassessed the situation and dropped to the cement sidewalk on my belly as well. "Wow, they are pretty!" I said. The plain old gardenias that I had walked by for days now seemed extraordinarily beautiful that day.

This small incident truly reminded me of the wonders God has created all around us. Most of the time I am too busy to notice them, but they are there. God has given us so much to be thankful for and to enjoy amidst all of the chaos. Sometimes, what we need to do is to stop and see the world through a child's eyes.

Roselie Bauman, LLUSM class of 1994, is an obstetrician and gynecologist in Riverside, California. August 14 is the birthday of her son Christopher.

August 15

There is a river whose streams make glad the city of God, the holy place where the Most High dwells. Psalm 46:4, NIV

The ambulance pulled in, with Code 3 lights and siren. Paramedics continued CPR while they rapidly wheeled the pale, elderly woman into the room. "One, two, three," the paramedic chanted to assist the team as they moved her from the ambulance gurney to the emergency department (ED) stretcher.

We all knew our roles. Airway, breathing, circulation . . . the resident put a tube in her to help her breathe, and the respiratory therapist squeezed a self-inflating bag to push air into her lungs. The medical student, glad to be needed, stood high on the bedside stool, rhythmically pressing his hands deep onto her chest wall, with adrenalin-enhanced strength. The monitor beeped in recognition of each thrust. Nurses started IVs and checked for a pulse as the chief resident barked out her orders.

"Her husband is in the waiting room," the charge nurse whispered to me. As the attending physician, I decided the patient was in good hands and went to find him. For many years, families were not allowed to watch loved ones undergoing CPR. Now it is commonplace to bring in the family to witness code teams in action.

I invited the husband to watch us work. I warned him that it did not look hopeful but that we were doing all we could. He nodded; he wanted to come but asked if he could go out to his car first. Puzzled, I said, "Yes."

A few minutes later, he arrived to a room filled with a flurry of activity. The octogenarian took in the entire room in a glance. His face registered recognition that his wife was not likely to survive.

He slowly walked over to the only empty spot on the floor and set down a tattered old case on the floor, placing it amid discarded medication boxes, syringes, and paper wrappers. He bent down and clicked the case open. "Continue CPR," I reminded the team. The man's gnarled hands brought up a violin. He carefully placed it under his chin and began to draw the bow across the strings. The charge nurse looked at me, unsure if she should allow this to go on. I nodded it was okay. The notes began to spill out in the form of a hymn:

> Shall we gather at the river, where bright angel feet have trod,
> With its crystal tide forever flowing by the throne of God?
> Yes, we'll gather at the river, the beautiful, the beautiful river;
> Gather with the saints at the river that flows by the throne of God.

The music seemed out of place, but the sounds coming from the violin brought a sense of peace to the entire ED. The whoosh of air being forced into her lungs and the rhythmic pumping on her chest were strange accompaniments. The man put the violin down, looked at all of us for a moment, and said, "It's okay; you can stop now. It is what she wants." I motioned to stop the attempted resuscitation.

"She wanted me to play this when she breathed her last. We always said we would meet at the river." The nurse reached up and turned off the monitor. We were all quiet, taking in the beauty of the moment—of a life well lived and the absolute faith that they *would* meet at the river.

Kathleen Clem, LLUSM class of 1989, is chair and a professor in LLUSM department of emergency medicine. She is the first woman to chair a department in LLUSM. August 15 is her wedding anniversary.

Dear friends, now we are children of God, and what we will be has not yet been made known. But we know that when Christ appears, we shall be like him, for we shall see him as he is. All who have this hope in him purify themselves, just as he is pure. 1 John 3:2-3, NIV

"Do you all really care what happens to me?" Her question pulled my frayed 4:45 a.m. thoughts into a single thread that was focused on the reality of the patient in front of me. She was asking me on behalf of our entire team. I had first seen this patient yesterday. Anticipating discharge today, she stood near the doorway of her room and, in between answering my mundane daily questions, reflected on her stay.

She told me how much she had appreciated the cute resident who checked on her progress each morning. She then discussed how she would care for herself at home. Finally, she asked the question that grabbed my attention—did we care what would become of her?

I avoided responding with, "Of course!" I wanted to be honest and sincere, not dismissive. Could I answer for the thoughts and motivations of others? Could I answer for myself? On the dark, chilly walk up to the hospital this morning, I had reflected on what made these early mornings worthwhile. Anticipating opportunities to interact with patients facing difficult times in their lives, I prayed for the ability to do my best, while tangibly bringing Jesus and His love into these interactions. This is Loma Linda University's mission, after all.

While I waited for the elevator that morning, the Scripture verse on a wall nearby reminded me that our hope is in God alone and His unfailing love; not just to save us, but to accomplish anything worthwhile through us. Nine floors up, however, all of this had slipped into the background. I had walked into this particular patient's room with my focus divided between what needed to be asked and examined this morning.

I quickly reflected on her question. Of course, we want good outcomes for all of our patients, for a mix of altruistic, utilitarian, and self-centered reasons. Without knowing my new team very well, knowing the tendency we struggle against—to get distracted by the details of pursuing excellent care for patients and lose focus on the person in our care—I decided I could truthfully answer her question. "Yes, we do care." As professionals and as people, we all want our patients to do well. We forget sometimes that our thoughts, priorities, and motivations can become discombobulated, but, underneath it all, we care.

Her question had not been meant as a challenge, but it challenged me. She reminded me not to leave my purpose behind as I strive to learn and apply vast amounts of knowledge.

I am grateful for patients who remind me of my purpose—patients who ask hard questions, tell me their faith stories, and offer to pray for their medical team before anyone offers them prayer. I expected, during this third year of medical school, to learn about disease processes by seeing patients with various etiologies. Patients have surprised me, though, by how often they teach practical lessons in spiritual care.

Staci Davenport, LLUSM class of 2014, is from Beltsville, Maryland. She graduated from Union College with a BS degree in international rescue and relief. She is a deferred mission appointee.

August 17

For you . . . joyfully accepted the plundering of your goods, knowing that you have a better and an enduring possession for yourselves in heaven.
Hebrews 10:34, NKJV

"**N**o, no. Not the brand new computer!"

It was the end of a long day of surgery at CURE Dominican, a pediatric orthopaedic hospital in Santo Domingo, the capital of the Dominican Republic. I was three weeks into the month I would be spending there during the summer after my first year of medical school.

I stared down at my backpack on the floor of the OR locker room. "Really? Three computers in one year?" I had bought the computer at the last minute (not at the best price!) the day before flying to the Dominican Republic, after an . . . um . . . unfortunate encounter between my previous computer and the concrete.

"*¿Alguien ha visto a mi ordenador?*" ("Has anyone seen my computer?"), I asked the two staff members left in the hospital, knowing full well I had put it into my bag before scrubbing in for the last surgery. They quickly assured me that nothing had ever been stolen from the hospital. They said all the staff was trustworthy, and I had most likely left it at home.

I walked the mile-and-a-half back to my rented room in record time, ignoring the sweat dripping down my face from the hot, humid Caribbean air. After confirming that I was not going crazy and had not left my computer at home that day, I stared again at my empty backpack.

"Why, God? What's the point of this?" My "go-to" Bible verses quickly popped into my head: "Do not be anxious about anything, but in every situation, by prayer and petition, with thanksgiving, present your requests to God. And the peace of God, which transcends all understanding, will guard your hearts and your minds in Christ Jesus" (Philippians 4:6-7, NIV).

"Thanksgiving . . ." I thought. "Well, thank you, God, that it is, just stuff; and, even though I lost travel pictures, you are in control, and my getting angry will just cause me distress without solving the problem."

A few days later, there was murmuring as I walked into the hospital office. The pastor pulled me aside: "The thief is turning himself in . . . and he's bringing your computer with him!" What a surprise! Although I had asked everyone to pray, I was already at complete peace about never seeing the computer or my photos.

I wish I could say that if you trust God, anything stolen from you will be returned. However, that is not the point of my story. (In fact, my bicycle was stolen two weeks ago, only about a year-and-a-half after the computer incident. There are no signs that I will ever see it again.) So here's my "take home" message: Everything we have is "on loan" from God. How can I complain if it is taken away when it was not really "mine" to begin with? If "my" things are stolen, I can let them go, knowing the thief cannot touch my real treasure!

Molly K. Lewis, LLUSM class of 2014, is from Fox Island, Washington, and graduated from Willamette University with a BA degree in Spanish. After completing medical school and residency, Molly hopes to serve as a pediatric orthopaedic surgeon in a Spanish-speaking country. August 17 is the day her computer was returned.

August 18

Oh, that you would be silent, And it would be your wisdom! Job 13:5, NKJV

Maybe it was the white coat I was wearing, the inexplicably long strides I was taking, or the fact that his eyes were glued on me as soon as I walked through the door. But everything felt too official. Unnatural. Completely the opposite of what I was expecting. Up until that moment, I had delusions of walking in, being greeted with a smile, and having an engaging, perhaps even cathartic conversation with the patient. Unfortunately, I had somehow forgotten that people stuck in a hospital—especially those who have been there for a long time—are, through no fault of their own, not jolly folk. They see a white coat and anticipate being poked or exhibited to an audience.

I attempted to introduce myself and received an abrupt "What?" in response. Of course, he was hard of hearing, I thought. I was certainly off to an inauspicious start. I tried again to explain my presence in his room, only to be interrupted again: "Are you here about taking me somewhere else?"

That was unexpected. Apparently the doctor had told him that morning that he would be going to a care facility before being sent home, and he was a little distraught. Eventually, with all the enunciation I could muster and the loudest voice I dared to use, I was able to introduce myself properly and to convince him that I wanted nothing more than to talk to him.

To my relief, his shoulders relaxed; his facial expression changed to what could be optimistically regarded as "resigned." On cue, I grabbed a chair, sat down, and began trying to fulfill the goals of my first class assignment—to "connect" and "listen" in earnest. I began to implement everything I knew about being a good listener: I leaned forward slightly, made eye contact, changed the subject when I felt it had run its course, and spoke softly and infrequently. I offered my condolences for his unfortunate situation and tried to commiserate with him about the uniqueness of "home." However, despite my efforts, the conversation gradually waned. After 15 minutes, I excused myself and walked out, far humbler and a little confused.

It has been a few weeks since that encounter, and I think I have a better idea of what happened. It would be easy to blame the fact that he had received disheartening news a few hours prior or that he had trouble hearing what I was saying. I could say that it was because I was four days away from my first patient interview class and was not armed with the full arsenal of interview tactics. However, I know now that it was something beyond my lack of technique. I was simply far too focused on what I should say than on how I should say it.

Without real empathy behind our words, our efforts can appear insincere at best, and utterly forced at worst. Without a calm, settled, and sincere soul, I run the risk of failing to be a truly empathetic physician. Although I should always strive to be the most competent physician I can be, exhibiting genuine empathy is the only way that I can help my patients feel at peace. I hope that the many humbling conversations that follow this one will continue to remind me of this fact throughout my career.

Michael J. Lee, LLUSM class of 2016, hopes to return to California's San Francisco Bay Area to practice medicine.

August 19

"You are My witnesses," says the LORD, *"And My servant whom I have chosen."*
Isaiah 43:10, NKJV

I heard a loud cry, shrill amidst the rhythmic serenade of synchronized ventilators and intermittent monitor alarms—sounds that reminded me I was in the intensive care unit. As a part of my daily pre-rounding, I walked in to examine my patient. There he lay, intubated and partially sedated—a stark difference from the vibrant baby that I had examined just days prior.

Prior to admission, seven-month-old Julian had been taken by his mother to another hospital. She had noticed a nonhealing wound on his upper lip and a sizable mass on his neck. In the emergency department, a complete blood count revealed hyperleukocytosis. He was later transferred to Loma Linda University Children's Hospital's pediatric intensive care unit for diagnostic evaluation to rule out possible malignancy. And he became my patient.

The diagnosis was acute myelogenous leukemia, with involvement of his central nervous system. Chemotherapy was started. I inquired about the prognosis: remission with high possibility of relapse. For me, this news was heartwrenching. Although unlikely, I had been hoping that the hyperleukocytosis was due to an infection, for which we would prescribe an antibiotic and then proceed to assure Julian's mother that he would be fine.

Now I was concerned—not so much for Julian because I knew that he was being taken care of by a scholarly pediatric oncologist and intensivist. But I was worried for his mother. How would she handle this news that her baby was terminally ill and that the therapies of medicine did not promise a cure? I searched for words to share that would ease her mind. What could I say?

For years, I had dreamed of becoming a pediatrician, a physician with the ability to make sick kids feel better—a healer. Now I realized that, as a pediatrician, my obligation was not only to the child, but also to the parent. I prayed for words of comfort to share with Julian's mother.

My friends and I conducted a weekly children's program for the community at the Del Rosa Seventh-day Adventist Church. I decided to tell the kids about Julian. They wanted to make get well cards and crafts for him. When I presented the cards to his mother, tears welled up in her eyes as she thanked me.

It was then that I realized that my call to become a pediatrician is not just a calling to heal; it is a calling to comfort, a calling to love as Jesus loved.

Michelle Y. Spencer, LLUSM class of 2013, is a pediatric resident in Gainesville, Florida.

August 20

Pride goes before destruction, And a haughty spirit before a fall.
Proverbs 16:18, NKJV

"**Y**ou did a great job on my first eye surgery!" "You are the best doctor!" "I'm so glad you are doing my second eye surgery, because I see 20/20 out of my first eye." "I'm telling all my friends about you!" "I see better now than I ever did my whole life!" "You're a miracle worker!"

These are some of the comments I have received from my surgery patients. After hearing such praises, it is easy to begin to believe them. But just when I start thinking I am a great surgeon, a complication will remind me how insignificant I am without God's help.

Not long ago, after returning home from a week-long vacation, I had scheduled 32 cataract surgeries on my first day back in the OR. The first seven surgeries went so smoothly that I began feeling quite confident about my abilities. On the eighth patient, I smugly thought about how long it had been since I had experienced any vitreous loss. Within seconds of that thought, my ultrasound probe went too far and poked a hole in the posterior capsule, which keeps the vitreous from coming into the front of the eye.

What normally is a 5-to-10 minute procedure dragged on for 40 minutes. Thankfully, the problem was successfully resolved, and I finished the remaining surgeries without any further surgical misadventures. However, the truth is that whenever I start thinking I am somebody really special, a surgical challenge brings me back to size. But the question remains—how do I stay humble in an environment of praise?

I believe the answer is gratitude—gratitude for patients who trust me to do their eye surgeries; gratitude that God has given me the talent, skill, and opportunities to be a good surgeon; gratitude for vibrant health from God; and gratitude for a wonderful staff that makes everything run smoothly so I can focus on surgery. I am grateful to be a member of a team of excellent medical workers in a Christian ophthalmology practice. This not only allows me to share my faith, but also to hone my surgical skills with high volume surgery as well. I am grateful for my training at Loma Linda University and its medical school and residency program, both of which allowed me to become an ophthalmologist. I would not be where I am today without all the help I received throughout my training. In addition, I am very fortunate to have a supportive wife and family that allow me to spend long hours at work, giving patients the best care possible.

So, whenever I start feeling that I am pretty good at what I do, I think about all the people who have helped me along the way, as well as those who are currently helping me care for my patients. My goal is to show gratitude to those who really deserve the praise— God and all my hardworking staff!

Paul Y. Chung, LLUSM class of 1991, is an adjunct assistant professor in LLUSM department of ophthalmology at Pacific Cataract and Laser Institute. He and his wife, Iris, LLUSM class of 1995, have five children and live in Chehalis, Washington. August 20 is her birthday.

August 21

Therefore we do not lose heart. Though outwardly we are wasting away, yet inwardly we are being renewed day by day. For our light and momentary troubles are achieving for us an eternal glory that far outweighs them all. So we fix our eyes not on what is seen, but on what is unseen, since what is seen is temporary, but what is unseen is eternal. 2 Corinthians 4:16-18, NIV

The sun was just peeking over the horizon as I headed to work. But even the breaking of a new day was not enough to lift my spirits. Stressors crowded my mind; I was not looking forward to my shift. As I sat down for report, Nurse Eva looked at me and sighed, "We've got a tough one!"

She went on to explain that Crystal had been admitted during the night. A loving mother of two precious little girls, she was battling metastatic breast cancer. And she had just received word that her husband was filing for a divorce. "The hardest part of this case is the smell," Eva continued. "She has lesions all over her body that are oozing—there's a terrible stench in there."

We finished report and I braced myself as I entered the room. Everything Eva had told me about the patient's condition was accurate, and it was difficult to stay in the room because of the odor. I introduced myself and started my assessment. A Bible lay open on her lap, so I said, "I notice you're reading a good book."

"Oh, I couldn't make it without this!" Crystal smiled. I shared with her that I also gained considerable strength from the Scriptures.

I turned next to check the medication record. A few moments of quiet ensued.

"Kathy, listen to this," she said, as I turned around and saw that her face was glowing. She read from Isaiah 40:31 (NIV), "But those who hope in the Lord will renew their strength. They will soar on wings like eagles; they will run and not grow weary, they will walk and not be faint." She paused, "Isn't that amazing?"

I had heard the words dozens of times before but never had they struck me like they did that morning. It was as if I was hearing them for the first time, and God was speaking directly to me. Suddenly, the stresses I was facing did not seem so bad.

"Thank you so much, Crystal," I said. "I really needed to hear those words today."

I continued on with my day's work. Several times throughout the shift, I had opportunities to talk with Crystal about the challenges she was facing. We both recognized that we had a shared trust in God's guidance in our lives.

As the shift ended, I made my way to her room. "I'm heading home now, but I'll see you in the morning," I promised. She extended her hand toward me, and I noticed a small card. "This is for you. I thought you might need it as a reminder," she explained. She had carefully written the Isaiah text for me.

As I prepared for work the next morning, I had one extra task to do. I found a 3" x 5" index card and wrote a promise on it for Crystal. And so it was, every day that I cared for her until her death, we were able to share Scripture promises with each other. Although Crystal was not healed of cancer, God used her to bring renewal to me.

Kathy McMillan is director of Employee Spiritual Care and Wholeness at LLUMC and a teacher in LLUSR. Her husband, James, is from LLUSM class of 1986. August 21 is the birthday of their twins.

August 22

Carry each other's burdens, and in this way you will fulfill the law of Christ.
Galatians 6:2, NIV

"I believe in God, only I spell it Nature."—Frank Lloyd Wright

This quote by the highly acclaimed architect expresses a common belief among many scientists, and physicians are no exception. Because modern medicine is grounded and steeped in science, many physicians either hold or develop atheist or agnostic beliefs throughout their study and practice of medicine. However, many patients and families rely on their spirituality during times of crisis. This divide between physicians and patients often results in lost opportunities for ministry and healing.

One of the most important skills I learned while at Loma Linda University was how to pray with patients. I distinctly remember an afternoon clinic spent with Harvey Elder, CME class of 1957. Although Dr. Elder had spoken about the topic in both formal and informal settings, it was seeing this skill in practice that reinforced his teaching. He skillfully navigated the patient's concerns, gently probed about the patient's spiritual beliefs, and unassumingly asked whether prayer would be helpful. His humble example and simple demonstration equipped me to share this powerful ministry with my patients.

Never was this more meaningful to me than during my clinical fellowship. I was caring for an elderly woman with a rare but very aggressive brain and spinal cord infection. Although she was clinically stable, it was unlikely she would recover. Late one night, I met with her many family members to discuss her prognosis. The meeting was filled with sadness, and there were more than a few tears shed.

At the close of the meeting, I gently asked about their spiritual beliefs. I asked them whether a prayer would be helpful. We closed our meeting with a short prayer. A few days later, her son and daughter-in-law told me how much that meant to them. When I asked them why, they simply replied, "We didn't think doctors believe in God." They were so grateful to know that a physician cared for their mother as one of God's children, and not just another patient.

While I pray only in select clinical situations and only with patients and families who accept the invitation, prayer has been profoundly powerful in my practice of medicine. We all have opportunities to show and share Christ in our daily work. I encourage you, no matter what your field, to share God in a real and tangible way with those you interact with today.

Cody A. Chastain, LLUSM class of 2008, is currently completing his fellowship in infectious diseases at Vanderbilt University Medical Center. He and his wife, Jamie, live with their triplet sons in Nashville, Tennessee. August 22 is Jamie's birthday.

August 23

Serve wholeheartedly, as if you were serving the Lord, not people, because you know that the Lord will reward each one for whatever good they do, whether they are slave or free. Ephesians 6:7-8, NIV

To illustrate the joy and great personal satisfaction of medical missionary work, I will relate one of the experiences I had while serving as physician/surgeon at Ubol Mission Hospital and Clinic in Ubol, Thailand (at the Lao/Cambodian Triangle), between 1953 and 1958.

Our township had a village of 12,000 refugees. They had a village chief who looked after their welfare. The mother of his large family of eight children had gone to the area's government hospital to deliver her ninth child.

Postpartum, she developed an acute abdomen, for which she underwent laparotomy for a supposed ruptured uterus. The abdominal exploration was "negative"; but post-op, she became septic and was not responding to treatments.

She was sent home to die because in their Buddhist culture the priest cannot chant the spirit into Nirvana while the patient is in the hospital. The person must be at home among family and friends. The husband came to me after the patient was home, worried that his wife would soon die. He wanted me to examine her, to see if her life could be saved. If she died, he would have to sell all nine of his children because he had no relatives to care for them.

I went to his village, examined her, and told him I would do everything I knew to save her, but he would have to bring her to our hospital. A family pow-wow was held to get permission for the *maaw-farang* (foreign doctor) to treat her. The family agreed, and she was carried by hand litter four miles to our hospital.

After x-rays, blood tests, IV antibiotics, and nasal oxygen, she survived that night. When I made rounds the next morning, she was sitting up in bed, wide awake! I asked the nurse, "What happened?" The nurse said that the patient called for the bedpan at 2 a.m., and she passed something. My astonished response, "I hope you saved it." She pulled the pan from under the bed. Upon lifting the cover, I could hardly believe my eyes! There was this large, golf ball-sized gallstone! It had eroded into her intestinal tract and had passed on out.

I took her to surgery and removed her gallbladder, closing a hole in her duodenum. She recovered without incident and was discharged after 10 days in our hospital. Her husband was ecstatic—now he would not have to sell his children!

From then on, every Friday exactly at noon, a servant delivered to my office a basket of freshly laid eggs. I told the husband that he needed those eggs for his children; I could buy eggs at the market. His response was *"Mai bpen rai, mai bpen rai."* ("It's a little thing. I must do it.") According to their culture, if a person does not show gratitude for favors, when he or she dies, the spirit cannot be chanted into Nirvana to start a new life in the lower echelons of eternity.

His response provided a wonderful opportunity to explain to him that Christians do not believe such actions are necessary since *phra yesu* (Jesus) has paid our debt for us. This story is just another example of why medical missionary work is so gratifying—providing many opportunities to both serve and witness.

George L. Juler, CME class of 1952, is a retired surgeon residing in Seal Beach, California.

August 24

But the very hairs of your head are all numbered. Matthew 10:30, NKJV

Thirty-seven years after graduating from Loma Linda University School of Medicine (LLUSM), I find myself reflecting on how the providential hand of God worked in the lives of my ancestors to lead me to the ministry of medicine. In 1866, my ancestors left the shores of India to sail across the *Kala Pani* to the Caribbean. The *Kala Pani* (black water) refers to the oceans surrounding India; and, in Hindu folklore, the *Kala Pani* was feared by the Indian people. Crossing the sea was taboo because it meant being cut off from the healing waters of the Ganges River.

However, like the Spirit of God hovering over the waters, my ancestors were moved by a force stronger than fear; by a hope more powerful than karma. My great, great-grandparents were some of those individuals who embarked on a journey aboard the ship *The Countess of Ripon*.

During their three-month voyage, my pregnant great, great-grandmother gave birth to my great-grandfather Gangaram. Soon after, my great, great-grandmother was stricken by an illness and was unable to care for Gangaram. Their voyage came to an unexpected end when *The Countess of Ripon* ran aground off the coast of Barbados, landing at Skeetes Bay.

After they were rescued, Gangaram was nursed back to health by an African woman who saved his life. Eventually, my ancestors relocated to St. Vincent in the West Indies. They came as indentured servants to work on plantations for the British. Their surnames were changed, as was much of their way of life; yet the Spirit of God continued to move in my ancestors' hearts. Two generations later, my parents embraced Christianity, with Adventism becoming the prominent faith of the Indians on the island.

As a boy growing up in a less-developed country, I witnessed the power of God's providence and the transforming power of His Spirit. Although I was raised with very few educational opportunities, I was determined to pursue a career in medicine. I graduated from high school at the age of 16 and became a teacher. At 18, I served as the principal of our Adventist school.

A year later I left for the United States to study at Andrews University. During the school year, I worked several odd jobs to supplement my tuition. In the summers I worked as a colporteur, selling Adventist literature in Alberta and Ontario, Canada. I am eternally grateful for the many strangers who took me in, expressing God's love through food and lodging.

During my third year of college, I met my wife-to-be, Delores; her father, the late John Ford, CME class of 1947, became my mentor. In 1971, I was accepted to LLUSM.

I look back at my life with a thankful heart for the way the Spirit of God has led me. I was placed to serve not only the families of Central Florida, but also many of my own relatives. There is no denying that the providential hand of God has been at work throughout my *entire* life.

Gideon G. Lewis, LLUSM class of 1975, is a family practitioner in Winter Park, Florida. August 24 is his birthday.

August 25

GOD *judges persons differently than humans do. Men and women look at the face;* GOD *looks into the heart.* 1 Samuel 16:7, MSG

"I understand your frustration," I overheard the charge nurse say. "I will have Dr. Chen come down and talk to you." That exchange was my first clue that something was awry. As I peeked around the door from the doctor's dictation room into the nurse's station, I saw an elderly gentleman standing in front of the desk, looking rather distraught.

"What room is your son in?" she asked, and then repeated the response aloud, "Room 2117."

"Of course," I thought to myself, "That would be the developmentally disabled 40 year old with sepsis who was admitted two days ago."

Communicating with this patient—a handicapped adult male with profound effects from cerebral palsy—was virtually impossible. I recalled nodding, somewhat patronizingly, to the caregiver just the day before, when she mentioned how well the patient was able to communicate.

As I walked down the hall to the room, the nurse updated me on the father's frustration regarding how we communicated with his son. What was going on? *The patient?* I thought again to myself. *He can't even understand what I'm saying to him.* I thought about the blank look the man had in his eyes when I saw him earlier that morning. I pretty much had directed my conversation to the caregiver his family hired to be with him. A caregiver stayed with him 24/7, even when he was hospitalized.

As I entered the room and introduced myself, the father respectfully, but directly, chided me for not explaining the treatment plan to his son. "He understands everything," the father stated, "and he never forgets anything. I wish I had a memory like he does. He likes to know what is going on, and have things explained to him. There's nothing wrong with his mind," his father went on. "People think just because of his 'condition' that he can't understand anything."

This patient's condition was quite pathetic, based on the standards of the general population. He was bedbound, due to his spastic quadriparesis. He was totally dependent on others for feeding, mobility, clothing, toileting, and access to anything of enjoyment.

Over the next 15 minutes, however, I watched an incredible display of love and devotion from an elderly father. Despite the bad hand life had dealt his son, and the challenges he and their family had faced over the past 40 years, he treated his son with the tenderness, patience, compassion, and love that a father might display toward his newborn child.

Despite my 22 years as a practicing physician, the last 15 of which have been as a hospitalist, I had once again had a momentarily lapse in my "judgment" of a patient, based solely on the patient's outward appearance.

Through this patient's earthly father, I was reminded how our Heavenly Father approaches us. Whatever deal life throws at us, we have a Savior who will stick by our side—with the tenderness, patience, compassion, and love that we need to get us through the most difficult challenges.

David Chen, LLUSM class of 1990, is an internist in Tacoma, Washington. This story took place while he was medical director of the MultiCare hospitalist program. He is currently the vice president of medical affairs at Good Samaritan Hospital in Puyallup, Washington.

And now these three remain: faith, hope and love. But the greatest of these is love.
1 Corinthians 13:13, NIV

It was my last "guaranteed" summer vacation, and I was in between my first and second years of medical school. While many of my classmates traveled around the world on mission trips, and some seized this last-call opportunity to take a three-month siesta, I reluctantly signed mine away for many hours in a room, crunching data for research.

I had developed a particular fascination with those creepy-crawly microbes during my undergrad years, and if I was going to have to sit indoors all day, I decided I had to be working in the specialty of infectious disease. That is how I found myself at the VA Loma Linda Healthcare System, on the service of Michael Ing, LLUSM class of 1990.

During my time working in the infection control office, I had the good fortune of tagging along on rounds some days; it was a way to break up the monotony of reviewing patient charts. It was on these rounds that I became witness to the incredible example of whole person patient care, an approach that made a particularly strong impression on me as a young medical student.

After listening to the exhaustive list of medical ailments that veterans almost invariably have, Dr. Ing would ask, "Is there anything else we can do for you?" One day a patient responded to this inquiry by stating that he was tired of the food at the hospital and was craving Del Taco burritos and Hawaiian Punch. That day, during our lunch break, Dr. Ing took another medical student and me to a Del Taco restaurant and purchased burritos, as the patient requested.

Of course Del Taco did not have any Hawaiian Punch, at which point it would have been perfectly understandable if my attending physician had said, "Oh well, the burritos are enough," and headed back to the hospital. But the doctor did not do that.

Instead, we went to Stater Bros. grocery store and searched for Hawaiian Punch; but they did not carry it, except for the powdered form. But Dr. Ing bought what they had and we left the store. Upon our arrival back at the hospital, he gave the bag of food with the powdered drink packets to another medical student to take to the patient. I was not present to see the patient's reaction, but I can only imagine his surprise and joy!

If you ask him why he does this, Dr. Ing will tell you that patients usually have simple requests and that he does his best to accommodate them because it makes their pain a little less. I will never forget this example of love and caring for a patient's happiness and well-being, beyond the illness that sent him to the hospital.

As medical students, we are pursuing the calling of a physician, to treat and alleviate illness. But it is also my hope that, no matter how successful we become, we never forget to take time to care about the seemingly small things that can actually make a big difference.

Christine Akamine, LLUSM class of 2015, is from Redlands, California. She graduated from Pacific Union College with a BS degree in biology.

August 27

I will give thanks to you because I have been so amazingly and miraculously made. Your works are miraculous, and my soul is fully aware of this.
Psalm 139:14, GW

O f the many areas in medicine, perhaps no area is quite as charged as cancer. When a patient first learns that he or she has cancer, a deadly race begins against both time and a sinister entity that is usurping what is good and natural. The treatment options for people with metastatic cancer largely revolve around chemotherapy, essentially a poison that affects both normal and cancer cells; it is a type of treatment that has potentially devastating side effects.

It was into this area of medicine that I felt called. I felt compelled to help vulnerable, often scared patients and their families. I soon began to understand that there was tremendous potential in the human body's amazingly complex and dynamic immune system that may be retrained to attack a cancer, and without significant side effects.

To study immunotherapy for cancer, I trained at the National Cancer Institute (NCI) within the National Institutes of Health in Bethesda, Maryland. This mecca of academic medicine, just like the city's namesake biblical pool, focuses on providing better health for the masses. The NCI is the leader in innovations in immunotherapy and continues to make immunotherapy a top priority.

Working with a cutting-edge laboratory, I began to apply my training to uncover the potential for the patient's own immune system to fight against cancer; I did this by running a large number of clinical trials. These clinical trials involved the use of therapeutic vaccines designed to retrain the patient's immune system to recognize and attack the cancer after the patient already has been diagnosed.

The potential of this technique is best demonstrated by one of my patients who had metastatic breast cancer. At the age of 32, she noted a lump on her breast. Diagnosed with poorly differentiated invasive ductal carcinoma, she underwent lumpectomy and radiation, but the cancer spread to the liver soon after this treatment. This was followed by chemotherapy and removal of her ovaries, as well as the part of her liver that was invaded by the cancer.

Despite this treatment, within one year the disease had spread to the lymph nodes of her chest. She came to see me at the NCI, and I enrolled her on a phase II study of a vaccine we had developed in the laboratory. She had a very good immune response to this therapeutic vaccine, and within eight months, her cancer was visibly smaller on CT scans. By 18 months, all evidence of the tumor was completely gone.

It has been more than five years since she started on the clinical trial, and based on our best imaging tests, she remains cancer-free. And the vaccines she continues to take give her no more side effects than a flu shot.

What an amazing immune system! What hope to unlock better treatments!

James L. Gulley, LLUSM class of 1995, PhD, is deputy chief of the Laboratory of Tumor Immunology and Biology and director of Clinical Trials Group at the Center for Cancer Research in Bethesda, Maryland. August 27 is his birthday.

But as for me, I am poor and needy; come quickly to me, O God. You are my help and my deliverer; LORD, do not delay. Psalm 70:5, NIV

A physician never knows what to expect when he or she walks into a patient's room. Not uncommonly, a chief complaint belies the major problem that needs to be addressed. Such was the case with Mr. S, who had a "genital problem." His examination was found to be normal; but after just a few minutes with Mr. S, I recognized that he was in a considerable amount of trouble. He was using 3 to 4 grams of cocaine and methamphetamine each week and suspected his wife was cheating on him.

The ability to prioritize his issues was not his forte. Instead of showing up for his court date, he kept his appointment with me, his doctor. He admitted later that this would lead to his incarceration. Obviously, his extensive problems would not be fixed in a 20-minute visit.

His drug use was at the center of his problems—perhaps causing some delusions, even mild psychosis, and poor choices. He was going to jail, so it seemed that anything I said or did would have little or no impact on his life. But I sensed that Mr. S was at the end of his rope, and that his coming to the doctor's office was a way of asking for help. Scripture speaks of this need, as seen in the verse above from Psalms: "I am poor and needy; come quickly to me, O God."

Many times people have to hit rock bottom before they look up. I asked Mr. S if he was a praying man. He said that he was a Christian but had not prayed in a long time. He accepted my offer to pray with him. After we finished, he fought back tears and apologized for the emotions that had overcome him. I told Mr. S he needed a new start. Life would be different once he walked out the door. After our prayer, I knew that a Greater Power would be at work in his life, in spite of all his previous bad decisions.

Visits like that have me on the lookout for the working of the Holy Spirit. It is not as if something like this incident happens every day. However, at times it seems that the Almighty orchestrates a special divine appointment to make a difference in a patient's life. I may not know what to expect behind each door for a patient visit; but if I heed the call of my Heavenly Father, I will have the opportunity to touch lives for Him.

D. Andrew Roquiz, LLUSM class of 2011, is completing his family practice residency at Kaiser Permanente in Woodland Hills, California. This story took place during his second year of residency. August 28 is his birthday.

August 29

Remember the whole way by which he has brought you these forty years through the desert. Deuteronomy 8:2, NET

It had been a frustrating day for me in my private practice. The patients all seemed difficult and unappreciative. Everyone seemed to have more questions than I had answers for. It was a relief to be home. Now, at the end of that long day, instead of relaxing, I was digging through an old drawer, looking for my son's social security number. I needed it for an application that was now due.

At the bottom of the drawer, I stumbled upon a "Thank You" card that was addressed to me. It did not look familiar at all, so I opened it and started to read. The first words I saw jumped out at me. "If ever there is a day when you ask yourself why am I doing this, remember me. There are a lot of people out there like me . . . Your actions saved my life." Who wrote this, I thought to myself as I continued reading.

"Each day I wake up, I am thankful to be here. I thank God and you for that." I mentally began to go back through the years, thinking of the hundreds of patient encounters I have had, and suddenly it all came back to me. This letter was written almost 20 years ago by a patient I saw while in my family practice residency. She had a 15-minute scheduled appointment for medication refills. It was supposed to be a quick "in and out" visit.

However, I sensed from the start that something was troubling her. I asked her point blank what was bothering her, but she said she was "fine." I was not convinced and continued to probe. I asked her about work, home, and family. She gradually started to open up. She was very distraught and confused. She admitted being suicidal. Her intention, in fact, was to overdose on the very pills she was requesting from me.

I stayed with her for some time, all the while empathizing, encouraging, but mostly listening. I finally was able to convince her to see a psychologist. She was briefly admitted to an inpatient psychiatric facility. I do not think I ever saw her again. The card I held in my hand was mailed to me several weeks after our encounter.

As I reflected back on that patient encounter, I thanked God that day for the privilege of making a difference in the life of a young woman. Then I thanked Him again for allowing me to find the letter on a day when I needed it most.

Tracey Wallace, LLUSM class of 1993, is a family practitioner residing in Norcross, Georgia.

August 30

For you have been called for this purpose, since Christ also suffered for you, leaving you an example for you to follow in His steps. 1 Peter 2:21, NASB

I am proud to say that I am the mother of a six-month-old girl. As I watch her tackle the motor milestone of flipping from her back to her belly, I look forward to watching her walk and become an adventurous navigator.

One of the most inspiring walkers I have ever seen during my training in physical medicine and rehabilitation was a boy named Ben. Every time I move from one workplace environment to another, I take with me a framed photograph of Ben. It is a picture of a two-year-old child during a triathlon, sporting a pair of sunglasses, and wearing his triathlon ID card on his chest—and he is my inspiration.

He was my attending physician's patient during residency. I first met him outside the clinic environment, during one of our PossAbilities events at Loma Linda University. This annual campus-wide event aims to promote wellness among individuals with disabilities.

Ben was born with a disease that affected his leg bones, weakening them so much that they could not bear his weight. After one year, the decision was made, with the permission of his parents, to amputate his legs in order to give him the chance to walk using prosthetic devices.

The "stubbies," or stilt-like feet he wears, have not impeded his strides. Ben is rambunctious, mischievous, and full of life! He will playfully chase after other children. When he falls, he does not cry, but just gets back up and charges on to play again.

This picture I have on my wall exemplifies how beautiful every child of God is and how our calling, as physicians, is indeed to "make man whole." In spite of missing his feet and knees, Ben is still a force of hope, joy, and abundant laughter. He reminds me that we have a duty to these children; we need to help them navigate this world. Sadly, too often it is a world where people with disabilities frequently do not have enough support or may be bullied and ridiculed for being different physically.

I hope to run into Ben again one day when he is older and causing even more trouble in the triathlon world. I also hope my own daughter will not take walking or her body for granted and will learn from Ben's story that fearlessness and hope, despite any physical challenge, are truly possible.

Giang–Tuyet N. Lam, LLUSM class of 2007, completed her residency in physical medicine and rehabilitation at LLUMC and a neuromuscular medicine fellowship at David Geffen School of Medicine at University of California, Los Angeles.

August 31

In thee and in thy seed shall all the families of the earth be blessed.
Genesis 28:14, KJV

Allia is very sick today and feels she may not have enough energy to speak with me. "I'll try," she says, as I ask her to become my teacher for a few minutes in my journey to become an excellent doctor.

She has been in the hospital for a week, and this is her second time in recent weeks. After getting better, things got worse again. Now she is a long way from home, unsure about her prognosis, and realizes she has no control over her situation. Yet despite all this, she is a woman of faith. "I trust God," she says. "Everything has a reason. God is with me."

Recognizing how important Allia's faith is to her, I reflect this to her, and I think that is where our connection really begins to deepen. She expresses her belief that God has been with her through both good times and bad. I ask her if she ever struggles with faith when she is ill.

"Sometimes I do," she says, "but I hold on." I learn that her faith is tied to her social support; she mentions her friends who pray for her, and her husband who visits her every day coming from far away. These visits must be taking a huge toll on her family. Perhaps it is keeping the husband from working. What are the costs associated with either local housing or tanks of gasoline?

I soon realize that her sickness is not just a disease of the person; it is an illness experienced by her entire social system. With this awareness in mind, I begin to see that the opportunity for her healing extends well beyond Allia; it includes those who care about her.

I also notice that Allia physically strengthens as she speaks about God. More life comes to her voice and she seems less tired. This reference to Him is definitely making her stronger. I think about what would have happened if she had not been hospitalized at a religious institution. Perhaps nobody would have taken an interest in this part of her wellness, and the potential empowerment this has brought her would have been lost.

It becomes evident to me that the doctors, who are providing her with a sense of courage and faith, are an important part of her emotional health. In fact, her trust in the expertise of the doctors seems to be determined by the way they treat her. Regarding physicians' attitudes toward patients, Allia encourages me to love my patients and always pray. She adds that love is the most important thing, as well as kindness and caring deeply for everyone.

Noticing that she is tiring, I ask her if she would like for me to pray with her; her face lights up. "Yes, please," she says. I grasp her hand and pray. She praises God throughout my prayer, thanking and worshipping Him. The beauty of this scene cannot be adequately described. "Thank you for talking with me," she whispers. *No, thank you, Allia, for teaching me.*

Casey Harms, LLUSM class of 2016, completed his MA degree in counseling psychology at Walla Walla University. He was president of his freshman class and currently is president of his sophomore class. August 31 is his wedding anniversary.

SEPTEMBER

"LET LIFE BE A PRECIOUS
COMMODITY IN YOUR BEING."

September 1

In all my prayers for all of you, I always pray with joy . . . being confident of this, that he who began a good work in you will carry it on to completion until the day of Christ Jesus. Philippians 1:4, 6, NIV

I am perhaps being more than a little presumptuous in suspecting that Dr. Carrol Small valued the text above as one of his favorites. Nonetheless, I would like to relate one of my many personal encounters with him.

Quite a few years ago now, Dr. Small asked me to do a favor for him—something in regard to a serious developing health problem. It was an honor to do so; and in return, he gave me a book, *The Chief: Dr. William Osler*. Dr. Small did not say much about this book, but somehow I think it was very important to him. In reading that glimpse into the personal life of Dr. Osler, I saw a number of similarities between two men whom I choose to call great.

I wondered as I read, and recently reread, if Dr. Small did not, in some ways, see William Osler as a role model. For instance, in Osler's essay on "The Student Life," he gave advice for the student "aflame with passion for knowledge."

I think Dr. Small would have all of us burn with that same passion. I think he would feel, as mentioned in the introductory text, that being a student is a lifelong undertaking— and his responsibility was merely to begin it; that our "good work" will only be completed when Jesus comes. I am absolutely sure he believed this, and I agree.

In his valedictory address at the University of Pennsylvania in 1889, Osler gave advice for personal equanimity, or imperturbability, in all professional activities—not only to "keep the trust of patients," but also to "pass gently through the trials of life."

In later years, as Dr. Small experienced sorrow and discomfort, we prayed he could be spared these trials; but he accepted them with equanimity. He was "Aequanimitas" personified. He earned the trust of all of us and; in spite of oppressive adversity, he "passed gently through the trials of life."

With his passing, we lost an articulate spokesman for and supporter of the Alumni Association and the Alumni Fund for the School of Medicine. But beyond that, we lost a brilliant mind, a consummate teacher, and an amazing repository of School of Medicine lore and alumni deeds. He had a subtle wit, was a legend in his own right, and was one of the most Christ-centered individuals I have ever known.

Those of us who knew him well at the Alumni Association felt we were part of his extended family. We miss the rare beauty of his character. One of his and our legacies that we must carry on is to make man whole, science and spirituality combined. It is Loma Linda's gift, a legacy that we must never forget which was embodied in Dr. Carrol Small.

Carrol S. Small (1910-1997), CME class of 1934, received the LLU Distinguished Service Award in 1984 and was LLU Alumnus of the Year in 1995. The Alumni Association building and the Carrol Small Amphitheater in Centennial Complex were named in his honor.

Hubert Watkins, LLUSM class of 1962, is an associate clinical professor in LLUSM department of dermatology and practices part time in Riverside, California, where he has practiced since 1968. He has been active in alumni affairs since 1980. He was honored with the LLUSMAA Iner Sheld-Ritchie Presidential Award in 2012. He and his wife, Dixie, LLUSAHP class of 1962, have four children, two of whom are graduates of LLUSM, and five grandchildren.

September 2

Let my prayer be set forth before thee as incense; and the lifting up of my hands as the evening sacrifice. Psalm 141:2, KJV

Her name is Crystal Glass; yes, that is her real name. The eldest of six children, born in a parsonage, she loved to sing; her entire family praised God in song wherever they were called to minister. The love of God, learned in the home of her youth, blessed many during her own years of motherhood. Unfortunately, she became a widow soon after her silver wedding anniversary.

Later, God brought back into her life a suitor from her youth, Ernest Glass, whom she married. They enjoyed life together until Ernest died when Crystal was in her eighties. By this time, her own health began to fail; she was evaluated, and began hospice. Somehow, that was not a good fit; her family was unable to manage her by themselves and arranged for her to be cared for by a dear Christian lady, Mrs. Rogers.

Mrs. Rogers kept Crystal clean and healthfully fed and encouraged her faith in the Lord. At times, the two ladies would harmonize in song to their loving Savior. Crystal's beautiful nature blossomed under such loving care. She often awoke with a song of adoration in her heart. Once, when her pastor came to the "care home," they ended up singing many songs of praise together.

Crystal's mind remained clear although the ravages of age immobilized her joints, dimmed her sight, and even hampered her ability to chew and swallow. She was almost never sick enough to need me, her physician, during those seven years of devoted care. Eventually, her personal financial resources came to an end and she was moved to a nursing home.

When Crystal, at age 95, came to the nursing facility, she was still praising God for a "lovely place to be and good food." I continued as her physician and heard her say kind things and compliment her aides, even while waiting for them to have time to bathe her, turn her, feed her, or meet her other needs.

The noises of other patients down the halls, or her roommate's TV have not changed her grateful, cheerful spirit. She spends long hours in her recliner or bed, singing in her heart or counting her blessings. I often stop by her room to make a quick visit and find her wide-awake in the dark, so glad to see me for even a short visit. She ministers to me with her kindness and gratefulness.

One day soon, she will fall asleep in Jesus, awaiting His return. Someday I want to meet Crystal by the Sea of Glass. We will sing our Savior's praises in the eternal light of His presence, and we will join the angel choirs in the place He has gone to prepare for each of us.

Rheeta Stecker, LLUSM class of 1963, is a family practitioner in Hot Springs, Arkansas. She served in Malawi, Africa, from 1964 to 1977 with her husband, Elton Stecker Jr., also LLUSM class of 1963. September 2, 2014, is her 79th birthday.

September 3

I no longer call you servants, because a servant does not know his master's business. Instead, I have called you friends, for everything that I learned from my Father I have made known to you. You did not choose me, but I chose you and appointed you so that you might go and bear fruit—fruit that will last—and so that whatever you ask in my name the Father will give you. John 15:15-16, NIV

One Friday afternoon, things were quiet enough at the hospital to allow me to get home around 5:30 p.m. Not having eaten since breakfast, I was anticipating a home-cooked meal. But as soon as I sat down to enjoy the wonderful food, my intrusive pager rang loudly. The screen displayed 911.

My heart sank, both because of the timing of the call and the fact that it was from the labor and delivery unit, a foreign place for a cardiologist. The obstetrician informed me that a 22-year-old patient of mine, with a history of atrial flutter, had just undergone an emergency C-section. Now the patient had no blood pressure, despite a heart rhythm. He added that the baby was doing fine.

I quickly gulped down enough food to quiet my stomach, made the 12-minute drive to the hospital, ran through the parking lot, and entered a crowded, but deafeningly quiet labor and delivery room. Several providers, nurses, and ancillary staff, probably 25 of them, were surrounding this ashen, motionless young woman, who now had a blood pressure of 45 systolic (normal 90-140) and a heart rate in the low 100 range.

As I joined the team effort to resuscitate this young woman, I thought of her normal vibrancy. "Lord, please help us and this young lady," I prayed. We were able to get her blood pressure up to the 90 systolic range, but an echocardiogram revealed a left ventricular ejection fraction of only about 5% (normal 55-70%).

She had pregnancy-related heart failure, so we rushed her to our sister hospital, where a heart bypass was initiated. Still unresponsive, and with her blood pressure in the 90s, she was flown to the Cleveland Clinic. Today she awaits a heart transplant, but is again vibrant, enthusiastic, and optimistic.

I have reviewed the events of that dark Friday evening several times. When entering that room, I felt a strong sense of impending death. A mighty battle ensued, and death lost. I praise God for showing His power that day, and I praise the medical team for its unified effort.

As health providers, we arm ourselves with knowledge, only to find that there is so much we do not know. We are called upon to be enthusiastic, attentive, and kind, when our cups are empty. And we are expected to do the miraculous for those who have lived by their own rules, and refused to cooperate with a better way of living.

But woven into all this concern are those times that renew us, instances when we see the hand of God. It is then we know for sure that He was the One who put us on His team. Those times refuel us—and we find that they really are not so few and far between.

Ronald McCowan, LLUSM class of 1980-B, is a cardiologist in Charleston, West Virginia.

September 4

I have fought a good fight, I have finished my course, I have kept the faith: Henceforth, there is laid up for me a crown of righteousness, which the Lord, the righteous judge, shall give me at that day: and not to me only, but unto all them also that love his appearing. 2 Timothy 4:7-8, KJV

My son was really frustrated. He wanted to practice dunking the basketball. He had just measured himself next to the rough edge "ruler" of the basement door, and had just crept past the last pencil marking. Surely he could jump higher today than yesterday. But as I watched him, I saw my husband stop his yard work to admonish, "Practice your free throws. It's all about the basics if you want to win games." Grudgingly, our son would practice a few of those unglamorous shots, until the cheering roar of his imaginary fans demanded he try to touch the basketball goal's rim in the last seconds of the game.

Too frequently, playing the game well comes down to "basics," no matter the task at hand. And while maybe not exactly like a basketball game, what happens in Urgent Care is rarely dull. One of the more surprising moments is when a patient sees a specialist for a problem, and then comes to my facility for a "second opinion."

For example, a 58-year-old gentleman, sitting quietly in the examination room, looked up from his phone when I entered. After the customary greeting, he began to summarize for me the story of his last 24 hours of medical evaluation: a visit to a nearby hospital emergency department (ED), where he had gone for an evaluation of his new onset of dizziness; the obligatory cardiac work-up, the mention of benign positional vertigo, and the phone number of a local ENT for a follow-up.

But he could not wait for that visit. So he sat in my office, looking expectant—hoping that I might accomplish something that the hospital ED had not been able to do. I rummaged in my pocket for my phone to make sure it was there. After I examined him, I could call and arrange a visit with the ENT sooner than the patient himself might be able to accomplish.

Stethoscope in hand, I listened to the heart and lungs—just like Leonard Werner, LLUSM class of 1981-R, had taught us all those decades ago. Finding nothing remarkable there, I grabbed my otoscope to see if there was an abnormality in the ears. I was surprised to have a huge cerumen (earwax) impaction greet my eyes as I entered the left auditory canal! Thinking "Naaa!" I finished the exam and asked the man if he would give consent to having his ear canal cleared. He was willing.

After the nurse emerged from the room, she gave me the "thumbs up." The man sat on the table, head down looking at his phone, towel draped loosely over his shoulder. He looked up as I entered and smiled. The dizziness was gone—he was so pleased! He then quipped, "I wish someone in the emergency department would have looked in my ears!"

The basics will always be important, whether in basketball, in medicine, or in our daily Christian walk. We need to set aside daily time to be with our Savior, take time to read his Word, fortify our faith by remembering how He has cared for and led us in the past, and, finally, recognize how He continues to move in our lives today. All these will be the basics that will carry us through to the awesome day when He will return to take us home. May we all then, like Paul, be able to exclaim, "I have fought a good fight, ... I have kept the faith."

Marcia Neil, LLUSM class of 1987, is a family practitioner in Illinois. Her great-grandmother Lottie I. Blake, AMMC class of 1902, was the first black Adventist female physician who trained under Dr. John Harvey Kellogg.

September 5

In peace I will lie down and sleep, for you alone, LORD, make me dwell in safety.
Psalm 4:8, NIV

The verse above is one I learned as a child and recited before I went to bed, after our family's last prayer of the day together. We learn by repetition, but sometimes we overlook the true meaning of the words until we see them in action—perhaps by personally experiencing a situation in which we develop a relationship with another person.

Such an experience happened to me while I was in my last year of medical training in northeast Mexico. I was working with two doctors in a rural area called Sabinas Hidalgo.

Mr. Gregorio had fractured his left tibia after falling from the second floor of a house where he and his brother were working. He was taken to the nearest hospital and had surgery with good results, but wound complications ensued. After IV antibiotics, he was discharged and instructed to go to the nearest clinic for follow-up treatment.

Two weeks later, his brother came to my office requesting a refill for the antibiotics. Since they had no car and it was a long journey, the patient had not come along. A volunteer drove back with the brother to pick up the patient. His wound was infected, so I cleaned it and changed the dressing. This continued for several months, until the wound finally healed.

One weekend during this period, I was resting at home. As I said my last prayer for the night, I felt an urge to go visit this patient. I decided to get dressed and stopped on the way to get him some food.

After arriving at the house where I thought he lived, I saw that it was empty. I called out and was surprised to hear a weak voice coming from a small, abandoned house nearby. Mr. Gregorio was living in a room that had only half a roof and no water or electricity. I found him resting on his dirty bed alone, scared, and hungry.

After I identified myself, he asked me why I was there so late. I could not answer him because I was surprised by why I had come. I believe that my impulse to go to him that night was God communicating with me. Mr. Gregorio told me that he had not had food or water for two days because his brother had not visited, and he had no money or any way to call him.

After I cared for his wound and provided him with food and water, Mr. Gregorio told me that I was an angel of God. I simply told him that God loved him so much that even in his circumstances, he was not forgotten.

When I returned to my house and went back to bed, I truly understood the meaning of this verse, "In peace I will lie down and sleep, for you alone, LORD, make me dwell in safety." As Christians and medical professionals, we have the opportunity to be instruments of God for people who are suffering around us each day.

Before you go to bed, ask God to give you peace of mind—the peace that will allow you to lie down and sleep because He makes you dwell in safety.

Samuel Rodriguez, a graduate from Montemorelos University, is a research assistant fellow in LLUSM department of surgery. September 5 is his birthday.

September 6

Jesus said unto her, I am the resurrection, and the life: he that believeth in me, though he were dead, yet shall he live. John 11:25, KJV

Doing short-term relief work as a general surgeon in a small mission hospital in Zambia was a wonderful experience. However, every day brought more challenges than I had ever anticipated. Three other doctors—a pediatrician, an ophthalmologist, and a family practice physician—were at that 60-bed hospital during my time there. Diagnostic and therapeutic capabilities were quite marginal, but still the hospital was a great asset to the local population.

We frequently had more than double our normal capacity, and the next nearest medical facility was too far for most of the people we served. These were people who survived in the bush, essentially as their ancestors had for thousands of years. Unfortunately, death was not unusual at the hospital, in spite of our best efforts.

Each day as I rounded on the male-patient ward, Mr. Banda, a pleasant gentleman in bed 1, smiled and greeted me in his native tongue. (It seemed that half the area's population was named Banda.) I smiled back, nodded, and said, "Good morning." He was not on my list but rather belonged to one of the other doctors, so I was not involved in his day-to-day care. I just said hello and moved on. He seemed to appreciate the recognition.

The medical students and nurses directed me, in this overcrowded ward, to the other patients I was to follow. Every bed was filled, and there were patients on mats under the beds, and sometimes on the floor between the beds. One man, thinking we had forgotten him, reached out from under a bed and tugged on my long white coat. "What about me?" he said in English. I rounded on him and went about my other duties.

Day after day, I nodded hello to Mr. Banda and moved on. He seemed to be recovering from whatever illness had brought him to the hospital and appeared about ready to go home. But one day, as I passed bed 1, Mr. Banda was dead—or so it seemed. He did not move. He did not nod or greet me. He lay still, barely breathing.

"What is going on with Mr. Banda?" I asked. "Oh, he is diabetic. He is dying," the nurse replied.

"Give him some IV glucose STAT," I said. Shortly after receiving the infusion of glucose, he began to arouse; and, by the time we finished rounds, he was awake, alert, and sitting up in bed. He nodded good morning in his usual way, but this time with a grateful smile on his face.

This episode reminded me of how it might be for some of us at the resurrection morning. We may be dead when that day dawns, but Christ will give us an infusion of life as He calls: "Awake, come forth, I am the resurrection and the life. Arise to new life everlasting." I look forward greatly to that morning!

James Simpson, LLUSM class of 1970, is a vascular surgeon in Riverside, California. In 1985, he served as a relief surgeon for three months at Mwami Hospital near Chipata, Zambia. September 6 is his daughter's birthday.

September 7

You therefore must endure hardship as a good soldier of Jesus Christ. No one engaged in warfare entangles himself with the affairs of this life, that he may please him who enlisted him as a soldier. 2 Timothy 2:3-4, NKJV

In Acts 14:22 (NIV), Paul—who had narrowly escaped being stoned to death—is encouraging his fellow disciples, with these choice words, to remain faithful in their preaching of the gospel: "We must go through many hardships to enter the kingdom of God."

As a physician, there have been, and continue to be, moments in my life where my faith and patience are tested. Perhaps many of you reading this can attest to what I am talking about. As doctors, we face the noncompliant patient, the unbalanced lifestyle between home and work, the pressure to spend more time with the kids, the lack of quality time with our spouse, and the need to be a role model in the community.

I had just been given the news that I would be deployed to Afghanistan. My heart sank to the floor as I speedily read the fine print of my orders, my eyes only seeing the portion that said "...450 DAYS." I pulled the orders up to my face and scanned that same line again and again and again. My mind was painstakingly trying to wrap itself around the math. 450 DAYS!

We were already stationed on Guam, an ocean apart from family; my wife was in her third trimester with our second child. We had just settled into our new home, and I was still a newly minted family physician. "Lord, why now? Lord, why me?" was my earnest prayer. I prayed for strength, to be shielded from the temptation to be angry or bitter, and for a hedge around my family. Through prayer, I reached the conclusion that this experience would be a prime example of what Paul was talking about.

After a tactical fixed-wing landing into Afghanistan, a helicopter flight into the southeastern region of the country, and a six-hour convoy excursion through some of the most dangerous terrain in the country, I was assigned as the sole physician to a small base deep in Taliban territory. Our small base took mortar and rocket fire regularly (with two instances of a direct hit a few hundred meters from where I slept). I went on over 30 convoy missions and was a first responder to dozens of wounded soldiers.

While getting home in one piece was my primary mission, God had a far bigger plan. During my time in Afghanistan, I was able to start a free clinic for children in the surrounding villages, train Afghan soldiers in basic first aid, lead out in Bible studies for fellow service members, and be a listening ear to those under intense personal stress—all while managing the medical clinic for the entire base.

Upon reflecting on this past experience, I have repeatedly expressed my gratitude to God for His infinite wisdom and mercy. I always knew He was there during times of comfortable living, but only when it was all taken away did He truly test my loyalty to Him and most clearly reveal His strength. To those who have served in the deepest jungles of Africa, in the most remote combat outposts in Afghanistan, or in the most picture-perfect suburban neighborhoods of the United States, may we continue to face our most trying of "tribulations" knowing that these are meant to prepare us for a life of eternity.

Michael Mercado, LLUSM class of 2004, was serving as head of the department of family medicine at the U.S. Naval Hospital Guam when this devotional was written. September 7, 2009, was the day that he was reunited with his family—his wife Gemma, also LLUSM class of 2004, and their two children— after a 13-month deployment during which he served as a clinical advisor to the Afghan National Army in Khowst, Afghanistan.

September 8

Jesus looked at them and said, "With man this is impossible, but with God all things are possible." Matthew 19:26, NIV

This story is about a CME disciple who lived an exemplary life. His name was Tadao Hata, CME class of 1931. He was born in Honolulu and was a general practitioner on Kauai for many years before taking an eye, ear, nose and throat residency in Pennsylvania. He returned to Kauai and retired in 1974. Multiple events relating to our family occurred which had lifelong consequences influenced by this man's kind, thoughtful and skilled professionalism.

To begin, my mother, Katherine Kam Lui, and her friend were traveling one rainy day on a muddy road that led over a cement bridge when the car skidded and was totaled. Good Samaritans took them to Dr. Hata's office. He examined the injured and repaired their wounds. Fortunately, there were no severe head injuries. Because there were no hospitals, Dr. Hata converted one of his office rooms to a hospital and took care of them until they recovered.

In another more critical event, my mother developed boils around the circumference of her trunk and developed septicemia; a condition that was sometimes fatal in those days. Gladys Weber, RN, wife of the pastor, skillfully cared for my mother in her home, with compresses, good hygiene, temperature control and all measures possible. Mother remained critically ill, so Gladys called Dr. Hata to come and see her. What happened next made a lasting impression on my mother, so much so that she wrote about it in a letter years later. "[Dr. Hata] came early in the morning to see me and brought his Bible. He read from the Scriptures, then knelt by my bedside to pray."

Drs. Hata and Burt Wade, CME class of 1932, from the other side of the island, consulted and did all they could to restore my mother's health, then asked the ministers and leaders of the church in Honolulu for special prayers. Their prayers were miraculously answered and my mother made a full recovery.

A year later, my third brother, Samuel Lui, CME class of 1949, was doing a tonsillectomy and adenoidectomy in Honolulu when he suddenly and unexpectedly lost his vision. Dr. Hata came immediately over to help him complete the case. Sam was found to have a pituitary tumor that involved the optic nerve. He went to Michigan where my brother Alfred Lui, CME class of 1945, was taking a surgical residency. Alfred arranged for a neurosurgeon to operate, followed by radiation, saving the vision of one eye. Ernest Zane, CME class of 1956, helped with Sam's vision for the rest of his life.

To a lesser degree, Dr. Hata also saved my right eye. I was cutting an ironwood pine tree with a cane knife when a piece of steel broke off and penetrated my eye. Fortunately, Dr. Hata came home for lunch and removed the steel, thus saving my vision.

God has been good to our family for all these years. I pray that we will remain faithful in serving Him—just as His servant Dr. Hata was.

Percy T. Lui, CME class of 1955, is a retired family practitioner residing in Redlands, California. In 1969, he and his late wife, Marjorie Low Lui, enjoyed working at Davis Memorial Hospital in Guyana where she grew up. They have four children, three of whom are graduates of LLUSM.

September 9

You knitted me together in my mother's womb. Psalm 139:13, ESV

F ew things are more awkward than sobbing in the presence of other people. That includes a first-time mother crying in the presence of doctors and nurses . . . or the intermittent sniffles, indicative of an extended period of crying, of one who leans limp and exhausted in the corner of an elevator.

My daughter was two days old when she was admitted to the neonatal intensive care unit (NICU) at Loma Linda University Children's Hospital. Her father and I, smug in the knowledge that we had brought this little life into the world successfully in the comfort of our own home, without the aid of medical intervention, were brought low by the discovery that she had Down syndrome. It was suspected first by our midwife and then later by our pediatrician, who directed us to go to the emergency department (ED)—immediately!

We arrived at the ED. Vitals were checked again. A nearby, self-proclaimed "nosy" nurse took notice of the numbers and she, too, was not pleased. Within moments, a team of ED doctors and nurses whisked us to an adult-sized gurney, upon which our not-even-six-pound baby was placed. And she cried for the first time.

I remember crying, too. From the time I was in the ED and on to the NICU, through our meeting with the cardiologist (who would ultimately inform us that our daughter had two congenital heart defects), through answering questions about my pregnancy and homebirth, and through being told about Down syndrome, I cried. When the lactation specialist escorted me to the pumps to collect my milk, because the act of nursing my baby would hurt her, I cried. My heart was breaking for my little girl.

In the end, she had to have two corrective heart surgeries. However, since that day, a vital piece of knowledge has surfaced amid the pain. This baby is not simply our baby. This baby is not just our own, but her father and I are stewards of her life. She was a gift from God, and it is to Him that she ultimately belongs.

I can no more boast in the triumphant success of my bringing her into the world than I should be devastated by her Down syndrome or heart defects. We thank Him for our pediatrician's intuition and initiative. We thank Him for the surgeons who brought our daughter safely through both of her surgeries. We thank Him for the NICU nurses and the pediatric cardiac nurses who cared for our baby when we could not. He gave us this little life, this little piece of His creation, and He did not—and will not—forsake her.

Kelly Nava's daughter continues to be a patient at LLUCH. Her sister, an employee, directed her to the Evening Rounds project.

September 10

Therefore, . . . let us throw off everything that hinders. . . . And let us run with perseverance the race marked out for us. Hebrews 12:1, NIV

While it is well known that physical exercise is essential for maintaining good health, exercise can be easy to neglect when one is faced with a busy schedule. When done right, walking and running can provide many health benefits—including cardiovascular health, prevention of obesity and osteoporosis, and better regulation of blood sugar. No wonder we see so many walkers and runners in Loma Linda, California—a city famous for healthy living and longevity!

When I took up running 10 years ago, I never imagined being able to run 26.2 miles in a full marathon. However, with the help of a great coach and regular training, I have now completed 26 marathons during that time. I have also enjoyed the health benefits that regular activity can bring. The back pain that bothered me for years has vanished; and, after my morning running sessions, I often feel refreshed and mentally ready to start my day.

The book of Hebrews admonishes us to "run with perseverance." Even if you feel pain and tiredness, you need to endure to finish the race. We may encounter obstacles in our spiritual life, but "You need to persevere so that when you have done the will of God, you will receive what he has promised" (Hebrews 10:36, NIV). Secondly we are urged to "[throw] off everything that hinders." When it comes to running, the lighter the shoes and clothes you wear, the better. If we are running toward Heaven, we need to throw off everything that weighs us down—anything that takes our attention away from Jesus.

Faith and confidence are also important. Half of completing a race is the belief that you can do it; the other half is physical endurance. As Hebrews 10:35 states: "So do not throw away your confidence; it will be richly rewarded." Training is the most important part of running a successful race. Running 26.2 miles should not be attempted without proper training. Paul advised Timothy in this way: "Train yourself to be godly. For physical training is of some value, but godliness has value for all things, holding promise for both the present life and the life to come" (1 Timothy 4:7-8, NIV).

One of the best rewards of running a marathon may be the feeling of fulfillment that occurs when crossing the finish line and receiving a medal. And when we finish our spiritual race and get to Heaven and meet our Lord, we cannot even imagine the joy we will feel when He gives us our crowns. Let us be faithful today so that we can declare, like Paul: "I have fought the good fight, I have finished the race, I have kept the faith. Now there is in store for me the crown of righteousness, which the Lord, the righteous Judge, will award to me on that day—and not only to me, but also to all who have longed for his appearing" (2 Timothy 4:7-8, NIV).

Timothy Jung, LLUSM class of 1974, PhD, is a clinical professor in LLUSM department of otolaryngology, head and neck surgery. September 10 is his wedding anniversary.

September 11

Yea, though I walk through the valley of the shadow of death, I will fear no evil: for thou art with me; thy rod and thy staff they comfort me. Psalm 23:4, KJV

Savoring the memories of visiting my mother's family in Norway, I waited for the landing announcement for Newark, New Jersey. Although quite jet-lagged, I calculated we should have landed 30 minutes earlier and worried about my 75-year-old mother and missing our connection to Los Angeles International Airport (LAX). When we finally landed just before dusk, the last light streamed under the gray storm clouds, creating a fiery glow on the picturesque Manhattan skyline.

From our left window view, I pointed out to my half-asleep mother the Empire State Building (which my grandfather had helped build) and the Twin Towers. But the plane that was supposed to take us to LAX had not landed yet because a hurricane, hovering 100 miles off New York City, had caused the postponement of flights all that day, September 10. I felt impressed to call my husband, David, and tell him we were exhausted and planned to stay overnight in Newark after our transatlantic flight. I said we would come home on September 11, 2001, after a good night's sleep.

On the phone, David paused and told me, "I don't know why I am saying this, because I usually am fine with your decisions in matters like this, Honey, but for some reason I feel strongly that I want you to stay at the airport until there is no chance of a plane coming to Los Angeles. Please come home tonight, if it is possible." This was a very atypical response from him, and I do not know why I listened.

We waited five hours for a plane to California and arrived at LAX about 2 a.m. PDT. We stumbled into bed on September 11, when passengers were boarding the United Airlines (UA) Flight 93 in Newark, the plane that crashed in Pennsylvania. Those passengers sat in the same boarding area where we had been waiting only hours before. We could have been booked on that tragic flight to San Francisco. At the very least, a different flight would have been grounded somewhere in mid-America, when all planes were ordered to land. We would have arrived home days later, along with thousands of other bewildered travelers.

Ironically, I returned to LAX on Sunday, September 17, when the first flights took off after the six-day moratorium. The somber atmosphere of waiting in long lines in the pre-dawn darkness in the tightened "airline security clearance" was numbing. Before I landed in Washington, DC, that afternoon, I saw the smoke still rising from the Pentagon crash site. Being present at the sites of terrorism was chilling.

Survivor guilt plagued me for weeks. I read every UA Flight 93 news release about the plane crash in the Pennsylvania field. Standing breathlessly with my mother at the Ground Zero Twin Towers memorial a few years later, we walked the entire fence line and looked at every photo before we could tear ourselves away. Why not us? We were spared and they were not . . . *we must never forget.*

Linda Hyder Ferry, LLUSM class of 1979-B, is an associate professor in LLUSM department of preventive medicine and an assistant professor in LLUSM department of family medicine. She and her husband, David, LLUSM class of 1976-A, reside in Yucaipa, California. September 11, 2014, marks the 13th anniversary of the terrorist attacks on the United States.

September 12

Work willingly at whatever you do, as though you were working for the Lord rather than for people. Colossians 3:23, NLT

P erhaps many of us have had times when we feel that what we are now doing is not what we envisioned when we decided to become physicians. We did not know that there would be compliance laws, unhappy patients, electronic medical records, and piles of paperwork. There are days when my clinic is not running smoothly, and I become frustrated that this is not what the practice of medicine is supposed to be. But one day, I read the Bible text above and it helped put things in perspective.

In Paul's letter to the Colossians, he includes advice on the everyday relationships of Christian living. One could assume that the above admonition was directed at church leaders or someone who had an important position. However, Paul is telling slaves to work cheerfully as though they were working for the Lord. At that time, slaves were not considered people, but rather things, similar to livestock.

Paul is encouraging them to work hard and cheerfully—instruction that would not be the natural inclination for a slave. Christianity was to change the way a slave approached his work. Christianity would provide the slave the physical and spiritual strength needed to approach difficult situations.

We who work in health care are not facing the same challenges that slaves had, but I think Paul's instructions are for us, too. I was recently at the Association of American Medical Colleges meeting in San Francisco and went to a lecture by Rachel Naomi Remen. She stated that meaning has the power to change the experience of work, but it does not change the work.

She went on to say that work can be experienced as a job, a career, or a calling. As Christian physicians, I believe we have not just jobs, but a calling to participate in the healing ministry of Jesus. When we experience our work as a calling, we are able to tolerate problems. Christianity provides us with the strength to perform our duties. We need to remember that we are working for the Lord, and that we are the hands of Jesus when we treat patients. It is certainly much easier for me to face the frustrations that arise when I remember that Jesus is my true employer; that is true for all occupations.

Paul does not stop without offering the slave hope for the future. He states, "The Lord will give you an inheritance as your reward" (Colossians 3:24, NLT). I know we look forward to the Second Coming when we will spend eternity with Jesus and will not be dealing with disease and death. We can experience rewards in our work now, when we remember that what we are doing is for Christ, and that He is blessing us as we minister to others.

May we always remember for Whom we are working, and may we always pray that we will fulfill the mission to which we have been called.

Sarah Roddy, LLUSM class of 1980-B, is associate dean for admissions and recruitment in LLUSM and an associate professor in LLUSM department of pediatrics. Her specialty is pediatric neurology. She is married to Daniel Giang, LLUSM class of 1983. September 12 is her birthday.

September 13

For all have sinned and fall short of the glory of God, being justified freely by His grace through the redemption that is in Christ Jesus. Romans 3:23-24, NKJV

Only a few months after his open-heart surgery, Mr. F came back in January with fever, chills, and shortness of breath. After replacing his infected aortic valve with a mechanical prosthesis and treating him with IV antibiotics for six weeks, his acute heart failure symptoms appeared resolved, his energy fully recovered, and "life was back to normal."

I was surprised to see him back in the hospital in September. He was supposed to have been "cured," and his mechanical valve was to last him a lifetime. This time, he could hardly breathe; and he was jaundiced, as well as swollen, with purple spots all over his skin.

He told me he had been using drugs again but sincerely promised not to once he recovered. Sadly, all we could offer him at that point was the promise that God loved him and had already forgiven him. A few days later, Mr. F—at the age of 40—died alone in a hospital bed with no friends or family next to him.

Mr. G had a different addiction. Alcoholism had weakened his body and suppressed his immune system. After his first aortic valve replacement for endocarditis, he promised to abstain from alcohol. However, in less than a year, he returned with a recurrent abscess that had eaten into his heart muscle. He survived a complex reconstructive heart operation but continued to drink, in spite of his family's efforts to help. It was after his third serious endocarditis event that he consented to intense professional counseling and he opened his heart to receive his family's unconditional love and support.

Miss L's heavy smoking habit contributed to her acute heart attack at a young age. After coronary surgery to bypass her clogged arteries, she put away the money she spent on cigarettes and sent a monthly donation in that amount to Loma Linda University Medical Center. This gift was her way of committing herself, on a daily basis, toward kicking her habit.

Perhaps any one of us can identify with one or all three of these patients: suffering from hard-to-break habits, failing repeatedly, or needing to make lifesaving changes. Fortunately, God's grace offers hope for a real "cure." It is the divine gift of transformation: "I will give you a new heart and put a new spirit within you" (Ezekiel 36:26, NKJV).

The healing power of a "new spirit" is often transmitted through a human link, such as a loving spouse, a supportive family, a caring friend, or a nurturing partner. If you are fortunate enough to have access to such a connection, be grateful, for like Mr. G and myself, you are truly blessed.

Anees J. Razzouk, LLUSM class of 1982, is chair and a professor in LLUSM department of cardiovascular and thoracic surgery and a professor in LLUSM department of pediatrics. He and his wife, Teresa Thompson, LLUSM class of 1990, reside in Redlands, California.

September 14

You are the God who performs miracles; you display your power among the peoples. Psalm 77:14, NIV

"I am having my surgery today. Can you come and pray with me?" The phone call was from my younger sister, Liza, who, for her entire life has been battling lupus; kidney failure; and, for the past 10 years hypertension and heart failure. Instead of dropping everything and rushing to her side, I said, "Yes, let's pray over the phone." When I hung up, I felt guilty.

After the surgery was completed, the surgeon called to talk to me about my sister's condition. I asked, "Is she all right?" He hesitated for what seemed an eternity and then asked if I could come talk to him in person. Immediately, I knew in my heart that something was very wrong, and I began praying that Liza was still alive.

As I arrived at the hospital waiting room later that day and saw the solemn look on the surgeon's face, I feared the worst. It was a surreal moment as he explained the process and technicalities of the surgery, and how it seemed to be a very successful surgery. But then he revealed the sudden crash of my sister's heart rate and blood pressure, indicating that despite attempts at resuscitation my sister had gone into a full cardiac arrest.

In careful detail, the surgeon described how they had been able to resuscitate her but thought she would not make it. As the doctors were asking us what her advance directives were, Liza coded once more. I was sobbing, "Please do everything you can to save her."

I remember crying out in prayer, "Dear Lord, I didn't listen to your voice and go into the hospital to pray with her. Please spare her. She is your child and wants to live for you. Please, God, give me another chance to pray with her."

The team of doctors directed us to go, two at a time, to say our goodbyes to her. Call it denial or faith, but I just did not believe she was going to die. The doctors and nurses, as well as science and medicine, said this was the end for her and that my talking to her was futile. I remember saying repeatedly, "Don't give up, Liza. You can make it." My husband whispered to my sister, "When you wake up, I will get you that latest iPhone you've been wanting."

A week passed. We had teams of doctors tell us she might be "brain dead," and there was nothing more they could do. However, my mother quickly reminded them that now the Great Physician would take over.

One day my sister woke up, and the first thing she said to my husband was, "So where's my iPhone?" She has since had other close calls, with a similar prognosis, but her life testifies that *He lives* and is evidence that miracles still happen today. Coincidentally, her Christmas card to thank her team of doctors read: "Believe miracles exist, because Jesus Christ was born."

Sheila Hodgkin earned an MS degree in marital and family therapy from LLUSBH in 1995. She is married to Steven Hodgkin, LLUSM class of 1990. September 14 is the birthday of her sister, Liza Jane Atiga.

September 15

Is anyone among you suffering? Let him pray. James 5:13, NKJV

It was my second week on the acute care surgery service as a third-year medical student and I was finally getting the hang of how triage and trauma worked. My role was to write down my resident's findings as he hollered out his physical exam and to piece together the patients' history by talking to the emergency medical technicians (EMTs) who brought them in.

This morning, a gentleman came in already intubated and sedated, with a rope burn near the angles of his jaw. I watched the man's thin, tattooed chest rise and fall with machine-induced breathing. The EMT gave a succinct report stating that the man was found hanging from a rope. They were able to administer CPR and re-establish a heartbeat, but his brain was likely without blood flow for over 10 minutes. After stating which medications the patient received en route, the EMT ended with, "his wife is in the waiting room and was the first person to find him."

I knew what this meant; I was the one who would be talking to his wife to get a full history. My mind raced, trying to find past experiences that would prepare me for how to converse with a woman who just witnessed her husband as he tried to kill himself. Blank. Then I thought of my classes in medical school pertaining to patient-physician interaction. Reflecting on active listening skills did not bring me much confidence. Then I turned my thoughts toward where I should have started: God. As I walked to the waiting room, I sent up a prayer for God to direct me in how to interact with this woman.

I called out her last name and saw a reddened face with swollen eyes look up. I introduced myself, and took her to a private room. Words slowly came out of my mouth as I worded questions as sensitively as I could to get a more complete history. Her response, in between sobs, was heartbreaking, "I heard the dog barking in the living room, I called my husband's name to see what the barking was about. When he didn't respond I walked to the room to find him hanging there. I ran over to try and hold him up, but it was hard, it was so hard!"

As I pictured her story in my mind, I began to get a gnawing feeling in my stomach and knew I had to offer a prayer for this woman. What if she thinks I am trying to use a vulnerable situation to push my religion? I decided to go for it, "I offer prayer to my patients, is that something you would be interested in?" She looked at the ground as she sobbed silently. Then she slowly began to nod her head and said, "Yes."

Frankly, I don't even remember what I asked God for in that short prayer, and I'm not sure that it mattered. Simply praying reminds us that God is present, especially during trying times.

Three days later I saw the patient's wife in the hallway, sitting on the ground with her back against the wall. She stared downward. I sat down next to her and asked how her husband was doing. She had just hung up the phone with the organ donation organization; the neurologists had pronounced him brain dead. Then she looked me in the eye, much calmer than three days ago, and said, "*Always* offer prayer to your patients. I would have never asked you to pray for me, but that is exactly what I needed." I told her I would, and then prayed that God would get her through the difficult times ahead.

God is powerful, and is able to do things through us, even when we don't feel prepared.

Blake Spitzer, LLUSM class of 2014, is from San Diego, California, and graduated from University of California, San Diego with a BS in human biology. He plans to specialize in general surgery and work in Latin America.

September 16

For I am the LORD your God who takes hold of your right hand and says to you, Do not fear; I will help you. Isaiah 41:13, NIV

It's been almost three years, yet the pictures in my mind are quite clear although the sounds are more muted. A very large propeller is coming straight down at us—full throttle. About 50 feet above us, it pulls up just enough to crash 70 feet away.

We were at the Reno Air Show for the first time after spending over 10 years trying to get there. Why God? But right then, all my mind could say was "Thank you God that my family and I are alive" and other than a scratch, and being covered in fuel, are okay even though we are surrounded by body pieces of those less fortunate. "What can I do Lord? Help me to help You," I think as I slide down the steps of the grandstand to the disaster below me.

No more P51 Mustang airplane. No more box seats. Fuel, gray dust, and what was left of seven disseminated bodies cover everything. No flames—"Thank you, God."

I know trauma from my time in the operating room; all the days and nights of trauma anesthesia kick in. My dear 100 percent non-medical husband, who is also a pilot, is right behind me. He is the first person holding on to me; I leave him with instructions for an injured pilot from Alaska who was running, screaming, gray, but very alive. Piles of bodies, feet, hands, unknown body parts, everywhere. A fireman grabs me next and does not let go for the next hour. Is this person alive? It's hard to tell. Everyone is gray. I think, "God, please help us!" Yes, no legs, but alive! There is nothing available to use that is not soaking wet and oily. People donate belts for tourniquets, shirts for compression bandages. "God, help me say and do what I can to help You help these poor people." There are so many amputations, head injuries, unknown abdominal injuries, poles, and chair pieces—it's hard to keep everyone calm and focused. I keep praying.

I feel that those who desperately need to be airlifted are miraculously being moved very quickly. I learn later that as I said "air" for the severely injured, around 20 of the injured were placed in a Huey helicopter that was there for the airshow. A Reno resident directed the demo pilot to one of the three trauma hospitals in the area—a true miracle!

Someone hands me three IV needles. I don't want to waste veins—these people have limited numbers as most are missing at least one limb. Gravel, plane debris, fuel, and who knows what else is on everything.

We are through the worst of the patients and I'm led to triage the "yellow group." My first patient is hardly breathing and blue. "Oh Lord!" I think there must be other doctors around but only learn of two. "There are so many injured dear God!" I now know there were 11 deaths. At least 73 people with severe injuries were transported in under one hour. All the OR's in the trauma centers were used for over 48 straight hours. Blood was flown in from Las Vegas.

As the last patient is taken away, less than an hour after the crash, an eerie silence settles over the airfield. There is a wheelchair and a few bodies that are covered. No other people except a few first responders are left. I am looking for my family, knowing that many lives are gone or have been changed forever, including mine. I have many questions God, but I know You were here. Your presence was here. I could feel it almost palpably. As a first responder, I felt lucky, guilty, overwhelmed, scared, but oh so thankful for my faith-based training.

Penny Kimball-Jones, LLUSM class of 1985, is an associate professor in LLUSM department of anesthesia. This story took place during the Reno Air Races on September 16, 2011.

September 17

Be still, and know that I am God; I will be exalted among the nations, I will be exalted in the earth! Psalm 46:10, NKJV

"I'm sorry, Dr. Chan. You have lymphoma." I was stunned as I heard these words over the phone from an on-call physician who was covering for my gastroenterologist. I had casually called on my day off to ask for the biopsy results. A colonoscopy had been performed for screening, but this was the last thing I was expecting to hear. Moments before, I had felt healthy, fit, and vibrant. The "C" word can change one's life in a split second.

For the next few minutes, while waiting for the fax of my pathology report and not knowing the grade or the type of lymphoma, I suddenly felt as if I was looking death in the face. I will never forget that moment. The fax indicated that I had Grade 1 primary intestinal follicular lymphoma of the terminal ileum, a rare, slow-growing tumor. I felt an incredible sense of relief within minutes of receiving the fax.

A "wait and watch" approach was recommended. A follow-up colonoscopy one year later showed a progression in cell type in some areas to Grade 3A, with concern for transformation to a worse form of the disease. As with many patients given the diagnosis of cancer, I made dietary changes. Now two-and-a-half years later, I am very grateful that without my undergoing treatment, there is no evidence of the disease. Spontaneous remission is known to occur occasionally with this type of tumor.

As an internist, I have had the solemn task of informing my patients of the diagnosis of cancer. Over the years, I have been taught countless powerful lessons about death and dying from patients. I would frequently wonder when it would be my turn to be the recipient of such news, and how I would deal with the process of dying.

The diagnosis of cancer can often make one see life in a different way. The prospect of one's death can, at times, be one of the greatest motivators to live a more meaningful life. I find myself appreciating the simple things of life immensely. I enjoy connecting with patients and others on a deeper level, and now I find a special kinship and bond with cancer patients. A few years ago, I came across these words that I found meaningful, "How happy a person is depends upon the depth of his gratitude."

My brother, Art Minagawa, LLUSM class of 1988, recently sent me a book by Kevin W. McCarthy entitled *The On-Purpose Person, Making Your Life Make Sense*. This book has helped me realize that my cancer is a gift. My cancer has helped me focus more sharply on the real purpose of my life. I exist to serve others by directing them to the grace and love of God.

My hope is to live each day that I am given to the fullest by spending time at the feet of Jesus and allowing Him to work through me. One day soon, I, too, will be a patient for the very last time.

Angela Chan, LLUSM class of 1983, is an internist. She lives with her husband, Terence Chan, LLUSM class of 1979-A, in Centralia, Washington. September 17 is her husband's birthday.

September 18

God created human beings; he created them godlike, Reflecting God's nature. He created them male and female. Genesis 1:27, MSG

Noticing an ambulance in front of our church in Calgary one Sabbath morning, I hopped out of the car to see who needed care, only to discover that Natalie, an 85-year-old close friend, had fallen and hit her head. I accompanied her to the hospital. While we were waiting in the emergency department, two large security guards dragged a young man of First Nation descent into the waiting room. As they plunked him in a chair, one of the guards said, in a voice loud enough for everyone to hear, "You are a disheveled, dirty, drunk Indian and you have a foul mouth. You need to remain in this seat until your turn to see the doctor."

Natalie became restless as the wait lengthened. I opened her Bible and read to her. As I read Psalm 23, the young man, from across the room, responded, "Amen!" When Natalie left for her CT scan, this same man moved closer to me. He returned my smile.

It was then I heard a voice speak to me, "Judy, I want you to sit by this man, hold his hand, and pray with him." I answered back, "Are you sure that's what you want me to do? I'm dressed to go to church, and he was just picked up from a ditch."

I hesitated for a moment but was impressed that God was the One speaking to me. It took every ounce of courage for me to stand up. Once I stood, God was so close to me that it was no effort to walk over and sit beside the man and take his dirty, sweaty hand in mine.

I asked him some questions; one of them was, "Do you believe in God?" He said, "Yes." He explained that he had lost a good job because he had taken one drink at a New Year's Eve party and had not been able to quit since.

I prayed with him for victory over alcohol and that he would trust God to help him turn his life around. He then told me that he had asked God to send an angel when the guards were so rough with him. He turned to me and said, "You are that angel." He hugged me as he left the room to see the doctor.

The deep spiritual thrill I received upon realizing that God had called on me in such an unusual way to serve one of His sons in need continues to lift my life experience. I pray for this young man, this man named Jason, and dream of meeting him in Heaven.

Judith Gimbel graduated from LLUSPH in 1979. She is married to Howard Gimbel, LLUSM class of 1960. They have five children and twelve grandchildren. September 18 is her birthday.

September 19

For the Son of Man came to seek and to save the lost. Luke 19:10, NIV

As a pediatrician, I like to tell people that I rescue kids every day. But what they want to hear about is the time I rescued two young children from a cave. This story really starts at a school retreat at Lake Britton in Shasta County, California. The speaker for the retreat was Pastor Carl Wilkens, Adventist Disaster and Relief Agency (ADRA) director in Rwanda. During that country's time of trouble, he helped with many miraculous rescues. After his talk, we went around the circle, saying what we hoped for, and, impulsively, I said, "I would like to rescue somebody."

Years passed, but then a call came on a busy day at the office. At Lava Beds National Monument in Siskiyou, California, two fifth graders were lost in Catacombs Cave. The sheriff was calling out cavers. The back half of Catacombs Cave is a maze of seemingly endless crawlways where people often get lost, including me on one occasion. But this incident was different. After 24 hours, these kids were still missing.

I had a hunch where they might be. There is an obscure room in the back of the cave not shown on maps. It is hard to reach, so searchers might easily miss it. I was working that day with Kay Henderson, LLUSM class of 1979-B, who immediately said, "Go. Go. I'll cover here." So off I went, leaving a schedule behind to go caving.

Two hours later, Russ Yoder and I arrived at the rescue site simultaneously. Russ, a fellow caver—thin, tough as nails—burrows through small holes like a weasel. "We're part of the rescue," we said, in order to get in. Next, I talked to the sheriff. "We have six likely spots in there we'd like to double check, and could we borrow kneepads?" I asked. He found some kneepads and said, "Okay, go in and do it." Another caver, Bill Devereaux, was at Entrance Control. He required: Name, Time in, Time out. "This won't take long," I said to Bill. He just smiled.

We went straight to that room. The final nine-inch high crawl space was almost too low. First, we found fragments of a sweatshirt. Then we found the two youngsters, huddled together in the obscure chamber.

Timothy and Kyra had been on a field trip from Grass Valley School. They were not injured, their lights worked, and they had warm clothes. But they knew they were lost and had decided to stay put. "We knew our moms would send rescuers," they said. Russ and I looked at each other. They had no idea how long they had been waiting in that cave. We said, "Lots of people are worried about you, so let's go."

Caver Jim Wolff had a radio at a junction point, and the news went out. "The kids are found. They're all right. We'll be out soon." At the cave's entrance, the two schoolchildren went up and out, and then went to happy reunions with their families. Many prayers were answered that day and the text above took on new meaning.

William Broeckel, LLUSM class of 1983, is a pediatrician in Yreka, California. He is married to Judy, LLUSM class of 1985.

September 20

Aren't five sparrows sold for two cents? God doesn't forget any of them. Even every hair on your head has been counted. Don't be afraid! You are worth more than many sparrows. Luke 12:6-7, GW

When Elder Don Roth from the General Conference contacted me in 1980 about going to Karachi, Pakistan, for three months to relieve Beverly Giebel, CME class of 1956, he said, "We really need a female physician in this specialty in a Muslim country; however, an elderly, white-haired male might do."

Shortly thereafter, I arrived at the Adventist hospital in Karachi. One late afternoon, I was called to the emergency department to see a young woman who was seven months pregnant with twins. She presented the typical picture of eclampsia or toxemia of pregnancy—frequent, severe convulsions and high blood pressure.

The patient was admitted to the hospital and the next 24 hours were spent at her bedside controlling her hypertension and convulsions. Early labor and the process of dilatation had begun, so it was elected to follow through with labor and delivery. With some assistance, 10 to 12 hours later, two beautiful baby girls arrived weighing just over three pounds each!

The babies were sent to the nursery and placed in incubators. The treatment for them was oxygen and nasogastric tubes for feeding. The mother had an uncomplicated postpartum course and left the hospital after one week, doing well. However, since the twins were born prematurely, they became anemic and jaundiced and required transfusions. After several weeks they were finally beginning to gain weight and it was felt they would continue to improve and survive.

When the twins were four to five weeks old, I received a call from the nursery one afternoon stating that the parents were there to take the babies home. I called my resident to accompany me to the nursery as I did not speak Urdu.

The parents had come from far out in the country and lived in a small, one-room shanty with dirt floors and no running water. We explained that the girls still needed medical care in our hospital setting. The parents stated they could not afford to keep them there. We countered by telling them that we would consult the hospital administrator (Eric Johanson from Australia) and take care of the expense. The husband stated, "We are going to take the babies; we don't want to leave them here any longer." Repeated efforts to keep the babies failed, so the appropriate papers were signed relieving the hospital, doctors, and nurses of any responsibility.

The nurses hesitantly and lovingly took the precious girls out of the incubators and gently removed their feeding tubes. Carefully and skillfully they wrapped the two little ones in blankets. As they handed the babies to the parents, they again reminded them that the twins would now have a grim prognosis. The father in turn said, " It doesn't make any difference, they are only girls." Needless to say, the entire hospital staff was heartbroken.

Certainly, if our Creator values sparrows . . .

Ronald Scott, CME class of 1943, is a retired obstetrician and gynecologist residing in Lincoln, California.

September 21

And God shall wipe away all tears from their eyes; and there shall be no more death, neither sorrow, nor crying, neither shall there be any more pain: for the former things are passed away. Revelation 21:4, KJV

She was a beautiful, happy-go-lucky two-year-old child, except that her eyes were a bit crossed. Her strabismus surgery to correct the problem went flawlessly, and our anesthetist extubated her without any difficulty. She was breathing spontaneously for about five minutes, but then her breathing rate slowed. *Everything* went downhill from there. She was masked, reintubated, given ampules of intravenous medications, and finally, CPR was initiated.

We did not have a defibrillator, nor did the Adventist Clinic in downtown Lusaka, Zambia. It took us half an hour to find an ambulance emergency service that did have one, and it took another half hour for them to arrive. But following a long two-hour battle with life, and after the ambulance arrived confirming an agonal heart rhythm (and eventually no rhythm), we pronounced her dead.

Although there is tremendous joy that comes from working in the mission field and bringing restoration of sight to many, I am acutely reminded of the risks involved when we leave our comfort zone to participate in God's work. I wanted to be a missionary doctor since I was 16. But when my husband and I came to Zambia in August 2011 to serve as medical missionaries, we had no idea how challenging it would be.

Some of the obstacles, including the obvious culture shock, involved uprooting everything we knew to live in a developing nation, dealing with insects and pests of every dimension, and learning to practice ophthalmology and dentistry in a foreign setting with very limited resources. Yet, despite all these challenges, it has been rewarding to know that we are part of a bigger work, an opportunity to serve as an active part of the medical ministry. We know that we are making a difference, not solely because of the talents and skills we bring to the table, but because God has chosen to use us for His purpose.

I may not ever completely understand why, in my first year of mission service, I had an innocent child die in my operating room. And as medical professionals, we may never fully understand why complications occur, even when we are doing our very best to help our patients. But, ultimately, it is up to us to leave these things in God's hands. We must trust that He is in control and that He will work in His time, in His way, for His purpose.

I take comfort in believing in a God who knows our pain and struggles, One who grieves as we grieve, and One who cares and loves humankind with all His heart. Despite some of the trials and tribulations on this side of eternity, I look forward to that glorious day when the trumpet will sound, and we will be taken to a place where there will be no more death, neither sorrow, nor crying, nor pain. It will be a place where peace and joy will reign, a place where our profession as physicians will no longer be needed.

Janie Yoo (née Lee), LLUSM class of 2006, is an assistant professor in LLUSM department of ophthalmology. She and her husband Paul, LLUSD class of 2008, are serving in Lusaka, Zambia. Janie is the medical director at Lusaka Eye Hospital, while Paul serves as dental director at Lusaka Adventist Dental Services. They are both deferred mission appointees.

September 22

But seek first the kingdom of God and His righteousness, and all these things shall be added to you. Matthew 6:33, NKJV

Throughout my first year of medical school, I heard many stories about how the second year of medical school was so much harder than the first. I wondered how that could be possible when I seemed so busy and was studying constantly during my first year. But with the approach of my summer break, I decided not to worry about it. That attitude really helped me to verbalize my faith in God. So when my friends would mention medical school, I would tell them how faithful God had been during my first year, and how I knew He would provide more strength for me in the second year to meet any additional challenges.

Now in my second year, I have experienced this belief to be true. Sure, it has been challenging; but God has poured out His blessing in so many ways to strengthen me. I have also learned this year how much my attitude impacts my enjoyment and experience in school.

I am not perfect; but intentionally focusing on the good and God's blessings has really helped to make my second year go much better. Philippians 4:4 (KJV) summarizes this optimism: "Rejoice in the Lord always: and again I say, Rejoice." Such a viewpoint often means living by faith, not feelings.

When medical school does seem overwhelming, it is not natural for us to rejoice. So, I decided to study all the verses in the Bible that talk about rejoicing. Over and over, I was reminded that the reason we rejoice is not because of our circumstances but because of God's goodness and character, His love for us, and His plan for our lives. This awareness reminds me that I can rejoice, regardless of my surroundings.

I can rejoice because my value comes from God—not from my academic performance. God sees me with potential, no matter how I see myself. He loved me so much that He sent His own Son to die for me, even when I did not care about Him. He has a plan for my future, despite what I see in the present.

And because my rejoicing is not based on my surroundings but, rather, on God's character—knowing He gives me value—I continue to trust Him with my heart, life, future, and career. Then medical school becomes a time to seek God first, just as stated in the verse above.

God will take care of the details of my life and future as I spend time with Him daily, encouraging those around me, and surrendering to His plan for my life. I am learning that medical school, more than anything else, is really about learning to trust God unconditionally, to seek His will for my life, and to share Him with others. Would you like to seek God first and experience the joy of knowing and sharing Him?

Debbie Beihl, LLUSM class of 2015, is from Saluda, South Carolina. She graduated from Southern Adventist University with an AS degree in nursing and a BS degree in physiology. She was class pastor during her freshman and sophomore years and currently is class pastor her junior year.

September 23

For if thou altogether holdest thy peace at this time, then shall there enlargement and deliverance arise to the Jews from another place; but thou and thy father's house shall be destroyed: and who knoweth whether thou art come to the kingdom for such a time as this? Esther 4:14, KJV

In 1934, Dr. Mollerus Couperus graduated from the College of Medical Evangelists. Not sure what area in medicine he wanted to practice, he pursued a mission opportunity at the Hydrotherapy Institute, a Seventh-day Adventist Mission in Jerusalem. At the time, Jerusalem was a part of the Kingdom of Transjordan. Dr. Couperus felt it was a place where God would lead him in his life of service.

One day, a call came from the palace in Amman, Jordan. King Abdullah was requesting an available doctor to come and treat a very sick baby in the palace. Dr. Couperus responded he would be willing to see the baby.

Soon a limousine arrived and off they went across the Jordan River into Amman, to the palace of the King. Upon arrival, Dr. Couperus was led into a building with a long hallway and many doors on either side. As he walked down the hall, he realized he was in the harem.

At the end of the hall, a door opened into a large room with a bassinet in the center. Inside it was a tiny infant with sunken eyes, poor skin turgor, and listless crying ... all signs the doctor knew were due to dehydration. He recognized that this baby was likely a prince. He asked the nurses what they were feeding the baby. They said another doctor had told them to feed him sweetened condensed milk. Dr. Couperus realized the concentrated milk had severely dehydrated the baby, and vomiting had compounded the problem. The young doctor told them to find a wet nurse and give this baby breast milk right away.

The door suddenly burst open and a man wielding a sword headed toward Dr. Couperus! Word had gotten out that there was an infidel in the nursery. The guards restrained the man and escorted Dr. Couperus back to the limo and drove him safely back home.

Several weeks later, he received a phone call from King Abdullah himself, stating that the baby had recovered, and thanking him for his wise recommendations. He kindly stated that the doctor could visit the palace anytime.

Years later, Dr. Couperus was a successful dermatologist on Wilshire Boulevard in Los Angeles, California. Late one afternoon, his receptionist excitedly reported, "There are some strangers in the waiting room asking to talk to you." Upon entering the room, Dr. Couperus found three men dressed in Arabic robes and headdress. They stated they were ministers in the government of Jordan and had been sent by the King.

They asked if he had been in Transjordan in 1935, and he nodded. They asked if he had treated a sick baby in the palace; again, he nodded. *They told him the baby was now King Hussein of Jordan!* The King had become aware that Dr. Couperus had treated him and wanted to reward him for saving his life. The ministers invited him to come back to Jordan at any time and they would honor him. Unfortunately, the doctor was never able to follow through on their generous offer.

King Hussein went on to become a respected king and a major stabilizing force in the Middle East. Perhaps history would have had a different course if God had not used a young Seventh-day Adventist doctor to save an infant in the harem.

Richard Catalano, LLUSM class of 1976-B, is executive vice chairman and a professor in LLUSM department of surgery. He is married to Patti Catalano (née Smith), LLUSN class of 1976. Dr. Couperus told this story to the Catalano family when they visited his home in Angwin, California.

He also said, "This is what the kingdom of God is like. A man scatters seed on the ground. Night and day, whether he sleeps or gets up, the seed sprouts and grows, though he does not know how." Mark 4:26-27, NIV

Steve grew up in Alabama, spent some time in the military, and then worked as a cross-country truck driver. Somewhere along the way, he got mixed up with drugs. He finally hit bottom in San Bernardino, California, where he lost his job and got involved with gangs for a time. Now he is homeless.

He is one of an estimated 2,000 men, women, and children living in San Bernardino without a place to call home. It is a city where one-third of the 200,000 residents live below the poverty level. The violent crime rate is twice that of California as a whole. Amid accusations of civil corruption, the city filed bankruptcy in 2012. The streets and vacant lots of San Bernardino at night are exactly the kind of place your mother always told you to avoid. It is the kind of place Loma Linda Street Medicine seeks out.

Street Medicine is what it sounds like. We are a team of doctors and students walking around with backpacks and headlamps to find the homeless in shelters or under bridges, in order to provide what care we can. We are trying to address the health care needs of those who would not or cannot access a clinic.

As our student-led outreach program only started in July 2012, we are still figuring out how to do the most good. The first few months involved considerable learning. Sure, we knew statistics about the community, but we did not really know the community in any meaningful way. We needed to know where the people were, their habits, their needs, and how we could best help. We needed someone to help us. We needed a guide. Enter Steve.

Steve took us, with our backpacks and good intentions, and led us. He introduced us to key people and to patients in need. He told us what to look out for and how to stay safe. He told us about his life, his rocky past, and how people survive on the street. He let us ask him all kinds of questions. He calls us when his cell phone has minutes available, and he is often waiting near our route with a smile.

Maybe that is the way of the Kingdom of God. We try to bring God with us to a dark and dangerous place, only to realize that He is already there, preparing good things. It was a sign to us that we found Steve, a man who has experienced so much of street life and is more than willing to take us under his wing. And we found him so quickly. It is a indication that our work is headed in the right direction. Although we do not know where the boundaries of His Kingdom are, or how His Kingdom is growing, it is a sign that in this city, marked by corruption, pollution, gangs, and poverty, God is not absent. He is building, even if we do not recognize it.

After all, it is in weakness that His power is made perfect. And is it not true that His grand plan of salvation was fulfilled on a cross? If He is there, in the gutter with a man who has a strange rash, in the dust under the bridge with men passed out drunk, and in the needs of the ancient diabetic woman who carries all her belongings on a walker—how can we stay away?

David Jasperse, LLUSM class of 2013, is a family medicine resident in Milwaukee, Wisconsin.

September 25

Look at the birds of the air; they do not sow or reap or store away in barns, and yet your heavenly Father feeds them. Are you not much more valuable than they?
Matthew 6:26, NIV

Learning to become a physician requires more than just book knowledge and test-taking abilities. That "something extra" is what we refer to as the "art of medicine" in practicing whole person care. While the medical school curriculum has changed through the years, the effort remains to develop the best possible physicians who will graduate from Loma Linda University School of Medicine.

One activity I always enjoy is teaching first-year medical students how to perform medical interviews with patients. These sessions are not graded but are intended only to be teaching and learning activities. I recruit patients from my clinic to be interviewed by these beginning student physicians. I ask each patient to recall a past episode of illness that the students could explore.

One Friday afternoon, I arranged for two of my patients to come into the hospital to have their stories investigated by two separate students. This meeting would be the first opportunity for these future doctors to actually talk to and obtain the medical history of a real patient. One or two other students would observe, and together the whole group would learn. I asked each student to try to elicit as detailed and accurate a history as possible.

The two students that day were a young lady and a young man. The first interview was given to the female student after I asked who wanted to go first. The first patient described his symptoms, which were related to a muscle condition. The student launched in and did a fine job. One hour later we were finished and as a group fully explored and dissected the patient's medical problem.

The next patient came in and told her story, which involved heart palpitations. It seemed that the male student did a reasonable job. Afterward, within the group, we discussed what aspects of the interview were done well, and ways it could have been improved.

At this point, the young man who had conducted the interview shared some information about what had occurred early that morning. He recalled having awakened at 2 a.m. with a strong premonition that he needed to study cardiac arrhythmias. However, he was still quite sleepy and decided to follow through later in the morning. Well, the morning passed without any review of cardiac problems. He even forgot about the incident until confronted with a patient who presented with heart palpitations.

We all pondered this for a moment. It was fairly obvious that God, who sees the future and knows all of the details of our lives, tried to help this young man prepare for his first encounter with a patient. My patients could have been switched, in terms of who went first, but that was not how it worked out.

God wants to help us through the difficulties of life. He *even* wants us to do well on the first patient interview of medical school.

Raymond Wong, LLUSM class of 1979-B, is an associate professor in LLUSM department of medicine, as well as clerkship director and head of the division of general internal medicine at LLUMC. He was president of the Walter E. Macpherson Society from 2003 to 2006. September 25 is the birthday of the author's wife, Lorna.

Then the King will say to those on His right hand, "Come, you blessed of My Father, inherit the kingdom prepared for you from the foundation of the world: for I was hungry and you gave Me food; I was thirsty and you gave Me drink; I was a stranger and you took Me in; I was naked and you clothed Me; I was sick and you visited Me; I was in prison and you came to Me." Matthew 25:34-36, NKJV

I sat in the waiting room, wondering if my wait was pointless. It was a Friday evening at the Loma Linda University Medical Center, and I was helping to continue a long-held tradition at the hospital.

For as far back as most can remember, students from Loma Linda University (LLU), joined by friends from the community, have brought songs and prayers to the bedsides of patients and their families on Friday evenings. Years ago, as a socially awkward teenager, I received my first introduction to the inside of the hospital through this ministry when I was brought there by my cousins who were medical students at LLU.

Now, as a freshman medical student myself, and designated leader for singing bands, I wondered if anyone else would show up. This activity was supposed to be singing bands, not singing solos! Time passed; and as I contemplated leaving, I noticed two people walk into the lobby. I went to talk with them and found out they had flown in from Tennessee to tour the University, and they just "happened" to hear about singing bands. Could they sing with me? I grabbed the well-worn song booklets and showed them the way to the wards.

Our small trio visited many patients that evening, but one that stood out was a family in the ICU. As we visited from room to room, a nurse directed us to someone who really wanted a visit. They were an Adventist family, and the patient had been in the hospital for a while; she missed being able to start the Sabbath with worship and singing, and she heard us singing in the hall. As we sang and prayed with them, it was easy to see how happy our short visit made her. Her Sabbath evening had been made; and I know that after seeing her reaction, ours had been made as well.

As we continued our rounds of the hospital, I began thinking about what had just happened. A few moments before, I was ready to give up and call it quits. Had I done so, I would have missed out on being part of a blessing. God knew that one of His children needed a visit that evening, and He had even sent reinforcements from across the country to make it possible. All He needed were some willing people to lend their voices and a lone medical student to stand faithful at his post.

Jonathan Martin, LLUSM class of 2013, is a general surgery resident in Detroit, Michigan. He is a deferred mission appointee and would encourage everyone to get involved with their own local mission field.

September 27

Gracious is the LORD, and righteous; our God is merciful. The LORD protects the simple; when I was brought low, he saved me. Psalm 116:5-6, NRSV

I had been frenetically busy, playing cardiologist during most of my working and waking hours. I noted a slight cough, but reassured my wife that it was nothing more than reflux. Did I feel perhaps a little more fatigued? The weekend was spent as usual, recharging body and spirit, and civilizing the acreage around our home by planting trees and moving heavy rocks.

On Sunday evening, I remembered I had retained a stethoscope that had surreptitiously shed its diaphragm. A search through a drawer of discarded relics found a potential replacement. A perfunctory self-auscultation to test the old stethoscope's functionality was followed by shock. What was this 4/6 harsh murmur emanating menacingly from my chest?

The annoying noise should not have been a surprise, since my father had received a prosthetic mitral valve at age 58 and my sister has severe mitral valve prolapse. Why had I deliberately ignored even the possibility of similar pathology? Perhaps doctors are allergic to the thought of joining the endless throng of patients. None of us enjoys being on the receiving end of health care, and certainly we do not want to be on the wrong end of a scalpel!

On Monday morning, an echocardiogram confirmed what was clinically apparent: a flail posterior mitral valve leaflet with multiple chordal ruptures. There was flow reversal into the pulmonary veins and the pulmonary arterial pressures had climbed to more than twice the upper limit of normal. A further delay in diagnosis would likely have led to further pulmonary hypertension, decreased left ventricular function, and poorly tolerated atrial fibrillation.

Thanks to the miracle of mitral valve repair, I was back in the office within a month. I was physically none the worse, and, spiritually, much improved by the experience. The broken stethoscope set in motion a healing cascade. Despite not pretending to understand the Lord's exact role in the case of the missing diaphragm, I remain deeply thankful. I do not believe that I was more worthy than any other for the grace bestowed upon me.

I am more mindful of my fragility and more aware of the need to introduce others to His Grace. The sense that I need to invite Him into the office visit and on hospital rounds has become more real to me. God is in charge of His universe. He is sovereign, both in the infinite cosmos and in our finite lives. His inerrant will is often opaque. Sometimes our snapshot view is capricious.

Were the movie of our lives revealed in advance, we would know that God is good all the time. How often we behave as if God rules the universe, but we actually take charge of our own work and lives. In this delusion, we deprive ourselves of many opportunities for healing of both body and soul from God. Thank God—He gives us so many repeat opportunities to introduce Him to others around us, and thus to grow His Kingdom here on earth!

Gary Marais is an associate clinical professor in LLUSM department of medicine and a cardiologist at Redlands Community Hospital and Beaver Medical Group. He graduated in 1973 from Stellenbosch University Faculty of Medicine and Health Sciences in South Africa.

September 28

There is a time for everything, and a season for every activity under the heavens: a time to be born and a time to die. Ecclesiastes 3:1-2, NIV

I will never forget the time I was called to interpret for a patient and her husband on Unit 4100 in the Loma Linda University Medical Center. They both were deaf. I was told the patient was awaiting a much-needed liver transplant and would be hospitalized until a liver was made available.

As it turned out, I checked on her daily. As time passed waiting for a liver, I grew fond of them both—and it was mutual. I not only was their link to the health-care team, but I was also their social outlet and now their friend.

During this time, we became better acquainted. They both knew of Jesus and recognized that I was a Christian; now they had a desire to know Him. I was thrilled to be asked to share my faith, knowing that deaf people make up the fourth largest group of people who have not been told the gospel. I used my gift of American Sign Language to lead them to His gift of salvation. They loved it when I would visit them after church, and they would ask me to "re-preach" the sermon to them. Those were beautiful times.

Then darkness came. Surprisingly, it was the first time in my career I had ever had to sign to a spouse of a patient, "Your wife only has a week to live." I cannot begin to explain all that happened to me from that moment on. Here, after three months, the end had arrived for my patient.

I vividly recall that final, sad day. I did not want to go to work, sensing it was time for her to leave us. I prayed and cried out to God, "Please don't make me go to see her die."

But then a beautiful, peaceful silence ensued; and the most unexpected, reassuring words came to my heart and mind: "Daphne, you don't realize the privilege it is to walk someone to the end of their journey." At that point, I loved God more than my brokenness, more than my sadness, or my soon impending goodbye; I could not say no to Him.

I obeyed His request, and I lovingly served her for Him.

Daphne Hunter is a sign language interpreter in LLUMC language services department. September 28 is the day the patient in this story passed away.

September 29

If you then . . . know how to give good gifts to your children, how much more will your Father in heaven give the Holy Spirit to those who ask him!
Luke 11:13, NIV

"If you're not laughing often, you're doing it wrong!" seems to be God's words to me in this season of life. It's a season of wearing many hats, not the least of which is being a doctor.

I really do think that I hear God laughing with me now, when I look back at where He and I have been over the last several years. It's been seven years since graduating from medical school at Loma Linda. Study, persevere, plan, graduate, repeat. So much of life had been wrapped up in accomplishing that set of goals. I now realize that was all just preamble to the abundant life that God had planned for me next—marriage, parenthood, and, oh yes, being a physician.

I never knew I could bear so many "burdens" simultaneously: love my husband, learn how to be married, raise a Godly son, keep learning medicine, be a good doctor, be Christ's light to the world, keep fit, maintain friendships, rest—and *not* do all of this under my own power or I will crumble. Sigh.

"[His] power is made perfect in weakness" (2 Corinthians 12:9, NIV) was the verse that was the theme for my life in medical school and residency. God made sure I learned it well. Now it has to be foundational, otherwise, the joy of this season of life would be totally absent.

Every day, I delight in seeing the world through my child's eyes. He's a preschooler in wonder—whether meeting new people, reading words on a page, tasting new foods, or, of course, testing limits. I try to delight in each moment, even the ones that make the veins stick out on my forehead! I am learning to love my husband in new ways as I see him in the role of father. And yes, I see how the Father loves each patient uniquely from His heart, as each is so different from the next.

I am overwhelmed at God's faithfulness every second of every day. I stand in awe of how much He loves each of us—my family, my patients, and me. He never stops giving us more of Himself. He's the source of all I need each moment, no matter how many hats I am wearing and no matter how many mistakes I've made that day. I get it now.

I love giving good gifts to my son—whether it's something he welcomes like a Lego set or something undervalued like discipline. I give to him because I cannot be compelled to stop. I delight in his mere existence because my heart knows he's my child. How much greater is the Father's love for me?

Kimberly Page, LLUSM class of 2005, is a family practitioner at a community health center in Utah where she lives with her husband and son.

September 30

Be assured and understand that the trial and proving of your faith bring out endurance and steadfastness and patience. James 1:3, AMP

Patients with advanced stage head and neck cancer need good communication by the treating team to maximize the possibility of long-term survival. It starts with the first visit, when the front desk staff and the nurses are cheerful and attentive. The physician imparts a first impression by the expression on his face and by the handshake that follows; and by showing kindness, compassion, and patience to educate the patient concerning his/her case, allowing time for questions.

When I first met Roger and Jan, they noted my New York accent and we talked about New York. The initial evaluation outlined the extent of his neck tumor. We discussed the treatment options. Roger selected chemotherapy and radiation. I gave him my home phone number with the comment to call anytime there was a problem or question that needed attention. My experience is that patients have rarely abused this opportunity to communicate.

Within months of completing therapy, it became apparent that he would need a radical surgery to eliminate the portion of the cancer that had not responded. The postoperative course was uneventful for the first year, but then he went to the emergency department (ED) with bleeding from his mouth and a bulging in his neck. His wife called, and within minutes I was in the ED opening the neck and draining the blood clot that was squeezing his airway. He was taken to the OR and the radiation-damaged ruptured blood vessel was removed, followed by an extensive reconstructive procedure.

Our prayers were answered, as he awakened with no evidence of stroke. But then, a few weeks later, he had some sloughing of his radiation-damaged skin, and I treated it with a diluted bleach solution. During one of these visits, I spilled the solution on his blue and white-checkered shirt, ruining what I learned was his "favorite" shirt.

Feeling bad that I caused this shirt problem, I told Roger to wear the same shirt to every visit, that way I would not be able to ruin any more of his clothing. Discussing this at home, my wife suggested that I buy him a shirt to replace what I had destroyed. Several weeks later, we found and purchased it at Nordstrom. I presented it to him after the wound had healed. He was gracious and ecstatic, and we parted that day as better friends.

Roger died from his cancer four years later, but the relationship with Jan continued with exchanges of greeting cards and phone calls. I have been blessed by this wonderful Christian family, who love the Lord and exercised faith that produced endurance and patience.

At age 89, Jan suffered a serious medical condition, and she told me that she was tired and asked if I felt it would be all right to ask God to let her go to sleep to await "the joy that will come in the morning." I assured her it was.

George Petti, LLUSM class of 1962, is a professor in LLUSM department of otolaryngology, head and neck surgery. He was an LLUSMAA Honored Alumnus in 2012.

OCTOBER

"There is great joy, along with the pain,
in being a wounded healer."

October 1

What is man, that thou art mindful of him? and the son of man, that thou visitest him? Psalm 8:4, KJV

Flying can be thrilling, and I love it! Looking down on the earth below from the window seat of an airplane, as it is taking off, can be quite revealing. I first notice how buildings and other objects progressively shrink in size, as the plane flies higher. Then I become overwhelmed by the "bird's eye view" of the vast expanse of land and water, seemingly endless, everywhere I look.

As the craft ascends beyond the clouds and mountain peaks to a cruising altitude, I can hardly make out clearly any identifiable man-made structures way down below, let alone the form of any individual man. Where did the teeming population of mankind go? What happened to the larger-than-life forms of the great and haughty? I squint in futility, trying hard to spot at least one VIP . . . and I see none.

At that point, I cannot help but wonder, like David in the book of Psalms, "What is man that thou [God] art mindful of him?" The greatness of man shrinks to nothingness; man is lost like a dust particle in cosmic matter from that high perspective. But the awesomeness of a Creator God shines forth in sharp contrast.

Yet the Bible tells us, "The eyes of the LORD run to and fro throughout the whole earth, to shew himself strong in the behalf of them whose heart is perfect toward him" (2 Chronicles 16:9, KJV). That means He notices even me? That is amazing, and it humbles me. How could a God so great stoop down so low as to seek communion with man who is so minute? His self-sacrificing love for "insignificant" humans is clear.

As our Creator God reveals Himself to us daily, guarding and guiding us as we cruise life's highways, fly Earth's skies, and while we are at work, school, or play, we ought to surrender all to Him in humility, knowing that we are nothing without Him. When our eyelids close in sleep each night, we can rest assured that we are safe in His arms, that He is always on duty, and that He does not overlook anyone as He conducts His "evening rounds."

Obinna Esiaba recently moved to the USA from Nigeria. His wife is a doctoral candidate in the graduate biology program at LLU.

October 2

For he hath said, I will never leave thee, nor forsake thee. So that we may boldly say, The Lord is my helper, and I will not fear what man shall do unto me.
Hebrews 13:5-6, KJV

When my mother was a child, my maternal grandparents immigrated to Mexico around the time of the ongoing Mexican Revolution. My grandfather, a physician and surgeon, had his office on Avenida Revolución in Mexico City. Pancho Villa, the famous Mexican revolutionary, was one of his patients.

Not only was my grandfather a well-loved physician in Mexico, but he was also a trick rider and sharp shooter. He could ride two horses at the same time, and he could also use pistols to blast coins out of the air and cigarettes out of the mouths of brave volunteers! Movies were made that documented these feats.

My grandfather owned a spotted fawn deerskin, given to him by the wife of the president of Mexico at that time. He attached leather loops to the tanned side of the skin and inserted his surgical instruments inside these loops, which were labeled in Spanish. When he was called to do surgery, he would roll up this deerskin with the needed instruments, go to the home of his patient, and perform the surgery. I am fortunate to still have that deerskin today.

My grandfather, in addition to being a skilled physician, was knowledgeable in the use of plants. Unfortunately, he died when I was five years old, so I never had the chance to learn from him about the traditional use of plants and herbs for medicinal purposes.

One evening, my grandparents went to the home of a patient with a severe head injury. They worked all night in an attempt to save the life of this patient, but the outlook was grim. Before each surgery, my grandfather would pray that the Great Healer would guide his hands for a successful outcome. In this case, as the sun arose, this patient, who was not expected to survive, did live to see another day.

As my grandparents entered the patient's living room that following morning, they saw a row of seated men, all with pistols in their laps. My grandfather inquired what this visit was all about. He was informed that if the patient had not survived, they were there to execute my grandparents! My grandfather was very thankful that he did not know their intention before starting to work on the patient, or he would have been so nervous that the outcome might have been different!

This is a true story, where prayer not only helped save the life of the patient, but also the lives of the physician and his assistant, my grandmother. It appears, in this case, that prayer was the only available "malpractice insurance" down in Old Mexico, as my grandparents were spared from paying the ultimate price with their lives.

E. A. (Billy) Hankins III, LLUSM class of 1964, is a retired dermatologist and curator of vertebrate zoology and chief preparator at the World Museum of Natural History, located on the La Sierra University campus. October 2 is his mother's birthday.

October 3

Before they call I will answer; while they are still speaking I will hear.
Isaiah 65:24, NIV

During the 18 years I did *locum tenens* at cancer centers throughout the United States, my wife, Mary Lou, and I lived full time in our motor home. Thirteen times we drove the Alaska Highway, towing a car to my Anchorage assignments. We fell in love with the state and the trip, enjoying God's creative greatness in the mountains, wildlife, and glaciers.

To understand why we especially appreciate the Scripture, "Before they call, I will answer," you have to know something about towing a vehicle on the Alaska Highway in the Yukon. First, the Yukon is huge—the size of the 11 northeastern states and extremely sparsely populated. It has only 35,000 residents, of which 20,000 live in one city, White Horse. To compare the area, it is like Pennsylvania with a population of 8,600 instead of nearly 13 million.

Obviously, few places exist where things can be bought or repaired, such as a tow bar for towing a car. As background information, a tow bar locks into place when you begin driving. But if the lock fails, the car's movement is uncontrollable. Also, tow bars have specific base plates on the towed vehicle and are not interchangeable.

Traveling back to Tennessee on Labor Day in 2008, after an Alaskan assignment, as we turned off the Alaska Highway toward White Horse I noticed the car moving from side to side behind the motor home. This swerving indicated that one of the tow bar locks had broken. I drove slowly down a steep hill and into the parking lot of the Canadian Tire store. I hoped to get a new tow bar there, but they had none.

Because of the holiday, we discovered no RV dealership was open. What should we do? Towing the car was not safe. If we could not repair or replace the tow bar, my wife and I would each have to drive a vehicle, separately, for more than four thousand miles. We prayed that God would guide our decisions and meet our needs.

Then we remembered that the Pioneer RV Park, where we had stayed previously, did limited RV repair work. Maybe they could help us. The mechanic said he had no parts to repair a tow bar and had no new ones, but he did have a used tow bar someone had left two years before. One of the telescoping arms was tight, but it still worked.

The owner had paid $900 for a new one and left the old one to sell for $300. It was the exact brand and model that we needed—a Blue Ox Aladdin! Two years before our tow bar had failed, God had placed that used one right where we would be when ours broke.

We have had many prayers answered while traveling across the country and in the wilderness. We know from experience that Isaiah 65:24 is true: "I will answer." Do you trust God enough to claim this promise for yourself?

Ronald Turk, LLUSM class of 1963, is a retired hematologist-oncologist who lives in Greeneville, Tennessee. October 3, 1953, is when he had his first date with his wife, Mary Lou.

God created human beings; he created them godlike, Reflecting God's nature. He created them male and female. Genesis 1:27, MSG

Coming in from the cold Romanian winter, I took off my coat for yet another long but rewarding day. Doditza raised his head as I entered the nursery for infant orphans, and I was immediately captivated by his apparent show of courage. At birth, he had been taken from his clinically "insane" mother and was now one of the helpless abandoned babies lined up in stark metal cribs, row after row. Many of his buddies lay listless, their muscles almost atrophied from being bound in mummy-like wraps and from lying on their backs hours on end. Most were abandoned because of the extreme poverty and desperation of their mothers.

I leaned down and gently scooped Doditza from his little bed. He was a tiny casualty of regulatory fallout during Romania's bid to join the European Union. He now had no hope of international adoption. I kissed his flushed cheek as he smiled, even though the soggy diaper he had been wearing for the past twelve hours was overflowing. I cringed as I saw the sores on his little bottom created from sitting endlessly in his own waste. My heart ached as I cleaned his sensitive skin.

I was shocked and angry when I first learned that hospital regulations allowed only one diaper change per half day. Initially, I defiantly overlooked this rule, but soon realized the government hospital was almost as desperate as the mothers who had abandoned their babies. I stopped being shocked, eventually, and started bringing in my own supply of diapers whenever possible.

With time, Doditza gradually came to enjoy our daily exercises. He became more flexible and responsive, no longer crying when I moved his stiff skinny limbs. Now he smiled, even laughed as he wobbled while trying to stand on my knees. Early in my time at the hospital, Doditza's mother came to give him a pair of socks and a banana. Even in her "insane" condition, there was love in her eyes. We did not speak the same language, but it was not difficult to understand her feelings.

She was not allowed to hold her son because of a previous escape attempt. In spite of the looks of scorn by others, I brought him to the door so his mother could touch his head and gently squeeze his tiny toes. Sometimes, on the last day of the required six-months waiting period for official abandonment, heartbroken mothers would come to see their babies for the last time, then be forever gone.

A hot tear sprinkled the top of Doditza's head as I bent down to kiss him goodbye. My months spent as a part of his life were over. I wondered what would happen to him and if my love would have any lasting influence on his life? But then I remembered, "Inasmuch as you did it to one of the least of these My brethren, you did it to Me" (Matthew 25:40, NKJV).

Thank you, Lord, for allowing me to cradle You in a Romanian manger. Amen.

Elizabeth Havice is the daughter of James and the late Nancy (née Wonderly) Simpson, both LLUSM class of 1970. Elizabeth volunteered in Romania in 2003 as part of her training as an international adoption consultant. October 4 is the day the author was adopted by the Simpsons.

October 5

Jesus said to him, "If you can believe, all things are possible to him who believes."
Mark 9:23, NKJV

The Varner, Sellas, and Stockton families have been friends for many years. But it was really when we three women, Nancy, Annie, and Cathy, were on the same cancer journey that we cemented the unbreakable bonds of love, joy, hope, and faith. Annie was ahead of Cathy and Nancy on that journey; her loving spirit, her faith, and her survivorship were a constant source of inspiration to the other two of us.

When we three went through our treatments, we did so with amazing love, support, and resources. We felt so blessed by God's grace and the love of family, friends, our churches, and our community. We quickly realized that it was not that way for everyone. And we knew, without a doubt, that we wanted to give back to others.

With that in mind, we formed a group of dedicated, passionate women to be known as Inland Women Fighting Cancer; and to them we pitched our "Walk" idea. We soon knew the event we dreamed of required extra assistance. We approached longtime friend and supporter, Jack H. Brown, Chairman, President, and CEO of the Stater Bros. Companies, a southern California grocery chain.

After prayers, discussions, and the incredible generosity of this one special man, we took the leap of faith, and the BELIEVE Walk was born. Since 2008, Inland Women Fighting Cancer has partnered with Stater Bros. Charities to present the Annual BELIEVE Walk in downtown Redlands, California, to benefit the Patient Resource Center at Loma Linda University Cancer Center, St. Bernardine's Women's Health and Wellness Center, Redlands Community Hospital, and other cancer-related facilities in the Inland Empire, California.

We are so thankful to have had the tremendous community support that has enabled us to already raise more than $1,800,000 to benefit cancer patients and their families in our community! And we have learned much along the way on this cancer journey.

We are grateful to God for our healing and for His loving presence in our lives each and every day. It is not about how long we live, but it is about who is in our lives and what we do with the time, energy, and gifts we do have. We all stand in an hourglass, the sands of time slipping through our fingers. Time—no one knows how much of it we have; that is what makes it so precious!

We three invite everyone in the area to celebrate life and to join us on the next BELIEVE Walk. Over these past five years, we have had the time of our lives! It has been an inspiring and amazing journey that pushed the boundaries of what we thought we could achieve. We look forward to what lies ahead, ready for that next bit of joy. We have learned two things for sure: friends never let friends go through cancer alone, and TOGETHER WE BELIEVE.

Nancy Varner, LLUSN class of 1978, is one of the founders of Big Hearts for Little Hearts Guild LLUCH. She is also a founding board member of LLUCH Foundation, where she has served continuously to this day. Annie Sellas is married to James Sellas, LLUSD class of 1983, an associate professor of LLUSD department of oral and maxillofacial surgery. She has been the office manager for his oral surgery practice since it opened 29 years ago. Cathy Stockton is the matriarch of a professional golf family. Her husband, Dave Stockton, a professional golfer, is an emeritus member of LLUCH Foundation board. October 5, 2014, is the date of the 7th annual Believe Walk in Redlands, California. For more information, please visit www.believeinlandempire.com.

October 6

Let us then approach the throne of grace with confidence, so that we may receive mercy and find grace to help us in our time of need. Hebrews 4:16, NIV (1984)

My appointment with my doctor was at 2:50 p.m., and I had left my work early in order to arrive on time. It was not easy leaving my busy office. We were short staffed, and I was filling in for a staff member on family leave. I left my co-worker somewhat on her own, thinking that I would be back before closing time to help with the end-of-day duties.

Arriving five minutes early, I checked in at the desk and noticed that the waiting room was full, and a few people had obviously been waiting for a while. So I joined the group . . . and waited and waited for about an hour before my name was called. The assistant said cheerfully, "It won't be too much longer," as she ushered me into the examination room.

I had plenty of time in the little room to look through a stack of magazines on the table. One local hometown magazine listed the doctor I was to see as one of the area's most respected doctors, one chosen by peers and patients. Worth the wait, I thought, as I waited . . . and waited.

I also had plenty of time to think about many subjects while I waited. Then I pondered the words I had read in the book *Too Busy Not to Pray* by Bill Hybels, and I thought: "I don't have to wait for an appointment with God!"

Not only is He, the most important and valued Person in the universe, *waiting for me* to seek Him out and to talk, but it is also true that *I never have to wait for Him. . . . He is waiting for me!* He has been voted, by Heaven and earth, the King of kings and Lord of lords! So why do I often find myself waiting to have an audience with Him?

What an honor it is to be able to speak to God. We never have to go through a secretary or a physician's assistant while waiting to see "the Doctor." We can boldly go straight into His inner office. Anytime, anywhere, under any circumstances, we can, as quoted above, "approach the throne of grace."

Bonnie Parker graduated from La Sierra University class of 1966. She is married to Richard Parker, LLUSD class of 1968. They are parents of three sons and six grandchildren. She is the office administrator for her husband's dental practice in Calimesa, California. October 6 is her birthday.

October 7

By whom also we have access by faith into this grace wherein we stand, and rejoice in hope of the glory of God. Romans 5:2, KJV

"This next patient is Maria, who is now nearly three weeks post-op from a ruptured spleen and lacerated liver sustained in an automobile accident. We did a splenectomy and repaired the liver. She had a rocky post-op course initially but now is doing very well, and we expect to discharge her in a couple of days." With clinical efficiency and detachment, the resident reported on the patient and we moved on to the next bed.

I was an intern, and the 6 a.m. rounds on the Los Angeles County General Hospital surgical unit began a long and busy day. After many hours on duty, and as we stood by the elevator waiting to go home, we were notified of a "code blue." Maria had arrested! We rushed to her bedside and engaged in frenzied resuscitation efforts, but none of our heroic measures could revive her.

I tried to make sense of what appeared to be an unwarranted death. What had happened? Maria was doing so well and was soon to be discharged. Trying to understand why this patient took such a sudden turn for the worse, I spoke with the woman in the adjacent bed of the six-bed ward. She observed that Maria was a "displaced person" from Latvia; and, while she could speak six languages, her English was "not so good."

After morning rounds, she had become depressed. She misunderstood the doctors' conversation and thought they said she would be in the hospital two more weeks instead of just two more days. She had said to her next-bed friend, "If I have to be here two more weeks, I just give up."

"No, you are doing well and will go home in two days, not weeks," her friend tried to reassure her. Maria, however, refused to be consoled and became increasingly despondent as the day progressed. Late in the afternoon she gave up and died.

It took some time to perform the autopsy, which revealed no apparent reason for Maria's demise. There were no pulmonary emboli, coronary thrombosis, infections, or anything else that could explain the sudden death. But loss of hope is not identified on an autopsy examination.

I learned early in my career the importance of hope in patient care. Communication is basic to our relationships, and volumes have been written about it; yet miscommunication abounds. Even my best efforts sometimes result in patients misunderstanding their true condition. Many of life's woes can be traced to such "misunderstandings." In Maria's case, it led her to give up hope.

In contrast to our human fallibility and imperfect communication, our Heavenly Father has done everything possible to avoid a misconception of the hope that is ours. He has taken great pains to communicate His unfathomable love for us. By giving His Son, He has proved His love, and in doing so has given us everlasting hope.

Jerome Niswonger, LLUSM class of 1962, worked from 1972 to 1978 in LLUMC department of gynecology and obstetrics before taking a second residency. He now practices ophthalmology in Paradise, California. October 7 is his wedding anniversary.

And I heard a loud voice from the throne saying, "Look! God's dwelling place is now among the people, and he will dwell with them. They will be his people, and God himself will be with them and be their God. 'He will wipe every tear from their eyes. There will be no more death' or mourning or crying or pain, for the old order of things has passed away." Revelation 21:3-4, NIV

I was on my second week of surgical trauma; and I was the only resident on call, with a physician's assistant and attending staff for backup. A 58-year-old female was brought into the trauma bay after a high speed, head-on collision. Her eyes darted around the unfamiliar environment, grasping for comfort in her state of fear. We performed the trauma ABCDEs and found a tense abdomen and the all-too- familiar seat belt sign. Her initial trauma films were negative, but the FAST (focused assessment with sonography for trauma) scan was grossly positive. We were going to the OR—emergently!

The patient coded in the elevator. As the only doctor with the patient, all eyes turned to me. I fumbled through the ACLS algorithm while jumping onto the gurney to start continuous chest compressions until we reached the OR. I would like to say the procedure was successful, but she had completely avulsed her mesentery and the injuries were irreparable. She coded three times during the exploration and was not expected to live.

We transported her back to the trauma ICU, intubated. When family arrived, they understood the gravity of the situation and agreed to comfort measures. They requested a priest to administer her last rites prior to removing life support. The on-call priest was busy and would not be available for a few hours. The family turned to me for guidance.

I was not sure where to begin. Sure, I was raised in a church and had led out in worship; but I had never led out in this type of service. Seeing the sorrow in the family's eyes, I began singing the first hymn that came to me—"Amazing Grace." I could not remember all the verses, so we sang the first one twice. When we finished, the family requested a reading from the Bible. I did not know what would be appropriate, but I felt impressed to read Psalm 23. I offered a prayer of thanksgiving for a life well-lived and a prayer requesting comfort in a time of pain and suffering for the family. When I finished, there were tears in everyone's eyes. The life support was then removed; and their spouse, mother, grandmother, peacefully slipped away. Another trauma activation was announced, and I was off.

Prior to leaving, each of the family members came up to me and gave me a hug, thanking me for taking the time to comfort them in their time of sorrow. I was speechless. Here I was, trying to be the doctor to the patient but actually found myself ministering to the family. It was the last thing on my mind that evening.

I truly believe that I was on call that particular night not to be a physician but to be an extension of the hand of God. This experience constantly reminds me of our mission on earth—to serve others in whatever capacity God has called us. There is no task beneath us when called by God to be His hands and feet.

Edmund Ko, LLUSM class of 2005, is an assistant professor in LLUSM department of urology. He and his wife, Grace, have two children. October 8 is their wedding anniversary.

October 9

If I take the wings of the morning, And dwell in the uttermost parts of the sea, Even there Your hand shall lead me, And Your right hand shall hold me. Psalm 139:9-10, NKJV

Pilots live by checklists. "Mixture rich, altimeter set, cowl flaps open, radios set and checked . . ." To miss one item could mean disaster. In addition to the list provided by the plane's manufacturer, I have added a final item: "Check with our Heavenly Co-Pilot." It is a prayer for wisdom and safety on the ground and in the air.

On the afternoon of June 20, 1996, there was a special reason I was glad I had not omitted the final item on the checklist. The plane I was flying, a Cessna P210—a pressurized, single-engine, six-seater—was just leveling off at 14,500 feet, heading to my mother's retirement home near Yosemite. Suddenly I was jolted by an ominous "bang" (later determined to be a blown cylinder)! It took only a split second for me to realize I had a very heavy (two ton) glider to land, rather than a plane capable of flying nearly 200 miles per hour.

No time for a printed checklist now. Only the automatic, often practiced emergency version would do. This time the final item on the pre-takeoff checklist had to be first: "Please guide me to a safe landing." I set up glide at 85 knots and radioed 121.5 "MAYDAY, MAYDAY, MAYDAY," a request to locate a potential landing site. It all took fewer than five seconds.

Air traffic control (ATC) responded on the emergency frequency and directed me to El Mirage Field to the northeast, but it appeared to be too far away for a certain landing. I could see three paved runways at an abandoned military airfield nearby (not on ATC's radar screen as a usable landing site). I exercised the "pilot in command" prerogative and headed there. I later discovered it was the Grey Butte Test Facility, a military research center off-limits to civilians.

The next few minutes were a blur: frequent checking with my "Co-Pilot," reporting to ATC, and estimating when to put gear and flaps down. Gratefully, I did not sense any panic, rapid heart rate, or sweaty palms.

As I approached the selected runway, a previously unrecognized radar antenna appeared just where I planned to touch down. So, it was necessary to divert to the north while losing precious altitude. With a final, "Help me, Lord," the wheels touched down on the abandoned runway, and the plane rolled to a safe stop.

A search-and-rescue sheriff's helicopter, having heard the distress call, landed next to the Cessna, ready to provide any necessary aid. They kindly flew me to an airport where I could arrange for transportation home.

The next morning, I was able to fly another plane to Yosemite uneventfully. At the small mountain church in Groveland, we had a praise service and renewed our commitment to follow the guidance of our "Heavenly Co-Pilot" each day of our lives.

Edwin H. Krick, CME class of 1961, is an associate professor in LLUSM department of medicine, division of rheumatology. He was LLUSMAA president from 1979 to 1980 and was the Association's 1998 Alumnus of the Year. He served as a missionary in Japan from 1962 to 1970 and was the third American to pass the medical boards there—which were in Japanese! October 9 is his wedding anniversary.

Let each of you look not only to his own interests, but also to the interests of others.
Philippians 2:4, ESV

She already knew. She primarily spoke Spanish. I primarily spoke English. But each day as I rounded, even in limited conversation, I could see that she was aware of what was happening.

She was young, a mother of two. She had already had extensive treatment. She and her husband wanted to know if the surgeons would operate. Surgery reviewed her CT scans and clinical records. Her cancer was very advanced. After discussing her case, the surgeons declined to proceed. As her primary team, we were responsible for breaking the news to her.

None of us wanted to talk about the fact that she was dying. But that day, I stayed into the early evening so I could meet with her and her husband. He sat at her bedside, close to her as I started. I gauged their understanding of the situation and then tried to gently break the news. Cure was unlikely. The surgeons deemed it in her best interest to forego an operation.

He crumpled before my eyes. Head in his hands, he wept.

"There's nothing more you can do?" he asked, looking up.

"There is always more we can do. But our goals look like they are shifting from cure to care." I told them about hospice and how we could establish her wishes and work toward them.

Her eyes filled with tears as she watched her husband. She extended a thin hand toward his head and ran her fingers through his hair, trying to comfort him.

I blinked hard.

After a few moments, she looked at me and said something in Spanish that I did not quite understand. As her husband was bilingual, I asked him what she had said. He lifted his head. "She wants to know if she can be an organ donor." At that point, my resolve broke. The three of us sat and cried together.

I now have children of my own, and I have some inkling of what she faced. I am able to turn away from it. She could not. But in that moment, she did not seem to think about herself. I can still see her reaching over to stroke her husband's bowed head. Her suffering was in seeing his pain.

That simple act was remarkable enough, and very touching. But that her thoughts would gravitate within minutes to how she could still help others was beyond my comprehension. I was stunned. I saw one who was in the fire, but shining like pure gold.

I was reminded of Jesus' final hours. Despite his agony, He ministered to the thief next to him. He asked John to care for His mother. He prayed for those who were crucifying Him. There is victory in reaching beyond ourselves—our own tragedy—to touch someone else. In giving and selflessness, we emulate Christ. That evening, I caught a glimpse of our Savior.

Julie Moyers, LLUSM class of 2005, practices radiology in Willits, California. She is married to Craig Robson, LLUSM class of 2005. They are the proud parents of two daughters. October 10 is the birthday of the author's mother.

October 11

He must labor, performing with his own hands what is good, so that he will have something to share with one who has need. Ephesians 4:28, NASB

We saw him in church every Sabbath morning, a slightly built man in a soft gray shadow-plaid suit and a black bow tie. In fact, his '88 Dodge was always in the parking lot before 9 a.m.

We also noticed, on the table in the church foyer and in the rack beside it, religious publications. All had their mailing addresses inked over. They obviously had come from the same person. I had wondered if that person was Jim Wright.

Then one Sabbath, during prayer time, Jim's daughter, Barbara, asked us, "Please pray for my dad. He fell at work; and although he didn't break any bones, he did pull some muscles and is in a lot of misery."

We knew about her father's work from an article in our Spokane, Washington, newspaper. Along with his picture, the story appeared in the *Spokesman-Review* last November: "At 94, this man's resume just keeps getting longer. Retirement was no goal for James Wright and no reward when it finally arrived. So 30 years later, at age 94, he's still happily pushing a vacuum, emptying waste baskets and collecting a paycheck." The article went on, commenting about his work history and his vegetarian diet.

Recently, I talked to Barbara about her father. "He is doing well," she informed me. "But he is very concerned that he may not be able to go back to work because he is a little unsteady on his feet."

"Did workers' compensation cover the cost of his doctor bills?" I inquired.

"Yes, they took care of that."

"Is his Social Security enough for him to live on?"

"Yes, he can get by on that." (Jim owns the house he lives in.)

"Then why is he so anxious to go back to work?" I asked.

"Well, the money he made by working went to many ministries of the church. And if he has to stop working, he will no longer be able to contribute to them."

So there you have it. At 94 years of age, his heart and efforts are still committed to spreading the gospel—may our hearts and efforts be as well.

Ruth Giem Edwards is a retired elementary school teacher. Her first husband, Ross Giem, was an LLUSM graduate, class of 1953-A. He passed away on August 7, 2013. They have five sons, three of whom are graduates of LLUSM.

October 12

Jesus answered, "It was not that this man sinned, or his parents, but that the works of God might be displayed in him." John 9:3, ESV

When Ruth was 55, her nurse practitioner advised that she should have a screening colonoscopy. During an office visit, the gastroenterologist prescribed preparation for the procedure: "Take four pills with eight ounces of water every 15 minutes, for a total of 12 pills." On the day of her prep for the colonoscopy she took the pills as she was told, but after the twelfth pill she began feeling strange.

She looked at the bottle of pills, and saw it had her husband's name on it, and the word, "diltiazem," a powerful blood pressure-lowering medication. She had a sinking feeling and realized she had made a big mistake. Being a social worker and somewhat involved with the medical field, she called a poison control center for advice and they told her to go immediately to the nearest emergency department.

I was the internal medicine physician covering unassigned admissions that day and received a call from the emergency department (ED) physician, who explained Ruth's situation. She was still alert and able to talk, but very weak. At her bedside, her husband was distraught. She was receiving blood pressure stimulants and fluids intravenously. The charge nurse was on the phone with the National Poison Control Center. Activated charcoal was given by mouth to bind the diltiazem. Calcium was given intravenously to try to increase her slow pulse and very low blood pressure.

Poison Control advised that we also give her a 100 unit per hour insulin drip, along with intravenous D50 (50% sugar solution). She was not a diabetic and this seemed excessive (a non-diabetic patient's pancreas might take several days to release 100 units of insulin). They explained that overdoses of diltiazem block the transport of calcium into heart muscle that is necessary for contraction. Insulin transports glucose into the cells and takes some calcium with it.

Standing at her bedside somewhat anxious, I was trying to comfort the patient, and also trying to hurry the stressed nurse who was doing all the work. The patient later told me she had an "out of body experience." She recalled feeling as if she was on the ceiling, looking down. She did remember my saying to the nurse, "Her blood pressure is 20. Can you hurry up with the calcium?"

Over the next 24 hours we depleted nearly all the hospital's D50. However, I was able to decrease the dose of insulin by that time. I was up late that night in the ICU, watching the nurse take finger pricks every 15 minutes, and push the D50. Just my being there was a comfort to the family and the patient.

She recovered, had no brain damage, and went back to work. She and I bonded during this "event" (as she calls it). The "event" gave her a different perspective on life and she seems to be more open to spiritual discussions. She still has not had her colonoscopy, but on her next visit I will bring it up, although I am not sure she is quite ready for that discussion yet!

David Allen, LLUSM class of 1981, is an internist in Sonora, California. He is an active volunteer in the prison system.

October 13

When Peter saw him, he said to Jesus, "Lord, what about him?" Jesus said to him, "If it is my will that he remain until I come, what is that to you? Follow me!" John 21:21-22, NRSV

The road to becoming a professional, at times, feels like a long, dark tunnel. And occasionally, those of us training to become ministers to others' needs desperately need others to minister to us.

On several occasions while in medical school, I have felt inadequate, hopelessly behind, and like a failure. These feelings were especially prominent one Friday, a week away from finishing my pediatric rotation, as I attended a practice exam and review session with my classmates.

Having studied daily for this clerkship, the low score I received on the practice exam shocked me. Confounded and demoralized, I asked the teacher to explain one of the questions. As she responded, I felt my face flush with embarrassment as everyone's eyes turned toward me—the guy who missed the easy question.

I clammed up and checked out mentally, my mind swirling in nauseating questions: Am I really cut out for this? Will I ever be competent enough with this amount of knowledge to be a responsible doctor? Should I have chosen a different career? Should I quit now—walk out, and not come back on Monday? These negative thoughts were further exacerbated by looking around at my talented classmates—many of whom had board scores several standard deviations above mine, seemed to always know the correct answer, presented better on rounds, or studied more diligently, I figured, than I did.

The review session ended, and I returned to the hospital to wrap up my last "to-do's" before the weekend. Busying myself with checking on patients and finalizing paperwork helped to suppress the depressing thoughts churning in my mind. Suddenly a page from the senior resident interrupted me: "Patient T is going home right now and his family wants to speak with you."

I was puzzled. What did they have to say to me? What should I say to them? I had started taking care of this patient only a day ago and had merely performed that morning's checkup to see how he was doing.

As I walked to T's room, I hurriedly prepared what I would say. I turned the corner and saw T and his mother just about to leave. I blurted out, "T! You're going home! Your tests were negative and you're gonna be oka—"

T's mother cut me off abruptly and pulled me aside; her forcefulness startled me! "When I found out T was coming home today, I drove here as fast as I could because I felt like God was telling me to tell you that you are where you need to be. You are in the right place, and don't let anyone tell you otherwise. Don't let anyone tell you that you aren't good enough." She continued, but her words and her face began to blur in my teary eyes and overwhelmed emotions. She hugged me, repeated herself, and then left. I was stunned, ecstatic, and humbled, all at once—and I came back to work on Monday.

Comparison and negative self-talk are corrosive, debilitating, and unnecessary. I am reminded to trust God more with my future. Becoming a professional takes an immeasurable number of baby steps, and if this is what God wants me to do with my life, then God's grace will get me there.

Marcus Heisler, LLUSM class of 2014, is from Sacramento, California, and graduated from Canadian University College with a BS degree in biology. This story took place during his third-year pediatric rotation.

October 14

Depart from evil and do good; Seek peace and pursue it. Psalm 34:14, NASB

One evening a few months ago, I was asked to consult on a baby in the neonatal intensive care unit. The infant had multiple medical problems and needed to be evaluated for heart surgery. During my assessment, I found out that this baby had numerous congenital anomalies. The tiny patient underwent several surgical procedures and was in need of more. Hundreds of thousands of dollars and hundreds of hospital days, yet we all knew, as health providers, that he would never be an individual who was even near normal. After deep reflections regarding this baby, I was not sure, as a clinician, if I was really in the right place to serve humanity.

Around 20 years ago, when I was a junior surgeon in Kuwait at the beginning of the Gulf War, I took care of an Iraqi soldier who was injured seriously on his right arm. He lost his brachial artery and the vascular repair failed. Rotating in orthopaedics at that time, I had to amputate his right upper extremity. A few days later, when he started to trust me, he began talking to me. I was shocked by his situation. He was 21 years old, newly married and had a newborn baby girl. He was supporting his two parents and six sisters and now he had lost his dominant arm.

The ethical challenges of the situations above have created a great debate in my heart and mind. I wanted to become a doctor to help people. I asked myself, "Am I really in the proper profession?" We spend long hours, effort and money to help a patient with multiple medical problems whom we know will never be normal or productive—and I am not against that at all. But, if we stop wars, we are saving healthy, productive people who are taking care of families. There are no winners in war because even if you lose one soldier, you have devastated the life of a family.

We human beings are contradictive to ourselves. Nowadays, we think we are at the top of civilization while I wonder if we are any better off than we were 5,000 years ago. In the last two centuries there have been more people killed than in the rest of the history of humankind. There are wars happening now and we know of only a very few.

I believe stopping wars is the most noble job an honest human can pursue. Can I stop wars? Or shall I just concentrate on what I was trained to do, that of doing my best to take care of patients?

I ask God for guidance and to lead us to peace.

Nahidh Hasaniya is an associate professor in LLUSM department of cardiovascular and thoracic surgery. Born and raised in Kuwait, he graduated from Kuwait University Faculty of Medicine in 1987. Rotating in orthopaedics when the Iraqis invaded Kuwait, he became one out of three orthopaedists covering the whole country—performing plastic surgery, trauma, and even obstetrics. He moved to the U.S. in September of 1991, a few months after Kuwait's liberation. He and his wife have five children.

October 15

May your father and mother rejoice; may she who gave you birth be joyful!
Proverbs 23:25, NIV

JANINA

It is not too often a father gets to see his daughter born thrice.

The first time at a C-section—with concerns for obstructed ureters, based on a pre-section ultrasound; but that worry was proven gleefully groundless within minutes of your birth when you prodigiously peed on the pediatrician! We were grateful for a skilled team who did an excellent job in assisting your transition to physical independence.

When you were held up, you were ALIVE! And I thanked God.

The second time on a river bank in Thailand, when you were baptized in brown water and came up to a life committed to furthering a relationship with Jesus Christ. We were thankful for a pastor who came especially to be there for you, getting in that brown water with you, and "drowning" you.

When you came up out of the water, you were ALIVE!! And I thanked God.

The third agonizing time happened when you had a physician father's worst nightmare— meningococcemia. We are forever indebted to the brother, the roommate, and the ED crew who worked in a rapid manner, and for Rocephin.

When you woke up in the morning, you were ALIVE!!! And I thanked God.

Thus, I have seen you, my daughter, born thrice. And each time offered its own unique opportunity to reaffirm the best of the past and the beginning of a new future.

I am a button-popping, proud papa, period.

I love you. And I THANK GOD.

Paul Betlinski, LLUSM class of 1973-B, is a part-time family practitioner, health officer at his community health center/county health department, and a county medical examiner in Tillamook, Oregon. October 15 is his daughter's birthday.

October 16

And we know that all things work together for good to those who love God, to those who are the called according to His purpose. Romans 8:28, NKJV

It was on a beautiful Saturday morning that I received a message saying, "Happy Birthday, I love you!" They may seem like five simple words; but to me, they contained a depth of meaning beyond what most of us have ever encountered. Encompassed in those precious words is Jenny's story.

Three months prior, Jenny and her siblings were hiking when she fell 30 feet onto the rocky ground below. She was airlifted to Loma Linda University Children's Hospital and admitted to the pediatric intensive care unit where I was training as a fourth-year medical student. I had recently started on that service and Jenny became my patient.

When I walked into Jenny's room, I saw a beautiful girl with more lines and tubes attached to her body than the nine summers she had lived. She had a large laceration above her left eye, and her left arm was painfully swollen. Her terrifying fall resulted in multiple skull fractures, several small brain hemorrhages, and left her in a coma. Her prognosis was uncertain, as it often is with traumatic brain injuries. The longer she remained in a coma, the probability for a meaningful recovery declined.

Jenny's coma persisted through the next week, despite the fact that she regained the ability to breathe on her own. Our medical team decided it was time to discuss with Jenny's parents the possibility that she might never wake up or recover further. Her parents, who rarely left her side, maintained their belief that Jenny would still improve. After 11 grueling days, their faith was rewarded. Jenny gave them a small, yet exhilarating eyelid flutter! That day signified the beginning of her remarkable and inspiring recovery.

An arduous three months defined the start of Jenny's rehabilitation. She relearned to walk, talk, eat, and navigate the simple tasks we take for granted. What made Jenny so special was her desire to live and her efforts to express her love for her family. Before she had relearned to talk, she had learned to sign "I love you" and was always offering hugs. When she could barely crawl, Jenny would try to sneak out of bed at night, going past the nurses' station to the physical therapy gym so she could play in the ball pit. Nothing was going to get in this girl's way!

Her recovery thus far has surpassed everyone's expectations. Within three months, she went from being in a coma with an uncertain future to being a happy girl. She is now home with her family, in school, and relearning to play her favorite sport, ice hockey.

Jenny's thoughtful birthday message of love and friendship for me symbolizes her ongoing achievements and reminds me of God's amazing power and grace. Medically, I do not know why Jenny woke up when so many others do not; Jenny's life is truly a miracle. However, I do believe in the Romans quote above, and I know "that all things work together for good to those who love God."

Andrea Chong, LLUSM class of 2013, is a general surgery intern at University of California, Davis in Sacramento, California. October 16 is the date Jenny went home, and it is the birthday of the author's mother.

October 17

Whoever exalts himself shall be humbled; and whoever humbles himself shall be exalted. Matthew 23:12, NASB

I was both excited and nervous on the first day of my first rotation as a third-year medical student. It was the ob-gyn rotation, and I was on the labor and delivery unit following a patient in labor. There is considerable "down time" when waiting for a delivery; and not knowing exactly what to do with myself, I spent time sitting at the nurses' station looking at the patient's chart.

My patient's nurse was obviously annoyed by my presence. She would take deep deliberate breaths and ask me, "Can I have my chart back?" She would then take it from me. I tried to be courteous and smile, but she must have been having a bad day. She never smiled and would not talk to me, other than to ask for the chart.

After a few uncomfortable hours waiting for the delivery, there was sudden activity with my patient. She was not progressing as expected, and the baby was in trouble. She needed an emergency C-section. My heart started to race almost as fast as the beeps from the baby monitor. I could not believe I was going to be in the OR on my very first day! My mind began trying to remember the OR rules we had learned, including how to scrub in and how to maintain sterile conditions.

The one problem was that the nurse who had been impolite to me all evening was going to be the OR nurse assisting with the C-section. I knew she probably was not going to make things easy for me. Adding to my anxiety, the attending physician on the case was none other than Elmar Sakala, LLUSM class of 1973-B. At the time, I did not know that much about him, but I knew he was very prominent.

I tried to stay calm and just follow what the resident doctor was doing. I scrubbed my hands and arms and entered the OR. I stood behind the resident, who stood behind the attending, waiting in line to be gowned and gloved by the nurse. The nurse gloved the attending and gloved the resident.

When I stepped up, she just walked away—leaving me standing there holding my hands up. Before I could think of what to do or say, before I could even feel embarrassed, someone quickly walked over to me. It was Dr. Sakala. The attending physician had come back to glove me!

I was relieved and grateful that Dr. Sakala saved me from an awkward situation, but that moment, that one act of kindness, also taught me many lessons. It was only later that I realized the full impact of what he had done. It is well known that a hierarchy exists in medical training, with the attending physician at the top. But in this case, Dr. Sakala was not just any attending physician; he was very accomplished with his many years of experience, prestigious titles, and a distinguished reputation. For him to have paid any attention to me, let alone care how I was being treated, was remarkable.

I was not a resident doctor, not even an intern, but just a lowly medical student. For him to step in and assist me with putting on my gloves, something the nurse would normally do, demonstrated such humility, compassion, and kindness. It did not matter to him that I was "just" the medical student. Leading by example, he demonstrated that everyone should be treated with respect.

Sharon Do, LLUSM class of 2005, is an assistant professor in LLUSM department of radiation medicine. She grew up in Orange County, California, married her high school sweetheart, and is the mother of two. October 17 is her daughter's birthday.

October 18

Jesus said to her, "I am the resurrection and the life. He who believes in Me, though he may die, he shall live." John 11:25, NKJV

Having sworn off medical school after graduating from college, I decided to go into law and was working as a patent examiner at the U.S. Patent and Trademark Office when I received this news: "Your father has brain cancer. It's a stage III anaplastic astrocytoma." It was June 20, 2008, when we received the pathology results from my father's craniotomy, and I became numb with disbelief. How could my father have brain cancer? No one in my family had ever had any kind of cancer. My life came to a halt.

Over the next five months, I took a leave of absence from work and practically lived inside the hospital as my mother and I became my father's primary caregivers. During that time, many of my encounters with physicians confirmed for me that I had made the right choice in shunning medicine. Their daily impersonal, five-minute interviews convinced me that a doctor's primary goal was to leave the patient's room as quickly as possible. I wondered if they ever really listened to us or if they understood just how their orders for the day could affect our lives for the next 24 hours.

Everything changed, however, when a physician who I can only describe as a true Adventist Christian stepped into our lives. In addition to managing my father's medical problems, he gave my father spiritual guidance and helped him work through difficult issues, such as depression and trusting in God.

After every visit, this doctor offered to pray with us and would kneel by my father's bedside. His heartfelt prayers would bring tears to my father's eyes. Although my father's cancer was still ravaging his body, I could sense that a far more important type of healing was taking place. In September, my father made the decision to rededicate his life to God; he wanted to commemorate the event by being rebaptized.

Unfortunately, on the day before his baptism was scheduled, my father suffered a grand mal seizure that left him in a near-comatose state. During the brief moments when my father was responsive, he let us know that his faith was in Christ. When my father passed away on October 18, 2008, I found myself thanking God despite my grief because I knew that He had healed my father on a much deeper level than I had asked.

After going through this experience, I was inspired to look at the practice of medicine again with new eyes. For the first time, I understood the impact a Christian physician could have on a patient's life. Looking back on my father's story, it became clear to me that a physician's daily interaction with patients could have eternal consequences.

I began to read *Ministry of Healing* by Ellen G. White, and I felt in my heart that God was calling me into medicine. After much prayer, I applied to Loma Linda University; and now, five years later, I find myself seeing patients as a fourth-year medical student.

As I go through my medical training, my constant prayer is that God will mold me into a physician after His own heart. I want to always point my patients to Christ, and I want always to remember that a physician's highest calling is not simply to heal the body, but also to save the soul.

John Shin, LLUSM class of 2014, is from Olney, Maryland. He graduated with a BS degree in computer science from the University of Maryland, College Park. He was his sophomore class pastor, senate chaplain his junior year and is currently senate chaplain his senior year. He is married to Elisa Shin, LLUSD class of 2008. For more of this story, refer to AMEN's journal, The Medical Evangelist, Fall 2013 or visit amensda.org. October 18 is the day that his father passed away.

October 19

Not only so, but we also glory in our sufferings, because we know that suffering produces perseverance; perseverance, character; and character, hope.
Romans 5:3-4, NIV

I was embarrassed. I had just received my physical exam results; and my HDL, or "good" cholesterol, was low at 32. As a preventive medicine physician, I did not think I should have a health problem that was lifestyle-related. But those results told me I was not exercising enough. I was broken. I needed to be fixed.

My response was to join the Loma Linda Lopers, a running and marathon training club. Soon, I was running 10, 12, or even 15 miles on a regular basis. And as I was running, I started sharing my life with the people I was running with. They all soon knew why I was there—to raise my HDL cholesterol.

And I knew why they were there—to lose weight, to accomplish a personal goal, to not have the same health problems their parents had, etc. We were developing a community, a group of people who shared and cared deeply about each other. But we were not there together because we were specimens of perfect health. We were there because we were broken and wanted to get better. We were connecting around our weaknesses.

Halfway through that first year of marathon training, my 13-year-old son, Stephen, was diagnosed with rhabdomyosarcoma—a rare type of muscle cancer that is almost universally fatal. I quit running and spent as much of the next seven months with him as I could. After Stephen died, my marriage fell apart; I found myself single, still with a low HDL cholesterol, and now with an extra 15 pounds of weight gained from trying to eat away my grief.

But that broken, running community I had known earlier gathered around me and said, "You need to start running again." They could all run faster than I could; but they stuck with me as I regained my strength and endurance, and they cheered me on as I gradually started shedding the pounds.

During the next year, I completed a marathon, surrounded by those who embraced my brokenness. At my next physical exam, my HDL cholesterol was up. I kept training and eventually lost 30 pounds and raised my HDL cholesterol to 56!

From being diagnosed with low HDL cholesterol, to losing my son from cancer, to going through a divorce, brokenness has been a reality in my life. But each time I recognized, admitted, and embraced an imperfection, I grew. And each time I did that in a community, I saw healing.

Trying to be perfect is the most tragic human mistake. Yet that is our natural tendency. We do not want others to know of our errors, our problems, and our weaknesses. But when we gather together as fellow human beings that acknowledge and, in fact, welcome our brokenness, we experience one of the core beauties life offers us.

Marion Woodman said, "God comes through the wounds." It is only when we, as communities, truly honor who we are that we really can become the people God wants us to be.

Wayne Dysinger, LLUSM class of 1986, is chair and an associate professor in LLUSM department of preventive medicine. He is also an assistant professor in LLUSPH departments of health policy and management, and health promotion and education. For more on the author's backstory, refer to his July 20 Morning Rounds devotional. October 19 is Stephen's birthday.

"For I know the plans I have for you," declares the LORD, "plans to prosper you and not to harm you, plans to give you hope and a future." Jeremiah 29:11, NIV

The hospital cribs were neatly aligned. Each one held a tiny infant, snugly swaddled in blankets and wearing either a pink or blue cap. It was a scene that was all too familiar to my sister and me as we watched our mother go to work. She started at the far end of the long line of cribs and began to examine the first newborn babe. Not too sure about what to think of this rude awakening and the strange person who was now laying a cold stethoscope on his chest, the infant let out a weak cry and began to squirm.

As our mother began to stretch this wiggling baby's legs to check hip rotation and reflexes, the little infant decided that he had been through enough and let loose a guttural cry of disapproval. Having completed her examination, our mother quickly scooped the baby up into her arms, and began wrapping him with blankets into what she liked to call a "baby burrito." Now back in his favorite curled up position, warm and snug, he calmed instantly and decided that he could come to like this strange person after all. Our mother would always tell us that her patented "baby burrito" technique was a huge success among the newborns. Later that day, I would practice my "baby burrito" technique on my favorite baby dolls.

My sister and I grew up with Loma Linda University Children's Hospital as our second home. Words like stethoscope, sepsis, and bilirubin were a part of our vocabulary; and the residents, pediatricians, and nurses always recognized us as we walked the halls of the Children's Hospital, hand-in-hand with our mother.

These early childhood experiences had a profound impact on me, and I have no doubt that God used these experiences as a part of His plan to guide my life toward a career in pediatric medicine and to kindle my desire to attend medical school at Loma Linda University. It is a school where whole person care is a priority and where faith and science are fused seamlessly into a first-class curriculum. It is also a place where each class begins with the acknowledgement of God's guiding hand, and where the students, faculty, and staff are genuinely kind, loving, and Christ-centered.

Now that I have been given the opportunity to study medicine at this University, which has meant so much to me over the course of my life, I have no doubt that this is the place and the career path to which God has called me. Every day I spend at Loma Linda University, I see more clearly how this institution continues to live up to its mission of training physicians to continue the teaching and healing ministry of Jesus Christ. I praise God for the promise of the above verse: "For I know the plans I have for you."

Paige Stevens, LLUSM class of 2016, grew up in Loma Linda, California. She graduated from the University of California, Riverside, with a BS degree in biology. She was social vice president of her freshman class and is the social vice president for her sophomore year. Her mother, Sharon Riesen, LLUSM class of 1982, is associate professor in LLUSM department of pediatrics and is director of the pediatric residency program at LLUMC. October 20 is the birthday of the author's mother.

October 21

Like the appearance of the bow that is in the cloud on the day of rain, so was the appearance of the brightness all around. Such was the appearance of the likeness of the glory of the LORD. And when I saw it, I fell on my face, and I heard the voice of one speaking. Ezekiel 1:28, ESV

Knowing God's will is the desire of all Christ's followers. At times, His will seems unknowable to me. During a dark time in my life, I felt alone and distant from God. Pleas to God for guidance seemed to go unanswered. An accident left me with severe and prolonged back pain; conflicts between science and religion tempted my faith; and I was being asked by my employers to help make difficult budget decisions that would negatively impact the lives of many colleagues.

While traveling in the rain along the Columbia River, my wife and I rounded a corner to see the sky filled with a double rainbow. As we drove on, the rainbow shrank to cover just the river, bank to bank. Within a few miles the rainbow moved before us to cover the highway in front of us, edge to edge. Finally, the rainbow appeared just over our vehicle, fender to fender. I exclaimed to my wife, "Isn't that awesome? I wish I had my camera!"

A week later, I was boating in the Puget Sound and was caught in a rainstorm. As sunlight broke through the clouds, a beautiful full double rainbow curved across the sky. The Cascade Mountains formed the backdrop. While I stared at this glorious scene, a pilot whale breached in front of me; and as it was perfectly framed by the rainbow, I thought, "I wish I had my camera."

The next day, traveling back to campus at Walla Walla and passing through the Hanford Nuclear Reservation desert, the gloomy rains came again. As before, the sky opened, allowing a shaft of light that matured into a full double rainbow. While watching this display of glory, I saw, on a rocky outcrop centered under this arch of color, three pronghorns mount the rocks and turn their heads, looking directly toward me. At that moment I was overcome with an overwhelming sense of God's presence. I pulled my truck to the side of the road and wept, recognizing that God had been trying to get through to answer my prayers.

In this case, God did not specifically tell me how to solve the issues at work or to resolve conflicts in science. But, more importantly, He encouraged my soul. He did this by demonstrating support through nature. He chose symbols that I value to assure me that He was there with me, even during times of despair.

Through His use of nature, He assured me of His creatorship, His commitment to me as a seeker, and His love for me as an individual. The three full double rainbows continue to remind me that God is the Pilot of my life.

Ronald Carter, PhD, serves as provost of Loma Linda University and as professor in the department of earth and biological sciences and the department of theological studies in LLUSR.

October 22

Be still, and know that I am God. Psalm 46:10, KJV

It was an unusually hot October day. I was driving home after a typically busy day of seeing patients in the clinic. During the drive, my mind was racing with a variety of thoughts. Did I make the right decisions on those difficult patients? Where should we go for dinner tonight? Should I come to clinic dressed up in a costume to entertain the pediatric patients for the upcoming Halloween day?

All these varied contemplations definitely distracted me from focusing on the duties of the drive. I was almost home when I rolled through the last stop sign without coming to a complete stop. Bad mistake! At the corner, on the other side of the street, was a sheriff waiting for someone to nab. Without mercy, he wrote a ticket for failure to come to a complete stop.

The next day, still reeling from my misfortune, I pulled into my parking space at the clinic. As I got out of my car, the security person greeted me courteously with a smile and complimented me on how nicely I was dressed. I began my day, continuing to provide care for my patients, while still trying to dismiss the negativity from the day before.

Without any particular reason, a mother of one of my first patients commented on how much she appreciated the way I treated her child. I finished the morning and drove to the hospital to make my midday rounds. After examining a newborn, I felt inspired to say a prayer for the baby. The parents agreed to my praying. After the prayer, the parents said that no doctor had ever offered to pray for them. They expressed their appreciation for my prayer.

Suddenly, I realized that my busy schedule had kept me from noticing, through encounters with people around me, the efforts from Above and God's desire to cheer me up and assure me of His blessings. It was when I stopped to pray that my worry was replaced by peace.

The monetary fine for that traffic citation was trivial, compared to the penalty for my failure to stop and acknowledge the Great Physician. Fortunately, His grace provides us the assurance that He will provide for our every need. That is the reason He encourages us to stop, be quiet, and know that He is God.

Samuel Catalon, LLUSM class of 1984, is an assistant clinical professor in LLUSM department of pediatrics. His daughter, Stacy Catalon, LLUSM class of 2013, is a pediatric resident at LLUCH.

October 23

If any of you lacks wisdom, he should ask God, who gives generously to all without finding fault, and it will be given to him. James 1:5, NIV (1984)

If one starts with the wisdom of God, an impossible dream can become reality. Divine intervention is real. In my mind, the proton treatment facility at Loma Linda University Medical Center (LLUMC) is a prime example of a dream becoming a reality; I think these few selected examples will show what I mean.

When LLUMC committed to build the proton treatment center, a large group that included some of the finest physicists in the world met regularly, at their own time and expense, to help our group at Fermilab (originally the National Acceleration Laboratory) in Illinois. At one such meeting at the Loma Linda site, a prominent East Coast radiotherapist said to me, "Did you ever imagine that the first meeting at Fermilab would become this group, all working together?"

During design and development at Fermilab, a dispute arose between Fermilab and Loma Linda Univeristy (LLU) personnel over the control system design. To ease tensions, the LLU group was transferred to Lawrence Berkeley Laboratory in California to continue its work. I was later told by a lead physicist at Fermilab that the transfer almost destroyed the entire project. But that did not happen.

Shortly after the proton accelerator was transferred to LLUMC from Fermilab, a design review session was held at Berkeley. A physicist at the meeting opined that LLUMC was eight years away from treating patients with protons. In fact, the first patient was treated eight months later.

By late summer 1990, LLUMC's industrial partner had not yet generated a beam in the proton synchrotron; this was nearly a year after the accelerator had been shipped to LLUMC. I charged three young engineers with the task of taking notes on every action, concept, and procedure involved in this effort, and to call me when they developed a possible solution to the problem. This they did—in less than two weeks. Soon they had the accelerator operating.

Shortly thereafter, the proton center was in operation, a faculty member said to me that the center, which had been more expensive to build that anyone had anticipated, would be the financial ruin of the institution. Nearly 25 years later, the proton center has become one of the important elements in the growing success of LLUMC, with over 16,500 patients treated to date.

When it opened, the LLUMC proton facility was the only hospital-based proton center in the world. It was the only one in the United States for more than a decade. Today, there are 34 centers worldwide, with 11 in the United States and 5 more facilities planned or under construction.

The wisdom of God is the foundation upon which all this rests. That is why I say, as I did in the commencement address to the LLUSM graduating class in 2008, that God's wisdom is available to all; one needs only to ask.

James M. Slater, LLUSM class of 1963, is founder of Proton Cancer Treatment Center of LLUMC, vice chair of the radiation research division of LLUSM department of basic sciences, and a professor in LLUSM departments of radiation medicine and basic sciences. He was LLUSMAA 1995 Alumnus of the Year and LLU 1994 Alumnus of the Year. October 23 is the date the first patient was treated at the Proton Treatment Center in 1990.

The angel of the Lord *encamps around those who fear him, and he delivers them.*
Psalm 34:7, NIV

Loud pounding African drums suddenly caught my attention. I was alone in a missionary's home in Goma, Zaire. My sister, Charlene Larsen Andersen, and my brother-in-law, Floyd Andersen, both LLUSM class of 1968, were in charge of the 100-bed Songa Mission Hospital. I had traveled to Africa to help them. In gratitude for my visit, they planned a safari near Goma.

When I heard the drums, I grabbed my tape recorder and headed toward the rhythmic sound. I crossed the dirt road outside the house, and followed a narrow dirt path into the African jungle. The deeper I went into the jungle, the louder the drumming became, and the more intense my excitement. My reason for this pursuit was that I wanted to take a recording of African drums back to my Sabbath School class.

The path abruptly stopped in the jungle at an opening about 50 feet around. There were three short African men vigorously pounding three large conical African drums about three feet high. They were bare-chested and wearing only small loincloths. Near them, about 25 more African men, who had been drinking banana beer—also bare-chested and wearing loincloths—were throwing dirt into the air, dancing vigorously, lifting their legs high, and chanting.

I froze in my tracks. All thoughts of a recording for Sabbath School vanished. Immediately, as if from nowhere, a very tall pleasant looking African man, with a beaming smile, approached me. He said, in perfect English, "You should not be here." I quickly said, "I know." He said, "Go back this way," pointing to a totally different trail in the African jungle. I said, "Okay," changed my direction and walked quickly down the trail he advised. I trusted him and never looked back.

My heart still pounding, I arrived safely at the mission home; my brain was racing as I pondered my plight. In contrast to the drummers and dancers, the man who guided me was very tall, spoke perfect English (not French or Swahili as normally spoken in Zaire), was wearing a clean white shirt, and had a radiant smile. I believe my Angel in Africa saved me.

"To His children today the Lord declares, 'Be strong, . . . and work; for I am with you.' The Christian always has a strong helper in the Lord. The way of the Lord's helping we may not know; but this we do know: He will never fail those who put their trust in Him. Could Christians realize how many times the Lord has ordered their way, that the purposes of the enemy concerning them might not be accomplished, they would not stumble along complainingly. Their faith would be stayed on God, and no trial would have power to move them. They would acknowledge Him as their wisdom and efficiency, and He would bring to pass that which He desires to work out through them" (Ellen G. White, *Prophets and Kings*, p. 576).

God is constantly watching over us and for that I am most grateful.

Lauraine Larsen Kinney, LLUSM class of 1971, practices family and geriatric medicine in San Diego, California.

October 25

Let your steadfast love become my comfort according to your promise to your servant. Psalm 119:76, NRSV

My father loves to tell the story of his visit to my husband's orthopaedic surgery office one Friday morning. The waiting room was filled with patients and the back office suite of examining rooms was full, too. My father had asked a nurse if he could wait in the back until the doctor might have time to take a quick look at his hurting elbow. The nurse kindly tucked my father into a room and informed the already overbooked doctor that his father-in-law had also been added to his schedule.

In an orthopaedic surgeon's office, most doors remain open. Privacy is not a big issue to people who sport huge casts and who have become accustomed to having several friends or relatives in tow to help wheel or push them around. If you stood in the middle of this doctor's back office area, you could see "the wounded" in almost every direction you looked. And they could all view each other. The door was usually closed only after the doctor had entered a room, when he needed to examine the patient's injuries more closely.

A little boy with crutches and casted leg was making his way to an examining room as the nurse stood in a doorway and beckoned him. The little boy was exactly in front of the one closed door in the office when the door flew open and the busy doctor emerged. The doctor was calling out pre-op instructions to the patient he had just examined and was bidding a hurried goodbye. He did not see the little boy on crutches.

Crash! The little boy started to topple to the floor and was saved only by the quick, long arms of the doctor himself. The doctor began apologizing profusely to the little boy and to his mother, who was not far behind the scene of the crash.

The mother's response was, "It's okay—he's easy to knock over! We're always accidentally knocking him over at home, too." The doctor smiled with relief, and every waiting patient and nurse within earshot began to chuckle.

Who of us does not remember a time in our own lives when we have been "broken" and how easy we were to "knock over" during the days and months that followed? If only we could remember during those times the promise that God will never allow us to endure more than we can handle, and that His quick, long arms from Heaven will save us from falling, whenever we really need them.

Carla Lidner Baum, LLUSD class of 1990, is an assistant professor in LLUSD. She is married to Bradley Baum, LLUSM class of 1982. October 25 is her father's birthday.

You keep track of all my sorrows. You have collected all my tears in your bottle. You have recorded each one in your book. Psalm 56:8, NLT

D riving to clinic one October morning, I prayed aloud, "Lord, I want to share your good news boldly with patients; but I'm afraid if I openly share and pray with patients, I may be fired. Shall I change jobs?" Trusting God would answer, I switched to my audio Bible for the rest of my drive.

My first patient was Katrena—a shy thirty-ish female. Her limp hair covered her eyes, while a reticent smile flashed flawed dentition. She had previously shared with me her struggles with drugs, alcohol, and abusive relationships. Her greatest challenge was staying off methamphetamine long enough to prove that she was a safe mother for her son.

During our earlier August visit, she had tearfully pled for my help in her recovery so she could redeem her four-year-old from foster care. I had queried, "Do you like poetry?"

When she nodded in the affirmative, I handed her a slip of paper on which I had handwritten Psalm 56:8. "This is one of my favorite poems about the God in Heaven who cares about us so much that He notices each tear. He wants to help you." I also handed her a red glass perfume bottle as a reminder of the promise. She accepted the miniature bottle appreciatively and allowed me to pray with her.

I had no idea what God had done in her life in the two months since our prayer. I greeted her, noting the medical assistant's input of her chief complaint: "Recheck blood pressure." Ahh! Her blood pressure was a much-improved 124/72, a hopeful clue that she had not recently used methamphetamine.

"I am so glad you are here," she confided. "Since you prayed with me last time, I started reading my Bible and joined a women's Bible study. I have been clean and sober for 56 days and am having supervised visits with my son!"

Smiling, I affirmed her choices and thought, "Lord, shall I tell Katrena what I prayed this morning?"

"Do it!" God prompted.

I said to her, "This morning I asked God to show me what He wants me to do about my job. I think He used you to answer my prayer!"

"Oh!" she gushed, "You need to be right here in this clinic praying for people like me. That gives me goose bumps—here I am just a baby Christian and God is using me to answer prayers!" She bubbled, "Is it okay to tell my Bible study group?"

"Absolutely!" We prayed again together, *Dear God, Thank you for Katrena. Thank you for showing her that You care about her very much, that You save her tears in Your bottle and write them in Your book. Thank you for her Bible study group and for keeping her clean and sober so she can be the mother she wants to be for her son. Thank you for answering our prayers and for using us to encourage each other. Amen.*

As our eyes flickered open, I squeezed her hand as she embraced me in a big hug. We were "sisters," and God was growing both of us!

Melinda Skau, LLUSM class of 1982, is a family practitioner in Oroville, California. Her classmate and husband, Randy Skau, is a general surgeon. They have two children.

October 27

I thank my God every time I remember you. Philippians 1:3, NIV

Sometimes, I feel as if I just cannot keep going. I get exhausted. In my conquest of medical school—and yes, it is a thing to be conquered—so many things wear me down: lungs, livers, upcoming research and boards, and a 6.9 percent unsubsidized loan that will not stop growing, no matter how many cherries I put on top of my "pretty pleases." Why am I even here at Loma Linda University training to be a doctor?

And then, I think of Mr. C. He was a patient recovering from a surgery to correct a bladder fistula. Essentially, there was a small hole allowing bits of fecal matter to slip into his urinary tract; the fecal matter would pass with his urine. And from what I understand, it is about as painful as it sounds! Nonetheless, he was still pretty upbeat about the whole incident. He told me: "I passed gas through my penis. Not many people can say they've done that!" I suspect he is right.

I had a chance to talk to him for a while, and he told me his story. He grew up on a large farm with his family in the midwestern United States. Eventually, he trained to become an electrical engineer, and worked various jobs until he retired about 12 years ago. He decided to go back to the farm life—in particular, to raising horses. He was simply an ordinary guy, no different from you or me, who wound up in the hospital due to an unfortunate circumstance.

He interrupted his story to tell me how thankful he was for his health-care experience here. The nurses were caring; the doctors were competent. "I'd be in a lot of pain without all of you," he admitted.

"Oh, not me," I corrected him. "I'm still just a first-year med student. I have a ways more to go before I become an official doctor. Have any advice?"

Mr. C lifted his head and looked straight into my eyes. "Don't forget your bedside manners," he warned me. "Also, be sure to establish the doctor/patient relationship." Then he relaxed into a smile. "It's hard, but just keep going. Once you start, don't quit. Pretty soon, you'll be helping people like me."

And while I know not every patient will be as grateful or as encouraging as Mr. C, when I am wearied and need a little hope, sometimes it is that one heartfelt "thanks" that can make all the difference. God knows just when to put Mr. C's into our lives.

And then, we can keep going.

Anthony Yeo, LLUSM class of 2016, is from Colton, California. He graduated from Pacific Union College with a BS degree in chemistry, emphasis in biochemistry.

So Abraham called that place "The Lord *will provide"; as it is said to this day,*
"On the mount of the Lord *it shall be provided." Genesis 22:14, NRSV*

In 1967, my husband, Orval Patchett, CME class of 1945, and I joined a medical tour to Asia. Afterward, we visited our friends in Saigon—Jess, CME class of 1952, and Juanita Holm. They showed us the city as best they could under wartime conditions, including a tour of the hospital. While there, we noticed the lack of essential equipment in every section. Finishing the tour, Juanita asked Jess to order IV solutions for the operating room. Supplies were low and war shipments were uncertain.

To her request, Dr. Jess gently replied: "I am sorry, but there is no money." Again Juanita declared her need. He smiled, touched her arm, and said: "The Lord will provide."

Upon our return to the States, we spent Sabbath in Hawaii with friends. They informed me I was already scheduled to give the mission story for church. Mission story? But this was a medical tour. Oh, no! What could I say? It had to be Saigon! But what could I say about Saigon? I really did not have anything to say.

I was miserable! I asked the Lord for help. I vowed I would *never* stay with friends again. How did I get into this? Why is it that my husband can never bail me out of these situations?

Sabbath arrived. There was *no* answer to my prayer. I was desperate and unsure as I slowly stood up. I smiled and said, "Greetings from your dear brothers and sisters in Saigon." That old cliché. I rambled through my memory bank of the city at war, along with conditions at the hospital. To fill up space, I relayed the conversation about the IV solutions. Mercifully, the time passed and I could sit down. I was utterly humiliated!

Later, I heard the rest of the story. Naomi Yamashiro—wife of Charles Yamashiro, CME class of 1950—had been in church that day. Naomi provided Friday night supper and worship every week for Adventist corpsmen stationed in Hawaii. A few days after my talk, her telephone rang. A corpsman mentioned that he had a large shipment of outdated IV solutions. Though perfectly good, they could not be used in any Navy hospital. Did she know of any Adventist hospital that could use them? Yes, she thought, in Saigon. But how could the shipment get there?

The next day, Naomi discussed the situation with an officer's wife who was planning to attend a Friday night reception at the Officer's Club that evening. While there, she met a captain whose ship had been delayed due to repairs. He was sailing for Seoul via Saigon the next day. Could he take the IV solutions? Yes, he would be happy to. But the solutions had to be at the dock by 10 a.m. the next day—*no later*.

At midnight, Naomi received the news from the officer's wife. Though it was Sabbath, Naomi called her corpsman, who then made arrangements to meet the morning deadline. Soon the solutions were on their way to Saigon. The Navy notified the hospital of their unexpected gift. In addition, they were delivered without any charge!

Just as Dr. Jess had said, "The Lord *will* provide."

Dorothy Patchett graduated from LLUSN in 1944. She served as a Loma Linda councilor for many years and was on the LLU Medical Auxiliary board from 1980 to 2000. Her late husband, Orval Patchett, was an ophthalmologist who practiced in Pasco, Washington. Four of his five children followed him into medicine. October was the month this story occurred.

October 29

For the eyes of Yahweh roam throughout the earth to show Himself strong for those whose hearts are completely His. 2 Chronicles 16:9, HCSB

"**M**edical ministry" brings to mind the ideal of following the Messiah's altruistic ministry to preach the gospel and to restore people to full health: physical, mental, emotional, and spiritual. Such a noble effort, often espoused in religion classes, inspired me to take on the rigors of medical school. But after two-and-a-half years of jumping through hoops, getting a taste of several clerkships in the hierarchy of medicine, seeing health care changes dominate national politics, and learning to use the electronic medical record, I found myself having misgivings. How could anyone pursue an altruistic model of medical ministry in the United States, where medicine is so commercialized and heavily managed?

As I prayed for an opportunity to see medical ministry being modeled, I remembered an appeal given back in January to join Dr. John Torquato and Pastor Wayne Kablanow in medical ministry in Spokane, Washington, the following October. Never had I imagined that my schedule would conveniently open up in October so I could respond to that appeal, but it did. I booked my flight that same day to Spokane.

Curiously, on one of the days after I arrived, Dr. Torquato told me to meet him in a grocery store. I was quite puzzled because he had informed me that he was only searching for a long-term clinic site closer to the medical evangelistic gatherings. As it turned out, this grocery store already had a rapid care clinic but it had closed down three years ago due to a sudden fallout with the investors.

The store was located conveniently beside a busy pharmacy that agreed to administer vaccinations and promote the clinic. The grocery store manager even offered to stock up on any supplies the clinic would need, just to get it started again. I had no idea these were the very specifications Dr. Torquato had prayed and searched for in order to provide for the needs of his part-time staff.

One of his struggling physician assistants had joined his practice at half pay and had a one-hour commute because she wanted to be a part of medical ministry. However, increasing demands at home were forcing her now to resign and accept a job offer at a nearby hospital. Dr. Torquato would not let her go that easily, knowing how she was called to this work.

He appealed to her to reconsider, suggesting a clinic might open up closer to her home and with the hours she needed. To everyone's amazement, this grocery store's rapid care clinic met her needs! It was half the distance from her home as the other one. Thus, she would have the hours she needed and could remain on staff while still being available for her family obligations.

Why I happened to be in Spokane to witness this turn of events is too much of a coincidence to ignore, and it served as a positive response to my own misgivings, as well. Through this group's obedience, I was humbled to experience the benevolent hand of the Almighty at work. I saw how He provided for all the needs of His workers and also affirmed my call to medical ministry.

Deborah Roquiz, LLUSM class of 2014, is from Avon Park, Florida. She graduated from Andrews University with a BA degree in music and minors in biology and chemistry. She is a deferred mission appointee.

*You've all been to the stadium and seen the athletes race. Everyone runs; one wins.
Run to win. All good athletes train hard. They do it for a gold medal that tarnishes
and fades. You're after one that's gold eternally. I don't know about you, but I'm
running hard for the finish line. I'm giving it everything I've got. No sloppy living
for me! I'm staying alert and in top condition. I'm not going to get caught napping,
telling everyone else all about it and then missing out myself.*
1 Corinthians 9:24-27, MSG

Have you ever run for a life? That includes "running for your life?"
Last night at 1:50 a.m. I received a 17-second call saying, "We are doing a
C-section. We can't get the baby out!"

I jumped out of bed, put in my contacts, leaped into scrubs and bolted. My amazing
wife, Sharlene, had the front door unlocked and open and I dashed out into the night.
Running down the hill I thought, "I should have recorded this run on Strava (an Internet-
and GPS-based personal training application for smart phones)!" It is just over 500 meters
from my front door to the operating theatre building. I flew.

I had sterile gloves on at 1:55 a.m. Malamulo's amazing team—anesthetist Edwin
Kachiwala, clinical officer Amy Chipinga, and nurse Esther—were able to get the baby out
through the incision just as I entered the room.

The baby's head had been trapped in the pelvic canal. She had a heartbeat, but was
gray and limp and not breathing. Edwin and I bagged and resuscitated the little one. At 30
minutes she gasped. At 45 minutes she was breathing on her own.

I ran to save a life. I named her "Grace."

---

*Ryan Hayton, LLUSM class of 2005, is an assistant professor in LLUSM department of surgery. A
deferred mission appointee, he has been serving at Malamulo SDA Hospital in Malawi, Africa, since
2010. He lived at Malamulo as a child (from ages 8 to 14) while his father, Bill Hayton, LLUSM class
of 1973-B, was a missionary obstetrician and gynecologist. To obtain international experience during
their five-year training course, fourth-year general surgery residents from LLUMC travel to Malamulo
to spend two months under his supervision.*

October 31

In all your ways acknowledge Him, And He shall direct your paths.
Proverbs 3:6, NKJV

Although I am not an alumnus of this institution, Loma Linda University (LLU) has had a profound influence on both my professional career and our family life. While a medical student at the University of Sydney in Australia—and having to request the rescheduling of Saturday exams—I often thought of the advantages of attending a Christian medical school.

After graduating and becoming a general surgeon (but still young and single), I stopped briefly at LLU on my way to England to become a Fellow of the Royal College of Surgeons. While visiting LLU, I met Ellsworth Wareham, CME class of 1942, who befriended me. This connection opened the way to my returning to LLU in a residency position a year later. I was leaning toward a career in orthopaedics, but Dr. Wareham offered a thoracic surgery residency. According to him, "Whatever branch of surgery you go into, you'll be that much better for this training."

About a year into the residency, he calmly announced: "I'm going to send you to Athens, Greece, for 12 months to help establish a continuing cardiac surgery program." This opportunity had little appeal to me; I did not know a soul there or a word of Greek. And this assignment would take me away from an ICU nurse I had met on unit 7100 of the Medical Center. We had only been on three dates, but the prospects seemed favorable!

With only a couple of months to go before departure, we accelerated the courtship, married two weeks before leaving, and had a fabulous honeymoon year in Greece. We have literally lived happily ever after!

Now, I look back over a very satisfying cardiac surgery career in California's Napa Valley, and my wonderful family. Adding to this is the continuing joy of now assisting with cardiac surgery and also teaching thoracic anatomy to the freshman medical students of LLU. For all this, I thank God; He has indeed "directed my paths." He can do the same for you.

Donald Wilson, MBBS, is an adjunct assistant professor in LLUSM department of pathology and human anatomy. He is board certified in surgery and thoracic surgery. He and his wife have two sons, one of whom is a graduate of LLUSM.

November

"All must be thanks giving."

November 1

For God so loved the world that He gave His only begotten Son, that whoever believes in Him should not perish but have everlasting life. John 3:16, NKJV

"**D**o you mean I'm going to die?" His eyes widened as his jaw dropped and the color drained from his face. He was devastated. I was startled by his response. I had just discussed the deterioration of his congestive heart failure and that his life expectancy had reached the six-month mark. It was time to consider a heart transplant. Options were limited for congestive heart failure in the 1970s.

As a cardiology fellow at a major heart transplant center, I wanted him to consider a transplant before his disease deteriorated past the point of being a candidate. We had become good friends during his clinical care, and he trusted my judgment. Thus we began the required preoperative evaluation.

We visited often during his hospitalization. My concern turned to his attitudes and beliefs about his life beyond this one, should the outcome of his surgery not be successful. I had encountered this discussion area before as a student and resident at Loma Linda University School of Medicine. And I confess it was a difficult journey for me to accept death, instead of healing, when all else failed.

The concept of "making man whole," as I learned, involved ministering to the total needs of the patient—both physical and spiritual. As a tribute to the dedicated physicians who trained me, I became more comfortable discussing the difficult area of a possible unsuccessful outcome.

When I asked my patient about his belief in God, he replied that, in spite of his being raised in the Church of England, he was an atheist and believed that God was in all nature. (I did not try to point out that he was actually a pantheist.) I asked him to accept a visit from my pastor. Earlier, when I was a resident at Loma Linda University Medical Center, I had support from the chaplain staff and my attending physicians; but now in a different environment, I had to take the responsibility to initiate the discussion on my own. Fortunately, he agreed to speak with my pastor.

He was accepted as a heart transplant candidate and, when a donor heart became available, I accompanied him to the operating room. The surgery was a success and he began the antirejection medication regimen. I visited him daily in his isolation room, and we became closer friends.

At our last visit, as I turned to leave, he stopped me with this statement, "Dr. Isaeff, I want you to know, I believe." I will never forget the look in his eyes as he spoke. And then, just the next day I found him covered with chicken pox. With his health compromised by the antirejection medications, herpes zoster attacked, and quickly spread to his brain, causing his death.

I am comforted by the promise in John 3:16 that "whoever believes in Him should not perish but have eternal life." My training in "making man whole" was a gift from God. Sleep in peace, my friend. We *shall* meet again.

Dale Isaeff, LLUSM class of 1965, is medical director of the coronary intensive care unit at LLUMC and is a professor in LLUSM department of medicine. This story was based upon a patient care experience while he was a fellow in cardiology at Stanford University Medical Center.

And call upon me in the day of trouble: I will deliver thee, and thou shalt glorify me.
Psalm 50:15, KJV

My first view of my husband post-op was in the ICU with wires and tubes everywhere. It was frightening to say the least, but a beautiful sight to me. He underwent surgery for a liver transplant at midnight and it was now 9:15 the next morning. I stood staring at him, so thankful as I tried to absorb all that had happened over the last five months.

In 2002 our son had been killed and my faith had been shaken to the core. I had been struggling, wondering where was God and why He allowed this to happen. Now to lose Marty would have been more than I could bear. For months I watched my husband's health spiral downward. Marty's acute liver failure began in May of 2008. He was not a drinker, had never done drugs and had no history of hepatitis, so we were shocked to hear the diagnosis of "mild cirrhosis." We insisted he be sent for a follow-up and second opinion. After his workup and an unexpected weeklong stay due to a kidney stone attack we were sent home. This was followed by numerous visits to various EDs where we live. He was finally hospitalized at one of our local hospitals for two months. Because it was not a medical center or a transplant hospital, all they could really do was administer pain medication as we watched him deteriorate over the next few weeks.

After Marty was hospitalized for several weeks, I was told that if he did not go to a transplant center soon he would die. I was shocked! We were a family of faith. We had been praying for healing, but now we had to put feet to our faith. We started calling every doctor and hospital we could think of, trying to get him transferred. A doctor that we had contacted had found a transplant center that would take him. Marty would be helicoptered to Loma Linda University Medical Center the next morning. Our family followed in the car for the three-hour trip. As we turned the corner onto Anderson Street and I saw the huge cross on the hospital, a peace came over me and the Lord spoke to my heart, "You are at the right place, at the right time, with the right people."

When we came onto the transplant floor that morning, the doctors had already done a pre-exam on Marty. They met us with grim news. If Marty couldn't be stabilized quickly he wouldn't live more than a few days. We told the doctors to do what they knew to do and we would do what we knew to do—pray. Hundreds of people across the United States joined us in prayer for Marty's life.

The hepatologist told us that Marty's liver was "shot" but inexplicably it was sustaining him. Then they discovered he had the CMV virus, a spot on his lung and was septic. Miraculously he remained stable that week while the doctors worked diligently. One night our friends and family held a prayer vigil. The next morning the spot on his lung was gone. The following day the virus was under control enough that he could be put on the transplant list. Miraculously within five hours he had a liver offer! We prayed the surgeon's hands be anointed and that it would be a textbook surgery. After the nine-hour surgery, the surgeon came out saying those exact words in describing what transpired in the OR.

I learned that God is a God of restoration and multiplication—not only for our family but also for all who went on this journey with us.

Lorna Jones is the wife of Marty, the liver transplant patient in the story. She loves to tell this story wherever God opens the door as a testimony of His goodness and mercy.

November 3

Then we which are alive and remain shall be caught up together with them in the clouds, to meet the Lord in the air: and so shall we ever be with the Lord.
1 Thessalonians 4:17, KJV

I still have a distinct memory of that night. I was on call on my pediatric rotation, when my father called to say that my mother was sick and had been admitted to the National Cancer Center in Tokyo. When I arrived in Japan, I joined my father and brother in the hospital. The doctor invited us into a small room where he told us that my mother had stage IV pancreatic cancer, and that there was no curative treatment. We were also informed that she, who had previously seemed to be in perfect health, had only one month to live.

Even after learning of her prognosis, my mother remained completely calm and told us that she had no worries, since God was always with her. She strongly urged us to take her home, and refused chemotherapy, so we complied with her wishes. Under the guidance of a visiting doctor and a nurse, I managed her everyday care, including checking her vitals, changing her IV line, and managing her pain.

Everyone knew that her health was declining at a rapid rate. My mother passed away one month to the day after we received the devastating news. On that particular morning, as I was listening to her heart, her heartbeats became intermittent and finally stopped. After her heart was silent, her body became cold in a short time. At that moment, I realized that she had indeed passed away.

In medical school, I had seen many cadavers during my anatomy class. At that point in my studies, death was always somewhat irrelevant and far away to me. I did not really understand how it felt to lose a family member. However, after my mother's death, I was able to relate to the pain people feel after losing a loved one.

I take pride in the fact that I put all my heart and soul into her care, and did what I could for her. Even though I tended to her for only one month, I learned many things from her including real patient care and how faith strengthens our body and mind.

While it pains me to think of the loss of my mother, as a Christian I hope to meet all my family members in Heaven. When I meet her again, I want to share many stories especially those I have experienced in the hospital and how the lessons I learned from taking care of her help me each and every day to become a better doctor.

Mutsumi J. Kioka, LLUSM class of 2009, finished an internal medicine residency in Los Angeles, California, and is completing a pediatric critical care fellowship in Detroit, Michigan.

Thy servant hath found grace in thy sight, and thou hast magnified thy mercy, which thou hast shewed unto me in saving my life. Genesis 19:19, KJV

God has always been a constant and awesome presence in my life. I know that He is in control, and that all things work together for good. Without Him, my life truly would be nonexistent. As a physician, I see miracles all the time, but here are four examples in which I was the patient.

I recall the first miracle that happened when I was 12 years old—when God saved my life. It was a sunny day, and my father was driving. My brother and I had fallen asleep on the back seat of the car, so we did not witness the collision. We were hit at a high speed by a drunk driver who was going in the opposite direction. We do not know how the three of us ended up outside the car, and, according to the hospital, suffered only minor injuries. The car was completely destroyed.

The second life-saving miracle happened when I was 16 years old. I was at a church swimming party and dove into the pool from a very high diving board. I hit something hard with my head and passed out. It took quite some time before someone noticed me under water. I was in a coma for three days, at the hands of the good people at Loma Linda University Medical Center, but woke up with no apparent neurological deficit.

God saved my life again, on a dark rainy night when I was 22 years old. A friend and I were driving back to Pacific Union College in Angwin, California. Visibility was low, and we took a corner too fast and drove off the road, rolling over many times down a cliff. The car was a total loss, but we were not, and the staff at St. Helena Hospital treated us with excellent care.

When I was 44 years old, I woke up one Sunday morning unable to move my right arm, which was also causing intolerable pain. My wife drove me to the emergency department, where a CT scan was done. My colleagues in the hospital and I spent a considerable amount of time looking at the scan. We found no reason for the paralysis and pain, which by then had completely resolved. However, we did find a neck mass, unrelated to the arm condition. It was later biopsy-proven to be cancer and was surgically removed. I believe that God saved me by giving me a temporary painful paralysis to draw attention to the tumor.

God's ultimate life-saving miracle is in giving His Son to die, so that we can all have eternal life. God performs miracles around us every day and, as Christians, we have a responsibility to share that good news. When a patient tells me that I am a good physician, I reply that God is the Good Physician—and that I am simply doing His will.

Osahon Osifo, LLUSM class of 1995, is an anesthesiologist in Oroville, California. He and his wife, Myrna, are blessed with two children. November 4 is the couple's wedding anniversary.

November 5

When the Lord saw her, He had compassion on her and said to her, "Do not weep." Luke 7:13, NKJV

Have you ever waited in a doctor's clinic to see a physician? Or have you ever waited anxiously for the surgeon to tell you how the operation went on one of your family members? I have and, as a general surgeon, I have learned invaluable lessons from being on "the other side of the fence."

Several years ago, my father was diagnosed with advanced colon cancer. Not willing to be defeated by the disease, my family and I decided to have him undergo a major operation, which involved excising several areas of metastasis in the liver, as well as resecting the primary tumor. I remember being in the office of the surgical oncologist with my father, discussing the case and reviewing the CT scan.

Having encountered similar types of cancer cases myself, I knew, cerebrally, that the odds were very much against my father. However, emotionally, for both of us, I needed to hear some hope of a cure from the expert, even if it was just a glimmer.

The day of the operation came. The rest of the family and I greeted our father with smiling faces that, with years of training, hid our fears and anxiety as we watched him being wheeled through the operating room door. Those six hours of operation felt like days. A thousand thoughts went through my mind. It was such a relief when the surgeon finally came to talk to us, telling us that our dad was doing well, and they felt they had taken care of the tumors.

After our father recovered from surgery, he still had countless clinic visits and chemotherapy sessions. I remember, on several occasions, having to wait our turn to see the oncologist. Yes, it was not unusual to wait an hour to have a 10-minute follow-up visit. The experience of waiting for doctors not only happens to my own patients, but it has become a norm in our society.

Although my father finally succumbed to the disease, I learned that it is essential, as a clinician, to try to connect with my patients on an emotional level. In dealing with patients who have cancer, it is important to emphasize the positive aspects of the disease process. To this day, I am very appreciative of the hope the surgeon gave us that day in his office.

I have also learned that patients' families are usually very anxious when their loved ones are undergoing an operation and, as a clinician, I can play an important role in bringing relief to those individuals. Just because I have performed an appendectomy a thousand times, this operation will be the first for my patient, who will experience a level of anxiety. In regard to the lengthy clinic wait, I have learned the importance of coming to clinic on time—and also decreasing the daily clinic load—in order to allow more time for each patient.

The next time I see a patient with cancer or take care of a patient requiring an operation, I will intentionally try to apply the lessons learned from "the other side of the fence."

On Wang, LLUSM class of 1989, is a general surgeon in Los Angeles, California.

November 6

You have heard that it was said, "Love your neighbor and hate your enemy." But I tell you, love your enemies and pray for those who persecute you.
Matthew 5:43-44, NIV

Come with me on a peace mission, deep into the remote desert of northern Kenya. Enter with me into the crowded room, filled with village leaders who are hoping that you can help them. Listen as our hosts tell the story of their pain. Understand and appreciate the privilege that is ours to be healers in this world beyond our imagination.

Here is the culmination of that event: a woman stands. She is a grandmother in her seventies, her hands broken by years of hard work, but she stands straight and proud. She wears a blue headdress wrapped around her sparse graying hair. Her wrap-around skirt is red-checked, with patterns of white.

She is unable to hold back her passion. She looks deep inside me with her eyes. She speaks with a pain that is beyond tears, and she keeps firing. I have never experienced a sermon like this. She speaks in another language, but I can hear every word.

She tells us how this conflict has escalated into something unheard of, where women and children are the targets. Women cannot draw water without an escort. She graphically describes how a woman was bending over to pick up firewood, when someone shot her from behind, ripping out part of her womanhood.

She points at me, her eyes pleading with me to do something. She is driving her pain deep into my soul. "God," I'm praying, "what am I supposed to do with this?" The chief tries to wrap up the meeting.

Now they want to hear from us. Would I like to say a few words? I clear my throat. I take a deep breath. Then suddenly, I cannot speak. A flood of emotion drowns me. I bury my face in my hands. The women are comforting me with their voices from across the room. A hand is on my shoulder. I recover.

I begin, "When I heard from my friends about how you were suffering, I could not pass up the opportunity to be here with you. I can only tell you how sorry I am for what you are suffering."

I choke for just a moment. The women are nodding. Their voices are encouraging me to continue speaking.

"We are here on a mission of peace. I know this is not easy. But I can't get these words out of my head—that we are to pray for and love our enemies. We may fail in this process, but if we fail, let us fail together. But let us not stop trying."

We make our way across the room, preparing to leave. The people are holding on to my hand, just for a moment longer, imploring me with their eyes, wondering if this crazy notion of peace will *ever* become more than a pipe dream.

As I walk away I am deep in thought, wrestling with what just transpired. If the roles were reversed, if I were the victim, would I be able to do what I had just admonished them to do—would I be able to find it within me to love my enemies?

Barry Bacon, LLUSM class of 1984, practices family medicine in Colville, Washington. This story took place in northern Kenya where he was helping to launch a peace initiative tied to primary health care. November 6 is when this story occurred.

November 7

Do not be overcome by evil, but overcome evil with good. Romans 12:21, NKJV

I inherited my Grandpa's Bible, his stethoscope, and his old prescription pad after his death two years ago. I treasure each item for its own unique reason: the Bible, represented Grandpa's love for God's Word; the stethoscope, his burden for helping patients physically; and the prescription pad, his passion for helping patients spiritually.

Prescription pads are not ordinarily associated with spiritual healing, but my grandfather, Russell Youngberg, CME class of 1949, was no ordinary doctor. Not only did he prescribe medicine, he also prescribed books. Grandpa believed in whole person care, in ministering to the physical, emotional, and spiritual needs of his patients. That is why he prescribed books.

It all started when Grandpa read *The History of the Unitus Fratrum*. This book describes the terrible persecution Moravian Protestants faced during the Counter Reformation. One particular story caught Grandpa's attention. Anton Koniash (1637), a Bohemian monk, was violently opposed to Christian literature being available to common people in their own languages. He risked his life to destroy the Bibles and books of the Moravian Protestants. At the end of his conquest, this man claimed he had destroyed over 60,000 books!

Grandpa was deeply moved by the story, and wanted to do something about it. He prayed God would use him to undo the damage by allowing him to give away 60,000 Christian books. The books he chose to distribute included the Bible, *Steps to Christ*, *The Desire of Ages*, *The Ministry of Healing*, and *The Great Controversy*.

Grandpa's primary mission field was his patients, so he started with them. He placed books in the waiting room of his office. He sent book "care packages" to interested patients after they were discharged home. He wrote prescriptions for books and sent patients to the local Adventist Book Center to have those prescriptions "filled," billing the cost to his office.

Book by book, Grandpa quietly worked toward his secret goal. No one knew the reason Dr. Youngberg was constantly giving away books, but many appreciated that he did. Toward the end of his life, Grandpa told story after story of patients, colleagues, and complete strangers, who had found hope and inspiration in the pages of their books.

Several years ago, while I was in nursing school, my 82-year-old Grandpa finally shared his secret. He was concerned he would not be able to reach his goal. "How many books do you have left, Grandpa?" I asked. "Oh, about 5,000 or 6,000," he replied. "Don't worry, Grandpa," I said. "You will finish. You just need some help from the younger generation."

It was a joy and privilege for my family to help Grandpa pass out his last 6,000 books. In the fall of 2010, just months before his death, Grandpa finally reached his goal!

I share Grandpa's story with the hope that it will inspire other health-care professionals to find creative ways to share God's love. Whether it is a book, a prayer, or an encouraging word, if we keep our eyes open, there are many opportunities to use our professions to continue the healing ministry of Jesus Christ.

Elise Harboldt is a registered nurse from Redlands, California. She co-authored the book Goodbye Diabetes *with Wes Youngberg, an assistant clinical professor in LLUSM department of preventive medicine and LLUSPH department of health promotion. November 7 is her grandfather's birthday.*

November 8

And the Lord turned and looked at Peter. Luke 22:61, ESV

"Doctor, I have a patient for you to see," said the Togolese health-care provider, who went on to describe a patient with unresectable cervical cancer, an all-too-common condition in this rural African mission hospital. At the time, I was covering for the missionary surgeon, who was in the United States on furlough. I was exhausted, emotionally spent, and reluctant to brave the noonday heat of 110 degrees. I patiently asked him to repeat his findings and his thoughts. He knew it was unresectable. I then asked why I needed to see the patient, since we both knew there was nothing I could do. He merely repeated, "You need to see this patient."

Grumbling, I pulled on my white coat as I walked through the heat and humidity. As I entered the examination room, I put on my professional, caring persona. I examined her. Indeed, there was nothing I could do in this African country for this unfortunate woman. I broke the news as gently and carefully as I could. She and her daughter collapsed into each other's arms, sobbing as the bad news impacted them.

Turning to write my note, I was startled when a clear voice within my head asked, "Is that all you have to offer them?" Silently, I enumerated my findings, and enlightened God as to the lack of chemotherapy or radiation therapy in this poor country. I made a solid argument. Clearly, I thought I should have convinced even Him.

But I heard the voice asking again, "Is that all you have to offer them?" Chagrined, ashamed, and somewhat angry at this unreasonable demand, I turned and began to talk to the patient once again. I explained that what I had told them was totally true, but that I had some hope for them nonetheless. Through the interpreter, I began to tell them of the true Hope of the world. My interpreter was born an evangelist and with the door now open, she bolted through it and the conversation ran without me!

As I turned back to write my notes, the tears in my eyes blurred the paper and I prayed fervently—both for the woman's salvation and for my own. I certainly needed to be rescued from my own blindness, self-centeredness, and narrow focus. I felt like Peter must have felt after his denial of Christ when Jesus raised his eyes and looked at him. God had weighed me and found me wanting. Forgiving and loving God that He is, He gave me a second chance to be used in His service.

During the past 15 years in the mission field, I have had many situations where I may not have been able to offer temporal physical healing, but I could always offer eternal healing. I only regret that I did not learn that when I was still a practicing physician in the U.S.

I challenge you to look for ways to share the "God News" that Christ is still the Great Physician—as Christ's messengers, we can and must *always* offer hope.

Bruce Steffes is an associate professor in LLUSM department of surgery and executive director of the Pan-African Academy of Christian Surgeons, a partner with LLUSM. November 8 is his wife's birthday.

November 9

When you walk through fire you shall not be burned, and the flame shall not consume you. Isaiah 43:2, ESV

My first foreign mission assignment, after completing a general surgery residency at Loma Linda University Medical Center, was a posting to Puerto Rico, to serve as staff surgeon at the Bella Vista Hospital (BVH) in Mayagüez. This hospital was a hub for medical training and caring outreach in the Greater and Lesser Antilles. Long before Bella Vista was founded, Loma Linda-trained physicians went to Puerto Rico to work for the sugar companies, caring for laborers as well as managers. They became the founders of our hospital and trailblazers for the many who followed.

Ivan Angell, CME class of 1950, was one of these mission-driven physicians based at BVH when we arrived there in 1973. He was also an intrepid mission-aviation advocate and participant. Since both he and I were licensed private pilots, I accompanied him on some of his flights to Haiti and the Dominican Republic, where he was actively supporting medical and education projects. Later, I made trips to those locations and others, piloting Ivan's Beechcraft Bonanza, carrying supplies, students, and staff to various locations.

Fuel management is always a factor in flight planning, and Ivan set up procedures to maintain supply and minimize cost. Fuel was expensive and scarce on the western side of the island, but abundant and cheap in San Juan, to the east. Since the Bonanza was equipped with two main tanks and two wing-tip tanks, we would calculate the fuel needed for the trip, but plan to arrive back in Mayagüez with all four tanks filled to maximum, having gassed up in San Juan on the way home. We would then off-load the fuel by hand pump into 50-gallon barrels, for storage.

One Sunday, when my son Doug and I went to transfer fuel, Ivan told me to use the new pump in the hangar. I was at the left wing tank with a hose in my hand while Doug stood at the gasoline drum, steadying the electric pump that conveyed fuel into the barrel. Everything was going well, but then Doug shouted, "Fire!" Seeing the flames lick across the drum lid, I grabbed the pump and flung it across the floor. As I attempted to beat out the fire with rags, my son raced toward the terminal to alert the firemen. The fire was out when they arrived, but attached to the pump was the charred hose that had dangled into the drum.

I believe Divine intervention is the only explanation why fire and fuel did not explode into a conflagration that could have destroyed the plane and hangar—and ruin my hands! A surgeon's hands are his most visible and viable tools. We like to think that we "are" Christ's hands, as we pray with patients and perform surgical procedures. But the greater truth is that we are all in His hands every moment. Hands—my patient's hands, my hands, and His hands—have all had profound meaning for me since that day.

Jack L. Bennett, LLUSM class of 1962, is a retired general surgeon. He served from 1973 to 1980 at Bella Vista Hospital. He has provided student mentoring and short-term relief for missionary surgeons in Nepal, Honduras, Haiti, Ethiopia, Guyana, and China. Presently, he is a clinical instructor for the LLUSM department of surgery. Past president of AIMS, he was named an LLUSMAA Honored Alumnus in 2013. He is married to Sharan, and they have four children, one of whom is a graduate of LLUSM.

November 10

And a great crowd of people followed him because they saw the signs he had performed by healing the sick. John 6:2, NIV

At times, I reflect on my career and wonder where all the years have gone. Recently, I was outside the Heart Transplant office, when I noticed a group of medical students gathered in animated conversation around a large portrait of some of our early heart transplant babies. I have seen this photograph, taken in 1989, in many places around the campus, and, also, in my travels around the world. It features Leonard Bailey, LLUSM class of 1969, looking down on 18 wiggly babies.

As I stopped to talk with these curious medical students, I realized that they too, were babies at the time this photograph was taken. Those little patients in the photo represent the beginning of heart transplantation at Loma Linda University Medical Center, and I enjoyed sharing their stories with the medical students. The story of heart transplantation did not stop with those babies. We were blessed with good outcomes and, since 1985, more than 500 children have now received new hearts at LLUMC!

These children came to Loma Linda from Japan and England, Spain and Italy, and from all over Canada and America, all with the same desperate hope—to be given a chance to live well. To achieve this goal takes a miraculous partnership with hundreds of individuals who are committed to excellence every hour of the day and night. Many of us in this Loma Linda University medical team have made a lifetime commitment to heart surgery and heart transplantation, and we have essentially "grown up" together.

In my 40 plus years with this team, I have been witness to many everyday miracles in the lives of these children. I have seen God's caring spirit in a colleague's tender touch or a softly spoken prayer. I have been aware of God's intervention when conventional wisdom seemed to have failed. And although we set out as a team of healers to help these children, we ourselves, as caregivers, have also been richly blessed in this process of healing.

As I said "goodbye" to these young medical students who are just beginning their professional careers, I hope and pray that their future in medicine will allow them to reflect back with gratitude and contentment, and that their profession will bring them closer to God.

Joyce Johnston Rusch, LLUSN class of 1971, is a heart transplant coordinator at the LLUMC Heart Transplant Institute where she has worked since 1985. She previously worked in the LLUMC cardiothoracic ICU. Her husband, Roy Rusch, LLUSM class of 1965, is an assistant clinical professor in LLUSM department of orthopaedic surgery.

November 11

Behold, how good and pleasant it is when brothers dwell in unity!
Psalm 133:1, ESV

This is the tale of two brothers who cared for each other. It begins in 1943, when Harvey Rittenhouse, CME class of 1943, waited for news about his involvement in World War II. Word came from the Federal Government: "Give them their medical licenses early; we need them."

Harvey was soon on his way to England to serve in the medical corps. His younger brother, Robert "Bob" Rittenhouse, CME class of 1949, an undergraduate student, waited anxiously for word of his brother. He saw the newspaper headlines of troops landing on Normandy Beach.

Meanwhile, Harvey narrowly missed injury when a German buzz bomb exploded a short distance away. He was sent with the troops to France, arriving in a landing craft on Normandy Beach not long after D-Day. Joining General Patton's 3rd army traveling across France, he was put in charge of a 200-bed tent hospital, triaging and treating the desperately injured and dying men. He oversaw the care of soldiers suffering from battle fatigue by placing them in a phenobarbital coma for two weeks to escape their terrible memories. Harvey was at the Battle of the Bulge, the battle that had more casualties than any other battle in United States history.

When Harvey returned from Europe, he was awarded the Bronze Star for meritorious service in France and soon began a residency in internal medicine. He later married musician Virginia-Gene Shankel, and they served as missionaries to Jamaica, where Harvey healed the sick with his medical knowledge and Virginia healed their souls with her music.

Bob, inspired by his brother, was accepted to the College of Medical Evangelists at the age of 18, the youngest of a wartime class, so young they were nicknamed "The Preemies." Bob followed his brother's example by serving in the Korean War as a physician on board the USS Tarawa, an aircraft carrier. With his military service completed, he and his wife, Peggy, moved to Massachusetts, where Bob worked as a family practitioner and Peggy taught nursing. Harvey and Virginia-Gene later moved to Massachusetts as well.

In 1977, Harvey was in a motor home accident and suffered head and spinal cord injuries. Not being able to practice medicine, he devoted his life to supporting his wife's music career. When Harvey's wife died; he was in his nineties and not well. Bob and Peggy moved to Harvey's lovely historic home to help with his care and rehab.

Gradually, Harvey, the old soldier, began to fade away. Bob, always the doctor, became a nurse. He patiently helped Harvey with his meals, and learned caring procedures from his nursing instructor wife. So now Bob, used to patient hospital rooms, sat by the bedside and watched Harvey breathe. When Bob and Peggy's children begged their parents to get help in caring for Harvey, they refused. Bob said, "He's my big brother. I want to take care of him." For nearly a year, Bob helped Harvey, and was with his brother when he took his last breath on February 11, 2012. To many, Harvey was a war hero. In the eyes of his family, Bob was no less.

Connie Rittenhouse Drexler, LLUSM class of 1983, is an associate professor of medicine at the University of Massachusetts Medical School. She is married to David Drexler, LLUSM class of 1988. They reside in Bolton, Massachusetts. The author submitted this in honor of her father, Robert Rittenhouse, CME class of 1949. November 11 is Veteran's Day.

November 12

How great is the love the Father has lavished on us, that we should be called children of God! And that is what we are! 1 John 3:1, NIV (1984)

The most amazing part of working in health care is that just by doing your job, you have the opportunity to help people on a daily basis. It is far too often shelved by the realities of work—routine, numbers and schedules. When that happens to me, God tends to send a reminder steering me back toward the mission of health care. Although I am still a newer ultrasound technologist, I have already experienced many such reminders. One of the most memorable occurred while I was a second-year sonography student attending Kettering College in Dayton, Ohio.

Looking back, it's almost comical to think about how we all waited for the boy. There were several of us: a guilt-ridden nurse who had organized the exam, the time-pressed cardiologist with her proud resident, the serious anesthesiologist, and the frustrated, yet patient, echo technologist with her overly excited sonography student. The pending procedure was a transesophageal echocardiogram, an ultrasound in which a probe is inserted through the patient's mouth and into the esophagus to obtain better views of the heart. It was ordered last minute for a pediatric inpatient and somehow all of the key players had arrived, except one—the patient!

We waited half an hour before the boy was wheeled into the room. I remember smiling at an assortment of stuffed animals and action figures that ran the length of his gurney. My instructor whispered that the boy was a very nervous 13-year-old with Down syndrome, as she and the nurse gently calmed and comforted him. Before long, in a blur of routine and professional steps, we began.

After a successful procedure, the echo tech and I made our way back to the lab. I commented on the toys lining the boy's bed. Smiling sadly, she told me that the toys had actually caused the delay. Apparently, when his nurse attempted to wheel him out of his room, he threw a fit until she realized he wouldn't leave without them. The tech explained that the boy was a ward of the state who lived in a group home and frequented the hospital. Our conversation was interrupted and the weight of it all didn't hit me until later that night.

Children don't belong in the hospital, but if they must go, they should have their family around them for comfort and support. This boy I had met earlier had come alone, a ward of the state, and government aside, his only family was the toys by his side. He had been scared about the procedure and of course he wanted them next to him: they were all he had.

I cannot wait until Jesus comes and this boy can have the family he needs and deserves. When that day comes, he will have a Father that will look him in the eyes with more love than he has ever experienced. But until then, I will strive in my daily work to show that love and support to the patients I serve.

Emily Unterseher (née Scofield) is an ultrasonographer at LLUMC. She and her husband, Mike, an LLUSM physician recruiter, live in Redlands, California, with their two rescue dogs.

November 13

Do not judge, or you too will be judged. For in the same way you judge others, you will be judged, and with the measure you use, it will be measured to you.
Matthew 7:1-2, NIV

I was putting gas in my car when a homeless man approached me, offering to wash my car windows. I hesitated, weighing in my mind if I should pay him and what he would actually use the money for. I said, "Yes," but then I added, "You can do something better than wash my windows. Will you tell me your life story?"

It seems to me that when people are not where they want to be in life, there is a reason. They may have made bad choices, or faced nothing but bad options which I have been spared. The reason does not matter. You can always learn much by listening to someone's story.

So, we made a lunch date for the next day. I met him at a Subway restaurant, and bought him a sandwich. By the look on his face, you would have thought I had taken him to a four-star restaurant! The everyday bounty of meat, cheeses, and vegetables amazed him. He exclaimed, "Wow, you can get anything on a sandwich here!"

We sat down and talked. His name was Joe. Now 61 years old, he had spent nearly half his life on the streets. He grew up in Louisville, Kentucky, with his mother, father, and three brothers. His father was a drunk and wife-beater. As early as when he was only five years old, Joe's mother and father would fight. The fight would scare Joe so much that all he could do was run to the window and scream for help. He thought he should have been able to protect his mother, but he could not. He still blames himself for not interfering, typical of the way young children react when they witness horrifying events they cannot explain or control.

Joe's father left soon after that. His mother was poor and had to work. Joe and his brothers were left at home alone all day. Joe started drinking when he was 13. And a few years after, he started using meth. He ended up in jail several times. His last arrest got him into a drug rehab program. He says he is doing better now, residing in a "sober-living" home in San Bernardino. But half his social security income pays the rent, leaving him little for groceries and cigarettes. Those items are what Joe panhandles money for, basic stuff some would take for granted.

Everyone has a story, and if a person does not take time to hear it, it is easier to think of poor or homeless people as dishonest, or dismiss their failures as deserved. But Joe did not deserve his fate, and I do not feel I am absolved of any responsibility to help him, and all the other Joe's out there. Stories matter. Unless I know their story, I am in no position to judge them.

I talked to Joe one other time after that day. He said he was still sober, and that things were going well for him. With a little help, maybe Joe's story will have a happy ending.

Bobbi Albano works in the public sector for First 5 San Bernardino. She is a frequent broadcasting contributor on KVCR-FM Weekend Edition. She previously worked for Loma Linda University.

My son, do not despise the LORD's discipline, and do not resent his rebuke, because the LORD disciplines those he loves, as a father the son he delights in.
Proverbs 3:11-12, NIV

Humility is one of those things you wish you could grow in, but hate when it slaps you in the face. I recall a time when I was looking up information in a patient's chart prior to seeing the patient in cardiology clinic, trying to figure out why the patient had developed syncope. As I was jotting down the information, the attending physician reprimanded me for copying the patient's history before talking to the patient himself. "Always talk to the patient first! Never copy from the H&P (history and physical)!" he barked. My heart sank.

"My apologies," I muttered. Why did he criticize me for something that seemed so *harmless*? Why did he have to do it in front of *everyone*? Questions like these raced through my mind as I walked sulkily toward my patient's room.

I entered the room. Before me sat Mr. AH, a 52-year-old Hispanic male—stout and dressed in a polo shirt and slacks. Realizing he spoke only Spanish, I pulled out my hand-held interpreter phone, dialed the number, and waited for a response. Meanwhile, mentally, I was still stuck in the other room, replaying, in my mind, the events that had happened five minutes ago. *I must be the worst medical student in the world.*

I decided that whatever had happened was probably for my own good. "Hello, this is Maria, the Spanish interpreter. How may I help you today?" With the help of the interpreter, Mr. AH told me that he had been arguing with his wife regarding recent calls made by his wife to men he did not know. He said that these arguments had caused him a lot of anxiety and stress, and sometimes fainting spells.

"What should I do?" he asked. Tears welled in his eyes, as he paused for an answer from me. Putting aside my feelings of insecurity from earlier, I told him that as physicians we do not always know all the answers, and that many times patients find it helpful when we physicians ask God for help.

He agreed, and firmly grasping his hands, I said a brief, one-minute prayer for God's presence to be with Mr. AH's health and situation. Every word I prayed was translated into Spanish over the interpreter phone.

"Father, Thank you for your child, Mr. AH." *"Padre, gracias por su hijo, Sr. AH."*

"Thank you that we can look to You in the midst of the storms." *"Gracias porque podemos ver a usted en medio de las tormentas."*

"Amen." *"Amén."*

The words of C. S. Lewis never rang truer than at that moment: "Humility is not thinking less of yourself, but thinking of yourself less." I will never forget the gratitude Mr. AH expressed verbally after the prayer. By the time I walked out of the room, I had forgotten what had distressed me earlier. Instead, I remembered why I was on this journey: to be intimately involved in the patient's lives, and to meet their needs physically, emotionally, and spiritually.

Brian Wong, LLUSM class of 2014, is from La Crescenta, California. He graduated from University of California, Los Angeles with a BS degree in psychobiology, and would like to be involved with providing quality medical care in underserved areas. November 14 is the date this story occurred.

November 15

Did this man sin or his parents? Neither. But God's glory will be revealed through this. John 9:2-3 (paraphrased by Shirley)

"This is the best time of my life."

A room of second-year medical students sits quietly as Shirley shares her story. As she begins, I vividly remember the details that led to this day. Last year she had a nagging cough. I noticed it too, as she visited my home. She looked tired, not surprising with all she was doing. For many years she was caught up in her husband's struggle with alcohol, trying to help him move to a different place in his life. She ended up raising four incredible children on her own, working long hours, while also going to school. As she had stood in my kitchen, with her four grown children around her, she beamed, "I am so proud of them!" Two are teachers, one is now in dental school at Loma Linda University, and the fourth is in graduate school. Shirley had done well. "And . . ." she smiled, "I am months away from being a nurse practitioner! I have only a few courses to go."

On November 15, soon after our visit together, Shirley discovered the reason for her cough. Stage four lung cancer with metastasis. One of her physicians suggested there was nothing she could do and gave her only weeks to live. Using natural remedies alongside medical treatment, she visited my home again 10 months after her diagnosis, having just climbed Half Dome. It was at this point she visited with the class.

"This is the best time of my life because I have gotten off the hamster wheel that I've been on for so long. I don't know why cancer would come just now, when I am almost finished with school and able to help my children financially, but it is giving me time to spend with them. That means everything to me. We've had so much fun together. I feel great and I have been able to spend more time with God. He has blessed me and is still blessing me. This is the biggest miracle of all. God is good, so incredibly good. He has given me this healthy quality of time in my life."

At 5:48 a.m. today (November 1), in the middle of this writing, I received a text from Shirley, "Saw my oncologist yesterday and found out that my cancer is growing again . . ." In a phone call she explains, "I will be joining a clinical trial and am hopeful, but I will spend most of my time going to lunch with my friends and family. I know what is most important in my life. By the way, I am having a party at my house on November 15, the day I was diagnosed a year ago.

"Every day I have I am going to live life to the fullest knowing that God did not cause my cancer, but that He works in every detail for His glory."

Carla Gober-Park, PhD, is currently the director of the Center for Spiritual Life and Wholeness, which Wil Alexander established to carry on the work of whole person care at LLU. She is director of the doctoral program in religion and health and an assistant professor in LLUSR.

Only in this way could he set free all who have lived their lives as slaves to the fear of dying. Hebrews 2:15, NLT

The first time I witnessed a code blue was during my third year of medical school. That day started by first meeting the patient in the emergency department, where he was transferred shortly to the intensive care unit (ICU). By the time I reached the ICU, they were already looking down his esophagus, staring at an ulcer bleeding uncontrollably. There was nothing they could do.

I watched as the heart rate went from 180 to 30 within just two minutes, and then the code was called. The medical team went through the motions of the code: administer chest compressions, give epinephrine, check the pulse, and continue chest compressions. No one expected anything, but this continued for several minutes—as a courtesy, and out of respect for the life that was leaving them. Finally, the code was stopped.

It was also the first time I watched someone die. My senior resident demanded the history and physical, and I, in a daze, said that I would go work on it. When she asked what was wrong, I murmured, "Nothing."

As I walked down the hall to the call room I thought about death. I had a distinct feeling of helplessness. The emotion reminded me of something, and then I realized it was the same feeling I had before a test that I was not sure I was going to pass. And just as I would study frantically and do everything I could to prepare myself for a major exam, I wondered if I was prepared for the "ultimate test"—the one that would eventually come—the one that had come for this man as I watched.

Would I pass *that* test? Had I done enough? No, I knew I could not pass, based on what I have done. But did I believe enough? What if my doctrine was wrong? Perhaps I had not read the Bible in detail and missed some crucial point necessary for my salvation. Maybe I did not really believe, but only thought I believed. What if I had been deceiving myself this whole time, and would only discover it when it was too late?

As I, in a short time, began to drown in my doubt, and give up any hope of ever surviving that judgment which comes with death, I, in the strangest of places, suddenly found comfort: I could not pass that test. I have nothing to offer God. All of my "studying," all of my efforts, all of my reasoning and searching for truth, and even all of my confessions and beliefs, fall short of the glory of God. When I come to the bargaining table with God, I have nothing; I have no chips with which to make a deal. All I have is His grace.

That was when this verse came to mind: "For by grace you have been saved through faith" (Ephesians 2:8, NKJV). From early in life, I had read that verse many times, studied it, memorized it, and believed I understood it. But when the weight of existence pressed hard on me, and I watched that man pass from life to death before my eyes, it forced me to consider death deeper than I ever had before. I finally realized that it was not just my deeds that are lacking in God's sight, but all that I am; and yet, it is precisely all of me that He forgives and desires.

Aaron Branch, LLUSM class of 2011, is a family medicine resident in Tulsa, Oklahoma.

November 17

Now all glory to God, who is able, through his mighty power at work within us, to accomplish infinitely more than we might ask or think. Glory to him in the church and in Christ Jesus through all generations forever and ever! Amen.
Ephesians 3:20-21, NLT

"We regret to inform you . . ."

My heart sank as I stopped reading the letter, and I could only stare at the floor. It appeared that my dream to go to medical school and become a doctor was at an end. I had been waiting for that letter from Loma Linda University School of Medicine (LLUSM) for so long—but it did not say what I needed it to say.

I was a recent nursing school graduate, and God had opened doors to help me finish my prerequisites, MCAT, and interviews in a short period of time. I felt sure that He had me destined to serve Him through medicine. But now my dreams were dashed and I did not know what to do next. I felt devastated, and was not sure what plans He had for my life, or if I was really cut out for medicine. I was filled with disappointment and uncertainty.

Moving on, I took a full time job as an RN in the pediatric intermediate ICU at Loma Linda University Medical Center. While on this unit, I gained valuable medical experience by working with patients and residents. But, at the same time, I was even more convinced that there was nothing else I wanted to do other than work as a physician. It was also during that time that I started dating a pediatric nurse, who would later become my wife.

With renewed determination, I reapplied to LLUSM and was accepted. If I had been accepted the first time I applied, I might not have met my future wife!

At the time, I felt as if I had made it into medical school by the skin of my teeth, and was just there to do my best to pass the courses. God again had other plans. I was pushed by my classmates to be sophomore class president and, by God's grace, I was re-elected as class president during my junior and senior years.

When I found out I would be our senior class president during the 100th year anniversary of the founding of Loma Linda University, there was no way I could have envisioned that for me, but God's timing was impeccable. Again, if I had been accepted initially when I applied, I would have missed out on that once-in-a-century opportunity.

Now I work in a field where God can use me to save the lives of children, and to teach others to do the same. I am able to pray with families, and I believe I am able to make a difference in many lives.

Whatever plans I had for my life, God blew them away with His own plans, and truly accomplished more than I could have on my own. I am certain there will be disappointments and setbacks in my life, but now I believe more than ever that God can turn those into amazing opportunities. God is waiting to do something phenomenal in you—just wait—it will be better than anything you could ask for!

Merrick Lopez, LLUSM class of 2005, is a pediatric intensivist at LLUCH. November 17 is the birthday of his older daughter, Mia Danelle.

You're blessed when you've worked up a good appetite for God. He's food and drink in the best meal you'll ever eat. Matthew 5:6, MSG

PROGRESS NOTE: Five-Year Follow-up of Angel A.

IDENTIFICATION: Nineteen-year-old from Cal State University majoring in hospital administration and business.

CHIEF COMPLAINT: "My experience at Loma Linda University has changed my life, my health, and my direction in life. This effect has spread to my mother, grandmother, sister and her family. And yet we have never been hospitalized at Loma Linda." Angel A.

HISTORY: "At 13 years old, I took two buses from Yucaipa to the Drayson Athletic Center at Loma Linda University to attend the Operation Fit Camp, run by the Pediatric Department. I was in an unhealthy state by being overweight and not knowing how to change this. Operation Fit is a day camp that lasts for five days. This experience taught me to 'exercise without exercising,' to read nutrition labels, and to choose health on a daily basis. My mom, who has a chronic illness, also attended the parent night.

"Over the next two years my habits for nutrition and physical activity changed. This influence of a healthy lifestyle spread to all of my family and we have never gone back to our old ways. At age 16, I became a volunteer at the main hospital at Loma Linda. Then at 18, I changed my volunteer work to the East Campus of Loma Linda. There I was added to the team of amazing administrators and clinical staff, where I was able to work for two summers with the Sickle Cell Support Group. The message that galvanized our team was, 'Find out all of the needs of the patients so that we can be complete in their care and home plan.' This has stuck with me as the ultimate in care giving. The staff has taught me to love the mission of Loma Linda University: To Make Man Whole. This mission statement is lived by the staff and shown in their patient care." Angel A.

Rx: Operation Fit Chili
  + 2 cans of black beans, drained
  + 2 cans of red kidney beans, drained
  + 1 diced onion, sautéed in small amount of olive oil
  + 2 cloves of garlic, sautéed with onion
  + 1 can of stewed tomatoes
  + Seasoning of oregano, bay leaves
  + Pinch of brown sugar and low sodium chili powder
  + 1 can of corn, stirred in before serving

(Angel still makes this healthy chili recipe from Operation Fit once a week and can recite it by memory. He made this as a child for family night.)

PATIENT PLAN: Continue current regimen of "exercising without exercising," low-sodium content foods, healthy choices in foods, and a commitment to mission statement of LLU.

BEST PRACTICES AND LESSONS LEARNED: Never underestimate the power of an experience for a child. Life can change over a chili recipe.

Marti Baum Hardesty, LLUSM class of 1979-B, is an assistant professor in LLUSM department of pediatrics. She and her husband, Robert, LLUSM class of 1978-A, reside in Redlands, California. For more on the backstory of Angel, refer to the author's November 18 Morning Rounds devotional.

November 19

Do not boast about tomorrow, for you do not know what a day may bring.
Proverbs 27:1, NIV

"I love you." How often do we forget to say it?

It was the holiday season and I found myself in the emergency department. No, I was not sick, but just an enthusiastic second-year medical student. For some reason, I was excited just to observe a variety of cases that day, everything from headaches to heart failure to necrotizing fasciitis.

Toward the end of my shift, I was told an ambulance was bringing in an older gentleman with chest pain. Not knowing what to expect, I waited quietly in the back of the trauma room, while the staff hurriedly prepared for his arrival.

The emergency department doors burst open and in came a gurney with a large man, surrounded by two paramedics, with a third performing chest compressions. The casual nature by which they had announced his transport made me believe he only needed some oxygen and nitroglycerin to relieve angina. But the way in which this scene exploded to life let me know that something was very wrong!

For the next 20 minutes, I tried to comprehend what was unfolding in front of me. Drugs were pushed, compressions were continued, even an electrical shock was given, all in a desperate effort to try to restart this man's heart. Nothing was helping. "This man is going to die right in front of me," I thought to myself.

Confirming my suspicions, the physician in charge looked up with a grim face and began announcing a time of death. Suddenly, a woman pushed her way into the room. "Stop holding me back; he's my husband!" she said. The physician seemed surprised by her abrupt appearance, but only for a moment, and then ordered another round of medications. "This happens all the time," the patient's wife said, looking at me. "Just give him some juice so we can get back to our holiday dinner."

This drama continued for another 10 minutes, with the staff looking around awkwardly, knowing what was about to happen. The physician finally stopped, walked over to the patient's wife, and gingerly began telling her that her husband had passed away.

I have watched this scene enacted on various television programs, but nothing could have prepared me for what came next. The room filled with the sound of sorrow, a cry of realization that her loved one would not be coming home.

Having never witnessed death before, I quickly left the room, holding back my own tears as sounds of anguish followed. I sat down at the physician's station, trying to hide my emotion, when the attending doctor sat down next to me and let out a big sigh. He quietly said, "You know, it never really gets any easier. But the thing that brings me back to work is knowing it does not always end like that."

Death is an inevitable part of life. But you never know where or when you are going to experience it. And though you may have heard it before, I want to say this again: Take time to tell your loved ones how much you care for them. Life is so precious, and you never know when or where it may change. Do not live in fear of that, but as the busyness of this holiday season approaches, take time to express those three precious words . . . I love you.

Ryan Babienco, LLUSM class of 2015, is from southwest Ohio and graduated from Andrews University with a BS degree in biology. November 19 is his birthday.

Love is patient and kind. 1 Corinthians 13:4, ESV

"Always try to be a little kinder than is necessary."—J. M. Barrie

One day, before Thanksgiving, I needed to find the Student Affairs office for the School of Medicine at Loma Linda University. Some of us who live in town were planning a Thanksgiving dinner for students who would be away from family, without a home in which to celebrate the holiday. Not knowing where I was going, I ended up in the registrar's office. A young woman interrupted her work to look in a directory for the secretary's name, and then gave me instructions as to where I needed to go. I thanked God for this genuine act of kindness.

Next, I had to park in the hospital lot which was very full at mid-afternoon. While I was looking for a space, a young woman was walking toward her parked car. She signaled for me to back up, and gave me her space close to where I was heading. Again, here was an act of undeserved kindness.

As I walked onto the ground level of the Coleman Pavilion, I stopped to look at the office directory. A young man approached, and asked if I needed help. He showed me the hallway that led to the office of the dean of the School of Medicine. Soon I was able to find the person I was seeking.

As I thought about this series of events, I felt profound gratitude for the people who had gone out of their way to help me—an older woman and a total stranger to the campus—get to my destination. And I was grateful that this spirit of kindness permeates Loma Linda University.

Wordsworth wrote: "[The] best portion of a good man's life, [are]/His little, nameless, unremembered, acts/Of kindness and of love." And to quote Mohandas Gandhi: "The simplest acts of kindness are by far more powerful than a thousand heads bowing in prayer."

May the students and graduates of Loma Linda University continue to show their spirit of kindness to demonstrate to the world God's graciousness and His love.

Joyce Reiswig previously taught at LLUSN and is married to Phillip Reiswig, CME class of 1961, an associate professor in LLUSM department of orthopaedic surgery. She has volunteered for many years in various capacities with Loma Linda University Medical Auxiliary.

November 21

Then two men will be in the field: one will be taken and the other left.
Matthew 24:40, NKJV

My most memorable experience as a medical school freshman took place during my first time at a San Bernardino outreach clinic. It is a place that allows students the opportunity to serve the needs of the local community. What made an impression upon me that day was not just the time spent with experienced physicians, or the needed reminder that my medical career will one day extend beyond my textbooks. Rather, it was in the actions and example of a fellow student—Jeffrey Cho, LLUSM class of 2014.

He was a fourth-year medical student who had been coaching me through the intimidating initial phases of doing a physical exam, and had proven to be a phenomenal teacher. When the clinic was over for that day, we volunteered to speak with the last patient, only to discover that her chief concern was not just her current sickness, but rather, the difficulty she was having in obtaining the paperwork needed to renew her prescription.

I listened to Jeff present his findings to the attending physician, and they both mulled over how there was nothing they could do—this was a problem for those who handled the paperwork. It was already 15 minutes past the time to go home, when I saw something light up Jeff's face.

I watched as he went to sit at the receptionist's desk (she had gone home). I stayed with him an additional 30 minutes as he called several different individuals, in order to expedite the paperwork the patient needed. Eventually, he walked back into the attending physician's office and showed him the documentation required to renew the patient's prescriptions.

Everyone went home with more than what they had expected to receive that day. When asked about what motivated him to labor so far out of the "scope" of his duties to fulfill the request of his patient, Jeff just looked at me and smiled.

I believe, over these next four years, I will discover that "extra mile" answer, just as I saw it in the light that illuminated the joy of our patient who went home fulfilled.

Morgan Green, LLUSM class of 2016, is from Rancho Cucamonga, California. He graduated from Oakwood University with a BS degree in biology. This story took place during his first year while volunteering at the SACHS clinic. November 21 is the birth date of his late younger sister.

November 22

He has told you, O man, what is good; And what does the LORD *require of you But to do justice, to love kindness, And to walk humbly with your God? Micah 6:8, NASB*

The practice of medicine can be grueling. It is my passion and what I feel I was called to do, but at times it is no more than a demanding "job" that takes me away from my other roles as wife, mother, friend. Sometimes it can feel all-consuming. In those moments, I sometimes forget that medicine is my "calling."

One busy weekend on call, I finally had a chance to go home and do some things around the house. It felt as if I had just arrived home when I was called back to the emergency department (ED). There was a "walk-in" patient who was hemorrhaging postpartum, and needed my help, which was fine. What annoyed me was that she had already been seen in an ED and released, *and* she had been seen in the office by her OB and was sent home. I was feeling frustrated and dumped on as I drove back in. I was *not* thinking about what an honor it is to serve God!

Upon my arrival, the patient was bleeding briskly, was hypotensive, and was already being transfused. But I was not afraid for her. I was confident that a curettage would slow her bleeding, and that we would stabilize her and be able to send her home. Then, I could go home, too.

As soon as I saw her face, however, I saw sheer terror—she clearly did not share my optimism! I tried reassuring her. She went on to tell me a story that changed my heart that day and taught me a lesson I will not soon forget.

Nine months earlier, she was so distraught to find herself pregnant that she purposely got into a car accident, hoping she would lose her baby. Over time, she began to feel better about having a baby but carried tremendous guilt about the accident.

When she began having bleeding problems after the birth of her daughter, she knew God was punishing her. She loved her daughter immediately but knew God would not let her live to rear the baby. She was certain she was going to die in the operating room.

In the time we had together before moving to the OR, I shared with her the truth about our loving God of forgiveness. I explained that God loves her and had no plans to harm her. We prayed and I saw her fear diminish. The curettage worked well. She received a few units of blood and went home.

I went home too, reminded of the honor I have to represent the Creator of the universe. I prayed for forgiveness for the attitude I had while driving back to the hospital that day.

I never saw that patient again. But months later, I received a letter from the patient's mother. She thanked me for taking care of her daughter that day and wanted me to know her daughter had not been the same since. She said her daughter had made a commitment to God and was happier than she had been in years.

I kept that letter. It reminds me that my work is my calling, and not just my job.

Tammy Hayton, LLUSM class of 1991, is an obstetrician and gynecologist who has been practicing in the Temecula/Murrieta area of Southern California for more than 17 years. She is married to Bruce Hayton, LLUSM class of 1984. They have three children, two dogs, and a cat.

November 23

And do not be drunk with wine, in which is dissipation; but be filled with the Spirit. Ephesians 5:18, NKJV

The year was 1987, and while I cannot remember the exact date, the events are indelibly fixed in my memory. In the emergency department of the Washington Adventist Hospital (DC) as the evening physician was leaving and I was taking over for the night, he mentioned a new patient in the holding room that had not been seen. A few minutes later, a nurse mentioned the same patient. I responded that I would check on him once I had seen a couple of patients whose problems seemed more urgent.

Only moments later, as I sat writing orders, a nurse rushed into the room with the news that the patient in the holding room had disappeared into the ceiling! I took a quick look, confirmed that the patient had indeed disappeared, and noticed that a large piece of the ceiling tile was no longer in its place. Apparently the patient saw potential for escape where the rest of us had seen nothing!

I asked a nurse to notify security and wondered what our options were. I knew I was not going after the patient. A short time later, I heard a noise and a light fixture fell from the ceiling. The large fluorescent light fixture was dangling by its electrical wiring with one end about six inches above the floor. But the patient remained somewhere in the dark void between the ceiling and the floor above. Undoubtedly, this upper space was a dangerous place, with electrical wires running through it in many directions as well as pipes for sewage, steam, and water.

Shortly thereafter, the patient was found lying face down on the floor and I feared the worst. What may have been simple intoxication might now be major trauma. To my great relief, an examination revealed no lacerations or major injuries. X-rays were negative for fractures and blood tests only revealed heavy alcohol intoxication. The patient received our standard "cocktail" of vitamins and careful monitoring and, upon regaining sobriety, was released uneventfully.

That busy night I had little opportunity to contemplate the futility of the patient's efforts. He was extremely motivated, but with a zeal "not according to knowledge" (Romans 10:2). Perhaps as I thought later, in God's eyes our efforts must often look similar. The apostle exhorts, "And do not be drunk with wine, in which is dissipation; but be filled with the Spirit" (Ephesians 5:18, NKJV).

For some of us, wine may have no appeal, but many of us are "drunken" with the cares of this life, such as our ambitions, our amusements, or our investments. We need to put away our pride and pray for an infilling of the Spirit. Only the Spirit can motivate us and guide us into a useful knowledge of truth (John 16:13). Then we will not fight "as one who beats the air" (1 Corinthians 9:26), but our efforts and our lives will become effective for eternity.

W. John Wilbur, LLUSM class of 1976-B, PhD, is a researcher at the National Library of Medicine in Bethesda, Maryland.

November 24

Jesus wept. John 11:35, KJV

Why would anyone choose a career in medicine? Not me! Too much blood and guts. Too many internal organs never meant to see the light of day. And yet, for several years, I helped medical students try to articulate exactly why they had chosen the field of medicine, as I helped them work on their personal statements for residency applications to be submitted all over the country.

The forms had tough questions. What will you bring to our program? Why are you the best candidate? Why should we take a chance on you? I remember helping students grapple with putting their commitment into words, just as they completed their first year of clinical rotations. One student named Karen still stands out.

That year, she was the first to call our office. With a deadline in November, she called in April. She was attending Loma Linda University School of Medicine, and at first I thought I had misunderstood what she wanted. But no, she was already pulling her papers together, and somebody had suggested that she call. Could I help her? Well, of course.

I will never forget her enthusiasm as we worked together to wordsmith her personal statement: as she described the joy of helping a family prepare to welcome their first child into the world; as she acknowledged the physical stamina her work would require; as she talked about grueling hours being overshadowed by shared ecstasy at a successful birth.

Already tapped as a talented candidate for residencies in surgery and gynecology/oncology, what she really wanted was a career in ob-gyn. And as we talked, I could almost imagine being one of her patients, even though my husband and I had never had children. I was almost as happy as she was when she finally accepted the offer of a residency right here at Loma Linda University.

We lost track of each other, as she moved into the rigors of those first couple years of residency. But I never forgot her passion. And when I became pregnant with our first child, I understood for myself what she had been talking about. Except that our son came way too early, and as my husband and I were rushed into a room in Labor and Delivery, after my water had broken at home, our ecstasy had turned to terror.

What a day that was! Early in the day, the resident doctor on call poked her head around the corner, and you guessed it. It was this young lady. The nurses were amazing. My doctor was out of town, and the physician taking call was phoning in for updates and to give instructions.

But it was Karen who became our touch point during each phase. Would they be able, would we be able, would God be able to save this precious baby? And when the answer turned out to be no, the doctor who held our son, who held our hands, who held our hearts, was Karen. As baby Eric breathed his first and then his last tiny breaths, 21 years ago, on November 24, Karen wept.

Elizabeth Sutherland (née Venden) is a facilitator and writer who worked for over 27 years helping LLUSM students create their CVs and personal statements for residency applications and working with faculty members on grant proposals and research articles. She and her husband have two children. November 24 is the date this story occurred.

November 25

It is the Spirit who gives life; the flesh is no help at all. The words that I have spoken to you are spirit and life. John 6:63, ESV

Slated for surgery the next morning for a congenital heart defect, he was having a full-blown meltdown. The CCU (coronary care unit) nurses were going crazy, because he kept tearing out his IV lines. He was supposed to be on bed rest, but he kept agitatedly pacing around his room. He was terrified of the potential of dying at age 23.

Having faced cancer for the first time when I was 24 years old, I had some idea how he felt. But not really. My first cancer was one of the few times that I actually experienced the peace that passes understanding. I was so thankful for the faith and precious friends I had found at Pacific Union College. Although I was very sad, I felt close to God and ready to sleep in Jesus if that was what my future held.

When I faced cancer the second time as a mother with young children, I was consumed with anger, depression, and fear. We walk through grief in different ways at different times. Through both experiences, I learned to more clearly understand and empathize with my patients.

My CCU patient eventually decided to sign out of the hospital against medical advice, forget about having heart surgery, and drive to the Grand Canyon, expecting to die . . . within hours to days, as predicted by his cardiology team. I was just an intern, but he let me pray with him. He then promised to wait until I ran home to get him a present. I came back with a tape recorder, several praise tapes, and the book, *Steps to Christ*.

He went ahead with his plan to leave, and I moved on to my next rotation. Later, our paths crossed again in the Loma Linda University Medical Center lobby. "Dr. Zimmerman, I had my surgery," he told me. "Thank you. I listened to those praise tapes while I was driving to the Grand Canyon. Then I read *Steps to Christ*, sitting there at the edge of the Grand Canyon, waiting to die. I decided that God didn't want me to die. I drove all the way back to Loma Linda, had my surgery, and here I am. He's given me a new life."

Is there anything more beautiful than seeing someone come alive in Christ? As physicians, we get to save people's physical bodies. What an honor it is when we have the chance to share our faith and see what happens when someone becomes filled with His Spirit!

Pearl Zimmerman, LLUSM class of 1994, earned her MPH from LLUSPH in 1984. From 1997 to 2001, she was an assistant clinical professor in LLUSM department of preventive medicine and LLUSPH department of promotion and education. Her mother-in-law, Grenith Zimmerman, PhD, taught biostatistics at Loma Linda University for over 40 years.

November 26

Your ears will hear a word behind you, "This is the way, walk in it," whenever you turn to the right or to the left. Isaiah 30:21, NASB

It was the day before Thanksgiving, and a call came in to the neuro-oncology clinic from one of our lung cancer specialists. A patient with leptomeningeal carcinomatosis had developed difficulty in talking and eating, despite brain radiation treatment. The oncologist's voice telegraphed his anxiety over the approaching long weekend, and we added the patient that afternoon to an already overbooked schedule.

When our secretary called the patient a few minutes later with the appointment, she accepted, but then changed her mind. The following Monday would be preferable. We reset the appointment and gave her my contact information.

When I saw her Monday morning, she was having nearly continuous focal motor right facial seizures, making speaking and swallowing a challenge. The seizures responded to a higher dose of her antiepileptic drug. I was surprised that she had been willing, or able, to get by for several days with this problem.

Why had she made a conscious decision to wait? Perhaps she made the correct choice. She had mentioned that relatives were arriving that afternoon. I could see her in the kitchen of her house, with facial seizures in full force, helping with preparations for what surely was to be her last Thanksgiving Day. She decided that her symptoms were not as important as the time spent at home with her family.

Perhaps also, she was fearful I would advise admission to the hospital. That would undo her hope for a family experience she wanted, more than any palliation of her symptoms. She set the priority she thought best, and acted upon it.

Physicians are constantly faced with providing the "right" answers to cancer patients. These questions usually involve interesting interplays between priority setting and hope. For instance, "Should I stop smoking?" is one question I occasionally hear from patients with newly diagnosed glioblastoma. It might seem that smoking cessation would not now be a patient's high priority, and the stress of quitting could impair the quality of the patient's life, but the answer needs to be, "Yes, you should try to stop smoking, if possible." Any other answer would send a wrong message about his or her doctor's expectations about health and survival.

Another question might be, "Can I interrupt my treatment for a week or two to fly to Hawaii?" If a patient is at ground level, it is not ideal to interrupt the schedule of brain cancer chemotherapy treatments. However, at the 30,000-foot level, the trip to paradise on earth is more important than chemotherapy in a patient with glioblastoma.

The physician's answer to such questions must seek a sensitive balance between the medical and psychological needs of mortally ill patients. Most patients easily set sensible priorities when given good advice, and act in reasonable self-interest.

An analogy arises. How does the Healer advise, and do we respond in reasonable self-interest?

John W. Henson, LLUSM class of 1984, is vice president of medical affairs and a neurologist at Swedish Medical Center in Seattle, Washington.

November 27

And one of them, when he saw that he was healed, turned back, and with a loud voice glorified God, And fell down on his face at his feet, giving him thanks: and he was a Samaritan. And Jesus answering said, Were there not ten cleansed? but where are the nine? There are not found that returned to give glory to God, save this stranger. And he said unto him, Arise, go thy way: thy faith hath made thee whole. Luke 17:15-19, KJV

The elevator doors slide open onto the 23rd floor of the medical center. The hallway is long and sharply rectangular. It is late, probably past 10 p.m., but there is a constant background noise. Pauses in time are filled with distant beeps, indistinct voices, shuffling of feet and bedding, fingers tapping lightly on keyboards, and the clanking of doors opening and closing. These are all familiar sounds in a hospital ward. The noise is familiar and in a way comforting.

This night, however, is somehow different; the voices are audible, but the speech is unintelligible. To my Western ear, the cadence and subtle intonation shifts of Mandarin transport no meaning to my mind. "This way please, follow me," brings me back into focus. It is Friday night and our kind Chinese colleagues lead us through the hallways of Sir Run Run Shaw Hospital in Hangzhou, China.

The CT scan is ominous, as the tumor extends to the skull base. The disease appears to be resectable, but should we attempt such a complicated surgery here in a foreign hospital? The reasons not to operate are myriad: the microscope does not release correctly, the plating system is severely lacking, and the cutting drill bit is the wrong size.

But the most concerning issue is that the staff has never done this particular procedure. It seems as if there are many opportunities for things to go wrong. And then we are reminded, "If you don't do the surgery, she probably won't get treated."

The group takes a turn into a dimly lit room. At the far end of the room our patient is resting comfortably; her head is wrapped in clean, white gauze that reveals a small amount of crusted blood that has soaked its way through. She is awake, surrounded by a small group of family members; and from a bedside chair, her husband springs to his feet.

Gratitude spills out of this man; it is spontaneous and uncontainable. His tiny frame dips his head repeatedly in that universal expression of thankfulness. There is no need for translation; it is unspoken gratitude that flows from the man's very soul. Tears spill out onto deeply furrowed skin as thick calloused hands reach out to grasp and hold our hands individually. He moves from one person to the next, then back down the line; the tears continue to course down his cheeks.

No words are spoken, no dialogue exchanged; and yet, each one of us present is deeply blessed by his expression of gratitude. As I step back into the hallway, I am humbled with the realization that the God of the universe—who holds the power to create life itself, who at the blink of an eye can heal the most broken of bodies—allows us to participate in the smallest of ways with the healing process.

Whether physicians or not, we are all given the opportunity to witness the miraculous, to see glimpses of His mighty power, and to experience His undeserved grace. Will I learn to respond with unfiltered, unsuppressed, and heartfelt gratitude?

Chuck Stewart IV, LLUSM class of 2000, is an assistant professor in LLUSM department of otolaryngology, head and neck surgery. November 27, 2014, is Thanksgiving Day.

November 28

One who is gracious to a poor man lends to the LORD, And He will repay him for his good deed. Proverbs 19:17, NASB

The plane *finally* landed in India, and we maneuvered our way through the airport. It seemed good to be off the plane after such a long flight. However, immediately upon exiting the airport terminal, we were set upon by a mob of beggars, many disfigured and filthy. We scurried as fast as we could into the waiting taxis.

We were members of Loma Linda University's Students for International Mission Service (SIMS). It was the early 1990s, and we had come to Calcutta to work with Mother Teresa. It was an amazing opportunity, and we were excited. However, having ultimately arrived, we faced the reality of what it meant to serve those she called "the poorest of the poor." The reality was overwhelming.

As we raced through the crowded streets in our taxis, heading to the compound, the sights of extreme poverty were everywhere. The odor of raw sewage filled our nostrils. The blaring of car horns and an endless mass of people going about their daily lives deafened our ears. We arrived and hustled into the safety (and sanity) of the four walls of the compound. We sat together in shock from the reality of Calcutta. I wondered how I/we would ever survive an entire month here, and whether we could endure the duration of our time sequestered in the compound.

Fortunately, Richard Hart, LLUSM class of 1970, arrived on the scene. A veteran of the mission field, he told us we were going for a walk. We exited the compound and walked together through the streets of Calcutta.

Eventually, we arrived at The Home for the Sick and Dying. This was where Mother Teresa began her mission. People who were sick came or were brought there. There were no doctors, no nurses, no medications. People were cared for in the most basic way: fed, hydrated, cleaned, and comforted. Some recovered and left. Many died, but died knowing someone cared about them.

When our group arrived, we were each given a task. My assignment was to feed an old, blind man. I sat next to him and served him spoonfuls of fish and rice. I hope that he found what I did for him helpful. I know that what he did for me changed my entire experience of Calcutta—and has continued to shape and sustain me in my practice as a physician. In caring for that one man, I found purpose.

Mother Teresa told us to return home and care for those in need in our own communities. "There is need everywhere," she said.

I became a psychiatrist and made it my mission to care for those suffering from mental illness. And, when I feel overwhelmed by so many who suffer psychiatric illnesses, I remember that old, blind man—and that my mission is to help that person sitting right in front of me.

Kevin Buchanan, LLUSM class of 1994, PhD, is medical director at Clara Martin Center, a community mental health center with various locations throughout Vermont.

November 29

Watch therefore, for ye know neither the day nor the hour wherein the Son of man cometh. Matthew 25:13, KJV

My wife, Betty, and I have made several trips to China recently, each time visiting different Seventh-day Adventist churches. Some have memberships in the thousands, while most are small home churches. They often ask Betty to tell a children's story. She has a favorite story that I would like to share.

Betty's father, Joseph, had come to the United States in 1947 to obtain a higher education. By 1949, with the escalation of China's civil war, Joseph was faced with the decision to either give up his educational pursuits and return to China or bring his family to the U.S. He opted for the latter.

After a year of nervous waiting, Betty's mother finally obtained a visa for a three-month visit to America. Betty, her mother, and brother Billy boarded the ship, *General Gordon*, on May 2, 1949, not knowing that it was to be the last ship to depart from Shanghai before the Communist regime took over the country. As the Chinese Nationalist government collapsed during their journey, a 14-day passage turned into 25 days, and they were suddenly war refugees.

General Gordon was a freight ship that made many stops to load and unload merchandise. At each location their layover time turned out much longer than scheduled. Honolulu was the last stop before reaching America. Joseph had written about his family's impending stopover to their friends, Stephen and Elsie Chang, who lived in Honolulu. They met Betty's family at the pier, prepared a delicious Chinese lunch, and showed them around Honolulu, including going to an amusement park.

Although the ship had announced it would depart at 6 p.m., it had never left any of the other stops on time, often delayed by days, not just hours, so they returned to the Chang's home for another delicious meal. As they approached the pier, they heard the familiar sound of a horn, a signal that a ship was leaving. Everyone got out of the car and ran, only to see *General Gordon* slowly pulling away.

Betty and Billy started to cry, "We won't get to America to see our daddy!" Fortunately, there were two American ladies (missionaries) who were passengers on the same ship and had also just arrived at the pier. They spoke with the authorities, but were told that the ship could not return to the dock. However, a small fishing boat would be able to take them to meet the ship.

As the fishing boat neared the large ship, a 50-foot rope ladder was thrown down the ship's side. Billy scampered up the ladder like a monkey, and Betty followed close behind. The missionary ladies took off their high heels and climbed up, trembling.

That close call has been a reminder to us that we should never be complacent while waiting for Christ's return. It is easy to become caught up with the cares and amusements of earthly life and often forget the most important appointment we have—to meet our Savior as He descends in clouds of glory to take us home.

John Wang, LLUSM class of 1960, is a retired radiologist and lives in Loma Linda, California, with his wife, Betty, LLUSN class of 1960.

Let your speech always be gracious, seasoned with salt, so that you may know how you ought to answer each person. Colossians 4:6, ESV

In the practice of anesthesia, our motto is vigilance, and our promise to each patient is to do no harm. We are the eyes, ears, and mouthpiece for our patients in the operating room. As such, we strive to gather information in the preoperative interview necessary to keep them safe and comfortable.

Our window of opportunity for conversation and influence is brief. With the pressure of productivity, EMR charting, and the plethora of verification steps, it is easy to "just do the interview." There are times when I come to work with personal distractions or burdens, but, invariably, my perspective is reset when confronted with the gravity or permanence of my patients' struggles. Each story is as unique as the coping mechanism of the patient.

During my internship, I had the opportunity to interview and hear the story of a patient who had recovered from Guillain-Barré syndrome. When he had the disease, his motor symptoms degenerated rapidly to the point of his being able to only blink "yes" or "no" in reply to questions. His being "locked in" was riveting and terrifying. Yet, it was one small frustration that caught my attention. He told of an agonizing few hours when, after being turned, he was lying on his bent ear, but unable to communicate his pain.

Fast forward to a day and a patient's surgery that I do not remember. However, I vividly recall standing at the bedside of Mr. Kamran for an interview. This exchange would not be the three-minute chat I could do in my sleep. Sitting next to him was a friend, an interpreter who was his voice actually. As a result of his neurologic disease, Mr. Kamran was "locked in," meaning he was able to experience life with all of his senses, except touch, and with none of his motor skills, except blinking.

He had devised a shorthand system, whereby the alphabet was divided into quarters, allowing for quicker spelling via his blinks. Communication would have been impossible without his interpreter. Far from being frustrated, angry, or dour, Mr. Kamran was full of grace, gratitude, and humor.

Our interview was far too short, and I went to the OR feeling humiliated for ever having a moment of self-pity. Truly he was an example of Christ, witnessing to me about grace and hope.

Grant me a clear mind and physical strength for the day/night, keep my patients safe, and may I always give You the glory. Amen.

Joyce Hoatson, LLUSM class of 1980-B, has been an anesthesiologist at Florida Hospital for over 25 years. November 30 is her birthday and the date she graduated from LLUSM.

DECEMBER

A Piece of Wholeness ...

"At this special season, sing as often as you can and wherever you can in worshipping Emmanuel, 'God with us.'"

December 1

You made my whole being . . . I praise you because you made me in an amazing and wonderful way. Psalm 139:13-14, NCV

Judy was 34 weeks pregnant and absolutely terrified when she was transferred to our high-risk antepartum unit. Her high blood pressure and pre-eclampsia symptoms were worsening. Her condition became even more serious when she was diagnosed with HELLP syndrome (a life-threatening condition thought to be a variant of pre-eclampsia).

She had previously experienced two miscarriages and could not stand the thought of losing this baby, too. She already did not feel well from the IV medications she was receiving and had one of the worst nights of her life worrying about her baby who still needed six more weeks to fully develop.

Both the perinatologist and neonatologist talked to Judy and her husband about the delicate balance between the risks to Judy's health if the pregnancy continued versus the potential major problems and challenges for a baby born too soon. When I started my shift on the morning of December 1, the unborn baby was showing signs of being in trouble and we immediately started preparing Judy for a C-section.

Fortunately, the delivery went smoothly and as soon as the umbilical cord was cut, the 3 lb. 11 oz. baby boy was whisked off with the neonatal intensive care unit (NICU) team. After he was stabilized, someone from the NICU was planning to come to Judy's room and show her a picture of the son she had not yet seen. However, when Judy was ready for transfer to her room, I decided to take a detour through the NICU. After rearranging chairs and tables, we were able to move Judy's stretcher right next to Tommy's isolette and I was privileged to witness the joy of mother and child meeting each other for the first time.

"I know Tommy is going to be okay because he was born on my birthday," I whispered to Judy.

As a gift, Judy gave me a glass angel and for years when I took it out with my Christmas decorations I prayed for Tommy and wished I could find my birthday baby. Years passed. I was unaware that the family had moved out of state and that Judy was remarried and Tommy had two little sisters.

While baking Tommy's cake for his twelfth birthday, Judy decided to look for me on Facebook and found my profile immediately. I was so excited to get her message—we had so much catching up to do!

Now, Tommy is a 16-year-old Eagle Scout who is active in his church and loves to play lacrosse. He is a handsome young man who is healthy, smart, funny, and thoughtful. Miraculously, Tommy did not experience any permanent negative effects from being born prematurely.

Max Lucado wrote, "Your place in this world was created by the love, purpose, and will of God—you are His incredible handiwork, His special creation, His ongoing joy!"

Lorrie Leno is a former labor and delivery nurse and childbirth educator who lives in Portland, Oregon. She is currently director for a company that offers homecare for high-risk pregnant women. December 1 is the baby's and the author's birthday.

If we confess our sins, he is faithful and just and will forgive us our sins and purify us from all unrighteousness. **1 John 1:9, NIV**

It was not my turn to do the needle localizations that day, but I came in to substitute for a colleague who had unexpectedly been called away. It was not too long before I knew the reason that I needed to be there. The young patient was diagnosed with breast cancer and was going to have lumpectomy surgery. Prior to surgery the cancer had to be localized by ultrasound imaging. Fortunately for the patient, the tumor was small, too small to be palpated by the operating surgeon. When the tumor is this small it is the radiologist's responsibility to image (ultrasound) the small mass and mark it with a needle, which guides the surgeon to the suspicious mass.

As I met with her that day and began to go through the consent procedure, she asked to speak to me privately. I sat down with her alone, sensing something was about to happen. Although I was a stranger to her, she began to pour out her heart. I listened as she told me about her inappropriate relationship with a co-worker at her school. She thought she deserved breast cancer. Cancer, she said, was the result of this infidelity. In addition she also felt that she had lost her salvation.

With a surgery time pending and others waiting, all came to a halt while the Holy Spirit divinely guided me through the plan of salvation: the fact that all have sinned, and that our God is a God of forgiveness and mercy.

First John 1:9 came easily out of my mouth, and I wrote it down for her. Tears of relief flowed from my patient.

As it turned out, everything went well with the procedure and all that followed. The most amazing part was that I was able to see her again years later, still doing well and reconciled with her husband!

I have never forgotten that "coincidence"; I know that God appointed the work arrangements that day. This experience taught me to be sensitive to opportunities in my life, both at work and at home, and to follow the Holy Spirit's guidance. We must not let our focus on a task blind us to a chance to stop and attend to the concerns and needs of others.

Bonna Rogers-Neufeld, LLUSM class of 1980-A, practices diagnostic radiology in Fresno, California. She was the first female president of an LLUSM medical school class.

December 3

Then you will call, and the LORD will answer; You will cry, and He will say, "Here I am." Isaiah 58:9, NASB

The setting was in the winter of 1948 to 1949. I had recently completed my internship at what is now known as Loma Linda University School of Medicine and had entered the Army as a way to pay back my medical education. I was living in a small rental house near Camp Breckenridge, Kentucky. I served in a station hospital, which consisted of a series of Army barracks joined by a boardwalk.

While I was on call in the emergency department one night, Sheila, a little two-year-old girl, the same age as my own little girl, was admitted, very ill. I quickly diagnosed meningitis and called the neurologists to take over her care. They soon confirmed the diagnosis of meningococcal meningitis, a very serious bacterial infection of the brain and spinal cord, and began treatment. The next day the child was comatose.

Her care consisted of an oxygen tent and antibiotic infusions. She was placed on my ward, even though I was not caring for her. This required me to be the link between the neurologists and the child's parents. I would report to her parents every day.

Every night I would spend a period of time in prayer for her, but she continued to deteriorate. After about three days, I had to tell the parents that, barring a miracle, their little girl would not survive the night. Her vital signs were almost nonexistent—it seemed to me that the specialists had given up on her.

That night, I prayed continuously until 11 p.m., pleading with God for her healing. Exhausted, I fell into bed. At 3 a.m., I was awakened by an audible command, "Get up; pray!" I rushed downstairs, fell on my knees in front of our coal heater, and pleaded with the Lord. "You called me. My guardian angel audibly commanded me to pray. I know You will answer my prayer!" At 3:30 a.m., my burden lifted, and I knew God had answered.

The next day I went to my ward fully expecting to find Sheila still alive in her oxygen tent—but improved. I quickly turned toward the tent. She was gone and the tent was folded up against the wall. Heartbroken, I turned to the nurses and asked, "When did Sheila die?"

"She's not dead!" they responded. I whipped out her chart: "3 a.m.—Vital signs barely perceptible. 3:30 a.m.—Child opened her eyes and sat up in bed." She was completely well. "Where is she now?" I asked. "Back in the pediatric room, in her crib," they said. We fed her and observed her for another day before she was sent home.

I am forever and profoundly grateful for this miracle in answer to my prayer.

Stanley (Jack) Wheeler, CME class of 1947, is a retired family practitioner residing in Denver, Colorado. He spent over 15 years working in Adventist medical institutions, both denominational and self-supporting ministries. He then continued a "lifestyle change" mode of practice until his retirement.

December 4

Precious in the sight of the LORD Is the death of His godly ones.
Psalm 116:15, NASB

It was 1959 when I first met Jack Irvine while attending Monterey Bay Academy in California. We played in the band and on the baseball diamond together. Our friendship grew and deepened over the years in spite of living some distance apart. We watched our children grow and our careers go forward. Besides our common love for family, jobs, and sports, we shared common spiritual interests.

I have always known that life is what happens while you make other plans. Early in Jack's career he developed testicular cancer, which was treated successfully. Part of his treatment included prophylactic radiation to his mediastinum. This procedure was done because the mediastinum is a common site for the spread of testicular cancer. Decades later, he developed alveolar cell carcinoma of the lung. This cancer threatened his life in spite of chemotherapy and surgical removal of one lobe of his left lung.

As his situation became more serious, with the cancer spreading to the other lung, my communication with him became more frequent. During the last six months of his life we talked nearly every day. At one point I went to his home and spent several days with him talking about life, death, and the future. Though his universe had shrunk to the length of an oxygen hose, he seemed to have a peace about him.

I asked him about his tranquility. He simply said that he only focused on the present moments he was given without worrying about the future. His desire was to pack the present with purpose and every moment with meaning.

I wanted to know more about his relationship with God in the face of his short life expectancy, so I asked if he was assured of his eternal future. We discussed everything from humans as possible victims of collateral damage to physician-assisted suicide. He told me that his hope was *not* based on present circumstances, the promise of eternal life or on an event such as the coming of Jesus. I asked him to explain further and he told me that he was certain of one thing: God would give him the desires of his heart. From our conversation it was clear to me that what he wanted was an eternal friendship with Jesus. As I watched him fighting for every breath, I could sense his soul breathing God's peace. His trust in God was palpable.

As I reflected on these conversations with my friend Jack, I was struck by the importance of maximizing meaningful living in the moments we have. It also became crystal clear to me that the desires of our hearts really matter. If the greatest desire is a forever friendship with Jesus, we can face whatever life brings with a calmness and peace that difficult circumstances, including death, cannot take away.

Trusting Jesus completely, as it pertains to our future, is the only thing that gives us peace. In many ways Jack not only showed me how to live, but also how to face my own mortality with hope and assurance.

David L. Wilkins, LLUSM class of 1970, is an associate clinical professor in LLUSM department of ophthalmology and a wellness consultant. He is the father of four and grandfather of six.

December 5

For he shall give his angels charge over thee. Psalm 91:11, KJV

The text above flashes across my mind in many scenes as I remember ways that God has led me, watched over me, and protected me. I may not recognize ordinary happenings, but I will remember one of God's most obvious interventions as long as I live.

In 1953, just a few years after I graduated from College of Medical Evangelists, God led our family to a total change. We left behind a busy practice in Oregon and went to the Belgian Congo as missionaries. Treating tropical diseases and performing urgent surgeries, many of which I was untrained for, presented dynamic challenges. Though the living conditions were very different, we made many friends and enjoyed Songa Mission Hospital for several years.

When the political upheaval of the early 1960s occurred, our family spent many months outside the Congo as refugees. When permitted to re-enter the Congo, with permission from church leaders and the U.S. State Department, I was once again able to treat patients. Early in December 1961 conditions improved and families of the missionaries were allowed to return to the church headquarters in Elizabethville. During the annual meetings there they joined relatives who had stayed at their posts.

At that time, the United Nations (UN) was trying to force the Katanga province to remain a part of the Congo Republic. Fierce fighting was generated in various parts of the city but we thought we had a safe haven as the office building was just across the street from the United Nations encampment.

One day, however, we began hearing machine guns and mortars going over us into the UN camp which provoked return fire by its defenders. We quickly gathered in the hall on the main floor of the office building as in that space we would be surrounded by walls that had a double layer of brick.

During a lull in the battle, my eldest son and I went upstairs to our room to pack a few belongings. While we were there the fighting started again; we dropped to the floor away from the windows. Suddenly, there was a loud explosion and the room was filled with a fog of plaster and ricocheting shell fragments.

After a few minutes of silence, we quickly sneaked back downstairs where the American Consulate directed us to a large school and then right into the back of the UN camp that had been shooting at us! From there, we were escorted by armored cars to the airport and flown to safety.

On this occasion, I simply believe God had more work for us to do and protected us. God is with us not only in dangerous times, but also in our daily tasks and in our contacts with others. Our growth in faith may occur when we experience God's dramatic intervention, but recognizing His hand in those times makes it possible to apply our trust in Him in various circumstances, even when immediate evidence of His presence is not visible.

Marlowe Schaffner, CME class of 1946, specialized in emergency medicine. He resides in Redlands, California. He served as a missionary for 15 years in Central Africa. December 5 is when this story occurred.

December 6

And as they were eating, Jesus took bread, blessed and broke it, and gave it to them and said, "Take, eat; this is My body." Mark 14:22, NKJV

It was late afternoon in December. Only a gentle glow from the low sun slanting on the windows lit the large room. Before leaving for Christmas break, I wanted to retrieve my anatomy lab textbooks, the ones that years later, still smelled like formaldehyde. Incredibly, those of us who studied anatomy in the pre-AIDS era did not use gloves, but coated our hands with greasy "liquid glove" from a tube each afternoon before lab. I opened my locker thinking of all I'd learned, but not yet fully appreciative of the extent.

So much more than knowledge took root that fall. Lifelong friendships crystallized in little alphabetical cliques around a shared cadaver—groups of students with last names beginning with "W" or "S" or "H." I met my husband. And the hard work ethic and demanding schedule of a physician's life began in earnest, the long hours far worse than those endured in college, not to let up for decades. The study was so intense it followed me home into my sleep.

One night I dreamt my cadaver was beside me—not in a horror nightmare sense, but reminding me very matter-of-factly that I really could follow this my chosen path. What a surprise it had been to learn that the scariest-sounding class of our training could be so fascinating and even enjoyable! How many of us who went into surgical specialties wished we could return to the lab to dissect a cadaver again?

I lingered alone, but not alone in the lab. As I gazed at the mounds on the tables in the dimming room, I knew that plastic and canvas covered broken bodies. Tendons, nerves and vessels were dissected like electric wires; even saws had been taken to those bodies to open the mysteries of the skull and thorax to the wondering students. Those cadavers were no longer whole, but deconstructed and spent.

Yet I realized in a moment of awe, that this was a scene of incredible peace. This was not a sad, frightening or violent place. The room was full of people whose life's work was finally complete. In death they had given of themselves in a way I knew I could not. They had given their all, literally, to help train a new generation of doctors. Their gift was priceless to me, my colleagues, our future patients.

Shattered temples of God—in their desecration had blessed us, walking beside us in the first steps of our transformation to become healers in His image. They were at peace at last, and I left the building in silent gratitude.

Kathryn Hayes Arct, LLUSM class of 1984, practices obstetrics and gynecology in Riverside, California. December 6 is the birthday of her husband, Mike.

December 7

Blessed be the Lord my God, who teacheth my hands to fight, and my fingers to war. My mercy, and my refuge: my support, and my deliverer: My protector, and I have hoped in him: who subdueth my people under me. Psalm 143:1-2, DRA

December 7, 1941, the date of the Japanese attack on Pearl Harbor, was an icy cold day in St. Louis, Missouri. The day remains a vivid memory though I was only 10 years old at the time. My father had arranged to pick up my brother and me at a nearby movie theater in the late afternoon. When he arrived, he told us with a grave look on his face, "We are at war, boys." But a 10 year old does not understand or perceive the horrors of war when the events are so distant.

At that time, St. Louis, Missouri, was still in the wake of the Depression and beleaguered by isolationist sentiments—all being fanned in the city by pro-Nazi organizations. This attack was a shock to my family as well as to my town and the nation.

My father was acquainted with war. He had been drafted into the American Army Air Corps in World War I and had emerged from the battlefields and airspace in France with no wounds. But he retained clear memories of all the havoc and chaos that war brings.

On that day the outlook was grim and his conversation reflected this emotion as he shared his thoughts with us. From ages 10 to 14, I saw the events of war loom ever more clearly as information from Europe and the Far East poured in. The war ended with weapons so powerful that man's future was threatened. However, there was an unprecedented euphoria and spiritual cohesiveness felt in the country at the end of the war that seemed unattainable in 1941.

Little did we realize that 60 years later there would be new confrontations and tragic events that would shape our national conscience. The unprovoked attack on our nation, repeated on 9/11, again aroused our moral culture and, to me, felt eerily similar to December 7, 1941.

Through these events, I witnessed how prayer provides strength to recover from seemingly totally destructive incidents, gives us the capability to prevent other human tragedies and, as a nation, inspires peace.

December 7 has a special meaning for me because it enabled me to communicate with my father as to what this threat meant to our nation, our peace, and our lives. The dialogue that took place on that wind-blown cold day safe from the terrors of war is a cherished memory.

Wolff Kirsch is a professor in LLUSM departments of basic sciences and neurosurgery and is director of the Neurosurgery Center for Research, Training and Education. He graduated from Washington University School of Medicine in 1955. December 7 is Pearl Harbor Day.

Why are you in despair, O my soul? And why have you become disturbed within me? Hope in God, for I shall yet praise Him, The help of my countenance and my God. Psalm 42:11, NASB

"Doc, be straight with me. How serious am I?"

Albeit not the most pliable question, the attending physician's response turned my mouth sour. He said, "What do you mean how serious are you? Are you trying to get me to tell you how much time you have left?"

I thought in my head, "I don't think that's what the patient is actually asking." But the attending went on, "I cannot tell you how much time you have left. You're asking me for something impossible." He then turned away from the patient to see the results of the pulmonary function test, turned back and spilled out the words, "You have severe COPD. Your numbers are critical. You're never going to get any better than this."

What takes a person who once committed himself to the ministry of healing to stoop to this point and utter such a prognosis? I have heard stories in my previous years of medical school where residents or attending physicians have said or done something that, even to the ears of a lay person, could easily sound unprofessional, not to mention inhumane. It was not the shock of the moment that I found so gut wrenching, but rather the treacherous process of such an attitude. After all, it is a subtle and insidious propensity.

A question was raised at a small group gathering I attended, "What do you say to a patient who asks, 'How hopeless is it?'" From consult to consult we sometimes encounter this exchange of opinions. And the immediate reaction may be to peruse the numbers, the facts, or the "reality." But the answer that followed gave me a sigh of relief: "I always have hope for the patient. It just may not manifest in the way I intend it to."

Can we practice a ministry of healing without the outlook of hope? After all, we will often encounter situations that demoralize us. If we allow ourselves to become callous to the secular "reality" of a terminal disease, then the patient indeed has a "terminal prognosis."

Later in the day the intern received a phone call from the patient's nurse telling us that the patient was very agitated. She added, "He told his wife that he was going to die." As I started toward his room I thought of what to say. I did not think it was appropriate, nor opportune, to negate the attending physician's words. And more than anything I sensed that what the patient needed to grasp was hope—not a wish that his lungs could be normal again or that he could garden with his wife without feeling out of breath. Rather, he needed hope that reassured him, in spite of his debilitative condition, that he could live to the best of his potential. This was not something that I, nor anyone in the hospital, could grant him.

If I am correct, prognosis means "to see" or "to know ahead" (*pro*—before; *gnosis*—to know). Without being pretentious, I wonder if part of our healing ministry requires us to be prophetic for the sake of our patients. And that requires us to engender hope.

I think I will choose that path.

Keeban Nam, LLUSM class of 2014, is from Riverside, California. He graduated from University of California, Los Angeles with a BS degree in psychobiology.

December 9

For I was hungry and you gave me something to eat, I was thirsty and you gave me something to drink, I was a stranger and you invited me in, I needed clothes and you clothed me, I was sick and you looked after me, I was in prison and you came to visit me. Matthew 25:35-36, NIV

He was my last patient of the day at the veteran's administration clinic and had been waiting a long time. He was upset and ready to leave. I called him into the clinic room and could sense a mixture of anger and hurt. He had come to the clinic because he wanted to stop smoking.

"I want to kill the person that did this to me," he seethed, as he pointed to the jagged scar line across his head.

"Sounds as if you're pretty angry about it," I said.

"Yes, I am. I'm going to kill the guy as soon as he gets out of jail in three months."

"How are you going to kill him?" I asked.

"I don't know yet."

"Oh, so you don't have a plan."

"No."

Then I saw him starting to fight back the tears as he began to relate his story. Three years before he had been hit violently in the head resulting in surgery on his skull. Ever since then he had trouble with his memory. He lost his job because he could not function well. He filed for disability, but was turned down.

Financially he was receiving only $127 a month for living expenses. He could not afford a place to live and was refused housing even in shelters because of a shady past. He had no family except an aunt he was not close to. He was now homeless and wandering the streets. He smoked because he was stressed and depressed about his situation. He had been free from alcohol and drugs for a long time and had tried to quit smoking, but could not. The tears quietly began flowing down his face.

Looking at the scar that ran across the top of his head, I imagined what it would have felt like to be struck in the head or to live on $127 a month. His anger was really an expression of a deep hurt and sadness. No wonder he was depressed. No wonder he smoked to relieve some of the heavy burden, even if it was a temporary fix. My heart went out to him.

I was taught to help people stop smoking so they would be healthier and to encourage them to rely on a Higher Power to help them quit tobacco. But how could I tell him to depend on God when this God supposedly did not even provide his basic needs? How could I preach to him to stop smoking when he was a broken man inside and the only way he knew how to fix the brokenness was to smoke?

I realized that to really heal this man I had to start with his greatest need while considering the bigger picture for him. As a team we referred him to those who could help him get back on his feet. I could see total relief on his face. Yes, God spoke to me that day. He said, "I needed clothes and you clothed me . . ." And I finally understood.

Dipika Pandit, LLUSM class of 2009, is a family practitioner in Loma Linda, California. She was the 2009 recipient of the Wil Alexander Whole Person Care Award.

December 10

Train up a child in the way he should go, And when he is old he will not depart from it. Proverbs 22:6, NKJV

I have wanted to be a missionary since I was in college. When I interviewed for medical school, I told them that I felt being a doctor opened the most doors for me to reach this goal; that was why I wanted to become a physician. However, if I did not get accepted into medical school, I would study something else and still be a missionary. With God's grace, I was accepted to Loma Linda University and made it through medical school and residency. While in school I married someone who shared my passion for missions.

My main concern about being a doctor and a missionary is what it would do to my children. I had heard stories of doctors' kids (DKs) and missionary kids (MKs) living troubled lives and leaving their walk with God. My kids would be both DKs and MKs. I finally decided that if God wanted me to be a missionary and I put Him first in my life, family second, and job third, it would somehow work out according to God's will.

Being missionary kids did have an effect on my two boys, but in a different way from what I was expecting. My wife was homeschooling our younger son, Ian, while I was working at Gimbie Adventist Hospital, Ethiopia. Ian was studying about farms using an American textbook and had to answer a quiz question: "Name two uses for cows." My son's very practical responses were: Cows are used for plowing and for eating the grass after it is cut. In Gimbie the farmers use their cattle to plow their fields and our gardener fed his cow with the grass he cut from our yard. I realized then, how growing up as a DK /MK may not be such as bad thing! My sons were learning how much of the rest of the world lives.

What finally convinced me that my children were going to survive being DKs/MKs was when I came home from the hospital one day concerned about a patient, as every doctor has at one time or another. My boys noticed I was distracted and asked me what was wrong. I told them I was worried about a patient in the ICU who might not survive. My older son, Christopher, exclaimed, "Well, why don't we pray for him. Jesus will help him get better." You know, we did pray for that patient and he did get better!

"Out of the mouths of babes . . ." took on new meaning to me and the promise of "Train up a child in the way he should go . . ." can be completed by the statement ". . . and when he is old he will strengthen his parents' faith." Never be afraid to step out in faith, trust in God's plan, and experience His blessings!

Nick Walters, LLUSM class of 1989, is a family practitioner in Thailand and has previously served in Singapore, Guam, and Ethiopia. He began his mission service as a deferred mission appointee on December 10, 1992. He and his wife, Phosfe, have two sons.

December 11

But those who wait on the Lord *Shall renew their strength; They shall mount up with wings like eagles, They shall run and not be weary, They shall walk and not faint. Isaiah 40:31, NKJV*

A phone call from my mother woke me up from my sleep. As I reached to answer the call, I glanced at my watch. It was 1 a.m. I knew something was wrong. She asked me to open the front door. About 15 other family members followed my mother into the house. I could tell they had all been crying. My mother asked me to wake up my other two siblings. The third was out of the country at this time. In the living room that night, my mother told us that our father had died.

For several months after this sad news, I was in shock. My father moved to the United States in 1996, and his plan was to bring us all to join him here. But it was not a fast process. In fact, we were separated from him for 10 years. And then, approximately 18 months after we were all joined together as one big family, he was dead. My first thought was, "God, this must be a cruel joke!"

Even at that moment, I believed there was a God, but I did not want to hear any spiritual consolations on how God had a plan in all this. We had struggled for 10 years while my father was away. My poor mother was both a father and a mother during those years. When we finally thought we would all be happy and fulfill our dreams together, our father and husband was gone. Suddenly, our only support and source of living in a new country was taken away.

Now I definitely know that as difficult as life can be sometimes, God is always present. We often blame God for everything that happens to us. We lose faith and doubt sets in. This situation reminded me of the story of Job and how he was tempted. He lost his sons and was struck with diseases, but he still believed in God. The walk is never easy, but I am constantly reminded that those who wait upon the Lord shall have renewed strength.

As time went on God provided for us more than we thought was possible. I never thought going to medical school would become a reality. But every step of the way God has provided, opened doors, and made many things that we thought were impossible, possible.

Oluwatobi Afolayan, LLUSM class of 2016, is from Lagos, Nigeria. He graduated from University of California, Riverside with a BS degree in biology. December 11 is his father's birthday.

December 12

I revealed myself to those who did not ask for me; I was found by those who did not seek me. To a nation that did not call on my name, I said, "Here am I, here am I."
Isaiah 65:1, NIV

The scene of swirling snow and subzero temperature outside the emergency department (ED) where I was working was like every other winter day in Kotzebue, Alaska. I was on call at the Maniilaq Health Center that evening when I met her. We both owed the blessings of that evening to Maniilaq.

Maniilaq, a native Inupiat (Eskimo) during the early 1800s, was a prophet who traveled extensively with the native Inupiat people of northwest Alaska. He broke the traditional influence of the shaman by speaking from a Greater Power who came to him in dreams. This Greater Power told Maniilaq to call Him "Abba" or "Father." He focused on the core community values of harmony, balance, and sharing.

Maniilaq was a healer and taught the people to have a day of rest; he himself rested on the seventh day of the week. He prepared the Inupiat for "white people" (missionaries) that would come in huge boats with white triangle tops that would tell them more about the Greater Power. When the missionaries arrived they were surprised to discover that the natives were already waiting for their message.

My patient, a proud descendent of Maniilaq, was in distress. After the initial patient history and unremarkable medical work up, she poured out her heart to me. With a voice filled with emotion, she then told me that her brother-in-law was an alcoholic who verbally and emotionally abused her sister and other members of the family. This led to the anxiety attack that she was experiencing that day.

We had a deep discussion about her pain. She realized that she could not change her brother-in-law, but she could change her response. She resolved to find ways to contribute in a more positive and loving way. Then we closed with a hopeful prayer for her and her family. As I opened my eyes, I saw tears on her face as she thanked me for addressing not only the mental and physical, but also the spiritual healing she needed.

I often look back and think about the God who reached out, through Maniilaq, to those who did not know to ask for Him in their isolated arctic. My thoughts turn to my patients today who have underlying hurt within their physical and mental diagnosis. They may not know to ask for healing, yet God knows what they need.

Lord, reveal Yourself to me today. Help me hear my patients' complaints and show me what they really need. Open my heart to them. And may whatever I say be from You. Amen.

Benjamin Riter, LLUSM class of 2004, is a family practitioner in Puyallup, Washington. Previously, he served the native population in Kotzebue, Alaska, for two years with his wife, Janella, and daughter.

December 13

Now faith is the substance of things hoped for, the evidence of things not seen.
Hebrews 11:1, KJV

I entered the exam room with a bit of trepidation. I was meeting a new patient. From my review of her old chart I learned that she had been diagnosed with breast cancer more than four years earlier. She had declined any medical intervention and was then lost to follow up. I was certain I would meet a very sick woman with wildly metastatic disease and only a few months to live.

Instead I met a vibrant, middle-aged mother of a 25-year-old son with whom she lived. Julia was a former teacher. Unemployed, she occupied her time with church activities. I found her to be engaging and personable with a quirky sense of humor. When examining her I could feel a large mass in her left breast and large lymph nodes in her left armpit. The mass was not attached to the underlying tissue, a situation which would have been indicative of a much more advanced stage. She otherwise appeared to be in good health.

In answer to my query as to why she had declined treatment so many years ago, she replied that it was not God's plan for her at the time. Next we commenced with imaging studies to determine the current stage of her disease. To my surprise and her reassurance, she did not have any distant metastasis. We discussed a treatment strategy to best manage her locally advanced disease. I recommended chemotherapy followed by surgical evaluation and possibly radiation therapy. She stated she would pray about it and let me know.

Eventually she did agree to chemotherapy, but stated that both surgery and radiation therapy were out of the question as God had not shown her that this was the route she should take. At the end of her course of chemotherapy, the breast mass was significantly smaller upon physical examination and the enlarged axillary lymph nodes had vanished. Imaging reports were consistent with the physical findings.

Julia was unfazed by this information. She simply smiled and stated that God had healed her. I felt that I was doing my job by trying to convince her of the opposite. "You still have disease remaining. The evidence is indisputable. Per protocol, you should proceed with surgery and possibly even radiation."

She listened respectfully, carefully considering my words. But she was firm in her stance. Did she not know that I had the strength of well-designed clinical trials to support my position? Did she not know about the unpredictable nature of cancer? Did she not know about my years of experience treating this disease?

Today, she continues to do well despite having forgone the recommended treatment options. I can still feel a lump in her breast. She insists she has been healed. I have been humbled by my experience with Julia. Her faith has trumped my medical training. Such faith is hard to argue with. As quoted above, the author of Hebrews wrote that faith is "the substance of things hoped for." It is indeed.

Laronna S. Colbert, LLUSM class of 1997, is assistant professor of clinical medicine in the hematology/ oncology department at Morehouse School of Medicine in Atlanta, Georgia.

Trust in the LORD with all thine heart; and lean not unto thine own understanding.
Proverbs 3:5, KJV

Albert Brown, CME class of 1933, was the one who advised me to go into family practice. I had worked for him in the clinical lab during my junior year. Upon graduating from medicine in 1957, I had already decided that I wanted to become a family practitioner. The thought of treating the entire family presented an enticing challenge and I enjoyed the close interaction with the patients. The rewards outweighed the long hours and, yes, even making many house calls during the middle of the night to care for sick children or the elderly added an interesting dimension I thought.

Several years after I began practicing, I was presented with a challenge that I had never faced. One of my regular patients came in for a prenatal visit during her first trimester. I had delivered her previous baby several years earlier and had cared for the family since that time. She had experienced a rash several weeks before and believed it was rubella since many of her friend's children had been diagnosed with it.

Being concerned about her pregnancy, she had gone to the University Hospital in Atlanta for help. However, they had denied her an abortion since there was no medical documentation to prove this was indeed rubella. So, in desperation, she returned hoping I would be able to help her by either giving documentation of rubella or terminating her pregnancy.

I kindly told her those things would not be options. (This happened before *Roe v. Wade*.) We spent considerable time discussing the issues of rubella, pregnancy, and potential risks that she would deliver a child with a deformity. I told her there were occasions, such as when severe deformities develop, when the mother spontaneously aborts.

Another important consideration was the fact that she may not have had rubella at all. We also discussed the emotional implications of having an abortion and the accompanying guilt of not really knowing if there were deformities. I told her I would be happy to see her through her pregnancy and help her accept whatever the outcome, or, she could seek termination elsewhere. I saw her in a few days for her prenatal checkup.

Her pregnancy progressed without any complications and she delivered a beautiful baby at full term without any defects whatsoever. Words cannot describe her relief following the delivery. She was elated! When she returned for her postpartum follow-up, her expressions of thankfulness and joy knew no bounds for she realized the decision to continue the pregnancy was the right one.

Whether or not she had rubella, only God knows. There are times in life when we must use our God-given judgment to do what is right, leave the results with Him, and He will see us through.

Howard Huenergardt, CME class of 1957, after 10 years of family practice, completed an orthopaedic residency followed by two years of mission service at Bangkok Adventist Hospital. He is now enjoying retirement with his wife of 50 years.

December 15

Blessed are those who mourn, for they will be comforted. Matthew 5:4, NRSV

I met Jane on the day her daughter died in her arms. The call came from a nearby hospital where the life of Jane's daughter, Carol, abruptly ended from a splenic hemorrhage after a fateful tumble over the bicycle handlebars while out riding with her father and brothers. Jane was not that hospital's regular patient, but the emergency department team contacted me, the on-call family medicine resident at Loma Linda University Medical Center. This mother has been my patient ever since.

Throughout my career I have had many opportunities to walk with patients on their grief journey, but my walk with Jane has been the longest. From the first moments of shock and visceral pain, through the throbbing, sobbing days that followed, I offered my phone presence and some benzodiazepines for less tortured sleep. When we met in clinic during the aching, hollow weeks that followed, we confirmed our common faith and sealed this unique bond.

In the months and years that have followed I have learned about a mother's grief and how it fits into a life that must keep on living. Because of Jane, I have a deep respect for well-run grief support groups, meaningful family celebrations of life, and covenantal marriage relationships that can survive the worst pain, as well as respect for the steady presence of true friends and a faith community.

The years have passed, even beyond that surreal moment when Carol has now been gone longer than her short 12 years on this earth. This year my eldest son turns 12 years old. I take pause—and breathe a sigh.

Many faces and phases of this tragedy have played out, but the story is still not over. In this time I have witnessed strength and resiliency that must come from God as He meets us in our greatest weakness, and the kind of peace that only He can offer, the kind that surpasses all understanding.

Michelle T. Opsahl, LLUSM class of 1996, is an assistant clinical professor in LLUSM department of family medicine.

Now may the God of hope fill you with all joy and peace in believing, that you may abound in hope by the power of the Holy Spirit. Romans 15:13, NKJV

"Sorry to disturb you, Doctor." The voice was soft and hesitant. I turned to see who might have bypassed the front registration desk. An obviously pregnant lady hovered just outside my door with an anxious expression clouding her eyes. "Please, Doctor, I'm not well." It had been a long week. There had been some sad cases and some frustratingly puzzling illnesses. My sympathy quotient was a bit depleted. But the patient pressed her case, "Please, doctor, I know I'm late. I've come from a long way and I'm not feeling fine." Her brown eyes certainly bore testimony that she was distressed.

My nurse was with her in the examination room, having already gone through the history of her current illness, when I entered the room. The patient was lying on the examination bed while the nurse tried to find the fetal heart tones with our handheld Doppler machine.

I sat down and looked over the provided written history and the antenatal card that indicated the patient had "G4 P0022 . . ." rather unusual—pregnant four times, two miscarriages and two living children but no actual deliveries . . . doesn't quite add up does it? I scanned further down through her antenatal card to the details of each of her previous pregnancies. Her last two pregnancies ended with fetal demise.

Empty static squawked out of the Doppler as the nurse moved it over her womb. She shook her head, frustrated. "Doc, I can't find it," referring to the heartbeat of the baby inside. Our patient became even more worried.

The nurse had charted under the heading of chief complaint "not feeling baby move." No wonder she was "not feeling fine." She didn't have a fever or headache; instead, her heart was filled with fear over whether another baby had died in utero.

It was the end of the day. The nurse had already spent several minutes searching for the heartbeat with the Doppler. I was not feeling very long-suffering. "Okay," I announced, "bring her over to the other exam room." Like the patient, I wanted an answer—now.

Between my limited French phrases and her much better comprehension of my English, we communicated and I took her to the other room where the traditional ultrasound machine was located. A few minutes later the machine warmed up and went through its agonizingly slow "in calibration" process and was ready to scan.

Suddenly the fuzzy black and white ultrasound image began to shake on the screen. Tears formed in the patient's eyes as she broke into sobs—tears of relief and happiness at seeing her baby's heart move! She didn't need to be a trained sonographer to know that a dark object moving rhythmically on the screen was her baby's heartbeat. All the anxiety, pent-up worry, and fear came crashing down in waves over her.

So often I have bad news to give patients; at best, I tell people that their illness will improve with patient effort and adherence to their treatment plan. It's not often that I can simply be the conduit of good news providing a definitive answer to alleviate the patient's fear.

After such a long day, I was touched and blessed to be a part of this patient's joy. A warm glow, a satisfaction, a thankfulness, encircled and hugged my soul, kissed my tired core, and left me with tingles of a glimmering gold that brightened the rest of my day.

Trixy Franke, LLUSM class of 2006, is a family practitioner in Buea, Cameroon, where this story took place. She finished her residency in 2009 and moved to Cameroon that same year as a deferred mission appointee. Her husband, Bill Colwell Jr., serves as the Health Centre's administrator.

December 17

And my God will supply every need of yours according to his riches in glory in Christ Jesus. Philippians 4:19, ESV

During my second year at Loma Linda University School of Medicine, my good friend, who was also a medical student, had her Honda Civic stolen from the Centennial Complex parking lot, the largest lot on campus. Over the recent, previous weeks, a few Civics in the area had been stolen and hers just became another statistic.

I knew that money had been tight for her lately and it seemed like the last thread had finally broken. A few days later, she learned that her car had been found in the impound lot, but the burglars had taken everything from her car, including tires, batteries, converters, and memorabilia. Even more disturbing was the discovery that the thief had torn up her Netter's *Atlas of Human Anatomy* and had strewn the pages all over the backseat. Also, the car smelled like gasoline and was barely driveable. She had to pay a significant amount of money to take the car from the impound lot and tow it home.

Knowing my friend, she was not one to ask for help. She would have placed the whole burden on herself even though she might not have been able to find the means to supply her needs. She would still try to act as if everything was normal, even in this bad situation. It hurt me to hear her say that she could not take out any more loans to fix the car. So, with the aid of some very generous and helpful friends and with answers to prayers, a series of incredible events occurred.

I received a random e-mail from my friend's father telling about a website where one could raise funds online. He had no idea about his daughter's situation or that I wanted to help her. He sent the e-mail out of the blue! This seemed to be a sign from God telling me to do something to help my friend.

We sent a message to anyone who knew her, asking them to donate whatever they could as a way of showing their love. We planned for the money to be a surprise for her birthday on December 17. In just one week, the response was amazing! Our goal was originally $650 to cover the cost of the parts, but God had a bigger plan for us. People offered to buy parts and others offered to fix her car for free. With gifts from friends and classmates from Loma Linda University, La Sierra University, Pacific Union College, Hawaii, and even anonymous donors, we raised $2,200!

Seeing all this money come in during the Christmas season was very heartwarming. It really reminded me of how God provides us with exactly what we need at the right moment—whether it be finances or just kind, loving people who are ready to help friends in their time of trouble.

Ariana Anugerah, LLUSM class of 2015, is from Norristown, Pennsylvania. She graduated from La Sierra University with a BA degree in music, cello emphasis.

December 18

I will give you a new heart and put a new spirit in you; I will remove from you your heart of stone and give you a heart of flesh. Ezekiel 36:26, NIV

"I hate my husband!" declared the mother of eight-month-old twins, seeming to mean every syllable. Problems and tensions were mounting between her and her husband, thus contributing to her stress level and pushing her to the point of postpartum psychosis.

My attending quietly locked eyes with his patient and nodded gently for her to continue, elaborate, and explore what she meant. Communication had broken down between husband and wife. They were sleeping in different beds for the past several months and she had come from a meeting with a divorce lawyer that very morning. The lawyer had suggested she see a doctor before making any permanent legal decisions.

Bending his head down to listen more carefully to the patient, my attending said, "Go on."

The patient said, "I really feel like I hate my husband." Her whole demeanor was tense and her lips were pressed together. She pointed out bitterly, "He never helps with the kids, and he leaves me alone with the babies and goes out with his buddies just for fun. The worst part is when we are together, all we do is argue," she ended dejectedly.

My attending paused for a moment before he responded in his kindly gentle manner. "Men sometimes think differently than women," he began. He gave her some advice on how to open the lines of communication and that instead of attacking the father of her children, could she have any positive regard for him? The attending helped her recall the good things about her husband. He offered an antidepressant expressing there is no shame in taking them while needed. Continuing, he said, "Many of the emotions and thoughts you are experiencing are not your fault, but instead may be due to chemical imbalances in your body."

After an extensive conversation where tears were shed, the patient calmed down. She was still angry but willing to attempt to talk things out in a civil manner. I believe my attending saved that marriage, at least for that day, and gave her a new perspective.

The office visit took more than the allotted 10 minutes. My attending said, "Ryan, sometimes when people in crisis come in, you simply have to drop everything and make yourself available to them."

A wise physician taught me whole person care that day by seeing a human being, not just a patient in an exam room for a 3:50 p.m. appointment.

Ryan Hill, LLUSM class of 2014, is from Yucaipa, California. He graduated from Walla Walla University with a BS degree in business.

December 19

Beloved, I wish above all things that thou mayst prosper and be in health, even as thy soul prospereth. 3 John 1:2, KJV

In just one day my relevance as a physician seemed to vanish into thin air.

The morning started off as most workdays had for the past 40 years. I had risen early, done my personal grooming, and grabbed a cup of coffee and a piece of toast. I headed to the office of the medical group I had called home for the entire duration of my practice.

But when I arrived at work that day, I saw some of my colleagues in the parking lot looking distraught and a sign on the office door. The sign read that the medical group had been disbanded; we were to retrieve our personal possessions and leave the premises. No explanations, no counseling. Just like that.

Because I was already 75 years old, I decided to retire from medical practice. It turned out to be the most difficult transition of my life. My family and friends encouraged me to pursue my various other interests—music, writing—but I was finding it a challenge just to get through each day.

I felt lost, missing the camaraderie of the office and the daily interactions with patients. In a clinical setting it is easy to see the results of a conscientious medical practice. But, retired and away from a physician's daily responsibilities—what now, I wondered? I loved my career in medicine, but would I leave a lasting legacy? Or is it true that "nothing lasts forever?"

Such was my frame of mind as I sorted through the mail at home one day. Among the usual bills and advertisements I noticed a cheerful red envelope with a handwritten address. The envelope contained a letter from a patient I had treated in the distant past.

This dear woman, now healthy and happy and in her eighties, had written a letter of gratitude. She thanked me for diagnosing and treating a hormonal imbalance that had threatened her marriage, her relationship with her children, and even her life. All three, she said, had been saved when the physical problem was addressed. She thanked the Lord for her restored health.

Though I had treated my patient's temporary physical ailment, the mental, emotional, and spiritual effects continue to bless her life. And through her letter I too, experienced the continued blessing of another's wellness.

My patient's letter reminded me that though earthly situations are temporary, human souls exist for eternity. The Lord has called us to be healers of the whole person. Each decision we make in the course of our careers can help bring others closer to Christ. Though our earthly medical practice must one day come to an end, we know that with the Lord's help, spiritual healing can and should accompany physical wellness—this is our legacy as Christian physicians.

Edward Dunn, CME class of 1961, is a retired family practitioner/dermatologist residing in Whittier, California. December 19 is his wedding anniversary.

December 20

For he was a good man, full of the Holy Spirit and of faith. And a great many people were brought to the Lord. Acts 11:24, NRSV

It was December—time once again for the unit's Christmas party, with its cold food and boring entertainment at 50 bucks a pop. The nurses said, "Let's do something else this year." (Okay.) As a "floating nurse," I had heard about another unit that had adopted a needy family for Christmas. (That sounded good.)

The nurses decided, "Let's go to St. Joseph's Catholic church for the name of a needy family. Robin, you brought it up. You go talk to them and let us know how it goes." (Bummer. Me and my big mouth.)

The receptionist nun was polite and reserved as she listened to our request. A big, rough male voice interrupted from a nearby room: "What does she want? Tell her to come back on Wednesday." (Yeah, sure, sounds just like some pompous authority figure. I was certain this would happen.)

On Wednesday, I met the voice. I sat across from the resident priest, a large character, rugged-looking, just like his voice. (Trepidation.) "Sorry I couldn't talk with you the other day. It's been hard this year for so many families in the parish and I needed to think about your request and pray about it." (He did?)

"There is one family with teenage children who will not have a Christmas this year unless someone helps them. The father cannot work because of a nervous breakdown. They are faithful members of the parish. Here's their name and address." (Hmmm.)

The nurses made an appointment with the family, found out the sizes of clothes for the kids, shopped, wrapped the gifts, and delivered them along with a big turkey dinner and all the fixings. When they arrived, the father was waiting for them in the front yard to ask, "I just wondered if it would be okay if we shared the dinner with our neighbors. They are worse off than we are." (What did he just say? My tears welled up when I heard the story.)

At this point I also thought, *Dear God, I am so very humbled. You spoke to the rough priest whom I thought to scorn and impressed him to pick the right family who in turn sought to bless others with their Christmas meal. God be praised for this righteous man. God be merciful to me, a sinner.*

Sometime afterward, I heard that the rough priest retired, a man much beloved to his congregation. He moved into a little 12-foot travel trailer, parked somewhere locally, so he could continue his mission projects within the congregation he had served for so long.

Robin Baldwin is an LLUSN graduate, class of 1979. She has worked at LLUMC for 19 years.

December 21

A merry heart doeth good like a medicine: but a broken spirit drieth the bones.
Proverbs 17:22, KJV

It happened in 1987 when I had been in private practice as an internist and gastroenterologist for about a year. The patient, JP, was an 83-year-old female sent to me from Rolling Fork, Mississippi, a small neighboring town.

Upon her arrival in the emergency department (ED) she presented with hematemesis, black tarry stools, and was anemic. I immediately inserted a large-bore intravenous catheter and gave an infusion of normal saline as volume replacement followed by a transfusion of a couple of units of red blood cells. Shortly thereafter, she was clinically and hemodynamically stable. I then performed an upper endoscopy that revealed a 15 mm gastric ulcer with a "visible vessel" appearing much like a tree standing in the middle of the ulcer base. I applied coagulation treatments several times directly on the bleeding vessel and was finally successful in cauterizing the lesion. Complete cessation of bleeding from the gastric ulcer was the good news; however, I was concerned about the size and shape of the ulcer. Could it be cancer?

With her gastrointestinal bleeding stopped, JP improved quickly in the days that followed and was able to be discharged to her home to recuperate. Because of my concern of the appearance of the gastric ulcer, I made a follow-up appointment and approximately 10 weeks later performed a second endoscopy. I was surprised to find that the ulcer had not decreased in size in spite of the treatment regimen. I then performed multiple endoscopic biopsies.

Unfortunately, the final diagnosis was adenocarcinoma (stomach cancer). I had the sad responsibility of relaying this to the patient and her daughter. JP agreed to have surgery to remove a portion of her stomach. The surgery went quite well and JP progressed rapidly postoperatively. One thing that I took notice of was that each time I made rounds on JP, her daughter was always present and always busy with a piece of handiwork she was creating.

Finally the day came for JP to be discharged. Just before she was about to leave the hospital, JP's daughter came to me and said she had a gift for me—to my utter amazement, it was the result of what she had so painstakingly and beautifully woven. The words worked into the cloth, stitch by stitch were: "A merry heart doeth good like a medicine. Proverbs 17:22"

I was overwhelmed by this act of kindness, so overwhelmed that I had the needlework framed and hung on the wall in my exam room at the clinic. Every time I see it and read the words, my mind goes back to the incident of 1987. I simply did what I was supposed to do—provide the best diagnosis and treatment for my patient, utilizing the best available techniques and knowledge at hand. I thought that was my duty as a physician. But when I was presented with a gift made by her hands as a form of thanksgiving, I was touched to the core of my heart. I lowered my head in humility and in tears.

Yoshinobu Namihira, LLUSM class of 1980-B, was struck by poliomyelitis in 1952 with residual weakness of his lower extremities. Nevertheless, to this day, he has been active in serving his patients in Vicksburg, Mississippi.

Who shall separate us from the love of Christ? Shall trouble or hardship or persecution or famine or nakedness or danger or sword? I am convinced that neither death nor life, neither angels nor demons, neither the present nor the future, nor any powers, neither height nor depth, nor anything else in all creation, will be able to separate us from the love of God that is in Christ Jesus our Lord. Romans 8:35, 38-39, TNIV

Some of my "vacations" were spent in remote locations. For instance, as a second year internal medicine resident, I spent my vacation in the Amazon portion of eastern Peru. We were based at a small airport with access to two single-engine planes that served numerous small Cauca Indian villages along the Ucayali River (on a lagoon near the city of Pucallpa). As traveling by canoe would take days, we flew from village to village providing medical support to the villagers.

Essentially, I was doing old-fashioned "house calls," using the black medical bag that belonged to my father, Hillis F. Evans, CME class of 1943. Amazingly, since it was full of donated medicines and even though I went through two different customs, it was the only bag never opened.

On one occasion, after flying to several small dirt landing strips and having "clinic" under the wings of the plane, we started back to the airbase. Following the winding river we suddenly heard the plane's motor sputter and then completely stop. As we glided down toward the Amazon jungle our pilot radioed the base to let them know our position and status. He noticed a small village to our left and guided the plane down to its short landing strip. After landing we were surprised to find an old petrol drum with a pump. So, we pumped enough aviation gas into the plane to fly gratefully back to base. The village's name was "Loma Linda"!

One Christmas vacation I went with a group of my medical students to several isolated villages in Chiapas, Mexico. The last village we visited was located 20 kilometers off the highway. To get to that location required driving across a small river 16 different times going in and another 16 times coming back out. My VW Rabbit was able to cross all the fords on the way in. We held a very busy clinic the next day.

Upon our return I cautiously drove through the river 15 times. It had rained the evening before and at the last ford, the water level was higher. In spite of water coming over the hood we were able to make it to the other side. But then the car suddenly stopped.

I know nothing about engines. Since this road was isolated, there was no expectation of anyone coming along to assist us. While we were standing and looking at the engine, suddenly there appeared a neatly dressed young man who asked me if I needed help. He soon found the problem and we closed the hood. I turned to thank him, but he had disappeared. That village was known as "Los Angeles"—"City of Angels"!

As the Scripture says, there is nowhere we can go, no situation that we might find ourselves in, that can separate us from the love of Christ Jesus, our Lord.

Dwight C. Evans, LLUSM class of 1973-B, is assistant dean for veteran affairs in LLUSM and an associate professor in LLUSM department of medicine. In addition, he is an associate professor in LLUSPH department of health policy and management, and chief of staff at VA Loma Linda Healthcare System. December 22 is the birthday of his mother (a 1940 graduate from CME's dietetics program).

December 23

He poured water into a basin and began to wash the disciples' feet and to wipe them with the towel that was tied around him. John 13:5, NRSV

I admit, I was overdoing the foot washing on this woman, but it was because a thought had suddenly hit me. No, this was not a Thirteenth Sabbath ordinance of humility foot washing ceremony. In the beginning I would have been much happier if that had been the case.

When I first looked out the clinic's window that morning I saw a lone African woman stirring on the grounds in obvious distress. I had the feeling that she was going to ruin my day.

Our family lived among villages with thatched roofed huts in the mountains of Lesotho. We provided a clinic for the locals, and, on Tuesdays, my husband, Rick (Richard) Lukens, LLUSM class of 1973-A, traveled down a dirt road to run remote clinics for Maluti Adventist Hospital. We also had a strong public health focus and considerable energy went into protecting the nearby springs so the people around us would have clean water.

A cursory exam showed that this woman was in active labor and there was no time to take her over that makeshift road to the hospital. Needless to say, we were not set up to do baby deliveries and now here she was on our doorstep. I was so frustrated because, it was almost Christmas, and I had plans. Now this interruption was going to mess things up.

It had been raining making all the paths muddy. And this pregnant woman had no shoes on. I figured she could have at least borrowed some shoes if she did not own any. Somehow, it just did not seem right for her to come here with such dirty feet to have a baby.

We placed her on the examining table. While Rick hurriedly looked around for gloves and suture, I began working on her feet. It was then the thought hit me. Mary probably had dirty feet when she delivered Jesus in the stable. The baby was coming and Rick wondered why I was spending so much time on her feet. I had finally realized whose feet I was washing—and I wanted to do a *really* good job.

Lorna J. Turner, LLUSM class of 1972, resides in Weimar, California, with her husband, Richard Lukens, LLUSM class of 1973-A. In 1989, upon returning from mission service in Africa, she took a residency in psychiatry and has just recently retired from practice. They return to Africa each year.

And she gave birth to her firstborn son and wrapped him in bands of cloth, and laid him in a manger, because there was no place for them in the inn.
Luke 2:7, NRSV

December 1974. Dhaka, Bangladesh. One California girl transplanted to the mission field—a new Seventh-day Adventist, a new bride, and now a new missionary. We had recently arrived in Bangladesh and I was barely making the transition. My husband, Walter, LLUSD class of 1974, was running the Adventist Dental Clinic where I helped. The work was so satisfying, but now that December was upon us, I saw no signs of Christmas in this Moslem country. I missed home.

One day Walter found a potted pine tree and brought it home to me. Our Christmas tree! My sister wrote that she had sent Christmas decorations to our address in Bangladesh. I was so excited, but my heart sank a bit, knowing how almost impossible it was to receive any package going through Customs. Everyday I hoped, but everyday the postman brought nothing.

Christmas Eve. I looked at my little potted Christmas tree on the veranda. I was grateful for it. At the last hours of the day, we had closed the clinic to celebrate. We lived at the back of the clinic where I went to wrap gifts. Suddenly, I heard a commotion. I opened the door, and there, coming down the veranda, was a tall man, someone I had never seen before. He gave me a huge smile—an American calling out to me, calling my name! Who was he? I had no idea, but he was so joyful, warm, and friendly. And in his hands was my sister's package to us—I was shocked!

He distinctly said that he wanted to personally deliver this special package to make sure that I received it by Christmas. Had the package come through a diplomatic pouch? But we were not entitled to that privilege, nor was it addressed that way. To this day, I have no idea how that package ended up in that man's hands. However, I do know that the messenger was as delighted to be making the delivery as I was to receive it. I was ecstatic! And on Christmas Eve, of all times! But who was that man? And how did he find me?

Even now, this man remains a mystery. I never saw him again, and when I asked about him, no one knew who he was. In that small American community, we fellow Americans would come to know each other, but no one knew this man. I asked about him for months.

We had a wonderful first Christmas together with our decorated tree and stockings made possible by a stranger coming to find me. But was he really a stranger? Every December, I remember my first Christmas away from home and the gift of an angel sent to amaze and delight a homesick missionary girl. To this day, that has been my favorite Christmas. An insignificant request was heard.

Thank you, God. You get my attention when I least expect it. I am Yours forever.

Beverly Hadley is a 1973 LLUSAHP physical therapy graduate. She and Walter, LLUSD class of 1974, served as missionaries in Dhaka, Bangladesh, at the newly-founded Adventist Dental Clinic from 1974 to 1977. He was the first permanent dentist to serve there. They reside in Pasco, Washington.

December 25

Jesus said, "Let the little children come to me, and do not hinder them, for the kingdom of heaven belongs to such as these." Matthew 19:14, NIV

The following is a Christmas letter from the author. It was written in 2005 during the time he was serving at Wazir Akbar Khan Hospital in Kabul, Afghanistan. His wife had returned to the U.S. for the holidays.

Dear Friends and Family,

Recently friends donated money asking that it be used to help the Afghan children; I used that money to buy gifts for boys named Wazir and Adequet. Wazir stepped on a mine and lost both legs. Adequet stepped on a mine and lost a leg; falling on a second mine, he lost his arm and most of his remaining hand. I purchased a flannel shirt, a sweatshirt and a hat for each; and a sock for Adequet. The shoe that Adequet has on his only foot is plastic. He loves to sit outside but he has no sock, so it seemed to be a very good gift for this time of the year. Both boys were extremely thankful for their gifts.

Not long ago, I stopped at the bakery to get something for lunch. A young girl was standing outside of the bakery with filthy clothes, torn and much too small. I stopped and looked in her eyes. She stared back but was silent. I said, "Salam." She said nothing. I entered the bakery and purchased a couple of rolls, and several pieces of candy. As I approached my truck I saw the girl begin to walk away carrying a filthy burlap bag filled with old cans. I called to her and she turned to me and stared. As I walked up to her and gave her a piece of candy, she continued staring. "Salam," I said again, but she just watched as I drove away. *My compassion will not feed this little one,* I thought . . . I fear what life has in store for her.

Three boys were standing at the hospital entrance as I approached. "Salam," I said as I reached in my bag and pulled out three pieces of candy. "Salam," they shouted with wide grins as they quickly unwrapped and devoured the candy. I waited to move through the door as the guard with his AK-47 slung over his shoulder searched the man in front of me. Another guard holding his AK-47 stood to the side watching.

What a strange world these kids are growing up in, I thought, as I saw them munching on the candy just feet from men with automatic rifles, searching people walking into the hospital. I noticed that the children don't even look up when a fighter jet screams past overhead. Yes, a strange world indeed.

The hardest part of being overseas is being separated from the people I love. Your accepting this announces you as one of them. I sit in the house Christmas night with no power or heat, feeling all alone with plenty of time to think of past Christmases. What memory will I have of this Christmas? Will it be of sitting here feeling alone, cold and lonely? Or will it be seeing two boys with one leg between them expressing much thanks in their eyes for a few pieces of clothing and a pair of socks.

I pray that this memory is for keeps.

Michael Mahoney is the executive director of operations for LLUHS. From 2005 to 2007, he was the hospital administrator of Wazir Akbar Khan Hospital while it was under the management of LLUAHSC.

December 26

Therefore do not worry about tomorrow, for tomorrow will worry about itself. Each day has enough trouble of its own. Matthew 6:34, NIV

It had been an exhausting day for me at a local hospital, and I realized that, even with a longer day, there was more work here than would be humanly possible to accomplish. Finally, rounds were done, ward work completed, and sign-out finished. It was time to start "spiritual rounds." After evening rounds, another team member and I often stayed to address the spiritual needs of willing patients.

On this particular evening, we visited an elderly female, who was having a relatively lengthy stay in the hospital, due to *Clostridium difficile* diarrhea. We had visited and prayed with her daily, and our supplications seemed to provide strength from which we all continued to move forward. She was not a Christian, but enjoyed the time we shared together and was increasingly open to spiritual things.

Unfortunately, she was deteriorating rapidly, despite medical therapy. Her abdomen was becoming increasingly tense and surgery had been consulted. We entered the room quietly for our nightly visit and found her sleeping. Not wanting to disturb her, we gently placed on her pillow a religious book with a picture of Jesus on the front cover and left the room quietly. We wanted her to see it when she awoke and be able to gain strength and hope to keep going.

Upon returning the next morning, we waded through the multitude of requests and responsibilities common to our pre-rounding duties. We headed toward the room of our friend to check on her progress with hopes to have a conversation about the book we had left the previous night. Instead, we found an empty room and a bed with clean linens awaiting the next patient. Commonly, patients are relocated to other rooms during the night hours, so we inquired of the nursing staff as to which room our friend had been moved.

The charge nurse told us the whole story. Overnight, this patient's condition significantly worsened, and it was decided to take her to the OR for emergent surgery. After two hours of surgery, she lost her fight with toxic megacolon and passed away. Our hearts were instantly saddened and heavy.

So many questions flooded our minds. Did she wake up and find the book? Did our visits help her find a peace that passes all understanding? Did she find Christ as her personal and loving Savior? Did she, like the thief on the cross, find the outstretched loving arms of the Savior ready to save?

How fragile life is. How precious the moments we have together with family, friends, patients, and each other. How important it is to never put off for tomorrow what we can do today, especially when it comes to spiritual things. This experience cemented my conviction that there is much work to be done to bring hope to people in need. Truly, today "is the day of salvation" for all of us.

Craig Seheult, LLUSM class of 2009, is an instructor in LLUSM department of medicine and a hospitalist for a local medical group. This story occurred during his third year of medical school.

December 27

Thus the heavens and the earth were finished, and all the host of them. And on the seventh day God ended his work which he had made; and he rested on the seventh day from all his work which he had made. And God blessed the seventh day, and sanctified it: because that in it he had rested from all his work which God created and made. Genesis 2:1-3, KJV

What does the Bible verse above, in these spare, elegant words, say to us? First of all, God, through creation, is at the beginning of all history, including human history. Here we find no theogony, no story about how the gods came into existence. God simply was present at the beginning. In keeping the Sabbath, we remember and celebrate this fact of creation. The Genesis 1:1 phrase, "In the beginning," is simple and direct. Although we do not understand how this occurred, we do understand that beginning and God are inseparable.

It is significant that God completed creation with the celebration of the Sabbath. In a sense, God created the Sabbath as the climax and fulfillment of creation. The Sabbath is thus the crowning jewel of creation and was to be celebrated with their Creator by all creatures, especially man. This is a different idea of rest than we are accustomed to. Why would man need physical rest, when Adam had just emerged from the perfection of creation?

Rabbi Abraham Joshua Heschel in his book *The Sabbath* made this dramatic statement on the value of this day: "Unless one learns how to relish the taste of Sabbath . . . one will be unable to enjoy the taste of eternity in the world to come." I would say that for many people, the "taste of Sabbath," to use Heschel's metaphor, has been lost.

For many, the Sabbath, instead of being a blessing, has become a burden, an obligation, an arbitrary command, its meaning forgotten and the day overgrown with cultural weeds. Somehow this treasure has slipped away. The Sabbath is often the first casualty of those who leave behind their Adventist faith. For some others, the day may be nominally observed, but is regarded as outmoded and archaic in a noisy, digital world of instant news, instant messaging, and continuous demands on our time and attention.

Relief from this noisy, restless, hyperactive culture of ours is one of many reasons I think we need to reconsider and restore the Sabbath. The Sabbath should remind us of who we are and where we came from. Weekly Sabbath observance, weekly "tasting" of this day, should fill us with admiration and worship for the Deity who longs for our presence. It is a longing that exceeds how much I used to look forward to seeing my overworked physician father at the end of his week at the hospital.

This is a God, who, the moment after He created us, provided a weekly date to spend time with his beloved kids. This is a God who Himself accepted the consequences of sin in His own body, so we will understand the high stakes in the decisions we make daily. This is a God who created us—real, physical, touchable, and embraceable humans. This is a God who made and loves the Earth and everything He created, including what we so inadequately call the Environment.

Our God desires our presence and plans a real physical resurrection at the end of our earthy sleep. This is the Sabbath rest to which He calls us.

Bruce Anderson, LLUSM class of 1964, is president of Adventist Health California Medical Group and practices psychiatry in St. Helena, Calistoga, and Clearlake, California.

If ye then, being evil, know how to give good gifts unto your children, how much more shall your Father which is in heaven give good things to them that ask him? Matthew 7:11, KJV

As a general rule, I offer to have a prayer with patients prior to beginning the anesthesia for their surgery. The majority of patients gladly accept the offer and most of those who say no are very polite, and at least appreciative that someone cared enough to offer.

One day, a middle-aged female patient declined by saying, "Nah. That's okay." There was no tone suggesting she was irritated by the request in any way. I went about my business thinking prayer was just not her thing and did not give it another thought.

After her surgery was over, her recovery room nurse wheeled her bed past me on the way to Phase II recovery. The patient pointed to me and asked the nurse, "Who is that guy?" The nurse, knowing my routine, replied, "That's the doctor who offered to pray with you." The patient's response startled both of us. "Prayer? He said, 'Prayer?' I would have said 'yes' to a prayer—I thought he said, 'Affair'!"

Many people have told me that I do not enunciate clearly and am quite difficult to understand. But to this day, what has confused me the most was how nonchalant her original response had been—if she actually thought I was asking her to have an affair!

From a spiritual context, how often are we offered the amazing gifts of Heaven only to decline them, because we do not pay enough attention to grasp the significance of the offer? The Majesty of Heaven has walked in our shoes. He knows exactly what we need for every situation we face. He has "all power" in the universe and He has promised to use it on behalf of anyone who trusts in His Word. The unfathomable purpose for which He created us can be easily attained through the power He longs to give us.

So why do we not have this power in our lives? Jesus' admonition to the last-day church provides a huge clue. He does not bestow the gifts, because we do not ask for them. We do not ask, because we do not think we are in need. He pleads with us to "open the door" when He knocks, and the Living God will come in and entwine our lives with His. He pleads with us to see our need; to buy of Him pure gold, clean clothes, and healing eye ointment.

The reward He offers His church for merely believing His Word and accepting the gifts that He offers today is that, in the eternal tomorrow, they will "sit with me in my throne, even as I also overcame, and am set down with my Father in his throne" (Revelation 3:21, KJV). With such an amazing prize, how sad it would be for any to come to the end of their race and wistfully say, "Sitting with Jesus on His throne? I'd have taken that. I didn't grasp the enormity of it all until it was too late."

May we all plead with God to use us as He sees fit today, assured that He will provide the power required to fulfill His plans for our lives. And, in that glorious tomorrow, may we all be reunited at the throne of God.

Brent Goodge, LLUSM class of 2000, was an anesthesiology resident at LLUMC from 2001 to 2004. Brent lives with his wife, Synnova, and their daughters in Dalton, Georgia.

December 29

Pleasant words are like a honeycomb, Sweetness to the soul and health to the bones.
Proverbs 16:24, NKJV

The news was almost more than we could bear. My loving mother had terminal stomach cancer and was not expected to live much longer. Adding to my stress was the fact that she lived 3,000 miles from me, as I was attending Pacific Union College (PUC) in California. Mother was the center of our family, the gentle, loving one, on whom my father and I relied for comfort, support, and caring. Our small family enjoyed many fun times, led an active church life, and invested much time in reaching out to others.

My mother was a seamstress who sewed beautiful clothes for my special Sabbath outfits. During my teen years, she taxied me to events and activities, such as choir rehearsals or skating parties, and she prepared refreshments for those same events. She nurtured my father for over 25 years as a devoted wife. Yet, here at the midlife age of 56, she was facing death. She never complained, talked often of seeing us in Heaven, and, despite the tragic prognosis, was able to make the trip from Detroit to Angwin, California, for my graduation from PUC in 1967.

It was the day of the onset of the infamous Detroit riots in 1967 that my mother became so ill and was rushed to Hutzel Hospital in an ambulance. As my father and I approached her hospital room the next day, prepared to take personal items to her, a nurse stopped us at the door. We were not allowed into her room, and, after a brief pause, a physician came out and spoke those fateful words, "I am sorry, but there was nothing more we could do."

I can still vividly remember my father's look of disbelief and bewilderment upon hearing the dire news. I heard him mumble, "I don't know what to do now." It was devastating. As we quietly and somberly headed back home, we drew sustenance from the memory of one who had lived for her family, who emanated kindness and gentleness in all of her dealings with people.

Children must have a space to sleep and to eat, but they also need a person who will emulate Christ in their lives. Mother was the one who taught by example in a gentle, quiet way, and I am so thankful for the short 21 years I was influenced by her.

It is because of the legacy of my mother's example of "giving back," that I teach and mentor social work students and travel to other countries with the Loma Linda University Behavioral Health Trauma Team.

As I reflect upon my mother's influence and my personal mission here at LLU, I am reminded of a contemplative phrase I once heard: "Speak kind words and you will hear kind echoes." Thanks, Mom, for all the kind echoes. I look forward to our reunion when Jesus comes.

Victoria Jackson is an assistant professor of social work and social ecology in LLUSBH and has been at LLU since 1994. She graduated from Pacific Union College and also from La Sierra University with an EdD degree. She is married to Craig Jackson, JD, dean of LLUSAHP, and they have three children.

December 30

Trust in the LORD with all your heart, And lean not on your own understanding;
In all your ways acknowledge Him, And He shall direct your paths.
Proverbs 3:5-6, NKJV

Accepting the call to serve as president of the Loma Linda University Medical Auxiliary was unthinkable.

Mother of three boys with the twins still at home, I was exhausted. I don't dress up. My husband does not even own a suit. I did not have any experience conducting board meetings and had never heard of "Robert's Rules of Order." Besides that, I definitely do not like public speaking. I already have plenty of stressors in my life; there was no need to add any more to my plate as a daughter, wife and mother.

Telling the nominating committee "no" three times was actually easy for this "pleaser." This is not my calling and especially not at this stage of my life. It would be crazy, stepping way out of my comfort zone to accept.

I was disturbed—God and the Holy Spirit kept nudging me. Loma Linda University had given us so much: a family history of education, careers, spiritual nourishment, friendships and spouses. With a heart full of gratitude for those who had come before and a belief and hope for the future, I conceded.

As the first Auxiliary event started falling together and our speakers for the year were lined up, I thought this is God's work, not mine! This is what the Lord has called all of us to do, step beyond our comfort zones, go away from the safety and calm waters of our shores. Many before us have done so, discovering and creating great things. LLU is the result of men and women stepping out and being the "crazy ones" in their time for the Lord.

At our fall event, the speaker challenged the Auxiliary by reciting the following prayer of an adventurer. It spoke to me and the room full of guests. I'm certain you'll find its relevancy has stood the test of time.

> *Disturb us, Lord, when we are too well pleased with ourselves, when our dreams have come true because we have dreamed too little, when we arrive safely because we sailed too close to the shore.*
>
> *Disturb us, Lord, when with the abundance of things we possess, we have lost our thirst for the waters of life, having fallen in love with life, we have ceased to dream of eternity, and in our efforts to build a new earth, we have allowed our vision of the new Heaven to dim.*
>
> *Disturb us, Lord, to dare more boldly, to venture on wider seas, where storms will show Your mastery, where losing sight of land, we shall find the stars. We ask you to push back the horizon of our hopes, and to push us into the future in strength, courage, hope, and love. This we ask in the name of our Captain, who is Jesus Christ.*
> —Sir Francis Drake (1577)

In the New Year, as we venture beyond the safety of our "shores," may we be used by God for His divine purpose.

Maggie Cotton (née Feldkamp), LLUSN class of 1995, is president of LLU Medical Auxiliary from 2013 to 2014. Her husband, Adrian, is a 1995 LLUSM graduate. They reside in Redlands, California, with their three sons.

December 31

I have fought the good fight, I have finished the race, I have kept the faith. Now there is in store for me the crown of righteousness, which the Lord, the righteous Judge, will award to me on that day—and not only to me, but also to all who have longed for his appearing. 2 Timothy 4:7-8, NIV

Some moons ago, Lyn Behrens, LLUSM class of 1963-aff, who at that time was the president of Loma Linda University, said to me when I was hinting at another try for retirement: "Wil, most of your lasting accomplishments have come through you since you turned 70."

I have been thinking about this as I now turn 92, and by God's grace and great love all around me, still seek to further the teaching and healing ministry of Jesus Christ. Not much is written about oldies like me, but recently I read somewhere about the last phase of life as that of "finishing well."

An unknown author notes: "This phase reflects a sense of fulfilling what you were born to be and do while reaping the fruit of a lifetime of faithfulness. Your focus is now more on your ultimate contribution—a godly legacy that you are to leave behind in people, resources, and accomplishments for kingdom purposes. This season is best spent investing godly wisdom in younger leaders using the ways of God you've gleaned from your life's journey."

If "finishing well" is your conscious goal, may I suggest the following:
+ Preserve a personal vibrant relationship with God right up until the end.
+ Maintain a learning posture, learning from all kinds of sources.
+ Display a Christ-like character evidenced by the fruits of the Holy Spirit.
+ Live in the truth you have learned, demonstrating to others, that the convictions and promises of God are real.
+ Leave behind one or more ultimate contributions as a lasting kingdom legacy.
+ Walk in a growing awareness of fulfilling your God-given destiny, in part or full.
+ Write over everything the initials SDG [*Soli Deo Gloria*] "To God only be the glory!"

Wil Alexander

For the bio on Wil Alexander refer to January 1.

Index of Daily Scripture References

Genesis
1:27 ....273, 291
2:1-3 378
5:24................................ 211
19:19.............................. 323
22:14.............................. 315
28:14.............................. 254
43:11................................17

Exodus
4:12................................ 141
15:1-2............................. 170
15:26.............................. 177
34:6..................................43

Deuteronomy
5:12................................ 171
8:2.................................. 252
10:17-18...........................89
31:6................................ 208

Joshua
1:9.................................. 116

Judges
6:36-37.............................57

1 Samuel
16:7................................ 248
18:3................................ 228

1 Kings
19:12.................................67

1 Chronicles
16:11................................16

2 Chronicles
16:9................................ 316

Esther
4:14................................ 278

Job
1:21................................ 179
12:12................................48

13:5.............................. 241
13:15................................97
29:3..................................69
38:4-6.......................... 136
40:3-5.......................... 151

Psalms
4:8.............................. 260
8:4........................49, 288
10:17................................65
16:9.............................. 119
17:15.............................. 142
18:35.............................. 217
23:4.............................. 266
28:6-7..............................72
28:7.............................. 222
30:11-12.............................3
31:24.............................. 187
32:8..................................68
34:7.............................. 311
34:14.............................. 301
34:18.............................. 144
37:5.............................. 103
41:1..................................50
41:2-3.............................. 135
42:5.............................. 133
42:11.............................. 359
46:1-3................................13
46:4.............................. 238
46:10..............36, 272, 309
50:15.......... 189, 205, 321
56:8.............................. 313
70:5.............................. 251
71:6.............................. 129
77:14.............................. 269
86:6-7.......................... 221
86:15................................99
91:2..................................11
91:5.............................. 154
91:11...................215, 356
91:11-12.......................... 139
91:15.............................. 101
93:4..................................96
103:2-5..............................5
116:5-6.......................... 282
116:12-13 35

116:15 355
118:1 186
119:18 125
119:76 312
133:1.............................. 330
139:9-10...................... 296
139:13 264
139:13-14 ....78, 352
139:14 ....158, 250
141:2.............................. 257
143:1-2.......................... 358
143:6................................30
147:3................................41
149:4................................32

Proverbs
3:5 365
3:5-6 381
3:6 318
3:11-12.......................... 333
4:7..................................44
4:23................................51
6:6-8 163
8:10-11.......................... 207
12:18...................140, 166
16:18.............................. 243
16:24.............................. 380
17:17................................92
17:22.............................. 372
18:24................................88
19:17.............................. 347
19:21.............................. 209
22:6.............................. 361
23:25.............................. 302
27:1.............................. 338
31:20, 31 81

Ecclesiastes
3:1-2 283
3:22.............................. 122

Isaiah
25:4 107
25:9.............................. 106
26:3................................87
26:4.............................. 182

28:15...................... 196
30:21...................27, 345
40:31...................... 6, 362
41:10..................112, 225
41:13..................206, 271
42:16...................... 149
43:1........................ 173
43:2........................ 328
43:10...................... 242
45:22.........................34
46:11...................... 231
51:3...........................85
55:8-9...................... 219
55:9...........................42
58:9........................ 354
58:14...................... 162
61:9........................ 174
65:1........................ 363
65:24..................197, 290

Jeremiah
17:7-8...................... 218
17:14.........................77
29:11..................143, 307
30:17...................... 111
31:3........................ 150

Ezekiel
1:28........................ 308
36:26..............4, 118, 369

Micah
6:8........................ 341

Zephaniah
3:17...................... 157

Malachi
4:6...........................39

Matthew
4:23...................... 109
5:3........................ 193
5:4........................ 366
5:6........................ 337
5:7........................ 233
5:8........................ 138

5:14-16.........................20
5:43-44...................... 325
6:14-15...................... 164
6:26.....................64, 280
6:33.....................61, 277
6:34..................195, 377
7:1........................ 175
7:1-2...................... 332
7:7...........................84
7:11..................210, 379
7:12...................... 216
9:12-13.........................70
10:30...................... 247
10:30-31.........................64
11:28-29...................... 203
13:44-46.........................66
13:45.........................10
14:14.........................59
18:3...................76, 237
18:5.........................71
19:14..................213, 376
19:26...................... 263
20:28...................... 152
21:22...................... 165
23:12...................... 304
24:40...................... 340
25:13...................... 348
25:34-36...................... 281
25:35-36...................... 360
25:37-38...................... 200
25:40.........................24
25:44.........................55

Mark
2:27.........................25
4:26-27...................... 279
9:23...................... 292
10:13-14.........................22
10:45...................... 145
14:22...................... 357

Luke
1:37...........................8
2:7........................ 375
4:40.........................18
7:13...................... 324
8:50...................... 224

9:23-25.........................79
9:48...................... 227
10:18-20...................... 100
10:41-42...........................7
11:13...................... 284
12:6-7...................... 275
12:48.........................91
16:10...................... 185
17:12-17.........................93
17:15-16...................... 201
17:15-19...................... 346
19:10...................... 274
22:61...................... 327

John
3:8........................ 130
3:16...................... 320
3:30...................... 204
6:2........................ 329
6:63...................... 344
6:68.........................46
9:2-3...................... 334
9:3........................ 299
9:25...................... 9, 180
11:25.......... 132, 261, 305
11:35...................12, 343
13:5...................... 374
13:15...................... 198
15:13.........................94
15:15-16...................... 258
16:33...................... 192
21:21-22...................... 300

Acts
2:21.........................58
4:13...................... 220
11:24...................... 371
16:9...................... 148
20:35...................... 202

Romans
3:23-24...................... 268
5:2........................ 294
5:3-4...................... 306
6:23...................... 212
8:28..................134, 303
8:35, 38-39 373

8:39.................................75
12:2....................................37
12:21............................ 326
15:13..............83, 169, 367

1 Corinthians
1:9.................................. 108
9:19.............................. 230
9:24-27......................... 317
10:31................................60
12:13............................ 155
13:3.............................. 156
13:4.......................167, 339
13:13....................29, 249
15:42............................ 214
15:58............................ 146

2 Corinthians
1:3-4 ....31, 137
1:9....................................86
2:15-16............................40
3:18..................................98
4:16-18.................56, 244
5:17..................................23
6:18.............................. 183
12:9..................160, 236
12:10............................ 172

Galatians
6:2................................. 245

Ephesians
2:4-5 82
2:8-9 115
3:20-21......................... 336
4:11-13......................... 104
4:16.............................. 168
4:28.............................. 298
4:32......................21, 121
5:18.............................. 342
6:7-8 246
6:11-12............................26

Philippians
1:3................................. 314
1:4, 6............................ 256
1:6....................................80
1:20.............................. 184

2:3 53
2:4 297
4:6-7 226
4:13.............................. 117
4:19............. 128, 178, 368

Colossians
3:12.............................. 229
3:23.............................. 267
4:6................................. 349

1 Thessalonians
4:14, 16-17 124
4:16-18....................15, 74
4:17.............................. 322
5:16-18.............................52
5:18.............................. 194
5:23-24......................... 235

2 Timothy
2:3-4 262
4:7-8 ....259, 382

Hebrews
2:9................................. 232
2:15.............................. 335
4:15-16......................... 131
4:16.............................. 293
10:24................................19
10:34............................ 240
11:1.............................. 364
12:1......................110, 265
13:5.............................. 188
13:5-6 289
13:7.............................. 161

James
1:3................................. 285
1:5................................. 310
1:17.............................. 176
5:13.............................. 270
5:14.............................. 147
5:14-15............................38
5:15..................................14
5:16.............................. 153

1 Peter
1:3................................. 113

1:18-19...........................45
2:21.............................. 253
3:8................................. 120
3:9....................................54
4:10..................................28
5:7....................................73
5:10..................................90

1 John
1:5-7 102
1:9................................. 353
3:1................................. 331
3:2-3 239
3:18.............................. 199
4:7,9................................47
4:18.............................. 114
5:11-12......................... 234
5:14-15......................... 105

3 John
1:2................................. 370

Revelation
7:16-17......................... 123
21:4......................181, 276
21:3-4 295

Index of Authors

Aagaard, Carla June 81
Achilefu, Samuel 194
Acuff, Calvin 187
Afolayan, Oluwatobi 362
Akamine, Christine 249
Albano, Bobbi 332
Alexander, Wil 2, 382
Allen, David 299
Allen, Kyle 134
Anderson, Bruce 378
Andrews, Thomas J. 97
Angulo, Jackeline 204
Anugerah, Ariana 368
Anzai, Alan 195
Arct, Kathryn Hayes 357
Atchison, Marvin 47
Aveling, D. Leigh 35
Babienco, Ryan 338
Bacon, Barry 325
Baldwin, Robin 371
Barcelo, Saul 179
Barker, Lewis 118
Bauman, Roselie 237
Baum, Carla Lidner 312
Beihl, Debbie 277
Belensky, Sarah 218
Bennett, Jack L. 328
Bennett, Sharan 17
Benson, Douglas L. 58
Betlinski, Paul 302
Bishara, Rima 236
Bishop, Douglas 180
Bland, David 39
Bond, Robert E. 216
Boram, Lola Aagaard 81
Botimer, Allen 72
Bowman, Anna Gomez 91
Branch, Aaron 335
Brandstater, Murray 52
Briggs, Burton 66
Broeckel, William 274
Buchanan, Kevin 347
Bussell, Rachelle B. 8
Cacho, Bradley 202
Calaguas, Daniel 133
Carlson, DuWayne 36

Carter, Ronald 308
Casiano, Carlos 5
Catalon, Samuel 309
Catalano, Richard 278
Chan, Angela 272
Chan, Claude 128
Chang, Shirley 85
Charles-Marcel, Zeno 155
Chastain, Cody A. 245
Chee, Vincent K. 140
Chen, David 248
Chinnock, Richard E. 168
Chong, Andrea 303
Choung, Andrew 184
Chow, Eric C. 158
Chung, John Y. 49
Chung, Paul Y. 243
Clark, Jane Yoon 60
Clem, Kathleen 238
Colbert, Laronna S. 364
Conley, Gene 55
Cook, Douglas W. 209
Cornejo, Amarilis 198
Cotton, Maggie 381
Cruise, James R. 149
Daniyan, Adegbemisola 61
Davamony, Padmini 120
Davenport, Staci 239
Davis, Arthur, Jr. 98
Dixon, Linda 124
Do, Sharon 304
Drexler, Connie Rittenhouse 330
Duerksen-Hughes, Penelope 29
Dunn, Edward 370
Dysinger, Wayne 306
Earle, Tiffany 59
Edwards, Lenoa 40
Edwards, Ruth Giem 298
Eggers, Ryan 19
Eiseman, Greg 69
Endeno-Galima, Elizabeth 193
Erickson, Carl 108
Erskine, Alyssa 200
Esiaba, Obinna 288
Estes, Molly 7
Evans, Dwight C. 373

Evans, Ronald.. 18
Fahrbach, Don C. 103
Ferry, Linda Hyder 266
Folsom, Lisal.. 74
Franke, Trixy 367
Giang, Dan.. 130
Gimbel, Judith....................................... 273
Gober-Park, Carla................................. 334
Gomez, Nephtali 199
Goodge, Brent 379
Graham, A. Richard 138
Graybill , Cassandra 171
Green, Morgan....................................... 340
Gulley, James L. 250
Hadley, Beverly..................................... 375
Hamann, Curt.. 174
Hamilton, Ted.. 45
Hankins, E. A.(Billy), III 289
Hanks, Brenden 156
Hanson, Keith.. 106
HansPetersen, Jeffrey T. 3
Harboldt, Elise 326
Harbour, Chad....................................... 121
Hardesty, Marti Baum......................... 337
Harding, Gary H. 219
Harms, Casey... 254
Hart, Elmer 112
Hart, Richard 71
Hartman, Matt... 90
Hasaniya, Nahidh................................. 301
Hasegawa, Hisanori 162
Haughton, Nicole 73
Havice, Elizabeth 291
Hayton, Bruce 113
Hayton, Ryan 317
Hayton, Tammy 341
Heidar, Helgi.. 27
Heisler, Marcus 300
Henson, John W. 345
Hernandez, Barbara Couden............... 94
Herrmann, Paul 10
Hewes, Robert.. 86
Hill, Ryan... 369
Hilliard, Anthony 229
Hoatson, Joyce....................................... 349
Hodgkin, Sheila 269
Holmes, Troy 20
Hon, Shirley 178

Horriat, Narges L. 22
Howe, Barry 161
Huang, Laura 192
Huenergardt, Howard......................... 365
Hunt, Haley 70
Hunter, Daphne 283
Hunter, Michael.................................... 109
Im, Tae-Woong 148
Isaeff, Dale 320
Isaeff, Wayne 189
Jackson, Victoria................................... 380
Jasperse, David 279
Javor, Edward... 57
Johns, Warren H. 110
Johnston, Chris 64
Jones, Dustin R. 213
Jones, Lorna... 321
Juler, George L. 246
Jung, Timothy.. 265
Jutzy, Roy 115
Kam, Nathan.. 129
Kelly, T. Martin 67
Killian, Sarah... 125
Kimball-Jones, Penny 271
Kinney, Lauraine Larsen 311
Kioka, Mutsumi J. 322
Kirsch, Wolff 358
Ko, Edmund 295
Koh, Shawn 41
Krick, Edwin H. 296
Krugler, Matthew.....................................4
Lam, Carrie... 165
Lam, Giang-Tuyet N. 253
Lau, Francis 68
Lau, Kathleen 78
Lee, Esther Chough 210
Lee, Michael J. 241
Leno, Lorrie.. 352
Leon, Yolanda 201
Levterov, Theodore N. 170
Lewis, Gideon G. 247
Lewis, Molly K. 240
Lewis, Priya G. 208
Liem, Caleb.. 54
Lohr, Jason 111
Longo, Lawrence D. 25
Lopez, Merrick...................................... 336
Loveless, William 147

Lowry, H. Maynard 186
Lui, Alfred H. F. 96
Lui, Percy T. 263
Mace, John 122
Mackett, Ted...................................... 212
Mahoney, Michael................................ 376
Manns, Ryan....................................... 143
Manullang, Wellington O. 220
Marais, Gary....................................... 282
Markoff, David.................................... 188
Martin, Jonathan................................. 281
Mayor, Raymond 173
McCowan, Ronald 258
McMillan, Kathy.................................. 244
McNulty, Norman L. 235
Meelhuysen, Delbe 144
Mercado, Michael 262
Merritt, Thurman 43
Michel, Alan 228
Miller, Gordon 9
Miller, Harley D. 215
Mitchell, Cory 65
Mitchell, Gayle V. 21
Moore, Pierce J. 50
Moores, Don.. 24
Moores, Tamara 83
Mosely, Thad 145
Moyers, Julie 297
Nam, Keeban 359
Namihira, Yoshinobu 372
Nava, Kelly 264
Neil, Marcia.. 259
Nelson, Scott....................................... 13
Ngo, Eric 203
Nguyen, Emilie 233
Nielsen, Karen Wat 48
Nilsen, Svein R. 107
Niswonger, Jerome 294
Norton, Leilani.................................... 102
Noyes, Edwin 153
Opsahl, Michelle T. 366
Osifo, Osahon 323
Page, Kimberly 284
Pajcini, Marlen 132
Palmer, Sharon Michael 181
Pandit, Dipika 360
Parker, Bonnie 293
Patchett, Dorothy 315

Paulien, Jon... 32
Peters, Marvin 146
Peterson, Donald 14
Peterson, Gordon................................. 154
Petti, George....................................... 285
Radoycich, Grace E. 211
Razzouk, Anees J. 268
Reese, James.. 84
Reeves, Mark 15
Regester, Willard D. 234
Reiswig, Joyce 339
Rice, Richard 46
Richards, Jon...................................... 172
Richards, Les 207
Richardson, Clare 79
Riley, Jean M...................................... 206
Riter, Benjamin.................................... 363
Robinson, William W. 221
Roddy, Sarah 267
Rodriguez, Samuel............................... 260
Rogers, John....................................... 26
Rogers-Neufeld, Bonna......................... 353
Roquiz, D. Andrew............................... 251
Roquiz, Deborah.................................. 316
Rosaasen, Amanda............................... 224
Rose, Kenneth 177
Ruckle, Herbert.................................... 28
Ruff, Lloyd 34
Rusch, Joyce Johnston 329
Samano, Daniel................................... 225
Sandoval, Mark 23
Schaffner, Marlowe.............................. 356
Schilling, Jonathan 135
Schleenbaker, Bradley........................... 151
Scott, Ronald 275
Seheult, Craig..................................... 377
Sellas, Annie 292
Shank, John 92
Sharp, Barbara.................................... 105
Sherwin, Brent 182
Shin, John 305
Shiu, Wilfred W. 99
Shrestha, Sherry................................... 152
Siebenlist, J. Barry................................ 82
Simmons, Jess S., Jr. 185
Simpson, George T. 163
Simpson, James 261
Simpson, Vicki J................................... 175

Skau, Keri 131
Skau, Melinda 313
Slater, James M. 310
Sloop, Jay.......... 141
Sloop, Richard.......... 142
Small, Mary 101
Smith, Jason C. 217
Sobrinho, Giovanna.......... 119
Spady, Robert 100
Spellman, Vincent M., Jr. 51
Spencer, Michelle Y. 242
Spitzer, Blake.......... 270
Stecker, Rheeta.......... 257
Steffes, Bruce 327
Stevens, Paige 307
Stewart, Chuck, IV.......... 346
Stewart, Katrina.......... 77
Stockton, Cathy 292
Stone, Erin.......... 37
Sumarauw, Cindy.......... 114
Sutherland, Elizabeth.......... 343
Swarner, Julia B. 166
Taylor, Zach.......... 80
Testerman, John K. 6
Thomas, Evelyan 30
Thomas, Tamara 183
Thompson, Walter C. 230
Thomsen, Russel J. 44
Thorp, Allison 76
Thorp, Jonathon 87
Thorp, Stephen 222
Tran, Mai-Linh 117
Tsao, Bryan 75
Tsao, Eric 116
Tsao, Juna.......... 89
Turk, Ronald 290
Turner, Lorna J. 374
Unterseher, Emily 331
Varner, Nancy.......... 292
Vassantachart, Janna.......... 169
Venden, Louis.......... 88
Verska, Joseph M. 226
Wahjudi, Ingrid.......... 31
Wai, Andrew 157
Wall, Wendell H. 139
Wallace, Tracey 252
Wallenkampf, Victor 53
Walters, Clifford A. 227

Walters, Nick.......... 361
Wang, John 348
Wang, Marilene.......... 160
Wang, On.......... 324
Wantz, M. Susie.......... 197
Warren, Mark.......... 137
Waterbrook, Stephen 56
Watkins, Dixie 214
Watkins, Hubert 256
Watson, Paul 42
Weismeyer, Marci 12
Westermeyer, Rick 123
West, Raymond.......... 38
Wheeler, Stanley (Jack) 354
White, David.......... 196
Whittaker-Allen, Janette.......... 231
Wical, Charles L. 11
Wilbur, W. John 342
Wilkemeyer, Jan 164
Wilkens, Keith 150
Wilkins, David L. 355
Williams, Deia 176
Wilson, Donald.......... 318
Wise, Gregory 93
Won, Daniel 167
Wong, Brian.......... 333
Wong, Raymond 280
Wonoprabowo, Jeffery 205
Wood, Virchel 232
Yang, Tony 136
Yeo, Anthony 314
Yoo, Janie 276
Zane, Ernest 104
Zimmerman, Pearl.......... 344
Zumwalt, Jonathan 16

Index of People Referenced

Aagaard, Carl 81
Aagaard, Earla Gardner 81
Abdullah I bin al-Hussein 278
Abelard, Pierre 25
Abou-Zamzam, Ahmed..................... 217
Ahmad, Borhaan................................ 183
Alexander, Wil 195, 198
Andersen, Bradley.............................. 228
Andersen, Charlene Larsen 311
Andersen, Floyd 311
Andren, Henry E. 27
Angell, Ivan....................................... 328
Ashwal, Steve 207
Baier, Aregane.................................... 71
Baier, Chandra.................................... 71
Baier, Charlie 71
Baier, Karl 71
Bailey, Leonard 145, 329
Bailie, Darrel..................................... 152
Bailie, Ira 152
Baker, Bob... 17
Barrie, James M. 339
Bazliel, I. R. 212
Beauclair, Teresa 145
Behrens, Lyn...............................207, 382
Bell, Rob... 80
Bennett, Doug................................... 328
Bennett, Jack..................................... 17
Brown, Albert F. 88, 365
Brown, Barbara 298
Brown, Emily Jane............................. 186
Brown, Jack H. 292
Brownsberger, Sidney 189
Bull, David.. 155
Buonarroti , Michelangelo 203
Burden, John..................................... 170
Cao, Jeff.. 217
Chan, Gloria 116
Chang, Elsie 348
Chang, Stephen 348
Charles-Marcel, Zeno 152
Chelliah, Bhaktaraj 101
Ching, Brent 85
Ching, Caleb 85
Ching, Hailey 85
Ching, Kristen Mautz 85

Chipinga, Amy.................................. 317
Cho, Jeffrey....................................... 340
Chung, John...................................... 60
Clark, Walter 27
Cochran, Werdna............................... 189
Coleridge, Samuel Taylor 25
Couperus, Mollerus 278
Crider, Frank 42
Davis, Kenley.................................... 155
Detloff, George.................................. 209
Devereaux, Bill 274
Drake, Dottie 96
Drake, Francis 381
Dunlop, Robert F. 155
Dysinger, Stephen 306
Elder, Harvey.................................... 245
Elgin, Duane..................................... 120
Enders, John F. 38
Evans, Dwight 152
Evans, Newton 48
Fahrbach, Alice.................................. 103
Fang, David....................................... 130
Fernandez, Leopold 96
Fernandez, Marsue McGinnis............. 96
Ferry, David 266
Ford, John 247
Francis of Assisi, Saint 43
Freed, Jon 148
Gandhi, Mohandas 339
Gardiner, Geoffrey 217
Gardner, Ethel Swing 81
Gardner, Jonathan Earl....................... 81
Gardner, Martha June......................... 81
George, Lewis.................................... 189
Giang, Daniel.................................... 235
Giebel, Beverly.................................. 275
Glass, Crystal 257
Gyatso, Tenzin 43
Hadley, Alphie................................... 130
Hadley, G. Gordon 48, 130, 161
Hamann, Carsten Robert 174
HansPetersen, Heidi 3
HansPetersen, Svea 3
Hart, Richard 8, 347
Harvey, Paul...................................... 40
Hasaniya, Nahidh.............................. 231

Haskins, Henry S. 185
Hata, Tadao 263
Hauck, Dale...................................... 189
Haynal, Peter..................................... 86
Henderson, Karen (Kay) 274
Heschel, Abraham Joshua............ 25, 378
Hewes, Judi.. 86
Holm, Jess 315
Holm, Juanita 315
Howe, Julian 161
Hoxha, Enver 17
Hszieh, George 116
Hszieh, Lena 116
Hussein bin Talal 278
Hybels, Bill 293
Inaba, Ethel Nakamoto 104
Ing, Michael..................................... 249
Irvine, Jack 355
Jacobson, Amy Feldkamp..................... 85
Jacobson, Ava Grace........................... 85
Jacobson, Erin.................................... 85
Jacobson, Jude.................................... 85
Jacobson, Ruthie...................................9
Jacobson, Taylor 85
Johanson, Eric................................... 275
Johns, Loretta 110
Johnston, Sarah 64
Kablanow, Wayne 316
Kachiwala, Edwin 317
Kam, Christopher 129
Kam, Serena Saw 129
Kambara, George............................... 189
Ketting, Effie Jean 42
Ketting, Samuel.................................. 42
Kido, Dan 217
Kim, Paul 82
King, Archie E. 171
King, Gerald W. 171
Koniash, Anton 326
Lewis, Delores (née Ford)................... 247
Limbong, Samuel............................... 165
Lombard, Ken 129
London, Jack...................................... 66
Long, Crawford 93
Longway, Ezra 116
Lui, Katherine Kam............................ 263
Lui, Pearl 96
Lui, Percy 104

Lui, Sam... 263
Lukens, Richard 374
Mace, Jan.. 122
Mace, John 207
Macpherson, Walter E. 48
Mayor, Wilma 173
McCarthy, Kevin W............................ 272
McElmurry, Lee................................. 206
McNulty, John 235
Miller, Arthur 163
Miller, Christina................................ 152
Miller, Harry 130
Minagawa, Art................................... 272
Mohamed, Ali 128
Mortensen, Raymond........................... 48
Nakamoto, Masao.............................. 104
Nelson, Bradley 148
Nelson, Rendon 217
Orr, Robert 222
Oshita, Hideo.................................... 104
Oshita, Winifred Nakamoto 104
Osler, William 256
Patchett, Orval 315
Pitman, Naomi 152
Pullen, Christopher 85
Pullen, Michael................................... 85
Pullen, Sydney.................................... 85
Pullen, Vanessa Feldkamp..................... 85
Redman, Matt 179
Remen, Rachel Naomi 267
Reynolds, T. Gordon 212
Rice, Alison....................................... 46
Richards, H. M. S., Sr. 58
Riley, Joe.. 206
Rittenhouse, Carol Anne 149
Rittenhouse, Harvey........................... 330
Rittenhouse, Peggy 330
Rittenhouse, Robert (Bob) 330
Rogers, Karl...................................... 166
Rommel, Erwin 103
Rosenquist, Betty............................... 130
Rosenquist, Robert 130
Roth, Daniel (Don) A. 275
Sargeant, Donald 152
Sauder, Jan 103
Schillinger, Robert 189
Schmidt, Judy 71
Schneider, Sanford............................. 207

Schweitzer, Albert.................................. 43
Shank, Donna 92
Shankel, Virginia-Gene....................... 330
Shaw, Run Run 130
Shearer, Robert 189
Shryock, Harold................................... 48
Sloop, Jay.. 142
Sloop, Jeff... 142
Sloop, Randy 142
Small, Carrol 48, 101, 256
Small, Lucile 101
Smith, Chauncey................................. 48
Smith, Douglas.................................... 217
Sparks, Vernon.................................... 215
Swarner, Steve 166
Teresa, Mother 347
Thorn, John... 209
Torquato, John 316
Turk, Mary Lou 290
Venden, Marjorie 88
Villa, Pancho 289
Wade, Burt.. 263
Walters, Christopher 361
Walters, Ian 361
Wang, Betty 348
Wantz, Mark 197
Wareham, Ellsworth............................ 318
Warren, Micah 137
Wat, Bo Ying 48
Watkins, Greg 214
Weber, Gladys 263
Werner, Leonard.................................. 259
Westermeyer, Ann 123
White, Ellen G.................. 23, 34, 43, 56,
            72, 133, 135, 170, 177,
            178, 185, 225, 305, 311
Whittier, John Greenleaf....................... 88
Wical, Crystal...................................... 11
Wilkens, Carl 274
Wolff, Jim... 274
Woodman, Marion 306
Wright, Frank Lloyd............................ 245
Wright, Jim... 298
Yamashiro, Charles 315
Yamashiro, Naomi 315
Yellon, Steven 25, 217
Yoder, Russ 274
Youngberg, Russell.......................152, 326

Zane, Ernest 263
Zane, Ronald...................................... 104

Glossary
A layman's guide to many of the medical terms used in this book

ABRUPTION: a premature peeling of the placenta from uterine lining

ABSCESS: collection of pus

ACLS ALGORITHM: rules for giving advanced cardiac life support

ACUTE: sudden or recent onset

AIDS: acquired immunodeficiency syndrome caused by infection with the human immunodeficiency virus (HIV)

ALPHA-FETOPROTEIN: a protein that when found in high concentration in amniotic fluid, indicates risk for certain birth defects

AMNIOCENTESIS: testing a baby's genetics by withdrawing amniotic fluid and cells from the pregnant uterus through a needle

ANEMIA: low red blood cell count

ANGINA: chest pain

ANTEPARTUM: before birth

ANTICONVULSANT: seizure medication

ANTIREJECTION MEDICATION: given to prevent the body's natural tendency to reject a transplanted organ

ANXIOLYTIC: anxiety treatment

AORTIC VALVE: one of the four heart valves that keep blood flowing forward

APLASTIC ANEMIA: low blood cell counts from failure to produce new blood cells

APNEIC: not breathing

APPENDECTOMY: removal of the appendix

ARRHYTHMIA: abnormal pattern of heartbeats

ASPIRATION: to inhale a substance into the lungs that doesn't belong there

ATRIAL FIBRILLATION: a type of abnormal heart rhythm

AUTOPSY: procedure to examine a dead body to determine the cause of death

AVULSE: to pull off or tear away by force

AXILLA: armpit

BABINSKI: an abnormal reflex of the foot that indicates damage to the brain or spinal cord

BENIGN: not likely to cause death

BENIGN POSITIONAL VERTIGO: dizziness brought on by sudden head movements

BENZODIAZEPINE: a type of anxiety medication

BILATERAL: both sides, left and right

BILIRUBIN: yellow product of the normal breakdown of red blood cells

BIOPSY: removal of living tissue for analysis

BIPOLAR: psychiatric condition with mania and depression

BOVIE: electrical cautery device that stops bleeding during surgery

BRADYCARDIC: slow heart rate

CACHECTIC: thin and emaciated from malnutrition

CADAVER: a dead human body

CARCINOMA: cancer arising from the surface or the lining of a body organ

CARDIAC ARREST: stopped heartbeat

CATARACT: clouding of the lens in the eye

CATHETER: a tube placed through an opening in the body

CAUTERIZE: apply heat to burn tissue, usually to stop bleeding

CAVERNOUS SINUS: a collection of veins in the middle of the head near the pituitary gland

CEREBRAL PALSY: a congenital condition resulting from damage to the brain

CHOLECYSTECTOMY: surgical removal of the gallbladder

CHRONIC: lasting a long time

CLEFT LIP/PALATE: birth defect caused by incomplete formation of the upper lip and roof of the mouth

CLOSTRIDIUM DIFFICILE: a bacterial infection in the colon

COGNITIVE: having to do with thinking and intelligent brain activity

COLONOSCOPY: to view the colon by means of a tube inserted aftward

COMMINUTED FRACTURE: fragmented bone

COMPOUND FRACTURE: fractured bone that protrudes through the skin

CONCUSSION: brain injury caused by a blow to the head

CONGENITAL: present at birth

CONGESTIVE HEART FAILURE: a weakened heart muscle struggling to pump enough blood to sustain life

COPD: chronic obstructive pulmonary disease

CORONARY: pertaining to the blood supply to the heart muscle

CPAP: continuous positive airway pressure, used to treat breathing disorders

CPR: cardiopulmonary resuscitation, attempting to save a patient who has no heartbeat or breathing

CRANIOTOMY: surgical opening of the skull

CROSSMATCH: testing of donor blood before transfusion to make sure it doesn't contain antibodies against the recipient or vice versa

CRYOSURGERY: use of extreme cold to destroy abnormal or diseased tissue

C-SECTION: Caesarian section, delivery of a baby by abdominal incision

CT SCAN: computed tomography—a radiology study that shows a cross-section of the body

CURETTAGE: a scraping procedure to remove tissue

CUT DOWN: use of a scalpel to locate hard-to-find veins or arteries

CYANOTIC: blue skin color from poorly oxygenated blood

CYSTECTOMY: removal of the bladder

DEBRIDEMENT: removal of scabs and dead tissue from a wound

DEFIBRILLATOR: device that shocks an abnormal heart rhythm

DELTOID: a shoulder muscle

DEMISE: death

DEMYELINATION: loss of the fatty insulation of nerves that allows rapid transmission of the nerve signal

DIALYSIS: kidney failure treatment to remove impurities and waste products from the blood with a filtering device

DISSEMINATED INTRAVASCULAR COAGULATION (DIC): bleeding caused by a clotting disorder that uses up all of the blood's clotting factors

DISTENDED: enlarged or bloated

DIVERTICULOSIS: condition of the colon where weak spots in its muscle wall allow the inner lining to protrude as a small sac

DO A SPINAL: either a spinal tap to remove spinal fluid or spinal anesthetic to numb for surgery

DORSAL: back side

DOWN SYNDROME: a genetic birth defect caused by an extra chromosome number 21

ED: emergency department

EFFUSION: extra fluid in a joint or other parts of the body produced by bleeding, injury, infection or inflammation

EKG: electrocardiogram, a tracing of the heart's electrical activity

ELECTROLYTES: dissolved minerals in body fluids such as sodium, potassium, chloride, and magnesium

EMACIATED: wasted away, with loss of muscle mass

EMANATE: to come out of

EMESIS: vomit or vomiting

ENCEPHALITIS: inflammation of the brain

ENDOCARDITIS: infection of the valves of the heart

ENDOSCOPY: use of a device to view the inside of the body

ENDOTRACHEAL TUBE: tube inserted into the airway to assist with breathing

ENT: ear, nose and throat

EPILEPTOLOGIST: subspecialist in neurology concerned with seizures

EPINEPHRINE: a medication to stimulate the heart to beat faster (aka adrenaline)

ESOPHAGUS: the swallowing tube between the mouth and stomach

ETIOLOGY: the cause of a medical or surgical problem

EXCHANGE TRANSFUSION: replacing the blood of one person with the blood of another

EXTENSOR TENDON: tendon that extends a body part (usually a limb)

EXTUBATION: removal of a breathing tube from the windpipe

FEMUR/FEMORAL: the thigh bone, or having to do with the thigh bone

FIBROID: benign tumor in the uterus

FIBROMYALGIA: chronic condition that causes pain

FISTULA: abnormal connection between two hollow organs or between one hollow organ and the surface of the body through which fluid or gas travels

FLAIL VALVE LEAFLET: a flapping heart valve that has ceased to perform its duty of preventing backward flow of blood

FLATLINE: when the heart stops, the electrocardiogram waves flatten

FLUCTUANT: having the characteristics of a fluid-filled cavity

FORCEPS: surgical instrument used for grasping things

GASTROENTEROLOGIST: subspecialist of internal medicine concerned with the digestive organs

GASTROSCHISIS: a birth defect in the abdominal wall that allows the internal organs to protrude

GASTROSTOMY: a tube placed through the abdominal wall into the stomach

GESTATION: pregnancy

GLUCOSE TOLERANCE TEST: test used to determine how well the body handles a large dose of glucose by measuring blood sugars afterward

GRANULATION TISSUE: the red, blood-rich tissue that grows on the surface of a healing wound

GUILLAIN-BARRE: a syndrome with progressive paralysis, often reversible

HEMATEMESIS: vomiting blood

HEMATOLOGY: the study of blood

HEMORRHAGE: bleeding

HEPATITIS: inflammation of the liver

HERPES ZOSTER: shingles

HYALINE MEMBRANE DISEASE: older name for respiratory distress syndrome of the newborn

HYPERLEUKOCYTOSIS: high white blood cell count

HYPEROSMOLAR HYPERGLYCEMIA: extremely high blood sugars

HYPERTENSION: high blood pressure

HYPOTENSION: low blood pressure

HYPOTHERMIC: low temperature

HYSTERECTOMY: surgical removal of the uterus

ICU: intensive care unit

IN VITRO FERTILIZATION: vitro=glass; fertilization of a human egg in a glass test tube

INOTROPE: a drug that increases the strength of heart contractions

INTERCOSTAL: between the ribs

INTRA-ARTICULAR: inside a joint

INTRAMEDULLARY: inside the bone, in the bone marrow

INTUBATE: to place a tube in the airway to assist with breathing

JAUNDICE: yellow appearance from excessive bile in the bloodstream

LACERATION: a cutting injury

LACTATION: production of milk by the breasts

LAPAROTOMY: surgery that opens the abdomen

LARYNX: voice box

LATERAL RECTUS PALSY: paralysis of an eye muscle causing crossing of the eyes

LEUKEMIA: cancer of the white blood cells

LUPUS: a disease where the body's immune system attacks the body itself

LYMPHOMA: cancer of the lymph nodes

MALIGNANT: likely to cause death

MANUAL: done with the hand

MASTECTOMY: surgical removal of the breast

MCAT: Medical College Admission Test

MEDIASTINUM: the middle of the chest between the lungs, containing the esophagus and trachea and the heart and its major arteries and veins

MENINGITIS: inflammation of the membranes covering the brain and spinal cord, usually from infection

MENINGOCOCCEMIA: widespread infection by a bacterium that causes meningitis

MESENTERY: the stalk in the back of the abdomen upon which the intestines are mounted that supplies them with blood and nerves

METASTATIC: physical spread of a disease, such as cancer, from its origin to another part of the body

METHADONE: a potent pain-relieving narcotic

MITRAL STENOSIS: narrowing of one of the four valves within the heart

MULTIPLE MYELOMA: a type of cancer of the bone marrow

MULTIPLE SCLEROSIS: a progressive disease of the nervous system

MYELOGENOUS LEUKEMIA: cancer of the blood from overproduction of a type of white blood cell

NASOGASTRIC: passing through the nose to the stomach

NASOPHARYNX: the back of the nose where it enters the throat

NEONATAL: newborn

NEONATOLOGIST: subspecialist of pediatrics concerned with care of newborn infants

NEPHROLOGIST: subspecialist in internal medicine concerned with kidneys

NICU: neonatal (newborn) intensive care unit

NITROGLYCERIN: a medication used to treat chest pain

ONCOLOGIST: subspecialist in internal medicine concerned with cancer

ONCOLOGY: the study of cancer

OPEN FRACTURE: a bone fracture that protrudes through the skin (see "COMPOUND FRACTURE")

OPHTHALMOLOGY: the study of the eye

OPIATES: pain-relieving narcotics

OTOLARYNGOLOGIST: surgical specialist concerned with the ears, nose and throat

PALLIATIVE CARE: emphasis on relief of suffering rather than on cure

PALPATION: touching and pressing on the body to feel underlying organs or structures

PALPITATION: a feeling in the chest that the heartbeat is irregular or abnormal

PAROTID GLAND: saliva gland in the cheek

PATHOLOGY: specialty of medicine concerned with the study of and identification of disease

PERINATAL: around the time of childbirth

PERINATOLOGIST: subspecialist of obstetrics concerned with care of mothers, fetuses, and infants during the period before and after birth

PERITONEUM/PERITONEAL: the inner lining of the abdominal cavity or the cavity surrounded by this lining

PET SCAN: a scan that shows function as well as anatomy

PHARMACOLOGY: study of medications

PIPETTE: a thin tube marked for drawing up and measuring precise quantities of fluid

PITTING EDEMA: swelling of the skin such that pressing on the skin produces a dent or pit

PITUITARY: the gland at the base of the brain that controls many other hormone glands

PLACENTA PREVIA: abnormal placement of the placenta in the womb that can cause heavy bleeding during delivery

PLATELET: small cells in the blood that initiates clotting

PNEUMONIA: infection of the lung

POSTERIOR CAPSULE: the membrane on the back side of the lens in the eye

POSTPARTUM: after birth

POSTTRAUMATIC STRESS DISORDER (PTSD): delayed psychological anxiety reaction to physical or emotional injury

POULTICE: a moist, soft, usually hot substance applied to the body to relieve symptoms of disease

PRE-ECLAMPSIA: a life-threatening pregnancy complication

PRENATAL: before childbirth

PROGNOSIS: outlook for the future

PROLACTINOMA: a benign tumor that produces excess prolactin, a hormone that stimulates milk production

PROPHYLACTIC: preventative measure

PULMONARY EMBOLISM: a blood clot in the veins that travels to the lungs

PULMONARY HYPERTENSION: high pressure in the blood vessels between the heart and the lungs

RBC: red blood cells

RECURRENT: a condition that went away and has returned

REMISSION: a disease that has improved, at least temporarily

RESECT: to surgically remove

RHEUMATOID ARTHRITIS: joint inflammation caused by the body's own immune system, which incorrectly attacks the joint as though it were foreign invader

RUBELLA: German measles

SCAPULA: shoulder blade

SEPSIS: widespread infection

SEQUELAE: bad results of a disease or treatment

SKIN TO SKIN: the time it takes to perform a surgery from initial skin incision to final skin suture

SPASTIC QUADRIPARESIS: condition resulting from spinal cord injury in the neck, causing weakness or paralysis and overactive reflexes of all four extremities

SPASTICITY: condition of overactive reflexes

SPECULUM: instrument used to expose a body part for direct viewing

SPLENECTOMY: removal of the spleen

STAT: immediately (from status post, which means it is already done)

STATUS EPILEPTICUS: a prolonged seizure that risks causing brain damage

SUBDURAL HEMATOMA: a collection of blood between the brain and skull caused by bleeding of injured veins

SUBLUXATION: partial dislocation

SUTURING: sewing

TACHYCARDIA: fast heart rate

THROMBOCYTHEMIA/THROMBOCYTOSIS: elevated platelet count

THROMBOSIS: clotting of the blood inside a blood vessel

TIBIA: the shin bone

TOXIC MEGACOLON: potentially fatal complication of colon infection or inflammation with dilation

TRACHEOSTOMY: a tube placed through the front of the neck into the trachea (windpipe) to assist with breathing

TRAUMA ABCDE: a mnemonic used to remember the important steps in assessing a trauma patient

TRIMESTER: the nine month human pregnancy divided into three equal three-month periods

ULCER: an erosion on the surface of a body part

ULTRASOUND: a diagnostic test that bounces sound waves off internal organs

URINARY DIVERSION: a place for urine to flow when the original route is not available

VASOVAGAL: a natural reflex that causes temporary low blood pressure

VITREOUS: the thick transparent gel behind the lens of the eye

NOTES

NOTES

NOTES